Praise for Neil Hanson's

UNKNOWN SOLDIERS

"In Neil Hanson's prose, the dark ceremonial of Remembrance Sunday [has] an almost unbearable poignancy. . . . A beautifully illustrated book that has all the somber grandeur of the Beethoven funeral march." —*The Sunday Times* (London)

"The books that are read most widely are . . . the ones that allow families to see the way the war invaded every household and left traces and wounds palpable to this day. This is the register of *Unknown Soldiers*, Neil Hanson's account of British and German families trying to cope with the loss of sons who had no known grave." —*The Times Literary Supplement* (London)

"Hanson builds on the experience of his three warriors to put WWI in haunting perspective. Their touching letters make you wonder: Will any future historian ever be able to put the same personal touch on what Americans in Iraq experienced?" —*St. Louis Post-Dispatch*

"One of the best books . . . on the insanity of life in the trenches." —*Daily Mail* (London)

"Hanson reconstructs these ordinarily extraordinary biographies. He shows us not only just how these young lives were abbreviated in the abyss of trench warfare, but how their 'people'—family as well as nation—came to terms with their loss." —*The New York Sun*

"[The book] is among the most memorable . . . in over thirty years of reading, teaching and writing about that disaster. And that includes Henry Williamson, Siegfried Sassoon, Robert Graves and a dozen other immortals. [Hanson] writes with passion, as anyone should who ventures into this appalling subject, but his passion is restrained—and therefore doubly effective—by the quality of his scholarship and by his exceptional gift as a writer." —*The Press* (New Zealand)

Neil Hanson

UNKNOWN SOLDIERS

Neil Hanson is the author of three acclaimed works of narrative history: *The Custom of the Sea*, *The Great Fire of London*, and *The Confident Hope of a Miracle*. He lives in the Yorkshire Dales in England.

UNKNOWN SOLDIERS

UNKNOWN SOLDIERS

The Story of the Missing of the First World War

Neil Hanson

VINTAGE BOOKS

A DIVISION OF RANDOM HOUSE, INC.

NEW YORK

FIRST VINTAGE BOOKS EDITION, MAY 2007

Copyright © 2005 by Neil Hanson

All rights reserved. Published in the United States by Vintage
Books, a division of Random House, Inc., New York.
Originally published in Great Britain by Doubleday,
the Random House Group Limited, London, in 2005.
Subsequently published in hardcover in the United States by
Alfred A. Knopf, a division of Random House, Inc., New York,
in 2006.

Vintage and colophon are registered trademarks
of Random House, Inc.

The Library of Congress has cataloged the Knopf edition
as follows:
Hanson, Neil.
Unknown soldiers : the story of the missing of the First World
War / Neil Hanson.—1st ed.
p. cm.
1. Hub, Paul, b. 1890. 2. Reader, Alec, b. 1897.
3. Siebold, George. 4. World War, 1914–1918—Missing in
action—Biography. I. Title.
D639.M56H36 2006
940.4'8—dc22
[B]   2005044506

Vintage ISBN: 978-0-307-27654-4

Author photograph © John Alexander
Book design by Soonyoung Kwon
Maps by Neil Gower

www.vintagebooks.com

Printed in the United States of America
10 9 8 7 6 5 4 3 2 1

In memory of Roger Goodman, 1933–2005,
another brave fighter

Farewell. You have known all the others who have been dear to me and you will say goodbye to them for me. And so, in imagination, I extinguish the lamp of my existence on the eve of this terrible battle. I cut myself out of the circle of which I have formed a beloved part. The gap which I leave must be closed; the human chain must be unbroken. I, who once formed a small link in it, bless it for all eternity. And till your last days, remember me, I beg you, with tender love. Honour my memory without gilding it, and cherish me in your loving, faithful hearts.

Letter written by German soldier Otto Heinebach,
the night before he was killed

Contents

Acknowledgements

My grateful thanks to the families of my three chosen unknown soldiers who have generously shared their memories and their family papers with me: Doug Goodman, Diana Goodman and the late Roger Goodman; Frau Brigitte Kostka; Bing and Nancy Seibold, Teddy Westlake and Grace "Bambi" Williams.

I am also grateful for the generous help of the following individuals and organisations: The American Aviation Historical Society; Debra K. Bade, Editor, News Research and Archives, Chicago Tribune; Ione Bates; Dick Bennett, President, the League of WWI Aviation Historians; Lorraine Brochu, University of Chicago; Dr. Erik Carlson of the McDermott Library at the University of Texas at Dallas; Bob Clarke; Richard Davies, Chris Sheppard and the staff at Special Collections, Brotherton Library, University of Leeds; Philippa Donovan; Jane Estevez; the late Pat Evans; Holly Fenelon; Andrew George, Principal

District Archivist, West Yorkshire Archive Service; the Rev. Dr. Neil W. Gerdes, Chicago Historical Society; Patricia Gnadt, Illinois; Paul Goodman; Phil Jarrett; Margaret Johnson; Jill Knight; Christian Kuhrt; Donna Ludlow at the Arkansas Historical Association; Franz Moegle-Hofacker and Judith Bolsinger at the Hauptstaatsarchiv Stuttgart; the Newberry Library, Chicago; Tim O'Gorman, Director of the Quartermaster Museum; Bob Pearson at internetmodeler.com; Holly Reed at the National Archives in Washington; Marvin Skelton, Jen Stebbing, Press and Communications Officer, and Dr. Tony Trowles, Librarian, of Westminster Abbey; John Thirlwell; Paul Tilston; Oscar Villalon of the *San Francisco Chronicle;* Simon Wilkinson at SWpix; David Wyka, University of Chicago, and the always helpful staff of the American Military History Institute; the British Library; the Brotherton Library, University of Leeds; the Chicago Public Library; the Imperial War Museum Reading Room; the London Library; the National Archives, Kew; the New York Public Library; the Muniment Room and Library at Westminster Abbey; and the many other archives and collections listed in the bibliography.

My thanks, as ever, to Ash Green, Luba Ostashevsky, Andrew Miller, and all the other members of the team at Knopf, Maria Massey, Soonyoung Kwon, and Christine Casaccio; to Kim Witherspoon and David Forrer at Inkwell Management in New York; and above all, to Lynn, Jack and Drew, without whom no books would be written and no books would be worth writing.

Introduction

At noon and four-thirty in the afternoon, today and every day, the plaintive wail of warning sirens echoes over the plains of Flanders and northeast France. There is a momentary silence and then the thunderous blast of explosions as piles of munitions, newly unearthed from the former battlefields, are destroyed, "an echo of the Great War which has continued to reverberate for eighty years." There is also an annual harvest of up to a quarter of a million kilos of scrap metal: shrapnel, shell casings, spent bullets, steel helmets, barbed wire, entrenching tools, buckles, buttons and all the other detritus of trench warfare.

Other legacies of the First World War surround us, from the less obvious inheritance of laws restricting aliens, sedition and espionage, cigarette smoking, wristwatches, paper money, and newspaper "In Memoriam" columns, to the memorials in virtually every town and city, graven with columns of names, and the fading sepia photographs of men in uniform that stand on shelves and sideboards, or turn up, with almost unbearable poignancy, in boxes of miscellaneous effects at auction rooms. Above all, there is the national memorial: the Tomb of the Unknowns in Arlington Cemetery, Virginia.

The bald statistics of the Great War—9 million soldiers dead or missing, 21 million maimed or wounded and at least 12 million civilians killed—tend to numb us to the fact that each one of those millions was a human tragedy, a young life cut short, a child orphaned, a woman widowed, parents robbed of their child. None were more tragic than the unknown dead, men lost without trace in the carnage of the battlefields or whose mangled bodies retained no form of identification. The grieving families of such men were deprived even of the consolation of a funeral and a grave site, and for them, the Tomb of the Unknown Soldier became the grave and gravestone of their lost loved ones. In almost every other combatant nation an unknown soldier was also buried at some national shrine and, just as in America, at once became the focus of a pilgrimage that continues to this day.

In the course of my research, I read literally hundreds of soldiers' diaries and letters. Out of all those unknown dead, I chose three men— a German, Paul Hub; a Briton, Alec Reader; and an American, George Seibold—whose stories spoke most strongly and movingly to me; in the end I felt that they selected themselves as much as they were chosen by me. *Unknown Soldiers* is based on the personal testimony contained in the largely unpublished letters and diaries they left behind—the "war memoirs of the dead." I have also drawn on the recollections of their families and the eyewitness testimony of scores of other soldiers present in the same trenches, aerodromes and battlefields, though I have sifted out, as one German soldier remarked, the views of "people who write fine-sounding letters [but] are mostly running around miles away from the trenches." Nothing has been invented or over-dramatised; every statement is underpinned by the personal testimony of those who were there, or knew the chosen men.

They are of different nationalities, backgrounds, personalities and circumstances. They are not clichéd stereotypes: Iowa farm-boys, chirpy Cockneys, Prussians with bristling moustaches. They are young men, barely beginning life's journey, each with their own hopes, fears, ambitions and dreams. Their tracks, faint as smoke in the wind, intersect time and again, but they are united only in death, for each was killed on the Somme, within gunshot sound of each other, and each—like 3 million of their fellows—has no known grave. They disappeared as completely as if they had "gone through a mirror, leaving only a diminishing shadow." No trace remained; the war had claimed even their names. Their story is the story of the Unknown Soldiers.

NEIL HANSON
November 2005

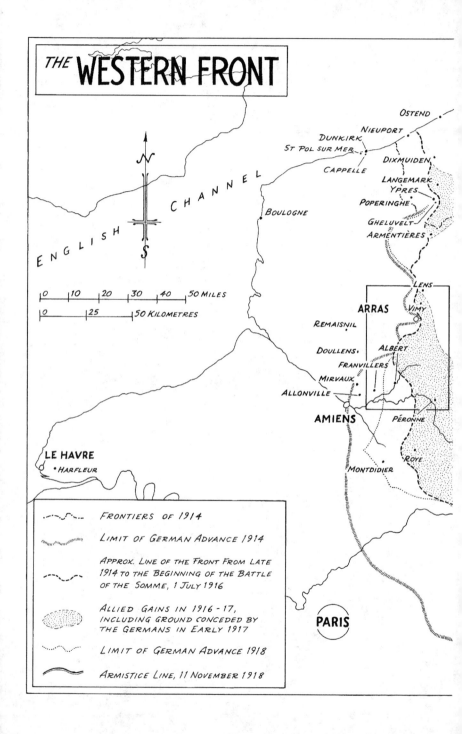

THE WESTERN FRONT

ENGLISH CHANNEL

N
S

0 10 20 30 40 50 MILES
0   25   50 KILOMETRES

OSTEND
NIEUPORT
DUNKIRK
ST POL SUR MER
CAPPELLE
DIXMUIDEN
LANGEMARK
YPRES
POPERINGHE
GHELUVELT
ARMENTIÈRES

BOULOGNE

LENS
ARRAS
VIMY
REMAISNIL
DOULLENS
ALBERT
FRANVILLERS
MIRVAUX
ALLONVILLE
AMIENS
PÉRONNE

LE HAVRE
HARFLEUR

ROYE
MONTDIDIER

PARIS

FRONTIERS OF 1914

LIMIT OF GERMAN ADVANCE 1914

APPROX. LINE OF THE FRONT FROM LATE
1914 TO THE BEGINNING OF THE BATTLE
OF THE SOMME, 1 JULY 1916

ALLIED GAINS IN 1916-17,
INCLUDING GROUND CONCEDED BY
THE GERMANS IN EARLY 1917

LIMIT OF GERMAN ADVANCE 1918

ARMISTICE LINE, 11 NOVEMBER 1918

UNKNOWN
SOLDIERS

THE SOMME, 1916

A burial party, led by an English padre, David Railton, with four soldiers conscripted for that day's burial detail, stands over a hastily dug grave, barely a spade's depth, just behind the front line. A score of other graves, marked by rough crosses of wood or scrap iron, reversed rifles from which a tin hat dangles, or "the usual inverted bottle, stuck in the mud, contain[ing] an envelope, blood-soaked and bearing his name," straggle over the devastated ground around them, a wilderness of mud and torn and cratered earth.

The endless bass rumble of the artillery is counterpointed by the crash of exploding shells. Dense clouds of black smoke drift over the battlefield, mixed with the fine yellow dust thrown up by shell-bursts. The smell of cordite cuts the air, but the all-pervading stench is of putrefaction. Here and there, scraps of frayed khaki and boot leather hang from the barbed wire and the white glint of bone can be seen protruding from the earth. Bullets whine and whistle around the five men, who are half crouching, keeping their heads below the line of the sand-bagged firing trench a few yards away. Their faces lined and haggard, these are men old beyond their years.

The burial service is brutally short—a few words, a muttered prayer—and then the soldiers begin shovelling the wet earth onto the crumpled body. Another crude cross—two angular shell splinters, lashed together with telegraph wire—is hammered into the earth with the butt of a rifle. Then they move on to the next body and the next.

That night, Railton "came back from the line at dusk" to his billet in Erquinghem, near Armentières. In the small garden of a ruined house, "only six paces from the door," was a grave. At its head stood a rough pinewood cross, inscribed "in deep black-pencilled letters, 'An Unknown British Soldier' . . . It was dusk and no one was near, except some officers in the billet playing cards. I remember how still it was. Even the guns seemed to be resting." Throughout the remainder of the war he could not erase that image from his mind.

THE REGIMENT OF
THE DEAD

On 20 October 1914, the 247th Infantry Regiment, known as the "Boy Regiment" because of the youth of its members, was pitched into the carnage of the First Battle of Ypres. Within days its nickname would be changed to "the Regiment of the Dead."

Among its ranks was Paul Hub, a twenty-three-year-old from Stetten-im-Remstal, in the far south of Germany, a few miles from the Swiss border. High in the valley where the upper Danube cuts through the Schwabian Alps, it remains a picture-postcard village of winding cobbled streets and whitewashed houses with brightly painted wooden doors and shutters. Rising above the red-tiled roofs, steeply pitched to shed the winter snows, is the slate-clad spire of the church where Paul was baptized. Born on 15 November 1890, he was the second of five children of Konrad and Friederike Hub. The Hubs were a prominent, well-respected family in Stetten, where Konrad was the teacher in the deaconry. Paul had three brothers and a sister, Helene, the youngest child, to whom he was devoted. Whenever he went away, he always brought her back a present of a necklace or a bracelet. She was just ten when he left to go to war.

Paul had angular features and a studious look that was heightened by the glasses he wore. He walked with a pronounced limp as a result of a childhood accident that left one leg shorter than the other, but none-theless he made the four-kilometre walk to and from the train station every day to attend secondary school in Stuttgart. A good student, serious-minded, "honourable, honest and very loyal," he had ambitions to be a notary public and was working as a clerk in the office of a Stuttgart law firm when war broke out. As befitted the son of a school-teacher, expected to set an example to the community both inside and outside school, Paul volunteered in August 1914 at the very outset of the Great War, joining the First Company of the 247th Infantry Regi-ment. His brothers Robert, an engineer, and Otto, a locksmith, also enlisted at once, in different regiments, perhaps on the advice of their father, who might have feared losing all of them in one disastrous bat-tle. The youngest boy, Alfred, was too young to enlist.

Paul would probably have shared the sentiments of a law student from Freiburg, who explained his decision to enlist to his mother. "You must not imagine that I [did] this in a fit of war-fever; on the contrary, I am quite calm . . . but you would not wish that your sons should show cowardice in the face of great danger and stay prudently behind." Many young volunteers were motivated by this simple patriotism and sense of duty; for others, there was a feeling that the war would create an oppor-tunity for adventure denied to them in their normal lives. "We had seen the generation before us grow old in security, and it seemed a wonder-ful dream to be permitted to fight for our country's greatness." The war also offered many the chance to "make a man of themselves." One seventeen-year-old was "setting out in joy and expectation, not in search of adventure and the spurious excitement of unknown experi-ences, but in the firm belief and hope that I shall become manly and firm, fully-developed, broadminded, full of power and strength, in readiness for the great life which will be waiting for me later on." But while there was a sense of excitement among the young volunteers, others had a more jaundiced view. The German War Minister, von Falkenhayn, told the Bavarian military plenipotentiary, "It is critical that we use the prevailing euphoria before it goes up in smoke."

Almost all men, on all sides, shared the certainty that the war would be short and victorious. Only a few, including the German General von Moltke, thought otherwise. On 28 July 1914 he spoke of the looming war as "a world war" and "a horrible war" that would "annihilate the culture of almost all of Europe for decades to come." Perhaps he was recalling the comments of U.S. General Philip H. Sheridan, who, while acting as an observer with the Prussians during the war against France in 1870–71, had commented that they had yet to understand the nature of modern war. Sheridan wanted to see "more smoke from burning villages" and so much French suffering that "the people must be left nothing but their eyes to weep with after the war." He concluded that while the Prussians understood better than any others how to defeat an enemy, they did not yet comprehend "how to annihilate one."

The one man with a precise and uncannily accurate view of how the war might develop was not a general or a politician, but a Polish banker. Had his views, expressed in a book written in 1899, been brought to the attention of the German, Austro-Hungarian or Allied generals, they would have been derided, for what do bankers know of war? More than many generals, it seems. "The war . . . will become a kind of stalemate . . . It will be a great war of entrenchments. The spade will be as indispensable to the soldier as his rifle. All wars will, of necessity, partake of the character of siege operations . . . Your soldiers may fight as they please; the ultimate decision is in the hands of famine . . . This is the future of war . . . the bankruptcy of nations and the break-up of the whole social organisation."

Just before his departure to begin his military training, Paul Hub became engaged to his childhood sweetheart, Maria Thumm. There would have been time for a hurried wedding, but Paul preferred to wait. Like most recruits on both sides, he expected the war to be over "by Christmas" but, in a characteristically self-effacing gesture, he also held back from marrying Maria because he did not want her to become a war widow. Two years younger than he, she was not yet twenty-two; if he was fated to be maimed or to die, better that she should not be burdened for the rest of her life by a cripple or "widow's weeds."

On 4 August 1914 Paul wrote a farewell letter to his parents. "My suitcase is all packed and at two this afternoon I'll be leaving Ulm on a troop train. My life as a soldier has begun. Maria's letters are in the engagement case, together with my watch chains and other keepsakes that remind me of the happy times I've had with her. Please look after them. I hope I'll be coming back . . . A final farewell to you all as a civilian. From this evening I'll be sending you greetings as a soldier."

After two months at the military training base at Munsingen, Paul was sent to the Western Front—one of the tens of thousands of reinforcements drafted into the depleted ranks to replace those lost in the first two months of fighting, when German troops swept almost to the gates of Paris, only to be defeated and driven back at the Battle of the Marne. When he crossed the Belgian frontier on 16 October, it was the first time Paul had ever left his native land. He wrote to Maria that night, "I never thought I would be wishing you a happy birthday from an enemy country! The whole time we were in Germany we were showered with presents at every station. That stopped when we got to Luxembourg. As soon as we crossed the Belgian border we were ordered not to wave at the locals, but to load our rifles instead."

Paul's regiment passed through Courtrai, crossing the River Leie in the shadow of the massive twin stone "towers of Broel" guarding the bridge, and reached the outskirts of Ypres on 20 October after a punishing four-day march during which, as one soldier complained, "we sweated like cooked herrings." It must have been four days of hell for Paul, limping along as best he could, but neither then nor at any subsequent time during the war did he ever refer to his disability or complain about the hardships he endured as a result.

The 247th had no time to become accustomed to life at the Front, for they were thrown straight into the battle that was to become known as "First Ypres." Crouched in the trenches, they had their first experience of being under fire, with the whine and crash of shells and the sound of rifle and machine-gun bullets "thudding on the sand-bag parapet. These ricochet off with varied noises—some with a high ringing note, others with the deep and savage hum of an angry hornet." They also suffered their "first losses; in the first night, the first dead." They were deployed "in an area of meadowland, covered with dead cattle and a few surviving, ownerless cows. The ruins of the village taken by assault are still smoking, trenches hastily dug by the British are full of bodies . . . a dreadful night comes down on us. We have seen too many horrible things all at once, and the smell of the smoking ruins, the lowing of the deserted cattle and the rattle of machine-gun fire make a very strong impression on us, barely twenty years old as we are, but these things also harden us for what is to come."

The warfare that they had now entered was so far removed from the lightning-fast "war of movement" of the early weeks of the war that some likened it to siege warfare. The network of villages, linked by tree-lined roads and stone walls, was so defensively strong that the attacking troops had to adopt tactics never used before, though all too familiar today: "clear the houses one by one, drag the enemy out of cellars and storage sheds, or kill them by throwing hand-grenades down at them. The casualties are always high." In open ground, troops began digging defensive trenches. "Part of our trench went right through a cemetery. We cleared out the contents of the family vaults, and used them to shelter from the artillery fire; hits from heavy shells would hurl the coffins and semi-rotted corpses high into the air." At Ypres, christened "the gateway to hell," even the noise of the bursting shells was distinctive. "Their shattering impact sent out a different noise to any before heard by me—a flat and battering, locked-in concussion." As well as the shelling, grenades and rifle and machine-gun fire, for the first time German soldiers also experienced a new horror of war—attack from the air—as French pilots dropped "shrapnel bombs loaded with thick knife blades and sharp hooks that ripped limbs from bodies."

Three days later, with fighting still raging, Paul wrote to Maria from "south of Terhand." "The morning of your birthday was our baptism of fire. So far we're fine, although we've been under heavy bombardment. Our adversaries are almost all Englishmen who got away from Antwerp. These dogs are almost on top of us and are costing us a lot of blood. They make swift raids from their trenches, then disappear into cover. Maria, this kind of a war is unspeakable; if you saw a line of stretcher-bearers with their burdens, you'd understand what I mean. I haven't had a chance to shoot at all yet, we're having to deal with an unseen enemy, but I'm slowly getting used to the noise and my hearing has come back after being deafened by shells exploding right next to me yesterday."

The rapid German advances in the early stages of the war had overstretched their supply lines, and to supplement their rations troops were ordered to live off the land, scavenging crops and livestock and confiscating whatever food they could find. Some took enormous risks to do so. "We kill and pluck any hens running loose and thus provide our own rations; our trusty gunners prove to be farmers and milk the ownerless cows; they don't get put off by the odd shells falling near them." On one misty moonlit night, the members of a German unit were pumping filthy water out of the trenches when one pointed to a tree in the middle of no-man's-land, miraculously untouched by shellfire and laden with ripe pears. "Before I could stop them, they had jumped out of the trench and begun—only one hundred metres from the enemy—to pelt the tree with bits of stick and lumps of clay. Imagine the scene, in the moonlight, close to the enemy, these foolhardy devils running round with no cover, shying at pears while bullets were whistling all about them. In a few minutes they had got every single pear off the tree and, loaded with fruit, we started back."

On 25 October, with fighting still raging around him, Paul wrote to Maria, "Everyone has to find their own food. Sometimes we manage to throw together a decent soup. You can find meat on the farms and we collect all sorts of things when we're requisitioning, but we just don't have enough bread. I've got a few pieces of chocolate and other tasty morsels in my rucksack that I got from you and our parents, and as soon as this battle is over (it's lasted a week already) . . . I'm going to open my rucksack and feast. But first I will ask for my post, because there's bound to be something there from my Maria. You just don't realise how lonely you get when you're cut off from the rest of the world like this. Now I understand why people were begging for newspapers at all the German-occupied train stations. God bless you, Maria! I hope he keeps an eye on me too."

His prayer was needed; Paul's regiment was now ordered to attack the village of Gheluvelt—"that louse's nest"—the last high ground controlled by the Allies in that area. The ridge was only sixty feet high, but that was a substantial hill in a region of plains and marshes at or often below sea level. From its summit, the entire Flemish plain was visible. General von Fabeck's orders, issued on 30 October 1914, stressed the strategic value of their objective. "The breakthrough will be of decisive importance. We must and therefore will conquer, settle for ever the centuries-long struggle, end the war and strike the decisive blow against our most detested enemy. We will finish the British, Indians, Canadians, Moroccans and other trash, feeble adversaries, who surrender in great numbers if they are attacked with vigour."

The fighting at Ypres was bloody and terrible in the extreme and losses on all sides were appalling. Many of the French troops were still wearing their peacetime uniforms of blue tunics and red trousers, and the sight of their dead, said one German soldier, made the field of battle "look like a mass of poppies, intermingled with cornflowers." The 247th Infantry Regiment was now earning its new nickname—"the Regiment of the Dead"—as the barely trained and woefully inexperienced troops were treated as cannon-fodder by von Fabeck.

On 31 October, an exhausted and dispirited Paul wrote to Maria, "I feel so terrible I'd really rather not write to you. That doesn't mean that I've forgotten you, though. Every day spent here makes it clearer to me how beautiful home is, and what a crowd of feelings that word 'home' brings out in me. I have lived through such horror recently, no words can describe the tragedy all around me. Every day the fighting gets fiercer and there is still no end in sight. Our blood is flowing in torrents. When I think of our 247th Regiment, my eyes swim with tears. The first and second battalions only have 250 to 300 men left, so more than half are gone. Today only a few of my comrades will still be standing. My company commander, Lieutenant Massbauer, had been at the Front for one hour when he was shot through the head. Pale and close to death, he was carried past me. Today, Sunday, I stood at his modest grave and joined in a prayer.

"That's just how it is. All around me, the most gruesome devastation. Dead and wounded soldiers, dead and dying animals, horse cadavers, burnt-out houses, shell-cratered fields, devastated vehicles, weapons, fragments of uniforms—all this is scattered around me, in total confusion. I didn't think war would be like this. We can't sleep for all the noise. At least thirty shells explode at once, the whole time. We called for reinforcements yesterday and again today. I hope they make it; there are only a few of us left." Already Paul well knew the truth uttered by another young German: "Nobody will come through this war without being changed into a different person."

A few soldiers created a refuge from the horrors of the trenches in the reserve area six hundred yards behind the front line, "a little wooded valley in which the most frightful hand-to-hand fighting has taken place. Trees and bushes are torn to pieces by shells and larded with rifle-bullets. Although we have already buried many, bodies are still lying all around in the shell-holes." From these unpromising beginnings, they created a garden. "First we built quite a neat causeway out of logs, with a railing to it, along the bottom of the valley. Then from a pinewood close by, which had also been destroyed by shells, we dragged all the best tree-tops and stuck them upright in the soil; they have no roots but we don't expect to be here more than a month and they are sure to stay green that long. Out of the gardens of the ruined chateaux of Hollebecke and Camp we fetched rhododendrons, box, snowdrops and primroses and made nice little flower beds. We have cleaned out the little brook which flows through the valley and some clever comrades have built small dams and constructed pretty little watermills, so-called 'parole clocks' which, by their revolutions, are supposed to count how many minutes more the war is going to last. We have planted whole bushes of willow and hazel with pretty catkins on them, and little firs with their roots, so that a melancholy desert has been transformed into an idyllic grove."

Their labours were wasted. By nightfall on 31 October, Gheluvelt, including their garden, was back in British hands and hundreds of Paul's comrades in the 247th Infantry lay dead among "the scabrous mud wastes and the stink of the captured dugouts of the Salient, piled up to ground-level with corpses, some feet uppermost, some heads, like fish in a basket."

The German trenches were also strewn with British casualties and Paul had his first sight of kilted Scotsmen among the dead and wounded. "Instead of trousers they wear a sort of short, warm skirt that only reaches halfway down their thighs. It is a strange sight and I'm amazed they don't freeze their backsides off, walking around half-naked like that, because they don't wear any underwear either. They do have a warm, heavy coat like the other English soldiers and the colour of their uniform is much more suited to the terrain than ours—a sort of dirty brownish green. Their hats and wrap-around things are the same colour. The English can move much more freely than us. With their practical clothing and their light packs, they can run like hares, a considerable advantage when under fire. But we're still going to win." Many of the young German troops had been sent to the Front still wearing their "Prussian blue" peacetime uniforms. Gradually these were replaced with field-grey, but soldiers on both sides continued to wear soft caps and forage hats until the mounting toll of men shot in the head by snipers or killed by head-wounds from shrapnel prompted the introduction of steel helmets.

On 10 November, yet more droves of boy soldiers marched to their deaths when the volunteers of the 206th Reserve Infantry Regiment, many of them students or members of the German Youth Movement, were annihilated at the Battle of Langemark. Stories circulated at the time of those boy-men, still wearing their student caps, singing "Deutschland, Deutschland, Über Alles" as they marched across an open field towards seasoned British troops, protected by barbed-wire entanglements and armed with machine-guns. Adolf Hitler, who faced action for the first time at Langemark, was later to claim he had heard the singing. He may have done so, but the real circumstances were very different. When 20,000 had been killed or wounded, the remainder fled the battlefield in panic and at that point some did sing the anthem, though it was not defiance of the enemy but the need to avoid being misidentified and fired upon by their own side that led them to do so. What is undisputed is that the battles of late October and early November 1914 left Langemark "a heap of rubbish" and killed or maimed a whole corps of German students. Some units lost 70 percent of their numbers in a battle that Nazis later celebrated as the "march of honour to Langemark."

In fierce fighting that day, "war volunteer Paul Hub of the 1st Company, 247th Infantry Regiment," was awarded the Iron Cross, Second Class, "for outstanding bravery in the face of the enemy." It was a genuine honour at the time, but Iron Crosses were later so devalued by the wholesale award of them that one cynical German soldier remarked that he had been "recommended for the Iron Cross—for playing skat [cards] well?" A total of 5.2 million had been awarded by the end of the war and staff officers joked that only through suicide could a soldier escape winning one.

The First Battle of Ypres continued until 22 November, when the onset of the winter frosts brought the fighting to an end. By then, 80,000 Germans and well over 50,000 Britons were dead, wounded or missing. German burial parties did what they could to clear the dead, both German and British. Where the fighting allowed, the bodies were moved to cemeteries behind the lines, sometimes on stretchers, more often "in a long strange bundle [suspended] from a pole . . . with two waxen yellow hands protruding from the wrapping." Some members of burial parties, their sensibilities not yet blunted by the sheer volume of dead, dressed the graves of their comrades. "We fetched some large glazed tiles from the roof of a summerhouse to put round the graves, and picked some lilac-blossom and branches of red and yellow leaves to decorate them . . . The lilac gave out its lovely scent and the coloured leaves glowed . . . we scattered the flowers and leaves over the dead and began to shovel in the earth. The last service I was able to render my dear Rudolf was to brush a little blue butterfly from his cold cheek."

In areas where fierce fighting continued, the dead had to be buried anywhere and by any means possible. "Burying the killed in No Man's Land had been rather dangerous, because the British started shooting right away and they were trigger-happy during the night. We buried as many as we could reach in ditches in No Man's Land, without coming too close to the British trenches. Having finished our work, we planted a white cross on top. Two days later we were surprised to see at daybreak a large white cloth, five to seven yards wide, fastened on two high poles on the first British trench—'We thank you for burying our comrades'—and the whole day they did not fire a single shot, even if they saw somebody moving about in our trench."

Many bodies had to be left to rot where they fell. "Lucky the few whom we or those opposite have been able to inter with some sort of decency, for fragments of human bodies are still hanging in the barbed wire. Only a little while ago, close in front of our trench, was a human hand with a ring on one finger. A few yards away was a forearm of which finally only the bone remained—so good does human flesh taste to rats." But even when buried, the dead had "no rest beneath the earth, for the shells plunge deep into the ground and blow up the graves."

The four months of fighting from September to December 1914 had cost the German armies 800,000 casualties. The Allies lost an even greater number; French losses stood at 854,000 and the much smaller British Expeditionary Force had been all but wiped out. Of 110,000 troops who had crossed the Channel to France, 86,237 had become casualties. Some battalions that had begun the war with a strength of 1,000 men were down to 30, commanded by a single officer. Meanwhile, politicians and generals on both sides continued to proclaim the certainty of victory, trumpet battlefield successes and downplay or suppress news of military defeats and the ever-lengthening lists of fatalities. German journalists were barred from the killing grounds and before the end of 1914 newspapers were banned from publishing lists of those killed. The public also remained in almost total ignorance about the defeat on the Marne and the resultant sacking of the Chief of the General Staff, von Moltke, but inevitably the real news from the Front leaked back in soldiers' letters. "Two cemeteries have been made here, the losses have been so great. I ought not to write that to you, but I do so all the same, because the newspapers have probably given you quite a different impression. They tell only of our gains and say nothing about the blood that has been shed, of the cries of agony that never cease. The newspaper doesn't give any description either of how the 'heroes' are laid to rest . . . it is pitiful the way one throws the dead bodies out of the trench and lets them lie there, or scatters dirt over the remains of those which have been torn to pieces by shells."

Right along the Western Front, the two sides had now begun to consolidate and fortify their defensive positions. As a Polish banker had predicted and as infantry veterans from the U.S. Civil War could have told anyone willing to listen, "one good man behind an earthwork was equal to three outside of it" and the spade had now "become as great a necessity as the rifle." As proof of that, the British Army's annual requirement for spades increased from 2,500 in the pre-war years to a total of 10,638,000 during the four years of war. The "War of Movement" had congealed into a war of attrition, a phrase already being used in October 1914, and summed up three years later as "the principle of the gambler who has the heaviest purse [to] force our adversary's hand and make him go on spending until he is a pauper." By December 1914 the trenches stretched unbroken from the Channel to the Swiss frontier; "we are a living wall . . . a fortress thousands of kilometers long."

The Germans prepared their trenches and dugouts with meticulous care. They constructed "the best trenches, the deepest, the widest, and with smooth, sloping sides that looked as though a mechanical digger had made them." Their concrete-reinforced deep dugouts, "as solid as a pyramid," thirty or forty feet below the ground, housed up to sixteen men in bunk-beds and often had floorboards, wallpaper, kitchens, curtained sleeping spaces, water taps, cupboards, mirrors, doorbells and electric light—albeit with a "black lattice of flies" hanging from each warm bulb, and "swarming and droning around the head of the passer-by." Living rooms, sleeping chambers and ammunition stores were connected by a network of tunnels, and in some sections of the lines, "one could traverse one's whole front like a mole, without once coming to the surface." British commanders spurned such refuges for their men. The lines of trenches gouged across the land were purely temporary, a mere punctuation mark before the next offensive, and to make them too comfortable might render the men less inclined to attack. "The result, in the long term, meant that we lived a mean and impoverished sort of existence in lousy scratch holes."

The men patrolling those trenches were also now coming to know one of the things that would forever colour the memories of all those confined in them: what one soldier, with admirable understatement, termed "a certain dampness"—Flanders mud—and "dread of the enemy is as nothing compared with dread of the mud." Ypres had once been a seaport and was now an inland city only because of the intricate network of ditches, dykes and canals that drained this low-lying land. Intensive shelling was already destroying the drainage system, and on 27 October the Belgians deliberately opened the sluices to flood large areas. "There is a soft whisper in front—water! It came suddenly. It gushed out of the ground. The sea has broken through again. We wade through water first knee-deep, then up to our waists, then again up to our knees . . . The way lies through the deep slough of a ploughed field. One's legs nearly stick fast in it, but they have to be dragged out, however much they seem disposed to stay where they are. Behind us the slough closes up again. The sheet of water is rippled by the wind. The pestilent smell of salt-water mud oppresses one's lungs." The result of the flooding was to turn much of the land into a morass of quaking mud—"all that muddy brown monotony, where blood's the only coloured thing"—that was neither wholly land nor water. "It was not like any mud I've ever seen. It was a kind of stagnant river, too thick to flow, too wet to stand."

One soldier described the conditions in a listening post in front of the trenches. "Two teams climbed over the top in the dark. Suddenly *rat-tat-tat-sim-sim:* machine-gun fire. I threw myself flat, then up and on. I staggered past a ditch full of water, crossed by a primitive bridge, then belly-crawled because of the fierce light of star-shells . . . A comrade disappeared down a hole, I fell after him. It was the outpost . . . I lay flat behind a tree-stump, rifle with fixed bayonet across my arm, and stared into the darkness ahead. We took it in turns until the grey of morning and then bright sunshine. One man stayed on sentry, the other crept into a hole at the side to sleep. There we sat, in the No Man's Land between the trenches, in a moated castle surrounded by water. We remained there for sixty-four hours."

In such conditions, even the simplest kind of activity—sentry duty, collecting the rations, moving up to the Front or back to the reserve areas—became an ordeal. "The trench was ten feet deep and about 200 yards long as the crow flies, but about 600 with the windings and zigzags of the trench (to prevent it from being swept from end to end by fire). It was two feet six inches wide at the top, narrowing to eighteen inches at the bottom . . . It took twenty men about one and a half hours to go that 600 yards. My first step was into two feet of liquid mud. After that I was nearly all the time up to within three inches of the top of my thigh boots in this mud. The bottom was worn with constant passage of feet to a 'V' shape and was composed of a thick, sticky, clayey mud.

"My sacks dangled in the water, the contents became sodden and a tremendous weight. My overcoat (thick) did the same. My upper half became plastered with mud, with constantly slipping against the side of the narrow trench. My rifle, wrapped in sandbags, became the same . . . We slipped and floundered and stopped for breath and shouted 'Step short in front,' as those behind lost ground . . . In some places deep and dangerous holes were left as a ditch is dug under them for [drinking] water(!). So at last we emerged into another trench and at last into the front line, more dead than alive. I had started with a load of about one hundredweight and finished with nearly half a hundredweight of water and mud in addition. [One officer reported that the waterlogged greatcoat of a member of his platoon weighed fifty-eight pounds.] On the way up, two men became delirious through exhaustion and one man went clean out of his mind.

"Eight of us, including a corporal, were told off to one sentry group. The post was a corner of the trench, over the knees in liquid mud and the slimy parapet and parados were collapsing, or had collapsed on all sides. In many places the parapet was entirely gone and the surface of the water practically open to German gaze. They were eighty yards away. The dugouts, needless to say, were hopelessly flooded . . . We did sentry continually as there was nowhere to sit, never mind lie. We were sodden and muddy and the temperature was considerably below freezing point, so sleep was out of the question. We threw our rifles down, and our equipment, and leaned against the wet earth or moved about in the water till daylight. The general feeling was 'If the Germans want this trench, we'll let them have it. They are welcome to it.' In the morning we had raw bacon and sopping bread as there was no dry wood obtainable for a fire . . . the tea ration was spoilt and the sugar had dissolved. Then happened the most pleasant event; one of the eight, my best friend, got a spent bullet in the calf and so his release from this submarine existence. I offered him ten pounds to hammer it into my calf so that I could go down with him but it was no use. How we envied him and how pleased he was."

Several men commented on the beauty of sunrises and sunsets over this flooded wasteland, the colours of the dawn or dusk reflecting from myriad pools and gilding the surface of the mud, but most saw nothing to eulogize. "Sunrise and sunset are blasphemous, they are mockeries to man, only the black rain out of the bruised and swollen clouds all through the bitter black of night is fit atmosphere for such a land." The Germans held the higher ground, but in winter even their trenches were often flooded. "In many places trenches and dugouts are so full that they are uninhabitable. However we have some electric pumps that pump huge amounts of water into the canal and they do their work well. We also play many a joke on the English, pumping the water into their front line trench so that they must either swim or drown in their own trench. Apart from that the English have to suffer more from the water than we do, because their positions are far lower than ours." In some areas, the height of the water table made it impossible to dig conventional trenches and "command" or "parapet" trenches were constructed instead: mounds of earth- or clay-filled sandbags raised seven or eight feet above the ground and as much as seven feet thick. And in the La Bassée sector, which lay below sea level, ferro-concrete emplacements were built.

. . .

Unlike so many of his fellows, Paul Hub had survived his baptism of fire at Ypres and he endured the winter in the front lines there. Early in March 1915, he received the terrible news that his younger brother, Otto, had been killed on 28 February, fighting the Russians on the Eastern Front near Warsaw. He had been at the Front for such a short time that he had sent only a single letter to his parents before his death. On 20 March, in response to the many messages of sympathy that they had received, "Head-teacher Hub, his wife and children" sent out cards expressing "our most heartfelt gratitude for your caring condolences on the occasion of the heroic death of our beloved son, Otto. May the Lord spare us from further sorrows of war." Within two months, they would be sending out more black-bordered cards.

On 22 April the German armies launched a surprise attack in Flanders. This Second Battle of Ypres was marked by the first successful German use of a new weapon of war—poison gas. The wife of Fritz Haber, the German progenitor of the gas, killed herself in horror at what her husband had unleashed. Gas warfare had first been used on a modest scale by the French in the Argonne and then by the Germans on the Eastern Front at Bolimov, but in weather so cold that the gas froze. Now at dawn on 22 April, following a brief artillery bombardment, chlorine gas was released from 5,700 cylinders. It formed a dense greenish-yellow cloud that drifted over the French lines along a six-kilometre section of the Front. It killed by asphyxiation and many of those who survived were temporarily blinded. Estimates of the dead varied wildly, from 200 to 5,000, but thousands of survivors fled in panic, leaving the German troops in their primitive respirators advancing into an undefended four-mile gap in the Allied lines. However, the Germans had deployed no reserves, thinking it inconceivable that such a breakthrough would be achieved, and a scrambled defence by British reserves stopped the German advance short of Ypres.

In a renewed and once more unsuccessful attack on 8 May, Paul Hub was so badly wounded by shrapnel that he was fortunate to survive. After emergency treatment at a dressing station and a field hospital, he was sent to the military hospital at Wunstorf, near Hanover. There he suffered another hammer blow: the news that his elder brother, Robert, had also been killed in action, on 5 May, fighting with the Southern Army in the Carpathian Mountains. Like Otto, he had been serving in the front lines for the first time. Paul wrote to Maria that night, "One more sacrifice and you will have to bury your love."

He remained in the military hospital for a further six weeks, but on 20 June he was considered well enough to be given home leave to convalesce. It must have been a very sombre reunion with Maria, his parents, his surviving brother, Alfred, and his two widowed sisters-in-law.

Ypres had not fallen to the German attacks and the shock value of gas warfare rapidly faded. The subsequent use by both sides was far less effective, and in the Battle of Loos in autumn 1915 a British attempt to release gas from 5,000 cylinders resulted in 2,632 British casualties when the wind blew the gas back into their own trenches. Such was the slaughter on the second day of the disastrous attack that German machine-gunners, after mowing down row upon row of advancing British troops, finally ceased firing out of pity for their enemies.

2

THE PLACE WHERE THE DIRTY WORK IS DONE

In August 1915, four months before his eighteenth birthday, Alec Reader went to war. Alec was born out of wedlock, on 8 December 1897, the eldest of five children. His parents, Fred and Rose, subsequently married and, ever conscious of his position in society, Fred avoided the stigma of having an illegitimate child by falsifying his son's birth certificate. Fred worked as the manager of the Clapham Bill Posting Company, a post with a certain status, reflected in the servants he employed and the family's detached villa, 4 North Side, overlooking a small green to the east of Wandsworth Common. The imposing, red-brick house with bay windows and a top-floor balcony still stands, though now serving as part of the premises of the Services Rendered club.

Known as "The Bastard" by subsequent generations of the family—a comment on his behaviour, not the circumstances of his birth—Fred had a certain charm, but he was a womanizing, hard-drinking, short-tempered and often violent man, and he treated his children and particularly his wife "like dirt." Rose was a sweet-natured, rather naïve woman, but she was not Fred's intellectual equal and, in his mind at least, she was also his social inferior. He made it clear to Rose on many occasions that he felt he had married beneath him. He also "made use of the female servants in a number of ways," fathered another illegitimate child and began an affair with the woman he had employed as housekeeper at 4 North Side. After the war he moved in with her, abandoning Rose, although he never divorced her.

Alec went to Lavender Hill School and then to Emanuel School in Wandsworth, where, according to his headmaster, he was "a splendid boy at school and gave promise of a bright future." He sang in the choir and had a good enough voice to be a soloist at St. Peter's Church in Eaton Square, SW1 (his upwardly mobile father must have been delighted by that address). He seems to have been a quiet, rather shy boy—there is no record of any girlfriend—but he had a mischievous spark and a very dry sense of humour. After he left school, he began work as a clerk with the Telephones Department of the Post Office, on the west side of Wandsworth Common.

From his birth to the age of seventeen, virtually the whole of his world had been encompassed by the Common, but in August 1915 he caught the train into London from Clapham Junction and walked to Somerset House in the Strand, the headquarters of the Prince of Wales's Own Civil Service Rifles, "where recruits can join any day between 10 a.m. and 7 p.m. . . . or later by appointment." Before the war, the regiment had been "recruited mainly from Civil Servants and their friends," but the ranks were now "open to all men of good character between nineteen and forty years of age . . . Pay is issuable to all men at usual Army rates . . . uniform and a complete free kit of all necessaries are provided immediately on enlistment."

"Bank clerks and clerks from the big insurance company offices were also joining the unit. That gives an indication of the kind of people that composed the Civil Service Rifles. To have obtained an easier time in the Army a clerk should have joined a unit composed of heavy manual labourers such as navvies, miners or heavy metal workers, for then there would have been openings for clerks with lighter duties in the orderly room or the quartermaster's stores." But neither Alec nor the rest of those eager volunteers thought in such cynical terms. They were joining to "do their bit" and fight the enemy, not hide behind a ledger while others did the fighting for them.

Alec was too young for active service—the minimum age for

recruitment was eighteen, and nineteen for service overseas—but like many thousands of under-age soldiers, he was accepted without question. Some lied about their age from the start; others, more naïve, gave their true age but were then encouraged with a nod and a wink from a recruiting sergeant to add the necessary years. Boys of sixteen, fifteen, fourteen—like Horace Iles, a member of the Leeds Pals—and even thirteen—like John Condon, the youngest boy killed in the war, who was only fourteen when he died—enlisted in this way.

Alec entered through a stone archway into a large open square "in which it was possible to drill several hundred troops." The Drill Hall, where recruitment was taking place, faced the Thames Embankment on a lower level, reached by a stone staircase. There he joined a crowd of other young men waiting in line for a medical inspection. By this stage in the war, the Army's voracious appetite for troops had progressively reduced the physical requirements. In August 1914, recruits had to be good physical specimens and a minimum of five foot eight inches tall. Inside three months, that had been reduced to five foot five, and on 5 November 1914, after a fresh avalanche of casualties, the height restriction had been reduced again. To qualify for active service now, recruits merely had to be five foot two inches tall, with a chest measurement of thirty-four inches, and even this was subject to some elasticity. At least one recruit was passed A1 even though he was below the required size, on the grounds that "no doubt training would increase my chest measurement."

Alec was nodded through the medical, given a New Testament to hold as he was sworn in and awarded the "King's Shilling" as Private 3623 of the 15th Battalion, Civil Service Rifles. A soldier's pay was a shilling a day (by the end of the war it had increased to two shillings a day), and for recording this payment he was issued with a pay-book with a brown cover. When serving abroad, pay days were not weekly as in England, but whenever the unit found it convenient, "and then we were paid only half the amount we were due, the other half being credited in the books of the Army Pay Corps, to be paid in a lump sum at some future date, possibly after the war."

The new recruits were issued with their khaki uniforms and their Army kit, including a cut-throat razor, toothbrush and towel. "Fit was somewhat approximate and was helped by exchanging between those being outfitted, but boots and cap had to be the right sizes." They were also issued with two identity discs, one red and one green, giving their name, initials and number, regiment and religion—"two in case he was killed; one to be buried with his corpse and the other to go to records. The indication of his religion was so that he might have the appropriate burial service."

By now it was late in the afternoon, and the fully equipped young soldiers were given a travel warrant and sent home for the night. No doubt Alec paraded in his new uniform for his goggle-eyed sisters and brother. He had joined up partly to get away from his over-bearing father, though he was also undoubtedly affected by the sense of duty instilled in him at school, and by the waves of jingoism and "foolish patriotism" that inspired a million more of his countrymen to join Kitchener's New Army. As Philip Larkin wrote, "Never such innocence again." One forty-nine-year-old man even committed suicide because of "worry caused by the feeling that he was not going to be accepted for service."

There were women already patrolling the streets, handing out white feathers to men of military age, but most of the volunteers needed no prodding to enlist, for these were "men of handsome and boundless illusions. Each of them quite seriously thought of himself as a molecule in the body of a nation that was really, not just figuratively, 'straining every nerve' to discharge an obligation of honour . . . All the air was ringing with rousing assurances. France to be saved, Belgium righted, freedom and civilisation re-won, a sour, soiled, crooked old world to be rid of bullies and crooks and reclaimed for straightness, decency, good-nature, the ways of common men dealing with common men." "'The freedom of Europe,' 'The war to end war' [a phrase first coined by H. G. Wells in a pamphlet published in 1914], 'The overthrow of militarism,' 'The cause of civilisation'—most people believe so little now in anything or anyone that they would find it hard to understand the simplicity and intensity with which these phrases were once taken among our troops, or the certitude felt by hundreds of thousands of men that if they were killed, their monument would be a new Europe not soured or soiled with the hates and greeds of the old."

Others played down such "pure" motivations, claiming to have enlisted solely because of "fighting spirit . . . and love of the old country. I don't remember ever hearing of stopping war for ever in 1914." Even the national sport of football was an aid to recruitment; by the end of 1914, half a million men had actually enlisted at football matches; and "the war, it was claimed, offered the chance to play 'the greatest game of all.' " But by the spring of 1915 there was an abrupt reversal of policy and professional football was banned, in the belief that many men were being deterred from enlisting because of reluctance to miss their teams' matches. Still other men enlisted under some form of moral or actual compulsion. Conscription was not introduced until 1916, but alongside the moral pressure voluntarily to "do your duty" came economic pressures. Some employers and organizations offered financial inducements to enlist, while others preferred the stick to the carrot and sacked men to force them into the Army.

For the next fortnight, Alec and his new comrades attended Somerset House daily to learn the rudiments of marching, squad drill and the other mysteries of Army life. "We had not been taught how to salute, nor did we know whom to salute. Strange to tell, we did not know an officer when we saw one and were likely to meet several as we passed back and forward along the Strand." At the end of the fortnight they were "taken from Somerset House by way of the Underground to Hammersmith, marched over the bridge south to Barnes, and handed over to the 3rd/15th CSR [Civil Service Rifles]." Their basic training took place in Richmond Park and "was necessarily on somewhat elementary lines owing to . . . the want of experienced officers and NCOs, lack of arms and equipment, etc." They soon had "the fine opinion of ourselves that we had gained definitely deflated. We were less than the dust and would now be shown what true soldiering was."

As well as marching and drilling—often with wooden rifles because the real things were in short supply—the recruits were also treated to a series of lectures, one of which, on the history of the rifle, began with the carbine. "The joke went round that the next lecture would be on bows and arrows." They were fed from field kitchens in the park and the notoriously bad Army food was actually welcomed by many, being as good as or better than the diet they had eaten at home. Alec had no complaints. "We're going strong down here, eggs yesterday and a kipper each today for breakfast." At first they lived under canvas in the park, often "under trying conditions of cold and wet," but as winter approached they were housed with local families in Barnes. Alec was billeted in the house of the Dubois family in Gerard Road—French exiles who had volunteered to take in soldiers as their contribution to the war effort. On 11 November 1915 the battalion transferred to Musketry Camp at Rainham for rifle training. The village was "about one hundred yards long. It takes five minutes to see everything," and his shooting in the bitterly cold weather was hopelessly inaccurate. "I felt quite lost without my mittens yesterday and messed up the firing."

In January 1916 he was given a few days' home leave. The photograph taken at the time shows Alec, a boy in a man's uniform, standing behind his seated family. He is tall and slim, with short dark hair, parted at the side. His face is pale and he has a sensitive, almost sad expression, heightened by the dark shadows visible beneath his brown eyes. His left arm is at his side, his right resting protectively on the back of his mother's chair. Fred, a much more stocky and powerful figure, sits arms folded, head back, fixing the camera with a confident, almost cocky gaze. Rose looks careworn, sad and perhaps a little fearful, gazing off to the side at something beyond our reach. Flanking them are Alec's younger brother, Arthur, fifteen years old and a mirror image of his father, and his three younger sisters, Lilian, eleven, Minnie, seven, and two-year-old Constance.

On his return from leave, his unit was transferred to the newly built Hazely Down Camp, near Winchester, the last staging post before embarkation for France. It was a huge camp, a mile long, "a new small town built for the military for a population of well over 6,000 men" but housing 14,000 troops when Alec arrived there. "More regiments are expected daily and when we get full up it will be some camp. I have not been down here long enough to know much about the camp but I can assure you it is far from being a 'home from home.' " He and his comrades were housed in wood-lined corrugated-iron huts, furnished only with a few wooden chairs and beds made from "three long wide planks placed on two six-inch trestles. A sack six feet long and three feet wide, moderately filled with straw, formed a mattress, and a bolster case also filled with straw served as a pillow." There was no mains drainage, only latrines. The food on offer was equally basic, both in quality and quantity, and as a result "the whole of our Army pay plus other money was spent on food."

There was a firing range nearby at Chilcomb, practice trenches on Fawley Down, about a mile away, and at the camp itself "there was plenty of space for digging and bombing and assault courses, as well as a good miniature range." On the ranges, lying "prone, we fired five rounds at various distances up to 500 yards, with the results being signalled from the butts. Finally we attempted fifteen rounds rapid, that is an attempt to get off as many as fifteen in one minute."

The intensity of the training increased as the time for embarkation approached. "We had a very novel route march on Tuesday, from 9 a.m. to 1 p.m. we climbed hills with a gradient of 1 in 3, and by the time we had finished, there wasn't much 'go' left in any of us. Last Monday we went to the [practice] trenches and had to dig solid chalk to a depth of eight feet. Some war!" Although Alec was unaware of its significance at the time, those conditions exactly mirrored the chalk bedrock in the area between the north bank of the Somme and Arras where his unit and countless thousands of other British and Empire troops were soon to be deployed in battle.

Alec had been told that he was to have three days' leave, but it was then abruptly cancelled when he was put on a draft for the Front. "I don't know when we are going or whether I can get any leave but I shall do my best to get home. The draft was only formed yesterday and we had to parade at 2:30 p.m. today for kit inspection." Training was further intensified and on 10 February 1916 Alec was "working very hard at present, trench-digging, bomb-throwing, bayonet-fighting, etc. We do all our work in full war kit (everything you take out with you) and I can tell you I am quite ready for the end of the day."

The following week "German measles has broken out in the camp and three huts are down with it. As the disease is spreading fast, the camp will probably be isolated shortly. The draft cannot be sent off while there is a risk of infection, so we should stay here for some time yet." However, on the morning of 20 February, "the draft was called out on church parade and marched to the Orderly Room. Of course we all thought we were going at once and so we did, but not to Southampton. We merely cleared out of our huts and have been put together in Hut Number 1A. As we have been taken away from the infected region, we are again fit for active service but rumour says we shall all get 24 hours leave, so I may come home any day. In case I can't get home, please send some money and a pair of socks."

Despite his hopes, there was to be no home leave. On the morning of 24 February, they marched to Winchester and took the train to Southampton. It passed straight through the town station and travelled "right on into the docks among the ships," where the men disembarked. Instead of boarding at once, they were each issued with a rifle— "We could well have done without these until we had left ship . . . but it was an easy way for the authorities to get the arms to France"—and then marched three miles out of town to a transit camp on a windswept common. Two red-capped military police tracked them all the way "to see that none of the Draft ran away."

Alec found the transit camp "a very dreary place, but we shall clear out as soon as the transfer boat comes for us. We sleep forty-five to a hut and from what I can see of it, there will be no room to turn round tonight in our sleep. I was very sorry indeed to be unable to get home, but although I kept asking for twenty-four hours leave, I was unable to get it. There are some old stagers here who say that the heavy fighting which is going to take place in March will finish the war one way or the other. Failing that, I shall be entitled to seven days leave in six months time, so all being well, you will see me at home before I reach the age of nineteen."

The following day he wrote a hasty postcard: "I expect to leave for [Le] Havre tomorrow. I shall stay there about a fortnight." As scheduled, he embarked for France on 26 February, but two days later he was again writing to his mother from Southampton. "I have had quite an exciting adventure. You read this morning about the P&O liner? [The 12,400-ton P&O liner *Maloja*, bound for Bombay (now Mumbai), went down off Dover after striking a mine. Forty-four people perished when the liner rolled over and sank almost at once.] Well, I embarked yesterday at five in the evening and hung about until seven. We were all given lifeboats [life jackets] and told to keep them on during the voyage. At 7:30 we were taken off the boat and marched back to camp and this morning we found out the reason. The above is an official secret at present and I have no idea when I shall cross. Please send me money (IN NOTES) as early as possible, as I'm not only broke, I'm bent."

Alec's battalion re-embarked that night and this time made a safe, if rough crossing of the Channel; "in fact there were only three blokes in the boat who were not sick. I had a very busy time dashing up to the tub and lying down again, all through the night, but nevertheless I enjoyed myself immensely." It was the first time that he had ever been to sea. They disembarked early on the morning of 1 March, and Alec wrote to his mother that night from "No. 11 Base Camp, Havre, BEF" (British Expeditionary Force), where he had been assigned to the 1/15th Battalion of the Civil Service Rifles, part of the 47th (London) Division.

The camp, "in fact, a town of about 10,000 men," was near Harfleur, a few miles east of Le Havre. The troops were all housed in bell tents with rough wooden floors and their days were spent doing their final training on a plateau reached by a steep slope from the camp. There they received "instruction in tactics and strategy . . . personal combat, both offensive and defensive, at a bomb-pit for the throwing of live Mills bombs and . . . time in a gas chamber." "After a lecture we were given 'Gas' helmets and marched into a room, the door was closed and the gas turned on from a cylinder. I hated my helmet at first, and thought I should never breathe, and the chemicals are awful—all the brass buttons, etc, went green—but I got used to it." A system of trenches had also been dug on the plateau and "there we would spend a whole day or a night to get some impression of what life in a trench was like."

Alec warned his mother that now he was on active service, his letters would be censored by his section officer. In many cases this was not an arduous task since most soldiers "had no clue on the subject of letter writing, and the average letter read, 'Dear Mother, I am glad to say I am all right and the grub is good. Your loving son, George.'" But "you have to be careful not to say anything of importance. I don't know how much of this letter the censor will pass but anyway I am still alive and want to hear from you. P.S. I have not said all I can. All I've done is to say what I think I am allowed to." The censor evidently agreed with Alec's judgement because the letter was passed without alteration. Once every two or three weeks, troops were also issued with a "green envelope" (actually a white envelope with instructions printed on it in green ink). Letters sealed in these were not read by the censor and troops were honour bound to use these only for personal messages and not to include "any censorable material."

On 6 March Alec was still at the camp and, despite "snow on the ground," he pronounced himself "like Johnny Walker, going strong. The food is not so bad as I thought it would be; we get tea and bread for breakfast instead of biscuits as it was when I first got here, meat and a spud for dinner, for afters we get *good* cheese and biscuits (I am sure Dad would like that). On Sundays, as a special treat, they give us tinned butter and we always have tinned jam for breakfast and tea. The camp is the best I have ever been in. It is two miles long and is full of YMCAs, SAs, Army canteens and cinemas! You get quite a good show for three shillings. The canteens supply anything from a bootlace to a wristwatch. They won't let us go into Havre, but that is Havre's loss. The place is in a filthy condition and considering they throw their refuse in the roads, I don't see how it could be otherwise. From what I've seen, I judge that they haven't got the water laid on in each house, although Havre is a big place, but they have pumps out at intervals in every street, even the main ones.

"We are kept very clean here. Every Monday we have a medical inspection and a *hot* bath and we are given time off to wash any dirty clothes we may have." Alec's first effort at laundry was not a success; as with most of his comrades, his mother had traditionally done all the housework. "I washed my dirty stuff and the shirt, which I left till last, was a tragedy when dry. I had merely washed it in places, and the dirty patches showed up very much. Still, I shall no doubt improve with practice. When you send a parcel, please put in an air cushion and some 'tabloid stuff' such as Horlicks, cocoa cubes but no Bovril or Oxo. Also don't put fags in as we get two ounces of tobacco and twenty fags given to us each week, and as I can buy fifty Wills for a shilling in the canteen. This is the longest letter I have written in my life, but even the longest must have an end. Love to all, your loving son, Alec. PS Please put some decent chocolate in the parcel such as Peter's Chocolate for *MEN*."

On 11 March, still at Le Havre, Alec was finding it "increasingly difficult to live on five francs a week with all these YMCAs and cinemas about, so please send what Arthur [his younger brother] calls 'filthy lucre' along. You needn't worry about Dad being called up, as from signs out here [the massive build-up of troops, guns and munitions in preparation for the Battle of the Somme], it is evident that the war will be over by the autumn. I am on a big funeral [burial] party this afternoon and it will be the first real evidence I shall have seen of the war. I expect to go up to the line any day."

The following day they were marched the few miles back into Le Havre and along the wharves over railway lines sunk flush with the stone surface. They "entrained in what seemed like a goods yard," "cast away in a quarter such as goods yards inhabit." The officers spent "hours in the train but in a first class carriage. The men were in trucks, poor boys," loaded into railway wagons, labelled as suitable for "Chevaux (en long) 8" or "Hommes 37–40" for a 180-mile journey that was to take them twenty-one hours, from 10 a.m. until 7 a.m. the following morning. "From far ahead, a crescendo clanging of couplings came back till it jerked your truck into motion. Hour after hour that train would bump and rumble along, with pauses and checks without number. It swerved into grassy sidings where boughs brushed its sides, and waited there so long that it seemed to have retired wholly from the world." The men slept "packed like sardines on the floor of the van" and were "accordingly rather cramped." For food they had only "bully beef and dog biscuits" (hard tack).

At the end of that marathon journey, followed by another few miles of marching from the railhead over roads "inches deep in mud, there is an advantage to this, your feet get less blistered," they were deployed in the front lines for the first time, "cheered on our way by ironical shouts of 'You're going the wrong way, chums!' from other troops watching us—as if we didn't know." Like most raw soldiers, Alec and his battalion were being "blooded" in a comparatively quiet sector, but the unfamiliar sights, sounds and smells of the trenches and the fear that all felt at being under fire for the first time made it a daunting, long-remembered experience for all. They entered the lines under cover of darkness, with a thick mist lying over the ground. "The stench of the front line assailed you miles before you could see it"—a noxious compound of excrement, urine, smoke, cordite, the chloride of lime and creosol used as crude disinfectants and, dominating all other smells, the stink of putrefaction.

A "trench-guide" was detailed to lead them through the network of zigzagging communication trenches leading to the support and firing lines. They groped their way forward, mud sucking at their boots, their feet stumbling and slipping on objects that might have been tree roots, spent shrapnel or half-buried bones. From time to time the darkness was torn apart by the explosion of a star-shell or flare. By its light they could glimpse crumbling sandbags on the parapet, and the scars of fresh shell damage, and every now and then the trench wall was "splashed with blood." The light of the star-shells diffused by the mist caused "a weird, pale-green glow all around. The machine-guns too, as is always the case in fog, are pretty busy.

"The Colonel appears up the dugout steps and wishes us good luck, saying that perhaps we mightn't find things as bad as we expected. In any case, we are fortunate to arrive when things are comparatively quiet. The Boche must have overheard this last remark as a 'big one' burst over the parapet not many yards away. I certainly am now feeling a bit weak at the knees. If this is a sample of 'quietness,' what is it going to be like when they get busy? Another terrific crash, but this time it is only one of our field batteries letting off behind us. Our dugout is in complete darkness but we grope our way down the steps and on arriving at the bottom, strike a match and light a solitary candle . . . Our new home from home requires very little description as there is nothing but four earth walls, into one of which is dug a recess, one earth floor, and an earth roof, supported by two wooden props. Pieces of stick are hammered into the walls supporting the belongings of the absent occupants . . . There are occasional dull thuds overhead and the candle flickers for a moment and revives." The feeble glow of candlelight could be unimaginably cheering to a man coming off sentry duty on the fire-step of the trench. "To feel the kind of warmth that came out as you pulled the gas curtain apart, and to see a candle burning, felt like home," but the air at the back of a dugout was often so foul that candles guttered and went out.

Like all fresh arrivals, Alec's battalion were put on immediate sentry duty, "to accustom them to the surroundings and presumably to get them used to being under fire." As a rule, new arrivals in the front lines suffered a disproportionate number of casualties. They "would herd together like sheep when under fire," and lacked the knowledge and survival instincts of the more seasoned soldier, who could "distinguish among the hubbub the one sound that endangers him, and the first whisper that heralds a shell gives him its whole trajectory." The rookies' familiarization process would also inevitably include their first encounters with the dead and wounded, and the horrific sights that would soon seem commonplace, like the "pair of boots, still containing someone's feet," that another soldier encountered in a pit used for filling sandbags.

While he was in the front line, Alec's horizons were confined to the dimensions of the trench and the long, narrow rectangle of sky directly overhead. To raise his head, even for a split second, was to invite death by a bullet from one of the ever-watchful snipers armed with rifles with telescopic sights. The parapet was "watched all day, from end to end, by eyes which hardly blink. The slightest movement on it—the mere adjusting of a sandbag from below—is met with fire." One officer of the West Yorkshire Regiment risked raising his head for a moment and was hit simultaneously by shots from two different enemy snipers. The only relatively safe view of the enemy lines was through a periscope—obtainable from the "Trench Requisites" departments of the larger London stores—or through a slit in a steel shield, and even these were hit by shrapnel or targeted by snipers, who were often accurate enough to put a shot through the loophole.

An English officer described how one morning he had "stood beside Sniper McDonald, and watched the enemy lines through my periscope. Suddenly, opposite us, a box periscope went up and, after a survey of our lines, was taken down and put up again further along. I told Mac to put it out of action next time. But instead of the periscope, a staff officer put his head up and looked around. I heard the ping of the sniper's rifle and saw Herr Von throw up his hands and fall back into his trench. Immediately another officer sprang up and shook his fist. Another ping and that was two he bagged that morning."

Alec would now have to get used to the strange, almost eerie fact that, though the enemy might be only fifty or a hundred yards away, they remained invisible. The only evidence that they were there at all was the crack of rifles and the whine of bullets zipping overhead and, apart from an occasional glimpse of a grey-clad figure diving past a gap in the enemy parapet, virtually the only time they would ever lay eyes on a German was during a raid or an attack. An officer of the 4th Oxfordshire and Bucks Light Infantry who arrived at the Front in May 1915 did not see his first enemy until 3 August. To the Germans, their khaki-clad enemy was "a brownish-yellow fleeting shadow" and the faint traces he left were "puzzled over as though they were the runes of a secret book or the spoor of some mighty and unknown beast."

Over the following days, Alec and his mates familiarized themselves with trench routine and an existence "like that of slum life" that was "the jealously close, exclusive contriving life of a family housed in an urban cellar." For an hour around dusk and dawn, the most likely times for an attack because mist or haze would often give some cover, everyone was on "stand-to," poised on the trench floor or the fire-step, ready to repel any attack. They remained on alert until it was full day or full night, when the order "stand down" was given. No one slept by night. Troop reliefs were made then, patrols and raids on the enemy mounted, casualties retrieved from no-man's-land, shell damage repaired, trenches and barbed-wire entanglements reinforced and saps and tunnels constructed. Soldiers also went back to the reserve areas and brought up ammunition, flares, barbed wire, sandbags, duck-boards, corrugated iron, tarpaulins, post, rations and water, carried in old petrol cans. It was "usually undrinkable except as a last resort, through the cans not being washed properly," and "if you'd been there long enough, you could actually tell by the taste of the water whether it was in a Shell or BP tin."

Drinking water had to be brought up from the rear because of the risk of contamination of groundwater and springs near the front lines "through so many dead being buried about," though some were prepared to take their chances. "One day the water did not arrive. An officer's servant came to me and asked if he could get some to make the officer's tea. The only water, I told him, was that gathered in a waterproof sheet which was stretched above our heads in the dugout to keep us dry. It was the colour of stout, and I was not very sure whether there were any dead Germans buried above us or not.

" 'Never mind; it will do fine. The officers will never know, as I will put plenty of tinned milk and sugar in it,' and off he went with his kettle filled.

"The following night he brought me a small mug of hot tea which I enjoyed very much, but suddenly I remembered the water had not arrived, and asked where he got it. 'Oh! just out of your sheet.' I flung the mug at his head and chased him along the trench."

After the dawn stand-to, troops would grab what sleep they could, but sentry duty—two hours on, four hours off—meant that no one had an uninterrupted rest. Around midday, hot rations—perhaps stew or rice and sultanas—would be brought round, carried in a sort of metal backpack the size of a milk churn. "A second man would bring rolls of currant duff [suet pudding]. These needed scraping from the hairs of the sacking in which they were carried."

In his next letter home, Alec attempted to reassure his worried mother about his safety. "It sounds silly I know, but it is a fact that out here I am as safe as you are at home. You couldn't have a safer place than a trench, provided you keep your head down. And it is a fact that more casualties occur whilst 'resting' than fighting. You underestimate my capabilities when you say I can't smoke a pipe; why there is nothing I am unable to do now, even work." Many men in the trenches smoked pipes because "you could cup your hand over the top and turn it upside down so the enemy couldn't see any light." "Of course," Alec added, "I don't mean to infer that I enjoy a pipe, but waste not, want not, has always been my motto, as you no doubt remember from the way I used to spread the butter and jam?"

He was already suffering from one of the banes of the trenches—lice. When resting out of the front lines, "much of the time was occupied by rifle inspections, feet inspections, scraping the mud and slime of the trenches from our clothing . . . a great part of the time, too, was spent in combating the ever-present tiny vermin. I never thought a man would be driven to such a state of frenzy by a louse." No bigger than a grain of rice even when fully grown, the lice fed up to a dozen times a day and the itch from their bites drove men demented. In any spare moment men could be seen scratching furiously, cracking lice between their nails, or trying to eliminate them by running a lighted match, a cigarette or the point of a bayonet along the seams of their clothing. In frosty weather some even tried to freeze them to death, putting their shirts out in the frost and then warming them by sitting on them before putting them back on, but, whatever the attempted remedy, the eggs would always survive and hatch and the lice returned almost at once. The Army's attempts to control them through "delousing units"—showers for the men when they were out of the trenches and the issue of clean clothing while their lice-infested uniforms were steam-cleaned or fumigated—proved no more successful. The words "lousy" and "crummy"—because lice looked like breadcrumbs—originally meant "louse-infested," but soon became, and have remained, slang words for anything bad or unpleasant.

Having explained the problem, Alec then added a rider to his letter: "Please don't send any Keatings [insect powder], as the following happened to a friend of mine. He had some trench powder sent out and sprinkled it all over him but omitted to put any on his neck. The consequence was that the livestock crawled up his body and collected on his neck and the poor fellow was in agony all night. Besides, when full grown they are a quarter of an inch long and so are easily caught."

On 13 March, his unit began a move to another part of the Front, the Carency and Souchez sectors near Arras, a modest train journey that took three days to complete. The creaking French railway system, with hundreds of miles of single-track lines and passing places, was unable to cope with the monstrous volume of men and matériel being carried to the Front. In addition to the daily supplies needed to keep hundreds of thousands of soldiers fed and watered, there were endless goods trains laden with guns, shells, ammunition, gas cylinders and all the other barbarous paraphernalia of industrialized warfare. All of these jostled for position with troop trains heading for the front lines and those bringing away the streams of casualties, for even in quiet sectors between major offensives a constant trickle of men were shot by snipers, hit by shrapnel or succumbed to disease.

After reaching the railhead, Alec and his comrades had a gruelling march, carrying all their equipment. "The stuff I carried weighed exactly 101 pounds and when I got off the train I had a ten mile march to get here. Fifty men had to fall out; it was too much for them." His battalion spent the night in farm buildings around the village. "This is the second time I have been billeted in barns but the first time it was spelt with a B [Barnes in southwest London]." The straw they slept on was often lice-ridden "and when this got too bad, the men would prefer to clear all the straw out and sleep on the bare earth." He shared his "billet" with "twenty-eight others. To reach it you have to climb up a rickety ladder with four rungs missing. There are several holes in the roof, one of which I am under." The latrine arrangements were "pretty primitive . . . The army set aside an area of a grass field at the edge of the village where the pioneer or sanitary men dug a dozen little trenches, three feet long by one foot wide and about three feet deep, and here, without any canvas or sacking or anything to hide the view, one dropped one's trousers, bestrode a trench, crouched and attended to nature. But, note, it was to the full view of the children of the village who stood around and conversed with us."

Alec found the village (probably Fresnescourt) "so-so; last night I went in a shop to buy a notebook and it took me a quarter of an hour to make the lady understand what I wanted. The French here are chronic. They treble the price of everything for us, and so I am glad of the ten shillings." On 25 March he was "still alive and kicking, though several of the draft have gone into hospital at various times with the flu, owing to the chronic weather we are having. It has snowed for two days here and as I have to stand perfectly still for an hour each morning while we are minutely inspected, you can guess at the state of my feet.

"It is a peculiar thing, but the nearer you get to the firing line, the more particular they are about cleanliness. In this place if you go on parade with a speck of mud on you, you are severely punished; I am now learning the meaning of discipline . . . I have to attend an instruction school here; a facetious person says that the instructors here have to go through a special course of voice production, but at any rate, if you have an eyelid off parade, one of them, in a voice like thunder, will ask you if 'you think you are still in the boy scouts?' or something to that effect. Their language is descriptive and sometimes it is lurid. We work all day every day here (no half day off on Sat) but as when I am not working I start thinking of home, which is the worst thing to do out here, I am glad to have my mind kept occupied. I shall be leaving here in a day or two for the place where the dirty work is done, but don't worry."

That place was a rural area of rolling hills and broad, wooded valleys stretching from the heights of the Lorette Ridge, across the Carency valley to the western slopes of the northern end of Vimy Ridge. The troops that they were relieving had maintained a precarious hold on the slopes of the ridge using a series of forward positions like the shooting butts on a grouse moor, but the Germans held "the Pimple"—the high point at the northern tip of the ridge. This overlooked both the British trenches and the rear areas in the Zouave Valley "along which the Boche could put down an almost impassable barrage."

The reserve units were billeted in the villages of Camblain l'Abbé, Villers-au-Bois, Estrée-Cauchie (known as Extra Cushy to the troops) and in barns and huts scattered through the woods of La Haie and Bouvigny. On 31 March, Alec's battalion moved up there, passing "a vividly painted crucifix, covered by a thatched roof, which is quite undamaged and so upholds the tradition that there is some special dispensation of providence which looks after such things. Probably the real reason in this case, however, is that it is built into a little hollow in a high bank and so is protected from direct fire."

On arrival in the reserve areas, Alec's battalion was "on a rest and will not go in the trenches for a day or two yet. Tonight I am on a working party and we are going in front of our trenches to erect barbed wire entanglements. We are in a fairly quiet part of the line so we shall be all right and will let you know what I think of it tomorrow." He was distinctly unimpressed, as he revealed in a letter to his mother the next morning. "[April] Fool's Day 11 a.m. Last night's affair was a wash-out. We were taken up the line in lorries and dumped in a ruined village. There we drew picks and shovels and marched up to reserve trenches for digging. We started out at 7 p.m. and got back at 3 a.m. Reveille at 7:30 a.m. this morning. The soil last night was awful. It was composed of sticky clay and flints and the only way to get it up was to pick it and then take it in your hands and throw it over the parapet. A spade was useless as the earth stuck to it and would not budge. Several large shells burst on our left and machine guns were very active at first, but towards midnight, things quietened down and it seemed as if hostilities had ceased for the night. Night lights are unceasing. They resemble Brocks' display of skyrockets and they give a brilliant white light which shows up everything for a square mile."

On 5 April Alec was "back at Fresnescourt for six days rest. Souchez is rather a hot part, but I understand the division is leaving this sector for Arras which is much quieter. Can't stop for more as a chap going on leave is taking this and he is just off." Alec's letter thereby escaped the censor, who would certainly have deleted the entire contents. Souchez was indeed "rather hot." As another soldier noted, the ground around the Bois de Souchez was "poisoned with human relics, limbs and bundles of clothes filled with rotted flesh, and even those poor remains of men which pious hands have buried are daily disinterred by plunging shells. Souchez itself is merely a heap of bricks and stones and it reeks to heaven of mortality." And if Arras was "much quieter" in the spring of 1916, it was not to remain so for long.

3

THE SUICIDE SQUAD

Alec Reader's platoon had a brief reprieve from the firing lines after measles broke out among them on 6 April 1916 and they were moved to an isolation camp, "so we look like having a soft time for a fortnight or so," though that still included "7 p.m. to 2 or 3 a.m. working party, next morning reveille at 6 a.m. and so on." The working party was a testing experience. "We marched up to a trench about thirty yards behind the front line and started deepening it. As there was heavy fighting in this part of the line last autumn, we kept digging up tunics, trousers, bones, etc. In fact it was quite a ghastly job. We had no sooner started than a battery opened fire only one hundred yards behind (they make the earth shake) and kept it up for two hours. After the first half hour the Germans tried to find it. The first shells burst a quarter of a mile away and then they gradually got nearer, until they burst not twenty yards in front. Then it got exciting. Every time we heard a whizz, down we had to go among the aforementioned tunics, etc, in order to dodge the splinters. This state of affairs lasted about three quarters of an hour—though it seemed a lot longer—and then our battery had to give up and clear out.

"Soon after this it started raining and after working for two hours in the downpour, we came back soaked to the skin, covered with slush, faces and all (for of course when shells burst near you, you get down as low as poss, in fact at first I was so nervy that I buried my face in that mud and I was not the only one, either). Got back from the working party at 2 a.m., whacked to the wide, and received yours and Arthur's letters. I was in the right mood to be told that I am homesick, I can assure you. After reading your letters I had so much cleaning up to do for today's parade that I didn't trouble to go to bed. The enclosed souvenir [probably a tunic button] I picked up in the trench. Just a little memento of my first exciting night in the line." Souvenirs were eagerly sought by men on both sides and corpses were soon stripped. Boots were ripped from dead men's feet, "the whites of their pockets turned out, their tunics and shirts undone. Revolvers were the best prizes, but money, watches, rings and the crosses of Catholics were also in demand . . . Front line soldiers were quickest in pursuit of loot; artillery and labour troops were slower and more methodical." Another soldier recounted his distaste at seeing a fellow soldier steal the boots from a dead German. "We thought that was terrible until one of the cooks took a chisel and a pair of pliers and knocked out his gold teeth for souvenirs."

Alec was now "camped in a wood [Bouvigny, below the Lorette Spur] that is under observation, so we have to stay under cover all day." No movement was allowed at all during the hours of daylight, pleasing the men, who could relax, undisturbed by patrolling officers and NCOs. "Shells come fairly close as there are two or three of our batteries nearby and the Germans keep trying to find them, but so far no shells have landed in the wood. This morning I had my first wash for four days, as when I was with the Battalion, the water was very scarce— one water bottle full a day. I have not had a bath for over three weeks now and as I shan't get one for another three weeks, I shall soon be dirty. On every possible occasion I have a strafe, which consists of searching my underclothes for livestock. I usually reap a harvest of from twenty to thirty."

Arthur Reader hero-worshipped his older brother, and had written Alec a star-struck letter urging him to great heights of bravery. He replied on 8 April. "You ask me to get the VC [Victoria Cross], well, let me tell you a secret. The only men out here who get distinction are those who lose their heads or have too many rum rations. The sensible ones get down into the bottom of the trench when things get a bit hot and they are the men who 'live to fight another day.' " Another soldier admitted, "No one wants to go back, not even *Daily Mail* heroes, really, not to the front line, if they've sampled it properly," and one assured his wife that he would "risk the Zeps [Zeppelin bombers over London] if we could only return."

Alec did not disappoint his brother entirely, giving him at least some tales with which to impress his schoolfriends. "Of course we all have to do dangerous work. I had to carry boxes of live bombs up the firing line with shrapnel shrapping all around. One of my pals stopped a bit with his leg and is now in England, I should think. Must pack up now as I haven't had any sleep for 24 hours and consequently feel a bit tired." He also wrote a rare letter to his father, heading it from "'The Promised Land.' The sun shines, the aeroplanes buzz, the guns bark and my unique collection of livestock bite; in fact, everything in the garden is lovely. Work (with a capital W) is the great thing out here and you are not allowed to forget it. After six hours work in a trench, one's feelings give the lie to that well known recruiting poster, 'He's happy and satisfied, are you?' Shellholes abound and coming back from a 'night out,' the language they cause is, to say the least, unparliamentary. 6 p.m. parade for working party, 3 a.m. return from same, 4 a.m. to 6 a.m. *SLEEP* (in spite of the fact that the guns were strafing like Old Nick)."

As well as lice, fleas, mud, shell-fire and shrapnel, Alec had also now encountered another bane of the trenches: rats. "Got a very nice parcel from Aunt Rachel yesterday, containing cold cross buns and bon cake. I ate the buns and was going to save the cake for today, but when I woke up this morning all I found was the paper, which the rats had been unable to eat." Rats were omnipresent—"like the poor they were always with us and we learned to take them for granted"—burrowing into the earth like their human neighbours, breeding in huge numbers, scavenging for food among the dugouts and trenches, spreading diseases like typhus, trench fever—caused by parasites in their droppings—and Weil's disease, and feasting on the casualties of war. "A sentry on guard at one part of our line could always see the prostrate skeletons of many enemy dead. They lay outside our wire, picked clean by the rats, so that the khaki fell in on them loosely—little heaps of bone and cloth half hidden now by nettles and grass."

The rats—both brown and black rats were present, though the

former were more common—showed little fear of humans, and in cold weather were sometimes even found clustered around sleeping men for warmth; "Having attached themselves to us for rations, [they] considered that billets might as well be included." "I was soundly asleep in my dugout with some outsize and friendly rats for close company—in fact close enough to keep me warm, if not too cosy." But in the hungry winter weather, when food was scarce and the seasonal lull in the fighting reduced the supply of fresh corpses, rats also attacked sleeping men. One sleeping corporal's nose was bitten by a rat, which clung on despite his shrieks until dispatched by a bayonet. Rats would also "eat through anything made of leather—they'd go for your shoelaces if you stood still long enough." In the fighting season when no-man's-land was daily littered with a new crop of dead and many more were buried in shallow graves just behind the lines, the rats grew fat and sleek on their diet of carrion, becoming so huge that "they would eat a wounded man if he couldn't defend himself." Some were so sated with their diet of human flesh that they spurned all but the most prized morsels; according to one soldier "they favoured the eyeballs and the liver of the dead."

They were hated and hunted relentlessly with guns, bayonets, shovels and pickaxe handles—soldiers often displayed their "bag" of rats in a row on the parapet of the trenches—but cats proved less successful. "We borrowed a large cat and shut it up at night to exterminate them, and found the place empty the next morning. The rats must have eaten it up, bones, fur and all, and dragged it to their holes." Even though soldiers displayed ever greater ingenuity in killing, capturing or evicting the rats, any success was purely temporary. "The front and back of the trenches were pitted with rat holes. Many times the boys would fill up a lot of the holes, leaving a couple open, and light pieces of sandbag, and when it smouldered, push it in the holes and we would wait at the uncovered holes and as the rats ran out, we would slice them with our bayonets, but it didn't do any good." "The old saying that 'Familiarity breeds contempt' never was more perfectly exemplified; they certainly were familiar, they bred—and how—and their insufferable contempt goaded us to measures that resulted in their discomfort and eviction. We put a dose of calcium carbide in one rat-hole, a little water to generate the gas, and then turf to keep the gas where it would do the most good. The next hole, a little petrol and turf, and so on until all the holes had been treated. One or two petrol holes were left open at strategic points and then fired. The resulting explosions of petrol vapour and gas seldom failed to clear the house and as the panic-stricken occupants hopped out, an enthusiastic reception committee of Gunners and dogs met them. Bon!" Others carried out "a great rat hunt" using the powder from captured shells and cartridges. "We shake the powder from the cartridges into their holes and light it. Rats as large and fat as guinea pigs pour out and are either shot with revolvers or killed with sticks."

Alec found the rats less troublesome than the endless working parties. "Digging trenches and repairing them is practically all we do. In fact, my answer to the question 'What did you do in the Great War Daddy?' will be 'Dug up half of France, sonny.'" For the ordinary soldier, war was often "the continuation of labouring by other means. The battlefield was a vast open-air factory where hours were long, unions not permitted and safety conditions routinely flouted." It was only later in the war that commanders began to realize that making men carry out gruelling fatigues every night on top of their military duties was counter-productive, leaving them sometimes too exhausted to fight or even mount guard adequately. In November 1915 the British High Command had addressed this problem in typically bone-headed fashion, by decreeing that in future the word "fatigue" was to be replaced by "working party." Having altered the nomenclature, they eventually took steps during the succeeding two years to lift part of the burden from the fighting troops by establishing construction units, many of them using Chinese coolies, to do at least some of the heavy work of trench-digging, road construction and repairing shell and bomb damage.

Alec had added a PS to his letter: "Keep your eyes open for news of the charge of the CSR [Civil Service Rifles], which is coming off shortly," and on 10 April they duly went into the front lines on the northern spur of Vimy Ridge. The entry to the communication trench leading to the Front was well disguised. "Passing through the remains of a cottage, down a flagged passage and through a stone archway, we find ourselves in the beginning of the trench, which proceeds to cut its way through the local graveyard. The church bell has toppled from the ruined spire and lies amongst a mass of fallen tombstones. A cheery start, indeed, to our journey. Owing to the nature of the country here, the communication trench is incredibly long, two and a half miles to be exact, and in daylight it is compulsory to keep to the trench all the way. The Germans, who are occupying Vimy Ridge in front of us, overlook our ground for miles, so it is difficult to keep proper cover." "We made our way in the darkness—you may not even use a flashlight as the ground is under observation from the Boche."

The communication trench was also "uneven and full of holes, taking a perspiring half hour trudge." The front lines were "close together, heavily guarded by thick belts of barbed wire" rusted to autumnal reds and browns, and, although the sector had been relatively quiet above ground, tunnelling companies from both sides were "working feverishly in the chalk subsoil to get into a position from which they could blow their opponents sky-high." Using nothing more than picks and shovels, short, wiry, hard-muscled men from the English and Welsh coalfields and the collieries of the Ruhr drove mines and countermines, hewing narrow, stifling tunnels through the solid rock. Close to the enemy lines, they cut lateral galleries from which a series of shorter tunnels were driven forward, each ending in a chamber packed with tons of explosives deep beneath the enemy trenches. When these were detected in time, a counter-mine would be driven and a "camouflet"—a small defensive charge—set to destroy the tunnel and kill the miners working in it, but others were missed or found too late and the mines were detonated to often devastating effect.

Above ground, there was a steady stream of fatalities. "Out in the tall grasses and weeds of the derelict cornfields, lay many dead beside the long rifles with the sharp-pointed bayonet. On quiet nights, parties of Riflemen would go out and bury those they could, bringing in letters and personal effects." "Little wooden crosses increased in number daily. Every man was buried where he fell, it was impossible to bear him away." In factories in the towns behind the lines, steam-saws ran day and night, turning out these wooden crosses. They were stacked in huge heaps in the yards outside the buildings, ready for the victims of the next offensive—a chilling sight for soldiers on their way to the front lines. "I watched the men as they passed by. Some smiled, others passed a joke, some wouldn't look. But I knew that they all saw and understood." Even more chilling to troops marching to the Front was the sight of the mass graves dug before the great battles of 1916 and 1917 had even begun.

Many of the men of Alec Reader's division killed in the front lines were buried by David Railton, "a good padre who was often seen in the trenches." Born at Leytonstone, in northeast London, in 1884, Railton was one of two sons of George Railton, the "first lieutenant" to Salvation Army founder General William Booth, and largely responsible for the "military metaphors and 'war songs' " adopted by the organization. His sons inherited a taste for militant Christianity but, to their father's intense disappointment, both became priests in the Church of England, not "soldiers" in the Salvation Army, though David was always "disturbingly conscious of the great gap that existed between the established churches and the great mass of people," and to experience real poverty for himself he even spent three months "disguised as a tramp," living from hand to mouth and sleeping in doss-houses.

Like his brother, Nathaniel, David Railton took an MA at Keble College, Oxford, in 1911, and after being ordained as a priest he became Territorial Chaplain to the Forces. When war broke out, he served as a padre with the 27th Northumberland Fusiliers—the Tyneside Irish—before transferring to Alec Reader's division, the 47th (London). Most chaplains had initially been content to minister to the troops in the reserve areas, and leave those in the firing line to their own devices. "There is only one Front here and few chaplains ever get there, and then not during engagements." It was an attitude that earned them only the contempt of the soldiers they were supposed to be serving. As one acerbic speaker to the TUC conference in 1916 enquired, "Why should these men who are so fond of talking about heaven be so afraid to go through its gates?" Particular vitriol was reserved for those who "declaimed with an almost Mohammedan fervour upon the bliss awaiting the dying warrior." Bishop Winnington-Ingram, the bellicose "Bishop of the Battlefields," had already issued a call to "jihad," urging his fellows to "MOBILISE THE NATION FOR A HOLY WAR," and was the leading voice among those who "prayed for victory and thundered from the pulpits for the enemy to be smitten hip and thigh, but did not believe in doing any of the smiting themselves."

The church made some effort to respond to such criticisms. Increasing numbers of clergy back in Britain volunteered for war work—some 4,000 found employment as mechanics, postmen, special constables, miners, stokers on merchant ships and munitions workers, and one even worked as a research chemist in a poison gas factory. As George Bernard Shaw remarked with withering scorn, "They have turned their churches into recruiting stations and their vestries into munitions workshops. But it has never occurred to them to take off their black coats and say quite simply, 'I find in the hour of trial that the Sermon on the Mount is tosh, and that I am not a Christian. I apologise for all the unpatriotic nonsense I have been preaching all the years. Have the goodness to give me a revolver and a commission in a regiment.' "

David Railton was one of the few chaplains willing from the start to serve alongside the fighting soldiers in the front lines and tend the wounded in battle. As one soldier remarked of another front-line chaplain, "It made us think a bit more of parsons to see how he walked quietly under fire, assisting the slow-moving wounded." A willingness to share some of the dangers faced by the men in the trenches even led the Reverend Robert Maurice Peel to go "over the top" with his battalion, though he was over fifty years of age and his pacifist principles meant that he was armed with nothing more warlike than a walking stick. He was roundly criticized for what many saw as a foolish, vainglorious gesture—"What on earth could a padre do in a fight? He was bound to be hit and there were certain to be quite enough casualties without having a wounded padre to attend to," but the criticisms "did not alter his determination to do what he felt to be his duty."

In July 1915 Peel duly went over the top at Festubert, walking stick in hand. Inevitably he was hit, wounded badly enough to be "a stretcher case." Undeterred, he returned to the Front as soon as his wounds had healed and was killed in 1917, "in the very forefront of some of the hardest fighting of the war . . . Those who argue that Peel threw away his life must by the same logic say that Jesus squandered his." Another chaplain, the forty-four-year-old Robert Callaway, went one further, resigning as a chaplain and then re-enlisting as a combatant. He was killed on the Somme in September 1916.

David Railton did not take his devotion to his men to quite those extremes, but he served in the front lines without complaint and was awarded a Military Cross for his own bravery in going to the aid of the wounded under heavy enemy fire. Even in the relative lulls between major battles, he had been forced to dispense with much of the traditional funeral service. "Yesterday I took my first burial . . . We buried the brave lad's remains just behind the trench. While they were preparing, I collected a few little blue flowers. A major came and sent off all the men except four as he said it would 'draw fire.' We had the burial service shortened. No Last Post! . . . No officers were there and just the four men joined in the prayer . . . I just dropped the flowers on to him and went back along the trench."

Chaplains were instructed to "bury for choice between 7 and 9 a.m., 'in the mist,' and if shelling took place, to take the men in, and not to look like a working party," to avoid increasing the chances of being shelled. There were also "many on both sides who took a malicious pleasure in sniping at burial parties." One chaplain recounted how he and his burial party, usually a corporal and two or four other men, moved "two by two and each file twenty-five yards from the next. As soon as I found a body (some in the older, disused trenches were terribly decomposed and had been out for months by all appearances), I dragged it, with the corporal, into the nearest new, or recent shell-hole." The body was searched and all personal belongings put into a small canvas bag and the name, Army number and unit—if known—were written in indelible ink on the bag. "(I stuffed my pockets with these canvas bags before sallying out), and then said the Committal words of the Prayer Book Burial Service and these additional words for the benefit of the corporal and for my own or anyone who might be present: 'Lord, we thank Thee for the example of this brave man who gave his life for his country. Grant him eternal rest and so teach us to number our days that we may apply our hearts unto wisdom, Amen.'

"Then I and the corporal each placed twelve spadesful of earth (only it was always mud up there) on the body, and beckoning to the next two men, who would be hidden in a shell-hole twenty-five yards away, went on to the next body. The two men behind shovelled twenty-four spadesful between them and so we went on." The place was marked on the map and correct map references made afterwards in reserve. "The manner of marking such graves is either to place the man's tin hat on a reversed rifle or to put a rifle alone in the ground—there are always heaps of rifles about—or to put his name on a piece of paper in an empty bottle, neck down and corked with something. Sometimes a rough cross can be made, if there is time or opportunity, either from the various pieces of revetting timber or of iron tied together with telegraph wire. It is surprising what a lot of odd pieces of iron and telegraph wire there are about on a battlefield. Later, when the area is quiet, the GRU [Graves Registration Unit] will come and put up their little official crosses with the man's name, number, unit and date of death, or date of burial if the latter was not ascertainable, on a strip of zinc stamped with capital letters, just as you stamp your name in the penny-in-the-slot machines at home."

David Railton had buried many men since his first one, "as reverently as we can here. Indeed it is wonderful to me, to stand there with a group of soldiers at such a time; the picks and shovels are put aside, we all stand quietly by and I lead the service. The Very lights go up now and again, lighting up our faces, and the guns keep up their usual squabbling with each other." At other times, fierce fighting meant that, if at all, men were buried where they fell and chaplains had to read the burial service crouching or lying flat on their stomachs. Every attempt was made to have a burial conducted by a chaplain of the same faith as the dead man, but often the dead were unidentifiable and sometimes mistakes were made. Railton and most of his peers took a pragmatic view of such incidents. "Bennett the RC was buried by one of our chaplains in mistake—but I don't suppose the Great Redeemer cares which chaplain buries a man as long as it is done reverently."

At 3:30 in the morning of Easter Sunday, 26 April 1916, David Railton was returning from yet another burial duty when the Germans detonated a huge mine. Alec Reader witnessed it at even closer range, for he was on sentry duty in his front-line trench on the northern spur of Vimy Ridge when it exploded "300 yards on our right. We were in a barricade about five foot high and the only shelter we had was a sheet of corrugated iron (some trench). When the mine went up it threw us all over and nearly shook the parapet down."

The detonation of the mine was followed by "a violent bombardment such as I have never heard or seen." Bizarrely, in the midst of this inferno of noise, the dawn chorus began. "All of us noticed at 3:30 a.m., how beautifully the birds were singing. They kept it up during the whole of the bombardment." The front line was broken and there were over one hundred casualties, including "one of our officers . . . buried alive and several men," but the still-smoking crater, promptly christened New Cut Crater, was immediately reoccupied and work began at once on fortifying the far lip.

As Alec noted, the Germans "sent over a lot of rifle grenades, trench mortars, 'minnies,' etc, just to celebrate the occasion." The "minnie"—*Minenwerfer*, literally a "mine-thrower"—was a "murderous instrument. They hurl huge shells about a thousand feet into the air and they fall almost vertically," blasting a crater as much as thirty feet across. Almost as fearsome was the improvised canister—a two-gallon drum with a cylinder containing "an explosive called ammonal that looked like salmon paste, smelled like marzipan and, when it went off, sounded like the Day of Judgement."

The explosive was surrounded by scrap metal, "apparently collected by French villagers behind the German lines: rusty nails, fragments of British and French shells, spent bullets, and the screws, nuts and bolts that heavy lorries leave behind on the road. We dissected one unexploded canister and found in it, among other things, the cogwheels of a clock and half a set of false teeth." Fired from a huge mortar like a medieval siege gun, "the canister could easily be heard approaching and looked harmless in the air, but its shock was as shattering as the very heaviest shell. It would blow in any but the very deepest dugout and the false teeth, rusty nails, cog-wheels, and so on went flying in all directions," causing horrific shrapnel wounds.

The German shelling lasted for an hour, as Alec wrote in his next letter. "The old chaps say that it was the worst bombardment they had ever been in. As I was on sentry during the strafe, of course I had to stand upright. Afterwards I was told that I had stood it very well. One of the chaps, about twenty-five years old, who came out on our draft, lost his nerve and lay in the mud groaning and crying the whole time. All in all, quite an exciting time." Strangely, it was often the newest in the front lines who showed the least fear under a heavy bombardment. "When on leave, acquaintances ask the customary question: 'I suppose you take no notice of them [shells] now?' One nods assent, so as not to rob them of a pleasant thrill, and also because one knows that they are quite unable to imagine the feelings of a man under heavy fire. But one would hesitate to tell the same yarn to an old soldier, for he knows well enough that even the coolest-blooded are bowled over every time a shell bursts . . . It is the newcomer who shows a more resolute bearing . . . at first far less overwhelmed by the bursts than one might expect. It is only when experience has taught him that these things can tear tree-trunks to matchwood, fling stone walls into the air, or slice a brain-pan like a cabbage-stalk, that he learns caution."

Alec had another "rotten experience" on Vimy Ridge the following night. "We were carrying rations up the line when shells started bursting about five minutes walk in front of us. We knew that if they didn't stop by the time we got up there we should all be 'goners' and it needed all my will-power to keep on walking. I felt like dumping my load and running. Luckily they stopped when we were about 300 yards from them."

Three days later, British miners detonated a camouflet to blow another German mine a few hundred yards north of the first one, creating Broadridge Crater, but the Germans then retaliated by detonating yet another mine between the first two, causing over eighty British casualties, principally to men of the 6th Battalion. Once more the craters, up to one hundred yards in diameter, were immediately reoccupied by "Crater Jumping Parties"—for some time, a General Order required that any substantial crater within sixty yards of the front line had to be occupied at once and fortified to prevent a German follow-up attack. A fresh frenzy of tunnelling then ensued as miners in listening galleries—tunnels driven forward from the British lines—estimated that no fewer than eleven German mines were being prepared.

The 176th Tunnelling Company at once began counter-mining, driving its tunnels forward at prodigious speed over the night of 2–3 May, while shifts of soldiers from Alec's division ferried pit-props to the workings and hauled mountains of earth away. "All worked themselves dead beat." At 4:45 p.m. on 3 May, four mines were detonated beneath the German lines. The tunnel leading to one had been inadequately sealed and the explosion blew back down it, barely disturbing the ground above, but the other three caused carnage in the German trenches and carved out a further three huge craters. Once more they were speedily occupied by troops of the London Division.

Alec Reader's early optimism was now beginning to give way to the fatalism and cynicism that gripped most soldiers in the front lines, daily confronted with the senseless, arbitrary ways in which some were killed and some survived. They used "such expressions as 'You never hear the bullet meant for you, so what's the use trying to dodge it?,' 'If it has your name on it you'll be hit by it in any case,' 'If you're for it, chum, there's no dodging it.' " Incidents such as the one where a man just back from honeymoon in England was given the safest job, "well in rear of our forward positions, and became our only fatal casualty that day from a stray shell" seemed to support the fatalists' beliefs. Even chaplains found themselves sympathizing with, if not accepting such views. As one admitted, "the broad fact remained that on the whole it was the best, and not the worst, who were killed, and that wasn't fair, at least not according to any philosophy of life which we had hitherto thought worthy of adopting . . . The shallow philosophy of life which did meet with a great deal of nominal acceptance was fatalism. The reason for this was that it did seem to explain the facts, even if it made no attempt to justify them."

Alec had now "undergone the various emotions caused by war, have seen most things that happen in war and don't think much of it. I have seen mines (three) go up, have been knocked down by the explosion of an actual torpedo [*Minenwerfer* mortar] (they kill by concussion at twenty yards), have seen men killed and wounded and have had to carry a mortally wounded man to a dressing station on a stretcher. The poor chap was dying fast and knew it; it was awful. A mine went up under the battalion on our right and caused over a hundred casualties. What a rotten game." The letter must have provoked renewed alarm at home, for in his next he made haste to explain that "my last letter to you was written shortly after we came out of the line and of course I was feeling whacked, fed up, miserable, etc, which is only natural after six days of nervous tension. You don't want to take any notice of that sort of letter, as we all have our rotten moments."

The following night he was back up the line with a working party, but had "a very bon time. Aunt Rachel sent me a parcel, another chap had one, while a third came along with a bottle of 'OO' [spirits]. We went to the line in lorries and then had one and a half hour's march to the scene of our labours. Every five or ten minutes word would come up, 'Halt in front, man fallen in trench or shell-hole,' upon which we would halt and wait for him to be fished out and then carry on again. Our bottle had several narrow escapes. We got in the trench, did a little work and then adjourned for supper. We had no sooner finished supper than it began to rain. This was about ten o'clock. Our party sat down in the bottom of the trench, passed the bottle round and told yarns until 1:30 a.m. (still raining). The word came down to get ready to move, which was a fine bit of sarc[asm] on the officer's part, as we had been ready at 10:30.

"The journey back was a farce; we had to hang on to each other's coat-tails, it was too dark to see. When one chap went down, he pulled about a dozen with him. I saved myself by catching hold of someone's leg, but in doing so I pulled him down and when we had stopped rolling, he was sitting in eighteen inches of water and I was on top of him, so had a dry seat. The guide kept losing the path and once we found that the rear had lost touch. We found them half an hour later in a swamp; they were up to their knees in the slime. My tin hat was loose and kept slipping over my eyes (a great drawback). We eventually got back at 4:30 a.m. and found hot cocoa waiting for us but—no pleasure without pain—I had to clean the dixie afterwards.

"This is a ragtime war! We get 'minnies,' high explosives and mines galore and yet in the front line we get one post and stuff from the canteen (tinned fruit, fags, sausages, etc) every evening. Sounds incredible but it's gospel, we fetch the stuff up with the rations." As Alec had noted, one of the strange incongruities of the war was that, even in the front line, there was usually a daily delivery of mail. Rose, like many other mothers, sent regular gifts of fresh food that normally arrived within forty-eight hours. One contained a parcel of eggs and a cucumber. "One of the eggs was a casualty and the cucumber was slightly wounded in the head (or tail). Still we had a grand feed and everybody is writing home for cucumbers, etc." It was the first fresh vegetable that he had eaten since arriving in France.

On 14 May Alec went back to the reserve areas to do a four-day training course in throwing "bombs"—hand grenades. "Ignoring all that at Aldershot they had learnt to be sacred," front-line troops had discovered that "so long as you stand in a hole deeper than you are tall you will never hit with a rifle-bullet another man standing in just such another hole twenty yards off. But also—divine idea!—that you can throw a tin can from your hole into his." "The most agile and daring fellows [were chosen] to go ahead as bomb-throwers" and it was now an invariable and essential element of trench raids and attacks. A bombing party, usually nine men, was led by two soldiers with fixed bayonets. Two bombers came next, followed by an officer to direct operations and four bomb-carriers and replacement throwers—a reflection of the short life-expectancy in that line of work. They cleared trenches from traverse to traverse—the buttresses built to prevent enfilade fire along the length of a trench. At each traverse the throwers would pitch a couple of bombs into the next "bay" of the trench and the bayonet men would then sprint round to finish off any survivors from the blast. Since the defenders of the trench would be operating on much the same principles, and the concussion of the five-pound bombs in the close confines of a trench was devastating, casualty rates were notoriously high.

The primitive bombs that had to be ignited by knocking against a hard object or striking on sandpaper like an over-sized match had been replaced in early 1915 by the more reliable and deadly pineapple-shaped Mills bombs, but supplies had not kept pace with demand. As a result, bombs were improvised from "old ham tins, wire, a little gun-cotton, a little time fuse, and some bits of sharp stone, old iron, or anything hard that came to hand that was lying about, with earth to fill in."

Every man in Alec's battalion had to go through a bombing course; and as he reported to his mother, the timing of his course ensured that he would "miss the next turn in the line (I know that the latter bit will please you). Throwing bombs from nine till twelve and two till four, with *all* the evening to ourselves, absolutely a rest cure. When the Batt comes out (so rumour has it) we all go back for a month's rest and then take over the part of the line where ten shells a day are considered a heavy strafe. In fact I am told that very often a day goes by without a shot being fired (quite a rest day)." The rumour mill was always active in the trenches and often generated spurious stories about moves to cushy sectors. They rarely proved true, but each fresh rumour was still eagerly believed.

Alec also expressed the widely felt envy for comrades who had got a

"Blighty One"—a non-fatal wound, but one serious enough to require the victim to be sent back to England for treatment. "By the way, my pal Cooper got a lovely wound last time up; a bullet went clean through his arm without touching a bone, but he will have at least six months in 'Blighty' [a Hindustani word for a foreign country, adopted by colonial Englishmen as slang for "home"] as the hole will take some time to heal." With conscription now introduced at home, Alec's father, Fred, was liable for military service and was awaiting his call-up papers. "I should think Dad would be the very man for the ASC (MT) or any Corps where his knowledge of engines would be wanted, but if the infantryman's life appeals to him the CSR are badly in need of recruits, I believe."

On the night that he returned from his bombing course, 18 May 1916, the Civil Service Rifles moved south with the rest of the London Division to the next sector of the line, below the summit of Vimy Ridge. Already the site of bitter fighting, the ridge was a cratered and devastated wasteland. Rocky outcrops along the heights made trench-digging even more backbreaking than usual, and "our new piece of front was not a satisfactory inheritance. Lately the scene of destructive mining, it was in a bad state of disrepair. No wire covered the front or support lines, and the front line consisted of disconnected posts, isolated by day [when troop movements were impossible because of the threat from enemy snipers, machine guns and artillery], and there were no shelters of any kind in the front system. Altogether it was a posting ill-equipped to counteract the increasingly aggressive efforts of the enemy, who lost no chance of inflicting casualties on our unprotected troops."

Alec had returned just in time for the next six-day rotation into the front lines. The German trench-mortars were "unusually active" and there was also a six-hour heavy-artillery bombardment of the trenches around "Ersatz Alley," beginning at five in the morning of Saturday 20 May. Each high-velocity shell "came suddenly with a shriek beyond expression, entered the mud . . . and rocked the earth and air." Being shelled was "the main work of an infantry soldier," and one described it as "the great leveller. Nobody could stand more than three hours of shelling before they started feeling sleepy and numb. You're hammered after three hours and you're there for the picking when he [the enemy] comes over. It's a bit like being under anaesthetic." Another, who had written to his parents in October 1914 that "I *adore* the war. It is like a big picnic . . . ," admitted after experiencing his first prolonged bombardment, "I can understand now why our infantry have to retreat sometimes, a sight which came as a shock to me at first."

The bombardment restarted at first light the next morning, increasing steadily in intensity as the day wore on. At 3:40 that afternoon a "box barrage" was laid down on Zouave Valley behind Vimy Ridge, breaking virtually all lines of communication between the front line and the reserves. Troops in the exposed, shelterless front-line trenches took heavy casualties. As Alec's battalion approached from the reserve areas six or seven miles away, "hanging over the area of the front line trenches on Vimy Ridge was a dense cloud of bursting shells, and to make the scene more weird, not a sound could be heard, either of guns or the explosion of the shells, although it was a beautiful, still evening." At 7:45 that evening the bombardment at last lifted from the front line, rolling on towards the rear, and the German infantry launched a frontal attack. In fierce fighting, the 7th and 8th Battalions of the London Division were driven out of the front line and back across two lines of support trenches to a tenuous position halfway up the rear slope of the ridge. Many of the shell-shocked survivors of the bombardment were captured as the trenches were overrun.

The 20th Battalion, holding the ground immediately to the left, fought bravely but suffered devastating casualties—"B" Company, 120 strong at the start of the fighting, withdrew from Vimy Ridge with only 17 men remaining. The Civil Service Rifles were "no sooner in position in the Miastre Line—a trench about two feet deep—than orders were received to move forward . . . The advance was along a very shallow and narrow communication trench and the scene of slaughter was approached through a barrage of tear gas." At ten-fifteen that night, the battalion reached the brigade headquarters, set up at the Cabaret Rouge, a ruined *estaminet* (bar) on the Béthune-Arras road.

The German barrage roared around them, "the most intense bombardment we had witnessed. He [the enemy] must have employed guns of every possible calibre. The air was just one solid mass of bursting shells. We had little or no information as to what was happening, and as darkness had now gathered and we were in entirely strange trenches, there did not seem much chance of finding out." So critical was the situation in the front line that three companies of the battalion were "at once loaded up with bombs [each one weighing five pounds] and an extra 100 rounds of ammunition per man," and sent forward to the Berthonval sector of the line. They arrived, exhausted, at one-thirty in the morning, having been on the move continuously since the previous afternoon. The "awful barrage" in the Zouave Valley had been negotiated almost without loss, but the battalion was now ordered to launch a counter-attack, beginning in just half an hour, at 2 a.m. on the morning of 23 May.

Captain Farquhar, commanding the lead company, "B" Company, was told that the attack would be supported by the 6th and 7th Battalions on his right and the 18th Battalion—the London Irish—on his left, but "where any of these troops were to be found was not vouchsafed to him. He was told that one of his flanks would rest on Ersatz Trench, but as he had never heard of Ersatz Trench, nor was anyone there to show him where it was, he might just as well have been told to rest his flanks on the Unter den Linden [in Berlin]. He was unable to find out whether there were any British troops between him and the Boche, or how much of the line he was supposed to capture."

It was also pitch-dark, the blackness broken only by the flash of explosions and the "fitful glare of Very lights," but nonetheless the attack was to proceed on schedule at two o'clock. The "Suicide Squad"—as Alec and his fellow bomb-throwers were christened, reflecting the appalling casualty rates among men who had to penetrate to within no more than fifty feet of the German lines before throwing their grenades—were to bomb the enemy trenches and carried "two boxes of bombs each."

At the designated hour, whistles shrilled to signal the men over the top. "B" Company led the way in two waves, over unfamiliar ground, not knowing where to find either friend or foe. They advanced without supporting fire from artillery, machine guns or Lewis guns, and came "under such a murderous and intense fire from enemy artillery, trench mortars, machine-guns and rifles that very few survived unwounded." Francis Alfred Martin left a terse description: "Moonlight on bayonets. Capt. Farquhar and Mr. Scott in front with walking sticks and revolvers. MG [machine-gun] fire hellish—chaps going down in dozens, twenty yards from the Boche." A handful of men may even have reached the barbed wire erected by the Germans after capturing the trench, but they could not penetrate it; "ordinary wire-cutters were useless," "the ordinary Army issue would cut only British wire." The surviving few, only thirteen out of the whole company, were forced to retreat and take cover in shell-holes. "I saw by the light of a flare, our platoon sergeant cursing some men . . . He was threatening them with his bayonet and shouting 'Get out you b——ds!' " Few heeded him. The survivors remained in their shell-holes throughout the rest of that night and during the scorching heat of the following day, before finding their way back to their own lines after nightfall.

"C" Company was ordered to support the London Irish, but since they could not find them in the darkness, they instead devoted themselves to fortifying a defensive position around "Granby Street," and trying to rescue some of the many wounded still lying between the lines. "D" Company was ordered to support "B" Company's attack and they advanced up the hill as far as the old reserve line, which they now converted into the front-line trench. Having remained silent throughout the carnage, the divisional artillery chose this moment to open up, raining shells down around this new front-line position. Vociferous complaints about "shorts" (shells falling shy of the enemy—what would now be known as "friendly fire") continued to be made at intervals throughout the following day. It was not a problem unique to British artillery units; the German 49th Field Artillery Regiment acquired the sardonic nickname "the 48½th" because so many of its shells fell short.

Daybreak on 23 May revealed that the communications trench up Ersatz Alley had been all but obliterated by the German bombardment. The London Division's artillery eventually fired over 32,000 shells in reply, but none had been fired during those crucial early stages when they were most sorely needed. That night, a further counter-attack by the 21st and 24th Battalions, who by now were at least aware of where friend and foe were situated, led to "great execution among the enemy they found in the trench and dugouts" and seven Military Crosses were awarded to men of the 21st Battalion for their parts in the attack, but they were then repulsed and nothing was gained from "this gallant and costly action beyond a few yards of our old front line."

During the hours of darkness, search parties went out into no-man's-land to find and bring in the wounded, and some of the multitudes of dead were also retrieved. In some areas, "the ground was covered with unburied dead and it became a matter of real military importance that the work of burial should be conducted, but it was no easy matter . . . to do so without getting fresh casualties among the burial party." Bodies often "remained a long time without burial, for who was going to risk lives for such a task? The dead would keep. They lay out there . . . yellow or grey or blue, with blood dried black on their skin and clothes. Sometimes a shell would hasten the indignity of slow decomposition. They were certainly not worth another life."

Those bodies that had lain there for some time were particularly unpleasant and difficult to handle. "Burying a dead man whose head comes off in your hands is a form of exercise not to be recommended to those with weak stomachs." "I once fell and put my hands right through the belly of a man. It was days before I got the smell out of my nails . . . As you lifted a body by its arms and legs, they detached themselves from the torso, and that was not the worst thing. Each body was covered, inches deep, with a black fur of flies which flew up into your face, into your mouth, eyes and nostrils, as you approached." In Artois a soldier described an immense "shimmering cloud" of flies "smelling of corpses . . . choking the combatants with its fetid odour." Bodies crawled with maggots, making "a noise like rustling silk as they gnawed their way through some dead man's guts." "We worked with sandbags in our hands, stopping every now and then to puke." Men could be forgiven for trying "to drown . . . with rum" such experiences.

Burial parties formed from troops in the reserve areas were supposed to bury the dead, but the sheer numbers overwhelmed them. "In some places the bodies were piled so high that one could take cover from shell-fire behind them"; and some dead were "buried in the trench, wrapped in an old blanket." In the sodden soil of Flanders the "swampy nature of the ground" also often made the "melancholy task [of burial] necessarily one of haste. The regulation depth of a grave was the length of a spade and unless the interment was immediate, the grave at once filled up with water."

A soldier on a work-party burying dead up in the Zouave Valley was one of "twenty-five of us and we were supposed to bury twenty men. We dug two holes seven feet by ten feet and five feet deep and had to go up to the front line for the stiffs. I made five trips up in all and I can tell you I was pretty tired. I think it's the hardest night's work I've ever done . . . The bodies were in a large shell-hole behind the parapet at the front line, piled three or four deep. There were over forty there that had been brought in, in the morning, from No Man's Land. Fritz [the Germans] helped them bring some of the bodies over. We had orders to pack them all out which was impossible in the time we had, as it took four men to a stiff, two at a time carrying them. We used home-made stretchers at first, but they were too awkward in the narrow trenches, so we used a pole and tied a body to it by means of a strap, etc. Some of them had been gassed, most had received machine-gun and shrapnel wounds, mostly in the face. It took us to 3 a.m. to carry twenty-nine down to the valley and bury fourteen of them. We quit then and went home, getting to our dugout in the reserves at 4 a.m. There are still a lot of bodies in No Man's Land to be brought in."

The Battle of Vimy Ridge was over for the exhausted and badly depleted troops of the London Division, who were relieved the following night. In all, 2,107 of them had been killed, wounded or were missing in action and "B" Company of the Civil Service Rifles had been almost entirely wiped out. As the official history of the division noted, with remarkable understatement, "It seems doubtful now whether our risky position near the crest of the ridge was worth holding at such cost . . . The magnificent spirit which refuses to yield to the enemy any ground, however useless, is worth much; but were the Higher Command justified in incurring the resulting losses?" It was a question that was to be asked with even greater force, after the next time the London Division was sent "over the top."

4

ONE GREAT CRY OF AGONY AND HORROR

Paul Hub made a slow recovery from the wounds he suffered at Ypres in May 1915. After several weeks in hospital, he convalesced at home in Stetten in the late summer of 1915, often sitting in the garden in the shade of the cherry tree. On returning to duty that autumn he was sent on an officer's training course in Ulm, where, "determined and assured," he showed "an array of solid skills" and was recommended for promotion. He then joined a reserve battalion at Ulm, which kept him out of the front lines for the remainder of 1915. But his strong sense of duty and his increasing guilt that, though fully recovered, he was in reserve while others were fighting and dying at the Front led him to make repeated attempts to be reassigned to his original regiment. Maria was horrified and tried to dissuade him, but in May 1916 Paul "tried again to be transferred yesterday. The Staff Sergeant of the battalion had already promised it to me. But when the Company Staff Sergeant found out about it, he was able to thwart it again. Now, obviously, any hope of going along is destroyed. Don't tell anyone at home.

You know that my parents don't think too highly of my volunteering, but with you I want to be open."

Knowing that she could not prevent him from returning to the front lines, Maria once more pressed him to marry her before he left. Paul remained doubtful. "How I wish you were here with me now to talk over your letter. A war wedding! I think about it so often. Every hour that goes by here is an hour of happiness lost for ever, but I can't think about marriage because . . . there's my worry about becoming a cripple. Maria, you say I shouldn't think about it, but I have to. If you were tied to me, what would your life be like? I know you would give up everything for me, as I would for you, but the sacrifice would be too great. You must believe me when I say that I would far rather marry you now, than put it off. But under the present circumstances it is too soon. Please don't be upset that I am replying to your dear letter in such a negative way."

Paul might have been surprised to discover how many priests shared his views. "Up till recently I encouraged and urged marriage during the war; never, never, never again. No, I would rather make a man, if I could, break off his engagement and never write again, than that he married till this is over. Even if men have been engaged for years, let them wait or break it off. On no account marry; it is more than cruel to the wives and children, it is agony to the men, often they have told me so . . . They can still be lovers and wait. At the end of the war, if he lives, they will receive their reward in the joy-life of marriage."

In early June 1916, Paul again applied to be transferred to active service and this time he was successful. He wrote to Maria at once. "I cannot forget how you wanted to make me promise that I wouldn't volunteer any more. Did I hurt you? Believe me when I say I understand you, but please try to understand me, too." He was granted a brief home leave and on 11 June, the eve of his departure to rejoin the 247th Infantry Regiment in "our old bloodbath—the Somme," he wrote to Maria again. "What are you thinking now? I feel as if your thoughts cross with mine. Last Sunday we parted, the last time I looked into your eyes, but it was not for the very last time. Maria, we will see each other again. It might be a long time before I can hold you in my arms again. But take comfort. Look to the future—we will see each other again. Dear girl, think of that beloved time and it will lessen the pain of parting. I would so love to be with you still, to comfort you and wipe away your tears. I know how hard it is to part. Yesterday evening, reading your words, I felt it all over again. The pictures that you sent brought back all those wonderful hours. After such happiness, parting is not easy. But I know that my brave girl will manage to stay strong, as always. I am so happy I spent my time with you. I can go, taking with me the memories of those beautiful days with my fiancée, and I can dream of the future which has helped me through so many dark hours. You should do the same. You know that I understand you. I am taking my ring with me. I cannot be parted from it. I also found leaving home very hard. It broke my mother's heart. Mine too."

The next day he began the long, slow journey north. Promoted to Second Sergeant with the Eighth Company of the 247th Regiment, he was now one of the few battle-hardened soldiers among a horde of raw recruits. For a while he allowed himself to be caught up in the excitement and patriotic fervour of his comrades, but a sense of foreboding soon returned. "We crossed the Rhine at Mainz. The singing! *'Es braust ein Ruf wie Donnerhall'* [There roars a cry like thunder] must have been heard by half of Mainz. Lord, the Rhine looked beautiful as we crossed, but after Aachen there was silence. All the men's cheering and shouting ceased. I entered enemy territory for the second time . . . We can hear firing in the distance."

He spent his first night back with his regiment at Audenarde, where he was shocked by the cynicism and near insubordination of some of the other sergeants, who had endured almost two years of trench warfare. "It's foul here and some of the Sergeants' behaviour is close to mutiny and treason. If any of we recently arrived Sergeants said anything, all hell was let loose, but I wasn't in the mood at all to put up with it. Sergeants who curse their men and eat their rations, get drunk and call the officers 'liars and swindlers who should be shot,' belong in prison."

The next day, the regiment began the long march to the Front. In the heat of early summer, nature had made attempts to reclaim the violated ground and a deceptive air of somnolence lay on the landscape. "The fields over which the scythe has not passed for years are a mass of wild flowers. They bathe the trenches in a hot stream of scent," "smelling to heaven like incense in the sun." "Brimstone butterflies and chalk-blues flutter above the dugouts and settle on the green ooze of the shell-holes." "Then a bare field strewn with barbed wire, rusted to a sort of Titian red—out of which a hare came just now and sat up with fear in his eyes and the sun shining red through his ears. Then the trench . . . piled earth with groundsel and great flaming dandelions and chickweed and pimpernels running riot over it. Decayed sandbags, new sandbags, boards, dropped ammunition, empty tins, corrugated iron, a smell of boots and stagnant water and burnt powder and oil and men, the occasional bang of a rifle and the click of a bolt, the occasional crack of a bullet coming over, or the wailing diminuendo of a ricochet. And over everything, the larks . . . and on the other side, nothing but a mud wall, with a few dandelions against the sky, until you look over the top, or through a periscope and then you see barbed wire and more barbed wire, and then fields with larks over them, and then barbed wire again."

The uneasy quiet of the early summer was soon to be torn apart, for the long-awaited British "Great Advance"—the Battle of the Somme—was about to begin. "To inspire the German troops with a spirit of martial fervour (not easily aroused to fever-pitch after the bloody losses before Verdun), Orders of the Day were issued to the battalions counselling them to hold fast against the hated English, who stood foremost in the way of peace . . . and promising them a speedy ending to the war." Such promises and appeals to patriotism might inspire the new recruits with whom Paul had travelled to the Front, but for him, as for another German soldier who had experienced the terrible realities of the war, "We, who have seen the dark side, must substitute for that enthusiasm a deep-seated determination to stand by the Fatherland whatever happens . . . We know that death is not the worst thing we have to face. Thoroughly to realise everything and yet to go back, not under compulsion but willingly, is not easy."

The British preliminary bombardment unleashed a weeklong firestorm, raining down one and a half million shells on the German lines— an average of one ton of steel fell on every square yard. "During that week the earth shook for miles around and there was a constant tremor in the night air of South-East England." From a distance, the battlefield had a strange and terrible beauty. "Some of the shells burst upwards as straight as poplars, others expand in mighty and irregular shapes like old oaks, others again shoot out low over the ground like dense undergrowth scoured earthwards by a storm."

"Heavy shells pass so high overhead that their flight is heard only as a sharp, long drawn-out sigh; then the crashes ring out." "Speech was of course impossible, one could only stand and *feel* the thousands of tons of metal rushing away from one . . . What I shall never forget was a substratum of noise, an unceasing, moaning roar, exactly like enormous waves on a beach." Another observer called it "a hurricane of hoarse and hollow banging, of raging clamour, of piercing and beast-like screams." All who heard that barrage agreed that the sound was not only louder but also qualitatively different from anything they had ever heard before. The noise alone must have unhinged many of those cowering in their dugouts, praying for the storm to pass. "To have to crouch under fire without cover, belaboured without a pause by shells of a calibre sufficient each one to lay a fair-sized village in ruins, without any distraction beyond counting the hits mechanically in a half-dazed condition, is an experience that almost passes the limits of human endurance." A soldier who suffered an even more prolonged barrage at Verdun confessed that "by the ninth day, almost every soldier was crying." If the noise of the shells subsided even for an instant, the air was filled with the buzzing of millions of flies disturbed from feasting on the dead, the terrifying, high-pitched screaming of the rats, and the most bizarre and incongruous sound of all: the singing of the birds, still marking their territory, even as it disintegrated in an inferno of noise, fire and smoke.

The German dugouts had to be flattened, "so that at the moment of assault, all the defenders, except a few survivors, and all the machine guns might be buried. Our second and third trenches were bombarded in order to prevent our bringing up reserves. For the same reason all the communication trenches . . . the main and side roads and all the crossroads were kept under fire so that approaching troops, munitions, supplies and provisions had to pass through several lines of fire . . . All places up to a distance of ten miles behind the front were brought under incessant heavy artillery bombardment, which often started actual fires, thanks to the incendiary shells used by the enemy.

"The battering down of our advanced trenches was almost exclusively left to the heavy artillery and trench mortars . . . They tore up our wire obstacles from the ground, poles and all, and threw them all over the place, crushing the dugouts if they fell on them, and damaging the trenches. In a very short time, great portions of our trenches had been flattened out, partly burying their occupants. This fire lasted for seven days, and finally there came a gas attack, also of an improved kind." "People seven to eight kilometres behind the front have become unconscious from the tail of gas clouds. Its effects are felt even twelve kilometres behind the Front. One only has to look at the rifles after a gas attack to see what deadly stuff it is. They are red with rust, as if they had lain weeks in the mud. And the effects of the continuous bombardment are indescribable."

The German forces were hampered in their reply by shortages of shells and artillery. As early as 22 October 1914, War Minister von Falkenhayn had warned that "unlimited amounts of ammunition" were already "a question of life or death for the Army," and he was furious that the arms manufacturer Krupp was still fulfilling foreign orders while German Army units on both fronts were suffering from shortages of shells. Even though output rose by 1,300 percent between August 1914 and October 1915, it was still far less than the German armies were demanding. Many gun-barrels were wearing out and needed relining or replacing and General von Gallwitz received reports of "an alarmingly large number of bursts in the bore, particularly in field guns."

The German artillery was also hindered by a lack of air observation. Whereas British squadrons were ordered to fly aggressive patrols, crossing the enemy lines and actively seeking ground and air targets, German pilots flew defensive patrols within and often well behind their own lines. This reduced losses relative to those of the Allies, but it left German front-line troops feeling exposed and abandoned. "You have to stay in your hole all day and must not stand up in the trench because there is always a crowd of . . . about eight to ten English machines overhead, but no one sees any one of ours . . . our airmen are a rotten lot." "The English are always flying over our lines, directing artillery shoots, thereby getting all their shells, even those of heavy calibre, right into our trenches. Our artillery can only shoot by the map as they have no observation. I wonder if they [the German pilots] have any idea where the enemy line is." As a result, the German fire was often dangerously inaccurate. "It is absolutely necessary that an observer from the front line should register the guns again. The men are quite unsafe. Perhaps the artillery are mistaking our trench for that of the English. From 10:30 to 11:30, our artillery sent over fifteen to twenty shots that fell short. Two hit the barricade and others the trench."

Every fresh artillery strike further pulverized the chalk, raising a pall of grey-white dust that drifted downwind for miles, settling "over what miserable traces of the undergrowth remain, so that they look as pale and sickly as if they had grown in a cellar." On the battlefield itself, the faces and uniforms of the dead were shrouded with the "grey dust that has settled on them during the bombardment and drunk up their blood."

Many men wrote "pitiful letters" describing the horror of that bombardment. "We are quite shut off from the rest of the world," one of them wrote. "Nothing comes to us. The English keep such a barrage on our approaches, it is terrible. Tomorrow evening it will be seven days since this bombardment began. We cannot hold out much longer.

Everything is shot to pieces." Those who survived had barely slept in a week, yet though some "shook all over and lay like one paralysed and prayed that I might be released from this hell," a surprising number were relatively unaffected by the noise, shell-shock or fear. "Young recruits who had just come into the field from home, fresh twenty-year-old boys, behaved in this catastrophic ploughing and thundering as if they had spent all their life in such surroundings, and it is partly thanks to them that the older married men also stood the test so well." They waited and waited for the bombardment to lift, knowing that it would signal a massed attack.

At dawn on 1 July 1916, the barrage lifted and the infantry attacks began. The weeklong firestorm on the Somme had guaranteed—or so the attacking troops were assured—that "not even a rat" would have survived, and the 100,000 attacking troops, struggling under the weight of the equipment they carried to refortify the "deserted" German trenches—a greater load, proportionately, than that authorized for Army mules—were ordered to walk rather than run across no-man's-land. This may also have reflected the patrician contempt of the commanders for Kitchener's New Army of largely working-class recruits, who were felt to be incapable of comprehending more complex tactics, even when these were as simple as advancing using the available cover or following close behind a creeping barrage.

Secure in their deep dugouts from even that terrible bombardment, enough Germans had survived to man their artillery, rifles and machine guns and mow down the attacking Britons in their thousands. One German machine-gunner was "very surprised to see them walking; we had never seen that before ... When we started firing we just had to load and re-load. They went down in their hundreds. You didn't have to aim, we just fired into them." The machine-gunners were also helped by the obliging way in which, in order to facilitate the advance, British commanders had had paths marked out with tape and gaps cut in their own barbed wire several days before the attack. The German machine-gunners merely had to register their weapons on these gaps and cut down the attacking troops as they funnelled through them.

As the torrents of machine-gun bullets ripped through the grassy slopes up which the British troops were advancing, the smell of an English summer—fresh-cut grass—filled the air. For thousands it would be the last scent they would ever smell. That "first day on the Somme" was to become a day of infamy. By nightfall, 57,000 British and Empire soldiers were killed, wounded or missing in action, and in places "one could walk across no-man's-land on British bodies without ever setting foot on the ground." The 1st Newfoundland Battalion lost 91 percent of its men within forty minutes—1 July is still a day of mourning in Newfoundland—and out of 900 men of the "Leeds Pals" (the 15th Battalion West Yorkshire Regiment), only 17 answered the roll-call that night. As a military consequence of the Somme, 10 percent of any battalion going over the top in any future attack were left behind, thus ensuring that, in the event of near-total casualties, there was at least a nucleus of experienced troops to train and "stiffen" the next influx of raw recruits.

The British commander-in-chief, Douglas Haig, continued to push the offensive with ever-increasing desperation. The grinding advance went on, yard by yard, and the haemorrhage of men continued for days, weeks and then months.

British and French losses on the Somme were to total over 600,000 and, although fewer, German casualties were also appalling. Some units lost "three-quarters of their number in casualties and our troops advanced over heaps of killed and wounded." The British artillery continued to maintain a bombardment "of considerable intensity of all portions of ground which are of any importance to us, as well as all artillery and infantry positions, all natural cover, rear slopes, hollow roads, and villages behind the battle front. Numerous aeroplanes flying very low assist in registration and the direction of fire. Bombs are frequently dropped by day and night," causing yet more casualties and further demoralization of the already battle-fatigued troops.

Letters taken from dead or captured Germans were "one great cry of agony and horror." "I stood on the brink of the most terrible days of my life," wrote one of them. "They were those of the battle of the Somme . . . the English wrote on our bodies in letters of blood 'It is all over with you.' A handful of half-mad, wretched creatures, worn out in body and mind, were all that was left of a whole battalion. We were that handful." Everywhere there were "heaps of corpses—a stench; I have to lie amid corpses." One company lost all its officers and 150 men, "but that is the same with every regiment and company on the Somme. I unfortunately could not get the much desired wound to send me home." Just as British soldiers dreamed of getting a "Blighty One," Germans longed for a *"Heimatschuss"*—literally a "home shot." "We meet parties of wounded—walking cases—each with a white label attached to their second button-hole. They are out of it now. They won't have to go up the line again. And so, in spite of their sufferings, they jog along quite merrily."

Despite the carnage among his own men, Crown Prince Rupprecht surveyed the results of the battle with apparent equanimity. "Our losses in territory may be seen on the map with a microscope. Their losses in that far more precious thing—human life—are simply prodigious. Amply and in full coin have they paid for every foot of ground we sold them. They can have all they want at the same price . . . It saddens us to exact the dreadful toll of suffering and death that is being marked up on the ledger of history, but if the enemy is still minded to possess a few more hectares of blood-sodden soil, I fear they must pay a bitter price."

However, the surviving German troops were inevitably affected by the pounding they had taken. "The only thing that really troubles me is the utter weariness of the troops. It is terrible how they are longing for peace." One captured letter showed the frictions over the possibly imaginary favouritism being shown to troops from certain regions. "All the Bavarian troops are being sent to the Somme (this much is certain, you can see no Prussians there), and this in spite of the losses the 1st Bavarian Corps suffered recently at Verdun! And how we did suffer! . . . To the devil with it! Every Bavarian regiment is being sent into it, and it's a swindle." In some units there was a complete collapse of discipline. "I collect my men, so as to lead them forward all together under cover, and spring forward. When I look back, not one, not a single one, has followed me. I go back, reason with them and order them to go with me. This time it has to be over open ground, as some parts of the trench have meanwhile been blown in. Now I spring forward again, leap through the shell-holes for about fifty yards, and throw myself down to get my breath. Two men have come with me . . . Another sergeant drives the rest forward with his revolver, until we have about forty out of the ninety we brought with us to occupy our 200-yard sector."

5

A NEW WORLD OF WAR

Alec Reader had survived his first experience of a full-scale attack at Vimy Ridge in May 1916 unscathed, but his attempts to describe his part in the action fell foul of the censor. "We have had a pretty rotten time lately but it's no use my telling you as you must have read the papers. We have been..." The rest of the paragraph was censored, though the words "... over the top and lost..." are still discernible through the censor's thick black pen. He tried again the next day, but this time "the regimental censor was so annoyed with the amount of *verboten* matter in my letter that he destroyed it." However, he did allow Alec to tell his mother in a subsequent letter that "the Batt. has had a rotten time in the line. We went 'over the top,' a most unpleasant job. Please send me some socks as soon as you can, as I lost all my stuff last time up. A shell apparently landed right on my pack; all I could find of it afterwards was one of the buckles. I have now got a casualty's stuff but he was very careless with his socks; they have all got holes in them." As in his previous few letters he also asked, "Has Dad decided yet?" as his father continued to vacillate over whether to wait to be conscripted or to volunteer, and if so, to which unit he would apply.

Alec's battalion was sent to the village of Calonne Ricouart to regroup and recuperate before returning to the front lines. Soon after arriving there, he was hospitalized with flu. Rose, who had read newspaper reports of the Battle of Vimy Ridge that, even with wartime censorship, conveyed something of the devastating casualties that the 47th London Division had suffered, immediately feared that he was badly wounded and concealing it by talk of "the flu." Alec at once replied, "You should know by now that the 'flu' was not a mistaken kindness. Unfortunately, the illness was far too slight to get me far back, I only had four days in hospital." He also managed to slip in an apparently innocent remark that escaped the censor's vigilance. "By the way, tell Alice and Bert that they are quite right about that little affair." This referred to two questions that his mother had asked in her letter: "A) Are you still in Arras? and B) Are you in the 47th Division?" His reply fooled the censor but also baffled his mother at first. She knew no one of those names and "it took me all day to grasp what he meant. He must have had a terrible time as the 47th Division was almost wiped out."

Among the items he asked his mother to send were "worm cakes if you can get them. The food we get is good (in quantity only). In spite of the lazy life I lead, I cannot get fat, and so have decided, as Dad decided long ago, that 'the kid's got worms.' Lastly I should like some money; I am very sorry to have to ask you again but while I am away from the line I enjoy life to the full, for which I can hardly be blamed, as anyone who has been will tell you. As this will *have* to be the last time I shall ask, please let me have as much as you can spare."

Wherever troops gathered in any numbers, "working women" were rarely far behind—one German officer expressed his disgust that when shelling a section of the French lines "a host of figures, mostly women in negligees," ran from the trenches—but it was unsurprising that men who "stood a good chance of being killed within a few weeks anyhow . . . did not want to die virgins." Even the fear of venereal disease was not the deterrent it might have been in peacetime; it "saved the life of scores by incapacitating them for future trench service. Base venereal hospitals were always crowded. The troops took a lewd delight in exaggerating the proportion of army chaplains to combatant officers treated there." Pay was deducted from troops who contracted venereal disease, a punishment also applied to other "self-inflicted diseases"— which included almost anything not caught on active service. American troops with venereal disease were given "extremely painful medical treatment which, it was suspected, was partly intended as a punishment and deterrent."

However, Alec's enjoyment of life to the full may have involved nothing more than gambling at cards and visits to the local *estaminet*, Au Joli Pêcheur, next to a picturesque watermill. "The French equivalent of the English pub," *estaminets* were usually "just the front room of an ordinary humble-looking house . . . [with] a tiled floor. Along one wall was a bench with a long narrow table in front of it. A few stools or wooden chairs completed the seating. Over by another wall there was a small counter on which, and on some wall-shelves behind it, were some bottles. Possibly madam was sitting at the counter, but more likely she was moving about serving her customers. The drinks sold were chiefly vin blanc and vin rouge; French beer was quite often available, though rather poor stuff . . . The estaminet was a place where letters home were often written."

On 12 June the division was sent back up the line, "a brute of a march, about fourteen miles," leading them to the quieter Angres sector, a few miles to the north of Vimy Ridge. But by 16 June Alec was again in a field hospital. "We went into the line the other night. It was raining in torrents, was pitch black and in many places the trench boards were floating. As you trod on them, down you went in from six inches to two inches of water. Of course by the time we got into the front line we were all soaked up to the knees. The Germans had apparently been dropping rifle grenades, trench mortars, etc, right into the trench, in a lot of places the trench was blown in and we had to climb over the top, while in other parts there were holes about three feet deep in the bottom which were not noticeable as there was water all along. Of course everybody fell into these holes and some unfortunates, myself included, slipped and fell full length. One I went into head first and was half-drowned before I could scramble out. To get wet through on the first night is the worst possible way of starting the eight days in, as you are sure to catch something before you finish. (A lot of chaps came to hospital with Peraxin [trench fever], flu, bronchitis, etc while I was there.)

"Well, we eventually got in our part of the line, took over, and then got a large rum ration which did us all a world of good. I did my sentry from 5:30 a.m.–6:30 a.m. and then went in this mine shaft for a sleep (we do sentry one [hour] in six in the daytime and one in three at night as a rule). Unfortunately the air was foul and I knew nothing more until

I came to, to find two chaps pumping oxygen into me. I am now in hospital recuperating. You might possibly see my name in the casualty list, so don't be alarmed, as I have given you fair warning. While down the shaft I caught my packet and in doing so was very lucky. I missed eight days very hard work, draining and repairing the trench, missed the possibility of catching something worse and am now having a very bon time."

The gas that had poisoned him was not from a German gas attack, but the odourless, colourless carbon monoxide left in the aftermath of the detonation of a mine. Heavier than air, it had remained trapped in the shaft where Alec encountered it. He was lucky to be found in time, but "the only lasting effect of it is to keep my face as white as the proverbial sheet, so when I come home, look out for someone who is 'pale and distinguished looking' . . . It makes you so beastly weak, however, that you are helpless. When I came to, my nose was running but I was too weak to put my hand in my pocket to get my hanky; I couldn't even move my little finger. It is called CO poisoning and the cure is fresh air and rest."

Rose had sent Alec the money he asked for, but it arrived just two hours before he went into the line, too late for him to spend it. It was "considered a very bad omen to receive anything valuable just before going in, and a lot of cases have occurred where chaps have been killed and thus deprived of the pleasure of spending their money. So you can guess I felt pretty sick; I jokingly remarked to a friend that when I was knocked out, he would find the money in my top right-hand pocket and he thanked me for the information. (It is also considered risky to wear anything valuable over your heart; surprising how superstitious everybody gets out here isn't it?) Well, when I came to, I asked a chap to see if my stuff was all right and he told me that all my valuables had been handed in at H'dqrs. Of course I felt horribly sick at that, as they never clear you out until they have given you up as a bad job. Just then our company commander came along and I told him I wanted my stuff back, so to humour me he sent a chap to get it, and that's how I won the Great War."

Despite Rose's regular gifts of cash, Alec was permanently broke. "My money usually lasts me two or three days, after which I owe until the next pay day. You know out here on pay days they don't say 'How much are you entitled to?' What they do is to ask how much you want, which is quite a different matter. When they make a balance (about once every three months) we all find that we have overdrawn more or

less. Owing to your helping hand and my luck I am only slightly overdrawn (a matter of ten or fifteen francs), but some are knocked to the
tune of 100 and 150. Here's a sample of my luck: I went down rather
heavily on a game of Solo, and arranged to settle on pay-day. Before
that day turned up, however, we went into a big affair and lost a lot of
men, my creditor being one of the lost (killed). I'm afraid that sounds
callous but one gets like that out here."

Alec's father had now finally made up his mind to volunteer for service
with the balloon companies, which "spotted" for the artillery. Fred
Reader was to become a member of the ground crew winching the balloons up and down on their steel hawsers. Each balloon was accompanied by a tender truck and a winch truck and a ninety-man crew,
including two dozen men operating as three-man lookout and machine-
gun crews, who formed a defensive circle around the balloon to deter or
attack enemy aircraft trying to shoot it down. Dangling in wicker bas-
kets below the hydrogen-filled "blimps" at a height of up to 3,600 feet
was perilous work for the observers—many of whom jumped or
plunged to their deaths as their balloons collapsed in flames—but far
less hazardous for the ground crews. Four or five miles behind the front
lines, Fred would occupy as safe a position as any could be in a war zone.

It was also entirely typical of him that he had taken the opportunity
afforded by his new surroundings to rearrange the sequence of his
Christian names. He had been christened Frederick John Hanwell
Reader—the third name probably the customary tribute to a wealthy
relative in the hope of "a mention" in the will—but he now instructed
his Army comrades to call him "Hanwell" and indeed, the official Army
records list him as "Hanwell John Frederick Reader." To Fred's ear, the
new first name must have sounded much more impressive, and certainly much more middle class, than plain "Fred Reader."

By June 1916 he was in training at the Richmond Park No. 2 Balloon Training School, prompting Alec to remark to his mother that
"Dad appears to be nicely settled for the duration and if he gets to Roe-
hampton, it *will* be a nice war, won't it? . . . It is nice to know that someone is having a good time. You need not worry about Dad, even if he
does come out here, because the nearest balloon is five miles from the
Line and the Germans leave it severely alone. In fact my job in the next
war will be Dad's."

Alec had been discharged from hospital on 26 June and rejoined his
unit just as his father was preparing to embark for France. The distant

rumble of the guns on the Somme was audible day and night to the men of the 47th London Division, but they had been fortunate to escape the full horrors of those notorious first days on the Somme. Their turn would come soon enough, but for the moment they remained in the Angres sector carrying out diversionary attacks and raids—the word "in the whole vocabulary of the war which most instantly caused a sinking feeling in the stomach of ordinary mortals." A few found those forays into a starlit no-man's-land an exciting, almost mystical experience— "stars and wet grass, and nothing between you and the enemy, and every now and then a very soft and beautiful blue-white light from a Very pistol; bright as day, yet extraordinarily unreal. You have to keep still as a statue in whatever position you happen to be in, till it dies down, as movement gives you away"—but for most it was simply a ter-rifying ordeal, stripped of even the illusory safety of the trench and hid-den only by the darkness from the guns of the enemy.

Noise was as much a giveaway as movement, and as well as bombs and pistols, many men carried improvised weapons—coshes, clubs, knives—to aid the silent killing of sentries. "We advance slowly, step by step, and everyone is careful not to brush the side of the trench and to avoid the clatter of metal." That was easier said than done. No-man's-land was littered with metal—barbed wire, scraps of corrugated iron, shell splinters, empty tins, upturned rifles and tin hats marking graves. To blunder into any in the dark or even to be betrayed by the creak of a boot or a leather strap was to guarantee a star-shell or a flare, followed almost instantaneously by the crack of a rifle or the dry, rattling cough of a machine gun.

Just after midnight on the night of 3–4 July, Alec's battalion, "with blackened faces," and armed with bombs, coshes and rifles with fixed bayonets, carried out a large-scale trench raid, aiming to "secure a live enemy" for interrogation. It was a moonless and windless night, and the darkness and silence increased the tension as they waited for the brief preliminary barrage to begin, but noise or too visible preparations had alerted the Germans. They responded immediately to the British artillery fire with a "box-barrage" of their own, preventing the attackers from "getting nearer than bomb-throwing distance." The raid was "a dismal failure . . . a forbidden topic of conversation in CSR circles," resulting only in fourteen casualties and a hasty and shambolic retreat back to their own trenches.

As one of the battalion's trained bomb-throwers, Alec would cer-tainly have been in action, but his only oblique reference to it came in his next letter to his mother. "We have been in the line for seven days now; the first four we spent in the 'line of resistance' and had a fairly rotten time, but now we are in nice deep dugouts and if it would only stop raining, all would be well. As it is the water drips through the dugout incessantly, everything is soaked but our spirits, which apparently can't be drowned." It was unusual for the British to have deep dugouts and these may well have been captured from the Germans during earlier fighting, leaving their captors marvelling at the "prodigious dugouts, arranged even in two storeys." Most British troops had to make do with "the cubby hole—a hole or cavity dug into the side of the trench a little above the trench-floor so that water could not run in. It was reinforced with any pieces of wood that one could lay hands on. One could sit but not stand up in a cubby hole, which one entered on hands and knees. It was wide enough to sleep three men side by side. A rubber ground sheet was put on the earth floor and another or some sacking was hung over the entrance hole for warmth or against bad weather . . . In a cubby hole one was protected from bullets, flying pieces of shell or trench mortar, but not from a direct hit by a shell."

Two days later, with the Battle of the Somme still raging, Alec was offered an unexpected chance to escape from the front lines. Arthur Markham MP, outraged that boy soldiers had not only been allowed and even encouraged to give false ages to enlist but were also serving at the Front in flagrant breach of military regulations, led a successful parliamentary campaign to force the government to allow all under-age soldiers the option of returning home or moving to reserve areas. The decision, communicated to the Civil Service Rifles by 8 July, placed Alec "in a very awkward position: An army order has been issued to the effect that 'Men between 18 and 19 are to be sent back, but any who choose can volunteer to stay with their Batt[alion].' The temptation to get out of this ghastly business is far greater than you can possibly conceive, but of course there's only one decent thing for me to do, that is to stay here, but oh! It's going to be very hard." His decision was probably prompted less by a sense of duty to King and Country than by the desire, shared by most front-line troops, not to let down or lose face with his mates. There was a widely held and often expressed view that "shirking" your duty, whether by evading the draft at home or ducking a stint in the trenches, for any reason short of physical incapacity, was a contemptible act, forcing another man to risk his life in your stead. Few could withstand the tacit pressure to keep bearing their share of the burden, even at the risk of their lives.

Within a week, Alec's father had arrived in France and joined No. 18 KBS (Kite Balloon Section) a few miles behind the lines, and he at once began efforts to have his son transferred to his unit, though Alec still had very mixed feelings about taking what might be seen as the coward's way out. "That transferring idea of yours is a jolly good thing, but it would be hardly the thing to leave the Batt now; it would look rather like running away from the advance, don't you think?" He also tried to make light of the dangers of remaining at the Front. "Every time we go in the line we expect to 'go over the top' and it won't be a bad thing in a way, as it will mean more rations. After the last big affair we were in, our platoon was only eight strong, and we had a tin of butter each, beaucoup bread and jam etc (some game). To resume, I have decided to stick it out here until I get knocked out as that is, in my opinion, the only thing to do. You ask how I like fighting Germans; well, it's no bon because all we do is, (1) when it's quiet, to carry up ammunition, bombs, trench mortars etc, and (2) when they strafe, to stick on the fire step waiting for something to hit you, and let me tell you that the waiting is by far the worst part, according to chaps who have been lucky enough to stop a bit."

Alec also enquired how his father—always very conscious of his position in society—was taking to Army life. "How do you like cook's fatigue, mess orderly, etc, etc? And how do you like being ordered about by NCOs who are obviously your inferior in civil life? (Our Batt SM was a policeman.) I am still employed on the digging up of half France and shall be out as usual tonight. It will take us three hours to arrive at the scene of action, we shall do two hours work (it gets light so early nowadays, thank goodness) after which we will make the return journey, which, although the same distance won't take us more than two hours. Five hours march for two hours work, and this in spite of the photographs of Tommies being carried to the firing line in lorries to keep them fit for their arduous tasks!!! Au revoir, *Brother in Arms* or, as the Church Army would have it, 'Fellow workers in the Lord.' "

Despite the jocular tone he had adopted with his father, as Alec continued to witness at first hand the full horrors of the Somme and saw the endless streams of bodies being buried in crude graves or abandoned to the rats in no-man's-land, for the first time he confessed to his mother his relief that Fred was persisting in his efforts to have him transferred away from the Front. "I wish you wouldn't talk all that bosh about bravery. This ought to show you what a 'brave' boy I am: I am very glad that Dad has asked for me, as I am horribly fed up with this game. I could never have applied myself, but am only too pleased to shelve the responsibility (compris bravery). You must excuse the writing as at present I am up a sap [forward trench culminating in an observation post] about forty yards from the Hun, and there are no facilities for letter writing. I am keeping fairly fit and am living in hopes. Did Dad state my age?"

Days and weeks passed and progress on the proposed transfer was painfully slow. A particular Army form was required and with the Battle of the Somme still in full spate, arrangements to move an individual soldier away from the front line would scarcely have ranked high on the scale of priorities at Headquarters. Yet despite this and the knowledge that his unit would soon be required to take their turn in the sectors where the fighting and bloodshed were heaviest, Alec's spirits remained relatively high at first.

On 22 July he wrote to his mother, "We have worked unusually hard lately (we have only had five nights in bed during the last month) but that very fact speaks well, as tired troops would not be used in an attack (bon eh?). We have been in the front line for several days past and Fritz has been on his best behaviour the whole time. We amuse ourselves at night by firing at the flashes of their snipers and they of course return the compliment, but it is surprising what a difference it makes when you can feel that you are getting a bit of your own back. Far better than sitting in a trench waiting for something to hit you."

Despite the appalling casualty rates, there was still widespread confidence—albeit greatest in units separated from the scenes of the worst carnage—that the Battle of the Somme would produce the decisive breakthrough. "I am absolutely sure that the war will be over by Christmas," Alec wrote, "so make a lot of puddings this year. Our crowd, being composed chiefly of Civil Servants is bound to be one of the first to be disbanded." He was also keen that his brother and sisters should have a present to remember him by, and wrote to Rose, "Before I came away I told you to be sure to buy everybody something from me, and although you did in Ivy's case, what about the others? And I feel almost certain that you have not got anything for yourself. If I am right, please rectify it at once as I derive quite a lot of pleasure from the thought of making presents." Perversely he then added a postscript: "I have just had a brainwave; please let me have ten shillings to carry it out."

On 26 July the 47th London Division was redeployed in preparation for a fresh wave of attacks in the continuing battle. They left Angres on the first stage of a march so protracted that it became known as "the Great Trek." The battalion began at a march but soon broke stride. Marching created noise and "one of the most important and profound rules of trench life was never to do anything that attracted the attention of the enemy." As an officer with the division noted, before the war, the landscape through which they passed had been a tranquil blend of wood, pasture and water meadow, and "frost-blue" streams dotted with pretty villages. "The marshes of the Somme and its little tributaries, planted with tall poplars and occasional elms, make beautiful glades in the summer time. Trees line the roads and stand in clumps on the slopes leading up to the hills on either side of the river. On the uplands, the lines of the landscape are large; in generous curves, the low hills covered with hedgeless fields billow away into the distance. Groves of verdure hide the villages, but the tall blue steeple of the church always emerges."

That timeless pastoral idyll had long been obliterated by the ugly face of warfare. "The monotonous rolling and pounding [of the artillery] seem to have become inherent in the landscape, and the clouds of fine dust, which vanish in the rays of the sun, give it a sullen and menacing air." "In the Angres sector we had seen the last of flowery trenches and pleasant, deserted villages with fruit and vegetables, a little way behind the line. Vimy had shown us the devastated result of concentrated shelling; such desolation was soon to be our normal dwelling-place."

Alec wrote to his mother that afternoon. "'Once more unto the breach, dear friends.' We had a brute of a march today and when we got here I found my feet were bleeding in one or two places. Consequently I had trouble in getting my socks off. Still, that is by the way . . . I got your letter of the 21st just after I had handed in my note to you. The news it contained is very welcome and the sooner the trans[fer] comes off the better, as before very long it may be too late. You have no doubt fathomed the meaning of my note."

That evening, as the order to move out was again given, he scribbled a further hasty note to his mother, fearing that the unit's long-heralded, much-dreaded commitment to the Battle of the Somme was about to begin. "Am not writing a letter as I have no time. We shall be very busy for some time to come, so don't worry if you don't hear from me regularly . . . the postal facilities are very poor where we are going. Can't stop now as we are moving in half an hour." It turned out to be a premature alarm—they merely marched a few more miles and then halted once more—but all were aware that their turn going "over the top" into the maelstrom of shot and shell that was the Somme battle-field had only been postponed and not averted. Over the following days, the unit continued its circuitous route to the Front. On 31 July, they were still "making a tour of the 'promised land,' and when it ends we are in for a very hot time, so the realisation of the brainwave will have to be postponed. The heat just now is terrific; yesterday we marched ten miles—only ten, but two chaps have died as a result of it, several are seriously ill . . ." Surprisingly the censor allowed that part to stand, but he obliterated the rest of the paragraph.

Even when they stopped for the night, the troops often had little or no rest. "We halted at the outskirts of a wood and were told to take our night's rest. We took off our equipment for a pillow and made a drink of tea with rags and whale oil to light it . . . Having rested a couple of hours, the order came and we were moving out again." Exhausted and spent men kept falling out at the side of the road, "in the state of a horse dead-beat, to whom any thrashing seems preferable to going on, or would march straight on as the road took a bend, tumbling, fast asleep, into a ditch. Some . . . walked as if they were balancing on a greasy pole, their boots slipping and sliding, struggling to recover imaginary losses of footing, pant and sweat and scrape desperately sideways with his feet . . . Down he would go time after time in the mud, each time as unable to rise of himself, under the weight of his pack and equipment as any medieval knight unhorsed and held down by the weight of his armour. Hauled up again to his feet, to be driven along like the spent cab-horses in Naples, just strong enough to move when up, but not to rise."

Men who could not cope with the rigours of the march were often punished to discourage malingering. "Our doctor is a terror! He fol-lows the march on horseback. If anyone falls out, he sends them back at once and they have to do an extra march in the afternoon or on the next day. Very few fall out when they know he is behind." At the end of a march by a Guards regiment during which many men had fainted or suffered fits, all those who had fallen out, for whatever reason, were forced to do a further five hours' march in full kit and were then con-fined to barracks for eight days.

David Railton also commented on the horrors of the London Divi-sion's march. "Orders were that no one was to fall out unless un-conscious. If so, he would be treated as a deserter. In spite of that, fifteen fell out of this battalion alone and many more out of the other battalions. Out of our fifteen, ten were unconscious, and the rest had feet so broken and bleeding that no more was possible. One brave lad-die held out to the end and then collapsed, and was found to have no skin on his feet at all, they were just raw."

The official history of the London Division—one of many unit histories written after the war, drawing on official documents but subject to all the constraints that such access entailed—painted an entirely different picture of an almost blissful country stroll. "We had hot summer weather for the journey and started early each morning from our billets to get our marching done before the heat of the day—a pleasant rest during the afternoon and evening in a quiet country village, a night under the sky in a green orchard, breakfast at sunrise and on the road again . . . These were pleasant days."

Alec's view continued to be rather more jaundiced. "The dust on the roads is three inches deep in a lot of places, and water carts are unheard of in our part of the country, so you can guess that our marches are a bit different from the Sunday morning appetiser. With my letters it seems to be a case of 'Oh! Listen to my tale of woe,' but we really have exceeded the limit during the past week, and if we don't slow up soon I shall soon—" he then put a row of ditto marks beneath the words "have exceeded the limit" and added "compris?" "Have not heard from Dad yet but live in hopes. Owing to the move, our post is very irregular and it may be more so in the near future . . . You will understand there-from that we are at *war*, the real thing at last. We are in an outlandish place miles away from anywhere (firing line included, thank goodness) and we move again tomorrow. Still we can't go far as long as this weather continues."

Despite a respite at Fortel, where "a delightful bathing place was discovered in the swift-flowing, icy waters of the River Canche," the heat and the marching proved too much for Alec's feet and by 7 August he was "in hospital once again; septic feet this time. I hope to stay here a day or two longer, and then—'back to the land.' The 'hospital' is situ-ated in a meadow; we live under canvas or in the open as we choose, we do nothing, eat plenty, and fully carry out the sentiment expressed by that well known poster 'He's happy, etc.' The only drawback is that they cut my feet about three times a day, causing me a small ration of pain, but it's worth it. Has anything transpired re the transfer? I have not heard from Dad and while I am here all my post is returned, so please let them all know."

Three days later, he was still anxiously awaiting news. "I have not heard from Dad, but no doubt his letter has been returned. Will you ask him to write again as I should like to hear from him." He was well aware that his stay in hospital would be brief and that he would be back with his unit before the looming battle but, whether genuine or simulated for his mother's benefit, he maintained an optimistic tone both about the progress of the "Great Advance" and his own prospects of returning home soon. "What do you think of the news? Quite the 'Johnnie Walker' spirit about it I think. Look out in the near future for news of the CSRs. In my humble opinion Fritz is practically 'NAPOOD' [a corruption of the French *"il n'y en a plus,"* "there is no more," the standard response of French bar- and shopkeepers to requests for items that were out of stock. By extension, it was applied to anything that was finished], and I put down the month of my return as October . . . Of course, I shall stand a very good chance of a 'Blighty One' during the next three weeks, so don't be surprised to wake up one morning to find me at the 3rd Lon. Gen. [London General—the hospital half a mile from Alec's home] Yours a la mort, Alec."

Many of the Army chaplains looked on this eagerness to be wounded with a "Blighty One" with helpless incomprehension, and each was forced to "examine without prejudice the original idea that his work lay primarily with the sick and wounded." At the start of the war, many chaplains had seen themselves as "an army of Crusaders, and . . . pictured soldiers crowding into barns to be converted. We dreamt continually of ministering to dying penitents. What an illusion it all was, almost a humiliation." "It is always assumed that a man will have more use for the ministrations of the clergy on his death-bed than when he is hale and strong. The experience of war ran counter to this presupposition . . . very few of those who were killed in the war were in a condition to receive much spiritual help when they were dying . . . The vast majority of the wounded, who had got a 'Blighty One' in France, felt they deserved our congratulations rather than our sympathy and the few serious cases were usually in too great physical discomfort to appreciate other than physical help."

Alec had heard nothing from his family while in hospital, since all his mail was sent to his unit. On 13 August he wrote to his mother, "I have received no post for over a week now, so when you write, please let me know the latest re Dad, the transfer, and everybody at home . . . It would be a jolly good idea if Dad or you would write to the CO. It couldn't hurt me and it might do some good . . . I told you two or three weeks ago that shortly my letters would be very few and far between; well, I was a bit premature, but the time is not far off now, and if I am lucky I shall be home within three weeks time telling you all what I did in the Great Advance. It is of no use you expecting me home yet on leave as chaps who have been out here twelve months are still waiting."

Rose wrote back that she had detected a change in his letters. His optimism had gone and any cheerful comments now seemed forced. He made no attempt to deny it. "You say that my letters are not so hopeful now; well when I get back I will explain all the whys and wherefores of the case. Still if I am not home for good by the end of Oct, well . . ." He did not complete the sentence.

Alec returned to his unit on 21 August. While he had been in hospital they had been stationed at a training area near Abbeville, but the day before he returned, the "Great Trek" resumed and he rejoined his unit just in time to be "back at the old game—marching." "The early part of the day was occupied in fighting a sham rearguard action, then we marched, marched, marched." "We are having rather a strenuous time but, with a bit of luck, it will soon be over." That night, the battalion was billeted in Mirvaux, "considered by many to be the most dilapidated village in Europe outside the 'forward areas,' and where one man pushed a wall down simply by leaning on it. Here there appeared to be a concentration of all the flies on the Western Front." These devastated villages just behind the lines, with their ruined houses and shattered church towers, were eerie places at night. In the darkness greyed by the distant glow of star-shells over no-man's-land, "the untended bushes of the waste gardens stand up as ghostly as in great cemeteries, motionless and stirred by no breath of air." In the intervals between the rumble and crash of shells, and the spitting of machine guns, could be heard "the scuttling of hundreds of rats, the hum of mosquitoes and the slow, silent tread of the men going to and from the line with rations, ammunition, relief parties."

The divisional artillery batteries stationed at Bottom Wood, Mametz Wood, Montauban and Caterpillar Valley had already been in action for a week and the infantry now began its preparations for the coming attack. At first, to Alec's sardonic amusement, this took the form of mock advances under simulated enemy fire. On 24 August 1916, he wrote to Rose, "We are still working very hard, marching from one place to another. The latest is that before we can enter a village we have to capture it, just as we did in England. When on the march an officer yells out 'We're being shelled,' upon which we all run into the fields and wait until the 'heads' decide that the shelling has stopped. It's a great game, playing at soldiers. Tonight we are going to dig, as they have decided that we don't know how to use a spade (this after six months of 'shifting France')." The rest of the paragraph once more fell foul of the censor. Before he enlisted, Alec had been talking of emigrating to Australia, but his experiences in the trenches seem to have cured him of any desire to see more of the world. "Arthur's letter of the 19th has just come; tell him that I shan't go to Austr[alia] after all. Once I get home I'm going to stick there like glue."

There was a tradition in the trenches that if a parcel arrived for a soldier who was in the thick of the fighting and not in a position to receive mail, it would be opened by his comrades, the food consumed and the other gifts and money shared between them. It was at least in part a pragmatic "waste not, want not" reaction to the knowledge that in any battle a percentage of the front-line troops would not be coming back, and by the time the survivors withdrew to the reserve areas any perishable foodstuffs might have been rendered inedible by the summer heat. Better by far that the rest of the unit should have the benefit than that the food should go to waste and the clothing and money be "returned to sender." But not everyone saw this redistribution of wealth in the same light. One soldier on the Somme complained bitterly, "not a single parcel received yet. I don't wish the swine who took them anything bad, only that they may choke at every mouthful or may their hands rot off."

Knowing what a struggle Rose had to afford the money, food and gifts she sent him, Alec told her not to send any more parcels. This both puzzled and upset her, and in his next two letters he endeavoured to explain. "The reason I don't want parcels is that the postal facilities in the sector of the line we are bound for are very poor, and it is highly probable that any sent would not reach me. There is another reason, and that I will tell you when I get home." Two days later, on 3 September, in response to another anxious letter from his mother, he tried again, but once more fell foul of the censor. "The reason I don't want parcels (once again) is that I stand . . . CENSORED . . . and my benevolence to the rest of the platoon does not exceed letter-pads and socks. To give you an idea of how firm my conviction is, I may tell you that I shall . . . CENSORED . . . within a fortnight. So why waste good stuff?" What Alec was trying to tell his mother was that he now knew that the long-awaited attack was to take place within the next two weeks and, as well as not wanting to see her hard-earned cash go to his comrades, he was probably also reflecting the superstition that it was bad luck to receive money or parcels from home just before an attack.

His certainty that the attack was now imminent arose from the new phase of training that had begun on 1 September, rehearsing the impending attack "on a flagged course," in an area behind the front lines near Franvillers, a village of small farmhouses just off the Amiens-Albert road. "A kind of 'finishing school' for troops in training for any particular phase of the battle of the Somme," it was laid out to resemble the ground over which they would be advancing and the objectives they would be attempting to reach. It was now known that the attack was to be on "a certain wood, but the name of the wood was so far kept secret."

Nor was the date of the attack yet known. "Wet weather set in and no orders came. Day followed day and on the fringe of the vortex that would engulf them in turn, the battalions continued serenely to train . . . Particular attention was given to night work. More than once in pitch darkness and blinding rain, companies were deployed in the stubble fields south of Franvillers to practise keeping touch and finally dig in as noiselessly as possible." As they practiced, "the horizon was lit by the flashes of the guns, dancing wildly in silence when the breeze was contrary, or accompanied by a deep-voiced booming that shook the air. Seven thousand tons of shells a day fed the guns."

Senior officers were now given their first sight of one of the Army's most closely guarded secrets: the first ever tanks, known as "Caterpillars" at the time, were to make their début in the same attack. First imagined by Leonardo da Vinci some 400 years earlier, the British tanks were devised by Ernest Swinton, an inventor, historian and war correspondent serving in the Royal Engineers. His idea for a "power-driven, bullet-proof, armed engine capable of destroying machine guns, breaking through entanglements and climbing earthworks" had languished unregarded at the War Office until Swinton lobbied Winston Churchill, who became an enthusiastic champion of tanks.

The first of them were now ready to enter battle. "Covered entirely with tarpaulins and guarded by sentries was a huddle of enormous, angular objects, perhaps eight or more feet high and tapering away at the tail like prehistoric monsters. They were not unveiled for our inspection but we were told to memorise their outline as we should shortly see them in action as a new and formidable weapon." Officers who had seen the tanks in practice manoeuvres reported that "walls were no obstacles, nor wire, banks, shell-holes nor any ordinary trench." Such was the determination to ensure that the arrival of these steel behemoths upon the battlefield would be a terrifying, debilitating shock to the German troops that the tanks remained shrouded and did not join the rehearsals for the attack. But the artillery, trench-mortar teams and even the ground-attack aircraft did so and at the end of their training "it was the widespread impression that the [London] Division had never been better prepared for battle."

Alec now knew that the battle would probably come before the transfer to his father's unit could be completed. In his letters to his mother he tried to maintain a cheerful front, but a darker, more fore-boding tone does intrude. "The transfer is going on all right and another month ought to see it through. You seem very optimistic re my prospects but, peculiar as it may seem, everybody hopes for a 'Blighty One,' more or less, it is one of the few things we have to hope for." Such a hope shows the depths of despair into which front-line troops had sunk, for while a wound might offer a passport out, for many it was a sentence of death. Penicillin had not yet been discovered and many of those exulting in their good fortune as they were carried back from the lines died of infection, blood loss or gangrene without ever seeing their homes. One such man at first "rejoiced at having got a 'Blighty one.' Gradually . . . he seemed to know that he would not see his home again. Before the end, his blasphemies rang out in the morning air. It is evi-dently very hard to die to the song of the lark." The purity and beauty of that sound, in the midst of the terrible obscenity of war, upset many men. "I used to hear the larks singing soon after we stood-to about dawn. But those wretched larks made me more sad than anything else out here."

Alec's younger brother, Arthur, wrote to tell him that he had seen a propaganda film of the front-line trenches, including an officer, sword in hand, exhorting his troops, and a cheery "postman" strolling along the parapet, delivering letters. Such films were almost invariably dra-matized and heavily sanitized, bearing about as much relation to the reality as the pristine "exhibition trenches" dug in Kensington Gardens in London. Arthur's comments showed that he treated the film with some scepticism but, perhaps worrying that he might soon be tempted to volunteer, Alec warned him not to be taken in by propaganda. "You mustn't believe all you see on the pictures; it is suicide to hold one's head above the parapet for long, so you can bet the 'postmen' don't walk along the top. Officers out here never wear swords as it would no doubt make them too conspicuous. The film you said was taken at Richmond Park, perhaps, but it certainly was never taken here."

Civilians on the home front were also treated to theatrical re-enactments of incidents from the war. The Tanzien Palast Theatre in

Berlin mounted a show climaxing with a U-boat diving into the "sea," and the Circus Sarrani staged *Europe in Flames* using "six field guns, two machine guns and a mock-up of a U-boat and a Zeppelin." Meanwhile, the Battle of Verdun, "in six scenes," was being staged for the delectation of Parisian audiences. None of these theatrical and filmed confections bore much relation to reality, but there was one notable exception: a silent documentary film of the Battle of the Somme, released while the battle was still raging and seen by an estimated 20 million British people—half the civilian population. Some of the footage was staged and filmed away from the front lines, but much of it was genuine.

No British audience had ever seen film of actual deaths in battle before and wherever it was shown, as the grey, grainy images of the troops going over the top on that terrible first day appeared on the screen, the cinema pianist stopped playing. A deathly silence fell upon the audience as rank after rank of men could be seen disappearing into an inferno of shells and machine-gun fire. Never again would the government permit an uncensored film of the fighting to be shown. In France, Abel Gance's film *J'Accuse*, though not a documentary, had a similar impact. Its most memorable sequence was of the war dead coming back to life. By a terrible irony, many of the soldiers he borrowed from the French Army as extras in that sequence later died in battle.

Alec concluded his next letter to his mother with a warning. "You remember what I told you nearly two months ago—that I shouldn't be writing very frequently? I was very premature, but the time has come at last and this will have to be my last letter for a week or maybe two. Of course I shall keep you posted with field cards [Field Service postcards, pre-printed with a series of bland phrases—"I am quite well," "I have been admitted into hospital sick/wounded and am going on well/and hope to be discharged soon," "I have received no letter from you lately/for a long time"—which were ticked, underlined or crossed out as appropriate]. But if you don't hear from me for a day or two you must understand that the postal facilities will be very poor and it is quite possible that our letters won't be collected for a week." Still he managed to end with a joke to lift his mother's spirits, and perhaps his own. "We are billeted in a farm and the lady of the house is skinning a rabbit for her Sunday's dinner. In a minute she will clear out the cowshed next door to us so I must pack up, as when she does start the air turns very blue and we have to wear our gas helmets. Yes! Here she comes, pitchfork in hand, so au revoir." The next day, 10 September 1916, he wrote to his father, who had at last replied to the letter Alec had sent him two months earlier. "Dear Dad, If you are hanging out near the place they spell with . . . CENSORED . . . you may see me shortly, but if not we shall have to wait until the transfer 'comes off' which won't be long . . . We have been told for the last month or so that we are going into the 'real thing' at last and other news calculated to produce 'wind up.' "

As the attack loomed, church parades became more frequent, conducted in the open air by David Railton and the other chaplains. The cross given to him by his wife before he left England was "fastened to a tree and the Union Jack and a fair linen cloth covered the Holy Table as usual." But any hopes Railton might have harboured that the imminence of the long-dreaded attack might have increased his flock's enthusiasm for the Word of God seem to have been dashed. Although he was personally liked, no more than a dozen men attended his "voluntary services," and even when turned out in force for compulsory church parades and exposed to "fire and brimstone" preaching—one officer recounted how, before an offensive, he had told his chaplain that he wanted "a bloodthirsty sermon . . . and would not have any texts from the New Testament"—the vast majority showed the same scepticism and cynicism as Alec. "While on church parade, we have hymns such as 'Nearer my God to Thee,' 'Forever with the Lord,' etc. They are trying to make us 'resigned to our fate.' Of course the beauty of the game is that although they are always trying to kill us, they can only succeed once. It would be painful if we had as many lives as a cat." He concluded his letter with the warning that, "This is absolutely my last appearance—on paper—for some time to come, as in the place we are bound for we shan't get time to sleep let alone write. Au revoir. Your loving son, Alec. PS If lucky I shall be in Blighty within a fortnight!"

Over the next two days, 11 and 12 September, the 47th (London) Division replaced the 1st Division in the front lines. As they advanced, entering Albert for the first time, they "walked into a new world of war." "Dawn had come as the battalion breasted the last long hill where the ragged screens of the old French camouflage still lined the road. Down in the hollow, the red brick houses of the once prosperous little town clustered round the remains of the red brick basilica with its shattered tower." The gilded statue of the Madonna, "holding out her child not to Heaven but to the endless procession below," had been toppled through ninety degrees after being hit by a shell early in the fighting, but remained stubbornly attached to the spire, jutting out like the figurehead of a sailing ship. A superstition had grown up that "when this figure falls, the war will end. If you have any faith in that, I might say that the war will last some years, because the figure is well-supported from inside by our own Engineers' work with iron girders." Albert itself was "a city of empty and ruined houses, some occupied by our troops, others barred and bolted as if a very plague had taken off the population."

"Beyond the valley, towards the rising light, stretched the grey slopes scarred by the white chalk of the old front lines." Sprawling over the lower slopes was "a vast armed camp, just behind the trenches and well within shell-fire." "As far as the eye could see, the hillsides were covered with parked wagons and limbers, ammunition dumps, RE stores, pontoons, bunches of tents, bivvies and shelters of every description, above which the observation balloons hovered in a huge 'S' that gave the general direction of the front. German eyes were on the scene also but apparently the target was too vast." Alec and his comrades must have shared the feelings of another soldier who wrote that "wearing the uniform of an army one feels a puppet, but here one shrinks to the size of a grain of sand on a mighty beach, with about the same helplessness individually."

In between the dumps of supplies and ammunition "in any old corner, were the big guns—huge monsters roaring incessantly." Gun positions were normally camouflaged with great care, to hide them from hostile aircraft, observation balloons and artillery spotters. "Guns were put in shell-holes and hidden from sight of aeroplanes. Ammunition was also taken up at night and covered over," and one German "Big Bertha" gun "making an ominous roar like the sound of an express train rushing through a tunnel" was even sited in a farmyard and disguised as a huge dungheap, but at High Wood—known by the French as Le Bois des Corbeaux (Ravens' Wood)—many of the British guns were fired from "scarcely concealed positions along the roadsides, in gullies or out in the open. Light railways fed each battery. Straight, dusty tracks crossed the countryside in every direction, steamrollers puffed where roads were being re-laid. Horses and mules thronged the water-points—large iron tanks fed by pipelines." "Up near the line, by Flat Iron Copse and the Bazentins, the ground was alive with field-guns, many of them hidden by the roadside and startling the unwary. All these things, later the commonplace of a successful 'push,' were new, but we never saw anything quite like High Wood."

"It was a scene of desolation—a desert of low ridges, scarred and marked by blurred lines of chalk trenches and shell holes . . . A confused blur showed where a village once stood, but only a heap of rubble and dust was left . . . In the dip below lay Fricourt, to the left, Thiepval and Pozières, where bloody fights raged on July 1st. Further away, the green mass of Mametz Wood, still providing excellent cover despite the 'thinning' it had undergone. Further on lay Contalmaison, Montauban and the Bazentins, with Delville Wood to the right, and there on the crown of the ridge, a little bunch of tree-stumps marked the wood that was to be our goal."

Clearly visible on the skyline, High Wood was a long, low hill, a natural strong point, the highest ground in this low-lying area. Densely forested when the fighting began, the months of incessant shelling had left it a wood in name only, reduced to a wasteland of shell-holes overrunning with water, its trees "splintered to matchwood," leaving smashed stumps "barely two feet above the ground," and shattered rock and churned earth, "like a sea all heaving in anger." A vast crater from a mine explosion stood just to the east of the wood and the soil was "poisoned with fumes of high explosives, the whole a mass of corruption." There was not a single landmark visible in the whole vast sweep of blighted ground, nothing but mud and bare, torn earth, shell craters and the ragged lines of trenches, like cracks in a dried riverbed. The shell-holes were "small lakes of what was no doubt merely rusty water, but had a red and foul semblance of blood." Dead trees, dead earth, dead water—nothing lived here except rats, flies and men.

"After weary weeks of training, this was to be the deciding point. 'Blighty or the other thing' was near at hand." The 7th Division had attacked High Wood two months before, on 14 July 1916, and a company of cavalry had briefly penetrated to the far side, but they were rapidly driven back and the Germans still occupied over half of the wood, repulsing nine further attempts "to get possession of the key to the ridge." Wave after wave of "costly and indecisive" attacks had achieved nothing but an ever-mounting toll of casualties. Now three army corps, the XIV, XV and the III, of which the 47th London Division was a part, were to be thrown into the battle, a final assault to break the German lines, but "it looked terrible country to fight through—naturally strong and made almost impregnable by German science and skill."

The areas where the troops were to bivouac spoke of the horrors to come. "The place stank of death and the residue of poison gas. The trenches had been cut, blasted and cut again by British and German troops in turn. To reach our concave wire-netting bunks in the lice-infested dugouts, we had to pass through trenches reported as 'cut through corpses.' As if to confirm this horrifying titbit, from the side of one there hung a hand and forearm." As in other parts of the Front, the dead were omnipresent; soldiers lived, fought and died literally cheek by jowl with them, their "boots and bones protruding from one's dugout walls."

"You can't *face* death . . . There's no facing it. It's everywhere. You have to walk through it, and under it and over it and past it. Without the sense of God taking up the souls out of those poor torn bodies— even though they've died cursing Him—I think one would go mad." Cutting a new trench exposed body piled upon body like the layers of an archaeological dig. "In one deep, sandy trench, I saw a man who had been buried and could not be got out. Also the black head of another man sticking out of the side of the trench quite low down at the bottom. I was told nearly everybody stumbles and trips over it at night. They found him when digging the trench and did not like to interfere with the head." Whole sections of front line were "more or less a graveyard. Many soldiers lie buried in the parapet and in some cases their feet project into the trench. We come across others as we dig. If you saw it all, you wouldn't know whether to laugh or cry." "Even the great shell-hole which we hazardously used as a latrine was overlooked by the sprawling corpses of . . . two flattened German bodies . . . tallow-faced and dirty-stubbled, one spectacled, with fingers hooking the handle of a bomb."

Bones, body parts and whole corpses were even used as building materials, reinforcing and shoring up trench walls—"it was literally true that trenches were built partly with the bodies of the dead." "Dead bodies were used to build the support walls for the fortified ditches; yellowing skulls, arms, legs could be seen packed tight into the dank, black soil . . . Soldiers tramped over dead men as they clambered along the earthworks. Men lived daily in the presence of death. They might pass through a doorway into the underground bunker in which they slept and ate, and the doorway might be propped up by corpses, pushed there to give increased protection to those inside."

Even when left undisturbed, the dead stubbornly refused to remain buried. Many were barely covered in the first place, since "burying a man who has been killed in the open is usually done by shovelling a few shovels of earth over the body where it lies, and the hands and feet are often left exposed." Bodies hastily interred kept re-emerging from the earth or glutinous mud, with hands, feet, limbs and heads continually appearing, like some hideous simulacrum of the Resurrection. As rigor mortis faded, distended hands moved in the wind as if waving farewell.

Many soldiers in their trenches hid these gruesome sights behind sandbags, or draped pieces of cloth or tarpaulin over them, or cut them off and buried them, but others left them exposed and used gallows humour to mask the horror that all felt. Every morning for several weeks, troops in one battle zone, where hands and limbs protruded from the broken soil like the first shoots of the harvest, took to shaking hands with one hand that had re-emerged from the earth and wishing it "Good Morning, old boy," in an excruciating parody of an English upper-class accent. But even when the bodies remained hidden from view, there was no escaping the stench of death, as prevalent and persistent on the Western Front as the endless bass rumble of the guns. "Everywhere like a pall, lingered the smell of corpses, or of the lime used to disinfect them."

On 12 September 1916, Alec wrote once more to his mother from this charnel house just behind the front lines at High Wood, but his tone was determinedly light, with almost no reference to the horrors he was seeing and experiencing. "Dear Ma, am now resting after a brute of a 'constitutional' this morning. We are in 'bivouacs' which were made for twenty and hold forty, so we take it in turns, half in at a time. For amusement, having no money, we do some small game hunting [killing rats with bayonets], attended with marked success as this place is unusually 'cutesy.' Now for a sleep, we were up at 1:45 a.m. and have been on my feet ever since (now 2 p.m.). Bon eh?! Au revoir, Your loving son, Alec."

6

A STORM OF SHRAPNEL

Paul Hub's regiment had been spared the furies of the initial phase of the Battle of the Somme, but by 10 July the 247th Infantry had marched to a tiny hamlet, "a little place of only two or three houses, to the south-west of Lille," where they were on stand-by, in the second line of trenches, just behind the firing line. Paul's dugout, which he christened "Villa Gretchen," was waterproof and relatively comfortable, if cramped. "I can almost stand upright in it, the walls and floor are boarded. I'm happily sharing my 'Villa' with Sergeant Sauter. I had both beds filled with fresh wood shavings, and there are only a few lice." They were further diminished as the regiment took advantage of a lull in the fighting to let Paul and his men use the filtration boilers of an abandoned sugar-beet factory as bathtubs. "They hold around thirty to forty men at a time and it was a strange sight to see a stream of naked men climbing down and disappearing inside these huge boilers. There are more rats and mice than lice, and unfortunately they're more difficult to catch. I've hung my bread bag from the ceiling in the middle of the shelter and hope it will be safe from them. The rats don't like the shooting at all. Right with the first shot, a huge beast jumped past my window. Armed with a hammer, I tried to track it down, in vain. A little while later, another one scuttled under the floorboards by the door."

On the night of 14 July, fighting erupted again in their part of the Front. "The English attacked the 248th, just about one hundred metres to our left, in a fire raid. I had my shift in the trench from ten to midnight and was looking forward to being able to sleep through the rest of the night. It was relatively quiet to start with and I and a few of the men were laying the five rolls of barbed wire allocated to me. [Units were routinely instructed to extend the barbed-wire entanglements in front of the trenches by a certain amount during each rotation into the front line.] But by the time we were setting out the second roll, the fire and the flares had increased and there was heavy fire from artillery and mortars on the trenches of the 248th. We abandoned the wiring and went into firing positions. From the safe haven of our section, it was eerily beautiful to watch. All the flares lit up the ground as if it was daylight, and the powder smoke drifting on the breeze was lit by countless flashes from bursting shells and grenades. The noise was terrible, though. At one in the morning the shelling stopped but the machine guns still rattled on and unfortunately, one man in my group was shot through the chin. I sent a comrade with him to the dressing station. This morning I found some bone splinters where he had stood. Our own artillery sent over a few salvoes of shrapnel shells, and then silence fell. From two o'clock we resumed putting out the rolls of barbed wire. It's not a cheerful business because the barbs rip your skin and clothes, and the men are quite scared of such work, so only one came to help me. My hands look as if I've been wrestling a dozen cats."

With the dawn, a beautiful sunrise on a clear, still day, the firing resumed. "The aircraft are in the air and busily looking for prey. Everywhere on the horizon you can see the little white clouds of shrapnels and the big birds circling in elegant arcs to avoid them. I watched the bursting shrapnels as if they were beautiful fireworks. It is unbelievable how much ammunition is fired away like that." That night, 15 July, Paul's unit were on stand-by in the "little forest of La Russie" when the British "released some gas or smoke to our right. We could hear thuds and bangs from their lines and saw a Very fire-glow and then huge, green-white clouds rose from their trenches and slowly drifted over our positions. Strangely though, there was no attack. Our section was extremely silent. Hardly a shot was fired the whole night through, but the silence is eerie and somehow almost more menacing than the din of shelling."

Paul and his men were huddled together in concrete shelters. "It is so gloomy that you need a light even in broad daylight and I share my shelter with fifteen other men. Eight two-man bunks have been put up, and I'm surprised that there's still room for so many rats. Last night they found my bread bag and feasted on my sausage and bread. Filthy vermin! I don't like it here at all—far better to be in 'Villa Gretchen.' There, I'm usually on my own, and I can dream away nicely in the sun on the little bench behind the Villa." He had his wish soon afterwards and on 21 July he wrote a hurried letter to Maria from there, complaining that "there's always so much to do when we're on stand-by in the second line. If there's any fighting going on in the front line, we have to jump in there; if not, we're 'the transport service'—boards, logs, rails, iron sheets, gravel, cement, rolls of wire, ammunition, food, everything has to be brought up by hand or on small, heavy carts. Another group is assigned to improve the paths and communication trenches that are under continuous fire. I was also helping the 5th Company to build another concrete shelter when shells started raining down around us. We took cover behind a three metre thick traverse, then moved back to the support line. When we came back in the evening, the whole of that traverse had disappeared, utterly destroyed by exploding shells."

Patrols also went out into no-man's-land every night, but Paul made haste to assure Maria that "people very rarely get injured on patrol. There are so many shell-holes, trenches and other pits between the lines that there's always somewhere to take cover, even from the fiercest fire. Plus, you have the whole night, and so, at your choice, you can move or wait until the firing stops. And as long as the patrol is out, we give covering fire, so it's never as difficult and dangerous now as it was back when I won my Iron Cross."

For the first time, Paul also saw a mine detonated. "It was accompanied by a fierce swaying of the ground, like a big earthquake. At the same instant, a brown-black column of earth rose into the air as high as a tower." It formed a huge crater that was immediately occupied by a British "Crater Jumping Party." The next morning Paul and two of his men were repairing shell damage to the parapet of their trench when "an Englishman shouted at me. I only understood the word 'Hey!' He had probably seen us shovelling earth and it was generous of him not to have shot—he could certainly have hit at least one of us. We didn't wait for a further warning and ducked down into the trench." Such gestures were not uncommon, but on neither side was goodwill banked for future credit. The very next day, "twelve men of the 7th Company stormed the crater occupied by the English. It was only manned by two men. One escaped, the other, about to have a wash, had taken off his shirt and tunic. He was injured so badly by shrapnel from grenades that he died soon after. Judging by the papers we found, they had only recently arrived from Egypt."

The following day, the German artillery shelled the English front line so heavily that "there were shell-splinters flying back even as far as our position. The English have the habit of letting off smoke when they attack so that they can avoid being enfiladed by fire from the adjoining trenches, and one of our shells must have landed in a store of smoke bombs because the whole area turned into a sea of smoke. It lasted for about two hours, and for most of that time we couldn't see anything of the English lines. We were on alert, waiting for a surprise attack, but nothing happened."

Maria had obviously poured out her worries for Paul's safety in her last letter to him, for he now chided her. "Why are you so lacking in courage? Don't you believe any more that we'll see this through? If you are wavering, think of the example of our men here. The 10th and 12th Companies will storm the enemy trenches in the next few days, a savage and perilous raid. Yet some ninety men from one company alone volunteered for it. If our company was taking part I would volunteer, too. When big battles are being fought at the Somme, then it is even more our duty to remain brave and strong. Become my strong woman again and share my optimism."

That would have been rather harder to do after Paul reported the results of that trench raid in his next letter, on 29 July 1916. "I haven't got much good news about the raid that we undertook the day before yesterday. We had big losses and achieved next to nothing—just two captives. The 248th had more luck. They took two machine-guns and almost thirty prisoners. Our men were probably two or three minutes too late leaving the trench after the artillery barrage. By then, the English had managed to reoccupy their trench and our men were met with the rattle of machine-gun fire. Only a few managed to get into the English trench, the rest retreated, taking with them the wounded. My heart bleeds for all those that were left behind—all dead, I think. Most of them were young men, an even greater loss for our Regiment, for these were the men responsible for much of the good spirit that has prevailed with us so far."

The second anniversary of the outbreak of the war passed almost without notice. "You don't really think any more about our entering the third year of the war, and still less about whether, and if so when, there is going to be peace again." Two days later, on 6 August, echoing his fears about the loss of morale that might result from the death of so many of the unit's youngest men, Paul admitted to Maria that "yesterday, there was a mutiny during the work detail. The Corporal responsible for transporting supplies into the lines announced at eleven o'clock that this was going to be his last trip of the day. When he and his men returned at twelve o'clock, another Corporal demanded a further trip. When they refused, he reported them to the Captain. He arrived, furious, took all of us NCOs to one side, and lambasted us for allowing such a mutinous atmosphere to develop. He told us the potential penalties and then ordered us to get on with the work. I made a real effort to get the men to come to terms with it, joining in with the work myself and heaving at the load as hard as I could. It had no effect. If the other Sergeants had supported me, I might have been successful, but instead they took the side of the men. In the end, they carried on with the work under the direct supervision of the Captain. I worry how this mutinous spirit will develop if the war goes on for another year. And such an attitude from my own men hurts me deeply."

Even when they pulled back to the reserve areas just behind the front lines, there was no respite from the shelling and bombing. "We are constantly being bombed. Today everything was all peace and quiet and I was reading a book when suddenly there was a terrible blast and a crash, and the whole building trembled. I thought the barracks would collapse. Splinters of brick and tile were flying everywhere. Some of the Russian captives of the 248th were killed by them—that's how close to the front line some of them are employed. The blast of each bomb is terrible, a storm of shrapnel shredding everything in its path. We fired at the aircraft but to no avail and they kept circling above our heads for some time before finally disappearing into the clouds.

"The division's saw-mill at Marquilles was also attacked. One bomb fell on a stack of oak trunks fifty to sixty centimetres thick. They went flying in all directions, smashed like matchsticks; the end of one was so shredded that it could have been used as a broom. Out of the three dead that I saw, two were terribly mutilated by shrapnel. One man had the whole side of his body ripped open, the other was missing his left arm and his neck had been sliced apart. The third was unmarked but killed by the shock wave from the blast. Today, Iron Crosses were awarded to the few men who escaped with their lives from the patrol on July 27. Wearing their decorations, they marched back to their divisions as a band played. They were hard-earned. I don't envy a single one of them."

On 16 August 1916, Paul was once more in the front line. "We started off towards the trench at seven in the evening. We were only marching in groups of fifteen, but even so we were targeted by aircraft and two bombs were dropped on us. I have more respect for bombs than anything else. The sky was overcast and we had no warning of the aircraft's approach. At the little forest at La Russie, we suddenly heard the familiar whistling sound and threw ourselves to the ground. They exploded fifty to a hundred metres away and completely destroyed the communication trench—beams, planks, gangways and sand-bagged walls torn apart. Only with great effort could we climb over the rubble. The aircraft was still circling above us, not very high up at all; but how powerless we are—we see death circling above us and can't do the least thing to avoid it. Our artillery didn't fire at it and though a machine-gun did start to crackle briefly, it didn't trouble the aircraft at all.

"The first night in the trench was very quiet. I don't even seem to notice the shelling and mortars any more—of course, when they go off right in front of you, then you do pay attention—but suddenly, just before seven, they began firing *Kugelminen* [heavy mortars]. They have an iron casing, thirty to thirty-five centimetres in diameter, and are packed with explosives. When the first one hit, I was just writing Mother's birthday letter and dreaming of peace to come soon. The explosion seemed like a mockery of that. My dugout shook so hard that I thought it was going to collapse on top of me. Half an hour later the mortar shells began coming in salvoes, exploding thirty to fifty metres from my dugout. It started to collapse and I ran over to the Commander's dugout, while the men fled in a panic into the concrete shelters. The enemy fired about sixty mortars in all, completely flattening a twenty-five-metre stretch of the trench. Today we're working on it relentlessly, but I hope we don't finish it completely so the 6th Company still have a job to do. On the day we relieved them, they fired 102 *Priesterminen* [small mortars] into the English positions and we were the ones to receive the retaliation."

The next day Paul's regiment took some revenge for the attack. "Our Russian 20.8cm howitzers [captured from the Russian armies and transferred to the Western Front] fired twenty-five shells into the

English positions, the shrapnel even reached our own lines and our men had to go into the shelters. It seemed to have worked, they only sent back one *Kugelmine*. Last night, I did my first patrol. I was ordered to find out what the enemy was up to. It was overcast and pouring with rain when, just before 11 p.m., I left the trench with four men and wriggled through the wire. Everyone had two hand grenades and a rifle, and I carried a revolver. The bright moonlight showed us the way. It was so quiet that I was certain we would run into an English patrol at any moment, but there was nothing. We inched forward, using every single trench and every shell-crater as cover, then lay still and listened. Every now and then there was a shot and we heard the British digging their trenches, though the sound of carts bringing up supplies was often loud enough to drown the noise of digging, but there was no sign of anything suspicious.

"My men weren't up to much, and after being out for only an hour, they wanted to go back, but instead, I took one man with me and crawled up the ditch of the 'French Way,' a road that leads to New Chapelle, but is now covered with grass. From there, I listened once more. I would have liked to have gone even closer to the British lines, but my one loyal man advised against it, fearing that we could be cut off by the sap [British forward observation post] that ran to the left. We finally arrived back in our own lines at 1 a.m., absolutely soaked to the skin."

On 26 August, back in reserve once more, Paul's regiment was still under fire. "The mortar battles are getting heavier and the English have now put my section under fire as well. I'd gone to bed after lunch, but suddenly there was a hell of a noise. A mortar-shell had exploded a few metres away and dirt and shrapnel battered the front of my shack. I jumped from my bed and looked out to see what was going on. Two men, pale with fright, ran past me; I can still see the terror in their faces. They didn't answer my questions, but just kept running towards the concrete shelter. I went to find out for myself and discovered that the mortar had made a direct hit on the shelter that my group usually used, but had left to another group this time. Of the four men who were in there, one, who had been sitting at the table writing, was horribly mutilated and stone dead. The other three had been asleep on their beds and escaped with shock.

"I had just reached the shelter when there was another bang. A second mortar-shell had exploded just a step from my 'Villa.' Luckily, I'd put up sandbags on that side some time before, otherwise it would be a ruin by now—the sandbags were completely torn apart. The door had been blown in as well, and my things inside were strewn everywhere. We expected another attack that night so we spent the night in a new concrete shelter, but there were no beds, so we had to lie on the ground. The shelling started again at 3 a.m.—mortar after mortar, shell after shell. We were surrounded by drumfire, but we weren't too scared, because the shelter was well protected. We lay there for forty-five minutes, being shaken like in an earthquake. Around 3:45 a.m. it started to quieten down. When I looked out, I was surprised to see that only a ten metre section of the front line had been battered down, though the communication trench was destroyed. My abandoned shelter had not been damaged, though my rifle that I'd left inside had been smashed by a shell-splinter. We started with the clean-up right away and by about 7 a.m., the main trench was clear again, but we didn't bother to rebuild it properly because we were anticipating yet more shelling."

As the remorseless attrition on the Somme continued, huge numbers of troops, including the 247th Infantry Regiment, were being drafted to fill the voids where the fighting was fiercest. On 29 August, fearing the worst, Paul Hub wrote to his parents. "We are moving out in the next few days, where to, nobody knows for sure, but there are probably difficult and bloody days ahead for us. Don't worry if you don't hear from me for a few days and, although we should be prepared for it, let's hope that the worst doesn't happen. God grant that I survive these perilous times. Again, many thanks for all the good things that you've done for me. Farewell! I remain till my last breath, your grateful son, Paul."

He also sent a farewell letter to Maria, full of foreboding. "We're moving out again and it seems very likely that we'll end up on the Somme. We won't stay there for very long. Usually, regiments are relieved after two or three weeks. Very few can cope with longer than that. Even if the losses aren't too great, men's nerves break down. God grant that I come back from this hell. I'm not particularly confident, but with luck, the worst won't happen; I want to be happy with you still, Maria. With this letter I send you my ring. I want to take with me as little as possible, because you never know what will happen. None of all your loving letters that always fill me with joy and that you, my love, dedicated to me alone, shall fall into the hands of strangers. I'll therefore send you them in the next few days. My dearest, accept my deepest thanks for all your gentle and loving words, and for all the good and blessed hours that I have had, thanks to you. I'm returning to the bloody battlefield. For myself, I have no fear, but I am worried about you and my parents; you may be alone again and my parents may lose a third son in battle. God grant that this will not happen. If only I could hold you in my arms again and tell you how dear you are to me, how full of love my heart is for you, I would console and encourage you. Take heart and be strong. Only this one more ordeal, then there will be quieter times for our regiment. We are forbidden to tell anyone where we are going, but I can't leave you in ignorance."

That night the 247th were relieved by "the Saxons who have been in the front lines on the Somme. Just before they arrived, the English sent over a few shells. It was the first time since I returned to the field that I'd faced shells of such heavy calibre. This was our farewell to our 'quieter' area—we had three wounded. Everyone was inside the seemingly safe concrete shelter, but the shrapnel burst through the door. How strange that the one worst hit was the one who'd been most afraid—Lance-Corporal Peter. My friend Anton Edelmann, with his nerves of steel, was standing in the entrance. The blast threw him to the ground, but he wasn't wounded.

"As we were being relieved, Commander Beck called me over to him. It was during a break and I was lying by the roadside. 'It's worth the effort for you to get up!' he shouted. I was preparing myself for a tongue-lashing and trying to recollect what I'd done wrong, but when I reported to him, he congratulated me and told me he was promoting me to Vice–Staff Sergeant and Provisional Officer. I was flabbergasted; I was the only Staff Sergeant to be promoted. I am glad and grateful that I now have the *portapee* [the sword and waist belt of an officer], and if I don't die first, I will become an Officer of the Reserve!"

The 247th moved out that night and, with his uneven gait, Paul suffered agonies on the long forced march to the Front. On 2 September 1916, he wrote to Maria during a rest stop on the outskirts of Lille. "We arrived at our so-called rest area at 0:45 a.m. It was a hellish journey. We marched from Le Willy almost parallel to the front line on the road, passing through Tournes on our way. My rucksack was very heavily laden and I was absolutely exhausted when we arrived. Many men fell out along the way and were left behind. We are now billeted in a former leather factory, where we Staff Sergeants have a room with good lighting, a big table and proper beds. There are baths and showers too, which refreshed me wonderfully after the march, but we had a depressing meeting with the Commander of the Battalion about the state of war. There are difficult days ahead."

By the next day, 3 September, as they prepared to move up into the front lines, "we could hear the thunder from the Somme. We couldn't distinguish the individual explosions, it was just a continuous thunder, eerie and incessant, and we couldn't begin to imagine how anyone could survive under such heavy fire. Is it surprising then, that I, like the rest, bade farewell to my life and everything that I held dear? That night we were loaded onto trucks and as we pulled out, the soldiers sang a few songs of farewell. On our way, we met innumerable convoys coming from the Somme and, at that time of night, with the rain drizzling down, they made a very forbidding and desolate impression. The thunder of the guns grew louder and louder and the line of the horizon was marked by a perpetual tremor. At 2 a.m. we reached Longuavesnes, where there was chaos because of the vast amounts of traffic. The few civilians still there were making ready to flee. The billets were very modest. Every shelter was crammed with people and some men were even put into henhouses.

"The next afternoon, we prepared our attack kit—overcoat, tarpaulin, weapons and ammunition, and everyone carried their food in an empty sandbag. We left our rucksacks and their other contents behind. You don't wash in the front lines, but I should have packed a second handkerchief; I had to make do with a piece of a sandbag after my only one became too awful to use. It was pouring with rain as we set off at 4:30 and marched on to Moislains, in a lovely valley, typical of the Somme region. How beautiful it would be, if not for the war. We were already within range of the enemy's heavy artillery and every now and then a shell crashed into the town, each one adding to the toll of casualties. How could it be otherwise when soldiers were so tightly packed together? We were billeted in a former dyeing mill and slept on the ground, so jammed together that a single direct hit would have wiped out half the Company.

"In the early hours of 6 September, I and the other platoon captains had to recce our front line positions, near Le Priez, so that we could lead our men there when we moved up to relieve the front line troops. The way led us past the devastated town of Rancourt, where the fifteen- and twenty-eight-inch howitzers of the enemy have done their work. All the roads were being shelled and we had to walk across the open fields. It was hard to find our way; it was a pitch-black night and there were many different paths, and shell-craters everywhere, big enough to swallow small houses. Eventually we were met by two Hussars, who led us to our positions just as dawn was crawling in through the fog. There was surprisingly little fire that morning, but our guides were still very nervous and couldn't understand our carelessness; later, we became more cautious, too.

"We all returned safely to Moislains. The Vaast forest just outside the town was bustling with activity. Many gun batteries were concealed there with mountains of discarded shells, and traces of the previous fighting were everywhere. The rear areas were so heavily shelled that the lives of the ammunition platoons had been made as hard as ours. In many places the hinterland has been so devastated that you can fall into a shell-hole at every step you take. Our last hours in Moislains were used to rest and replenish our provisions and ammunition. Everyone was trying to get some sleep, as rest could not even be thought of in the days to come. Everyone took another hearty ration of provisions, bread and two bottles of water. Before we set off that night, we were supposed to receive two more bottles, have our canteens replenished, and be given some chocolate, tobacco and cognac but, like the water, none arrived. There was ammunition in abundance and everyone took four hand grenades, though many were lost or even thrown away on the way—that's just the way people are."

At 10 p.m. they left Moislains, reaching the front lines after a further three-hour march, laden with equipment and "under constant gunfire, the last hour and a quarter in a narrow communication trench, and the last 500 metres from the communication trench into the front line in the open, from one shell-hole to another." It was "hardly endurable . . . we lie down in an unfinished sap, exhausted and almost sick. Our uniforms are dripping with sweat . . . The trenches look terrible, all shot to pieces. Numerous bits of equipment belonging to our dead and wounded are lying about. There are a large number of corpses and we can hardly bear the smell . . . Many here—nearly all—have gone mad and have had to be taken away. No wonder, for with such a bombardment, one gets no rest. Our tongues are hanging out of our mouths with thirst and not a mouthful of water is to be had."

Paul's company was divided into four platoons, "three combat platoons, and the fourth—mine—had the task of collecting the rations from the supply troop and bringing them up to the front line. I thought this would be an easy job, but soon realised my error. Only a few hundred metres from the crucifix on the Rancourt-Manacourt road, between the Vaast and Vaux forests, we came under fire and lost one dead and three wounded. The houses in the area had all been flattened and shells were continually raining down on Combles, in the bottom of the valley. Whenever a 28-inch projectile struck, the ground shook for two kilometres around. Nobody could survive in the town, or allow themselves to be seen by daylight anywhere. We took cover in the underground shelter on the southern edge of Combles, but some platoons had to lie up in the devastated brickyard.

"My shelter had two entrances; if all underground shelters had done so, we would have been spared many losses. Often the only entrance was blocked by artillery fire and the people in the shelter suffocated, as happened to Staff Sergeants Berger and Sauter, and another two men. And twenty-three men died in the shelter of my former platoon captain, Lieutenant Köperle. My shelter had been used by the artillery; there was an abandoned battery of guns and many unused shells still lying around it. It was eight metres deep and eight metres long, and quite dry. There is a one-metre surface layer of clay soil, but below that the chalk layers begin. There was no chance for us to wash, and dwelling in these caves, we soon looked like millers or plasterers, covered in fine grey-white dust.

"The artillery fire usually started around 10 a.m. and increased hour by hour until, from 4 p.m. onwards, it had evolved into a continuous drumfire. This lasted until around 6 p.m. or 7 p.m., and then the nightly attacks were launched. Every day, my men and I received the rations by the crucifix and distributed them to each platoon. Food was plentiful and quite good—bread, tinned pork sausage, ham, bacon, and lots of butter—but water was often very scarce. Every man was allocated two bottles—not enough in any case—but many were smashed on the transport up to the lines or drunk by the men bringing up the rations. Some of them were utterly without conscience when they came under fire—as happened at regular intervals—and just threw away the sacks they were carrying and ran. They certainly weren't thinking of their thirsty comrades lying in the trenches. On one occasion, they dumped our sacks, each containing ten bottles of water, in the trenches of the 6th Company on our right flank, and fled. Of course the bottles were taken by the men of the 6th Company. So we weren't short of unedifying moments, though fortunately my troops had enough understanding of the situation not to blame me for their thirst.

"If you showed yourself in daylight, you were inviting immediate shelling. The enemy had occupied the heights to the west of Combles and could watch over the whole area. We would normally have urinated and defecated in a latrine well away from the shelters but in this situation, we had to stay under cover and use empty cans instead. The enemy aircraft made our situation even more unbearable. They dominated the area right up to our second line. Why do our planes allow the enemy to fly as low as fifteen metres above our trenches, watching over every single man and every single cut of a spade? Nothing made us more nervous than this. We could see some of our aircraft in the early mornings high in the sky, and there were often dog-fights, but as soon as more enemy planes appeared, ours fled back to our third line. And as long as we're not ruling the air, we're taking one backward step after another. The enemy artillery could fire at will, the fighters marking their targets for them as they could see every single man in our trenches, but our artillery couldn't even fire back because that would have given away their positions and attracted immediate heavy fire. What sort of conditions are those for us infantrymen?

"Even after dark, our artillery fire had far less impact, and though stormy, overcast weather is better, even bad weather doesn't keep the enemy aircraft away. Some of their pilots perform unbelievable acrobatics. I saw one going down in a nosedive after coming under fire, and we had already shouted our 'Bravos' for his fall and crash, when he pulled out of the dive at the very last moment and escaped. The enemy also outnumber us at least fivefold in observation balloons and you can imagine the difficulties that creates for our artillery. We had to watch enemy companies marching up the Combles Heights and deploying in compact order without being able to do anything about it. And during attacks, we saw enemy troops advancing across open ground while their aircraft almost dipped their wheels into our trenches, and yet our artillery could hardly fire at all. Our field artillery might have made a difference but they had it almost as bad as we did. Their batteries were in the open without a shred of cover or shelter, and the enemy aircraft soon found them, causing huge losses of matériel and men.

"On the morning of 10 September, we changed our billets to the brickyard and I put my men into the disused furnace—there was no other space available. In the afternoon, heavy fire set in." Hardened to years of trench warfare, Paul, like many others, had even begun to describe being under fire in the neutral, impersonal way he would have talked about the weather. Some men said "it was shooting" just like they would say "it was raining." In the dark and claustrophobic interior of the old furnace, the men "went crazy under the heavy fire. When part of the furnace collapsed because of the ground movement as the shells detonated, they scrambled out and squeezed themselves into the only available shelters, already packed with wounded men. Men in the front line were even worse off. There were a few scattered shelters, but mostly they just lay in shell-holes waiting for another shell-burst to bury them. Those without nerves of steel simply couldn't cope with the psychological pressure. As we waited our own turn in the front line, wounded and shell-shocked men were continually coming back with pitiful, terrible tales of what they had been through. I really don't know how we're going to survive.

"On the night of 11 September, our relief, the 3rd Battalion, arrived. We were happy to be able to escape this hell-hole, but we went straight from the frying pan into the fire. We pulled back to the Priezferm [a ruined farm] but there was not enough space in the shelter for the whole company, so I and my platoon dragged ourselves back to the Vaast forest. The men put up their tents and we three Vice–Staff Sergeants moved into a modest shelter originally built by the artillery-men. There followed the only pleasant time we had on the Somme. There were five bottles of wine in the ration sacks and we kept one for ourselves and shared the rest among the men. Then I collected the post. There were parcels with honey, pears, *zwieback* [bread buns], chocolate, sweets and a tin of bean salad. We took it all into the forest and sat among the trees in the warm sunshine, and afterwards lay down and went to sleep. After what we had gone through, I'll never forget this peace and quiet, though even here, that was a relative term. Ahead of us always was the rumble of heavy drumfire, while the nearby road and the twenty-seven-centimetre gun battery 200 metres behind us were under constant fire, so we were woken up more than once, but compared to what had gone before, this was perfect peace.

"We were not to be left to enjoy it for very long, however. In the evening, the first platoon was moved forward to help with digging entrenchments while I took my platoon to collect the rations from the supply troop. We had to wait until 2 a.m., when the carriers at last arrived with soup in four metal pots; the first and the last time we got hot food. But our men were so exhausted by the endless shelling that they didn't care about eating and most of them just tried to snatch some sleep. Only two of the four pots of soup were eaten, the other two were left where they were and were then blown to bits or buried by shell-bursts. The food carriers hadn't bothered to wait for them; they'd already left at high speed.

"A one hundred metre stretch of the communication trench was completely flattened by the shelling and we had to dig it out again to make it relatively passable. We were working until about 5:30 a.m. and

I was very lucky to survive. A shell exploded right next to us, wounding two of the infantrymen in front of me. But I got away with shock and none of the following salvoes hit me either, though I've still got the ringing sound in my ears. On the way back from the front line we had yet more shell-fire. We've been six days in this Battle of the Somme and there's still no end in sight. The enemy artillery keeps battering our positions, shaking the ground and our nerves with it, but so far, I've been looked after mercifully, often miraculously. The enemy attacks are incessant but their infantry are very poor; one machine-gun and a few rifles is usually enough to repel them. But the artillery fire never ceases, pounding us day and night. I don't know how we will endure the next twelve days. We look and live like pigs, eating cold food if and when we can, and I'm so thin that my uniform is hanging off me."

The next night, 13 September, was another dispiriting night for Paul. "Around 8 p.m. the provisions carriers were spooked by some alarm and disappeared, taking my men with them—real heroes they were—and the Staff Sergeant let them take my equipment and my gun with them. I could have punched him. I was forced to go first to Mana-court, then to Etricourt, looking for my men. Of course, I didn't find them. I arrived back at 1 a.m., completely exhausted, and half an hour later the shame-faced supply carriers and my platoon reappeared. Shortly afterwards we were ordered forward to reinforce the company. We reached the Front at 6 a.m., where many of the underground shel-ters, including those packed with men, had been shattered by shells. Yet more men had to be crammed into the few that were still intact. I found a modest refuge on the stairs of a machine-gun shelter, but it was too narrow and uncomfortable to rest there for long."

On the following day, 14 September, "the enemy guns fell suspi-ciously quiet. We didn't like that at all. The artillery fire only started around 1 p.m., but then increased continually until by 6 p.m., I don't think I've ever been under heavier fire. The men crawled into the very bottom of the shelters, but because I knew for certain that nobody would want to observe during that sort of bombardment, I did the observation duty myself. Time and again I used my binoculars to search the area and yet none of the endless shell-splinters hit me. I had the strong, secure feeling that somebody was watching over me, and it didn't leave me throughout the long hours of the night."

Cowering in their shelters, trenches and shell-holes, the German troops heard "nothing but the drumfire, the groaning of wounded comrades, the screaming of fallen horses, the wild beating of their own hearts, hour after hour, night after night." Another German soldier, in the front lines just to the north of Paul's unit, described the scene at daybreak. "I looked around me; what a ghastly picture. Not a trace of a trench left; nothing but shell-holes as far as the eye could reach—holes which had been filled by fresh explosions, blown up again, and again filled. In them we lay as flat on the ground as if we were dead, for already flocks of enemy aeroplanes were humming over us. We were absolutely at their mercy, and with remorseless accuracy, they directed the English heavy guns, shell after shell, into our line, and themselves fired with machine-guns at everybody who made the slightest move-ment . . . The fire increases to such bewildering intensity that it is no longer possible to distinguish between the crashes. Our mouths and ears are full of earth; three times buried and three times dug up again, we wait—for night or the enemy."

—

7

THE ROTTENEST PLACE
ON THE SOMME

The military form that would have extricated Alec Reader from the battle of High Wood never arrived, and during the night of 14–15 September he and his comrades of the 47th London Division moved up to the firing line. "Greatcoats and packs had been handed in. Gas masks were worn rolled up and stuffed into the breast of the tunic. Extra ammunition, two sandbags, pick or shovel, besides entrenching tools were carried." Infantrymen carried 200 rounds of ammunition, bomb-throwers only 50 rounds, in recognition of the weight of the bombs they also carried. Each man also had a waterproof sheet in his belt, an empty sandbag in his right tunic pocket, a field dressing and iodine, emergency rations "including a biscuit," and "wire-cutters, as many as possible." An officer described the scene that night. "It was almost dusk when we reached the dangerous gap through which all traffic to and from High Wood must pass . . . here on the threshold of stark tragedy, all lightheartedness fled. Till recent days this gap had been a popular target for our gunners. Now the road was ours and we were the target.

Only one platoon at a time went forward. The rest stood silently with grounded arms at the sheltered approach."

For days the German artillery batteries had been laying down fusillades of shells upon the gap at unpredictable intervals, causing carnage among supply trains carrying ammunition and supplies to the front lines. "The stench of dead mule almost overwhelmed us. The bloated bodies of these wretched beasts sprawled in grotesque postures and hampered our progress through the cutting. One animal still showed movement and was shot by its driver. Here lay the wreck of a gun limber and there an overturned ambulance van. With unhurried urgency we skirted the carcasses and the craters and gave a wide berth to any dud shell."

"I wondered what it might feel like to be wounded—to be killed! All through that night I never had a wink of sleep. My stomach would insist on rising to my throat to choke me each time I thought of some lurid possibility . . . I find myself engaged in calculating the chances of escape. Surely a quarter of our number will remain unscathed. I have one chance in four of coming out none the worse. And the other chances, what are they? Maybe they are three to one against being killed. There is some comfort in that. One chance in four of being wounded, which means a respite, and one in four of being taken prisoner—almost as good as escaping scot free . . . Where we had been lying in bivouac the noise of the guns had been an incessant thunder. We had found time to pity the poor devils who were already in the thick of it. Now we found ourselves approaching the monster. Gradually, as we moved, we were enwrapped in that almost homogeneous sea of sound, and shells burst nearer and nearer.

"Stumbling along in the inky darkness, the intensity of which was preserved by frequent explosions, I can hardly attempt to describe my thoughts and feelings . . . Two horses dashed madly past us towards the rear, released from their load by a shell which had killed their driver and shattered their wagon. With a crash, one of them collapsed within a yard of us, showing horribly plainly that even horse-flesh cannot be disembowelled and live. We continued going forward. Then the darkness was temporarily relieved. A dump of Very lights had been exploded, and a firework display, enough to confuse the most carefully contrived artillery signals, shed a fantastic light upon this hell on earth. Darkness may be awful, but when duty tells you to go and be killed and, in the going, to walk past wounded men, right and left, in the eerie light of military fireworks, the horror of it becomes almost unbearable . . .

My strength was in my three to one odds. It was all chance. Oh for a Blighty one. Even the fourth chance, death, was becoming less dreadful. It would take me out of it all, whatever else might happen."

The attack had not yet begun, but snipers, mortars and artillery were reaping their usual harvest among the soldiers lining the trenches and a steady stream of casualties was being borne away from the front. "Stretcher bearers with expressionless faces picked their way through the rubble, their burdens hidden under greatcoat or blanket. A shell screamed above us and burst dully over the hill. Still in step, we plodded on . . . The last lap led us, in fading light, along a road cut in the side of a hill which lay between us and our old enemy. At the roadside I recognised a huge, dark object concealed under a canopy of tarpaulins. We slithered down a slope and, under cover of darkness, entered a maze of communication trenches, where we squeezed unceremoniously past the men we were relieving. Their cold, wet garments brushed against our hands."

They moved into the firing trench by the eerie light of flares fired from the German side, which threw strange, lengthening shadows as they dropped to earth, making the skeletons of the trees seem to grow to a monstrous height. High Wood was already infamous among British troops—"ghastly by day, ghostly by night, the rottenest place on the Somme"—and the superstitious among Alec's comrades would not have liked the omen of being assembled in Black Watch Trench, for the men of that regiment had died in droves during an unsuccessful assault on High Wood at the end of July. In those cold, dark hours before a dawn that they knew would be the last that many would ever see, few of the men in the crowded trenches would have been able to snatch even a few moments' rest. The only ones "who got any sleep were those who crept out into No Man's Land to lie down in shellholes."

The rest remained awake, brooding on what the daylight might bring, thinking of their families and making last-minute pleas to their friends that, if the worst happened, they would take a final word or a keepsake to their loved ones. As the night wore on, men retreated deeper and deeper into themselves. "One by one they realised that each must go alone, and that each of them already was alone with himself—helping the others, perhaps, but looking at them with strange eyes, while the world became unreal and empty, and they moved in a mystery, where no help was."

Most had some talisman or lucky charm—white heather, a shamrock, a treasured picture, a lock of hair, a lucky coin—and countless times in that long, dark night their fingers must have strayed to it, seeking the reassurance of that familiar object. Others obsessively checked their weapons. The Mills bombs for Alec and the other bomb-throwers were lined up in canvas buckets, ready to be carried forward, two at a time. Others "felt for their grenades and tried the pins with a delicate touch. They crammed their magazines with cartridges, one over the other and gently drove the top one home in the breech. We threw up a star shell to see where Fritz had put his wire and get a dekko of the rising ground. A sniper's bullet pinged and whistled over our tin hats and we stepped down again because we'd seen the wire and the rising ground and there didn't seem to be anything left to do except to stand back against the trench and yawn and ask the time and go to sleep without knowing it, and wake up again and ask if anyone knew the time."

The 47th London Division was deployed in and around High Wood itself. The 15th Battalion—Alec Reader's Civil Service Rifles—and the 7th Battalion—"the Shiny Seventh"—were to mount the initial attack at zero hour, 6:20 a.m., on the morning of 15 September. The 7th would advance on a line clear of the eastern fringe of High Wood, while the Civil Service Rifles straddled the eastern side, with two companies inside the wood and two just to the east of it. Their objective was to capture High Wood and their allotted sections of the "Switch Line," the trenches extending through and to either side of the northern quarter of the wood. The 7th Battalion was also under orders to give assistance by mounting a flanking attack on the wood if the Civil Service Rifles experienced difficulties in taking the German trenches unaided. The fact that this was written into the brigade orders shows how strong that probability was. The Post Office Rifles and the 6th Battalion—"the Cast-Iron Sixth"—in turn would then pass through their lines to continue the advance to the next objectives on the downward slope of the ridge, the "Cough Drop," also known as "Leicester Square," and the "Starfish Line." The London Irish and the Poplar and Stepney Rifles were to lead the advance to the west of High Wood, before being succeeded by the 19th and 20th Battalions. "The postmen from quiet little hamlets or clerks who had spent their lives hitherto in snug offices, talked about these future regimental mortuaries with the homely names with astonishing calmness . . . The chances of success or of a 'Blighty One' were discussed, while the other chance, more than probability for one man in four, was quietly ignored."

Across the whole battlefront, it was hoped that the infantry, aided by the British secret weapon—the new tanks—would punch a hole two

(*Above*) A chaplain leading the burial of some of the thousands of British dead on the Somme, 23 September 1916. The numbers present and their relaxed and upright posture indicate that the burial is taking place well to the rear of the front lines.

(*Right*) The Reverend David Railton, a chaplain with Alec Reader's 47th London Division and the originator of the idea of burying an Unknown Soldier in Westminster Abbey.

(*Below*) The grave of one of the three million soldiers of the Great War.

(Left) Alec Reader with his family on his last home leave in January 1916.

(Below) The Civil Service Rifles training in England, before their embarkation for France.

(Background) Kilted Scottish troops going over the top near Arras during the Battle of the Somme.

(Left) Dead bodies laid out awaiting burial in an Artois field seem almost to merge with the earth on which they lie.

(Below) British troops huddled in "cubby holes" carved out of a trench wall in Thiepval Wood.

(*Left*) Paul Hub, photographed in August 1914, shortly after enlisting in the 247th Infantry, known as "The Regiment of the Dead."

(*Above*) Paul Hub and Maria Thumm on their wedding day, 11 June 1918. No longer the young, carefree couple of four years earlier, they now carry the effects of war etched on their faces.

(*Left*) German troops reading and writing letters in their trench during a lull in fighting, ca. 1916.

A wounded German soldier, 8 May 1915, the day that Paul Hub was so badly injured at the Second Battle of Ypres that he was not expected to survive.

(Background) A shell exploding in the devastated landscape near Ypres, photographed in August 1917, after three years of almost continual fighting.

(Below) The defeated German armies straggle homeward after the Armistice.

(*Above left*) George Seibold photographed in Chicago in 1917.

(*Above right*) George Seibold in his aviator suit.

(*Above middle*) Grace Seibold (*left*) and Grace Coolidge walking in Washington, D.C., near the Reflecting Pool. The first lady's friendship with Grace Seibold influenced the parsimonious President Coolidge to fund the Gold Star Pilgrimages to the battlefields.

(Left) An American aviator with a Lewis gun.

(Below) Pilots and ground crew of the 148th Aero Squadron testing the engines of their Sopwith Camels, at Cappelle air base, near Dunkirk, on 6 August 1918. The pilot leaning into the cockpit of the lead aircraft, D9516, is George Seibold.

(Background) A squadron flying in close formation over northeast France.

(Right) American pilots relaxing between missions.

THE ILLUSTRATED London News

MEMORIAL NUMBER

TO THE UNKNOWN WARRIOR.

(Above) "The Dead's Man's Penny"—the bronze medal presented to the next of kin of all the British dead.

(Inset) Walter Eberbach, "Verdun: Die Waltblutpumpe," a satirical medal showing a skeleton pumping the lifeblood out of Europe.

miles deep and three miles wide in the German lines. A force of five cavalry divisions would then mount a charge through this gap, turning a German retreat into a rout. That was the theory and the way that the battle had been rehearsed among the white marker tapes in the reserve areas but, as in every phase of the Somme campaign, the plan might rapidly unravel in the face of the bloody realities of actual combat.

On the orders of the British commander, Sir Henry Rawlinson, a three-day artillery barrage had been mounted. "All along the skyline our heavy shells and shrapnel were bursting continually, so that the smoke never ceased. Now and again it would slacken, only to break out again with double intensity. Behind and around us the 'Heavies' boomed and roared, whilst in front in every little valley and hollow, even in the open without pretence of cover, our eighteen-pounders snapped and barked viciously, alternating with the deeper notes of the 4.5s and the sixty pounders. Between whiles one heard the heavy 'crump' of the Hun shells."

Such a prolonged barrage was the British custom before launching an offensive, but whatever value it had in "softening up" the Germans was often outweighed by the advance notice it gave of an impending attack. Just as on the first day of the Somme, they would weather the storm of shellfire in their deep dugouts and then emerge to fire on the attacking British troops. In addition, the opposing front lines were so close together in High Wood that a barrage could not safely be deployed against the German positions without risking the destruction of the British front-line trenches as well.

The tanks and a creeping artillery barrage—moving over the German reserve trenches to prevent reinforcements reaching the front line—should still have given the men of the Civil Service Rifles some protection as they went over the top in High Wood, but the corps commanders had decreed that no creeping barrage was to be employed within the wood itself in order that the four tanks to be deployed there should have a clear path for their advance. Yet the most cursory glance at an aerial photograph, let alone a visit to High Wood itself, would have demonstrated the sheer folly of sending tanks in there at all. The wood was a morass of massive tree-stumps, shell craters and churned and pulverized ground, crisscrossed by trenches. The thirty-ton tanks travelled at a maximum of two to three miles an hour over firm, level ground; they could advance no more than fifteen yards a minute—barely half a mile an hour—"over badly crumped ground," and in terrain like High Wood they would be fortunate to make any progress at all.

The London Division's commander, Major General Charles Barter, had argued that the attack would be better served by first withdrawing Alec Reader's battalion from the front line to allow an artillery barrage to take place and then using the precious tanks to advance over the easier ground to either side of the wood. His suggestions were noted and ignored. The tanks were to go through High Wood, not round it, and the infantry were to hold their positions until zero hour and then attack.

The officers' watches had all been synchronized at midnight at brigade headquarters. An hour before zero hour, just as "the cold disturbing air and the scent of the river mist marked the approach of the morning," the men were issued a rum ration. Alcohol was the traditional aid to courage and fighting spirit—when one teetotal general outlawed the rum ration among his troops, it resulted in "the heaviest sick-list that the battalion had ever known," and one medical officer even claimed that without "the rum ration, I do not think we should have won the war"—but it sometimes proved too successful. After a raid on the enemy trenches, the men of one unit, "by way of reward or celebration, were all treated to a tumbler full of strong army rum. As a result of this potent and generous libation on empty tummies, our lads soon became fighting mad to such an extent that afterwards it was remarked with a certain degree of truth that there had been almost as much fighting going on as during the actual raid itself. There were quite a few casualties as a result, one or two of which even proving fatal." French and German troops were issued with brandy as an aid to morale, and some German soldiers dosed themselves with an even more fearsome spirit, probably wood alcohol. "After a few glasses it acts as a complete narcotic . . . Last night [one of the soldiers] riddled warrant officer K's long boots (they share a dugout) with revolver shots, in the belief, apparently, that he was rat-hunting."

At High Wood, "as the sky was turning grey . . . I wasn't cold, but shivering all the same, when they passed a water-bottle of rum from hand to hand." Just before six o'clock, officers sent word among their men to wait for the creeping barrage to pass. "It'll last about twenty minutes. Keep your eyes on me; and remember, over the top together. Give him no target. Keep in line with even spaces. Leave no gaps. Keep walking and listen for orders. Look out for gas. Senior man present takes charge"—an oblique reminder that many of those poised in the firing trench were now only minutes from death. "When you get the first line, hold it till the second wave passes. Remember, over together; and good luck."

One of the soldiers about to go over the top knew that "in a few minutes we should endure the supreme test. Furtive peeps over the parapet revealed nothing of the enemy trenches, for a mist lay over all. What if our artillery had failed to cut 'his' wire? Were his machine-gunners waiting to mow us down as we struggled to break a way through his entanglements? The monotonous hammering of these questions must have had different effects on different men. In me, strangely enough, they induced feelings of utter weariness followed by spasms of fatalistic carelessness, which I could have wished to last the whole war through. But our emotions come and go like clouds in the sky, and my new-found peace of mind was short-lived."

For another two minutes there was silence, then "breaking the deadly stillness came three singular gun shots from one of our heavy guns behind. This was the signal for the barrage to open, which it did like one huge earthquake." "Out of the void, a warning, ineffable yet menacing, a soundless movement of atmosphere and a tremor that seemed to disturb some elemental law of equilibrium. And in its wake a whistling and a vast tearing of the air and a tremendous roar as from hundreds of thousands of hidden barrels, the first shells crashed and burst before us and to left and right, so that the earth heaved and rocked while shells followed shells in agonised flight through the early morning air. Shells of almost every calibre, down they rained in a mighty curtain and blasted their high explosive or flung hot, jagged fragments among the first lines of the enemy. And as our gun teams fell into the rhythm of their task and the tempo reached its appointed measure, so the thunderous concatenation of unbridled sound resolved itself into one sustained and monotonous roar."

High Wood was eerily still, a tiny eye of calm in the midst of this hurricane of shellfire. To either side the scream, crash and roar of an endless stream of shells continued to tear the last of the darkness apart, but none fell in or ahead of the wood itself, the channel through which the four advancing tanks were to pass. Most of the troops remained on the fire-steps, positioning short trench-ladders for the officers and cutting footholds for themselves in the face of the trench, but the crookedness of their assembly trenches compelled "B," "C" and "D" Companies of the Civil Service Rifles to creep forward and lie in no-man's-land, to form a line with "A" Company. As soon as there was sufficient light, the exposed men became the target of "a murderous fire from a multitude of machine-guns and rifles in the German front-line trenches. At the same time, down came the German artillery barrage on the assembly trenches."

All was now in place, save for the arrival of the tanks. Moving forward from their holding areas at dusk, they were scheduled to move through the reserve lines during the night and advance through High Wood so as to reach the German front-line trenches at one minute to zero hour, giving their guns three minutes in which to wreak havoc among the German defenders before the infantry of the Civil Service Rifles arrived to storm the trenches and overwhelm the last resistance. The tanks were then to continue their advance, reaching the Switch Line at zero plus thirty-two minutes—6:52 a.m.

Tanks were to prove formidable weapons against infantry but vulnerable to heavy weapons like artillery. They were also ponderous in the extreme, difficult to manoeuvre because of the limited visibility through the narrow, forward-facing slit in the steel armour, and their 105-horsepower engines were prone to mechanical breakdown. The deafening noise, furnace heat and sickening fumes of the cramped interiors also made conditions for the eight-man crews close to intolerable. Forty-two tanks had been allocated to the entire front; over a quarter of them broke down or got bogged down before the attack had even begun. A few minutes before zero, "company commanders received a message telling them to send an officer to guide the tanks, if seen. Thus the Civil Service Rifles were handicapped at the start, for the tanks were neither seen nor heard." All of the four tanks allocated to the High Wood sector were late in arriving, having lost their way before even reaching their start-points. Like a bemused motorist on a touring holiday, one tank commander even went into the Civil Service Rifles' battalion headquarters to ask the way to High Wood.

The tanks were still some way from their starting positions as zero hour was reached and their contribution to the subsequent battle varied from negligible to farcical. Only one actually managed to reach the German lines and it was destroyed by an artillery shell while machine-gunning the German support trench. One tank broke its rear axle and was immobilized, though its crew continued to fire its gun at the enemy. The other two fared even more ignominiously. One grounded on a tree-stump within fifty yards of entering High Wood. As helpless as an upended tortoise, it was abandoned and eventually destroyed by German shellfire. The fourth tank proved more damaging to British forces than to the enemy. Forced off course by the shell craters and tree-stumps, its disoriented commander sent it blundering out of High Wood near its southeastern corner and, having mistakenly shelled some hapless troops of the London Division, he then ditched the tank in a British communication trench, where it "materially interfered with the removal of the wounded." After almost being shot by the furious soldiers they had fired upon, the crew spent the next fourteen hours trying to dig out their useless tank.

In the unnaturally restrained language of the London Division's official history, the infantry, "thus disappointed of the tanks' assistance, were also deprived of the support of the guns, which were afraid to fire near the tanks." That "disappointment" and "deprivation" left them to advance alone and unaided into an inferno of fire. The distance they had to cover to reach the enemy lines was no more than one hundred yards and as little as fifty in places, but very few of them achieved even this.

Suddenly the noise of the guns eased off. For a second or two there was quiet and then, at precisely six-twenty, the barrage to either side of the wood lifted and began to creep forward. "The fury of our barrage dropped like a wall of roaring sound before us." As it did so, the shrill blasts of whistles signalled the attack, though few could have distinguished the sound in that inferno of noise. The men of the Civil Service Rifles and the rest of the attacking battalions rose from the ground or clambered out of their trenches and, with the discipline ingrained through months of training and practice, marched in orderly ranks towards their own funerals. "By some means the signal to advance was given and understood and we found ourselves walking forward into the mist, feeling utterly naked. Who can express the sensations of men brought up in trench warfare suddenly divested of every scrap of shelter?" As one New Zealander later wrote, "So many men strolling over the open ground, within a few yards of the German lines, as if they were going across a paddock in New Zealand." According to one British general, soldiers dying for their country met death "as a bridegroom who goes to meet his bride." If so, grooms must have gone to the altar in the grip of terrible fear or numb stupefaction, for that is how most men advanced to meet their fate at High Wood.

One of them "stumbled into a mist that seemed to grow ever thicker. So great was the noise that the order to keep in touch with one another was passed only by means of shouting our hardest, and our voices sounded like flutes in a vast orchestra of fiends. All at once I became conscious of another sound. A noise like the crisp crackle of twigs and branches, burning in a bonfire just beyond my vision in the mist, made me think I must be approaching some burning building. I realised, when my neighbour on the right dropped with a bullet in the abdomen, that the noise was machine-gun and rifle-fire." Others went into an almost dreamlike state in which all sounds, even the tornado of artillery fire, dwindled to a meaningless blur. "The din must have been deafening (I learned afterwards that it could be heard miles away) yet I have only a confused remembrance of it. Shells which at any other time would have scared me out of my wits, I never so much as heard, not even when they were bursting quite close to me. One landed in the midst of a bunch of men about seventy yards away on my right. I have the most vivid recollection of seeing a tremendous burst of clay and earth go shooting up into the air—yes, and even parts of human bodies—and that when the smoke cleared away, there was nothing left. I shall never forget that horrifying spectacle as long as I live, but I shall remember it as a sight only, for I can associate no sound with it."

Such was the weight of German shot and shell-fire that many died before they had taken a step. The machine guns, firing from unscathed, steel-reinforced concrete fortifications—each occupied by two machine guns, gun crews and spotters housed in subterranean bunkers—mowed down rank after rank of men. Alec and the other bomb-throwers of "the Suicide Squad" of "A" Company had been sent forward to the Switch Trench, within fifty feet of the enemy. They made some inroads into the German lines and reached the first objective, the Switch Line, albeit "in reduced condition" due to heavy casualties. "Before we knew it, we were in the ruin of what only minutes before had been the enemy's foremost trenches, among ghastly and unforgettable carnage, mutilated bodies, gory, amputated limbs and a horrible head still encased in its grey helmet. We leaped down for sanctuary among this unspeakable horror and crouched there awaiting orders."

Supported by "bayonet men," they now began to bomb their way along the trench, clearing it of the remaining German defenders. The horror of this close-quarter slaughter with bomb and bayonet, perhaps the most terrible of all the forms of combat that the war had fathered, was captured by a survivor of the battle. "Sackfuls of bombs are passed along to the front and used up with inconceivable speed. Bomb after bomb circles aloft into the silvery clouds of smoke and explodes in a blaze of fire . . . The trench is broken into a zig-zag by frequent, massive traverses. Between every two there is a straight run of about eight metres. The thing is to land a bomb in this space. A single one suffices; for if the fragments of the bomb are not fatal, the mere force of the explosion in this confined space is so violent that nothing can withstand it. Thus the storming of the trench is punctuated by short rushes. There is a leap forward to duck behind the massive block of the traverse, during which one throws the bomb, hoping by judgement and guesswork to land it in the trench further on, and then there is another rush forward almost simultaneously with the explosion, which long experience enables one to time to a second.

"In this sort of fighting, you never see your enemy, though never more than ten or twenty metres from him. At most you might catch sight of a shadow or two sneaking round a traverse, and those you try to outreach at once with a bomb, so as either to cut off their retreat or to make them run back into the jaws of death . . . Behind nearly every traverse, we come upon a dead body, with the blood oozing from numerous wounds caused by thin, sharp [shell] splinters. It is a brief glance only, for our eyes are more in the air than on the ground . . . It is a strange feeling to leap forward over these dead, whom you have never seen alive."

Dugouts were cleared with smoke bombs, "so that they must either choke or come out . . . They are half-blinded and choked with poisonous smoke and you station a man at the entrance to receive them, but as you only have a party of nine, it would be difficult to spare men if you took them prisoners, so the instructions are these poor, half-blinded devils should be bayoneted as they come up. It may be expedient from a military point of view, but if it had been suggested before the war, who would not have held up their hands in horror?" Such accounts bear out the comment of one senior officer who claimed "No man in this war has ever been killed with the bayonet unless he had his hands up first." Both sides were guilty of such conduct. Robert Graves recounted the story of a wounded officer, O. M. Roberts, who had lost consciousness in an earlier attack on High Wood and come round in time to see "a German staff officer working round the edge of the wood, killing off the wounded with an automatic pistol." The German fired at him twice, missing once and hitting him in the arm with the other shot. Before he could fire again, Roberts dragged out his own pistol and shot the German in the head.

In the aftermath of the battle, every shell-hole was "full of German stick-bombs and the black, oval, grooved bombs of the English . . .

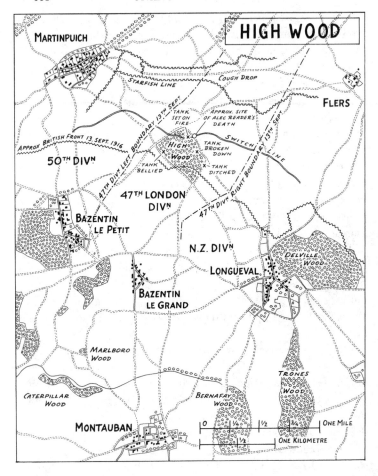

Everywhere among the shell-holes are to be seen the shallower, charred depressions where bombs exploded in the stampede of hand-to-hand fighting. The effect of the bursts, which at this range can fling a man in the air to come down like a sack, can be seen from the dead bodies lying all about, beside and over one another, just as death cast them down. Their faces and bodies are riddled by [bomb] splinters and their uniforms burnt and blackened by the flame of the explosive. The faces of those that lie on their backs are distorted, and their eyes wide open as though fixed upon a disaster from which there was no escape. Horror is fixed there like a mask—and one that no fantasy could devise . . . In their last moments they saw themselves cut off by a flaming and concentrated annihilation. One of them still clutches a stick-bomb, showing that as they ran, they let them fall behind them to cover their retreat with a barrier of fire, but that did not suffice to ward off their fate."

"A" Company had been expecting to link up with "B" Company, but "B," "C" and "D" Companies had all been halted in no-man's-land, where all three lost four-fifths of their men, all but one of their officers and most of their NCOs. "A" Company fared little better. Like the rest of the Civil Service Rifles they had been annihilated, and Alec Reader was among the dead. There is no way of knowing when he died or what happened to him in the last hours, minutes or seconds of his life, any more than we can discover the individual fates of hundreds of his comrades. So many were lost that there were precious few left alive to tell the tales of any of the ranks of dead and missing. Alec may have been killed within seconds of zero hour, rising from the trench only to be cut apart by machine-gun fire or blown apart by a shell; he may have performed heroics, mowing down several German soldiers before himself falling to a valiant death; he may have lain shaking and whimpering with fright until a German shell or bullet brought a merciful end; he may have been buried alive by a shell-burst and condemned to a slow death by suffocation; or he may have been one of the hundreds of wounded littering the battlefield, the life slowly ebbing from him with the light of this, his last day on earth. If his death was not instantaneous, his last thoughts must have been both for his beloved mother and for the simple bureaucratic error—the wrong form sent by some overworked or indifferent clerk at Headquarters—that had condemned him to death.

— · —

8

A MILLION BLOODY RUGS

On every side in High Wood were scenes that might have been torn from some hellish vision of Hieronymus Bosch: "the falling and burning trees, the dead and dying, aircraft bombing us, the deeds of bravery and . . . loss of nerve . . . I was ordered to take a machine gun party to the strong point at the north-east corner of the wood . . . I found no one to relieve, all were dead and the defences obliterated." The handfuls of survivors of the Civil Service Rifles could only crawl back to their trenches and re-form, where they became entangled with the support battalions preparing to launch their own attacks. Even though well fortified with rum, the men of the Post Office Rifles must have been almost unhinged by the carnage in front of them as they awaited their own turn to attack. "Assembly trenches on the High Wood front were so congested with the dead, wounded and unwounded soldiers of the first abortive attack, that the press of men for the second attack made them almost untenable." The frustrated commander of the 19th Battalion climbed out of a rear trench, calling to his men to follow him as he led their advance. All those who did so, including the commander, were immediately cut down by machine-gun fire.

When the whistles sounded, the men of the Post Office Rifles in turn rose from the trenches, screaming and shouting. "The yells were soon death-screams as man after man went down before that awful machine-gun fire . . . Within fifty yards of the trench we left, there was but a bare handful left of half a company. I looked behind to see the second half of the company come on, led by the company officer who, I remember as he neared us, shouted 'Get on, damn you!' Just then he fell dead . . . Men were falling on all sides, some in death agony and, between the groans and cries of men and the eternal, awful fumes of cordite, that hundred yards to Fritz's lines is the most fearful memory of France I have . . . Germans were lying all over and at the back of the trench, a group of six or seven had been hit together by a shell. They were the bloodiest and most battered human beings I had until then seen. Some of the less severely wounded put up their hands, while their comrades in the trenches behind kept up machine-gun fire and rifle-fire among friend and foe alike."

The advance by other divisions was proceeding to either side of the wood, aided by the creeping artillery barrage. It was "clockwork warfare. These troops had been drilled to move forward at a given pace. They had been timed over and over again in marching a certain distance, and from this timing, the creeping or rolling barrage which moved in front of them had been mathematically worked out." The barrage advanced at fifty yards a minute, leaving the ground behind it "fine powder; shells did not so much make shell-holes but merely moved them. Of the German trenches there was no trace."

At midmorning five battalions—or what was left of them—were still engaged within High Wood and, hours too late for the dead who already carpeted the wood, the divisional artillery and mortars were at last brought into play there as well. The artillery laid down a barrage on the western and northwestern sectors of the wood while the trench-mortar battery fired over 750 rounds in less than twenty minutes into the German lines near the crater on the eastern side, an astonishing feat of sustained rapid fire. One soldier even claimed to have seen eight or ten of the cylindrical mortar shells in the air simultaneously, following close upon each other like the carriages of a train. The barrage was followed up by bombing parties attacking the German flanks, and at last their resistance began to crack. At one that afternoon, following two months of almost constant fighting, High Wood was finally reported clear of the enemy.

"The German Switch Line was found to be practically obliterated by the British artillery," but the attempt late in the afternoon to take the next objective—the Starfish Line, some 700 yards away on the down-slope of the hill—resulted in more appalling carnage as German batteries laid down barrages on their own former trenches. The 1st Battalion, advancing with their rifles over their right shoulders "just as if they were on parade," suffered almost 90 percent casualties. The 24th fared little better. A handful of soldiers reached the Starfish Line; the rest of the survivors dug in well short. Some of them returned to the British lines under cover of darkness that night, "a mere handful, a few whimpering, a few crying like babies. Poor devils, they had it rough."

They left behind a battlefield strewn with dead and wounded men. They had been ignored by their advancing comrades, who had been issued with the standard warning that to give aid and succour to the wounded rather than continuing the advance would be construed as cowardice in the face of the enemy. "No man was to halt to attend to a wounded comrade or for any other reason. It would be regarded as a crime which would be met by the sternest penalty . . . The wounded must be left to look after themselves." Military policemen were often stationed in communication trenches during a battle to enforce compliance with such orders and arrest or shoot those in breach of them.

By day, the screams and groans of the wounded and dying had been drowned in the deafening clamour of the battle. At nightfall, though still counterpointed by the rumble of the guns, their pitiful cries and pleas for help could be heard echoing through the shattered wood. None who heard it would ever forget that terrible sound. "I saw men in their madness bayonet each other without mercy, without thought. I saw the hot life's blood of German and Englishman flow out together . . . I saw men torn to fragments by the near explosion of bombs, and—worse than any sight—I heard the agonised cries and shrieks of men in mortal pain, who were giving up their souls to their Maker . . . The cries of those poor, tortured and torn men I can never forget; they are with me always. I would I had been deaf at the time."

With the darkness, "the melancholy work of the burial of the dead was begun. The special party told off for this work dug graves in High Wood itself, and all the dead who could be found were buried side by side there." "As one looked on the weary band of tired and muddy comrades who had come to fulfil this last duty to their friend, one felt in a way one seldom does at an ordinary funeral, that . . . [the dead] really were to be envied, since for them the long-drawn agony of war was at an end." "Many men who have stood it all, cannot stand this clearing of the battlefield . . . No words can tell you all I feel, nor can words tell you of the horrors . . . several men went off with shell-shock . . . caused not just by the explosion of a shell nearby, but by the sights and smell and horror of the battlefield in general."

Retrieving the dead and wounded was often hugely difficult. Even if nightfall, mist or fog gave the stretcher parties some protection from German snipers and machine guns, the pulverized ground, shell craters, barbed-wire entanglements and the endless mud, or fine dust like quicksand, often made it "almost impossible for an armed man to move himself, let alone carry a wounded comrade." Eight men were required per stretcher, four carrying and four as a relief, and "many a time it had to be decided to carry only those who had a reasonable chance of survival." "In many cases a man badly wounded was put on a stretcher but if on the way we found another man who seemed more likely to survive, we changed them over; such was the shortage of stretchers and carrying parties."

The two sides would sometimes co-operate in rescuing the wounded, though this could come with strings attached. On one occasion on the Somme, the Germans allowed the rescue of a British sapper buried up to his shoulders as the result of a mine explosion, but only on the condition that he was then handed over to them as a prisoner of war. He could not extricate himself, so the alternative was to let him die, and the deal was therefore agreed. "A couple of Sappers armed with picks and shovels went down to the man and were joined by a German Red Cross party with a stretcher. They dug him out, finding one of his legs badly broken and sundry other damage. He handed over the contents of his pockets, dictated a letter to his wife, shouted 'Goodbye' to his watching pals and was carried off by the Germans. The war then started again."

The work of clearing the dead from High Wood and finding and aiding the wounded went on all night, amid "the ceaseless wail of the field guns, echoing over the wilderness. Listening to them on that night, one could almost imagine that they, too, were mourning for the gallant fellows who had lost their lives that day, and who were now being laid to rest. To many who were there, the peculiar echo of the field gun ever afterwards brought back vivid memories of those terrible nights in High Wood." "The trailing processions of wounded, English and German, on foot and on stretchers," left "so much blood that some of the tracks were flamboyantly marked for miles across country." A few wounded men were still being discovered long after the fighting had ended. "The dead lay where they were killed, lying in the mud and the debris of war. There were many wounded who had been lying in the open for days. On our return from the front line one night we found a man who had been out for nearly ten days, living on his iron rations of biscuits, bully beef and chocolate, and raw potatoes from the earth nearby. After the war I made enquiries and found out that he survived."

Many of the dead at High Wood had been lost without trace, blown apart by artillery fire or buried in collapsing trenches and shell-holes. Their bodies—food for the omnipresent rats—simply disappeared into the pulverized earth of the battlefield. But those men whose bodies could be retrieved were given the semblance of a Christian burial by David Railton and the other divisional chaplains, who were at their grisly task "the best part of three days." "We are now burying the bonny comrades who were with us before, it is dreadful," Railton wrote. On 24 August, he had handed a young Scots officer a piece of white heather that he had been sent from home. "His eyes seemed a bit full as he popped it away in his pocket and said 'That's going over the top with me.'" Among the multitudes of dead buried by Railton after the battle of High Wood was the Scots officer. "The sprig of white heather was still in his pocket, but it had brought him no luck."

Months after the Battle of the Somme, the dead still "lay three or four deep" in no-man's-land, and "the bluebottles made their faces black." Some burial details were semi-permanent, carrying out the gruesome work for weeks and months on end, advancing and retreating with the ebb and flow of battle. "I was attached to a company of about 150 men and our task was to search for dead bodies and bury them. Two issues of raw rum were served out to us daily, to kill the dangerous germs which we might inhale"—and to give them the courage to do the work at all. "It was a ghastly job and more than ever I learned what war meant . . . For the first week or two I could scarcely endure the experiences we met with, but I gradually became hardened and for three months I continued the job. We worked in pairs and our most important duty was to find the identity discs. After our morning's work was over, a pile of rifles and barbed wire stakes would mark the place where we had buried our gruesome discoveries. There they lay, English, Germans, Australians, South Africans, Canadians, all mingled together in the last great sleep."

Troops were given canvas bags in which to gather what they could and "often have I picked up the remains of a fine, brave man on a shovel, just a little heap of bones and maggots to be carried to the common burial place. Numerous bodies were found lying submerged in the water in shell-holes and mine-craters, bodies that seemed quite whole, but which became like huge masses of white, slimy chalk when we handled them. The job had to be done; the identity disc had to be found. I shuddered as my hands, covered in soft flesh and slime, moved about in search of the disc and I have had to pull bodies to pieces in order that they should not be buried unknown. And yet, what a large number did pass through my hands unknown, not a clue of any kind to reveal the name by which the awful remains were known in this life.

"It was painful to have to bury the unknown, be they British or German. Very often my chum and I would collect small stones and pebbles and work out some epitaph above the grave, as a last worldly tribute to men who would probably be living today if the world had really striven for peace in the opening years of this century. In those three months I assisted in the burial of over ten thousand dead, known and unknown. The womenfolk of those thousands who may be yet mourning their loss in British and German homes can rest assured that we carried out our work with reverence and care for friend and foe. For months after I relinquished this job, the smell of the dead was in my nostrils."

Alec Reader's body was found and he too was hastily buried and the grave marked with a rough wooden cross or an upturned rifle. Like all his fellows, he was buried facing towards the enemy as if, even at the Resurrection, these long-dead soldiers would rise once more and resume the fight. Army form "SS 456 Burial of Soldiers" required the officer conducting a burial to complete a return to the Director of Graves Registration and Enquiries giving "Number, Rank, Name with Initials, Battalion, Regiment, Date of Death and Exact place of burial by reference to the official name of the cemetery, the 1/40,000 map, or an accurate description. The difficulties with which Officers Commanding Units are confronted are fully realised, but it is to the advantage of the relatives of deceased officers and men that details regarding burials should be sent as soon as possible after the burial has taken place. This will enable relatives to be informed with as little delay as possible that the grave has been marked and registered and that crosses have been erected by the Graves Registration Units."

. . .

Fabian Ware, a former editor of the *Morning Post*, who was working for the Red Cross in France, had begun the recording of the graves of the war dead on his own initiative in the early stages of the war. His amateur "Graves Registration Commission" was recognized by the War Office in 1915 and became an official arm of the government the following year when the numbers of dead threatened to overwhelm Ware's cash-starved organization. A leaflet, "The Care of the Dead," was also issued in late 1916, in an attempt to assure relatives that their loved ones had received a Christian burial, but it included the risible claim that "everything is done as tenderly and reverently as if the dead man were in an English churchyard." The Graves Registration Units were "continually reminding padres that it was their duty to bury the dead in [proper cemeteries]; what they did not always realise was that this was often quite impossible and the best the padre could do was to bury the dead near where they lay, sometimes using a disused trench for the purpose." Only the bond felt by all serving at the Front and the knowledge that their wives and families, too, might one day be waiting for news of where they were buried can have persuaded burial parties to adhere as far as possible to the correct bureaucratic procedures in the midst of the hell of the battlefields. On many occasions they must have been quietly forgotten.

By nightfall on 15 September, the day of Alec Reader's death, the already depleted ranks of the Civil Service Rifles had been reduced from around 450 men to two officers and fewer than a hundred men, and almost the only rations the survivors were given that night was another issue of rum. Yet over the following three days, with a "small reinforcement of fifty-three men," they attempted further advances under heavy shelling. Two days of incessant rain turned the area to a sea of mud, choking their rifles and Lewis guns; "dirty cartridges, rifles whose clogged-up mechanisms wouldn't work any more; the men pissed in them to make them fire."

At three in the morning of 20 September, "a skeleton of a battalion" was withdrawn from the front lines. "When the relief did come it was due more to sheer fatigue than self-control that we refrained from running out of the trenches." The reading of the battalion roll-call must have broken the hearts of all who heard it—"a hollow square of jaded, muddy figures . . . the afterglint of a sun that set red; mist begins to float up the valley, but the glint of light on some clouds high up has still the hardness of silver. A strong voice . . . calls one name after another from a Roll lit by a fluttering candle, shaded by the hand of one of the remaining Sergeant Majors." Name after name went unanswered; each silence, another man wounded, missing or dead. In all, 380 of the 450 or so soldiers who had advanced into High Wood five days earlier had not returned.

One of those relieving the forlorn remnants of the Civil Service Rifles and the other ravaged battalions saw "hundreds of wounded men, some in a deplorable condition, helped along by those less severely hit . . . We finally reached a sunken road, a left turn off the main road. This was about the worst sight ever I witnessed. There must have been nearly a battalion lying dead . . . and bearing a piece of paper to signify who they were, and a vast number who happily were not dead, but unable to move." Another man serving on the Somme described seeing such men "shuffling past . . . haggard, bloodshot-eyed, slouching past in loose file, slouching on, anywhere, anyhow . . . slavering and rolling their bare-teethed heads, slobbering and blowing, blasting brightness behind their eyes, supported by listless cripples."

In total, the 47th London Division had lost over 4,500 men in order to secure a hundred yards or so of German territory—every inch had cost a life. "It has been a great victory, but the cost was and is too much to bear." Even by the ruling standards of the Great War, the death toll was so extreme that a scapegoat was deemed to be necessary. The London Division was officially criticized for its "lack of push" and the divisional commander, Major General Charles Barter, was dismissed for the "wanton waste of men" entrusted to his command. The verdicts were cruel libels on both the division and its commander. Deprived of the promised tanks and artillery, the men of the London Division had been thrown, unprotected, into the furnace, but Barter was not the man responsible. The decisions taken were not his and his vehement opposition to them had been ignored. After the war's end, the incandescent Barter was exonerated by an unofficial investigation—the government and the Army refused his demands for a public enquiry—and he was subsequently knighted and sent to Petrograd as part of a British military mission; both of which smacked of official attempts to stifle his protests and spare his superiors further embarrassment.

Having defiled the reputation of the London Division and its commander, British propagandists led by Philip Gibbs, the celebrated correspondent of *The Times*, then heightened the outrage by perverting the story of High Wood to glorify the role of the tanks. In Gibbs's fantastic version of events, the troops saw the advancing tanks "to their great joy . . . 'It was like a fairy tale,' said a Cockney boy. 'I can't help laughing every time I think of it.' He laughed then, though he had a broken arm and was covered in blood. 'They broke down trees as if they were matchsticks and went over barricades like elephants. O Crikey, it was a rare treat to see! The biggest joke that ever was! They just stamped down the German dugout as one might a whops' [wasp's] nest.' " Lord Northcliffe, publisher of *The Times* and a leading govern-ment propagandist, even contrived to reduce the German machine guns that had killed so many tens of thousands of British men to some-thing no more threatening than children's toys. "Now and then we heard the brisk note of a machine-gun, which sounds for all the world like a boy rasping a stick along palings, or the rattle which policemen carried in mid-Victorian days."

Such fabrications might have fooled some of the people at home, but not the survivors of the London Division and the other units on the Somme, who had watched their comrades being scythed down by machine-gun fire and seen for themselves the dismal failure of the four tanks sent into High Wood. But "little it mattered in London what he or I saw . . . what the soldier said was not evidence." The "tame" war correspondents—and they were the only ones allowed in France, let alone near the front lines—were "embedded" with staff officers well away from the front lines and, "when autumn twilight came down on the haggard trench world of which they had caught a quiet noonday glimpse, they would be speeding west in Vauxhall cars to lighted chateaux gleaming white among scatheless woods." Their reports car-ried always the "brisk implication that regimental officers and men enjoyed nothing better than 'going over the top'; that a battle was just a rough, jovial picnic; that a fight never went on long enough for the men; that their only fear was lest the war should end on this side of the Rhine.

"This, the men reflected in helpless anger, was what people at home were offered as faithful accounts of what their friends in the field were thinking and suffering. Most of the men had, all their lives . . . taken the Press at its word without checking. Bets had been settled by reference to a paper. Now, in the biggest event of their lives, hundreds of thousands of men were able to check for themselves the truth of that workaday bible. They fought in a battle or raid, and two days after, they read, with jeers on their lips, the account of 'the show' in the papers. They felt they had found the Press out. The most bloody defeat in the history of Britain . . . on July 1, 1916, and our Press came out bland and copious and graphic, with nothing to show that we had not had quite a good day—a victory really. Men who had lived through the massacre read the stuff open-mouthed." As one young soldier complained, "It is rubbish like this which makes thousands of people in England think that war is a great sport." Widespread distrust of the media originated in the press coverage of the First World War—a name first given to the conflict by Colonel Charles a Court Repington in 1920.

Photographers were subject to the same official constraints and, in many cases, the same self-censorship. Very few photographs of British dead were published during the war and those archived were edited when the conflict was over to remove images that might prove too graphic, but the harsher realities could not be forever concealed from those at home. "Runlets of news and rumour came trickling from France; wounded soldiers talked and could not be censored; they talked of . . . Staff work that hung up whole platoons of our men, like old washing or scarecrows on uncut German wire; of little, splendid bands of company officers and men who did take bits of enemy trench, in spite of it all, and then were bombed to death by the Germans at leisure, no supports coming, no bombs to throw back."

High Wood had been arguably the most ferocious and terrible battle of even the bloody Somme campaign—"the Great Advance," the largest battle in history, but christened with rather more accuracy "the Great Fuck-Up" by the British troops who survived it. If, like the Battle of Agincourt fought 500 years before in that same treacherous terrain, it had symbolized the final extinction of the old ways of combat—one of the last British cavalry charges was mounted at High Wood—and the emergence of the monstrous war machines of the industrial age, the machine gun, the howitzer, the ground-attack aircraft and the tank, it also encapsulated the profligate, murderous futility of the Battle of the Somme and of trench warfare as a whole.

As an Australian officer remarked, with more honesty than many of his British counterparts could summon, "Let us not hesitate to confess that strategically the battle was a failure. Of course we are now threatening the communications of Bapaume, Vely and Achiet after *four months*. We had meant to do that in as many hours." "Despite the optimistic public claims made on behalf of the offensive, its real achievement was to bring mourning into nearly every household in Britain." Those who had fallen were the once living, now dead proof that "in modern warfare, the actual troops themselves count for less and less. Given the right sort of officers, you can make almost any physically efficient human material perform almost any task. If they are naturally brave, they need little but leading; but with stern discipline and driving, timorous troops can be made to do just as well."

Brave and timorous alike had advanced side by side towards the German machine guns and been cut down in their thousands. And inevitably most of the victims were the young. Of men aged between thirteen and twenty-four when the war broke out, 30 percent were killed and another 20 percent disabled. "In the school library, a huge map of the Western Front was pinned on an easel, with a red silk thread running across on a zigzag of drawing-pins. Occasionally the thread moved half an inch this way or that, each movement meaning a pyramid of corpses." The most poignant part of one Army chaplain's account of "those indelible days" was that "after two long years of stalemate on the Western Front, he should have felt that an advance of only a few hundred yards should have been sufficient justification for the reading of the Thanksgiving for Victory."

As autumn faded into the winter of 1916, the final indignity for those British troops left alive on the Somme was that "the appalling weather and tremendous German artillery concentration, left units at the front with neither the time nor the opportunity to revet the sides of the battered trenches. The front line was reduced to a series of mud holes and remained that way throughout the winter."

The totals of dead, wounded and missing were visible enough, but the Somme also had an inevitable impact on the morale of the survivors. "In the training camps in 1914, the safe working presumption about any unknown man was that he only wanted to get at the enemy as soon as he could. Now the working presumption, the starting hypothesis, is that a man wants to stay in out of the rain, as long as you let him." The daily sick parade was a sure barometer of morale. Writing in the aftermath of the Somme, Captain J. C. Dunn observed that "a year ago, it was very exceptional to see a dozen 'sick'; now nothing was too trivial a pretext for 'going sick' and sixty was the daily average." However, sick men were also returned to duty with increasing rapidity, often with serious and even life-threatening conditions. Men who had lost toes to trench foot or were suffering from heart disease or tuberculosis were routinely returned to front-line duty—a sentence of death for many. Shell-shock—today we would call it Post-Traumatic Stress Syndrome—was also widespread but was acknowledged only with reluctance. Severe cases were often diagnosed as NYD(N)—Not Yet Diagnosed (Nervous). Less serious ones—and few soldiers who served in the front lines for long were not suffering some symptoms—were merely ignored or disparaged for displaying cowardice or "funk." Many of the soldiers executed for desertion may simply have been too traumatized to continue or even unaware of what they were doing, driven only by the need to get away from the endless whistle, crash and thud of shells and the crawling fear that the next one would be the one to kill them.

The Army's response to the increasing numbers reporting sick with shell-shock or displaying its symptoms was simply to enforce stricter rules about what constituted the condition; three times as many men were diagnosed with shell-shock during the Battle of the Somme than during the arguably even more traumatic Battle of Passchendaele the following year. Yet despite all constraints, soldiers continued to report sick in large numbers, and discipline in some sectors collapsed to the point where there were the first recorded instances of what became known as "fragging" during the U.S. war in Vietnam—the deliberate killing of officers by their own men. Such incidents were elliptically acknowledged by R. H. Mottram, who noted "a new spirit of taking care of oneself among the men, which ended in late 1918 in a few rifles being fired."

The "lions led by donkeys" view of the First World War—a term first used by Prussian officers to describe the enemy troops in the Franco-Prussian War—has become unfashionable in recent years as revisionist historians have attempted to argue that, despite the mountains of corpses, Douglas Haig's conduct of the Battle of the Somme and the war as a whole was the most militarily effective and indeed essential means to victory. However, what may seem necessary and even inevitable in the rarefied air of a military staff college almost ninety years after the event can seem considerably less so in the wider world outside, let alone to those who lived through it. At lower levels of command, "it is easy to make a fool a Sergeant, but he is still a fool," and many junior officers simply lacked the training and experience to lead effectively in the terrifying new world of total war—though casualty rates in the front lines admittedly meant that few had time to garner much experience. But the belief that a public school education was all that was needed to fit a man for command was demonstrably false. "When you are given an infant earth to fashion out of a whirling ball of flaming metals and gases, then good humour, some taste for adventure, distinction at cricket, a jolly way with the men and an imperfect digestion of thirty-nine partly masticated articles may not carry you too far."

At the higher levels of command, it would perhaps be unfair to say that men such as Haig were indifferent to the mountainous levels of British casualties, which, he said, "cannot be considered severe in view of the numbers engaged and the length of the front attacked." Others were more forthright. One chaplain overheard a corps commander remarking, "The men are much too keen on saving their own skins. They need to be taught that they are out here to do their job. Whether they survive or not is a matter of complete indifference." But then, as an American writer mordantly observed, "Generals dealt with war at the wholesale level, but troops fought it retail."

British commanders were willing to sustain the losses almost indefinitely because of their obsession with the same "attack at all times and all costs" policy that had led them to dismiss the idea of making trenches and dugouts more permanent and durable. The machine guns that wiped out tens of thousands of his men were "much overrated" weapons, according to the British commander-in-chief Douglas Haig. Like many of the Allied commanders, Haig still believed that "morale," "spirit" and "elan," as expressed through attacks by massed infantry and cavalry, were the crucial elements in battlefield success. He preferred to ignore the brutal lessons of the American Civil War and the Russo-Japanese War, let alone Britain's own colonial experience at Ulundi—where the Zulu forces were virtually wiped out by artillery and Gatling guns—and Omdurman, where 2,000 Dervishes were slaughtered by artillery and the withering fire of the new Maxim machine guns.

One British soldier bitterly observed, in the aftermath of the Somme, that a senior officer would usually come down to a battalion a couple of weeks after a battle, "to thank it for its gallant conduct, and fancies for a moment, perchance, that he is looking at the men who did the deed of valour, and not at a large draft that has just been brought up from England and the base to fill the gap. He should ask the services of the chaplain and make his congratulations in the graveyard." As one of the handful of survivors of the 22nd Manchester Rifles remarked, "Our battalion attacked about 800 strong. It lost, I was told in hospital, about 450 the first day, and 290 the second. I suppose it was worth it." To Haig it apparently was, and with the exception of lulls in fighting imposed by the onset of winter, offensives were only interrupted long enough to clear the dead and wounded, replenish the ranks with barely trained men, and furnish the supply dumps with fresh mountains of shells and ammunition. Haig's grasp of the new realities of modern warfare can perhaps be best understood with reference to his comments, written a full eight years after the war had ended, when, even with the benefit of hindsight, he still insisted that "aeroplanes and tanks . . . are only accessories to the man and the horse."

The British blockade of the North Sea coast and the vast and ever-widening disparity between Allied war production and that of Germany would inevitably have led to a German defeat, albeit in a slightly longer timeframe. There was nothing efficient or necessary about the meat-grinder of the Somme, yet the worst that some modern apologists can find to say about Haig's conduct of the battle was that he "over-estimated the ability of his army in July 1916, in effect trying to make them run before they could walk." It is a grotesquely infelicitous phrase, given the notorious orders to the troops on the infamous first day of the battle to advance at a walk rather than a run, because "not even a rat" would have survived the preliminary bombardment. As F. Scott Fitzgerald remarked, the reality of the Somme was more like "a whole empire walking very slowly, dying in front and pushing forward behind. And another empire walked very slowly backward a few inches a day, leaving the dead like a million bloody rugs"; and one of those "bloody rugs," trampled underfoot, was Alec Reader.

9

THE PLACE OF JUDGEMENT

At dawn on the morning of 15 September 1916, Paul Hub had heard "the alarm raised; the enemy were attacking"—part of the assault against the German positions just south of High Wood, where Alec Reader's lifeblood was ebbing away. "At first we could only make out a few people, then they came in bigger and bigger groups, advancing towards our left wing. We moved left to reinforce the troops under attack, but suffered heavy losses ourselves in the enemy's box-barrage. A fighter kept circling above us dropping flares [to mark their position for the artillery] and within a few seconds a storm of shells was unleashed on us. The enemy also had twenty-six observation balloons up and it was no surprise that, when our own artillery remained silent, we infantrymen were the idiots being shelled without respite. Fortunately the enemy infantry is no good. I saw the men attacking the Priezferm who were so fearful and faint-hearted that I had to laugh. Whenever we fired at them, even though there were very few of us left alive and unwounded, they always flooded back towards their own lines. Despite the three day artillery barrage, if there had still been even ten men in the Priezferm, the attack would have been repelled. But it was under so much fire that no-one could have stayed in it and lived, and it was no surprise when the enemy eventually captured it.

"The Battle of the Somme is mainly a battle between the enemy artillery and the German infantry. The enemy infantry usually only attacks trenches that contain dead or wounded, and I don't regard those as brave attacks. On our left wing, beyond the curtain of shell-fire, Vice–Staff Sergeant Kany and another nine men were killed during the attack, the remainder of his unit were wounded, but despite outnumbering us twentyfold, the enemy didn't dare penetrate our position and we inflicted heavy casualties even though we ourselves were under heavy fire. However, the enemy advanced slowly into the Priezferm. We couldn't possibly avoid it, because most of them could operate out of our sight within the little Anderly Wood. They must have had heavy losses themselves on the Combles Heights where Lieutenant Schirmer held on with a few survivors and a machine-gun, but our Company suffered forty per cent losses that day. Many others were so exhausted and intimidated by the artillery fire that they weren't of much use, but a link had to be made with the 1st Battalion lying to the left of the Priezferm, where a 300 metre gap had opened and the enemy could have broken through. We set up relay posts—two-man posts with machine-guns twenty paces apart—and closed the gap again. The men dug themselves in inside shell-holes; we couldn't dig a trench because of the aircraft; when our relief regiment did so later, despite our warnings, they paid heavily for it."

Under the relentless bombardment morale grew more and more fragile. "A Staff Sergeant who I stopped from sneaking away from the battle threatened to shoot me; I arrested him and he'll face a court-martial. At first our Battalion Commander wanted to start a counter-attack on the Priezferm, but at least two enemy companies were spotted by our patrols and on top of that, we could hear a machine-gun rattling in our direction. Against so much force we couldn't do anything, especially with our depleted companies. Around midnight parts of the 74th Regiment arrived as our relief and we gathered the remnants of our troops together, but we were then given orders to dig in on the open fields of the Combles Heights. Despite all the persuasive efforts of another Vice–Staff Sergeant and myself, we managed to take only a few men with us. When we got them out of one shell-hole, they disappeared into the next. When we had most of them out, a fresh burst of shelling set in and they were all gone again. After all that they had already been through, I couldn't really blame them.

"The Combles Heights was dangerous territory. Lieutenant Schirmer and his platoon had been there for two days. On the first night some of them fled because they couldn't stand the shelling any longer. The few that remained were almost completely wiped out. Most of them, including Staff Sergeant Sauter, were buried alive, and because there was no trench, it was impossible to go to their aid. In twos, threes or fours they just lay in shell-holes with nothing but canvas over them, waiting for the shell that would kill them. My men knew about these conditions and no-one wanted to face near certain death. In the end we set out with only six faithful followers. At about 2 a.m. we found a hole half a metre deep, and hid beneath a tarpaulin covered with straw and thistles. The others did the same; anything to avoid being seen by the enemy aircraft."

The remaining days until they were due to be relieved must have seemed an eternity to Paul and his surviving comrades, but on 17 September, after ten terrible days in the front line, they were withdrawn. "The shelling never ceased and the enemy attacked every single night. Our company has been terribly depleted, but we've held out bravely. Most of my equipment has been blown into pieces, but the shells never touched me, though I am more tired than I have ever been in my life." Sheer exhaustion and the stress of being continually under fire pushed many men up to and beyond their physical, mental and emotional limits. "It was a horrid feeling to get far beyond the tired stage to that of extreme exhaustion, and only those who have felt it know what it means. I remember sitting down ... and crying like a child." Some struggled through somehow, others succumbed to shell-shock, catatonic depression or madness.

On 19 September Paul and his men were in reserve, "lying in a shed inside a wood, a few kilometres behind the front line. The rain is dripping through all the gaps." It proved to be a very brief respite, for "tomorrow we'll have to move up to the Front again to take back from the enemy a few positions that the Saxons have lost to them. For now the food is good—we're getting warm meals again—I've washed for the first time in twelve days, and I don't think I've got any lice. So far I've been mercifully protected from all dangers, so I'm hopeful of getting through the coming days unscathed."

Two days later, now at Nurlu, where among the troops ranged against them were the remnants of Alec Reader's Civil Service Rifles,

Paul had just "taken up my position when a heavy mortar hit the parapet of the trench, burying me and two of my company. I can't describe what it felt like to be buried alive under such a mass of earth without being able to move a muscle. Thankfully, my steel helmet slid forward over my face and stopped my nose and mouth from being blocked with earth. Even so, I was having difficulty breathing, but luckily help was at hand. When someone called out asking if there was anyone underneath, we shouted 'Yes!' and they started digging us out right away, first the men next to me, then, finally, me. I felt as if my legs had been cut off. I was kneeling down when the trench collapsed, with my back against the wall and my feet pulled up underneath me. The weight of the wet earth had pushed my head right forward and torn my neck and back muscles, and strained my pelvis.

"Tomorrow we'll probably be relieved. Many of us are ill. We've done enough here on the Somme. My company has lost fifty-seven per cent of its original number in the last ten days." Inside he must have felt the way that all those who had long endured the slaughter in the trenches came to feel. "Everybody who looks daily into the cold eye of death and gazes on so many dead faces bearing the stamp of suffering and renunciation, becomes certainly callous, but also old, very old." The next night they were duly relieved and the remnants of the regiment marched—or shambled—back to Clary to regroup and recover. "The Battle of the Somme is over for us now. We're now busy cleaning the dirt of the Somme from our equipment and slowly, we're starting to resemble human beings once more. We came here on foot and though I didn't have any baggage to carry—everything was destroyed by enemy shelling—I did suffer quite a bit on the march; the bruising on my pelvis made it painful to walk. However, I'm glad to have got away that lightly." Many others were not so lucky; Paul was one of only twenty-three men from his company, out of a notional strength of over 200, to escape death or serious wounds.

Every front-line unit had suffered horribly. "We stood and sat on bodies as if they were stones or logs of wood. Nobody worried if one had its head stuck through or torn off, or a third had gory bones sticking out through its torn coat . . . A heap of five corpses lay just this side of the barrier; we were constantly having to tread on them to try and squash them down into the mud; because of the gunfire, we couldn't get them out of the trench. Suddenly I noticed with horror that one of the supposed corpses, lying underneath three others, was beginning to move . . . He must have lain insensible all night beneath the corpses.

We dragged him out, screaming with pain. I gave him a drink, but we couldn't do anything else for him, and he soon sank back into a coma. Our feelings gradually became quite blunted." "The night passed. We sat on corpses without worrying—as long as one didn't have to sit in the mud." Some men also became "blunted" and even indifferent to the dangers of the front lines. As a young German soldier remarked, "Life here isn't worth a damn; one thinks nothing of losing it. Today, for instance, I walked for half an hour through violent rifle-fire, just to have a wash and because I hoped to get one or two cigarettes."

By the time the British offensive "suffocated in swamp and blood" in the mud and snows of winter, there were half a million German casualties. The losses prompted the Kaiser to make a tentative move towards peace. On 12 December 1916, Paul Hub's 247th Infantry Regiment and all the other German units were assembled to hear their officers read a proclamation from the Kaiser. "Soldiers! Conscious of the victory which you have fought for and won by your courage, I and the Allied rulers [the German allies] have made an offer of peace. Whether the associated objective is achieved by this, remains undecided. Your duty continues to be this: with God's help, to stand firm!" However, the Kaiser's terms fell well short of the total German withdrawal from all occupied territories that was the minimum that Britain, France and their Allies could accept. His offer was rejected and the brief hope of peace stillborn.

For the third time, the troops spent Christmas at the Front. German soldiers in their deep dugouts "snap their fingers at the Somme and sing away at Silent Night . . . embroiled in this great battle, we are quite particularly moved. Everything round us has been shot to pieces. Where trees, and avenues of trees, used to stand, there now remain a handful of stumps a few inches high, but in spite of that, our men have put up Christmas decorations in their dugouts—a soldier can always get hold of something. Since mail arrived last night, every man has some little present from home lying in front of him."

The customary seasonal lull in the fighting was even more prolonged during that winter of 1916–17—the worst in twenty years. Soldiers "lying at each listening post were freezing stiff, and would take half an hour's buffeting and rubbing on return to avoid becoming casualties." Many men on both sides died of frostbite and hypothermia, and in conditions where even survival was a daily battle, both sides restricted their aggressive actions to sporadic sniping, artillery duels and small raids on the enemy trenches.

One man recorded "a lull in the fighting here last night. Yes, I counted the time—it was a clear moonlight—for exactly twelve seconds I heard neither gun, machine or rifle." It must have been as startling as the sudden roar of a plane overhead in a quiet country lane, for normally the din of shelling and firing "never stopped for one moment—ever." He also bemoaned "this bitter, bitter winter . . . I never knew the terrors of winter before. Even when I used to appeal for the poor, I did not know how fearful it was for them—I thought I did; I did not—never properly dry, never really warm . . . Today there was an inspection. The men were not kept there long. Still two of them fainted from cold . . . Even the Sacred Wine in the Chalice froze on Sunday. Our men are very, very brave. To me it is unspeakably dreadful, what must it be to them? Some of them could not bear their boots on this last time up the line. They put sandbags around their feet . . . We have thirty degrees of frost out here."

A soldier in the reserve areas "had to light a fire of paper in boots frozen hard before they were pliable enough to put on. One learnt the lesson that it was necessary to sleep with one's boots in bed with one and, strange to believe, make them part of one's pillow. Bed here, means bare floor, with possibly one blanket and one's greatcoat, with as many pieces of sacking as one could acquire." In the trenches, even a bare floor and a blanket would have seemed like luxury. Men slept—if they could—fully clothed and booted, huddled together for warmth in a dugout or "a 'rabbit-hole'—a burrow under the firing step," carved out of the trench-face.

Yet a few reluctant soldiers on both sides did not allow even the extreme cold to distract them from their self-appointed task of avoiding work and, above all, combat whenever possible. One anonymous soldier whose diary was found on his corpse was stolid, unimaginative, lazy, moaning, skiving, debt-ridden, scrounging and thieving, and yet, for all that, a strangely likeable character. He was German but could as easily have been British, French or American. Far from heroic—"only just managed to be left behind for a draft today, because of my acting, our Lieutenant made an exception in my case but I don't know how long it will last"—he wanted nothing more than to survive the war and be back at home dozing in his chair by the fire with a stein of beer at his elbow and a well-filled paunch straining the buttons of his waistcoat. Instead he was cold, hungry, uncomfortable, louse- and flea-infested and wishing himself anywhere but there.

In mid-January 1917, with bitter frosts and two feet of hard-frozen snow on the ground, he noted that "our watchword is still 'Let's rather freeze stiff than be worked stiff.' No one can disturb our tranquillity, however cold it is." In an attempt to combat the cold, German troops were given "a lot of Schnapps," just as the British were issued with extra rum. "The men always got their tot about 4 a.m., and I can assure you they needed it. Standing about day and night wet and half-frozen, it always put new life into them." But the effect was very temporary.

On each succeeding day the temperature dropped steadily lower, and the German soldier's misery was compounded on 26 January, when, to show their disrespect for the Kaiser's birthday, "the Tommies started a barrage at 6:30 a.m. which lasted till midnight." By 1 February his malingering had caused him to be sent "with several of my company to the detention prison at Bapaume." He was fortunate that his punishment was no more severe. Summary justice was often meted out to men of both sides at the Front, with draconian punishments for offences that, in other circumstances, would have been regarded as trivial. Five days later, no doubt to his great satisfaction, the anonymous German soldier "went sick on account of my feet. It was impossible to bear it any longer in this cold weather."

Others endured the misery of the frozen trenches with as much stoicism as they could muster. One soldier "was suffering badly from frost-bitten feet. My hands had swollen to twice their normal size and frequently my arms were completely numbed up to the elbows. For nearly a month I had not had my boots off and most of my companions were in the same miserable state as myself, owing to the intense cold . . . Putting the backs of my swollen hands to the barrel of my rifle, I could feel nothing, and I could only lift it up by holding it between my elbows. God help us if we had been called upon to defend ourselves. Fifty yards away [the enemy] were, no doubt, thinking the same thing. Frostbite was a terrible enemy, how terrible only those who lived in the trenches for weeks on end knew. Men were actually being frozen to death and others were fighting against sleep and cold until they could fight no longer."

Both sides suffered equally and, not for the first time, the front-line soldiers undoubtedly felt more of a bond with the men in the enemy trenches than with almost anyone else. Most Allied soldiers would have agreed with the sentiments expressed in a card that Paul Hub sent to Maria, featuring a quotation from Charlotte, Queen of Württemberg: "Patriotism does not consist of hatred towards other peoples but of the love of your own." Hatred was felt more for staff officers in the rear areas well behind the lines, and for the *Drückeberger*—draft-evaders—and *Etappenhengste*—war profiteers—living it up at home, while their fellows suffered and died in the trenches. Such feelings were as true on the British side of no-man's-land as on the German.

Henry Ford might have returned his $29 million war profits to the U.S. Treasury—a gesture that received a strangely muted acknowledgement—but there was no sign of any British industrialist or speculator doing the same. Rates of dividend on ordinary capital in industries such as iron, coal, steel, motors, shipping, textiles and oil were running at 4 to 6 percent in 1914. By 1918, the rate had risen to between 13 and 33 percent, and "the fortunes from swords were soon ploughed back into shares and honours," to the disgust of fighting troops. "All we want to hear is that the cads who have been trying to shirk it come out and put their noses well into the thick of it, which is simply unimaginable." "There are moments when even the bravest soldier is so utterly sick of the whole thing that he could cry like a child. When I heard the birds singing at Ripont, I could have crushed the whole world to death in my wrath and fury. If only those gentlemen [politicians] could be transported to this spot . . . there would be peace tomorrow."

Although some of the rigidities of the class system survived even the enforced intimacy of the front lines—when resting on the march, officers invariably fell out on the opposite side of the road from their men—front-line officers did at least share most of the discomforts of their men, and went over the top with them, and they often shared the views of their men about those having it easy a safe distance from the place where the real fighting was done. "GHQ had heard of the trenches, yes, but as the West End of London hears of the East End—a nasty place where common people lived." "Battalion commanders did not soon tire of telling how in the busiest days of big battles, the unseen powers would pester them for instant returns of the number of shovels they had, or of the number of men who in civil life had been fitters, or had been moulders."

As if in confirmation, on 1 July 1916—the first day of the Battle of the Somme—the 1st Londons had received a message asking them to nominate a man to serve as the divisional drummer. Later that month an exhausted runner arrived in the trenches, having survived an artillery bombardment en route, to bring the vital message to the unit commander that "your old mare is suffering from an attack of the strangles." The nightly spectacle afforded by departing leave trains at London's Victoria Station must have further infuriated all fighting troops.

While the men sat squashed "five a side in badly-lit compartments," staff officers travelled in a separate train with "two dining cars and all the carriages were first class. Obsequious myrmidons . . . guided red-hatted and red-tabbed officers to their reserved seats. It was nearly six-thirty and the waiters in the dining cars were already taking orders for drinks."

Even greater vitriol was reserved for those who paraded about in army uniform without ever setting foot in a combat zone, or even in France. "London to any open eye, was grotesque with a kind of fancy-dress ball of non-combatant khaki; it seemed as if no well-to-do person could be an abstainer from warfare too total to go about disguised as a soldier." But fighting troops also regarded the rare presence of staff officers and other high-ranking personnel in or near the front lines as at best a nuisance and at worst a positive danger. "The Duke of —— visited our Kemmel Hill sector to see something of a special bombardment by our guns staged for the occasion, but unfortunately our guns ran out of ammunition, just when the German batteries were plastering us thick and heavy in retaliation, with the result that we suffered far more damage and casualties than the Germans did, and that we 'blessed' the Duke in no uncertain terms, especially after we'd had to 'blanco' our web equipment in his honour with such improvised means as crushed grass and clay. In fact our morale by then was at its lowest, after such a vain and deliberate waste of lives and ammunition and war matériel."

The simmering resentment against staff officers, generals, profiteers and politicians alike might grow into something larger and more dangerous in time, but for now the rumbling discontent was sublimated to the war effort. "There was a bad smell about; the air stank of bad work in high places . . . They would not try to throw off the lead of the asses just then; you cannot reorganise a fire-brigade in the midst of a fire . . . 'We've got to win first. Then—? But we've got to win first.'" "The war will end and next will come a day of reckoning. Do they know it at home? They will." "They were almost exactly the words in which most German prisoners, till 1918, expressed their own feeling about the old rulers of Germany."

By contrast, enemy troops were more usually regarded with respect, understanding and sometimes even affection. "I will go on fighting as long as is necessary," one Englishman declaimed, "but I will not hate Germans to the order of any bloody politician . . . When you are lying at rest and hear a bombardment going on, you can't help thinking of the poor devils of infantry in the trenches on both sides with sympathy. You are none the worse soldier or fighter for that." Another spoke for many when he wrote, "For the Hun, I feel nothing but a spirit of amiable fraternity that the poor man has to sit just like us and do all the horrible and useless things that we do, when he might be at home with his wife and his books," and most soldiers "thought us all equally fools, the Germans and us, to be out there pasturing lice." Whatever their nationality, soldiers were the same—ordinary men, with families, wives or sweethearts, who all exhibited "the same mixture of cowardice and courage, the same devotion to country, the same numbness in the cogs of the military machine, the same love of home and wife and children." No amount of lurid propaganda or fire, brimstone and vitriol from their own politicians and generals would convince them to think any different.

Some propaganda was successful. The Kaiser's alleged description of the BEF as "a contemptible little army," which led them to call themselves "the Old Contemptibles," was actually the creation of a British War Office civil servant; and stories about "Huns" raping Belgian nuns and crucifying Canadian soldiers had an undoubted impact on American public opinion. There were other reasons for a pro-British or, at the least, anti-German bias in the U.S. media, including the fact that 25,000 Americans were serving as volunteers with the Allied forces. A British ship had severed the deep-sea cables between Germany and America on the second day of the war, breaking direct communication between the two countries. European correspondents of U.S. newspapers were based in London, giving the British government a further propaganda advantage over the Germans.

It was fully exploited. The *New York Herald* ran a story claiming that a German soldier had been seen carrying a bag of ears, and the findings of the Bryce Report into German atrocities—effectively a propaganda document itself—were taken as gospel and avidly serialized in American newspapers. However, myths like these, and tales of the German "corpse factories" where dead British troops were supposedly rendered down and their body fat used for the manufacture of explosives, candles or—a nice touch—boot polish, were treated with contempt by most British soldiers. And German trenches, when captured, "never contained the right things—no poison to put in our wells, no practical hints for crucifying Canadians; only the usual stuffing of soldiers' pockets—photographs and tobacco and bits of string and the wife's letters."

The one myth that was widely believed perhaps says as much about the soldiers' longing for any escape from the trenches as their credulity, and it also offered a more palatable explanation than the awful reality for the disappearance of the countless men missing in action. Told with relish up and down the lines, the story claimed that an army of deserters from both sides were living in abandoned dugouts, trenches and mine-workings in no-man's-land. This army of the undead would emerge at night, like rats or feral dogs, to rob the dead and dying, scavenge food and prey on any soldiers unwise enough to stray into their domain.

10

THE FURNACE

Paul Hub saw out the rest of the terrible winter of 1916–17 in the front lines on the Somme. "Through all those wet, snowy, cold days, we were lying, wet through and with chattering teeth in the mud and filth of holes that we had dug ourselves in the ground." There were now no more than a handful of his original fellows in the 247th still serving. Most had gone, the "fortunate ones" with a wound serious enough to send them home, the remainder rotting beneath the frozen earth. On 3 March 1917, now one of the oldest and most battle-hardened men left in the regiment, Paul was promoted to lieutenant. Nine days later, on 12 March, the German armies began a planned withdrawal to the "Siegfried Line"—a hastily constructed but formidable series of defensive ditches, barbed-wire entanglements, trenches and steel and concrete fortifications. In the territory that they were abandoning to the Allies, "every village was reduced to rubble, every tree felled, every street mined, every well poisoned, every creek dammed up, every cellar blown up or studded with hidden bombs, all metals and supplies taken back to our lines, every rail-tie unscrewed, all telephone wire rolled up, all combustible material burned; in short, we transformed the land into which the enemy would advance into a wasteland."

Small squads of troops remained behind in the trenches, firing off mortars, flares and weapons to give the impression that the line was still defended. Delayed-action bombs were planted—one destroyed the town hall of Bapaume after the British had occupied the town—and booby-traps were also laid, often with considerable ingenuity. "A new shovel lying among old ones would be wired to a bomb, a duckboard out of place awaited a neat-minded Englishman, an innocently open door, a closed door, fountain pens on a desk."

Maria remained frantic with worry about Paul and he did his best to offer reassurance, together with another mild rebuke. On 26 April 1917, with the winter at last behind them and the "fighting season" beginning, he wrote to her, "Again your letters are full of fear and anxiety. You don't realise how well things are going now. You write about blood, death and terrible battles, but the fighting isn't like that. At the moment we are several kilometres behind the Front and are not thinking of death and the horrors of war. Why are you obsessed by it? If a battle is taking place somewhere on the Western Front, it doesn't necessarily mean we are in the thick of it. My dearest, your continual worrying is depressing me. Here I am, enjoying some peace in my comfortable lodgings, full of the joys of spring, and there you are at home worrying. I understand your worries only too well, but you shouldn't believe what they write in the papers. If you read about a battle, tell yourself I am not there. Ninety-nine times out of a hundred you will be right. So don't worry unnecessarily, because you only make me nervous. It makes me admire all the more my sorely tested parents."

In August of that year, Maria was given fresh cause for concern when Paul's regiment was moved south to "Robbers' Castle" near Verdun—"the place of judgement" in its German code name. Knowing the ancient citadel's huge symbolic importance as "the heart of France," the German Chief of Staff, Erich von Falkenhayn, had vowed to "bleed France white" there in the First Battle of Verdun in 1916, drawing ever more French troops into a defence that would end with their annihilation. In fact both sides found themselves sucked into a brutal war of attrition in which German losses were almost as great as those of the French—377,000 Frenchmen and 337,000 Germans were killed, wounded or missing in action. "We all had on us the stench of dead bodies. The bread we ate, the stagnant water we drank, everything we touched had a rotten smell . . . the earth around us was literally stuffed with corpses." It is claimed—with some hyperbole—that 250,000 Frenchmen are entombed behind the glass-walled ossuary built at Verdun after the war, though how it was possible to distinguish French from German dead in an area where, in places, a thousand soldiers had died per square metre was not revealed.

Fourteen million shells were fired there—200 for every casualty—and the intensity of the artillery bombardment often made Verdun glow like a furnace, visible to all approaching soldiers from miles away. It was searing even for those who, like Paul, had experienced the trenches of Flanders and the Somme. "Our dugout . . . entrance was like that of a fox's hole. At the end of a short passage, some broken steps led down into the place we occupied for four days. Dead bodies were lying under the soil, one with its legs protruding up to the knees. There were three separate chambers down there: one was full of rockets and detonators; another—as big as our kitchen at home—in which we were housed, also contained French ammunition; the third was full of French explosive. It was pitch dark the whole time, as we had only a few candlesticks. There was a horrible smell down there too, the reek of decomposing bodies; I could hardly eat anything the whole four days." They lived in the "constant expectation of death, either through being buried alive or of being blown into the air if a shell should happen to fall where the explosive was stored."

In one trench at Verdun, German soldiers came upon "a great, bloody heap of mangled human bodies, dead and wounded; on the top a corpse without a head or torso, and underneath some who were still alive though with limbs torn off, horribly mutilated. They looked at us with bleeding, mournful eyes. The crying and moaning of these poor, doomed enemy soldiers went to our hearts. We couldn't get out of the trench to avoid this pile of bodies. However much our hearts shrank from trampling over them with our hob-nailed boots, we were forced to do it . . . I also came upon a young War Volunteer lying dead, still clutching his rifle. Facing him lay a French Corporal. They had run each other through simultaneously and their bayonets were still sticking in each other's bodies." The stuff of the blackest nightmares, men carried such horrific sights and sounds with them to their graves.

Verdun also saw the introduction of phosgene gas—which ate away the lungs of those unfortunate enough to inhale it—and the first large-scale use of flame-throwers, lending combat in the caverns and passageways of the forts and citadel a particularly hellish quality. "The air was suffocating. A mixture of the horribly sweet smell of putrefaction, phenol and iodoform, the stench of human excrement, explosive gases and dust, took our breath away." One incident in which perhaps 800 Germans were killed was entirely self-inflicted. A group of soldiers in the underground passages beneath Fort Douamont were heating coffee using oil from flame-throwers mixed with powder from hand grenades, next to a store of captured French fifteen-centimetre shells. The volatile mixture exploded into flame, burning several of the men, who dropped the blazing pots and their burning uniforms near the shells. The resulting explosion left hundreds dead. Still more were killed when dazed survivors, their faces blackened by powder burns, staggered through the passageways. German soldiers, fearing they were French Senegalese attackers, hurled hand grenades among them. The dead were walled up where they lay in the abandoned passageways. Above ground, Verdun was a pitted and pulverized wilderness of shell craters, littered with the dead and dying, on whom regiments of rats fed. One Württemberg unit—possibly Paul Hub's—counted 25,000 rats while camped at Montfaucon.

Paul Hub survived the horrors of the Second Battle of Verdun, which raged from 20 August to 15 December 1917. It was summarized by another German soldier: "Heroes become victims, volunteers slaves; death is a mere trifle; we are all screws in a machine that wallows forward, nobody knows where to." But by the end of the battle, "police measures" were necessary to maintain discipline among the demoralized German troops. Even so, they were less rebellious than the French *poilus*, many of whom had made *baa*-ing noises as they went, lambs to the slaughter, to Verdun. They had mutinied in May of that year, in the aftermath of a disastrous attack ordered by General Nivelle. Some troops simply stayed in the reserve areas and refused orders to go up to the front lines, others walked away from the Front en masse, singing and firing off their weapons. Officers who attempted to stop them or force them to return were beaten or killed. Widespread rioting broke out, an artillery regiment tried to blow up a munition works and several trains were derailed. At the height of the mutiny, fifty-four divisions—three quarters of a million men—were involved.

It might easily have led to the total defeat of France, but the German High Command remained unaware of the extent of French disaffection and disarray, and Nivelle was at once replaced by Pétain, who restored order with brutal efficiency. His pledge that there would be no further suicidal offensives, combined with offers of improved leave entitlement and conditions of service, removed the mutineers' prime grievances, and they were then cowed by thousands of courts-martial that saw 432 men officially executed—countless others were shot without trial or sentence—over 100 ringleaders shipped to the colonies, and 250 subjected to the exemplary punishment of being herded together and blown to pieces by their own artillery. The remaining men in the most mutinous units were then sent to the most dangerous sectors of the Front where the relentless daily attrition of wounds and deaths eliminated many more. Pétain had now stopped the rot, but there was no question of the French being involved in any further large-scale offensives that year, and perhaps ever.

German soldiers were also showing dangerous signs of disaffection. So disciplined at the start of the war that even seriously wounded men were required to "lie to attention," ramrod straight in their hospital beds, if a senior officer approached, 18,000 Prussian soldiers were now under arrest for indiscipline and 300 men of the Third Army Corps had been arrested after refusing to board the troop trains carrying them to the front lines. The bloodied remnants of the 247th Infantry Regiment remained loyal. Freed from the furnace of Verdun, they were sent north at the end of October 1917, just in time to join the "deadly attack" on Dixmuiden in Flanders, in the closing stages of "Third Ypres"—the notorious Battle of Passchendaele that had been raging since the end of July.

Paul Hub and his men were housed in deep dugouts in the front lines. The dugout roofs were twelve to twenty-four feet thick, formed from reinforced concrete or from layers of crisscrossed tree trunks, covered with earth and stone. On 1 November 1917 Paul wrote to Maria, "We live in a concrete dugout, deeply buried in the ground . . . a good two-storey block of concrete. The ceiling consists of seven long rail tracks cemented solidly together. The only window has been plugged up with sandbags, and our stovepipe runs between them. We don't even have to fear fifteen centimetre shells, but it is all the more gloomy as a result. We live on the ground floor, and fire our shots from the first floor . . . At least, the dugout is dry. We are right in the middle of a flooded area and only the few roads rise above the water like small dams. Between them is only swampland. The huge holes caused by mines and shells all fill with water and the dams are under persistent fire."

The incessant shelling had reduced the waterlogged ground to "a sea of mud, churned up to a depth of fifteen feet or more by the daily barrage of the English six-, eight- and eleven-inch shells, one crater touching another. To this the never-ceasing rain adds a finishing touch!" "One could see nothing anywhere, in fact, but a brown waste of mud blasted into ridges and hollows like a frozen sea, littered with debris and melting on all hands into the prevailing haze."

Passchendaele would now take its place in the pantheon of infamy, alongside the battles of Verdun and the Somme. Obsessed with the need for a successful large-scale offensive before winter, Haig and his staff ignored all warnings about the disastrous unsuitability of the terrain and sent troops, tanks and artillery forward into ground that was literally impassable in wet weather. Attempts by the Tank Corps to alert GHQ in memos and maps were greeted with the curt rejoinder, "Send us no more of these ridiculous maps."

The German supreme commander, von Hindenburg, had received intelligence of the impending British attack with barely concealed delight. "I had a certain feeling of satisfaction when this new battle began . . . It was with a feeling of absolute longing that we waited for the beginning of the wet season. As previous experience had taught us, great stretches of the Flemish plain would then become impassable, and even in firmer places, the new shell-holes would fill so quickly with ground-water that men seeking shelter in them would find themselves faced with the alternative, 'Shall we drown or get out of this hole?' " That the British High Command was equally aware of this was demonstrated by a diary entry from General Charteris, Haig's trusted—and notorious—conduit of information, disinformation and outright lies to the press. "Every brook is swollen and the ground is a quagmire. If it were not that all the records in previous years had given us fair warning, it would seem as if Providence had declared against us."

Nonetheless, the attack went ahead with predictably disastrous consequences, though as usual the unholy alliance of Charteris and the "embedded" war correspondents ensured that only reports of "great victories" appeared in the British newspapers. Dozens of tanks became bogged down before even reaching their start positions, and those that made the start line fared little better; an anti-tank gun fired from a single German pillbox accounted for no fewer than seventeen. Many guns could not be hauled into position at all, and those that were brought up often sank deeper and deeper into the mud each time they were fired, ensuring that the artillery barrage was both inaccurate and inadequate. Even shells falling in the right areas tended to bury themselves deep in the liquid mud before detonating, or sank without trace and did not explode at all. The troops struggling to advance through the cloying mud were left far behind by the creeping barrage that was supposed to protect them and, hopelessly exposed, they were cut to pieces by German machine-gun fire.

Meanwhile tanks, guns, horses, carts, men—everything—sank into a mire that was often the consistency of quicksand. "Boots were torn from the feet of men held fast in the octopus of the mud. Horses and mules remained to die, stuck fast." "We produced ropes with which we pulled out men who could not move, and with one man we unfortunately pulled too hard, and his leg snapped with a loud crack, broken just below the knee." Some men were immovably trapped. They might be found two days later, "sunk lower in the mud and with their minds gone." One was eventually released from his torment only when "one of his comrades mercifully put a bullet through his skull." A Guards battalion lost sixteen men to the mud in a single month. "They drowned in mud. Their graves, it seemed, just dug themselves and pulled them down."

As von Hindenburg had predicted, those who sought refuge in shell craters fared little better. The water was invariably contaminated with human excrement and putrefying flesh, and the oily residue of mustard gas often covered the surface. Bodies lay or floated in this filth, "a khaki-clad leg, three heads in a row, the rest of the bodies submerged, giving one the idea that they had used their last ounce of strength to keep their heads above the rising water." And each crater with its surface water tinged with the brown-black coloration of spent blood, spoke of yet more men entombed, invisible, beneath it. The misery of the men was compounded by the inevitable outbreaks of flu, respiratory infections, gas gangrene—caused by bacteria from the fecal matter in the soil—dysentery and trench-foot, though some welcomed even that horrific condition, often accompanied by the loss of several toes, as a way out of the nightmare of mud and death.

Within a couple of days of the start of the offensive, the Tank Corps sent another unwelcome memorandum to GHQ: "From a tank point of view, the Third Battle of Ypres may be considered dead . . . From an infantry point of view, the Third Battle of Ypres may be considered comatose. It can only be continued at colossal loss and for little gain." That assessment proved entirely accurate but once more was ignored. The battle continued through late summer and autumn until winter finally brought it to a close. Men returning from the front lines were coated from head to foot in slime and their faces were death-white—they looked, as one observer memorably remarked, "like men who had been buried alive and dug up again"—but while his men were floundering and drowning in Flanders mud, Douglas Haig's sole concession to the conditions was to have the track near his headquarters sanded to help his horse keep its footing during his morning canter.

Ypres was now "simply a desolation. You cannot imagine it being rebuilt. We walked through the streets and found not one house which was not a mere mass of ruins or just a big heap of bricks." "Scarcely any stone [was] left upon another. The best preserved part of the town, ironically, was the municipal cemetery." Third Ypres—the Battle of Passchendaele—was finally halted on 20 November 1917, after the capture of the eponymous tiny village that allowed Haig and the British press to proclaim it as a victory, but Lloyd George later summed it up with rather more accuracy. "During the whole battle we recovered less ground, we took fewer prisoners, we captured fewer guns (about one quarter) than we did in the despised Nivelle offensive [which had led to the wholesale mutiny of French troops], and that with nearly three times the casualties we sustained in that operation, which was always alluded to by the Staff as a 'failure' . . . So much for the bovine and brutal game of attrition on the Western Front."

Unable to sack Haig, who, helped by mendacious press coverage, was widely regarded in Britain as a hero, Lloyd George and his War Cabinet took steps to reduce the flow of men to the Front, hoping by this means to deny him the resources to launch another bloody and futile offensive. "The War Cabinet felt, not without reason, that if given another 100,000, he would stake them to gain the next shell-shattered hilltop . . . the obvious moral was 'Keep back the men.'" In that they were successful, though the shortage of men arguably played its part in the initial success of the next great German offensive in the spring of 1918.

If censorship ensured that civilians at home remained ignorant of the full horrors of Passchendaele, conditions on the home front were harder to conceal and food shortages were a source of constant popular grievance. German U-boat attacks on British merchant shipping had greatly reduced the availability of imports, and priority in the supply of foodstuffs was in any case given to the armed forces, with the result that, though there was no domestic rationing, meat and fats were in perennially short supply and tea, sugar and potatoes were often unobtainable. Shops that had—or were rumoured to have—stocks were marked by huge queues. Coal was also very scarce, and petrol unobtainable at any price. Buses, trains and taxis were always overcrowded. The aggression of would-be passengers fighting for a space on buses and trains, and the avarice of taxi-drivers, joined the shortage of tea and meat as staples of food-queue conversations.

However, conditions were far worse in Germany. Over three years of war and the British blockade of the Channel and North Sea ports—illegal under international law—had left the German economy in ruins, with every raw material and even the most basic foodstuffs in desperately short supply. Crucial materials for the war effort—high-grade iron ore, manganese, bronze, brass, copper, tungsten and nickel—were so scarce that regular appeals were launched for old telephone wires, doorknobs, candlesticks, pans and kettles, brass handles and ornaments, copper piping and copper roofing from churches and city halls. Churches also gave up their bells—the Old Prussian Synod alone "donated" 10,312. Ersatz substitutes were found for other strategic materials, including saltpetre, gun cotton, glycerine, sulphur, alcohol and rosin, but, despite experiments with *Benzolspiritus* ["gasohol"], alternative supplies of oil and rubber were much less easy to find or synthesize. Petrol stocks were a third below military demand and rubber was in such short supply that the Army even requisitioned the cushions from billiard tables.

German farmers had produced 90 percent of the country's food needs before the war, but they did so only with the help of 2 million tons of imported nitrogen and phosphate fertilizers, 6 million tons of fodder and 1 million foreign seasonal workers. When the war and the Allied blockade stopped these, food production fell by a quarter. The civilian population was neither fed nor clothed adequately and domestic fuel was also very scarce. As a result, mortality rates were rising sharply. Malnutrition, rickets and tuberculosis, which increased by two-thirds compared to pre-war levels, were rampant—death rates among children and women doubled in Germany during the war years—and there was an inevitable impact on civilian morale. "The women who stood in pallid queues before shops spoke more about their children's hunger than about the death of their husbands."

In the allocation of food, troops at the Front received priority but the quality was often appalling and even they were so hungry that no potential source of food, no matter how unappetizing, was ignored. "In earlier days, when a horse was shot, it lay where it fell, rotted, and poisoned the whole neighbourhood until somebody threw a sack of quicklime on it. Today it is as though we were in the tropics, where vultures are at home. At first great pieces disappear from the hams and shoulders, and within the day nearly all the flesh is removed from the bones . . . So it was today, H, like a regular freebooter, was one of the first to hear of this windfall and brought the tongue along. We found it excellent." Troops could also forage and plunder during an advance. Civilians had no such opportunities, unless they turned to crime.

There had been food shortages in Germany as early as the autumn of 1914 and they reached critical levels in 1915 and the "turnip winter" of 1916–17. There were no eggs, cheese, butter, fats, cooking oils or soap. Beef and pork were replaced by horsemeat, and before long even that was unobtainable. Nettles were added to stews in place of vegetables. Ersatz products such as bread made from barley, ground peas, beans or potato flour, "war sausage" (described as "a mouthful of sawdust"), butter made from curdled milk, sugar and food colouring, "Hindenburg fat"—turnip paste—and coffee ground from acorns, chicory and beech-mast were unpalatable, and others, made from chemicals, were also potentially poisonous. Albert Speer was "often so hungry that in secret I gradually consumed a whole bag of stone-hard dog biscuits left over from peacetime."

Government action often made the situation worse. When farmers ignored restrictions on using grain as animal feed, 9 million pigs were compulsorily slaughtered in what became known as the "*Schweinemord*" (pig murder). Farmers retaliated by withholding pigs from market, leading to escalating shortages and prices. By 1916, German civilians were reduced to a diet of black bread, fatless and sometimes meatless sausage, three pounds of potatoes a week, and a single egg. Only turnips—mere animal fodder before the war—were in plentiful supply. "Faces like masks, blue with cold and drawn by hunger" were too common a sight to be worthy of comment. There was often no fuel either for lighting or heating. "One of the most terrible of our sufferings was having to sit in the dark. It became dark at four in the winter. It was not light until eight . . . we were left shivering with the chill that comes from semi-starvation, and which no additional clothing seems to alleviate."

Ration cards or vouchers were needed for almost every item of food or clothing and black marketeering was rife. For those without money, long queues, and then food riots, became commonplace. The first in Berlin had occurred in October 1915 and there were also wild-cat strikes calling for "Peace and Bread." Some 55,000 Berlin workers downed tools in the summer of 1916 to protest at the arrest of a social-ist who had made an anti-war speech, and 40,000 Krupp workers and 75,000 coal miners struck the following spring. Order was restored only when the Army subjected factories to "militarization" and shipped strike leaders to the front lines, but not even such draconian solutions could stifle industrial unrest and domestic discontent for long. In January 1918, war-weariness, hunger and cold provoked a further wave of strikes. By the end of the month 350,000 were on strike in Berlin alone, aircraft, gunpowder, artillery and ammunition plants were at a stand-still and martial law was declared in Hamburg and Brandenburg.

The unrest forced a rapid conclusion to the protracted peace negotiations with Russia, but 1 million German soldiers remained in the East to enforce the peace terms that stripped Russia of all its former western territories including the Ukraine, Finland, Poland, Latvia and Estonia. The new territories were plundered for food and resources—even the official German figures show that 150,000 head of livestock and 50,000 tons of grain were appropriated from the former Russian territories—but whatever domestic peace that brought was very short-lived.

11

A TEST TO DESTRUCTION

George Vaughn Seibold had been married for precisely twenty-four hours when, on 22 July 1917, he went away to war. Born in Washington, D.C., on 6 February 1894, George was the son of George Gordon Seibold, a proofreader and linotype operator for the *Washington Star* and secretary of the Columbia Typographical Union, and Grace Darling Whitaker Seibold, the daughter of a distinguished Civil War general, Edward Washburn Whitaker. Prominent in Republican politics—Grace was a friend of Grace Goodhue Coolidge, wife of President Calvin Coolidge—their influence and George senior's union position made the Seibolds one of the first families in Washington to have a telephone installed, at their house in Rock Creek Road. The imposing house still stands today.

George was the eldest of three children, with a younger brother, Louis, and a sister, Theodosia—Teddy for short. She would later tell her own children that George was the perfect older brother, kind, protective and great fun to be with, and "no siblings anywhere can have been as close." They were a talented and self-confident family—Theodosia was a champion tennis and basketball player and a leading suffragette who also worked with handicapped children, and George was a good student and sportsman, popular both with his classmates and with the opposite sex.

He attended Central High School but, rather than George Washington University, he then went on to graduate from McKinley Manual Training School. After working at the Government Printing Office in 1912, he served as Congressman Thomas Nelson Page's secretary before moving to Chicago and joining a relative's patent law firm. Patent law was evidently too dry a subject for George, who soon began work in real estate for Aldis and Company of Chicago, remaining with them from 1913 to 1917. A surviving photograph from that era shows a handsome, confident man with a strong jaw, dark hair and a neatly trimmed moustache. His gaze is penetrating and a smile plays around his lips. His family remember a man of immense, easy-going charm with "a wonderful sense of humour." With his personal qualities and background, and the family's Washington connections, a career in politics beckoned, had it not been for the U.S. declaration of war on 2 April 1917. George had already trained at Officers' Training Camp in Plattsburgh, New York, the previous year. The draft for the first batch of conscripts for the Army was due to be held on 20 July 1917, but he did not wait to be drafted. Earlier that month he undertook further training at the Officers' Reserve Camp at Fort Sheridan, Illinois, and then volunteered for the Aviation Section of the Signal Corps.

There was a widespread belief—albeit one belied by the background of many American flying aces—that to become an aviator, a man "had to know somebody, say like a governor or a senator, or at least a judge." George certainly had those connections, but there is no record that he made use of them. A pilot was required to be "naturally athletic and have a reputation for reliability, punctuality and honesty. He should have a cool head in emergencies, good eye for distance, keen ear for familiar sounds, steady hand and sound body with plenty of reserve; he should be quick-witted, highly intelligent and tractable. Immature, high-strung, overconfident, impatient candidates are not desired." It was a list of qualities that few European air aces could have matched, but George evidently fitted the bill and duly became "the first member of the Fort Sheridan unit to do solo flying, as flying alone is called."

While working at Aldis and Company in Chicago, he had met and fallen in love with another company employee, Kathryn Irene Benson, the "tall and beautiful" daughter of Mr. and Mrs. Paul Benson of Lake Forest, Illinois. Knowing that he could be called up at any point for active service, George and Kathryn accelerated their wedding plans, announcing their engagement on 18 July 1917. The couple, both twenty-three years old, were then "quietly married in the Chicago residence of the bride's mother" just three days later, on 21 July, after the sudden arrival of orders for him to report for military training to an air base in Canada.

The wedding was arranged with such haste that George's father and mother did not attend. Their absence may have been because of difficulties in travelling at such short notice, but it may also have been partly motivated by a touch of parental disapproval. George senior and Grace were both devout Baptists and Grace "would not have been thrilled by the news that her future daughter-in-law was an Episcopalian." Nor would the separation between Kathryn's parents have endeared them to the elder Seibolds—Paul Benson, an insurance broker, who also did not attend the wedding, was still resident in Lake Forest, but Susan Benson was described as "of Chicago" in the wedding announcements.

George and Kathryn had just one night together at 4321 Hazel Avenue, Chicago, before he was posted to his training unit at Long Branch in Canada, where many of his countrymen, including a number of "pseudo-Canadians" who had joined the British Royal Flying Corps at its recruiting office in Fifth Avenue, New York, were already based. George underwent ground-school training in engines, airframes, navigation, Morse code and primary flight training, progressing from the basics of "feeling controls" in his first week to dual-control landings and take-offs in his second. He then began solo flying, learning the handling of his aircraft—spirals, figures of eight and touching down in a fifty-foot circle—before moving on to more complex manoeuvres like steep banks, glides, vertical turns, loops, Immelmanns, Chandelles (abrupt climbing turns, converting momentum into altitude), formation flying and stalls. He also began to acquire the military skills like bomb-dropping, machine gunnery and aerial photography at "other schools in different parts of Canada."

At the outbreak of the war, aircraft had been regarded solely as a means of reconnaissance, replacing the cavalry traditionally used in that role but rendered obsolete by the trenches that prevented their movement and the machine guns that slaughtered cavalrymen and horses alike. On 2 September 1914, a French aviator, Corporal Louis

Bréguet, was the first to report that the German armies were swinging to the east, rather than the west of Paris as the Schlieffen plan had required. The Allied armies were quickly redeployed and inflicted the Germans' first defeat at the Battle of the Marne. Bréguet's report, confirmed by other pilots, was the first positive demonstration of the value of air observation. Pilots also supplemented "kite-balloon" observers in carrying out target-spotting for the artillery, but their use in air combat and ground attack came later. An Act of Congress of July 1914 showed the low priority given to aviation by establishing what was to become the U.S. Air Service as the aviation section of the humble Signal Corps. Its authorized strength was precisely 60 officers and 260 enlisted men, and there were only two commissioned ranks in the pay scale. When the United States actually entered the war, the aviation section had only 13 officers and 1,000 enlisted men.

At first the other combatant nations were little better prepared for air war. Early scout planes did not even carry weapons but pilots then began taking pistols, carbines and grenades aloft with them. One bizarre British experiment even involved trailing a 150-foot length of cable with a lead weight attached to entangle in an enemy aircraft's propeller. The first attempt to fit a Lewis gun to a British aircraft had to be abandoned as those early planes were so underpowered that it "adversely affected their performance," but as more powerful and durable aircraft were developed, fitting a machine gun to two-seaters became standard practice. Single-seaters remained either unarmed or equipped only with homemade arrangements to allow the pilot to fire a rifle, and their inability to fire forwards for fear of damaging the propellers was a serious obstacle.

A Frenchman, Roland Garros, devised a means of firing through the arc of the propeller—but only by cladding the rear of the propeller blades with triangular sections of armoured steel so that the bullets hitting them would be deflected away. It was crude and potentially dangerous to Garros as well as to his opponents but he succeeded in shooting down three German aircraft with this system. However, on 19 April 1915, Garros was forced to crash-land behind the German lines and he and his machine were captured. The Dutch engineer Anthony Fokker, who was working for the Germans, then made a quantum leap by designing an interrupter gear that used the revolutions of a camshaft attached to the engine to interrupt the fire of a machine gun whenever the propeller was in front of it.

By the late summer of 1915 "numbers of sinister looking monoplanes"—Fokker Eindekkers—were taking a heavy toll of British and French aircraft. The British were still experimenting with guns mounted to fire above or below the arc of the propeller, their only line-of-sight guns being employed on aircraft mounted with a propeller at the rear, which were comprehensively outflown and outfought by the German Fokkers. As the losses of the RFC (the Royal Flying Corps, which merged with the Royal Naval Air Service on 1 April 1918 to form the Royal Air Force) rose to alarming levels in 1915 and early 1916, frantic work led to the development of an efficient if still slightly imperfect interrupter gear, designed by a Romanian engineer, Constantinescu. "When correctly adjusted, all bullets passed between the propeller blades. When firing in a steep dive, however, the propeller could overrun the gear, resulting in some bullets striking the blades." Before the end of April the first production models were being fitted to British aircraft and the "Fokker Scourge" ceased to be such an overwhelming factor in the battle for air supremacy. By the time George Seibold qualified as a pilot, all combat aircraft had long been fitted with interrupters and forward-firing machine guns, though "British gunsights were at that time still designed for 100 mph targets"—inadequate against Fokkers dropping from cloud cover at twice that speed.

After completing his primary flight training, George was posted directly to Taliaferro Field, Fort Worth, Texas, one of several Texan airfields used for RFC flight training during the Canadian winter. George underwent further flight training there and subsequently became an instructor of cadets, flying the Curtiss "Jenny," which was the standard training plane for the USAS throughout the war. In November 1917, he narrowly escaped death when his aircraft fell from 1,500 feet during a training flight. That crash may have been the cause of the scars on his right cheek and right hand, noted in his military records.

On 1 December 1917, he was commissioned a first lieutenant, and early the following year he was sent overseas, sailing from the Cunard docks at Hoboken, New Jersey, on 24 January 1918. There were no fanfares, no bands, no crowds of friends and loved ones waving farewell. On a cold and misty winter morning, with not even a blast on its foghorns, the great grey ship slipped its moorings and slid away from the docks down the Hudson River. George's last sight of his native land must have been a brief one, before the mist clinging to the water obscured everything from view. Once clear of the Hudson, the ship tracked the coast northeast, making for a rendezvous two days later off Halifax, Nova Scotia, with the rest of convoy HX-20, where George's ship took up station directly astern of the *Tuscania*. They then ran east-wards, by day ghost shapes as grey as the ocean swell that surrounded them, and at night as black as the overcast skies, every glimmer of light from portholes and companionways shrouded by heavy drapes.

George and the other officers were housed on the upper decks, enjoying better and more sanitary conditions than the enlisted men of the ground crew in the ship's bowels. "Sub" drill was practiced every afternoon, reflecting the threat from the lurking U-boat packs. A week's steaming brought them near to the Irish coast, the danger zone where scores of ships, including the *Tuscania*'s sister ship, *Lusitania*, had already been sent to the bottom by U-boats. The convoy's escort was further augmented by destroyers, and every captain remained on the bridge, eating and even sleeping within a hand's grasp of the helm, while every man aboard every ship was ordered to carry his life-preserver with him at all times.

At two o'clock on 5 February 1917, a crisp winter's afternoon lit by a watery sun, "we passed, some hundreds of yards to starboard, a round, dark, bobbing object which some observers thought was a floating mine. Others thought it might be the head and shoulders of a human body held upright in a life-ring. Whatever it was, our ship gave it a wide berth, sheering off from the object in a sharp swing. Almost at the same moment upon our other bow, at a distance of not more than one hundred yards from the crooked course we were then pursuing, there appeared out through one of the swells a lifeboat, oarless, abandoned, empty, except for what looked like a woman's cloak lying across the thwarts. Rising and falling to the swing of the sea, it drifted down alongside of us so that we could look almost straight down into it." The sight and what it might portend unsettled everyone. No doubt there were a few forced jokes and strained smiles, but a deeper silence settled over the ships of the convoy.

The long ocean swell now began to change to the shorter chop of tidal waters and the coast of Northern Ireland was dimly visible ahead, catching the last rays of the setting sun. The flashing beam of a light-house seemed to offer a glimmer of reassurance, but at 5:42 p.m. there was a dull concussion. A water spout and a column of oily black smoke rose into the darkening sky. A German U-boat, *UB-77*, had tracked the convoy and fired two torpedoes. One missed its mark, but the other struck the *Tuscania*'s bows. The rest of the convoy at once took evasive measures. There was no question of going to the ship's aid; standing orders in the event of U-boat attack were to ensure the safety of the other vessels, but as George's ship swept past the stricken *Tuscania* and made full speed ahead, all shared the thoughts articulated by Irvin Cobb. "We could feel our ship throb under our feet as she picked up speed. It made us feel like cowards. Near at hand a ship was in distress, a ship laden with a precious freightage of American soldier boys, and here we were, legging it like a frightened bird, weaving in and out on sharp tacks. We knew that guardian destroyers would even now be hurrying to the rescue, and we knew land was not many miles away, but all the same, I think I never felt such an object of shame as I felt that first moment, when the realisation dawned on me that we were fleeing from a stricken vessel instead of hastening back to give what succour we could."

The *Tuscania*, now ablaze with light, fired off three distress rockets, bursting in showers of red sparks against the night sky. It remained visible for another hour, a diminishing blur of light on the western horizon as the convoy headed on into the North Channel of the Irish Sea, before at last it disappeared from view. It went down at ten o'clock that night, with the loss of 230 American lives, the first U.S. troopship to be sunk. It must have had a sobering effect on George Seibold and his peers. If they had been in any doubt before, they now knew that this war was not just some great adventure but a brutal matter of life and death.

George's unit disembarked at Liverpool and then entrained for Oxford, where, billeted in the comfort of Queen's College and "paid the munificent sum of $100 a month," they undertook a ground course "identical to the one we had just completed" before leaving the United States. The course included military drill and discipline—not always the American contingents' strongest point—and it was "a mental and physical strain which was something of a test to destruction, thirty per cent or more being failures." The belief that American pilots could go straight from the Curtiss Jennys that George had been flying in Texas to British aircraft without further training had been discredited by the death of a U.S. flying instructor earlier that year. As a result, all the American pilots were also sent to British flying schools to train on the unfamiliar British aircraft: Avros, Sopwith Pups and Camels. George was to join the 22nd Aero Squadron in flight training on Salisbury Plain.

One of George's fellow pilots observed with a mixture of delight and disbelief that the training regime appeared to have been based on the theory that, since pilots "didn't have any sense and couldn't be approached by any normal disciplinary measures, so their procedure was to have absolutely none whatsoever . . . Nobody had to do anything except you had to fly, and everybody wanted to fly." After completing their additional flight training, the American pilots were sent for a week's gunnery practice at the machine-gun school near the Turnberry golf course in Scotland—a privilege not extended to the pilots of two-seater aircraft or bombers, who "were to endure at least as much contact with the enemy."

The presence of the famous golf course right next to their airfield was too much temptation for the Americans, who took to buzzing the golfers on the links. One hapless group was pinned in a bunker "all day," as George's fellow pilot Harry Callahan claimed, probably with some hyperbole. The siege was lifted only after the over-excited Callahan ploughed his aircraft right into the edge of the bunker in which the golfers were hiding. "The plane proceeded to do a somersault and ended upside down on the green, directly over the hole." To their own and the golfers' relief, George and the rest of the U.S. pilots were transferred to Ayr shortly afterwards for the School of Aerial Fighting, after which their formal training was complete and they were regarded as ready for active service.

British flight training had improved a little since the black days of 1915 and 1916, when pilots were sent overseas with as little as five hours' flying time under their belts, a policy that a future air marshal, Sholto Douglas, described as "sheer murder," though with breathtaking complacency the director of the RFC felt able to remark that "short training was a consequence of the number of casualties and not the casualties of the shortness of training." However, training remained "quite inadequate, designed by senior officers who . . . had no experience of war in their new element" and were primarily concerned with producing the numbers needed to replace those pilots being lost every day in France. Even in April 1917—"Bloody April" as it was known, in reflection of British aircrew losses—large numbers of raw and barely trained novice pilots were still being sent to almost inevitable death at the Front, and it was widely believed that fatal crashes in training were averaging one hundred a month.

Hidebound official attitudes had originally led the British to refuse to allow NCOs to become pilots—there was "a bias towards horsemen and countrymen"—though by 1917 the wastage of war had forced changes, and one British flight commander had started life as "a barber's lather boy." The use of parachutes for aircrew was also rejected, not merely because of their weight but because they might diminish the pilots' "fighting spirit." Pilots feared death by fire or mid-air break-up of their aircraft more than any other fate, "the two situations which no self-reliance or skill could control. It was these that made the feeling about the non-issue of parachutes so deep and bitter." A soldier on the ground noted the effects on one pilot, who fell "like a stone. We watched him all the way down . . . his body had driven almost six inches into the ground. I think that every bone of his body was broken, for we can roll him up just like a carpet."

However, the commander of the RFC, General Hugh Trenchard, was unmoved and his " 'considered attitude to this innovation was characteristically spartan. His balloon observers, being defenceless, were issued with [parachutes] as a matter of course, but never his airmen. He was more interested in armouring vulnerable parts of their machines against bullets so that they could fight with easier minds' . . . as a result hundreds of lives were thrown away in support of a doctrinaire opinion." "In common with neglect of most life-saving measures for the flying men . . . there appeared to be little effort in France to establish a useful daily weather forecast"—vital and easily obtainable information for aircrew.

In 1918, despite some improvements in both the quality and the duration of pilot training, it remained "very spotty. We seldom had more than a fifteen minute hop, as training airplanes were scarce and there were not many instructors." The huge losses of men and aircraft sustained during the German advance of spring 1918—1,032 of the 1,232 aircraft on the strength of front-line British squadrons were lost in the four weeks from 21 March—meant that even the most inexperienced pilots were being rushed to the Front.

Instruction was little more than a set of rules that pilots were supposed to follow, "like when you got up and flew, you were not allowed to fly straight for more than a hundred yards. They were up against the proposition of having to produce a great many pilots as quickly as possible and didn't care very much how they did it." Even advanced instruction tended to be crude and although, as an instructor, George Seibold was already an experienced pilot, as one English aviator remarked, most new pilots had only fifteen to twenty hours' flight time and "can't even fly, let alone fight."

Regulations laid down that every pilot must have:

1. Undergone instruction at a School of Military Aeronautics.
2. Had twenty hours solo in the air.

3. Flown a service aeroplane satisfactorily.
4. Carried out a cross-country flight of at least sixty miles successfully—during which he must have landed at two outside landing places under supervision of an RFC officer.
5. Climbed to 8,000 feet and remained there for at least fifteen minutes, after which he will land with his engine stopped, the aeroplane first touching the ground within a circular mark of fifty feet in diameter.
6. Made two landings in the dark assisted by flares.

All this was designed to ensure that pilots had at least a measure of competence in handling their aircraft, but the rules were frequently bent and in any case none of it, not even the School of Aerial Fighting at Ayr, really prepared them for air combat against battle-hardened opponents. Their only training for that was in mock dogfights among themselves, and, with so few experienced instructors, that was based on guesswork as much as on experience. It would have to do, and at least one of the Americans believed that their idiosyncratic flight training might have been more effective than it appeared. "There's no way to check on what another person does in the air . . . It's very easy to say that your guns have jammed or your engine isn't going quite right and say you have to go home, but that was not what they wanted. So in that way, they managed to find the people that were suited to fighter work."

The ground crew were the first to taste the harsh reality of air war. On the night of 22 March, a detachment of ground crewmen were ordered to camp in pup tents near the railway station at Chaulnes. At about eight in the evening, they were attacked by a German Gotha bomber, whose "aim might have been helped by a small fire" they had lit to boil water. There were eighteen casualties, ten of whom died. They were buried at Chaulnes, their graves marked with "rude crosses." As a sergeant in the ground crew of the 148th noted with remarkable restraint, it had "proved most costly in human lives not to have been warned about making a fire near the front lines." The death toll before the squadron had even fired a shot in anger was to prove more severe than in all the months of combat ahead.

VANISHED FROM THE
FACE OF THE EARTH

Paul Hub had been stationed near Dixmuiden throughout the winter of 1917–18, and the weather and the exhaustion of the troops on both sides after the bloodletting of Verdun and Ypres confined them to patrols into no-man's-land and occasional trench raids, but by early March 1918 he was back in the familiar slaughterhouse of the Somme. All the original combatant nations were close to exhaustion—the British Army was 80,000 under strength at the start of the year, and the French and Germans were in even more desperate condition—but knowing that a massive force of American troops would soon be thrown into battle on the Allied side, the German field commander, Ludendorff, prepared to launch a final desperate offensive. Officially titled "Operation Michael" in honour of Germany's patron saint, it was also known as the *"Kaiserschlacht,"* or "Battle for the Emperor."

The German troops were intensively trained for the coming battle, to be fought over the doubly devastated landscape between Albert and Montdidier, battered by the British during the Battle of the Somme, and then razed to the ground by the Germans during their withdrawal to the Siegfried Line. If the advance was successful, German railway engineers would have to lay new lines through the wilderness to connect with the French railways to the west. The flat plains and shallow valleys of the Somme and Ancre would provide good conditions for an attack only in dry weather; heavy rains would turn the clay soils into a quagmire. The aim of the attack was to seize the strategic city of Amiens and drive a wedge between the British and French armies, fatally weakening both of them. Even if it were not enough to win the war, the German High Command at least hoped to enter peace talks in a dominant position.

From mid-February to 20 March, 10,000 trains, running mostly at night, brought men and matériel to the front lines. Meanwhile a "decoy plan" was carried out. Forces in other sections of the Front increased their artillery bombardments, aerial reconnaissance and bombing, and marched their forces to and fro to confuse Allied reconnaissance aircraft. Thousands of meaningless radio messages were transmitted and hundreds of carrier pigeons, including captured enemy birds, were released carrying false orders. The civilian populations from areas behind the lines were also dragooned into huge formations to simulate the massing of German reserves.

"We are already imagining what it will be like when the order comes '*Protzen heran!*' [prepare to move]. We are most conscious of the greatness of the moment, and have got into a terrific state of tension, and even when we have time for any rest, we genuinely can't sleep any more, not for a second." On 19 March, another German soldier confided in his diary, "Handed in our one blanket, so it looks as though the show starts tomorrow. We . . . are in the first assault. We must have better weather though; it is raining almost continually now and it's hardly possible to get through the mud." It was still raining the following day, but such conditions hampered enemy observation and barely affected the German preparations, and on 20 March a communiqué informed troops that the Kaiser and Field Marshal von Hindenburg had arrived at German headquarters to take personal command of the battle.

At four-forty the next morning, 21 March 1918, "a green Very light was the signal for 'annihilation fire,' " and "with a crash, our barrage begins . . . From tens of thousands of gun-barrels and mortars, a barrage that sounds as if the world were coming to an end." As well as high explosive shells, the Germans fired "Blue Cross" shells, containing diphosgene gas, and "Green Cross" shells, holding a mixture of high explosive and a gas that could penetrate the Allied gas masks and cause uncontrolled sneezing and vomiting—forcing the troops to remove their masks, and thus making them vulnerable to the diphosgene. "The gunners stand in their shirt sleeves with the sweat . . . dripping off them. Shell after shell is rammed into the breech, salvo after salvo is fired." After a barrage lasting only five hours, but of such incredible intensity that the ground around the Allied lines seemed to "boil," the creeping barrages began and sixty-three German divisions advanced along a sixty-mile front held by twenty-six British divisions. They were led by stormtroopers—heavily trained assault battalions, armed with machine guns, flame-throwers and trench-mortars—instructed to advance at all costs, ignoring any pockets of resistance that could be left to the following troops to mop up. They were supported by ground-attack aircraft, strafing and bombing the Allied lines.

Fog shrouded the battlefield until midday and the soft ground slowed the attackers so much that they fell well behind the creeping barrage that had been designed to protect them. Some spoke of trenches filled with "dead Tommies" and reported that the survivors "begged for quarter and showered us with cigarettes, food and the like," but most units managed only half of the six-mile advance that had been planned and casualties of 78,000 were the highest for any day of the entire war. However, on the following two days, despite further heavy losses, significant breakthroughs were achieved, and within five days the Germans had rolled up all the British gains from the bloody, attritional campaigns of the previous three years. One German soldier marvelled, "However did we people, who have been enduring a starvation blockade for a good four years [sic], manage to do the very thing that the men over there couldn't do in some fifty pitched battles?"

Some 1,300 guns and 90,000 prisoners were taken, and many more were deterred from surrendering only by the threat of summary execution. Lieutenant Colonel Graham Seton Hutchinson recounted with obvious pride how he had come upon a group of British soldiers who had raised their hands to surrender. "If there does not exist on the spot a leader of sufficient courage and initiative to check it by a word, it must be necessary to check it by shooting. This was done. Of a party of forty men who held up their hands, thirty-eight were shot down, with the result that this never occurred again"—unsurprisingly, since only two were left alive. Killing two to inspire thirty-eight might have been regarded as good leadership; killing thirty-eight to inspire two was a war crime.

As well as prisoners and equipment, the Germans also captured hundreds of thousands of postcards that Haig had had printed, outlining "Britain's war aims"—actually a collection of pious platitudes, suggested by Bishop Gwynne, that were more reminiscent of slogans from an election campaign: "Better homes where the children could grow up healthy and strong, better education which gave a child full opportunity for developing the faculties implanted in him by God; a fair deal for labour, giving to the worker a fuller life; justice for women and a resolute stand against prostitution; a discipline which keeps a man at his best and maintains holy matrimony as the ideal of family life." Even the most obtuse front-line soldiers might have wondered how the forty-two months of carnage they had endured were helping to realize any of these war aims, but in the event few had the opportunity to read them. Those who actually received them were far too busy fighting or retreating.

Haig had rather more pressing things to worry about than the fate of the postcards. The monthly average of British casualties had steadily increased in every year of the war, from 19,000 in 1915 to 44,000 in 1916, 56,000 in 1917 and 75,000 in 1918, and these new huge losses threatened Britain with defeat. Haig's headquarters "broke down in an avalanche of orders and counter-orders" as German troops crossed the Ancre River and approached the outskirts of Amiens. Only the lack of artillery support and ammunition as the attackers outran their supply train prevented the advance from penetrating even deeper into France, but the threatening thunder of gunfire was once more audible in Paris, and Haig was forced to issue a "backs to the wall" appeal to his men, stressing the crucial juncture that had been reached and urging them not to yield another inch of ground, even at the cost of their lives.

German morale was now sky-high. On 24 March, Paul Hub scribbled a hasty note to his parents. "We've already advanced quite far into the English territory, here in our Somme region. We are full of confidence. Today we finished off English tanks. It was superb. For a few days now, we've been spending the nights outdoors. It is cold, but mobile warfare is an excuse for everything." Five days later, he reported that "in battle, we've now already passed our first position of 1914. Am still in good health, though our offensive so far has been a downright shiver and freeze tour! On average, I am freezing twenty hours a day. I hope we get back to being camp followers or civilians soon."

By 2 April, for the first time since the attack began two weeks before, he was able to write more than a brief note to Maria. "You are curious about where I am, aren't you? Oh, it must have been a hard trial of your patience to endure such a long time without letters. Today I'll try to give you some details. I'm writing this letter on my lap, sitting on a broken chair that has been fixed again by a private. Next to me there's an open fire and the smoke is driving tears to my eyes time and again. Lieutenant Schurr is next to me, kneeling on the floor. One thing right at the start: Don't expect any tales of heroics. You'll find those in the papers. The rubbish that they write only brings a smile to our faces. Oh Lord, what sort of ideas will you all be getting about the 'Kaiser-schlacht'! I would love to chase those newspaper people over the Ancre down to the Avelny Forest. They would stop fantasizing soon enough.

"We stayed in Ostkamp until 10 March . . . At four o'clock in the morning we set off, nobody knew where to—there were rumours about Cambrai. The train went via Ghent, Courtrai, Roubaix, Tourcoing to Iwuy. We unloaded there in the evening. Now we knew it—we were really going to Cambrai. We marched there in the evening . . . So many soldiers! Everyone rushing to and fro, everything militarised. The enemy didn't seem to take note, only the station was under heavy fire. We stayed in Cambrai until 19 March, the whole time off-duty, then on the evening of the 20th, we marched to Lesdain. The town had been flattened, but the accommodation, on wooden bunks with sawdust mattresses, was decent and the enemy left us undisturbed. In the evening we moved into our start position, a half-fitted trench west of the Vaucelles Forest.

"On 21 March . . . at 9:40, under cover of a dense fog, a division from Württemberg lying in front of us attacked the enemy. We were told to be ready to move up time and again, but the order to advance was not finally given until four in the afternoon. By then the fog had lifted and the sun was shining. We weren't told how the attack was going ahead of us . . . The stone bridge over the Schelde river was under heavy fire and we crossed by the artillery footbridge. There were convoys everywhere, and continuous heavy shellfire. It was only with great effort that I and my three machine-gunners forced our way through the press of people.

"We spent the night in a small forest to the west of Honnecourt. What a freezing night! I lay in an underground shelter with Lieutenant Gailsdörfer, Faber, Wirt and Walker. Everyone was groaning with cold and all around us gun batteries were blasting. What a din! On the evening of the 22nd, we reached the first English position. The newspapers talked about a large funnel-shaped field, with levelled trenches filled with dead bodies—the writers can't have been anywhere near the Somme, nor Champagne, nor in front of Verdun, nor in Flanders—but hats off to our infantry, they took the trenches. Bands of prisoners marched past us. Here and there lay dead Englishmen, and here and there also our own dead.

"We were still at least three kilometres behind the front line, so we could make ourselves comfortable. The English dugouts, some of them quite primitively built, were still full of gas, so Faber, Walker and I lay down in a trench, pulled a canvas sheet over the top and slept well and warm. The horizon was ablaze—the English were blowing up their ammunition dumps. That fire, coupled with reports that Reims had fallen and 29,000 prisoners had been taken, filled everyone with excitement—people believed every rumour that was circulating, even though nobody really knew how it was looking on the other fronts.

"At seven o'clock on the 23rd we marched on, not even stopping for coffee, through Heuticourt, Fins, Equancourt and Etricourt. The English had converted these villages into encampments and, to our great delight, a huge amount of supplies had been abandoned there— jam, tinned food, clothes, and shoes. If only we hadn't had to carry all this ourselves! The trailing convoys were much better off. Even though I tried to keep it as light as possible, my pack was weighing me down, and on top of everything else, my unit had to carry the machine-guns and ammunition; it was a huge effort." Others, less scrupulous or less heavily burdened with military equipment, profited handsomely from the stores they found: "Living like princes. We are eating Tommy's rations all the while—butter and some bread—and we eat mostly meat." "Plenty of oats for the horses and tinned food, bacon, cheese and wine for us . . . the wonderful British supplies even include biscuits, ginger, whisky and English cigarettes."

At Etricourt, Paul's regiment "finally got to the very front line. Vicious machine-gun fire hissed around our heads as we stormed the enemy line at Quatre-Vents, causing the first losses. But the blasting of the ammunition dump in Itres was a tremendous sight, the whole area crimson with continuous explosions. I spent the night of the 23rd/24th with Private Bauer (from Nürtingen) in a small trench—just another one of those simple pleasures—and in the morning we blundered on through the fog, with shrapnel whining around us, to an old position near Barastre, where a shelled English supply vehicle yielded lots of cigarettes and tinned meat. All of a sudden there was a tank alert and I saw our front line retreating. I had an uneasy feeling and it took a lot of effort to calm my men down. There was heavy fire from machine-guns and artillery and one of my men was shot in the arm. All at once, a tank appeared about 250 metres away. Two of our machine-guns opened up on it, destroying the tank's machine-gun, and our artillery and mortars then took care of the rest. Within two minutes, the tank was destroyed and its surviving crew members captured. The remaining tanks turned tail and more were destroyed as they fled.

"That evening we bivouacked on the outskirts of Sailly, which I knew from the [Battle of the] Somme. We hadn't seen a kitchen in a day and a half and were very hungry and thirsty, but we spent another of those cold nights in the open and then, without coffee, we continued the advance at five o'clock the next morning, the 25th. All the old shell-holes were overgrown with grass, and the deeper ones filled with water. The main roads used by the English were good, the rest hopeless. The heavy artillery couldn't carry on, the lighter only with great difficulty. From Ginchy we advanced around the Vel-Ville forest towards the Foureaux Forest. Our infantry had already cleared both of them of enemy troops."

They were now advancing through or around High Wood, taken by the British at such terrible cost but back in German hands once more. The grave-markers of Alec Reader and many of his comrades were probably destroyed in the course of this German advance. Finally they reached Bazentin, occupying ground that had been abandoned by Alec's old regiment, the Civil Service Rifles, as they retreated the previous day. "Despite all our maps, orientation was difficult. New roads and tracks had been cut, old ones obliterated; there were no villages, just huts, and the woods and forests were reduced to stumps. We linked up with the 5th Regiment in Bazentin le Petit. Furious machine-gun fire ripped over the crest of the hill and the enemy was also generous with shrapnel and light grenades. What a pity that our artillery hadn't been able to keep up with us; it would have spared us some of our losses. Schurr and I spent all afternoon trying to find our battalion and it was astonishing that none of us were hit by shrapnel. I hadn't been in the midst of fire like this for quite some time. A grenade exploded two metres away from Faber, Walker, and me, and although we were standing upright, by a miracle it didn't harm any of us . . . I wasn't happy with how things had gone that day and the long search for the battalion left me in an ill-humour. I didn't start feeling happier until I saw our artillery building up on the heights behind us [along the ridge of High Wood].

"The night was terribly cold. We slept in an abandoned English tent and moved off again at nine the next morning, 26 March. We were told that the enemy had retreated even further, across the Ancre. Soon we reached Pozières and contrary to our expectations, the heights there were unmanned . . . The 247th were the first to cross the Ancre. If only the artillery had made it too. If it wasn't for the terrible state of the roads, we could have advanced twenty kilometres further . . . Only English aircraft—many of them—harried us, strafing us with their machine-guns . . . Our own fighting squadrons came howling in overhead just before dusk. Within ten minutes, three enemy aircraft had crashed down in flames. It was even better in the late morning of the next day, the 27th, seeing several more enemy aircraft crash, all in flames." However, the Allied aircraft were inflicting heavy losses on the advancing German troops. "In an advance you are quite helpless against being bombed from the air, and it is a much more uncomfortable feeling than being bombed in static warfare, when you have decent dugouts. The casualties were correspondingly higher."

Paul was now suffering badly from rheumatism, exacerbated by the nights spent sleeping in the open. "We spent the night in a small narrow pass—the coldest night of all. My left leg and right arm felt as if they had been cut off from my body and I could hardly move them. But once more we carried on with the advance and on the morning of the 28th, despite heavy enemy fire, we crossed the Ancre at Aveluy. We picked off a lot of Englishmen but we also suffered losses and the numbers of enemy machine-gun nests didn't allow us to advance further. Rain set in overnight and the next morning, 29 March, we were pulled out, completely exhausted. Now it's all much calmer, i.e., we are bivouacking in holes and under tents."

On 5 April, "East of Albert," Paul wrote a further letter to Maria. "We have suffered quite heavy losses. Twenty of our officers are down, five of them dead . . . We have been sitting in the same spot for eight days now. We lie piled on top of each other like sardines to keep warm. We wouldn't have put up with these conditions in the trenches, but in a war of movement anything goes. We will be setting off again soon—I get tired of lying around doing nothing—and with luck, I will be fine just like before. Your dream where you saw me wounded was just that— a dream. Sometimes when I see the lightly wounded going home, I think that I would gladly swap places with them, if only to see you again. But it's great to take part in this kind of war of movement . . . that's when we find booty. The English tins of meat are fantastic compared to ours and English sugar tastes so good, but unfortunately, we've finished the English cigarettes and biscuits."

While such plunder was very welcome, the difference between British rations and the meagre supplies on which the German troops had been forced to subsist, and the clear evidence that the German High Command had lied when claiming that the British were starving and on the point of surrender, only served to lower German morale. Scavenging stocks of food, and especially alcohol, also caused serious disciplinary problems and on occasions had actually stopped the German advance in its tracks. One German soldier recounted that "on account of shortage of food" he and another soldier had gone absent without leave from their unit "to snaffle some bread; unluckily got caught out by the company commander." And Colonel von Thaer complained that instead of pressing the attack, "entire divisions had totally gorged themselves on food and liquor."

Although German pilots had reported no Allied troops between Albert and Amiens, the German advance stalled at Albert, where another witness saw men who "looked very little like soldiers and certainly showed no signs of advancing" moving away from the Front, driving cows and hens before them, and "men carrying a bottle of wine under their arm and another one open in their hand . . . Men with top-hats upon their heads. Men staggering. Men who could hardly walk." Crown Prince Rupprecht admitted that his troops had abandoned the advance on three separate occasions to loot stores of French wine. "Repulsive scenes of drunkenness" had ensued.

On 9 April, Paul again wrote to Maria, his tone markedly less optimistic than that of a few days earlier. His regiment was still "just east of Albert. We put up our tents yesterday in the pouring rain. We don't like all this waiting around. We like our mobile war but wish it were one hundred times more demanding. But of course we can't rush. The terrain is more difficult in this godforsaken part of the Somme." Perhaps he also had a premonition that the German advances could not long be sustained and Maria's dream might yet become a reality, for he added a footnote to the letter. "I am sending you all my letters today. If anything happens to me, I don't want them to fall into strangers' hands."

Two days later, he wrote to his parents from Montauban, after "an agonising wait" for a letter from them. "I am still fine. Mobile warfare brings with it infinite exertions, but when you're moving forward, you gladly accept them. The cold and the wet were our worst enemies and because of my rheumatism I could hardly move my arms at times. However, it has almost gone now that I've been sleeping in the warm for a few nights. I was lucky to come through each of the skirmishes we fought, at Etricourt, Bus, Barastre, Bazentin, and Aveluy, without any harm, but the regiment suffered severe casualties, including a significant number of officers, eight of them killed. For the past fortnight things have come to a standstill and everyone wants operations to continue soon; the Somme region does not have a very uplifting effect on us. The towns exist only on the maps; they have literally vanished from the face of the earth. Only the roads that the English used are in good condition. You can imagine how longingly we look over to the land on the other side of the Ancre."

Despite Maria's repeated pleas, Paul had always refused to consider a wedding before the end of the war, but now, in the spring of 1918, he at last changed his mind. Perhaps, having already survived so much, he now felt confident of reaching the war's end alive, or perhaps he was fearful of losing her, the one bright light in the bleak, dark world he inhabited. In the same letter to his parents he added a postscript: "Father, if I've still got money with you, then feel free to credit it as a war loan for me. However, I am hopeful of a wedding leave and must have about a hundred marks available for that. Otherwise, just do what you feel is right, I leave my money and its management completely to you. I'm going to give Helene [his sister] a watch for her confirmation. Please buy it for me when you get the chance. You can take the money from my next remittance [his army wages were sent to his home]. I am thinking about spending between thirty and forty marks, though I don't actually know how much watches are these days."

By 15 April, Paul's elation at the early German advances had given way to profound depression and pessimism. "We feel so abandoned here. We can't go very far because we are now surrounded on all sides. The first few days we went pigeon-hunting. I shot some too, they tasted delicious. There were many sheep here, but the Prussians ate them all. Some of our infantrymen said that dog tastes just as good and brought one in. Of course it's all a matter of taste." As his comments indicated, rations were becoming more and more meagre, and in another letter to Maria he showed that he was well aware of the even more desperate situation at home. "Sometimes I go out foraging, but I'm not very good at it. One of my men found a pound of soap today. I have put three large pieces of soap and a bundle of string in a parcel for you. I don't know when I'll get to send it, but you do need this kind of thing, don't you?"

News of the plunder German troops had found in captured Allied dugouts and stores had even reached Berlin, where the items were enumerated with a mixture of envy and fury. "Stacks and stacks of food, cases of biscuits, jam, tobacco, corned beef, milk—all that a poor starved German's imagination could desire in his wildest dreams. Then clothes, mackintoshes, leather waistcoats, silk socks." As well as food shortages, leather, rubber, cloth and fabrics were virtually unobtainable in Germany. Wood and paper took the place of leather for shoe soles, and paper and nettle fibres were substituted for wool and the unobtainable cotton in cloth manufacture. Paul Hub's mother asked him to keep an eye out for woollen yarn for mending the family's threadbare clothes—there was none to be had at any price in Germany—but her son had little more success. "There hasn't been much loot for us here, well, not for the fighting troops at the front anyway. Those coming behind us had better luck and after two days, even the biggest stores have been cleared. When I get the chance again, I will stock up, but Mother, so far I am unable to find any." Despite the privations there, Paul longed for nothing more than to be allowed to return home. "What bliss it will be to go home! It will soon be four years since I became homeless, moving from one ditch to another, dirty and crawling with lice, dead tired and so sick of it all that I don't know what to do with myself. Can you imagine how I long for ordinary family life?"

On 17 April Paul's regiment moved up the line near Méaulte "under heavy fire. The route across open fields was quite arduous in the dark. We were dead tired at the break of dawn when we reached Mamete and moved into the dugouts of the 3rd Machine-Gun Regiment. We had to crawl in on all fours and can hardly sit upright on the floor. The weather is lousy again." Even the villages and houses that had not already been completely devastated by shelling were almost impossible to defend. "It is no longer possible to hold villages under the fire of the enemy's new heavy artillery . . . Houses burnt fiercely after being struck by just one shell of the heaviest type. The smoke and the flying debris from shattered walls as they were blown apart, drove the troops from the villages." As a result, Paul and his men were forced to seek shelter where they could.

Five days later, on 22 April, still in the Méaulte area, they were "lying in an old clay pit. Our accommodation is as ever, boards of corrugated iron against the walls, but at least they protect us from the wind and keep us dry. Two small ovens—one at each of the open entrances—allow us heat during this cold weather and through the night. Nobody can see us in here, so that we can move around freely, if only within the pit. It's not a lot, but at least we don't have to keep our ears pricked all the time. On sunny days like today, we sit on the green bench outside our dwelling and enjoy the Spring. It's so good for our exhausted bodies . . . we work only at night as the enemy's artillery is always active."

Paul's letter also revealed the tacit arrangements between the warring sides in many areas of the Front for the "ritualisation of fire" that allowed both a brief daily respite from the otherwise incessant shelling and sniping. "There was another massive skirmish at Albert and to the right of it yesterday and early today. Judging by the flares, the English did attack, but probably to no avail. Tommy is quiet only between seven and eleven o'clock in the mornings. Then we can just wander around, and even drive vehicles on the most visible streets that are usually subject to constant, heavy fire, and the Tommies don't shoot. It's always been like that with them but the French are less reliable." A stretch of the front lines on the Chemin des Dames Ridge became known by German soldiers as "the sanatorium of the West" because the lack of fighting made it a rest cure for anyone sent there, and there were several other areas where firing was restricted to occasional token bursts of rifle or shell fire, sometimes even said to be targeted on empty fields rather than the opposing trenches.

In many areas temporary truces were also agreed to bury the dead of both sides. Officers often intervened to halt the practice, but on more than one occasion during the course of the war such arrangements developed into a de facto cease-fire. The Christmas Truce of 1914 is well known, but the truce in another part of the Front that started on New Year's Eve of that year was even more indicative of the war-weariness that was already setting in. "An English officer came across with a white flag and asked for a truce from eleven o'clock to three to bury the dead. The truce was granted, it is good not to see the corpses lying out in front of us any more. The truce was moreover extended. The English came out of their trenches into No Man's Land and exchanged cigarettes, tinned meat and photographs with our men, and said they didn't want to shoot any more . . . That couldn't go on indefinitely so we sent across to say that they must get back into their trenches as we were going to start firing. The officers answered that they were sorry, but their men wouldn't obey orders. They didn't want to go on. The soldiers said they had had enough of lying in wet trenches . . . Naturally we didn't shoot either, for our communication trench leading from the village to the firing line is always full of water, so we are very glad to be able to walk on the top without any risk. Suppose the whole English army strikes and forces the gentlemen in London to chuck the whole business!"

The truce ended only when "an English officer came across and said that the Higher Command had given orders to fire on our trench and that our men must take cover. The artillery began to fire, certainly with great violence, but without inflicting any casualties." In the summer of 1915, on the Vosges, German and French troops agreed to another impromptu cease-fire. "At first we threw bombs at each other, but then we agreed not to throw any more and not to go on firing. Latterly, we exchanged cigars, cigarettes, money, letters, etc. We looked out over the parapet in broad daylight and gazed innocently at one another . . . If a Frenchman had orders to throw bombs several times during the night, he agreed with his 'German comrade' to throw them to the left and right of the trench." That truce came to an end only when the two units were relieved. In other sectors, the deployment of American troops who insisted on firing at the enemy infuriated some French forces. "When one labours for four years in Artois, at Verdun and other bad sectors, and one has the good fortune to find a quiet and wooded spot, what bad luck to see some idiot excite the sector." Americans felt that "it was perhaps high time that the stagnant ambitions of getting either a flesh wound (to be sent home to safety) or being placed in a *bon secteur* where the shelling was by timetable and mutual agreement only, were replaced by energy, initiative and individualism."

The German advance of April 1918 was now moving, if at all, only at a snail's pace. One soldier described passing through the devastated landscape abandoned by the Germans in 1917. "This was really a place where no bird sang and not even a rat or a mouse would find anything to eat . . . We passed a combined French-German cemetery with graves dated 1914, 1915, 1916, 1917, and 1918—there is one cross inscribed '*Für sein Vaterland*' and another bearing '*Mort pour la Patrie.*' They were all doing their duty to the same degree; we feel that all this murdering is unworthy of the human race."

Paul Hub was now one of the few surviving soldiers on either side to have served since the opening days of the war. The vast majority of his contemporaries from those far-off days of August 1914 were gone—dead, wounded, crippled, blinded or mentally unhinged by shell-shock and battle fatigue—and war-weariness and homesickness were now constant themes of his letters. "Yesterday I read the obituary of Alfred

Weinland [his former instructor]. He died in battle. That's how, little by little, and one after another, the old friends crumble away . . . I don't know if you can comprehend, but for almost three quarters of a year, I've been living in burrows, all dirty and soiled, with lice creeping up me, surely, it's no wonder that I want to go home, home, home! So you'll understand how much your letters cheer me up, for each one brings a piece of home with it. And when I think of home, I can even forget about the war for a short while—it's my only recreation."

All leave had been suspended since well before the start of Operation Michael on 21 March. Paul was desperately looking forward to the day when he could take his wedding leave but, like soldiers on all sides, he was also prey to the semi-superstitious fear that he might die before he could use his precious entitlement. That he also had good reason for his fear was shown on 25 April, when he had "a very close call. I was sent up from the reserve area to the front line in Ville with the machine-guns, through areas that were under constant artillery fire. One man sprained his ankle during the march and when I walked over to have a look at him, a shell struck the ground right in front of me. Luckily, it was a dud, otherwise . . ."

Rations were now even more meagre and at every opportunity Paul and his men were out scavenging for food. "Pigeons have become scarce and shy here now, but today I was able to shoot one; it made a good lunch. My people were grinding wheat all day in a coffee grinder. Tomorrow they want to reap the benefits of their work and cook beans with the flour. I'm intrigued how that'll work out without meat broth."

Ludendorff continued to launch fresh German attacks but the advances were rapidly losing momentum as casualties mounted, supplies ran low and the weeks of fighting brought his men to the point of exhaustion. By the end of April, Operation Michael had reached the furthest limits of its advance. During the forty days since the attacks had been launched, British casualties had reached 240,000 men and the French had lost 100,000, but German losses were even higher—350,000 men, including many of their most seasoned and effective fighting troops. Superficially, there had been substantial German gains but tactical and strategic blunders by the German High Command, who had twice shifted the focus of the attack in an unsuccessful attempt to capitalize on perceived Allied weaknesses, had blunted the impact of the offensive. Furthermore, the chaotic response of the Allied leaders during the opening days of the attack had at last forced them to recognize the need for a unified command. General Foch (he was not made a

Marshal of France until 7 August 1918) was appointed "General in Chief of the Allied Armies in France" on 3 April.

With the failure of Operation Michael had gone the last German hope of victory, and the depleted and sorely over-stretched German armies were now very vulnerable as the Allies weathered the storm, regrouped and began to counter-attack with increasing ferocity. News of the early advances had been greeted with wild enthusiasm in Germany, where the illusion of impending victory persuaded citizens to contribute 15 billion marks to the latest war bond, more than at any previous stage of the war, but the optimism was no longer shared by any in the front lines. Ludendorff continued to claim, at least in public, that Operation Michael had been a brilliant success, but others, including Colonel von Thaer, saw through the bluster. "Every battalion and company leader, and therefore every rifleman and gunner, clearly understands that the hope [of victory] has been dashed."

Paul was by now so exhausted that after lying down "just to have a bit of rest, when I woke up it was 12:30 the next afternoon. I slept through the evening meal and even a heavy exchange of fire. I heard nothing." On 5 May, now based at Cournay, he found a rare moment of inspiration among the death, destruction and desolation of war. "There's nothing left standing here. Just the ruins of one house. The trees are all stumps. But every night, from what's left of the wood you can hear the nightingales sing! It's so beautiful! Just imagine, in the middle of the battlefield, nightingales. Just a few kilometres away, one shell after another, continuous firing." However, his black mood could not be lifted for long. "My dear friend Lutz from Plochingen is dead— hit by a bullet, killed instantly. We buried him yesterday. I cried as I threw earth on his body; another of my closest friends is in his grave."

Two days later his unit had moved again, this time to Dernaucourt, from where he wrote to his parents on 7 May 1918. "For a few days now, my company leader Lieutenant Schurr has been so ill that all the work of the company is on my shoulders. Last night I went back into position [in the front lines]. Of course it was raining cats and dogs and in the darkness of the night I couldn't see a thing, so I arrived here absolutely drenched and covered in mud. Static warfare with all its stupidity has restarted . . . We've reached the point now that we need some rest and I don't know why the relief is taking so long. I'd love to change my clothes and sleep in a real bed for twenty-four hours nonstop. We were given the opportunity to have a bath recently, but the delousing unit had not been completed . . . Daily louse hunts and washing have almost become a routine, and when I itch, I scratch furiously. But why should I have no lice when everybody else suffers? How sick I am of this war and how I long to be at home! My thoughts are always with you and when I get such nice letters from you, homesickness grips me . . . Father, I thank you very much for the 100 Marks that you credited to my account as a war loan. You know that one day, when I'm older and earn more money, I will maintain you, too."

By 12 May, his unit was once more in transit, somewhere in the Ancre valley, and he wrote to his parents "on the railway platform. A parcel with six eggs—what riches! And what a welcome addition to my meat pie. I should have made it last the whole day but it didn't even survive past breakfast . . . We're still waiting for our relief, but the war won't be over for a long time yet, so the relief can take its time. Now some good news—we are at last being allowed home leave again. It's being restricted to farmers at first, but perhaps in the long run somebody will have pity on us other mortals. 'Chin up, don't lose patience, wait!'—a song that we've been singing day in, day out, for years now— it's becoming almost mind-numbing."

With front-line morale in steep decline, restrictions on leave had been eased and troops now had at least the prospect of a few precious days at home with their families. The initial restriction to farmers was to ensure help with the gathering of early crops that might improve Germany's desperate food situation. Farm work was hampered by the shortage of horses, donkeys and mules, for tens of thousands had been taken by the Army and the rate of attrition among animals bringing up supplies equalled that of the soldiers at the Front. But every staple of life was now equally impossible to obtain. As well as the chronic food shortages, shoes and clothes fell apart for want of the materials to mend them, and cars were abandoned because there was no petrol, tyres or spare parts. Paul continued to send whatever he could find to help Maria and his family, but with the battle-lines again static, there was precious little to be scavenged. On 18 May, he sent home some parcels. "One of them contains dirty and ragged socks, the other some rubber from a battered English motorcycle. If mother is missing rubber bands for her preserving jars, she might be able to cut some out of this. The cords are from an English laundry bag that I spent some spare time undoing. The other two parcels with sack ticking will have reached you. There's lots of that stuff lying around here.

"The fighting is constant now. Reserve areas and communications trenches are under continual fire and planes are airborne night and day.

The leave issue seems to be tailing off again." The pessimism of that footnote proved to be unfounded and on the last day of May 1918, even as the tide of war continued to turn decisively against Germany, Paul was finally granted a few precious days' wedding leave. "If everything goes to plan, I'll arrive in Stetten on the fifth or perhaps even the fourth [of June], but please don't make too much of a fuss, I'd like to enjoy this time with you in peace and quiet . . . I'll tell you everything else when I see you."

The journey to Stetten took two days. The train was stopped at the German frontier while all troops had their hair cut short and were stripped and scrubbed down with foul-smelling disinfectant and their uniforms fumigated to kill the lice. As Paul neared his home town, he must have been struck with the same fear that beset all men going on leave. How many times in the heat of battle and the dark nights in the trenches had they thought of their homes and families, and one fear always gnawed at them: Would everything be the same as in that familiar mental picture? For some the homecoming was a brutal trauma. One German soldier, Kurt Rohrbach, had been granted a brief weekend's leave to visit his ill father. As he entered the house his mother rushed to embrace him and then broke the news: "He died two days ago. His last words as the doctor laid a cool hand upon his burning forehead were 'There was a letter from Kurtchen today,' and then he died. That was my homecoming. Now I am back in Flanders in the trenches."

Paul Hub's return home was a much happier one, though the empty places at the family table were a poignant reminder of the two brothers he had lost. On 11 June 1918, he and Maria were at last married in a "war marriage" in the Castle Chaplaincy in Stetten. Their wedding photograph shows Paul in his dress uniform, helmet gleaming, hands resting on the hilt of his ceremonial sword and the Iron Cross proudly displayed on his jacket. Maria, in white dress and veil, stands alongside him, her arm through his. The years of hardship, strain and suffering have etched their mark on both of them. No longer the carefree, happy couple who became engaged four years earlier, their pose is suffocatingly stiff and formal, and both look gaunt, severe and unsmiling, their gaze not meeting ours but fixed on a point beyond our sight, as if contemplating a bleak, uncertain future.

13

THE LONESOMEST
FEELING

George Seibold was briefly assigned to the British 22 Squadron, but on 30 June 1918 he and his fellow pilots reported to one of the Air Ministry buildings in London—de Keysers Hotel at Blackfriars or the Hotel Cecil in the Strand—where they were issued with their full kit, including gas masks, and were given a final briefing at "an inconspicuous office in Mason's Yard, off St. James." They then flew, or in some cases were ferried, across the Channel to France to join two newly formed squadrons—the 17th and 148th Aero Squadrons—exclusively staffed by American pilots and ground crew, but flying RAF aircraft and operating under overall British command as part of the 65th Wing of the 5th Army Brigade. The flight, on a hazy summer's day, was the first time that George or any of them had flown out of sight of land. As one of them remarked, "It is the lonesomest feeling to be flying straight out to sea on a smoky day. There is no horizon and you feel exactly as if you were flying into limitless space. The dim yellow line that marked the coast of France was a very welcome sight."

The 17th Aero Squadron was based at Petite Synthe; the 148th Aero (also known as the 148th Pursuit Squadron), to which George was posted, was at Cappelle, on the outskirts of Dunkirk, under the command of First Lieutenant Morton "Mort" L. Newhall. A former Harvard quarterback and "an older man than the average flyer," Newhall had won his command after seeing heavy action with the British 3rd and 84th Squadrons. The 148th Aero Squadron had actually been activated some months earlier, on 11 November 1917, at Kelley Field in Texas, but in the intervening period all its ground crew had been seconded to other squadrons for training and its roster of pilots was similarly dispersed. Only in July 1918 did the ground crew and combat aircrews finally come together for the first time. All the pilots had trained in England but only a handful, those who had already flown on active service with other RAF squadrons, had any combat experience. They were now to be pitched into battle against the massively experienced and battle-hardened pilots of the German *jastas* (squadrons).

George and his fellow American pilots were to fly elderly British Sopwith F1 "Camels," nicknamed for the humped fairing in front of the cockpit, housing the breeches of twin Vickers machine guns, synchronized to fire the 750 rounds of .303 ammunition through the wooden propeller. "Like all mechanisms of its day, this was subject to fits of illness; precise adjustment was necessary or the shooting pilot would blow his prop blades full of holes, or worse yet, shoot off the blades entirely. 'U' Camel of 'C' Flight went the longest without such a mishap and fired 6,700 rounds before putting one through a blade."

The Camel had a top speed of about 115 miles per hour in level flight and, in addition to its guns, it also carried four 20-pound Cooper bombs on external racks along the sides of the fuselage—a wire-braced wooden box-girder. There was aluminium cladding on the fuselage around the engine, but to save weight the cockpit was clad in plywood and the rest of the fuselage in canvas. The propeller, engine, fuel tank, guns and ammunition, and the pilot's cockpit, were all contained in the first seven feet of its nineteen-foot length. That and the torque from its nine-cylinder rotary engine—the whole engine spun with the propeller around a fixed crankshaft—gave the Camel its extraordinary manoeuvrability but also led to its equally legendary "unforgiving handling characteristics."

In a right turn the nose would drop sharply, and rise equally sharply in a left turn. And without the "coarse use" of the rudder to control it, the aircraft could go into a spin without warning. The instructions issued to new pilots on "Flying and Fighting the Sopwith Camel" listed a few of the potential perils. "Always wear a belt or harness when flying the Sopwith Camel as there is a tendency to leave the seat when diving vertically. Do not turn to the right under 1,000 feet until you know the machine thoroughly as the nose has a tendency to go down and lead you into a spin . . . Do not 'buzz' your engine whilst doing 'S' bends near the ground. If you put your engine on whilst doing a right hand turn, you are liable to sideslip and nosedive to earth, or to stall on a left hand turn." Some U.S. pilots did not receive even those rudimentary instructions. According to Harry Callahan, the only guidance that he was given was "'Don't get into a right-hand climbing turn.' That's all they told you."

The Camel had a number of other defects. The rotary engine always ran at full throttle, requiring "constant blipping with the cut-out button" on the control stick to regulate the power. The position of the top wing and the cockpit gave the pilot a poor "fighting view," and both pilot and guns "suffered from the cold." The Camel was also unstable and prone to savage vibration, making accurate shooting difficult. It was "so tiring" to fly, the cockpit was "inexcusably draughty" and the guns often froze. The average interval between engine overhauls was only twenty flying hours, and castor oil rather than the usual engine oil was used in the rotary engines, because it was not miscible with petrol and so would not dilute the fuel-air mixture in the crankcase. This had an unfortunate side-effect, since castor oil fumes had a similar laxative impact on a pilot's digestive system to a spoonful taken orally.

Despite the drawbacks, some pilots loved the Camel. It turned with such speed that USAS instructor Charlie Meyers said that "it could bite its own tail" and, aided by the torque from its rotary engine, many pilots would even turn 270 degrees right rather than 90 degrees left. "Not only did they believe this to be faster in combat, but it was tactically confusing to an enemy." One British pilot declared that the Camel was "unquestionably the greatest plane at the front—and that includes the German planes"—and they were responsible for more "kills" of enemy aircraft—1,694—than any other Allied plane, but many pilots loathed them with a passion. Another pilot with George's squadron, though agreeing that a Camel "could turn inside a stairwell" and "was deadly below 5,000 feet," also claimed that "a Camel pilot had to shoot down every German plane in the sky in order to get home himself, as the Camel could neither out-climb nor out-run a Fokker." That view was confirmed by fellow pilot Lawrence Wyly. "We couldn't dive, we couldn't run, we couldn't climb; all we could do was turn a tight circle and dogfight." Two American pilots who had never flown Camels

before joining the squadron remedied this defect with typical noncha-
lance by getting the ground crew to explain the controls and then trying a few take-offs and landings. "When we thought we were good
enough to get on the ground by the third bounce, we went on back to
our airdrome."

George Seibold reported to his new squadron on 4 July 1918. A
grainy, black and white film taken at the time shows his Sopwith Camel
D9516 drawn up at the head of a line of the squadron aircraft. The pilot
glimpsed for a few tantalizing seconds, strolling round the tailplane and
leaning into the cockpit, is George. With pilots Lawrence Wyly, Walter Knox and Jesse Orin Creech from Harlan, Kentucky, George was
assigned to "A" Flight, under the command of Field Kindley, from Pea
Ridge, Arkansas.

In training, Kindley had seemed an unlikely pilot, let alone a flight
commander. His British flight instructor, Captain Howard, described
him as " 'very slow on learning . . . one bad landing . . . heavy on controls . . . very bumpy . . . very bad landing,' and as if he didn't have
enough disadvantages, he was also unlucky and accident prone . . . in
one week of training he had mechanical failure on seven out of ten
flights . . . It's really a toss-up whether he eventually destroyed more
Allied or German planes." After he wrecked his fifth aircraft, one of his
comrades pointed out that he had already accumulated enough "kills"
to qualify as a German fighter ace. Kindley even survived a collision
with the white cliffs of Dover in dense fog, and yet he went on to
become one of the finest of all American pilots with a victory record
that, in terms of "kills" per mission flown, stands comparison with any.

Elliot Springs, from Fort Hill, South Carolina, commander of "B"
Flight, was "no less a fine pilot and flight-leader, but more impetuous,
more willing to take chances, the last to leave a fight and the first to
commence one." The "C" Flight commander, Henry Robinson Clay,
from Fort Worth, Texas, was a much cooler and more calculating type
and for that reason was usually preferred as patrol leader. "Because of
his wonderful knowledge of aerial strategy and his even temperament,
because he knew when to attack, when not to attack, how far into
Hunland to go and still get back safely, and because of his intrepidity,
Clay . . . was generally chosen to lead the Squadron or the lower flight,"
which led the attack with the other two flights following behind.

All the aircraft carried the squadron identification insignia—
a white equilateral triangle just behind the RAF roundel on either
side of the fuselage, and a squadron romantic soon christened them
the "Knights of the White Triangle." The three flights were distin-

guished from each other only by the streamers carried by their flight commanders—like the favours of medieval knights preparing for a joust—and by the differing colours of their wheel hubs. "A" Flight had red wheel covers with a white centre spot; those of "B" Flight were all white and "C" Flight's were blue. The flamboyant Elliot Springs, not content with streamers, hung "various coloured silk stockings" from his aircraft.

The men's quarters, mess and recreation areas were all in Nissen huts but "very comfortably and attractively arranged," with white-painted walls, chintz curtains, wicker chairs and a phonograph and a piano. American-style informality was the rule; the pilots and ground crew called each other by their first names, and outsiders assumed discipline to be chaotic or non-existent. "They must have a great outfit in 148. They are all First Lieutenants and every one bawls everybody else out to suit themselves. And they have about six different bosses and get orders from all over the world," but Mort Newhall ensured that discipline, morale and flight- and ground-crew training were excellent. The U.S. High Command later cited the 148th as the best-drilled squadron on the Western Front.

George and the men of the 148th spent their first few days in France in relaxed mode and even found time to fit in a Fourth of July baseball game against the other American squadron, the 17th Aero, and spent some of their evenings exploring Dunkirk. By day, they flew the largely empty skies, familiarizing themselves with their aircraft and the landmarks of the surrounding area. The flat coastal plains were often subject to ground mist in the early morning, but the breeze off the sea would soon disperse it. From the air, the flat terrain was "an immense, irregular patchwork of light and dark green, interspersed with the grey and brown of well-tilled fields." Long lines of poplars marked the Route Nationale to Calais and the pilots also noted the prominent landmarks of "the spire of St. Eloi at Dunkirk, not far from the city's network of docks and shipbuilding yards, and, to the east, the many-moated, star-shaped and battered Nieuport, on the Yser canal." Even without enemy action, the aircraft remained temperamental in handling and prone to mechanical failure, and George was one of two pilots to crash on the airfield on 9 July, though both escaped unhurt.

British regulations stated that "no pilot was to cross the lines until he had been three weeks in France and, in addition to showing marked proficiency in flying and manoeuvring, had flown a certain number of hours on line patrol and had fired successfully a certain number of rounds from the air into a fixed target." To achieve this last aim, they practiced singly and in full squadron formation, "diving and firing on the silhouetted plane in the marsh nearby at St. Pol." The target received so much fire that "there was nothing left of it but shreds." When Elliot Springs made a practice attack for the first time, he couldn't find the target at all for a while and then "saw a rotten attempt at a silhouette of a plane over in a corner of a field, and I dove on it and emptied my guns into it." When he returned to base he discovered that an apoplectic Belgian major had telephoned to complain that a Camel bearing Springs' identification number had been shooting up the Belgian mess hall.

At four o'clock on the morning of 10 July 1918, just as the summer dawn was about to break, George and fourteen other pilots of the squadron flew their first "line patrol." George's excitement at his first combat patrol would have made it hard to sleep the previous night, but in any event there was little opportunity to do so, for he and his comrades were woken at 2:30 a.m. "after two to four hours sleep, ate a nauseating fried egg slapped down by a dirty-handed orderly, tested their guns and lurched off the ground in semi-darkness." Before taking off they had queued to hand over the contents of their pockets to the squadron's orderly officer, ensuring that they carried nothing of potential intelligence value to the enemy.

As they climbed towards their "ceiling" they met the first rays of the rising sun, but long after it had climbed above their horizon the earth below them remained in shadow, with sinuous trails of mist tracing the course of each river. The beauty of the scene and the prospect of engaging the enemy heightened still further the pure exhilaration of flight that all pilots shared: "The way the earth looked, falling . . . the scream of wires; stars between wings, grass blown down when engines were run up; the smell of dope [thick varnish used to cure the aircraft canvas], and castor oil and varnish in new cockpits; moonlight shining on struts, the gasps before the dive; machine guns."

The rising sun had little effect on the arctic cold of the upper air. "Although 17,000 to 18,000 feet was the usual compromise between extreme discomfort and the upper hand over the enemy, there were several shows which started at 19,000 feet, resulting in occasional touches of frostbite on the face where goggle- and chin-masks met, and sometimes a rim of blood round the lips." The terrain they overflew was mostly low-lying marshland, almost impossible for ground troops to traverse, and for that reason the front line there had remained virtually static for almost four years. There was consequently little enemy air activity in the region and the patrol leaders "took their charges up to the edge of that awesome place 'Hunland' and let them look it over." To their disappointment, they returned without sighting a single enemy aircraft.

George's jubilation at making his first combat patrol might have been tempered by a better knowledge of the odds against his survival. The majority of U.S. pilots began flying combat missions only in the summer of 1918, just a handful of months before the war ended, yet of the 210 Americans who trained with the Royal Flying Corps/Royal Air Force in England, 51 were killed, 30 badly wounded, another 14 became prisoners of war and 20 cracked up under the mental strains. According to one pilot, the average life expectancy of a scout (fighter) pilot on the Somme was three weeks and even if he survived, six months of combat was as much as the average man could stand. Another showed the mental stress. "My ears are afire until I hear what we are to do the next morning. Then I can't sleep for thinking about it all night. And while I'm waiting around all day for the afternoon patrol, I think I am going crazy. I keep watching the clock and figuring how long I have to live."

A British Medical Research Committee reported in 1918 that "war flying exposes the human organism to a greater strain than it has probably ever been exposed to before," and noted a disturbing number of cases of fainting, falling asleep in the air and hallucinations. Some pilots became ill with ulcers, insomnia and mental problems, others responded to the stresses with cynicism or black humour, or found solace in heavy drinking. Another pilot with the 148th Aero Squadron remarked that "a lot of fellows in our squadron couldn't fly unless they were at least half-drunk," but, whatever their private thoughts, most pilots affected a studied insouciance among their peers, treating air combat as one more "wonderful game . . . just like rugger, which continued irrespective of injuries to the players." This was particularly true of Englishmen steeped in the public school ethos, for many of whom, it seemed, war was the continuation of sport by other means. In wartime England, schoolboys had even been taught that "playing for one's school is much the same thing as fighting for the Empire," and the attitude was taken to its logical conclusion by an English officer, Captain W. P. Nevill of the 8th East Surreys, who distributed four footballs among his men and, as the Battle of the Somme was launched, set off kicking one of them towards the German lines. He was killed while the ball was still in the air.

On the evening of 10 July, George and nine other pilots of the 148th were caught in a dramatic thunderstorm, with cloud from 100 feet all the way up to 18,500 feet. Another patrol landing as the storm burst had to do so "at full throttle to remain on the ground." It was a potentially lethal situation. The rapid pace of aircraft development during the war had produced increasingly efficient fighting machines, but the need to minimize weight still left them fragile, prone to mechanical and structural failure and very vulnerable to extremes of weather. One storm destroyed "half the fragile aircraft of the RFC's No. 6 Squadron on its flying field in France," but on this occasion the skill of the 148th's flight commanders and pilots and a measure of good luck ensured that all returned safely to base. There was another alarm soon afterwards when three of the squadron pilots lost their way while trying to fly back to base by moonlight. After "flitting around like the bats in a belfry tower," they saw an aerodrome beneath them and landed safely miles from their own airfield. The worried officers and men of the 148th were still "firing Very lights up into the darkness and lighting large gasoline flares" to guide the pilots home, when they arrived by road in a borrowed truck.

The practice line patrols continued over the next few days with "no attempt yet at offensive work," but on 11 July George and his comrades experienced their first "Archie"—anti-aircraft fire—which looked "like snakes' tongues as they burst." "A burst near you sounds like a loud cough and as soon as you hear it, you start zigzagging . . . The battery has your range and the next one is sure to come closer unless you fool him and sideslip, zoom, turn or throttle down. Then he fires where you should have been but weren't . . . The best thing to do is to change your course every twelve seconds. That gives you time to get out of the way of the one that's coming up at you at that moment, and doesn't give the gunners time to get your deflection for the next shot." Two days later the squadron recorded its first kill, when George's flight leader, Field Kindley, shot down a German Albatross D-3 at 12,000 feet between Poperinghe and Ypres. This "blooding" of the all-American squadron was duly celebrated in a congratulatory telegram from British Brigadier General Ludlow Hewitt, chief staff officer at the RAF's French headquarters, "for marking up the first point scored against the enemy by the American Air Service."

Patrols did not take off in poor visibility or bad weather, and as it was raining for much of the next few days there was little activity by the 148th. Despite the occasional wail from "Mournful Mary"—the Dunkirk air-raid siren—immediately echoed by those at Coudekerque and St. Pol sur Mer, there was also a brief respite from enemy bombing raids. "You watched the sky in the evening and, if a star came out as it grew dark, you were sure to hear someone remark 'Well, I guess old Jerry will be over tonight.'" The German Gotha bombers raided Dunkirk on "every clear night and it's gotten tiresome already." The city was just twenty miles from the front lines and its harbour and the three canals emptying into it made Dunkirk "just as easy to find in the moonlight as in the daylight."

"The strictest rules were enforced with regard to lights" but, since the base at Cappelle was on the city outskirts, flanked by two of the canals and with railway sidings running across a third side, "on which hospital trains belonging to the French Medical Corps were drawn up, waiting for sudden calls from this or that part of the Front," bombs often fell on the airfield and around the men's living quarters, sending them sprinting for the dugouts or the ditch at the edge of the airfield. In wet weather this could be waterlogged, as one private discovered when he dived into "a little water, about enough to cover the neck from the feet up."

On the evening of 19 July, General Salmond, "Commanding General of the RAF," made an inspection of the 148th and, even though combat patrols had actually begun nine days earlier, he announced that they would officially go into action the next day. The following evening, Sergeant "Spike" Irvin of the ground crew duly recorded in his diary that "real war flying started today."

For much of the remainder of the month, George and the others were night-flying on reconnaissances and providing fighter escorts for British DH 4 and DH 9 aircraft carrying out bombing raids on German-occupied Belgium. The fighters would give the flights of "twelve, fourteen, even sixteen" DH 9 bombers thirty-five minutes' start and then rendezvous with them at 15,000 feet over Dunkirk. The bombers flew on at 14,000 to 15,000 feet with the 148th's Camels at 16,000 feet and sometimes even as high as 19,000 feet, providing top cover against attack by German fighters. The pilots had no cockpit canopy, no oxygen and little in the way of protective clothing, and those long flights were a miserable, cold ordeal, made worse by the ferocious "Archie" fire from the German anti-aircraft batteries. Those on the coast at Middlekirke were reckoned to be "the best and most accurate that the 148th ever encountered," filling the sky with whorls of sooty smoke and "the white blossoms of the ever-rising, ever-drooping star-shells."

The outward route took the squadron along the coast past Ostend and Zeebrugge, where the mole and "the two British concrete-laden battleships" (used to blockade the harbour) provided instantly recognizable landmarks. The island of Flushing marked the turning-point where the squadrons of bombers and their fighter escorts swung southwest to begin their bombing runs over the railway marshalling yards, ammunition dumps and docks around Bruges, some twenty-five miles behind the German front lines, "which they bombed twice a day regularly for weeks." Once free of the weight of their bomb-loads, the DH 9s were faster than their escorts, and they would streak for home, leaving the Camels to bring up the rear, maintaining height over the marshes of the Yser and beginning their descent only when the front line was safely behind them.

They also flew offensive patrols behind enemy lines to protect the British BE2C artillery observation planes, "a pretty sorry lot; slow, unwieldy and practically helpless . . . most of Richthofen's victories were over this type. When I first arrived we were sending one flight of five machines to do this work and as we were always in enemy territory, the Hun usually outnumbered us, and we changed to two flight and squadron shows." Some went further in their criticism of the hopelessly slow BE2Cs, describing their use for artillery spotting as "a reckless waste of human life."

On the last day of the month a patrol of the 148th was attacked by enemy aircraft—"Lt. Forster's machine shot up by Fokker, Lt. Clement's machine hit by German AA"—but both returned safely to base, and on Saturday, 3 August, the "A" and "B" Flights returned from their morning patrols claiming four victories between them, but only two were confirmed and formally credited to the pilots. Pilots serving in the French sectors operated under looser rules and could claim a victory if the enemy plane was last seen spinning out of control, even if there was no confirmation that it had hit the ground, but the British squadrons, including those staffed exclusively by Americans, had stricter criteria. A victory would be confirmed only if there was corroboration that the enemy aircraft had crashed. If the battle reports were inconclusive or unconfirmed, the claims were almost invariably rejected.

On the same patrol, George Seibold's aircraft was either hit or suffered engine failure and crashed, but he escaped with nothing more than slight injuries. It may have been his first experience of being under fire from an enemy aircraft, a terrifying rite of passage for every pilot. "If you heard reports you could be sure that you yourself were being shot at . . . it sounded like a wood fire crackling, only more so."

———

14

GOING OUT
LIKE CANDLES

On 18 June 1918, just a week after his wedding, Paul Hub parted from his new wife and family and returned to his unit on the front lines of the Somme, near Amiens. There he "reluctantly had to take over command, because my own commander stayed behind at Mons." The depression at being parted once more from his loved ones was heightened by a deep sense of foreboding, as all the ground gained in the German spring offensive was once more being yielded to the Allied counter-offensive.

The last desperate throw of the dice had begun three weeks earlier, on 27 May, when, after an artillery bombardment that saw 2 million shells fired in four and a half hours, the Germans attacked the French forces on the Marne and advanced to Château-Thierry, just fifty miles from Paris. Once more the German guns were clearly audible in the capital and the anxious population poured into the streets, sifting the rumours sweeping through the crowds and scanning the eastern horizon for whatever portents it might hold. A soldier who returned to the front lines after being all night in the streets of Paris spoke of "the silent crowds blackening the boulevards through the few hours of midsummer darkness; other crowds on the skyline of roofs, all black and immobile, the whole city hushed to hear the bombardment, and staring, staring fixedly east at the flame that incessantly winked in the sky above Château-Thierry—history come to life, still enigmatic, but audible, visible, galloping through the night."

On 11 June, French and U.S. troops, engaged in significant numbers for the first time, and eager to show how "superior" American forces would rescue the "tired Europeans," drove the Germans back in ferocious fighting at Château-Thierry and Belleau Wood. The U.S. Marines added a new chapter to their formidable legend at Belleau Wood but the casualty rates were heavier than any they had ever experienced. At the time of the U.S. declaration of war on 2 April 1917, "the U.S. regular army was on a par with that of Chile, Denmark or the Netherlands," and German commanders may well have assumed that the prime U.S. contribution to the Allied war effort would be financial and logistic rather than in combat. The vast numbers of U.S. troops now entering the front lines and the ferocity of their fighting spirit showed how foolish that presumption had been, even though American commanders proved themselves as willing as their British and French counterparts to squander the lives of their men. Just like the British on the first day of the Somme almost two years before, the American dead at Belleau Wood "lay in beautifully ordered lines where the traversing machine-guns had caught them."

Before the American declaration of war, the Germans had released a propaganda document, "The Archives of Reason," suggesting that Americans who contemplated joining the fighting should first "dig a trench shoulder-high in your garden; fill it half-full of water and get into it. Remain there for two or three days on an empty stomach. Furthermore, hire a lunatic to shoot at you with revolvers and machine guns at close range." Now Americans had experienced trench warfare for themselves and realized that the German propaganda was small exaggeration of the bloody reality. Officers fresh from West Point had not even studied the Great War raging on the other side of the Atlantic, let alone assimilated its lessons. "While the French army bled to death before Verdun, the cadets at West Point inspected Gettysburg . . . The instructors continued to emphasise cavalry tactics and made no attempt to teach the cadets anything about trench warfare." Despite all the bitter experience of the previous four years, American troops "carrying rifles over open ground had marched against men firing machine guns. The war had become a classroom in which the teachers were dumb and the students deaf."

In June 1918, for the second time in the war the German forces had been stopped "at the gates of Paris." There were now no reserves to throw into the fight, and the remaining exhausted, malnourished and battle-weary troops faced an enemy that possessed air superiority, a massive preponderance of guns, ordnance and tanks—in the closing stages of the war Germany could field only forty-five tanks against the Allies' 3,500—and hundreds of thousands of fresh American troops to throw into the battle. Slowly, remorselessly, the Germans were driven back.

On 28 June 1918, near a village he identified only as "D," Paul Hub wrote a bleak, despairing letter to his parents. "Before we went on leave, when our relief arrived and we marched away from the Front, we bade farewell to the Ancre valley with joyous hearts. Our hopes were high that we would never see it again. That didn't last long. Today I'm sitting in the same dugout that I left a few weeks ago. Back from leave straight into the Ancre valley! Can you imagine how I felt? I would have liked to have had another day to get used to this again and to recover from the long, arduous journey, but as the company had to move into the front lines on the very day that I arrived back, I had to go with it, for better or worse.

"Some time will probably pass until I've completely got used to the war again and immediate problems begin to bury the thoughts of home, but for now, my mind is still dominated by them. I took some relief from the fact that the fighting has calmed down a little around here, both by day and night, compared to how it was a few weeks ago, but the village of 'D' has sunk even further into misery. Many a shell must have rained down in the meantime. The pretty fruit and espalier trees, then in bloom, have now become sparse and sickly, because of the phosgene gas fired into the village. What a pleasure it would have been if we'd been able to fill our bellies with nice ripe fruit!" He made a transparent effort to lighten his tone before ending the letter. "I've been welcomed back joyously. If all the sincere and cordial blessings that people have given Maria and me become reality then we'll always be fine. How are you? Please send my regards to Maria's loving parents and siblings. This letter is for them, too. In grateful love and my heart-felt regards, Your Paul."

The false note of optimism was unlikely to have erased the impression created by the rest of his letter and events on the battlefield would only have increased his pessimism. Although better fed and munitioned, the French and British troops were in almost the same exhausted state as the Germans. Half the British infantry at the Front were now younger than Alec Reader had been when he died; all would then have been illegal combatants. But the rapidly growing numbers of fresh American troops and the ever-increasing imbalance between Allied and German war matériel were causing a decisive, terminal shift in the balance of power on the Western Front. Allied losses—of men, guns, tanks and aircraft—were massive, but were constantly renewed, whereas every German resource, including its reserves of fighting men, had been depleted to the point of exhaustion.

Ludendorff launched one final desperate offensive on 15 July, as "the terrible brazen roar starts up again from the mouths of thousands and thousands of guns," but it ended in failure. Losses during Operation Michael had now reached 688,000 men, and the German Army had effectively defeated itself. A French, British and American counterattack—the Second Battle of the Marne—now forced a chaotic German retreat. "It looks as though we are being thrown into the largest enemy offensive of all time—and it was supposed to be *our* offensive. We couldn't even have dreamed that this would happen—never." As if even the gods had turned against them, dozens of thunderstorms lashed down on the retreating German soldiers, and in the darkness and confusion none could see the man in front of him. "You shouted into the darkness, trying not to lose touch, but in spite of this the unit got separated into different parties . . . We arrived soaked to the skin after ten hours on the road, having managed to travel fourteen whole kilometres."

The "skeletal [German] divisions, manned by badly clothed and undernourished soldiers . . . outnumbered and outgunned in the air and on the ground," that had driven the Allies back to the outskirts of Paris could now do no more, and they stared with dumb horror at the whirlwind they were now reaping. "The word 'hell' expresses something tender and peaceful compared with what is starting here and now . . . It's as though all the barrages one had ever known had been combined . . . You can hardly see anything because of the smoke, you have to keep throwing yourself flat on the ground, and you can't understand why you haven't been hit . . . the very earth was rumbling and it seemed as though the world were coming to an end."

Like the troops themselves, morale and discipline were close to collapse and reserves taking their places in the front lines were even met with shouts of "strike-breakers." The German forces were still ceding the ground that had been gained that spring, and each withdrawal was only the prelude to another battle and another defeat. The Allied artillery and ground-attack aircraft kept up relentless assaults on the German positions, denying the exhausted soldiers even the consolation of rest and sleep. "Planes are coming over at us, thirty, forty and fifty at a time in waves close behind each other . . . the bombers come over as well, throwing down their revolting cargo in the broad light of day . . . a dreadful day is drawing to its close."

Paul's regiment now found itself in continuous action, without prospect of relief. On 17 July 1918—nineteen days after his previous letter—he snatched time for a brief note. "Our battalion still has to fill the gap that has occurred in our neighbouring regiment. The usual resting days seem to have fallen by the wayside completely and Tommy's getting increasingly angry. I don't know how long this can continue. Time and again we suffer losses in surprise raids, shelling and gas attacks. The Spanish flu has seized me, too, but because Lieutenant Bosch is on leave, I've had to stay out here despite a very high fever." Paul was one of half a million German soldiers infected with the flu who had no choice but to remain in their trenches. Another 80,000 were so ill that they had had to be taken out of the front lines. Many, their condition exacerbated by the long years of combat stress, exhaustion and near-starvation rations, were "dying off in the hospitals, going out like candles because they have no physical reserves."

On 25 July, Paul found a few moments to send birthday greetings to his father. "I cannot shake your hand firmly this time, as German men usually do, but the telepathy that knows no boundaries should therefore be all the more effective. Look after your health and may God bless you. That builds a bridge across anything, no matter how unpleasant. I wish you such a bridge, firm and without breaks, to carry you safely over all ravines, and the rocky and hard places that the way of life leads through." How fervently he must also have wished that for himself.

"How often do I think back to my wedding leave? A full month has already passed since then. Five more months still lie ahead before my next leave—and I'm already longing for it." He managed to conclude with a feeble joke but it was clear that he was close to despair. "Last week I was rested in Carnoy. The Spanish flu that I caught so badly in the trenches is now gone. After three very long and painful days, I drove the subsequent diarrhoea away with five tanalbin pills that I took in one go . . . this resolute approach had quite an impact!" Paul was lucky to shake off the flu so easily. The pandemic had a death rate as high as one in three of those affected and claimed an estimated 21 million lives worldwide in the course of the year—more even than the harvest from four years of Great War slaughter.

The German retreat continued, and on 1 August 1918 Paul wrote to his parents, "Tonight, we'll leave the Ancre area for good. The bridgehead that we won in battle this March will be evacuated and left to the enemy. Our position in a valley with the enemy occupying the heights has been a hazard for so long now—constantly under fire and suffering losses again and again—that we have decided to give up the ground. It will be interesting to see how the enemy deals with this, and whether we profit from it a little. But what a waste of all the work we've done; all the shelters we dug, the cellars and lodgings, will all be blown up. We've already spent the last few days removing ammunition, tools and anything else that could be of use to the enemy. In the last few days, by day at least, the fighting has been relatively light, but during the night Tommy fires like there's no tomorrow. Every night I fear for my food carriers who have to cross the area under fire to fetch our rations."

Two days later, on 3 August 1918, with the pull-back safely negotiated, Paul found time to reply to a letter from his brother Alfred, still a student at home in Stetten and training to be a teacher, like their father. Once more, the vicious impact of the Allied blockade on Germany's already war-ravaged economy was only too evident from Alfred's plaintive plea for any pair of boots that could be scavenged. "Alas," Paul wrote, "the battlefield's been cleared and there's nothing to be found. Buying army boots isn't possible because I've no vouchers left. I've already bought the two pairs I'm allowed for 1918 [a rule in force since January of that year] so it'll have to wait till next year. The army boots that you say civilians at home are wearing must have been stolen; it happens all the time around here. So, I'm very sorry, but I can't raise any hopes for you though I have posted you a pair of rubber soles. You'll surely make some use of them, as soles, heels or something else. The parcel also contains strong, waterproof English canvas. Perhaps you can have a pair of shoes made out of the canvas and the rubber soles?

"I'm glad to know that you're fine otherwise. I envy you your four weeks' holiday, but do work, too! I don't want to discover any grey hairs on my wife's head because of you! She's got enough trouble looking after you already. Send mother and father, Helene and Maria my regards. And if you've got a nice apple spare, you know where I 'reside.' As a reward I'll go for a walk with you on the Kernen on my next leave. And after the war—you know it, I've told you already—on the Feldberg."

Paul was due to be pulled out of the front lines for a ten-day training course in Mons on "the machine-gun pistol. I don't yet know what sort of thing that is, but I'm really looking forward to being able to escape this shambles during that time. I'm hoping to get a decent civilian bed and a relatively comfy den." However, his hopes of a respite were to be dashed by a fresh Allied attack. He was too much of a realist not to be aware of how much the tide of battle was now running against his country, but if he needed any further confirmation it was supplied on 8 August 1918, when a massive combined assault by British, Australian and Canadian forces was launched east of Amiens, with the French mounting a supporting action further south. Having at last learned the lessons of earlier disasters, the British did not telegraph the impending attack by a prolonged preliminary bombardment; instead they used disinformation and fake radio signals to suggest a build-up of troops elsewhere.

Dense fog in the early hours of the morning also helped the attackers to achieve surprise. The attack began at four-twenty in the morning, just as the first grey light of dawn was beginning to pierce the darkness. Following a brief but ferocious artillery bombardment, the first wave of troops overran the German front-line trenches and many of the enemy gun positions. At eight-twenty that morning, just as the fog was beginning to lift, a second wave of infantry and cavalry was launched, supported by tanks and armoured cars. Many tanks were lost to shell-fire but, freed from the morasses of the northern Somme and the impossible terrain of High Wood, the remainder proved devastatingly effective, sapping the morale of defenders who, once their artillery was silenced, stood virtually defenceless against them. A third wave of infantry and cavalry followed, smashing right through the German rear, their advance slowing only as they outran their artillery support. By nightfall a fifteen-mile gap had been punched clean through the enemy lines. German losses on the day were estimated at 30,000—five times the Allied casualties. This was Ludendorff's *"der schwarze Tag des deutschen Heeres in der Geschichte dieses Krieges"*—"the black day for the German Army," and the seriousness of the defeat was compounded by a further collapse in morale that saw 16,500 German troops surrender.

Discipline among the remainder was increasingly fragile and many soldiers simply deserted. British troops had sometimes done so earlier in the war, particularly at Ancre in 1916, where one officer claimed to have "direct evidence that British troops deserted in considerable numbers." Now the tide of battle had turned irreversibly and German troops were laying down their weapons in ever-increasing numbers. "In almost every single order of the day, warrants were issued for deserters," and, according to Ludendorff, German deserters in neutral countries numbered in the tens of thousands. Many more, "unmolested by the authorities," simply went home; Colonel von Thaer claimed that there were nearly 30,000 in Cologne alone. Trains carrying wounded men back from the Front were even commandeered by rebellious troops. An entire trainload of troops transferring from the Eastern Front refused en masse to enter the front lines, and an estimated 40,000 German soldiers abandoned their trenches and voluntarily surrendered to advancing American troops. Those who did remain in the trenches either "feared the shame of ridicule" from their comrades or punishment by their officers, or stayed "from a simple sense of duty . . . [but] most of us from habit." Had the choice been offered, "not a man would have remained voluntarily at the Front," and, on both sides of no-man's-land, "men endured the horrors and privations of trench warfare because their self-respect and their sense of duty would not allow them to give in."

Paul Hub's troops, facing the northern arm of the attack, were not routed like some of the other German units, but they too were driven back from Amiens. He outlined the day's events in a letter written to Maria the next day, 9 August 1918. "Yesterday started with an enemy barrage followed by a ground attack. We only lost a small amount of ground. It sounds like it's really bad south of the Somme. I hope it doesn't get too terrible here. Our neighbouring division has lost most of their ground. The shooting went on all day. We were forced out of our lovely position in the most horrible manner. But then the night was unexpectedly quiet . . .

"Please don't worry if you've read about attacks in our region in the papers recently. The situation isn't perfect, but it's not that bad. It could have been very serious for me, but I was protected and guarded with mercy and my commander has provided me with a relatively safe area with the regiment. Last night, the situation was critical, but today it seems better. So don't worry. Please tell our parents not to worry, either. I don't get a chance to write very often." The Allied attacks continued and the next day, contradicting his claims of a "safe area," Paul told Maria that his regiment had "fought brilliantly in the last three days. Our losses are heavy, like the last time on the Somme. But the enemy hasn't made much ground. Their gains are all down to their tanks. We can't do anything against them, the armour plating is stronger than on the old ones. Our M6s [anti-tank guns] have no effect whatsoever. To the left of us it looks even worse. We desperately need reinforcements. We just need to hold our nerve and everything will be all right. I will write more when we're out of this mess. Please let my parents know how I am."

On 15 August, Haig called a halt to the advance to allow his troops to regroup and resupply, but by then German officers from General Ludendorff to Lieutenant Paul Hub could hardly avoid recognizing the inevitability of final defeat. The transfer of troops from the Eastern Front after the disintegration of Russia in the October Revolution of the previous year had not been enough to offset the huge advantage in men and matériel that the Allies now enjoyed. German reserves had been further depleted by the need to sustain the war effort of its partner, Austria-Hungary, whose armies had almost ceased to exist as a fighting force. German troops might arguably be said to have been superior in training, discipline and fighting ability to all their enemies, but they were exhausted by four years of war and there were nowhere near enough reserves to fill the gaps in the ranks, nor enough guns, aircraft, tanks and shells. The outcome was now inevitable; the only question was for how long the German commanders would choose to delay it.

15

GROUND ATTACK

Sensing victory, Allied commanders were now throwing every resource into waves of attacks. George Seibold and his fellow pilots of the 148th Aero Squadron had been hampered by low cloud, ground mist, poor visibility, rain and showers for much of July and throughout the first week of August, but by the afternoon of 8 August 1918 a change to high summer had begun with bright sun and clear skies—perfect flying weather. That day had seen the launch of a British offensive led by 450 tanks on a twenty-five-mile front along the Somme between Albert and Roye, aiming to retake the Amiens Salient, seized by the German armies during the spring offensive. The advance began under cover of mist that kept aircraft grounded until 9 a.m., but 1,904 British, French and American aircraft, including those of George Seibold and the rest of the 148th Aero Squadron, were then marshalled in support of the attack. They were faced by a heavily outnumbered force of 365 "EA" (enemy aircraft) that rose to fight only in concentrated formations.

The first day's fighting saw the ignominious surrender of hundreds of German guns and thousands of soldiers; the tide of the ground war was now turning decisively in the Allies' favour. Whether in celebration of that success or because they had received their moving orders that day, or simply because they had managed to obtain a few bottles, the men of the 148th held a champagne party that evening.

George and his comrades were now regarded as fully trained and ready for a more "active" sector of the Front. They were accordingly transferred from the 10th to the 5th Army Brigade, requiring a move from the base at Cappelle to Allonville—also known as "Horseshoe Woods" after the feature that was its most distinctive landmark—ten miles northeast of Amiens. The pilots made the seventy-five-mile transfer in less than an hour. Their long-suffering ground crew took two days to make the same journey, travelling in a convoy of twenty lorries over the clogged and war-battered roads. They had to camp for the night in a wheat field before finally reaching the new base at three the next afternoon, where they at once "got busy with the war again."

The grave of the "Red Baron," Manfred von Richthofen, was just outside the airfield at Horseshoe Woods and the pilots of the 148th all made the pilgrimage to pay their respects to the great aviator. After he was shot down and killed—"no words will suffice to do justice to his deeds, or to describe the grief which every German feels at the loss of this national hero"—his body was retrieved by RFC personnel and buried with full honours. The grave was outlined with white stones, and a four-bladed propeller cut in the shape of a cross stood at the head. A copper plate had been fixed to the hub, inscribed with his name and war record and a brief epitaph. Such was his fame that "it was no strange sight to see twenty or thirty soldiers and civilians gathered about the grave." But not everyone came to pay their respects, and in the closing weeks of the war the grave was robbed of its inscribed propeller-cross.

Accommodation in the front areas was rather more spartan than George and his fellows had been used to in Dunkirk—most now slept in bell-tents—and Horseshoe Woods was "a hot spot within a few miles of the front lines. Many of the finest squadrons in the German Air Force were based in this area," and as soon as they arrived, the pilots of the 148th began familiarization flights to ready them for operations over the front lines between Albert and Roye. The flight leaders went up first to memorize the local landmarks, and they then took their flights up, leading them "up and down the lines until they get the compass bearings of all roads and canals, know all the woods and the villages, and get the position of all salients, and then we are ready for battle."

At first the daily operational reports recorded only "EA slight," and "very few EA seen," but the mental stress of even a routine offensive patrol was considerable. The tension was overwhelming, especially when acting as "bait" for a trap to be sprung by another flight lurking in the skies above. "Nobody in the squadron can get a glass to his mouth with one hand after one of these decoy patrols . . . I don't know which will get me first, a bullet or the nervous strain. This decoy game is about the most dangerous game in the world. I know I'll never be able to shoot at a bird again. I know too well how they must feel." There were also lasting physical effects. "My eyes are so sore that it's getting hard to write. You can't wear goggles when you are out hunting and the wind blows your eyelids when you sideslip or skid. And our ears are ruined forever. The sudden changes of altitude play hell with them. Going up in an elevator a few hundred feet used to affect mine. Now I dive five thousand at a crack and they ache all night."

At 1:50 p.m. on the afternoon of 13 August, another fine, sunny day, George was on observation patrol with "A" Flight north of Roye, flying at a height of 5,000 feet, when they sighted a flight of six enemy aircraft approaching from the east. There were four Halberstadt two-seaters and two Fokker DVII biplanes—recently introduced by the Germans and by common consent the best and most feared combat aircraft on the Western Front, with an edge in power, speed, height and armaments over all the British aircraft facing them. "It was not long before that stark, square-rigged outline became an object of foreboding to the RFC. Cases of turning away and avoiding combat, of 'suspected engine failure' or 'guns jamming' came to be recorded with increased frequency."

The markings of the different German *jastas* were diverse and colourful. Some had red, black, blue, white or orange tails, some broad bands of the same colours across the fuselage, some black and green camouflage, some black and white stripes or checkers, and others spots of yellow and green camouflage. The 148th had little regard for the "Black Tails," "White Tails" and "Black and White Checkered," who were all regarded as "dud" opponents, but the "Blue Tails" were seen as even more formidable opponents than the dark-red aircraft, "about the colour of veinous blood," of the Red Baron's legendary "Flying Circus."

George and the other pilots of "A" Flight turned northwards to give the Germans the impression that they had not been seen, and then banked around, using a drift of cumulus "fair weather clouds" as cover. They re-emerged into clear air and "zoomed up" into the German aircraft, achieving complete surprise. George, flying Sopwith Camel

D8203—not his usual aircraft, which must have been under repair after being damaged in a previous sortie—selected his target and "fired 150 rounds into one scout at fifty yards range, which was diving down to get away, apparently out of control, and followed him down to under 2,000 feet, when I saw him crash."

It is possible that his victim was Staffelführer Lothar von Richthofen, brother of the Red Baron, and himself an ace with a formidable fighting record of forty confirmed victories. Richthofen had attacked a British two-seater "and was about to finish off his opponent" when, looking over his shoulder to ensure that he was being covered by his pilots, he was surprised to find several Camels coming down on him. He broke away and half-rolled, but "suddenly there was a terrible pain in my right leg. I almost got away. It was the only shot [to hit] the whole machine. I had such pain that I was unable to work the rudder. My right leg was stuck on the rudder bar and I couldn't move it. I had to pull it free with both hands." Losing height, he managed to force-land, but although he survived the impact it was his last combat flight. Field Kindley, who shot down another German aircraft in the course of the same engagement, also claimed that it was Richthofen's. However, his "Combats in the Air" form merely describes the aircraft as "Unknown. Two-seater. Had no extensions but appeared somewhat like Fokker biplane," and since the Fokker DVII was a single-seater, it seems improbable that his victim could have been Lothar von Richthofen.

Elliot Springs penned a lyrical description of the contrasting emotions that must have gripped George Seibold after this, his first victory. "It was the most dangerous of all sports and the most fascinating. It got into the blood like wine. It aged men forty years in forty days. Men came out of the trenches after three years of hell and became pilots. After their first fight in the air, they felt the same grip on their hearts as downy-faced youngsters facing their first adversary. No words can describe the thrill of hiding in the clouds, waiting on the human prey. The game is sighted, then a dive of 5,000 feet, thirty seconds of diabolic evolutions, the pressure of triggers, soundless guns, an explosion, a pillar of flame and the adversary hurtling downward in a living hell. What human experience can compare with it? No man could last six months at it and remain normal. Few could do it two months. The average life of a pilot at the front was forty-eight hours in the air [i.e., forty-eight flying hours], and to many that seemed an age."

On George's return to the airfield, he completed his combat report,

Form 3348 "Combats in the Air," and his commanding officer, Mort
Newhall, then stamped it with the words "DECISIVE AMERICA,"
confirming the kill. In total the 148th claimed four confirmed and two
unconfirmed victories that day, with Lawrence Wyly another to record
his first confirmed kill. Elation at that success was marred when he
failed to return to base and was listed as missing in action, but the next
day a signal arrived from an infantry unit, reporting that he had suffered an engine failure and had been "obliged to dead-stick to the
ground," but had managed to land just inside British lines with only
slight damage to his aircraft. When Field Kindley commandeered a
touring-car and went to collect him, he found that Wyly had
befriended an anti-aircraft machine-gun company and "was having the
time of his life popping away at Hun planes as they came within
range. He didn't seem to mind the fact that Hun shells were dropping
near their position every now and then and it was only after some
persuasion . . . that he was induced to climb into the car and leave that
fascinating machine-gun."

Two days later, on 15 August, "A" Flight was again on observation
patrol east of Chaulnes, and this time George Seibold was in his normal
Camel, D9516, flying at 11,000 feet, giving top cover to "B" Flight
below them. The weather was fine with good visibility and it had been
a quiet day in that sector with very few enemy aircraft sighted, but at
4:30 that afternoon twelve biplanes, the much-feared Fokker DVIIs,
attacked the lower flight. They "came down like a ton of bricks and
sounded like a 4th of July celebration. We started twisting and turning
to spoil their aim and then the top flight came in." Waggling his wings
as the signal to go, Field Kindley led "A" Flight to the attack. As they
came down in a "power on" dive to intercept the Fokkers, George
"fired about 200 rounds at one EA [enemy aircraft], who immediately
went into a spin. I followed him down and fired another 100 rounds at
him but had to pull up at 8,000 feet as two EA were on my tail. I
climbed up to 11,000 feet again, in the sun, and dived on one EA on the
edge of the scrap."

By now the sky was full of aircraft, twisting, banking, looping, diving and climbing as they sought to engage a target or escape an attacking aircraft. George had no time to take in the bigger picture because
he was immediately attacked by two other enemy aircraft. "I turned up
at them and one turned east and the other zoomed up above me, missing me at 25 yards. I fired about 75–100 rounds at him, when he did a
series of stall turns and turned over, dropping down from side to side. I

followed him down and fired about 75 rounds more at him as he stalled down. My pressure pump had seized so I glided west across the lines but saw EA crash NE Chaulnes while gliding down." On his return he claimed two EAs—one destroyed, one driven down out of control. Both were confirmed. In total, the squadron recorded six victories that day, but Lawrence Wyly was again posted as missing in action after his petrol tank was holed and he went down in flames over Rossières. To everyone's delight and amazement he walked into the base next morning, suffering from nothing worse than a bullet wound in the right forearm.

The next two days saw little enemy activity, and only one "kill," with another large Fokker formation turning tail to avoid an engagement. On the evening of 17 August, the 148th again received moving orders and the next morning the squadron was transferred once more, from the 5th to the 3rd Brigade, and began operations from a base at Remaisnil, six miles west-northwest of Doullens. Screened on all sides by woods, the airfield was well hidden from enemy bombers and, though it was covered with shell-holes, "through the constant work of the Chinese coolies, of whom there were thousands in France, the holes had been filled in . . . and the Airdrome was quite smooth and good for landing." However, the huts that the Germans had occupied before being driven back by the British advance had been reduced to matchwood, and pilots and ground crew were once more housed in bell-tents.

Some thought the base "a most disagreeable place" but, at least in the warmth of summer, it was not significantly worse than those they had previously used, and when bad weather or poor visibility grounded the flights, the pilots could amuse themselves by playing cards around a battered old green baize table or pitching horseshoes in the dirt at the edge of the airfield. Like his comrades, George was also beginning to look forward to the two weeks' "home" leave in England awarded to all pilots within three months of their first combat missions. They had now been carrying out operational flights for almost six weeks and some of them could reasonably expect to be going on leave within the next month. It was an enticing prospect, but one that also seemed to heighten the dangers of every combat mission. The closer to leave time, the more nervous pilots became, fearing not so much the loss of their lives as that of their precious leave. As a result of that superstitious fear, pilots were always excused patrols the day before they were due to go on leave.

The 148th Aero Squadron was now to begin patrolling the front between Arras and Albert in preparation for the Battle of Bapaume and the British advance on Cambrai. During the course of the war, this ground had been fought over as fiercely and repeatedly as any on the Western Front. In consequence the entire swathe of territory was a wasteland. "If you have ever seen the pictures of 'No Man's Land' taken from an airplane, showing the overlapping shell-holes, the torn trenches, the barbed wire and the terrible desolation wrought, you have but to multiply that picture many thousands of times, thirty miles wide and many more in the other two directions, to get some small idea of what this territory looked like to those who flew over it every day. As far as the eye can see across that rolling plain, nothing but the havoc of war is apparent. All habitations have vanished or lie in ruins, almost level with the ground, the trees like gaunt spectres, blackened and shorn of their foliage and branches."

On 17 August 1918, the day that George and the 148th Aero Squadron had arrived at Remaisnil, the weather began to break, with low cloud and high winds. For most of the next week the skies were overcast, and even though the temperatures remained suffocatingly hot, the morning mists and heavy overnight dews gave a first hint of the approaching autumn. As a new offensive was launched in the killing ground of the Somme, the 148th were switched to ground attack— "low work, the most dangerous of any" and "an expensive business, justified only in extreme emergency or for attainment of a vital objective." It was also "a severer test than most fighting of a pilot's stamina and skill, and of the rigging and fitting of his machine."

Casualty rates among pilots were already terrifying. Like Sir Douglas Haig, the commander-in-chief of British land forces, General Hugh Trenchard, commander of the RAF, had ordered an attack-at-all-costs policy. Trenchard, a large man with a voice so powerful that his nickname was "Boom," had declared in September 1916 that "an aircraft was an offensive and not a defensive weapon" and later added that "British and American pilots have only one policy, one method of fighting—to go and find the Hun and make him fight." This led to the vast majority of dogfights taking place over German lines, with the inevitable result that even if they survived being shot down—and most did not—his pilots and their machines often ended up in German hands. "Trenchard's policy of 'the offensive at all costs,' [though] willingly agreed by the fighting pilots who needed restraint rather than urging," also resulted in patrols neglecting the protection of ground-attack aircraft and "seeking the enemy too far afield, leaving their charges almost defenceless, particularly in conditions of cumulus cloud cover."

Despite Trenchard's protestations—delivered while perched on a shooting stick—that "just because I'm condemned to drive round in a Rolls Royce and sit out the fighting in a chair, you mustn't think I don't understand," there was as great a gulf between aircrew and their senior officers as there was between the soldiers in the trenches and staff officers miles behind the lines. Few senior officers had ever flown in combat—Trenchard's principal staff officer had not even flown as a passenger. "It was hardly surprising therefore, that sometimes unrealistic orders were given which suggested incomprehension of the vastness of three-dimensional space and the effects of atmosphere and cloud conditions on war in the air, resulting in uselessly high casualties." Of 1,437 British pilots sent to France between July and November 1918, only 11 percent were still serving with their units at the time of the Armistice and it was claimed that pilots lasted barely three weeks during heavy fighting. One squadron lost its entire flying strength almost six times over in the space of two years and four months, "206 flying crew (that can be traced) being killed, wounded or missing from its flying strength of thirty-six."

Even the official historian of the RFC permitted himself an implicit criticism of Trenchard's policy: "Whether or not the air casualties on the Western Front would have been fewer had the policy which directed employment of the squadrons been different, is a matter which may be argued." Others were rather less restrained. "Most leading German pilots were generous in their appreciation of the spirit of the RFC; few could refrain from commenting adversely on its policy. Nor . . . should the good effect on German morale at the daily evidence of numerous crashed British aircraft be discounted . . . Single-minded and stubborn and seldom able to admit himself in error, it was a tragic irony that his [Trenchard's] fixed ideas on air warfare should have been aided and abetted by those of whom so many were its victim."

The appalling casualty rates were even higher among those operating in the ground-attack role. Bombs had to be delivered from well under a thousand feet to achieve any sort of accuracy, and flying at these and even lower levels to bomb and strafe enemy troops not only put the pilots within range of ground fire—"a proof of the low altitude at which the enemy's aviators flew is furnished by the fact that aeroplanes were shot down by infantry"—but also made them desperately vulnerable to attack from above by enemy aircraft. Despite the dangers, the congestion among the German troops and supply vehicles on the roads behind the enemy lines "gave us an opportunity of doing greater damage to his morale and matériel by attacks on moving infantry and transport than we could ever have accomplished by devoting all our attention to his scouts [fighters]."

Ground attacks were carried out "without cessation . . . shooting up convoys that became a wild confusion of broken lorries and runaway horses, and scattering infantry from the roads into the fields, inflicting on them many casualties." The impact on German men and morale was undoubtedly substantial, and reflected in the bitter comments about the increasingly outnumbered German pilots. "During the day one hardly dares to be seen in the trench owing to the English aeroplanes. They fly so low that it is a wonder that they do not pull us out of the trench. Nothing is to be seen of our German hero airmen . . . One can hardly calculate how much additional loss of life and strain on the nerves this costs us."

None of this impressed a future American president serving as an officer with a gun battery, who complained—with more hyperbole than justice—that "they fly around a couple of hours a day, sleep in a featherbed every night, eat hotcakes and maple syrup for breakfast, pie and roast beef for supper every day, spend their vacations in Paris or wherever else suits their fancy, and draw twenty per cent extra pay for doing it. Their death rate is about like the quartermaster and ordnance departments and on top of it they are dubbed the heroes of the war. Don't believe it, the infantry—our infantry—are the heroes of the war."

While Captain Harry S. Truman was fulminating against them, George Seibold and the other pilots of the 148th would go out "in pairs or alone and make three or four trips a day." Sometimes another flight or squadron was detailed to provide top cover, but often they went in unescorted, praying that they could hit their targets and return without being intercepted by the Fokker DVIIs prowling the skies above them. A modified version of the Sopwith Camel, the TF1—Trench Fighter 1—fitted with armour and two downward-firing Lewis guns, had been tested in the ground-attack role but it proved unsatisfactory, and the only protection for Camel pilots—and even then it was supplied only to a few of them—was a small piece of armour-plate fitted underneath the pilot's seat.

In the daily orders received from Wing Headquarters, only the names of the targets would change. Every plane that the squadron could put into the air was to take off at dawn, drop its bomb-load on a specified village, crossroads, railhead, communications trench or other German strongpoint, and then seek targets of opportunity for its machine guns before returning to base to refuel and reload. The flights would continue as long as weather and visibility permitted. Most feared of all ground-attack missions were attacks on railheads up to ten miles behind the German lines, thick with anti-aircraft batteries and defending Fokker DVIIs.

George and his fellow pilots would aim to cross the lines at a height of 4,000 or 5,000 feet, continuously scanning the sky above and ahead of them for the almost invisible dots that revealed the presence of enemy aircraft. As they started to descend towards the target, anti-aircraft fire began to spot the skies with puffs of oily black smoke. The fire increased in weight and intensity as they approached the target until it seemed as if there could be no possible way through the forest of flak-bursts and the searing flashes of phosphorous tracer as the machine-gunners and infantry added their fire. The pilots dived to under a thousand feet, levelled out for the few seconds it took to sight their objective, aim and jerk the bomb-rack control, and then roared away on full power, bucking upwards in a long, climbing turn as the deadweight of the bombs fell away.

The four bulbous brown 20-pounders dropped in clumsy, wobbling arcs until the weight of the tip and the rush of air on the metal guides straightened their flight and then they would plummet earthwards. The slipstream made the propeller on the nose of the bomb spin, twisting it off and exposing the trigger-tip that detonated on impact in a brief flash of murky orange flame, instantly engulfed by the cloud of dirt and debris that rose around it.

The new offensive was launched at dawn on 21 August, with a fierce artillery barrage and an advance by tanks and infantry, supported by ten squadrons of aircraft. To prevent any possibility of compromising the secrecy of the attack, none of the pilots had been informed that it was to take place until after they had landed from the last of the previous day's sorties. Aircraft were then kept flying along the front lines throughout the night, to drown the noise of the assembling tanks, and diversionary flights also took place over the neighbouring sectors of the Front to keep the Germans guessing about the true focus of the Allied attack.

After the experience of the early stages of the offensive in the

Amiens Salient on 8 August when, in contradiction of Paul Hub's complaint about their impotence against the new British tanks, a single German anti-tank gun knocked out eight tanks in succession and brought the advance in that sector to a grinding halt, all pilots were directed to pay particular attention to targeting anti-tank guns. The position of hostile guns was predicted by studying large-scale maps and aerial photographs, and likely sites were then to be bombed and strafed "until the tanks had run over the emplacements . . . As each of our aeroplanes had only about 2,000 yards of front to watch, the result was that all likely places were periodically bombed."

However, thick mist and light rain kept the aircraft grounded as the attack began at 4:55 a.m., with a "big drive towards Bapaume . . . a terrific barrage." If it hampered the air support, the mist also helped to conceal the attackers and their tanks, and they swept over the German front line in the first rush. The mist had begun to lift between ten and eleven in the morning and the 148th and the rest of the Allied squadrons then flew sortie after sortie, returning to base only to refuel and reload before taking off again.

Four of George's fellow pilots "each got a Hun" while flying offensive patrols in support of the attack, and all the men of the 148th had "a grandstand seat" as the advance continued. The rolling artillery barrage obliterated the few buildings still standing. As the shells hit them they "would rise about twenty feet in a mass, then disintegrate, muck fly about and then, as it settled, I would hear a dull thud and my machine would wobble from the concussion . . . Shells were bursting everywhere, shrapnel in the open spaces with its white puffs, and high-explosive with its cloud of dust and debris on the trench parapets. Here and there were tanks, some belching lead and some a mass of flames, or a misshapen wreck, hit by field guns. I was right down on the ground and saw very few dead bodies but any number of dead horses. The ground was all pockmarked and what little vegetation remained was a light straw colour from the gas. Further down I saw the Huns using gas, a thin layer of brownish-green stuff was drifting slowly along the ground from a trench about three hundred yards long. But no men were to be seen anywhere, only dead horses and tanks."

On the ground, "the force of the gas being discharged could easily be heard by a hissing sound." It formed "curious greenish-yellow clouds [that] moving before a light wind, became a bluish-white mist, such as is seen over water on a frosty night." Each kind of gas was marked by a distinctive odour—chlorine smelled of pineapple, phosgene had the stench of putrid fish and mustard gas had a rich, sweet, almost soapy smell. "Gas gongs"—empty brass shell-cases hung at intervals along the trench—were banged to warn of the danger. "The gas was so strong that it turned all our buttons olive green, stopped our wrist watches and turned the rats out of their holes by the score." Fortunately, the design of gas masks had improved greatly since the first gas attacks when "Gas Masks Type I" were "squares of blue flannel, just large enough to cover the mouth, with a tape on each side to tie round behind the head . . . Anything more futile could never have been devised . . . On the whole, we preferred to resort to the face towels dipped in our own urine, which an earlier order had suggested might be a temporary palliative."

Despite the gas, by that evening the advance had penetrated two or three miles into the German lines. The night was fine and clear and the night-reconnaissance and bombing squadrons were in constant action, attacking German airfields and dumping twelve tons of bombs on the Cambrai railway junction. Thursday, 22 August, dawned fine, though very humid, and the ground attack resumed at 4:45 a.m. The 148th Aero Squadron was again in heavy action during the advance, which saw Albert at last fall to the Allies. Heavy bombers again concentrated on the rail junction at Cambrai and the lines radiating out to the Front from there, while the 148th and the other squadrons flew offensive patrols and carried out ground attacks in support of the advancing infantry. On one sortie George dropped four bombs and fired 500 rounds into German infantry near Gueudecourt. Elliot Springs personally accounted for "three decisive Huns" in dogfights, and another pilot survived, injured, after being wounded and crash-landing on the Allied side of the front line.

The heat and oppressive humidity of the day continued into the evening and that night many of the airmen and ground crew followed the example of Spike Irvin and slept out under the trees, "obtaining much relief." The night was clear and moonlit and the Allied night-bombers were again in constant action, hitting the railways at Cambrai, Valenciennes and Somain, where an ammunition train was destroyed. Other squadrons carried out harassing attacks on Bapaume and the surrounding villages where German troops were billeted, ensuring that few of them enjoyed an undisturbed night's sleep.

16

THE LOSSES WE HAVE SUFFERED

On 16 August 1918, as the Allied advances continued unabated, Paul Hub wrote to Maria, "We have lost our forward positions and need to dig new trenches . . . Tommy hasn't attacked for a few days, not here anyway, but if I allowed myself to think of the losses we have suffered I would have gone crazy by now. I will see how it goes. Hopefully we can grind our way out of defeat. The last letter from my father was so full of praise for you. I hope you are not too shocked by this! You know I am always delighted when my little wife is praised."

Late the following night, 17 August, just over two months after their wedding, he began another letter to Maria. "I almost forgot to write to you today. That has never happened before. I usually find some quiet time for you. I'm always uneasy when I can't, because I really don't want anything to come between us. We were shot at today and unfortunately one of my men was killed, torn apart by a direct hit. The shelling is really horrible, sometimes just one constant bombardment. As the dugout shakes, I think of how peacefully you sleep in your beds back home. Last night was very noisy. There were constant explosions around the dugouts and more shooting this morning when one of our men went too close to Tommy. You seem to be very busy, judging from your letters. My parents must be so happy to have your help. Please remember what I said in my last letter." There was no last message, no valediction from him, but that letter was the last that Maria would ever receive from him.

Even during the prolonged fighting, Paul had somehow managed to scribble a series of hasty field service postcards to his parents, though all contained no more than a couple of lines: "Tommy is planning more foolishness. But all's fine"; "Don't expect any letters, later! later! I am fine"; "It's getting better, the enemy is quieter"; and, "If Tommy doesn't thwart me, I will be able to keep my promise tomorrow. In the meantime, I'm asking for your patience."

Finally, on 20 August 1918, after twelve continuous days of fighting, retreating, digging in, fighting and retreating again, he found time to write a brief letter. "There's nothing much new to tell you. Tommy's attacks seem to have faded for now. Admittedly, he's still firing off plenty of shells, but that has been his speciality right from the start. Our hopes for a relief are not being satisfied, though we're all in desperate need of rest. Constructing a completely new position is a lot of work to complete with so few men, but at least it's less unpleasant than lying idly in a hole in the ground, which I've already had to so many times and for so many years. How are you? Have you completed the harvest? Now the wind already blows over the stubble field . . . ! In grateful love, my heartfelt regards to all of you, Your Paul."

Paul Hub had endured almost four years of fighting on the Western Front. He had fought at Ypres, Verdun, the Somme and Passchendaele—names of infamy with death tolls in the hundreds of thousands. He had been seriously wounded by shrapnel, buried alive by a shell-burst and had seen an artillery shell land at his feet and miraculously fail to explode. He had lived through advances, retreats, endless poundings from artillery, mortars, bombs, snipers, machine guns, gas attacks and vicious hand-to-hand fighting in the trenches and, while almost every comrade from "the Regiment of the Dead" was now dead, wounded or missing in action, Paul had somehow survived.

He knew in his heart, as every German soldier probably knew by now, that the war was lost, and his letters show how much he was yearning to put those bloody, terrible years behind him and return home to live out his days with Maria. "Over by Christmas" was a phrase that had been used by every side, in every year, since the war began. This time it carried the ring of truth, if only because the decimation and demoralization of German troops, the famine and growing social unrest among the civilian population and the transfusion of mountains of war matériel and American soldiers into the Allied ranks argued for no other outcome. Paul had only to survive for a few more months and, for better or worse, the war would be over.

By 25 August, his unit had retreated twenty miles east of Amiens and dug in around the village of Maricourt. The Allied attack on Bapaume, a few miles to the north, had already been raging for four days and the constant bass rumble of the guns was counterpointed by the shriller whines and crashes of the shells pounding the remnants of the 247th Regiment, as they took what shelter they could find among the craters and rubble heaps that were all that remained of a once-thriving village. Paul and his demoralized and hungry troops suffered not just continual shelling but the horrors of bombing and strafing— "night and day aircraft come and lay their 'eggs,' yesterday seventeen men killed here"—while the machine guns and snipers' rifles continued to exact a daily toll.

On 26 August 1918, after furious fighting, Maricourt fell to the British. As they advanced through the smoking ruins of the devastated village, they passed the blackened, already bloating corpse of Paul Hub. He and his exhausted troops were being relieved and were pulling back towards "a slope of the Somme valley." They had paused for the distribution of rations when a direct hit from a shell caused severe shrapnel wounds to Paul's head and legs. He died soon afterwards. For the third time, Paul's parents were left to mourn the loss of a son. And Maria Thumm, who for four years had begged her fiancé to marry her, was now a widow after just ten weeks as a wife.

17

A DIMINISHING SHADOW

On Friday, 23 August 1918, George Seibold and the 148th Aero Squadron were involved in a further massive Allied attack, across a front stretching thirty-three miles from Soissons in the French sector in the south all the way to the outskirts of Arras, in the north. The weaknesses now apparent in the German armies, with reports that "a Bavarian Division fled in panic, carrying back with it another division which was advancing to its support," persuaded Sir Douglas Haig to announce that "the most resolute offensive action is everywhere desirable. Risks which a month ago would have been criminal to incur ought now to be incurred as a duty. It is no longer necessary to advance in regular lines and step by step. On the contrary, each division should be given a distant objective which must be reached independently of its neighbour and even if one's flank is thereby exposed for the time being."

The renewed offensive was launched at 4:45 a.m. that Friday, and George and the other pilots were again engaged in "low strafing all day . . . Pilots hit ground targets in and around Bapaume," as the advance rolled inexorably forward. They were aided for the first time by intelligence collected and distributed by the wireless Central Information Bureau (CIB) that had been set up near Villers-Bretonneux. Observers who spotted enemy formations of aircraft or targets suitable for ground attack by Allied aircraft fired a red flare from a Very pistol to attract any aircraft in the area, but they also sent a wireless message to the CIB, giving the number, height and position of the enemy aircraft or the co-ordinates of the ground target and a brief coded description: infantry, artillery, munitions and so on. This information was then transmitted to the neighbouring squadrons, which would either scramble aircraft to intercept or, if they were already airborne, indicate the direction of the threat or target by laying a large white arrow on the airfield pointing in that direction. This crude method proved surprisingly effective in bringing the Allied squadrons to bear on targets.

The offensive was resumed in the dead of night, at 1 a.m. on 24 August, but low cloud and intermittent rain kept the squadrons grounded until lunchtime. As the cloud lifted and broke up, they took to the air and resumed their attacks, "hitting ground troops and much transport around vicinity of Bapaume" as the Germans tried to relieve their hard-pressed front-line troops. At 2:15 that afternoon, flying at 700 feet over Ecourt-St. Menin and Moreuil, George dropped four bombs and "fired into infantry and horses." He fired 500 rounds in all, returned to base to reload and refuel and five hours later was north of Haplincourt. There he saw a *Drachen*—a German artillery observation balloon—being prepared and "dropped bombs near same and fired into men standing by same. Thinks he killed two." Tethered by a steel cable to a winch-truck, the *Drachen*s were dangerous targets, always surrounded by anti-aircraft machine guns and "fearsome devices known as 'flaming onions' that formed a curtain of fire around the balloons." George returned to base safely but Lieutenant Kent Curtis of the 148th was posted as missing in action when he had not returned at eight-twenty that night. By nightfall the whole of the Thiepval Ridge was in Allied hands and several thousand more Germans had surrendered. The night was clear and moonlit and bombers were again active against targets around Cambrai, Douai, Somain and Valenciennes.

The following morning, 25 August, it was turning much cooler, with the haze obscuring the sun promising a change of weather. The Allied advance continued with Favreuil, Spaignies, Behagnies and Mory falling in the course of the day, and it was another day of frenzied air activity by both sides. The 148th's pilots reported the "sky full of Huns" as they continued bombing and strafing around Bapaume. George carried out another bombing raid and fired at a balloon at 4,000 feet over Rocquigny, and at ten past six that evening, south of Haplincourt, he claimed another kill, "probably a Hannoveraner," another much-feared enemy plane. "The flight below us dived on a formation of two-seaters. I dived down on an all-black two-seater and fired about 500 rounds, when he dived towards Haplincourt and crashed on road S of Haplincourt. I then turned back towards the flight and dived on a greyish two-seater, and fired all my rounds, but failed to get him and had to return as ammunition was all gone."

It was George's fourth victory in the space of twelve days, and an RAF report covering the period 1 July to 25 August cited him for "distinguished service." Among the other pilots of the 148th, only the leader of "B" Flight, Elliot Springs, had achieved as many victories in the same period, and one more confirmed kill would have given George "air ace" status—though that term did not win acceptance among British and American pilots until much later, and the German practice of "starring their airmen was a matter of mockery in the RFC." Three other pilots of the 148th also recorded victories that day and there were no losses of men, though two were forced to crash-land on their way back to base.

The morning of 26 August dawned overcast with rainstorms sweeping in on strong southwesterly winds that "grew stronger and gustier as the day advanced. Low clouds, with gaps of blue between them, streamed thickly up from the south-west . . . The little wood was full of the noise of the wind, blowing in fits at seventy or eighty miles an hour." The weather prevented operational flying until the afternoon, and it was so windy that ground crewmen had to hold tightly to the wingtips of each Camel to prevent them being flipped over as they were turned into the wind for takeoff. Despite the conditions, there was ferocious air activity on that part of the Front. Bapaume was on the brink of falling and aircraft attached to the 3rd Brigade, including the 148th, flew a total of thirty-six reconnaissance and seventy contact and counter-attack patrols, firing 42,500 rounds and dropping fifteen tons of bombs.

As soon as the cloud began to lift, even though the wind was still "blowing furiously into Hunland," men of the 148th were dispatched in teams of two, to carry out bombing and strafing operations. George Seibold, flying his usual Camel D9516, took off with Walter Knox and set a course for Bapaume, where fierce ground fighting was still taking place. But the same slight easing of the weather conditions also allowed the German Jagdeschwader III to get airborne, and Jasta Boelcke, commanded by Oberleutnant Bolle, and Jasta 27, led by Leutnant Hermann Frommherz, began defensive patrols at high altitude over Bapaume.

Protective cover for the ground-attack planes of the 148th was to have been provided by the 17th Aero Squadron, based at Auxi-le-Château, but when George and Walter Knox arrived over Bapaume there was no sign of their fellow Americans and they began their bombing and strafing attacks without top cover. At about ten past five that afternoon, "George spied three Huns down below. The rest of the formation was pretty busy and lost track of him for a moment. In the meantime he had downed one of them and was engaging the others most valiantly . . . He had gotten another Hun" when they were jumped by a flight of five Fokkers coming down from high altitude out of the sun.

Hermann Frommherz, from Waldshut, in Baden, a formidable flying ace with "a chestful of decorations" who was to end the war with a tally of thirty-two victories, led the attack. He flew "a gaudy Fokker, marked with the unit's yellow nose and tail markings, and red and white chevron-pattern stripes on the upper wing to identify him as a Staffelführer." As Frommherz dived on him out of the sun, it is probable that George did not even see his assailant until too late. He took no apparent evasive action and his aircraft was hit "after an engagement of short duration" and began "coming down in a slow spin." Frommherz pursued him all the way down, pouring fire into the first of three victims he was to claim that day.

German ground troops would also have fired at George's aircraft as it came down—the entirely understandable reaction of both sides to an opportunity to take revenge on the aircraft that caused them so much misery and death. A soldier in the British lines recorded the delight at a German fatality in the same area. "About 7:30 p.m. an aeroplane fight began. It got nearer and nearer until in the full glow of a glorious evening sunset, the Boche came lower and lower and fell in Bazentin-le-Petit Wood, bursting into flames. As he got near the earth, every rifle and Lewis gun opened on him and as he fell, everyone burst into a cheer."

The nine aircraft from the 17th Aero Squadron had appeared just seconds too late to help George Seibold. Responding to a warning that "some of our 'low-strafers' were in trouble on the Cambrai-Bapaume road," they arrived to see "five Fokkers, climbing east of Queant at about five o'clock." "Immediately afterwards one Camel was seen being attacked . . . at 1,000 feet. The patrol at once went down to the assistance of this Camel (afterward identified as that of Lieut. George Seibold of the 148th Squadron) and attacked the enemy machines. Several other flights of Fokkers were then observed coming down through rifts in the clouds from 6,000 feet . . . A general engagement occurred in which two other separate flights of Fokkers came down from higher up."

A German account of the same incident suggested—probably more accurately—that the 17th only began to engage the enemy after George's aircraft had already been shot down. "First sortie of the whole *Geschwader* in the afternoon. Frommherz dived and shot down a Sopwith. We had barely assembled again when strong enemy single-seater units dropped on us. Frommherz and Klimke rushed at them with perfect timing, while I missed the proper moment. Terrific dogfighting followed, in the course of which Frommherz downed two opponents. Klimke and I followed another one. He manoeuvred so smartly that it was nearly impossible to close in. Occasionally he would rush one of us and fire. Finally, when he flew straight for a moment to run home, Klimke and I got behind him and he plunged down burning."

The engagement capped a day of disaster for the U.S. squadrons. The Fokkers had baited a classic trap and "a cloud of fifty to sixty German machines" had ambushed the 148th and 17th Squadrons to devastating effect. The 17th's losses were the heaviest in any single American fighter engagement throughout the war. At seven-thirty that evening, with nightfall approaching, seven American pilots had not returned and all were listed as missing in action. Among them was George Seibold, shot down on the same day that Paul Hub was killed.

As the stricken Camels had gone spiralling down, the gale-force westerlies had driven most of them across the German lines and their crash sites could not be identified. However, Jesse Orin Creech had seen George's engagement as he carried out ground attacks near Bapaume, witnessing a dogfight between "11 Camels and Fokkers. Saw one go down in flames and saw four others crash." His own aircraft was badly shot up and he was "too far to distinguish" whether George's stricken Camel was an Allied or enemy aircraft, but he marked the site where it came down on his map. It was unusual for a pilot's end to have been witnessed in this way. "The pilot lived and died very much alone, and when a friend 'went west' over the lines, his moment of fate was rarely seen in the confusion of high speed fighting and it was as if he had gone through a mirror, leaving only a diminishing shadow."

18

AT THE ELEVENTH HOUR

On or soon after 26 August 1918, Paul Hub's body was hastily buried as his regiment retreated. Within days the Allied advance had swept over the site and the German retreat began to resemble a rout. They were steadily driven back during the autumn of 1918, with both sides suffering horrendous casualties that only one could now afford. On 9 November the Kaiser's abdication was announced—the Kaiser himself was not made aware of this until after the proclamation had been issued. German military commanders were then led through the Allied lines under safe conduct, and taken to the forest of Compiègne, near Paris, where Marshal Foch gave them the humiliating terms of their surrender in a railway carriage that had been used by Napoleon III during the Franco-Prussian War. (After the Germans conquered France in 1940, they forced the French to sign their surrender in the same carriage. It was then transported to Berlin, but was destroyed during the Allied advance on the city in 1944–45.)

Germany was to cede all occupied territory on the Eastern and

Western Fronts, including Alsace-Lorraine, taken from the French in 1870. The Allies would also occupy Germany west of the Rhine and bridgeheads thirty kilometres deep on its eastern bank, and Germany was to hand over a vast quantity of military equipment, including 10 battleships, 14 cruisers and light cruisers, 160 U-boats, 2,000 aircraft, 5,000 field guns and other artillery pieces and 25,000 machine guns. In all, 5,000 locomotives, 5,000 goods wagons and 150,000 railway carriages were also to be confiscated and Germany would be required to pay reparations for her aggression in cash, coal and other goods. As a further indication of Allied intransigence, the blockade of Germany would remain in force until the signing of the final peace treaty, and even though the German commanders begged for hostilities to be suspended while they obtained their political masters' approval of the cease-fire terms, Foch insisted that the war would continue until the Germans completed the formalities of their surrender. As a result, thousands more soldiers of both sides would die and countless German civilians starve. There had been no American representation at Compiègne, but the commander of the American Expeditionary Force, General Pershing, whose attitude to President Wilson's earlier peace proposals bordered on insubordination, wholeheartedly approved the continuation of hostilities. "There can be no conclusion to this war until Germany is brought to her knees."

At 5:10 on the morning of 11 November 1918, the German commanders signed the Armistice, which would at last bring four years of slaughter to an end. News spread rapidly through the ranks on both sides that the war would officially cease that morning—at the eleventh hour of the eleventh day of the eleventh month. However, celebrations in many parts of the Allied lines gave way to disbelief and then despair as it became clear that, Armistice or no Armistice, the attacks already scheduled for that morning were to go ahead as planned. A minority of front-line commanders allowed common sense and common humanity to prevail and called an immediate cease-fire. The rest, including the commanders of nine of the sixteen U.S. divisions on the Western Front, ordered their men forward in one final, futile assault.

Some did so simply because the previous orders to attack had not been rescinded and prudent soldiers did not question commands from their superiors; some because, as career officers, they saw it as their last chance for glory, medals and personal advancement before the peacetime ossification of the ranks; and some—reflecting the belief of their supreme commander, General Pershing, whose "thin, crescent-shaped mouth . . . turns down like a bulldog's and makes him look as if he had never smiled in his life"—from a desire to inflict the maximum possible punishment on German troops.

The Armistice was announced on the radio in the United States as soon as it had been signed, but while late-night revellers and early risers in New York, Boston and Washington, D.C., were spilling into the streets to celebrate, American soldiers were still fighting and dying on the Western Front. At ten, ten-thirty and even ten fifty-nine, the guns were still blasting off every available shell, partly fired by the determination—at least at officer level—to punish "the Hun" to the very last second, but primarily, one suspects, because the gun crews knew that otherwise they would be given the back-breaking task of carrying the unused shells back to supply dumps behind the lines. And, knowing that the war was all but over, men still kept rising from their trenches, only to be met by a murderous hail of artillery and machine-gun fire. By the time the guns finally fell silent, 11,000 more casualties were strewn across no-man's-land. The day's total was greater than the number who fell on D-Day in Normandy in 1944.

Even in the First World War's four years of remorseless attrition, never had there been such needless slaughter. The terms of the Armistice required Germany to cede all occupied territory, and every inch of ground gained at such human cost that morning would have been handed over anyway within two weeks. Who could possibly have explained to that day's fresh crop of grieving mothers, widows and fatherless children why their men's lives had been sacrificed? It was a day that reflected in perfect microcosm the whole weary pointlessness of the "war to end all wars." "The retaking of Mons, site of the first British retreat of the war, might be seen as poetic closure. It could also symbolize futility. The British army was back where it started on the Western Front, some 700,000 lives later" (a figure that does not include the more than 300,000 soldiers of the British Empire who also died). The first British and Empire soldier killed in the Great War—Private J. Parr, killed on 21 August 1914—and the last—George L. Price, 28th North West Battalion, 2nd Canadian Brigade—were buried in the same cemetery. "Their proximity in dust and the fact that they share a burial ground with four years' worth of German dead bespeak the military futility of their actions."

After the Armistice finally came into force, the German armies were allowed to march home, still bearing their arms and with their colours

flying. They were greeted as if they were the victors, lauded and gar-
landed with flowers in every village, town and city through which they
passed, but the demeanour of the majority of those returning heroes
showed the reality of their situation and what they had endured. "The
soldiers marched quickly, in close formation. They had stony, expressionless faces. They looked neither to right nor left, but straight ahead,
fixedly, as though magnetised by some terrible goal, as though they
were gazing from dugouts and trenches over a wounded world. Not a
word was spoken by those haggard-faced men . . . One platoon passed,
the ranks close, a second, a third. Then a space. More space. Could this
be a whole company? Three platoons? God! How terrible these men
looked—gaunt, immobile faces under shrapnel helmets, wasted limbs,
ragged, dusty uniforms . . . Did they still carry terrible visions of battle
in their minds, as they carried the dust of the mangled earth on their
garments?

"The strain was almost unbearable. They marched as though they
were envoys of the deadliest, loneliest, iciest cold. Yet they had come
home; here was warmth and happiness; why were they so silent? Why
did they not shout and cheer; why did they not laugh? The next company advanced. The crowd thronged forward again. But the soldiers
trudged on rapidly, doggedly, blindly, untouched by the thousand
wishes, hopes, greetings which hovered round them. And the crowd
was silent. Very few of the soldiers were wearing flowers. The few
which hung on their gun-barrels were faded. Most of the girls in the
crowd were carrying flowers but they stood, trembling, uncertain, diffi-
dent, their faces pale and twitching, as they looked at the soldiers with
anxious eyes.

"The crowd pulled itself together. A few hoarse shouts were heard,
as though from rusty throats. Here and there a handkerchief was
waved. One man murmured, convulsed, 'Our heroes, our heroes!'
They passed on unmoved, shoulders thrust forward, their steel helmets
almost hidden by bulky packs, dragging their feet, company after company, little knots of men with wide spaces in between. Sweat ran from
their helmets down their worn grey cheeks . . . Not a flag, not a sign of
victory. The baggage wagons were already coming into sight. So this
was a whole regiment."

Paul Hub's body was exhumed from the temporary grave at Maricourt
after the war and moved to the German military cemetery near
Péronne, on the Somme, but the location is unknown. Shamefully for a

man who had served his country with such distinction for four full years, "neither at the German military cemetery in Rancourt nor in nearby Fricourt does Paul's name appear on the lists of dead soldiers."

Maria remained childless and never remarried in the half century she lived without him. After the war she became a nursery school teacher in Reutlingen, Cannstatt and Stuttgart and it's tempting to see in the children she cared for at least a slight palliative for the lost family that she and Paul had hoped to share. She died in 1963 at the age of seventy-three.

Like Alec Reader and George Seibold, Paul Hub's life and death reflected the experience of millions of fighting men: the naïve patriotism and optimism buried by the appalling realities of trench warfare, the dogged struggle for survival, the grim fatalism and black humour, the often surprising compassion and common humanity, the acts of individual and collective heroism, the moments of weakness, self-doubt and despair, and the numbing futility of the expenditure of countless human lives for the temporary conquest of a few yards of mud and slime. They fought within sight and sound of Agincourt and Crécy, but these twentieth-century battles were fought with the weapons of the industrial age, by field-grey- and khaki-clad "workers of war," and the slaughter was on an industrial scale.

Until the Great War, the bloodiest campaign in history had been Napoleon's war on Russia, including the corpse-strewn retreat from Moscow. That had cost 400,000 lives—200,000 fewer than had been killed in the Battle of the Somme alone, and barely half the number who died at Verdun. In total, 1,081,952 British and Empire soldiers had died in the Great War. That massive death toll was actually less than the numbers who had emigrated from Britain in the decade prior to the war, but if the "Lost Generation" was to some extent a myth, it was widely believed to be true and the sense of loss experienced by all who lived through the 1920s and 1930s was unarguably real. Almost half of the British dead, 499,000, were listed as missing in action, of whom 173,000 had been found but not identified. Those unknown dead had "given even their names" for their country and it must have been hard for the relatives of the lost men not to feel stigmatized; unmarked graves had long been "associated with punishment, barbarity and victimisation."

It was a feeling many millions across Europe would have shared, for even the huge British losses were modest in comparison with those of France, Germany, Russia and Austria-Hungary. Over 2 million German soldiers were killed; in 1918 there were half a million war widows and a million fatherless children in Germany. In total, over 9 million men of all combatant nations were killed and over 21 million wounded—and one in eight of those eventually died of their wounds—and 2 million more soldiers were listed as missing. Shell-shock also affected as many as one in every four combatants. Even these appalling totals contain no figure for civilian fatalities. These included not only the multitudes killed when caught up in the fighting, but those starving to death, particularly in Germany during the Allied blockade, those without shelter who succumbed to hypothermia and pneumonia, those without sanitation who died of dysentery and cholera, and those killed in war industries. Many munitions workers died of TNT poisoning. The disease started with coldlike symptoms, then the hair turned ginger, and the faces and hands became bright yellow. With black humour, they were called "canaries," and they died as readily as the caged birds in mines. In total perhaps 12 million civilians died as a direct result of the war, with another 3 million succumbing to plagues and diseases that were, at the least, exacerbated by the wartime conditions.

Even some of the survivors were to remain forever unknown. A handful of soldiers from each of the combatant nations remained alive but without identification, and so shell-shocked or mentally traumatized that they had lost all knowledge of their identity. Some of these "living unknown soldiers" were subsequently claimed by their relatives, but a small group were never identified. It says much for the grief and despair of the bereaved relatives of the war dead that literally hundreds of them tried to claim these pitiful human remnants of the war as their missing sons, fathers or husbands, despite the lack of any physical resemblance or any supporting evidence. These living unknowns had at least survived, for what it was worth to them. The millions of unknown dead of the war had simply disappeared into the fog of gunsmoke and the mud of the battlefield, never to be found.

19

THE COINAGE OF
REMEMBRANCE

Alec Reader had died on 15 September 1916, but word of his death did not reach his mother for another three weeks. Families of men killed in action were informed with varying degrees of urgency, the class system prevailing even in the means by which the news of a soldier's death was communicated. When an officer died, a telegram was sent, giving the next of kin almost instant notification; when a common soldier died, a letter was thought sufficient, and with so many deaths for army clerks to record, it was rarely a speedy process. The lack of any letters or field service postcards from Alec must already have made Rose Reader fear the worst, but it was not until 6 October 1916 that his mother received in the post Army Form B 104-82, the official notification that her son had been "killed in action in the field . . . I am to add that any information that may be received as to the soldier's burial will be communicated to you in due course." Enclosed was a printed letter from the Secretary of State for War: "The King commands me to assure you of the true sympathy of His Majesty and The Queen in your sorrow. He whose loss you mourn died in the noblest of causes. His Country will be ever grateful to him for the sacrifice he has made for Freedom and Justice."

It was a form of words designed above all to reassure the recipient that their loved one had not died in vain and carried the implicit exhortation to the bereaved to make sacrifices of their own—albeit in less extreme form—in order to be "worthy" of the dead. (Little altered, the message continues in use to this day.) Many of the recipients of such letters must have felt, like Ernest Hemingway, that "the sacrifices were like the stockyards of Chicago, if nothing was done with the meat except bury it." In her grief, Rose must have echoed the sentiments of the former British Prime Minister Henry Asquith, who also lost a son in the war. "Whatever pride I had in the past, and whatever hope I had for the far future—by much the larger part of both was invested in him. Now all that is gone."

A week later Rose received a rather less impersonal letter, hand-written by Captain George Gordon Bates, one of the few surviving officers in Alec's battalion. "It is with extreme sorrow that I write to say that your son Alec Reader has been killed in action. During the time he was with my company, he proved himself a good soldier and will be greatly missed. Please accept my sincere sympathy and regret at being unable to write more at present. I have been unable to write before. PS His body was found and properly buried and the grave registered by the Graves Registration Committee." The letter had originally been dated "29 September 1916" but had then been overwritten "12 October." The delay was understandable; only two of the Civil Service Rifles' officers remained alive and unwounded, and between them they had written 380 letters of condolence to the families of those killed, wounded or missing in action at High Wood. They were unusually diligent in so doing, for many officers did not write such letters as a matter of course.

"If an officer was killed, the CO and usually one or more of his company officers were pretty sure to write to his home and give details. But in the case of other ranks, this was by no means always the case. Thousands and thousands must have been killed on active service under circumstances which were perfectly well known to their comrades, whose next-of-kin received nothing more than the cold official fact notified to them by the War Office." When letters were written, they usually contained only "three stock messages: the man in question was loved by his comrades, he was a good soldier and he died painlessly." However, officers had to be "very careful in writing these letters [of condolence] and it was well to keep a duplicate of them. Accuracy was essential and it was quite rightly forbidden in any way to go beyond the official announcement as to the man's fate. For instance, if a man were reported merely as 'missing,' it was absolutely forbidden to say that 'he might be presumed to have been killed' or, in the case of the dead, that if he had lived, 'he would probably have been awarded a decoration.' The reason for these restrictions, hard as they may seem, was obvious . . . though nearly all took the letter simply for what it was, a mark of sympathy, some few did not scruple to use such letters as grounds for making claims on the War Office." Despite the need for accuracy, some parents—those of Robert Graves among them—were notified that their sons had died and only discovered later that they were in fact merely wounded and recuperating in hospital.

The bare statement of facts and a few platitudes about the dead man did not begin to satisfy the hunger of bereaved families for details of how their loved one had met his end. David Railton complained to his wife, rather peevishly, that "they almost invariably write and ask if he 'said anything under the operation' or if he 'left any message,' when you've carefully told them he was unconscious from the time he was brought in. And when you've said the Chaplain took the funeral, they write and ask 'if he was buried respectable?' " More personal details would only, if ever, be provided by a friend or comrade of the dead man, visiting the family when on leave or at the war's end, in fulfillment of a promise made in one of those long, dark nights before the attack began. But many, many families must have remained forever in ignorance about the last moments of their dead husband, father or son.

If there was any comfort to be drawn by Rose in those bleak, terrible days, it must have been the knowledge that her son had at least been given a Christian burial and his grave marked, though even when the war ended there was no possibility that she would be permitted to bring his body back to England. An order had been issued in 1915 forbidding the return of the bodies of fallen soldiers for burial, and it would remain in force until the 1960s. It was partly a matter of priorities and logistics—there was neither the spare manpower nor the resources to ferry the dead back to England, even if their bodies could be found among the battlefield morasses. It was also a matter of ethics—the Red Cross strongly insisted that it was inequitable to allow the luxury of having their dead returned to England for burial only to those who could afford the expense; either all should be returned or none. But it was also a matter of propaganda and morale. The sight of wounded, maimed and gassed survivors arriving in England was already shocking enough, hard though the authorities tried to conceal them from public view—most of the hospital trains disgorged their pitiful cargoes during the hours of darkness. But "the sight of hundreds of men on crutches, going about in groups, many having lost one leg, many others both legs, caused sickening horror." The prospect of an endless procession of coffins passing through the ports and railway stations and filling to overflowing the cemeteries of every town and village, like the plague dead of 250 years before, would have had a devastating impact. "In the absence of corpses, it is easier to justify death and killing."

Even without those bodies, the number of women wearing full mourning could not be hidden and told its own sorry tale. Each was "a tragic, almost frightening figure in the full panoply of widow's weeds and unrelieved black, a crepe veil shrouding her (when not lifted) so that she was visibly withdrawn from the world . . . In the summer of 1915, and thereafter, widows in mourning became increasingly frequent in the streets." A *Times* reporter at St. Paul's Cathedral for the service commemorating the first anniversary of the declaration of war revealed that his eyes had filled with tears when he saw that most of the congregation were in mourning dress.

Although, as early as the opening days of the war, there had been suggestions that mourning dress should not be worn for those killed in action, most women "followed scrupulously the customary usage in the modification of [their] outdoor costume, the shortening and abandoning of the veil, the addition of a touch of white at the proper calendrical moments. It would have been unthinkable at that date for a respectable woman to do otherwise." But by the later stages of the war, "mourning succumbed before the vast numbers of the dead; faced with this, family mourning and its conventions were an insufficient comment," and "the full panoply of public mourning became exceptional rather than general . . . The holocaust of young men had created such an army of widows; it was no longer socially realistic for them all to act as though their emotional and sexual life were over for good, which was the underlying message of ritual mourning . . . There was too, almost certainly, a question of public morale; one should not show the face of grief to the boys home on leave from the trenches." Nor did the traditional mourning customs resume after the war, perhaps because the war had "identified these practices with a morbid and antiquarian outlook and left people exhausted with death."

Many of the dead remained where they had fallen on the battlefield or were interred in hastily dug graves behind the trenches. Where time and military operations allowed, the remainder were buried in large "concentration cemeteries"—a phrase that had unfortunate resonances even in those years—a safe distance behind the front lines, but at the war's end there were still 1,200 patches of ground containing marked British soldiers' graves in France alone. On 29 December 1915, the French government had promised a permanent resting place for all her war dead—though after the Armistice, many families grieving their loss and infuriated that three years were to elapse before the French military cemeteries would be constructed, ignored all restrictions and "came in great numbers to dig up their dead" and reinter them in their home villages. Many gravediggers were willing to pocket a bribe to exhume a body or turn a blind eye while someone else did so, and some entrepreneurial Frenchmen even set up a commercial service, undertaking to exhume and return bodies to their home villages for a fee of two francs fifty centimes a kilometre, plus a handling charge.

Neither edicts and prohibitions from the French government, nor the promise of an annual visit to the battlefield cemeteries at government expense, had more than minimal success in stamping out the practice, and "this form of private enterprise infuriated the Army, which had to deal both with bribery and churned up cemeteries, as well as the anger of poor parents, irate at the crassness of the rich." In the end, bowing to force majeure, the French government decreed that all families who so wished could claim the bodies of their loved ones and have them shipped home at government expense, but the process of claiming the dead could be fraught. There were inevitable disputes between widows and mothers and, as was also to be the case in the United States, mothers were adjudged to take precedence. Around 40 percent of the identified dead were eventually removed; the rest remained in the battlefield cemeteries or the great ossuary at Verdun.

Following the lead of the French government, Britain had also pledged to provide a grave for every one of her fallen soldiers on French and Belgian land given to the British government in perpetuity. The great architect Sir Edwin Lutyens had visited some of these concentration cemeteries in 1917 on the invitation of the Director of War Graves: "For miles these graves occur, from single graves to close-packed areas of thousands, on every sort of site and in every position—the bodies laid to face the enemy—in some places so close one wonders how to arrange their names in decent order."

On 1 December 1916, Rose Reader wrote to the War Office asking for details of the site of Alec's grave. When the war ended, she might at least be able to walk the battlefield where he had fallen, kneel by his grave and say her farewells to her son. The reply, dated 9 December 1916, was not encouraging. "Private BA Reader is reported as buried at a point just north-east of High Wood, north-east of Albert. For military reasons it is not at present possible to make a thorough search in this neighbourhood, but if at a later date the officers of the Graves Registration Units in that area are able to locate the grave, I will inform you at the first possible moment. I am very sorry not to be able to send you a more satisfactory reply." Rose could at least draw consolation that the letter was a standard Army "Form D," sent out to all bereaved enquiring about grave sites, and she had Captain Bates's reassurance that the grave had been properly marked and registered.

On 22 February 1917 she received a further communication that must have seemed almost an insult to her son's memory. "War Office Effects Form 45B" informed her that "the Command Paymaster . . . has been authorised to issue to you the sum of two pounds, six shillings and twopence, being the amount that is due on the settlement of the accounts of the late No. 3623, Private Bertram Alec Reader." Two pounds, six shillings and twopence must have seemed a very modest price for her son's life.

On 5 July of that year, the whereabouts of Alec's body still preying on her mind, she again wrote to the War Office, asking for further details of the location of his grave. A reply from the office of the Director of Graves Registration and Enquiries was not forthcoming until five weeks later, and it contained heartbreaking news. "I am much afraid that heavy shelling may have obliterated all trace of his grave, but you may rest assured that if at a later date I receive any further information, it will be transmitted to you." Although the graves of Alec and his dead comrades had been marked with wooden crosses, these were destroyed, if not by German shelling in the months following the Battle of High Wood, then by the vicious fighting that again swept over the Somme in the spring and summer of 1918. "In the newspapers, you read 'Peacefully they rest on the spot where they have bled and suffered . . . while the guns roar over their graves, taking vengeance for their heroic death.' And it doesn't occur to anybody that the enemy is also firing, that the shells plunge into the hero's grave; that his bones are mingled with the filth which they scatter to the four winds; and that after a few weeks, the morass closes over the last resting-place of the dead soldier."

At the war's end, the whereabouts of Alec's grave, like so many others, was unknown. The War Office set up a Special Commission to "ascertain as far as possible the precise location and identity of British soldiers hitherto unaccounted for . . . the public may rest assured that all that can be done has been done." But even where bodies remained intact—and tens of thousands had been blown to pieces—and a precise death site was known, the devastated state of the battlefields meant that the chances of locating the missing were often vanishingly small.

Even those who knew the last resting place of their loved ones faced difficulties and restrictions in commemorating them or visiting their grave. When the war was over, travel to the former battlefields was expensive and difficult—there was virtually no infrastructure of any sort—and potentially dangerous; there were millions of items of unexploded ordnance. Attempts to personalize graves were also strongly resisted. "We must make every effort to . . . prevent them from becoming eyesores on the countryside of France through the hideous effigies relatives often have a tendency to erect." An Army General Routine Order of May 1916 had banned "permanent personalised memorials" in any military cemetery, and a further requirement that all headstones be of uniform design had also been imposed after a "highly charged debate" in Parliament in May 1920. Rudyard Kipling, a member of the War Graves Commission, suggested the standard inscription from the Book of Ecclesiasticus, "Their name liveth for evermore," but relatives could add their own inscription of a maximum of sixty-six characters. They were charged for the privilege—threepence halfpenny for each letter and space—so that the popular epitaph—"At the going down of the sun we will remember them," from a poem by Laurence Binyon published as early as September 1914—cost a bereaved and often severely impoverished family fourteen shillings and sevenpence halfpenny.

Some time in 1919, like the next of kin of all British and Commonwealth dead, Rose had received a stiff card folder containing what was soon christened "the Dead Man's Penny"—a circular bronze plaque of Britannia and a lion, four and three-quarters of an inch in diameter, and inscribed with the name of the deceased and the words "He died for freedom and honour." Many grieving families made small domestic "shrines" in their homes centred on these plaques and any medals of the deceased man. Others undoubtedly felt that the satirical medal produced by the German artist Walter Eberbach at the time of Verdun, showing a skeleton pumping the lifeblood out of Europe, would have been more appropriate.

Under separate cover, Rose had also received a cardboard tube with an official stamp. Inside was a printed letter bearing the facsimile signature of George V—"I join with my grateful people in sending you this memorial of a brave life given for others in the Great War"—and a commemorative scroll. The original wording had referred only to men answering the "call of their country," but the King had insisted that "the sovereign be specifically mentioned." Sir Cecil Harcourt-Smith, Director of the National Gallery and a member of the subcommittee that had chosen the wording, "could hardly control his irritation at the amendment," but it was duly made. The final form of words was: "He whom this scroll commemorates was numbered among those who, at the call of King and Country, left all that was dear to them, endured hardness, faced danger, and finally passed out of the sight of men by the path of duty and self-sacrifice, giving up their own lives that others might live in freedom. Let those who come after see to it that his name be not forgotten."

Many next of kin were also given the opportunity to claim the original wooden cross that had first marked their loved one's grave, but few took up the offer; perhaps it was simply too poignant a memento. Many crosses, though unclaimed, were nonetheless returned to Britain, where some were honoured in church services and then buried in the churchyard, and others were hung on the walls of the church or placed in the vestry. There was outrage when some crosses were burned, compounded when one of the tabloid newspapers published a photograph of crosses lying on a rubbish heap.

There was no surviving wooden cross or grave to mark Alec Reader's passing, but his parents refused to give up hope of finding his grave. On 2 August 1923, almost seven years after Alec's death and nearly five since the war ended, Fred (signing himself "H. Reader," showing that his change of Christian name was now permanent) wrote again to the successor of the Graves Registration Service, the Imperial War Graves Commission, pleading for a search to be made for his son's grave. Once more, when the reply arrived, the Readers were to be disappointed. "I regret to have to inform you that although the neighbourhood of Albert, in which Private BA Reader was reported to have been buried, has been searched, and the remains of all those soldiers buried in isolated or scattered graves reverently re-buried in cemeteries in order that the graves may be permanently and suitably maintained, the grave of this soldier has not yet been identified.

"As you will understand, in many areas military operations caused the destruction of crosses and grave registration marks, and completely changed the surface of the ground, so that the work of identifying even those graves of which the position was accurately known has often been extremely difficult. I need hardly say that any further information which may be obtained will be communicated to you at once, and I greatly regret that it should be necessary to send you this reply. I may add that it is the intention of the Commission to erect memorials to those officers and men whose graves cannot be found. You may rest assured that the dead who have no known resting-place will be honoured equally with the others and that each case will be dealt with upon full consideration of its merits as regards the site and the place of the memorial." It was clearly intended to be the last word upon the subject and for many years afterwards, despite frequent further pleas and enquiries, Rose could not even discover if Alec had been commemorated in any way at all.

In 1928, the tenth anniversary of the end of the war, she and her surviving children made a pilgrimage to the battlefields. Rose stood gazing up at High Wood, where, among a few blackened, splintered tree-stumps somehow still sprouting green leaves, the saplings planted after the war's end had already grown tall enough to shade the overgrown trenches and shell-craters where Alec and so many more had died. Perhaps, like thousands of others, Rose also scoured the ground for a memento—a spent bullet, a button, a pebble, a seed or a little phial of the soil on which her son had breathed his last. Such items had become "the coinage of remembrance, a currency that crossed all borders." She paused and bowed her head before the memorial to the London Division, beside the Martinpuich-Longueval road, and paced along the neat rows of carefully tended graves in the nearby cemetery, where cornflowers and Flanders poppies were in bloom. Rose knew that Alec's grave had never been found, but she would not have been human if her eyes had not scanned each headstone, hoping for some miracle—a misspelt name, an untended grave in a forgotten corner—that might yet reveal his last resting place. And each time she passed a grave inscribed only "A Soldier of the Great War," the thought must have gone through her mind, is this the one? Is this Alec's grave? That thought must then have faded with the awful, numbing repetition of grave after grave, row after row. There was no miracle to be found.

Later that day or the next, like 100,000 other people in one three-month period of that year alone, she visited the Menin Gate Memorial, opened the previous year, and searched through the 55,000 names listed there—all soldiers who have no known grave—but found no trace of Alec's name. She stood there still as a lone bugler completed the nightly ritual by playing the Last Post as the sun went down, then she took her children and returned home. Ten years later, in 1938, she made a final visit to the battlefields, but once more her searches failed to find any trace of a memorial to her son, let alone his last resting place, and she went to her own grave, on 26 May 1954, never knowing where her son lay and believing that his sacrifice had been forgotten.

Only in the late 1980s did two of her grandchildren, Alec's nephews, Roger and Doug Goodman, discover that Alec's name had been inscribed on pier and face 13C of the Thiepval Memorial just two miles from High Wood. Completed in 1932, it lists the names of another 73,411 soldiers killed in this part of the Somme alone, who have no known grave. And Thiepval is only one of the hundreds of Great War memorials dotting the plains and low hills of Flanders and northeast France.

20

MISSING IN ACTION

There was little doubt about George Seibold's fate. His aircraft had been pursued all the way down by Hermann Frommherz, who kept pouring machine-gun fire into it until it hit the ground. The Squadron War Diary for 26 August 1918 merely noted that George had "not returned at 7:30 p.m.," but Spike Irvin recorded in his diary that night, in the block capitals that he reserved for fatalities: "LT SEIBOLD WENT 'WEST.' " However, members of the 148th still overflew the site the next day, hoping against hope that he might somehow have survived the impact. They could find no sign of George or his aircraft. Either the wrecked aircraft had been removed or the continuing heavy shelling had obliterated all trace of it.

After their return, George's commanding officer, Mort Newhall, filled out RAF Form 2370/2, used for all combat casualties and MIAs. The same day, 27 August 1918, a letter was despatched from "Major General, Commanding Royal Air Force in the Field" to the "Chief of Air Service, American EF [Expeditionary Force], Tours, France. Major

H Fowler U.S. Air Services c/o GHQ 1st Echelon. The following casualty is reported for your information: Lieut. GV Seibold, USAS, 148 Squadron RAF, MISSING 26/8/18. Next of kin: Wife Mrs. GV Seibold, 4321 Hazel Avenue, Chicago IL, USA."

Although the U.S. authorities therefore knew within twenty-four hours that George was missing in action, neither his wife, Kathryn, in Chicago nor his parents in Washington received any notification. On 2 September, 2nd Lieutenant Louis W. Rabe was drafted from the pilots' pool to replace George, but he was not formally struck off the strength of the RAF until 16 September. Nothing further was known about his fate until around 23 October, when a chance meeting took place in No. 14 General Hospital in France, between two wounded pilots, Errol H. Zistel of the 148th's "C" Flight and James Bruce Edwards of 64 Squadron.

Zistel had been hospitalized for a month following an accident on 24 September when, following a patrol in which he had recorded his third victory, he and his fellows were celebrating by hedge-hopping back to base when his aircraft struck a 150-foot wireless pole, severing the right wing. The plane lurched violently to the right, hit another pole, and then crashed. During his last days in hospital before returning to duty, Zistel struck up a conversation with Edwards, a South African pilot, who had been forced down with a badly damaged engine near Bapaume on 26 August, the same date and location where George had been shot down.

Edwards was already on the ground when he saw George crash. "On the 26th of August, at 5:10 p.m., I saw a flight of Camels attacked by a Hun formation of Fokkers. After a short but sharp scrap, one Camel came down out of control, followed by the Hun, who was firing the whole time. The Camel eventually crashed about 200 yards from me, being absolutely wrecked. I rushed out to see if I could aid the pilot in any way, but unfortunately he was dead. I believe he was killed before he hit the ground, as he was stone cold when I touched him."

Edwards "could not look into his pockets, because the machine was on its back and he was doubled up inside, and also on account of the shell fire, which was extremely heavy." He "looked to see if he had any valuables on his person, but the only thing I could find was a ring inscribed 'From ?? to G.V.S., July'; I cannot remember the other person's initials." The other initials were K.I.B.—Kathryn Irene Benson; it was the ring she had given George on their wedding day. Edwards had kept it for such a long time because he could not find anyone who recognized his description of the squadron insignia on the aircraft's fuselage—the white triangle of the 148th. He now handed the ring to Zistel and it began a slow progress up the ranks of the USAS, but it was to be many more weeks before it was returned to the Seibolds.

The U.S. authorities now had absolute confirmation both that George was dead and that his aircraft had come down behind Allied lines, making the prospect of finding his grave a little brighter, but still his wife and parents remained in ignorance of his fate. George had written to his wife and mother almost every day that he was overseas, so there was immediate concern when his letters ceased. In his last letter to Kathryn, written on 24 August, he had written that "if by giving his life, he could help only just a little, he would be glad to do so."

Despite increasingly anxious enquiries, nothing further was heard until 11 October when Kathryn arrived home to find a cardboard box that had been left on her doorstep. It was marked "Effects of deceased officer 1st Lt. GV Seibold," and probably contained the possessions left in his quarters at the 148th Aero Squadron base. It was not of itself proof that George really had died, nor was it the worst example of official insensitivity and incompetence. The Adjutant General, War Department, wired the family of Kent Curtis, the pilot of the 148th posted as missing in action on 24 August 1918, two days before George's death, that he had been killed in action. Cleveland newspapers carried reports of his death. In fact, although his plane had been shot down behind enemy lines, he had survived the crash and been taken prisoner, and he returned home safely at the end of the war. Even more appalling was the case of a man from Trenton, New Jersey, who arrived home to discover that his son's coffin had been left on his doorstep. The unexpected and unexplained arrival of George Seibold's effects had a similarly devastating impact on Kathryn. Horrified, she wired his parents, who now began even more frenzied attempts to discover their son's fate.

George's mother, Grace, had already been visiting wounded soldiers in Washington hospitals as part of her charitable work, but she now toured every hospital in the district, hoping against hope that her son might be there, wounded and unidentified. Her search was unavailing, and nothing further was forthcoming from the U.S. authorities until 30 November, when, in response to an intervention from Senator Owen of Oklahoma, who may have been prompted to act by George's former employer, ex-Congressman Thomas Nelson Page, now serving as U.S. Ambassador to Italy, they were notified that Lieutenant Seibold was missing in action, "last seen flying east of Bapaume." It was not until 13 December that a letter arrived at the Seibolds' Washington home, informing them that George had been officially reported as "Killed in Action" and "had fallen in the enemy lines," and this was confirmed in a letter dated 23 December 1918 and received on Christmas Eve.

The day before, Grace Seibold had received a letter from George's close friend Captain James A. Keating. They had volunteered together and gone through their training in Canada, Texas and England at the same time. Keating was then posted to 49 Squadron but he had pieced together the story of George's last hours and sent it to Grace in the hope that it might give her some consolation to hear of the brave death of her son. "I cannot imagine a more fitting end to a valiant life and you and your husband are sincerely blessed to have had such a son. George made, as you realise, a good fight, and I assure you he always did his duty bravely and well."

Their hopes for his survival finally extinguished, George's parents instead turned their attention to finding their son's grave. The parents of Alec Reader, Paul Hub and tens of thousands of others, from countries right around the globe, were embroiled in the same heartbreaking and usually fruitless search. Only a handful of officials and military personnel were involved in the mammoth task of locating and identifying the dead strewn across northeast France and Flanders and buried, sometimes four, five and even ten deep, beneath its heavy soils. Like so many others, the Seibolds found their enquiries met with at best helplessness, at worst obfuscation and indifference.

George's uncle Louis, a journalist for the *New York World* and a future Pulitzer Prize winner, used an assignment to Paris in early 1919 as an opportunity to enlist the help of the Provost Marshal's office in the search, but to no avail. Family frustrations came to a head after a report published by the Red Cross suggested—correctly—that George's aircraft had come down in Allied lines, greatly increasing the likelihood that he might have been found and buried by a British unit. At this point Grace's father, the redoubtable General Edward Washburn Whitaker, entered the fray. A Civil War general at just twenty-three years old, and a Congressional Medal of Honor winner after leading a charge against the Confederate forces at Reams Station, Virginia, in 1864, Whitaker had served as Chief of Staff to General George A. Custer, and had carried the flag of truce through the Confederate lines to arrange the meeting between Generals Ulysses S.

Grant and Robert E. Lee that secured the surrender of the Southern armies. He kept the flag, and later gave the major portion of it to Mrs. Custer (who subsequently donated it to the National Museum) and bequeathed the remainder to his daughter, Grace Seibold. General Whitaker was now almost eighty years old but he had lost none of his fire and retained a powerful circle of acquaintances. On 8 February 1919, he wrote to Newton D. Baker, U.S. Secretary of War.

"Sir, I have the honour to solicit through General JJ Pershing, commanding United States Expeditionary Forces in France, an order on the Commandant of the Air Service there during the month of August, 1918, to submit for my information, through you, a prompt and detailed report from his records of the loss in an air battle on or about August 26, 1918, of First Lieutenant George Vaughn Seibold, with his airplane, of the 148th Aero Squadron, with a full explanation of the reasons for failure to promptly report for information of relatives. The Red Cross having recently reported that the Lieutenant fell *inside of our lines*, the delay in the partial and conflicting reports is astounding to one like myself, who served from Bull Run to Appomattox, under officers of the Regular Army, and learned to admire their intelligence and strict enforcement of army regulations requiring promptness and accuracy in reports from all branches of the service.

"I am the proud grandfather of this brave young officer and am sorely disappointed in the conduct of the officers over him. If he did not fall in the lines of the enemy, as first we were informed, why no information of the location of his burial? What has been done with his airplane and his personal effects? His sad parents and brother and sister should be informed, as well as his wife. I am confident you will concede that I am not asking too much, nearly two months after the armistice and nearly five months after the battle." He signed it with a flourish, "EW Whitaker, Late Inspector General and Chief of Staff, Cavalry Corps, Army of the Potomac, at muster out in 1865."

The prestige of a man of Whitaker's record and the influence he and his daughter could wield in Washington were considerable, but even so it was over a month before the letter, having been passed down the chain of command, produced a reply from George's squadron commander, Mort Newhall. "1st. Lieut. Seibold, in company with 1st. Lieut. Walter B Knox, A.S., of this squadron, left our aerodrome on the afternoon of August 26th, 1918, on 'low strafing' duty. Lieut Seibold did not return and 1st. Lieut. Jesse O. Creech, A.S., also of this squadron, saw one of our machines shot down by three enemy machines and pinpointed the place where it crashed." Newhall also enclosed the statements he had obtained from Errol Zistel and James Bruce Edwards, giving their accounts of events, and said that while the squadron was stationed near Bapaume in October 1918, he had personally made efforts to find George's grave, without success.

Undeterred, George's wife and family persisted with their efforts to find his grave-site and there was a brief flicker of hope in April 1919, when a letter from the Graves Registration Service reached Kathryn, now living at 1437 Thome Avenue in Chicago (though, with crass insensitivity, George's surname had been misspelt and his squadron misnumbered). The letter offered the options of leaving his body buried in France or having it returned to America for burial there and, unaware that such letters were sent as routine to all next of kin of war fatalities, she took some comfort from the belief that his body had been found.

Under an Act of Congress of 17 July 1862, all those who fell in defence of the Republic during the Civil War were to be interred in one of the seventy-three national military cemeteries that were ultimately established. The fallen of the Spanish-American War and the Philippines Insurrection had also been repatriated and reinterred, and at the declaration of war on Germany the Wilson administration had once more pledged that the bodies of any soldiers killed in action would be brought home. As even the briefest experience of trench warfare would have demonstrated, it was a promise that could never be wholly fulfilled, and in any event many next of kin preferred their sons or husbands to be buried with their comrades on the battlefields where they had fallen. However, as the death toll mounted, U.S. politicians came under enormous emotional pressure through petitions from grieving wives and mothers and the cynical lobbying of the Purple Cross, a newly created body representing American funeral directors, that was anxious to ensure that the profits from such lucrative windfalls of war should not be denied to them by burials in France. Some funeral industry organizations and publications discussed openly the profits to be made from the repatriation of 55,000 dead U.S. servicemen, and even offered to send legions of embalmers to France to ensure that every fallen "American Hero" could be brought home in "a sanitary and recognizable condition a number of years after death."

The War Department rejected such self-interested offers and entrusted the care, transport and burial of the dead to the Graves Registration Service. When the commander of the AEF, General John "Black Jack" Pershing, expressed concern that attention or resources might be diverted from the task of winning the war, it was acknowledged that repatriation of the dead could not begin until hostilities were at an end. Meanwhile, although the Graves Registration Service would handle the relevant documentation, individual army units were to have the principal responsibility for burying their dead.

After the Armistice, passionate arguments were advanced both for and against leaving the American dead in the soil in which they had perished. Some claimed that the "sacred dust" of the bodies would make those cemeteries forever a symbol of America's sacrifice and her growing international power and status. There were also considerable financial and practical implications in the exhumation and return of the bodies that, though rarely discussed in public, certainly occupied government and military minds. Meanwhile, proponents of repatriating the bodies painted alarmist pictures of the French government holding the American dead as "hostages" that would require the United States to intervene in any future Franco-German conflict, and of avaricious Frenchmen waiting to rob the bereaved American relatives of their hard-earned dollars as they made pilgrimages to the graves of their men. The Bring Home the Soldier Dead League demanded nothing less than "an American tomb, in America, for every American hero who died on foreign soil."

In 1919, Secretary of War Newton D. Baker brokered a compromise, offering the next of kin of war-dead the choice of whether the body would be returned to the U.S. at government expense, or re-interred in one of the eight U.S. military cemeteries that were being established in France, Belgium and Great Britain. The War Department, the U.S. Commission of Fine Arts and General Pershing were united in insisting that, as in the British war cemeteries, all men were to have identical tombstones and were not to be separated by regiment or rank. The symbolism was obvious—the dead had submerged their individual identities in a collective national cause.

Christian iconography was very prominent in the American cemeteries—the result of a conscious decision to portray America as a Christian nation. Jewish dead were allowed a Star of David upon their tombstones, but no other religions were so acknowledged and the cemetery chapels made no attempt to accommodate Jewish or any other non-Christian denominations. As the architect of the chapel at the Suresnes Cemetery revealingly remarked, although the chapels were non-sectarian, "they were Christian." Private or state monuments that commemorated troops "from a particular locality" were also discouraged; the memorials and monuments were to play their part in nation-building, and only national monuments were welcomed. The Belgians showed no such reticence and "monuments shot up like mushrooms" there, commemorating everything from the "twenty-eight operators of fun-fair stands who had died for their fatherland to the . . . footballers who had made the supreme sacrifice." Many were in such execrable taste that King Albert, who had the painful duty of unveiling the majority of them, was said to have described them as *"les horreurs de la guerre."*

In the U.S. government, if not the military, there was also an awareness that an over-lavish commemoration of the American dead would offend Europeans whose nations had suffered infinitely higher casualties. Americans might remark among themselves that they had "saved Europe" by their intervention in the war, but Europeans who had noted America's enrichment on the proceeds of Europe's slump from the world's greatest creditor nations in 1914 to the world's greatest debtor nations just four years later—all were deeply in hock to the United States—did not view the belated U.S. involvement in the war in quite the same light.

Seven out of ten American next of kin remained immune to all arguments for burial overseas, and opted to have their dead returned to their homeland. It was a process that occupied several years: in March 1921, though 14,849 bodies had already been returned and 500 were at Hoboken "ready for shipment," a further 3,293 were still waiting at French ports and 3,577 more were at "concentration points" in the former battlefields. Like 31,000 other bereaved American wives and mothers, Kathryn Benson Seibold felt that it would have been George's wish to remain among the comrades who had also fallen in battle and she gave instructions that the body should remain where it lay. In so doing, she was consciously or unconsciously echoing the sentiments expressed by George Seibold's former mentor, Thomas Nelson Page, and by Theodore Roosevelt, whose youngest son, Quentin, also a pilot, was shot down and killed in France on 14 July 1918. Roosevelt was outraged at suggestions that his son's body should be exhumed and returned to the United States, and wrote to the Army Chief of Staff, General Peyton March, "Mrs. Roosevelt and I wish to enter a most respectful but most emphatic protest against the proposed course as far as our own son is concerned. We have always believed that where the tree falls, let it lay."

Kathryn's letter to the War Department was couched in equally emphatic terms. After requesting that the errors in George's name and squadron be corrected, she concluded, "I protest against the remains of my husband being brought back to the U.S." The force with which she expressed her wishes was perhaps indicative of the poor state of her relations with her parents-in-law. The indomitable Grace's belief that the bond between mother and son superseded all others would not have been well received by George's wife, who must already have been smarting over the failure of his parents to attend the wedding. It seems clear from the correspondence that Grace was determined to bring George's body home for burial and Kathryn equally insistent that, as George's widow, her views must prevail.

Kathryn and the Seibolds were soon made aware that George's body remained missing, and they continued their independent efforts to locate his grave. On the anniversary of George's death, General Whitaker again wrote to the Secretary for War, "It seems incredible that your great department with all the appropriations and organisations, has thus far failed to locate the grave of my grandson killed in action August 26, 1918, *a year ago today*! Will you now order an investigation and report?" If it provoked a fresh flurry of action in the War Department, it did not yield any substantive results.

In June 1920 the Seibolds sought the help of Clayton Bissell, now serving in the Office of the Director of Air Service in Washington. His enquiries produced a tantalizing clue, but no tangible outcome. A report from Colonel Charles C. Pierce, Chief of the Cemeterial Division, dated 29 March 1920, stated that "commune list 1144-2670 shows this officer's grave to be located in C1144, Commune of Bapaume (Pas de Calais)." However, that reference was to a temporary, battlefield burial site and there was no record showing to which of the permanent "concentration cemeteries" the bodies from C1144 had been moved after the Armistice. It was "thought likely that this body would have been moved to Cemetery 721 or 443, which are the nearest to the Commune of Bapaume," but a further search revealed no useful information.

The report added that a "Sgt. Young states that he remembers . . . that a detachment of men, including himself, was sent . . . to locate the body of an unknown aviator, probably Seibold, but without success. He also states this territory was occupied by the British, and that they might have reburied this man . . . the British Air Service probably knows something about this matter." But a letter of 19 June 1920 reported that "careful search was also made in the British Military Cemetery near Bapaume," without result.

Captain Charles Wynne then wrote to George's father in September, offering the hope that at some future time a definite answer would be forthcoming. "This is not an unusual case as there are in the battle area some bodies buried as 'unknown,' the complete and absolute identification of which we will attempt to establish on the exhumation of these bodies. The dead were at times buried under battle conditions which precluded absolute identification. At other times, the wounded were received in hospitals without identification and their deaths at, and burials from, said hospitals necessarily caused them to be buried as 'unknown' dead . . . The case of your son has been recorded for special attention at that time when we commence the exhumation of the 'unknown' dead. We earnestly hope to be able to give you, ultimately, some definite information."

Before the end of the month George's father received a further letter, requesting George's full dental records "to include fillings, crowns, bridges, etc. . . . The information requested to be used in matters of identification." The reason for the request became clear the following month, when a memorandum from the Cemeterial Division of the Quartermaster General's Department offered fresh hope. "It is now the opinion of this office that, in all probability, the body of Lieutenant Seibold is contained in Grave 151, Row 3, Plot A, American Cemetery 176, Villers Tournelle, Somme." The body was subsequently disinterred and checked against the dental records supplied by George's parents, but once more their hopes were dashed. The body was not that of their son.

Kathryn Benson had meanwhile attempted to put the past behind her and build a new life, but suffered a further terrible tragedy. Having lost the man who had been her husband for only a day before he left for the war, she fell in love with George's former flight commander, Field Kindley, who had visited her in June 1919 to express his condolences and tell her more of how George had met his end. Kindley already had Chicago connections. He had done his ground training at the School of Military Aeronautics at the University of Illinois at Champaign, and had also had a girlfriend in Chicago—his wartime instructions to his cousin in the event of his death included notifying Miss Constance Miller of Lake Park Avenue in Chicago—but that relationship had not survived the war. Now a strong mutual attraction developed between Kindley and Kathryn Seibold. By the end of the year they had become engaged to be married.

Kindley was a decorated war hero with twelve victories, a Distinguished Flying Cross and a Distinguished Service Cross and Oak Leaf Cluster. He was "just about everything you'd want a Flying Ace to be, charming, charismatic, well-liked and respected, tough, humble, quick reflexes, a deadly shot, tall, handsome and dashing, blue-eyed, brave and cool-headed in a crisis. What he lacked in formal education he more than made up for in common sense." His resourcefulness and self-reliance may have owed much to his upbringing—his mother died when he was three and when his father took up a job in the Philippines, Kindley was shuffled between his grandmother and two aunts. Before the war he had owned and run a movie theatre in Coffeyville, Kansas, and he had had the opportunity to get even closer to the movie business after the war, but turned down an offer to star in a filmed reconstruction of his war service, at least in part because he thought it might interfere with his career as a flyer. "It is not a lasting proposition and . . . I do not feel like taking it."

However, his celebrity and his skills as a pilot led the Air Service to use him to promote the military value of the aeroplane. With four other American air aces, he appeared before a House of Representatives subcommittee on 12 December 1919 to urge the creation of an independent Air Department, and he took part in numerous air shows—doing "aerobatics, mock dogfighting, 'balloon busting' and air-to-ground target shooting." He also flew in several air races and had a narrow escape during the New York to Toronto race in midsummer 1919. His former colleague from the 148th Squadron, Elliot Springs, crashed on landing at Albany and the crowds rushed to see what had happened to him, blocking the runway just as Kindley made his approach. "To avoid hitting the crowd, he kicked the rudder and deliberately crashed his SE5 [aircraft]. He was unhurt but his plane was a washout."

In January 1920, Kathryn accompanied Kindley to Kelley Field, San Antonio, Texas, where, as the new commander of the 94th Aero, the "Hat in the Ring Squadron" previously commanded by Eddie Rickenbacker, he was to take part in an air display in honour of General Pershing. At one-thirty on the afternoon of 1 February 1920, as Kathryn watched from the grandstand, Kindley was practicing aerobatics in his SE5 biplane at the head of a flight of four other aircraft. The display was to include live firing at a ground target and, concerned that a group of enlisted men were sitting dangerously close to the target, Kindley made three low-level passes over them, trying to warn them off. On the third pass, as he began a right climbing turn, an aileron control cable snapped. The aircraft dropped from a height of between seventy-five and one hundred feet, smashed into the sun-baked earth and burst into flames. Kindley was probably killed instantly, but so fierce was the heat that it was several minutes before his body could be removed from the burning wreckage.

For the second time in three years, Kathryn found herself bereaved. On 5 February 1920 she attended Kindley's funeral at Gravette, Arkansas, where he was buried with full military honours, and she then returned to Chicago. She picked up the threads of her life and in 1922 she married for a second time. Her husband was an Illinois artist, Charles Vedder Sutherland. The Seibold family lost contact with her soon afterwards and my research enquiries have failed to trace her descendants, but it is to be hoped that she was able to find fulfillment and happiness with her new husband and put the past tragedies behind her.

That was something Grace Seibold was unable to do. The anguish that she felt at the loss of her son was repressed, buried deep within her, and her son, Louis, and daughter, Theodosia, were required to show similar stoicism. There were to be no open displays of grief, no sharing of their burden, something that Theodosia was to regret to the end of her life, but Grace's refusal to accept that her son's grave would never be found tells its own story. True to her father's example, Grace Darling Seibold was not a woman to allow obstacles to stand in her way. She was "a very giving and kind woman," but also energetic and opinionated, a devout, slightly bigoted churchgoer at her local Calvary Baptist church, an indefatigable worker for charity, and a member of the North Star Union, the Women's Christian Temperance Union, the American Legion Auxiliary, the Daughters of the American Revolution and the Ladies Auxiliary of the International Typographical Union.

She now threw her formidable energies into locating her son's grave, even though it was entirely possible that there was no grave to find. Direct hits by artillery shells could obliterate human beings as if they had never existed, as one soldier's description indicates. "A shell came over us and three of the boys were blown to pieces. Nothing of them was found—not a shred." In his more pessimistic moments, George's nephew, Bing Seibold, who has spent many years researching his uncle's fate, leans to this belief. "Ground troops and artillery men hated pilots," because of their ground-attack role, bombing and strafing trenches and gun positions. "The plane was in No Man's Land and the artillery just zeroed in. So perhaps there were no remains."

The American and British Graves Registration Units did put

enormous efforts into identifying bodies. In the case of aviators, they would even try to trace "the serial numbers of fuselages, engine cylinders, and even rubber tyre rims in order to find the base from which a downed, and lost, aviator came, so that his name could be preserved near his flight's point of origin." No trace of George's aircraft was discovered but in the spring of 1923 hopes were raised again when an unidentified body was exhumed from "Grave 29, Plot 8, Row B, Queant Road, British Military Cemetery, Commune of Queant 8, Department of Pas-de-Calais." A War Department official at once wrote to Grace, informing her that the body of "an unknown American aviator" had been "exhumed from the same vicinity where your late son . . . was reported buried." It was "found to have had an India rubber plate of thirteen teeth in the upper jaw. The Department will appreciate your advising this office whether you recall your late son having such dental work." Once more it was a cruel and unnecessary raising and dashing of Grace's hopes, for the dental records supplied to the War Department three years before proved that the body could not have been that of George Seibold.

Kathryn had also been notified and, reading between the lines of this latest disappointment, she wrote a dignified letter of reply. "My late husband, Lt. Seibold's body will not be found, I believe, from the information gleaned from your letter, but I should like to have a detailed report from the War Department of what information they have on the case, including the name of the 'vicinity' in which this officer was reported buried. PS. By information on the case, I mean where he fell, on what day, during what offensive, who found him etc. I have never had such a report and I feel I am entitled to one."

The War Department promptly supplied copies of the accounts of George's death and the finding of the ring from Errol Zistel and James Bruce Edwards, but it is a revealing sidelight on the unyielding, unforgiving side of Grace Seibold's character that the information that came into her possession in early 1919 had never been communicated to George's widow. Nor did Kathryn ever receive the wedding ring inscribed with her own and her husband's initials, taken from George's body after his death and eventually passed on to his mother. According to members of the Seibold family, it remained in Grace's possession and was left to Theodosia after her mother's death.

In the early summer of 1923, a further body was exhumed but in circumstances that made identification all but impossible, for it was that of an unknown "headless aviator," though other documents refer to the body as being "jawless." Although James Bruce Edwards did not describe George's body as mutilated in this way, Errol Zistel's report to his commanding officer, Mort Newhall, had said "his machine landed on its back, thus horribly mangling the pilot." A handwritten note dated 5 July 1923 scribbled to a "Mr. Davis" by a War Department Official, C. Scott, states: "Do not know what further to do with case. [The American officer] in Europe is inclined to believe the headless aviator is Seibold. He [an official at the War Department?] questions it? Yet we have no other body so far discovered that will suffice. Please suggest what to do?" The cynicism of the penultimate sentence is shocking, implying that any body that could be passed off as George Seibold's would do, if it would get General Whitaker, Grace Seibold and Kathryn Benson Seibold off their backs. A further note in another hand then remarked, "There seems nothing further to do on case at present, pending further reports. This aviator without head is doubtless George Seibold."

The next day Scott again wrote to Mr. Davis giving further details. "The headless aviator comes from very near the location where we would expect Seibold. (The man with the rubber plate investigated by Swindler is a different unknown and does not come from the location we want, hence that case is eliminated.) To date we have no record of any other unknown aviator from this British sector which will check with Seibold. This jawless man is the only one that could so far be accepted . . . It is possible this may be the man, inasmuch as records indicate the machine fell on its back and him. His head may have been crushed and yet held together by the flesh . . . We might advise Seibolds re facts that headless man is son but that there is no means of iden[tifying] it, except fact he is an aviator and comes from co-ordination [i.e., the correct map co-ordinates], and that we believe it to be the body, and ask their views, suggesting if it meets their approval, we will so designate the body and mark grave with his stone. Otherwise the body must remain an unknown and their son must be buried without a grave." He ended, "Am inclined to believe they will agree with us," but once more his conclusion appears to have been based on a cynical calculation that the grieving parents would seize upon any proffered unknown as their son.

The chance to accept this body as George's and close that painful chapter must have been a massive temptation to Grace and her husband, but without definite proof or positive identification they felt unable to do so. Grace continued to hound the military and government bureaucracy for information, calling in favours and arm-twisting politicians, and made the first of two voyages to France, travelling alone and at her own expense—her family still have the suitcase she took, plastered with steamer and train labels. Her liner sailed from the same Cunard pier in Hoboken as George's troopship had done in 1917. In France she spent weeks interrogating local officials in Bapaume and the surrounding towns and villages, and pacing the rows of white marble gravestones in the war cemeteries of the Somme, reading the endlessly repeated inscription, "Here rests in honored glory an American soldier known but to God," searching always for some trace of her son, no matter how insubstantial. Nothing was found. The American Graves Registration Service formally abandoned efforts to locate George's grave on 19 April 1927, when a memorandum to the Quartermaster General's Office stated that "unless precise burial data is available or can be obtained, at this time it is believed further physical search should not be made until more definite information as to grave location is furnished." No such information would ever be forthcoming.

At last, all hope spent, Grace returned to her home in Washington, "totally devastated. She went through a period of depression for several years; in fact she never really got over his death." However, she hid her emotions so skilfully, even from her close family, that "had we not known what she'd gone through, I don't think we'd have guessed from her actions." It may be a sign of at least a partial, subconscious acceptance that her son's body would never be found, that Grace had written to the Secretary of War in August 1924, requesting an American flag. "Had his body been returned, his casket would have been covered with the United States flag. I would appreciate receiving one of those flags as a memento of my son's service." However, one of her granddaughters suggests that the family never wholly accepted that George was dead and gone. "I always expected that one day there would be a knock at the door and there would be Uncle George." Grace now began sublimating her considerable energies into a cause that would both commemorate her son and give comfort to countless other war mothers, widows, and wounded and shell-shocked war veterans. In so doing, she realized that "helping the returning veterans who were still coping with physical and emotional hurts caused by the war, eased her own grief over the loss of her son."

21

A HOUSE FOREVER DESOLATE

Since the first American troops had sailed for Europe, every American family had been entitled to display a blue star service flag, for each husband, father or son serving with the U.S. forces. Thousands of women sewed a blue star on to a piece of white fabric and hung it in their windows. On 28 May 1918, concerned at the negative impact that the sight of thousands of American women in traditional mourning dress might have on public morale, President Woodrow Wilson had approved a proposal from the Women's Council on National Defense that the mothers or wives of dead American servicemen could display a gold star service flag and wear a black armband with a gold star to symbolize the honour and glory accorded for the supreme sacrifice for the nation.

Some American servicemen viewed such emblems with contempt. As one of George Seibold's fellow pilots in the 148th Aero Squadron remarked, "They have issued special rules about Service Stars, regulating how people may proclaim to the world at large that a member of their family is a hero. A man is killed in action—certainly somebody ought to be able to swank about and get his glory! But I don't think they go far enough ... Let the bona fide wives of dead heroes wear a gold star with an edging of mourning. Let the war brides of lucky cannonfodder wear two gold stars and gold mourning. Let the would-be wives of eager and successful belligerents wear a single plain gold star and black stockings. Thus every woman could swank, mourn and advertise all at the same time, and the itinerant doughboy would be saved much curiosity and vain labour."

Such sarcasm and cynicism would have horrified Grace Seibold. Seizing on the emblem of the gold star as "the last full measure of devotion and pride of the family in this sacrifice," she became one of the driving forces and the first president of the Gold Star Mothers. Initially established in her home city of Washington, D.C., but expanding steadily throughout the 1920s, the Gold Star Mothers dedicated themselves to the support of U.S. war veterans and the bereaved families of fallen servicemen. Under Grace's powerful direction, and helped by the political influence of her friend Grace Goodhue Coolidge, the Gold Star Mothers and its sister organization, the American War Mothers, which was open to mothers of all men who had served in the war, became a vocal and effective lobby for the rights of war mothers and widows.

As early as 1919, bereaved mothers had begun lobbying for subsidized visits to the battlefields and cemeteries of France for the mothers of American soldiers buried there. New York Congressman Fiorello La Guardia introduced a bill to Congress that year, but it failed, partly for lack of support after intense lobbying by funeral directors, but partly for more reputable reasons. Some congressional opponents of the bill argued that the total destruction of the infrastructure of roads, railways, hotels and power and water supplies made such visits impractical, while the scarred landscape of the Western Front, still strewn with battlefield debris and even human remains, would have been too traumatic a sight for grieving mothers and war widows. Flanders was then "nothing but a deserted sea, under whose waves corpses are sleeping." "The emptied land was devoid of identifying landmarks, except for painted signposts indicating the sites of former villages, churches or farmsteads," which "the pestle and mortar of war had so ground into dust, red and white, that each separate brick went back at last, dust to dust, to mix with the earth from which it had come." The first post-war pilgrims found battlefields and trenches still littered with bones. Not all visitors displayed the proper reverence for the war graves; souvenir hunters gathered everything from spent bullets and tunic buttons to bones and skulls, and in the summer of 1919 a magazine published a picture of people picnicking in the uncleared battlefields.

Even before the Armistice, servicemen had been put to work clearing the battlefields of bodies that were often weeks, months or even years old, and exhuming and reinterring the hundreds of thousands buried in makeshift shallow graves. All solitary graves and small war cemeteries had to be cleared; it had been agreed with the French that the minimum number of graves that could constitute a permanent cemetery would be forty. Each body had to be identified, a grisly, nauseating task of sifting the remains for identity tags or personal items like letters—often carried into battle in defiance of standing orders—but vast numbers remained unidentified. Some thousands may have been buried as unknown soldiers simply because the burial parties were hasty or careless, or did not know where to look for the identity tags. Miners from the coalfields of Yorkshire, Lancashire, Northumberland and Durham were used to fixing their colliery "tokens" to their braces during working hours, and tended to fix their army identity tags in the same way, rather than around the neck. If they were killed in action, "when the burial party came along to identify the body, they would open the neck of the tunic to remove the identity disc," find it missing, and bury the body as an unknown soldier.

Despite incentives that included promotions and double pay, few could stomach the work of exhuming and reburying the dead. Before receiving his demobilization papers, one man who had already spent a harrowing three months in a burial party was ordered to appear before the colonel of his battalion. "He had sent for me to ask me to remain in the army for another year. He explained that the work of collecting dead bodies and burying them in the cemeteries which were to be laid out in the vicinity of the battlefields was to be commenced, and men with some experience of that work were needed. I gently but firmly declined to remain in the Army for any purpose. He made a personal plea and spoke of the high pay that was being offered, but I was adamant."

American burial parties made extensive use of black troops, who had often been spurned during combat. Although the very few all-black U.S. combat units and the African-Americans serving with the French forces gave the lie to the racist view that black troops were indisciplined and cowardly—units like the 369th Infantry, the "Harlem Hellfighters," repeatedly proved their valour in combat—most had been kept away from the front lines and given menial, manual work in the reserve areas, or digging trenches, clearing unexploded ordnance, barbed wire and destroyed military equipment from the battlefields. A disproportionate number of them were then employed in the burial parties clearing the battlefields of corpses.

Even with 30,000 workers—that was the official figure, though it was suspected that many civilian contractors were padding their payrolls with "ghost employees"—the last battlefields were not fully cleared until 1922, and even then the dead kept reappearing, dug up by the plough or rising from the earth as it settled around them. Men searching for bodies worked alongside those engaged in the mountainous and often perilous task of clearing the battlefields of spent and unspent ordnance and restoring the ground to cultivable condition. In places, there were as many as five unexploded shells per square metre and levelling operations unearthed "as much as 5,000 kilos of shrapnel and detonators per hectare, not counting the shells and larger pieces." Scrap-metal dealers made fortunes from carting away the brass cartridge cases and non-ferrous metals until the glut and the post-war recession produced a slump in prices.

Men of the U.S. Graves Registration Service laboured in Flanders and northeast France on the mammoth and often impossible task of tracing the graves of American servicemen. There were an estimated 2,400 sites where American soldiers lay buried. Many grave markers had been destroyed in subsequent fighting, or removed by farmers squatting on their ruined land in primitive shelters and desperate to begin ploughing and replanting. As a result, all trace of tens of thousands of graves had been obliterated, and most of those U.S. war dead who had been found had yet to be exhumed, identified and reinterred in ordered military cemeteries.

The growing political power of women, reflected in the passing of the Nineteenth Amendment in 1920, extending the suffrage to women, ensured that Gold Star Pilgrimages remained a live issue, even though congressional opposition and continued lobbying by U.S. funeral directors kept legislation from the statute book until almost the end of the decade. However, the Gold Star Mothers set the agenda for congressional debates. War mothers testifying before the House Committee on Military Affairs repeatedly hammered home the same message: "I want to begin by telling you that you are all men and you have not and cannot feel the way a mother feels. It is a part of her body that is lying over there." "It was the mothers who suffered to bring these boys into the world, who cared for them in sickness and health, and it was our flesh and blood that enriched the foreign soil." "Without Mothers, America would have had no men to go forth and save our country and the most beautiful flag in the world." In speech after speech, Congressmen went out of their way to echo the Gold Star Mothers' view that the bond between mother and son was somehow stronger than that between father and son or even wife and husband.

The grief of war mothers on both sides of the Atlantic was heightened by a profound social change that had occurred over the preceding forty years. Infant mortality was an accepted part of life in the early to mid-Victorian era. Virtually every family grew used to burying small children—often several in the same family—who had died at birth or in infancy from one of the multitude of diseases and deprivations that assailed them, but from the 1880s onwards infant mortality rates had dropped sharply, reflecting improvements in nutrition and health care. For the first time in human history, it had become the expectation and the general rule that children would outlive their parents. Increased affluence and the more widespread use of methods of birth control—crude though they were—had also led to a fall in the birth rate. Parents now were more likely to have much smaller families, and their hopes and dreams were vested in one or two children. The death of a child had always been a tragedy, but now it was often an utterly devastating blow. "Every spare farthing had been spent on his upbringing since childhood. He was to be the pride and assistance of his parents when they attained old age . . . A house had been left forever desolate."

General Pershing gave the Gold Star Mothers' campaign only qualified support. He declared himself "interested in every movement in any way connected with our soldier dead, realising as I do the great sacrifice which they themselves made and the irreparable loss which their families sustained." But he abhorred the idea of pilgrimages becoming nothing more than a glorified "sightseeing tour." Uppermost in his thoughts would have been the shaming annual convention of the American Legion held in Paris in 1927. Far from a respectful pilgrimage to the battlefields and war cemeteries, it had degenerated into a drunken free-for-all characterized by a souvenir illustrated with "a picture of a drunken American soldier, balancing a champagne glass in one hand, kissing a naked Frenchwoman."

Despite such unfortunate precedents, the Gold Star Mothers won powerful backing for their own campaign from the American Legion and were eventually granted a Federal Charter on 4 June 1928 by a Republican administration seeking electoral advantage among newly enfranchised women and the 1 million members and women auxiliaries of the American Legion. The Gold Star Mothers were duly incorporated as a national organization and, no doubt helped by her friend the First Lady, Grace Seibold was instrumental in persuading the famously parsimonious President Calvin Coolidge to sign one of the last bills of his term of office on 2 March 1929, allocating $5 million to fund "Gold Star Pilgrimages of Remembrance." These would enable mothers of servicemen who had fallen while serving in Europe between 5 April 1917 and 1 July 1921, either as fighting troops or as part of the post-war U.S. Army of Occupation, to travel to France at U.S. government expense and see for themselves the places where their men were buried or commemorated. "Widows who had not remarried also received invitations, but only as an afterthought." It was probably mere coincidence that this limitation excluded Kathryn Benson Seibold, who was now Mrs. Kathryn Sutherland. In all, 17,389 women were declared to be eligible, of whom around 40 percent eventually took advantage of the scheme.

The Gold Star Pilgrimages were in marked contrast to the experience of British mothers travelling to the battlefields and cemeteries, who received no government support at all. The St. Barnabas Society was founded in 1919 to help bereaved pilgrims, many of whom were "vaguely wandering about in search of cemeteries and with no signposts to guide them." The society placed wreaths on behalf of relatives who were unable to travel and, like the British Legion and the Empire Service League, it also arranged subsidized pilgrimages for those too poor to pay their own way. They were extremely cheap but "devoid of comfort and luxury. There were no lights in the train, one veteran recalled, just travelers sitting up all night in the dark on wooden benches, talking about the war." The St. Barnabas Society ended such pilgrimages in 1927, partly because most relatives who wished to do so had by then visited the grave or memorial site of their loved ones, and partly because pressure from commercial tour operators and their clients on scarce facilities was driving up the price of food and accommodation beyond the level the society and its pilgrims could afford.

Despite the generous treatment given to American Gold Star Mothers, controversy still dogged the pilgrimages. Fathers, stepmothers, adoptive mothers, remarried widows and children were all specifically excluded by the terms of the legislation. The official reply to the heartfelt plea of one grieving widow was typical of many. "As the Act of March 2, 1929, does not contain any provision for any member of the family to make the trip except the mother or unmarried widow . . . it is regretted to have to inform you that while your feelings with regard to taking your little daughter to her father's grave are appreciated, she is not eligible to make the pilgrimage." Racial prejudice was also evident, though that would not have surprised the majority of the African-American troops who had served in the war. The members of the Gold Star Mothers were predominantly white, Anglo-Saxon and Protestant, and it was alleged that they "granted membership only to qualified members of the Caucasian race." Although white mothers on the Gold Star Pilgrimages travelled cabin class in ocean liners and stayed in the best hotels, African-American mothers were rigidly segregated and given more spartan travel and accommodation. One shipping line even claimed that if black women travelled on their liners, they would have to be taken out of service, stripped and redecorated before their white customers would consider using them again.

At 11:30 on the morning of Friday, 7 February 1929, in the Red Room of the White House, Mrs. Lou Henry Hoover, wife of the newly elected president, drew one of fifty-four envelopes from a silver bowl, each one representing a U.S. state or overseas territory. The first one drawn was Nebraska, and Gold Star Mothers from that state were the first to make the pilgrimage. Three months later, on 6 May 1930, the first group of 231 women set sail from Pier 4 at Hoboken, New Jersey, aboard SS *America*. Many of their sons and husbands had left from the same pier in 1917–18 to go to war.

All the pilgrims' expenses were met, though money was disbursed in a rather grudging and suspicious manner. One pilgrim receiving the modest sum of $2.50 to cover her "meals and incidental expenses from your home to New York" was warned in strident capitals: "UNDER NO CIRCUMSTANCES MUST THIS CHECK BE CASHED AND USED FOR ANY PURPOSE OTHER THAN THAT SPECI-FIED." A military liaison officer, doctor and nurse accompanied each group of pilgrims, special access and facilities were negotiated for them and a number of "rest-houses" were even constructed, to spare them the horrors of French plumbing. Each woman was given a wreath to lay at her son's or husband's grave or memorial, and a photographer was on hand to commemorate the occasion. The liaison officers were also patronizingly reminded of the necessity to "prevent over-emphasis of the sentimental side in order to prevent morbidness or hysteria . . .

Many of them will become hysterical, I have no doubt, upon the least provocation."

Nineteen more vessels—all ships of the United States Lines—followed SS *America* during the course of that summer, and over the next four years almost 7,000 mothers and widows availed themselves of the opportunity to see their men's graves. Among them was Grace seibold, who made the pilgrimage in June 1931. Her husband, George senior, accompanied her but paid his own way. There were seven days in Paris—pilgrims could choose a week in London if they preferred—including visits to the Sacré Coeur, Notre Dame, the Louvre, Napoleon's Tomb, the "Colonial Exposition" and the Arc de Triomphe, where Grace laid a wreath on behalf of the Gold Star Mothers, but, perhaps surprisingly, the pilgrims spent just three days visiting the battlefields and cemeteries.

There was some friction on the trip and the Seibolds clearly did not enjoy the warmest relations with the party's liaison officer, who described them in her report after the pilgrimage as "nuisances of a difficult kind." Grace was also refused permission to call a meeting "for purposes of organising Gold Star Mothers . . . on the ground that we could not appear to sponsor any particular organisation. For another reason, Mrs. Seibold has displeased many members of the party because foreign and colored mothers are said to be excluded from her organisation."

Whatever the truth of that allegation then, the organization that Grace Darling Seibold founded—"loyal, capable and patriotic mothers who, while sharing their grief and their pride, have channeled their time, efforts and gifts to lessening the pain of others"—has now long been open to women of all races and origins, and the Washington, D.C., chapter—one of 200 across America—is still named in her honour. The Gold Star Mothers continue their work with bereaved wives and mothers and disabled or impoverished veterans to this day; the war in Iraq has reaped another bitter harvest of sons, husbands and fathers.

Like Grace, George's sister, Theodosia, also had "a lifelong devotion to his memory." She talked constantly of him and never lost hope that one day his grave might be found. On her own deathbed, many years later, she told her daughters that she could see a male figure standing at the foot of her bed, and the last words she ever spoke were, "Oh! There he is."

After the end of the war, avenues of trees were planted in Washington, D.C., dedicated to the memory of men from the District of

Columbia who had died in their country's service. A plaque mounted on a stone in Gillson Park, Wilmette, Illinois, marks a grove of thirteen trees planted in honour of local "heroes of the First World War," including George V. Seibold. Beneath the neat rows of headstones in the Somme Cemetery at Bony in France are the last resting places of several of George's fellow American pilots of the 17th and 148th Aero Squadrons, and George's name is inscribed on a Tablet of the Missing set in the stone walls of the chapel there, along with those of 332 other U.S. servicemen killed in that area whose graves have never been found. That stone inscription and the plaque in Wilmette are the only official acknowledgement of George Seibold's service to his country. His name does not appear in the British lists of American personnel who lost their lives while attached to the RFC and RAF, and most books on First World War aviators do not credit his victories at all or, when they are listed, cite them as just two, or in one case three.

Official British records stored in the National Archives at Kew in southwest London show that the true total of confirmed victories is four, but according to his close friend James A. Keating, a pilot with 64 Squadron, George had also secured two more victories in the fighting on 26 August just before he was shot down and killed. If confirmed, they would have taken his tally to six, one more than the five necessary for official "air ace" status. The point is academic, but there is little reason to doubt the claims. It was the duty of returning pilots to complete the form W3348 "Combats in the Air," which was the basis for their tally of confirmed victories. On the day that George died, six other American pilots of the 148th and 17th Aero Squadrons were listed as missing in action. In those bleak circumstances, few would have had the appetite to register their own claims, let alone file them on behalf of a missing, probably dead friend and comrade. As a result, George's last two victories went undocumented.

Almost ninety years have elapsed since George Seibold died, but it has been a lifelong regret for his surviving relatives that "we never knew where he was." Perhaps all traces of his aircraft and his lifeless body were indeed obliterated by artillery shells during the Battle of Bapaume, but even now his nephew and nieces still maintain hopes that a grave marked only "An Unknown Aviator" might yet be unearthed, or some long-forgotten document identifying his grave-site be found, and they are still continuing the search. For them, if for no other reason, proper official acknowledgement of George Seibold's record as an American air ace should now at last be made.

22

THE CENOTAPH

David Railton had remained on the Western Front until the Armistice on 11 November 1918. Throughout the long, weary years of the war, he had continued to brood on the grave of that one unknown soldier on the Somme that had so moved him. "How that grave caused me to think . . . What can I do to ease the pain of father, mother, brother, sister, sweetheart, wife and friend? Quietly and gradually there came out of the mist of thought this answer clear and strong, 'Let this body—this symbol of him—be carried reverently over the sea to his native land.' And I was happy for a few minutes."

Curiously for an event that left such a deep impression upon him, Railton did not mention the incident in any of his letters to his wife, even though they do refer to a burial carried out earlier that day. But though he "told nobody; yet I could not throw the idea away. Every Padre serving with infantry brigades was bombarded after each publication of casualties with at least this request: 'Where—exactly where— did you lay to rest the body of my son? Can you give me any further information?' . . . To all these questions we were allowed to send a map reference only. Oh those letters of broken relatives and friends! They reinforced the idea so that I could never let it drop."

After the war, Railton became vicar of St. John the Baptist Church, Margate. He took his wartime pledge—"If God spares me I will spend half my life getting their rights for the men who fought out here"— sufficiently seriously to "devote much time to visiting his poorer parishioners" and, at the time of the General Strike, even "gave up a comfortable living to work for two years for the Industrial Christian Fellowship." He was also determined to do what he could to ensure that the body of one "Unknown Comrade" would be brought home for a symbolic burial that would also lay to rest the hundreds of thousands of missing men of the British forces who had no known grave. He was well aware of the difficulty of the task he had set himself. Throughout history, kings, emperors, chiefs, powerful warriors and great men had been buried in magnificent tombs, built to stand as their memorials for all time. Monuments had also been constructed to honour past British war heroes—Blenheim Palace was the gift of a grateful nation to the Duke of Marlborough, and Nelson's Column was erected in commemoration of the great admiral killed at the Battle of Trafalgar. Nelson's body had famously been carried back to England, preserved in a barrel of rum, and buried after a state funeral—but his dead sailors were simply wrapped, weighted and thrown over the side; and the concept of an unknown soldier or sailor being buried with honour was unheard of.

The ancient Greeks and Persians had built shrines of helmets, armour, swords and shields after great battles, and the Romans erected obelisks and triumphal arches, but these were to commemorate victories more than to honour the dead. The first monument to dead soldiers was erected in Lucerne to commemorate the members of the Swiss Guard killed in the Tuileries on 10 August 1792, but a proposal to the House of Commons in 1815 to erect a monument naming all those who had died at Waterloo attracted only modest support.

In Britain, senior military commanders were always drawn from the upper echelons of society and were accorded funerals befitting their status. The last rites for the Duke of Wellington, the victor of Waterloo, organized by Prince Albert, were as lavish as those for a king, with 200,000 filing past the body as it lay in state in the Great Hall in Chelsea. Even the less exalted junior officers at least had a certain aura of raffish glamour, but rank and file soldiers had always been seen as the lowest of the low, the sweepings of the gutters. They were mere cannon-fodder and their names and exploits were very rarely recorded or memorialized. At Waterloo and in the Crimean War, most men were buried in common graves, and though a small minority of Crimean War memorials mention individuals of all ranks, most of the 45,000 British dead were simply "shovelled into the ground and forgotten." In 1880, 962 British soldiers were killed at the Battle of Maiwand during the Second Afghan War, but only Major Blackwood of the Royal Horse Artillery and a pet dog named Blackie that had later been shown to Queen Victoria as a survivor of the battle were commemorated.

Railton's idea was no longer unique; a French plan to reinter their own *poilu inconnu* in the shadow of the Arc de Triomphe was already under consideration. Monsieur Binet-Valmer, the thrice-wounded and thrice-decorated president of the League of Section Heads and War Veterans, had made the original proposal, and a journalist, Gabriel Boissy, had then suggested the addition of an eternal flame to symbolize remembrance. In response to reports of the French plan, the *Daily Express* had also launched a campaign to bury a British unknown soldier beneath the Cenotaph to be erected in Whitehall—"the dust of one soldier, unknown and undistinguished, would lend it a sacredness worthy of so great a monument"—though rather contradicting the purpose of the monument, since "cenotaph," from the Greek words *kenos* and *taphos*, means "empty tomb." The Comrades of the Great War supported the proposal, which was both raised in Parliament and proposed directly to the government in the autumn of that year, but it was turned down because it would not be "consonant with the symbolic character of the monument."

Perhaps because of this precedent, Railton was afraid that a too hasty approach to the British authorities might result in an irreversible refusal. He pondered the wisdom of writing to Sir Douglas Haig, Prime Minister Lloyd George or the Archbishop of Canterbury, but was afraid that none of these "great men would be likely to heed the request of an ordinary Padre . . . a failure to get the idea accepted might be final." Railton also thought of enlisting the help of one of the newspapers, but "who is there that would risk so great a matter becoming a newspaper 'stunt'?" He even contemplated writing direct to the King, who would, "I felt somehow sure, agree, because he understands the hearts of his people. But I feared his Majesty's advisers might suggest an open space like Trafalgar Square, Hyde Park or the Horse Guards for the Tomb of the Unknown Comrade. Then the artists would come and no one could tell what weird structure they might devise for a Shrine!

There could be only one true shrine for this purpose . . . Westminster Abbey—the Parish Church of the Empire." It was a surprisingly homely description of a building that another referred to as "Death's Cathedral Palace, where Royal ashes keep their court."

Beset by doubts, Railton continued to vacillate until August 1920, when his wife told him, "Now or never." Stung into action, he outlined his idea in a letter to the Dean of Westminster Abbey, the Right Reverend Herbert Ryle, and also "made bold to suggest that a real 'War' flag in my possession be used at such a burial rather than [a] new flag of no 'Service' experience." Ryle replied within three days, declaring himself "warmly inclined to favour the idea . . . However I must not move, or talk, too fast. The idea shall germinate."

Railton heard nothing more from Ryle until 19 October, almost two months later, but the Dean had not been inactive in the meantime. He first took soundings within the church hierarchy, where the idea was received with enthusiasm, at least in part because it helped to soothe "ecclesiastical misgivings" about the secular, non-denominational nature of the Cenotaph designed by Lutyens. On 4 October 1920, Ryle then wrote to Lord Stamfordham, George V's private secretary: "I am desirous to approach the King upon a matter . . . There are thousands of graves, I am told, of English 'Tommies' who fell at the Front—names not known. *My idea* [emphasis added] is that one such body (name not known) should be exhumed and interred in Westminster Abbey." Displaying a rather un-Christian egotism, Ryle had now adopted the idea as his own; Railton's authorship of it is never mentioned in any of Ryle's correspondence with third parties. As a result, Ryle's official biographer felt able to comment that "it is not possible to say to whom the credit is due for the original idea of such a service" and *The Times* went even further, stating categorically that "the idea of paying the last honour to an Unknown Warrior originated with the Dean of Westminster."

The King rejected the proposal at once, finding it in poor taste. "His Majesty is inclined to think that nearly two years after the last shot fired on the battlefields of France and Flanders is so long ago that a funeral now might be regarded as belated, and almost, as it were, reopen the war wound which time is gradually healing." However, Ryle then wrote to the Prime Minister and that shrewd and very modern politician Lloyd George saw its potential for validating the sacrifice of so many lives—"Nations must justify mass killings, if only to support the feelings of the bereaved and the sanity of the survivors"—and of cementing his own reputation as "the architect of victory." However, no one, not even a Prime Minister, could impose a meaning unacceptable to the public on any memorial, which "by themselves remain inert and amnesiac, dependent on visitors for whatever memory they finally produce."

Lloyd George was also motivated by fear of "a war-torn and hungry proletariat with a huge preponderance of voting power"; the 1918 Representation of the People Act had increased the size of the electorate almost threefold, from 7 million to 20 million. In 1914, on the eve of war, the country had been riven by dissent and unrest. The suffragettes were waging "this woman's war," as Emmeline Pankhurst had described it, with houses, churches and public buildings burned and riots outside Buckingham Palace. Labour unrest had led to strikes in schools, mines, railways and building trades, and a threatened general strike in the autumn had been averted only by the outbreak of war. The unrest continued at a lower level throughout the war. Some 200,000 Welsh miners struck in 1915 and were only talked back to work by Lloyd George himself, whose gift for persuasive oratory was backed up by the cash to settle most of their demands, and in 1918, 100,000 engineering workers struck in Birmingham, and were joined by 12,000 from the aircraft factories of Coventry. The Minister for Munitions, Winston Churchill, eventually forced them back to work by threatening to conscript them, but unrest continued and even members of the Metropolitan Police staged a strike that summer.

There had been a brief period of domestic quiet after the Armistice—"like the noise of the machines, in the testimony of the factory worker, which only becomes unendurable when they are silent; so humanity is still stunned, not by the noise, but by the silence of the guns"—but the returning soldiers were now making their voices heard. The result of the war might have seemed straightforward to schoolboys and those who believed exactly what they were told by the press—"We had beaten the Germans. The retreat from Mons had been a wonderful thing. Angels had appeared for us there. We had won the Battle of the Somme. Sir Douglas Haig was a great hero"—but veterans of the conflict had a very different view. Many of them, who had left Britain naïvely imagining that they were going to fight the "Great War for Civilisation," had returned sharing Ezra Pound's conviction expressed in his poem "Hugh Selwyn Mauberley," that they had not been battling for civilization, King, country, home and family and the British way of life at all. Britannia was a poisonous old hag and the society over which she presided was nothing more than "a botched civilisation." "The land for heroes turned out to be a land in which heroes were selling boot-laces and matches, going with their families into the workhouse and tramping the heedless countryside in vain search for work." And there was often bitter rancour between those who had fought and those who, for whatever reasons, had stayed at home. "The fight that always occurs between the generations was exceptionally bitter at the end of the Great War . . . For several years the old-young antagonism took on a quality of real hatred. What was left of the war generation had crept out of the massacre to find their elders still bellowing the slogans of 1914."

George V shared Lloyd George's fears that the returning soldier would take full note of "the inadequacy of his present position to the sacrifices which he made, and the promises of the rulers of his country that these sacrifices would be more than recompensed." "Many san-guine well-to-do people [had] dreamt, in the August of 1914, that the war, besides attaining its primary purpose of beating the enemy . . . would even have as a by-product a kind of 'old time Merrie England' . . . For any little expense to which the war might put us, the Germans would pay, and our troops would return home to dismiss all trade union officials and to regard the upper and middle classes thenceforth as a race of heaven-sent colonels—men to be followed, feared and loved." The "flame might still flicker on in the minds of a few tired soldiers and disregarded civilians. Otherwise it was as dead as the half-million of good fellows whom it had fired four years ago, whose credulous hearts the maggots were now eating under so many shining and streaming square miles of wet Flanders and Picardy." Now "the pre-war virilists, the literary braves who felt that they had supped too full of peace, have died in their beds, or lost voice, like the cuckoos in June, and a different breed find voice and pipe up . . . They have seen trenches full of gassed men and the queue of their friends at the brothel-door in Bethune. At the heart of the magical rose was seated an earwig."

Republicanism was a growing force. Even while the fighting was continuing, H. G. Wells had written to *The Times* asserting the need to shake off "the ancient trappings of throne and sceptre." And men who had seen "cities pounded to rubble, men who with little aid or guidance from their own rulers have chased emperors from their thrones, are pretty fully disengaged at last, from the Englishman's old sense of immutable fixity in institutions which he may find irksome or worth-less." There was a widespread feeling, articulated by Edmund Gosse, that "we are passing through dreadful days in which the pillars of the world seem to be shaken. All in front of us seems to be darkness and hopelessness." There was still a residue of respect for the King, whose most inspired act of public relations during the hostilities—other than changing his family name from "Hanover-Saxe-Coburg" to "Windsor" in 1917, after outbreaks of anti-German hostility that included burning shops with Germanic names and stoning dachshund dogs in the streets—had been to announce in 1915, under pressure from Lloyd George, that he was giving up alcohol for the duration of the war. In public at least, he adhered to that pledge and "the one good word that the average private had for his 'betters' during the latter years of the war was for the King. 'He did give up his beer' was said a thousand times by men whom that symbolic act of willing comradeship with the dry throat on the march and the war-pinched household at home had touched and astonished." Just the same, the King was "daily growing more anxious about the question of unemployment . . . The people grow discontented and agitators seize their opportunities; marches are organised; the police interfere; resistance ensues; troops are called out and riot begets revolt and possibly revolution."

After four years of war, the least of George V's subjects could not but be "dimly aware how surprisingly little there is to keep us all from slipping back into the state we were in when a man would kill another to steal a piece of food." "Seven hundred thousand of the beauty and pride of Britain who might have changed the world a little for the better, lie silent and cold among the 'unanswering generations of the dead.' Of the many of those that remain, the sense of duty and hard service has been shaken by the shaking of the solid ground, by the knowledge of how hazardous and transitory is the life of man." "Civilisation itself, the at any rate habitable dwelling which was to be shored up by the war, wears a strange new air of precariousness," and "the hills about Verdun are not blown to pieces worse than the whole social structure and intellectual and spiritual life of Europe. I wonder that anybody is sane."

The physical evidence of what the soldiers at the Front had endured was everywhere. *The Times* printed its daily Roll of Honour until well into 1919, as men continued to succumb to their wounds. In almost every street there were blind men, turning their sightless faces to the light, the maimed and disabled, standing with the arm of a jacket or a trouser leg flapping empty or hobbling on crutches down the street, and scarred or disfigured ex-servicemen—the French called them "men with broken faces" and sculptors made metal masks to cover their ravaged features. Such sights were so familiar that they barely attracted notice. And for every visibly damaged war veteran, there were a score more who carried physical or mental scars that were never to heal.

The dimensions of the problem were staggering. Some 2.7 million Germans had either been disfigured or suffered amputation of one or more limbs by the end of the war, and there were almost a quarter of a million British amputees. In 1928, 2.5 million British men were still in receipt of war pensions because of wounds, disability or shell-shock, and in that year alone 6,000 new artificial limbs were issued to war-wounded men. A further ten years later, on the verge of another world war, despite the millions who had died as a result of their wounds in the two decades since the Armistice, half a million disability pensions were still being paid to men wholly or partly disabled because of their service in the Great War. Widows and orphans faced an almost equally bleak future. Wartime separation allowances and widows' pensions were never above subsistence level and, like disabled pensions, were further eaten away by the inflation of the 1920s. During the war, a German widow's pension was barely a quarter of the average skilled worker's wage, and the position of the half million German widows and 1 million orphans steadily worsened under the Weimar Republic. Britain was not hit by the same hyperinflation, but prices did rise significantly faster than incomes, and war widows and disabled veterans alike struggled to make ends meet.

There was a widespread belief that even the able-bodied, battle-scarred soldiers would never again "be found serving ribbons to ladies in drapers' establishments, following the plough in the bleak, lonely winter fields, tending the machines in the vast factories, adding up other men's accounts in the cellars of great city offices by the aid of artificial light." "Bolshevism" at home and abroad was now a powerful and growing force, and industrial unrest was spreading. Miners and railway workers mounted strike actions in 1919 and a general strike was threatened if the British military intervention against the Russian Bolsheviks escalated into a formal declaration of war. Thirty-five million working days were lost to strikes in that year alone. The Guards Division had been hastily brought back from France to be on hand in case of serious disturbances, but though the loyalty of the Guards was unquestioned, other units of the Army were now "threatening, insubordinate and mutinous."

The troops forming the British Army of Occupation in Germany were doubly discontented; aggrieved not to have been demobilized and appalled at the suffering they were daily witnessing. The Armistice had come into force at eleven o'clock on 11 November 1918, but it had to be renewed every thirty days and the formal end to the Great War did not occur until the signing of the Treaty of Versailles on 28 June 1919, the fifth anniversary of the assassination of Archduke Franz Ferdinand in Sarajevo. To maintain the pressure on Germany during the negotiations, the British naval blockade was continued until the treaty had been concluded; "the guardian of the peace was hunger." The result, compounding Germany's misery, was to condemn further thousands to death from disease and starvation, to the horror of the Allied troops. "When all the great and good at Paris were making peace, as somebody said, with a vengeance, our command on the Rhine had to send a wire to say that unless something was done to feed the Germans starving in the slums [250,000 Germans died of malnutrition in 1918 alone], it could not answer for discipline in its army; the men were giving their rations away, and no orders would stop them . . . While these men fought on, year after year, they had mostly been growing more void of mere spite all the time, feeling always more and more sure that the average German was just a decent poor devil like everyone else."

This discontent, coupled with the pressure of public opinion at home, had forced the British Army into a demobilization that was "felt to be dangerously rapid." Many ex-servicemen returned home with their rifles, fanning fears of unrest and even armed insurrection, but the "last in, first out" system of demobilization that had initially been adopted to ensure the rapid return to industry of "key" or "pivotal" men, provoked fury among long-serving soldiers. Perhaps anticipating troubles to come, policemen, whether old hands or new recruits, were the first to be demobilized. "There was a notice at headquarters saying that anyone who wished to join [the police] who was six feet tall and in good health, could put his name down and go home straight away . . . So the police went back first, then we agricultural workers and then the miners."

The delays in demobilization for long-serving soldiers led to demonstrations in Brighton, Dover, Folkestone and in Whitehall, and in January 1919 Sir Henry Wilson warned Lloyd George that "we dare not give an unpopular order to the troops, and discipline was a thing of the past." Even while the fighting had still been going on, there had been mutiny and rioting at the notorious "Bull Ring" training base at Etaples, put down only by attacks on the alleged ringleaders by "break-up patrols" armed with pick-axe handles, followed by mass arrests.

Now troops in several areas rioted, soldiers looted *estaminets*, held up cars and lorries, and even robbed trains, and a mutiny in Calais by 5,000 troops was suppressed only after Haig had their camp surrounded by loyal troops armed with machine guns. The ringleaders were arrested and Haig was narrowly persuaded against having them all shot.

Winston Churchill, hurriedly transferred to the War Office on 10 January 1919, at once scrapped the former method of demobilization and introduced a more acceptable system, with priority given to those with long service or war wounds, but once demobilized, many ex-servicemen struggled to find lasting work. There was a short-lived boom in 1919, but by Armistice Day 1920 total unemployment stood at half a million; within three months that figure had doubled, and by June 1921 it had doubled again, to two million. While others had been gaining industrial experience and building their careers, a huge number of servicemen had neither apprenticeships nor work experience in anything other than trench warfare . . . and there was no longer any demand for that. The "last in, first out" system that caused such friction in the Army also applied in industry, so that many of those ex-soldiers who found work in 1919 lost it again within two years. Two-thirds of the male unemployed were ex-servicemen, and ex-gratia payments of twenty-nine shillings a week to unemployed ex-soldiers came to an end in March 1921. For many of those returning to "a land fit for heroes," "the greatest indignity was having to watch their children line up at soup kitchens."

Britain's already war-ravaged economy had been dealt a further series of blows by the Bolshevik regime's repudiation of all Tsarist debts and its nationalization of all foreign investments—in both cases the vast majority were British. The post-war recession in manufacturing was also deepened by the impact of reparations imposed on Germany. So many German ships and liners were transferred to British, French and American flags that domestic and export demand for new ships from British yards was wiped out. Export markets for British coal were similarly shrunk by the millions of tons of German coal that the French took in reparations. In addition, while British industry had been wholly devoted to the war effort, rival nations had taken the chance to build their own domestic manufacturing base. British engineers and textile firms in particular found their former markets subject to ferocious competition, led by America and Japan.

Even those soldiers with no political or ideological agenda tended to feel alienated from their fellow countrymen who had not served at the Front. Soldiers of all eras share something of the same ambivalence and the same bittersweet feelings when their war service is over: relief that they have survived, but regret and even guilt about those who did not, and a less tangible feeling of loss for the bond with fellow members of the same troop or cadre who, in the friendship forged in the crucible of the trenches, were as close, if not closer, even than their own families. Many who had no reason to remember the Great War with fondness were nonetheless to describe it years afterwards as the high point of their lives, a time when every impression, every sensation, every emotion, was more vivid and immediate than it had ever been before or was ever to be again. "We remember it always and know, without proof, that while the rapture was there, we were not drunk, but wise; that for a moment some intervening darkness had thinned and we were seeing further than we can see now into the heart of life." In Siegfried Sassoon's words, the survivor of the Great War was "everlastingly differentiated from everyone except his fellow soldiers," and R. H. Tawney said that "between you and us, there hangs a veil." "The dead are less dead than the living . . . where the war has spared, it has slain," and the veterans were no less bereaved than those who had stayed at home; they had all lost many friends and comrades.

Despite the unrest among troops awaiting demobilization, the Commissioner of Works, Sir Alfred Mond, suggested that returning servicemen would be a stabilizing force in industry, since the burning hatred of men at the Front for wartime "strikers" and "shirkers" back home was well known. As one soldier put it, "To me the most contemptible cur in the world is the man who lets political influence be used to keep him away from the Front. For he lets another man die in his place," and the term H.S.B.—Home Service Bastard—had been specifically coined for those not in the front lines. Lloyd George's government also attempted to calm the fevered atmosphere with some palliative measures. Supplies of food, beer and spirits were increased and restrictions on fuel and lighting lifted. Football, horse-racing and other sports popular with the working classes were encouraged and great efforts were made to rekindle wartime patriotism. George H. Roberts, Minister of Labour, advocated marching demobilized soldiers through towns and cities to stir public opinion "to the highest pitch" of patriotism, and "brass bands . . . flag-waving . . . [and] everything possible should be done to work up a high patriotic feeling."

One of the ways Lloyd George hoped to stir such public feelings was by a Victory Parade. The Treaty of Versailles was signed in late June, but the official Peace Day in Britain was set for 19 July 1919. In celebration, a Victory Parade was duly arranged in London on that day. With a mixture of hideous snobbery and penetrating accuracy, Virginia Woolf dismissed it as "a servants' festival; something got up to pacify and placate 'the people' . . . there's something calculated and politic and insincere about these peace rejoicings." Two march-pasts were organized, one reviewed by the King in front of Buckingham Palace, the other before the Prince of Wales, passing through the East End on a route that also went south of the river. Borrowing from the French plans for their celebration, Lloyd George, who "deprecated a national rejoicing which did not include some tribute to the dead," also proposed the erection of a temporary "catafalque"—a decorated structure on which a body or effigy would be laid during a funeral or lying in state. Draped with a pall, it was also used to represent the body at a post-interment requiem mass. The catafalque would stand beside the parade route so that the marching soldiers could pause to salute the dead.

The proposal was controversial. Memorial Day, honouring the Civil War dead, was well established in the United States, though there was concern that, far from being an occasion of national reconciliation, supporters of the Confederacy were using it as a rallying point. In Britain, virtually the only pre-war precedent was the annual "Lady-smith Day" parade in Liverpool in memory of the Boer War siege and the men of the city who had died in the fighting. During the Great War, it had become the custom to commemorate the anniversary of the outbreak of the war on 4 August—it was known as "Remembrance Day" until superseded by 11 November after the Armistice—and as the war progressed, what began as a patriotic rally began to assume the character of a commemoration. In many areas a commemorative element, often including the reading of the Roll of Honour, was also grafted onto church festivals and secular events such as Trafalgar Day. But several of Lloyd George's Cabinet colleagues thought the idea of a catafalque in poor taste. Lord Curzon described it, with withering Anglo-Saxon snobbery, as "rather foreign to the spirit of our people, however much it might be in harmony with the Latin temperament"—ironically, the French catafalque was removed immediately after the parade since it was deemed to be "too Germanic"—but the Prime Minister forced it through. Britain's most distinguished architect, Sir Edwin Lutyens, who had already been informally consulted by Sir Alfred Mond, was commissioned to produce a design for a suitable temporary structure.

Lutyens, who made no charge for his work, took his inspiration from the ancient world. The ancient Egyptians prepared at least two tombs for a pharaoh, one of which was destined to remain empty. The Greeks also attached great importance to the proper burial of the dead and even if the body was missing, a burial service would be held and a cenotaph erected over an empty grave. At the turn of the century, Lutyens had designed a garden seat for Gertrude Jekyll that was christened the "Cenotaph of Sigismunda"—the first time he had been aware of the word—but he was not the first in Britain to adopt the idea as a commemoration of the war dead. In 1916 it had been agreed that a marble cenotaph would be placed in the northeast transept of the new Anglican cathedral in Liverpool as a memorial to the war dead of the city, but Lutyens now put forward the idea of an empty tomb awaiting the return of a missing soldier to commemorate all the British war dead. That imagery had a potent emotional force, and the absence of any figurative representation of the dead avoided an otherwise inevitable controversy. Lutyens's later cenotaph for the City of Manchester did include a representation of a soldier's body, but set so high on a towering plinth that it was barely visible. By contrast, A. G. Walker's memorial to the Men of Limehouse, or Charles Sargeant Jagger's Royal Artillery Memorial at Hyde Park Corner, clearly depicted dead soldiers and provoked fierce criticism both for the "gruesomeness" of their design and for the artists' perceived intention of "forcing home on the minds of the public, the horror and terror of war."

Lutyens's simple, elegant and neutral design for the Cenotaph avoided such problems by creating a blank canvas that allowed each individual to project onto it his or her own thoughts, feelings and emotions. Haig chose to describe it as the "symbol of an Empire's unity," and The Times could claim that "it speaks of the qualities of the race," but for most people it was free of all nationalist, imperial and warlike connotations. In the same way, the chosen inscription: "THE GLORIOUS DEAD"—a term first coined by Lloyd George—was neutral, almost blank, a commemoration of the fallen, not a celebration of victory. Even today, the Cenotaph continues to be open to a variety of interpretations. On May Day 2000, while still encircled by wreaths laid to commemorate the anniversary of Gallipoli, the Cenotaph was defaced by rioters with the slogan "Why glorify war?" in red paint.

Lutyens was given no more than two weeks to design and build the structure, but he produced a sketch "in less than a couple of minutes" and, "still in a great state of excitement," reproduced it "in pencil and coloured chalks on the back of an advertisement" while dining with his mistress, Vita Sackville-West, that night. By ten o'clock the following morning, he had completed the half-inch and full-size working drawings. Based on the Greek principle of *entasis*, in which slightly curved surfaces create the illusion of linearity, all the apparently horizontal planes are actually curved, forming parts of spheres 1,801 feet, 8 inches in diameter, and the vertical lines, if extended, would converge at a point the same distance above the ground. The same principle was used in Lutyens's design for the Stone of Remembrance placed in each British war cemetery. The detailed technical drawings for the Cenotaph required a manuscript book of thirty-three pages, but though the "mathematical precision" of the design would remain undetected by all but the most acute observer, all could respond to the emotions evoked by that empty tomb. Since it was not intended to be permanent, the temporary Cenotaph was constructed like a theatrical set, from wood and plaster, painted to resemble stone. It was so fragile that even the weight of a ladder against it might have been enough to topple the whole structure, and the fire brigade was accordingly summoned to erect the banners adorning it.

Curzon saw it as "an Imperial monument, commemorating men of many races and creeds," and Lutyens's design was deliberately non-denominational, containing no cross or other Christian iconography (to the fury of one correspondent of the *Catholic Herald*, who thought it pagan and an insult), so that all the troops of the Empire—Protestant, Catholic, Jewish, Hindu, Muslim and Sikh—could share in the memorial, though not all ex-servicemen felt inclined to do so. In Chertsey, several hundred boycotted the Victory Parade in protest at not having secured their pension rights, and in other areas ex-servicemen stayed away in protest against British troops being sent to fight the Bolsheviks in Russia and growing militarism at home; "our pals died to kill militarism, not to establish it here." In Merthyr Tydfil, 25,000 people attended an alternative ceremony offering a thanksgiving for peace and ending with a unanimous call for higher pensions for ex-servicemen and their dependants. In Luton, ex-servicemen were refused permission to stage their own memorial service and responded by setting fire to the town hall and then holding the police and fire brigade at bay until the building was completely gutted. When loyal troops eventually arrived to disperse the rioters, they found them staging an impromptu singsong around a stolen piano. Luton remained under military occupation for several days.

Despite some unrest around the fringes, the Victory Parade proved hugely popular and was mirrored by smaller-scale celebrations, including parades, bonfires and fireworks, in almost every community throughout the country. Prime vantage points in central London were occupied before daybreak and, despite the overcast skies and the forecast of heavy rain, by eight that morning Trafalgar Square was impassable and the sculpted lions guarding Nelson's Column were buried under masses of people. So dense were the crowds that it was estimated that only a twentieth of them actually saw the parade; most caught glimpses only of those on horseback and the gleaming tips of polished bayonets as the ranks of troops marched by.

Lutyens's "temporary but fitting monument" had been erected in Whitehall the previous day, 18 July 1919, and people at once began laying wreaths and flowers around it. These were cleared away before the parade, when Haig, Foch and Pershing led a silent march-past by 15,000 Allied soldiers to salute the dead—"the most impressive sight I ever saw," according to the King. All the Allies were represented by contingents of troops; after the French and Americans came Belgians, Italians, Portuguese, Poles, Romanians, Serbs, Japanese and Chinese. Bringing up the rear were the British and Empire troops. As they passed, the crowd showered them with flowers, cigarettes and sweets. When the Americans passed the Treasury, pound notes began floating down through the air. There was no explanation of why or from where they had come, but apparently reliable witnesses described seeing it happen. "Pound notes also fluttered down from the upper windows of public houses, but that is more easily explained." Each serviceman was rewarded for his participation with "an eight-ounce meat pie, two ounces of cheese, four ounces of biscuits and a bar of chocolate, plus some cigarettes" for his homeward journey.

As soon as the parade had passed, thousands of bereaved mothers, fathers, widows, children, friends and relatives of the war dead again began laying wreaths and bouquets around the Cenotaph. Within an hour, they were piled high around its base. Despite the heavy rain that began falling at five that afternoon, people continued to lay flowers and wreaths until well after nightfall. Press reports the following day accorded the Cenotaph an almost mystical significance. The *Manchester Guardian* claimed that "a light was shining in the daylight like a light on an altar," the *Daily Mail* claimed that "you could scarce see the Cenotaph for the *aura*, the halo, the throbbing air that encompassed it," and another reporter heard "moments of silence when the dead seemed very near, when one almost heard the passage of countless wings—were not the fallen gathering in their hosts to receive their comrades' salute and take their share in the triumph they had died to win?" J. M. Barrie wrote to Lutyens, "The Cenotaph grows in beauty as one strolls down alone o'nights to look at it, which becomes my habit. I stand cogitating why and how it is so noble a thing." Over the succeeding days, despite the hostility of the Church of England, expressed through an editorial in the *Church Times* denouncing the powerful public sentiment as "a cult" and "cenotapholatry," more and more flowers were laid at the Cenotaph. Many of the people visiting it were accosted by hawkers in Whitehall selling flowers and postcards. Some were disgusted by this, feeling that it was "a desecration of a sacred spot," but many thousands of people bought postcards of the Cenotaph, perhaps adding them to the personal "shrines" to their dead that they maintained in their homes. Several applications for permission to manufacture and sell small models of the Cenotaph were also made to the Department of Works.

The subject of a permanent memorial was now aired in Parliament, where twenty-three MPs signed a memorandum to the Commissioner of Works, requesting that one be erected on the same site. The press took up the theme. "Simple, grave and beautiful in design, [the Cenotaph] has been universally recognised as a just and fitting memorial of those who have made the greatest sacrifice; and the flowers which have daily been laid upon it since the march, show the strength of its appeal to the imagination." Although Sir Alfred Mond opposed making the Cenotaph permanent, suggesting that it might be "of too mournful a character as a permanent expression of the triumphant victory of our arms," there was otherwise near universal agreement on the need for a lasting memorial, though some favoured a quieter, more contemplative site, well away from the roar of Whitehall traffic. Lutyens emphatically disagreed. The current site had been "qualified by the salute of Foch and the allied armies and by our men and their great leaders . . . no other site would give this pertinence." It had also, said a correspondent of the *Daily Mail*, been "consecrated by the tears of many mothers."

Such arguments were persuasive and the Cabinet took the decision to place a permanent memorial on the same site since "the Cenotaph in its present position had memories which could not be uprooted." As Lutyens later noted, "The plain fact emerged and grew stronger every hour, that the Cenotaph was what the people wanted . . . It was a mass feeling too deep to express itself more fitly than by the piles of good fresh flowers which loving hands laid at the Cenotaph day by day. Thus it was decided, by the human sentiment of millions, that the Cenotaph should be as it now is." That human sentiment was on a massive scale. It was estimated that, in the last week of July alone, half a million people paid their respects at the temporary Cenotaph, and so many flowers were laid that the Department of Works had to employ two "custodians" to deal with them.

The public response should not have surprised anyone, after the reaction to a temporary war shrine—"a large, white Maltese Cross . . . with a spire twenty-four feet high," draped with purple and white cloth, and decorated with the Union Jack and the flags of the Allies, that had been erected in Hyde Park in August 1918 to mark the fourth anniversary of the outbreak of the war. The prime mover in the erection of the shrine was Bishop Winnington-Ingram, who won support from the Lord Mayor and private benefactors. On the first day, 4 August, it was besieged by tens of thousands of Londoners, many dressed in mourning, and by 15 August it was claimed that 200,000 floral tributes had been laid there. It remained in Hyde Park for fifteen months, during which time it was patched up on several occasions, but the final removal of the by now severely dilapidated edifice in October 1919 provoked an angry response. One woman complained that it was an "outrage on this small sacred spot . . . is this how we poor broken-hearted Mothers are to be treated?"

The powerful response to the Cenotaph from press and public alike accorded with Lloyd George's determination to give the population not only "bread and circuses" but also patriotic, unifying (and for the Prime Minister, self-aggrandizing) symbols and rituals, stressing that "the war was an experience where everyone sacrificed and some died, not as members of a separate group, but as citizens of a whole community." Armistice Day fulfilled all these criteria. It was not a "universal ritual . . . oriented to all human beings killed in wars, [but] for the dead of a specific area, and of a particular nation state." The temporary Cenotaph was left in place for the Armistice Day commemorations on 11 November 1919, when, despite the opposition of Sir Alfred Mond, who considered that "the placing of flowers, memorial wreaths, etc., at all times on the Cenotaph should be discountenanced," preferring a commemoration that would "exalt the dignity of sacrifice without the tears," large numbers of people again laid their wreaths and floral tributes around it. The crowds were even bigger than those that had assembled for the Victory Parade that summer and the police, who had only seventeen constables on duty, had to issue a hasty call for reinforcements to help maintain order. Mounted police were also needed to clear a path for the French Premier, M. Clemenceau, and Lloyd George through the crush surrounding the Cenotaph, where Lloyd George laid a wreath of orchids, white roses and laurels at its base. The commemoration was again marked by protests from unemployed servicemen. In Manchester, the organizer of the local branch of the National Association of Employed and Unemployed Ex-Service Men and Women was refused leave to address the Armistice Day crowds on the subject of "the case for the living, in honour of the dead."

The Cenotaph in London continued to draw a stream of pilgrims, with crowds in mourning dress gathering there at Christmas to lay wreaths of red-berried holly. The structure was now badly dilapidated, but a Ministry of Works announcement that it was to be demolished in January 1920 provoked a furious response, one newspaper describing those taking the decision as being "utterly without soul or sentiment or understanding." A hasty statement was issued, pointing out the fragility of the wood and plaster structure after six months' exposure to the London weather, and the demolition proceeded on schedule, but, "to spare the feelings of those to whom the structure is especially sacred," it was first surrounded by hoardings so that its destruction was concealed. A Department of Works official also suggested that "since the ground upon which the Cenotaph had been built has been consecrated, it would be highly undesirable to let the traffic again move over that portion of the road."

Lutyens had already been commissioned to produce a permanent memorial, to be unveiled by King George V on Armistice Day 1920. The stones were cut and laid with such precision that the joints are no more than one-sixteenth of an inch wide, and the design was virtually unaltered from the temporary Cenotaph, though Lutyens had to intervene to prevent the addition of life-size bronze statues of sentries at each corner. He felt that this figurative element would have detracted from the abstract, neutral symbolism of the monument itself, and would also "prevent living sentries being posted on days of ceremony." The Cenotaph "could refer to the dead without images of the Allied victory being invoked, thus appealing to people who did not accept the traditions affirmed by that victory . . . When the meaning of the war was questioned in the years following it, therefore, the memorial itself was not doubted." But Lutyens was unsuccessful in attempting to replace the silk flags that had adorned the temporary monument with stone carvings. He complained that the silk flags increased "the speci-

ficity of patriotic and nationalistic sentiment," but for Lloyd George
that was exactly the point.

Buoyed by this popular success, when Dean Ryle's proposal to bury
an Unknown Warrior in Westminster Abbey reached his desk in mid-
October 1920, Lloyd George then succeeded both in changing the
King's mind and in persuading the Cabinet to adopt the idea, though in
his diaries, Sir Henry Wilson, Chief of the Imperial General Staff,
claimed the credit for winning over the initially sceptical Cabinet.
"After some discussion, in the course of which the Chief of the Imperial General Staff informed the Cabinet that the Army might be
assumed to be unanimously in favour of the proposal, which was
regarded as the greatest honour that could be paid by the nation, the
Cabinet agreed a) to accept in principle the proposals and b) to appoint
a Committee composed of: Lord Curzon, Lord Lee of Fareham, Mr.
[Winston] Churchill, Mr. Walter Long, Mr. Short and Sir Alfred
Mond, with Colonel Storr (Cabinet Office) as Secretary." Foreign Secretary Curzon, though an initial opponent of the whole idea, was a
former Viceroy of India, and the talent he had shown there for lavish
public ceremonials such as the Delhi Durbar—in Curzon's own admittedly biased view, "one of the most solemn and awe-inspiring ceremonials ever held"—was now to be unleashed on London. Curzon
"possessed unrivalled skill and imagination as a master of ceremonies,
as a stage-manager of spectacle, as an inventor of traditions." His vision
would ever after dictate the form of public remembrance of the war
dead.

Lloyd George's secretary wrote to Dean Ryle that night, 15 October 1920. "Your memorandum . . . was considered this afternoon by the
Cabinet, and accepted in principle. The Prime Minister has already
notified the King of this . . . I should add that the Cabinet would prefer
that the first announcement of the adoption of this proposal should be
made in Parliament. The Prime Minister asks me to thank you for this
impressive suggestion." There were now barely three weeks before
Armistice Day and the Cabinet Committee was convened with un-
accustomed haste to examine the feasibility of completing the arrangements in the available time. The opinions of the commanders of the
three branches of the armed forces were also sought. The committee
noted that "objection has been made a) That it is too late—But not too
late if carried out about the same date as the Cenotaph. b) That it is
sensational—But any appeal to national sentiment is open to this
charge. The *advantages* would be that it would generally be acceptable

to the people; that it would do honour to the great mass of fighting men; that it would furnish a Memorial to them in Westminster Abbey, without singling out for such distinction *any one known man*. At present Westminster Abbey has no memorial of the Great War."

Railton's recommendation that the body be known as the "Unknown Comrade"—an idea suggested to him by one of his relatives—was discounted. Railton found it "more homely and friendly," but the Russian Revolution of 1917 was too fresh in Cabinet and military minds for "Comrade" to be an acceptable honorific, though the committee felt, and was "warmly supported" in their view by Field Marshal Sir Henry Wilson, that rather than "soldier," it should be "a neutral word like 'warrior' so as to include Navy and Air Force as well as Army." The committee's suggested inscription was:

A BRITISH WARRIOR

WHO FELL IN THE GREAT WAR

1914–18

FOR KING AND COUNTRY

They concluded by resolving that "the remains of one of the numerous unknown men who fell and were buried in France, should be exhumed; conveyed to England; if necessary, cremated; escorted by soldiers as a military funeral procession to Westminster Abbey, and there, after short, impressive funeral service, be buried in the Nave, a central position having been granted by the Dean, fairly opposite the great West Door, so as to be easily seen and identified by people in all future times."

Sir Henry Wilson wrote to Dean Ryle to express his delight, though in his enthusiasm he neglected his previous inclusiveness towards the other two services. "I am heartily glad to think that your proposal is going to be carried out . . . May I once again give you my warmest congratulations and thanks for the great honour you are doing to the Army." Ryle continued to accept the plaudits offered to him as "the originator" of the idea, though he did at least express his "warm acknowledgement and thanks" to David Railton, albeit in a private letter rather than a public forum.

Public and press reaction to the idea, following Lloyd George's announcement in the House of Commons, was also enthusiastic. *The Times* editorialized that the Unknown Warrior, "the silent ambassador of the legion dead to the courts of the living," was "an emblem of 'the plain man,' of the masses of the people who in every age, have borne their full share in all our national wars. For the first time . . . it has been decided to recognise this share by the highest honours which Church and State pay to the illustrious dead." At an individual level, the interment of a single Unknown Soldier ("strange," as Andrew Kelly remarked, "that this should always be capitalised when lower case would be more universal") also offered the millions of bereaved relatives and friends of the missing a symbolic chance to lay their loved ones to rest. "Those mourning at home had lost a human being. But there was no visual object for their mourning, no corpse to which they could say a last farewell." The Unknown Warrior—the only one of the million British and Empire war dead who would ever be repatriated—was now to fulfil that role for all the wives, parents and children of the missing.

A minority of people, including the poet Siegfried Sassoon, were sickened by what they saw as the sentiment and hypocrisy of the proposed ceremonies at the Cenotaph and the grave of the Unknown Warrior.

> The Prince of Darkness to the Cenotaph
> Bowed. As he walked away I heard him laugh.

In his poem "The Horizontal Man," W. H. Auden contrasted the pious platitudes about honouring the returning soldiers—the "vertical man"—with the reality of their post-war predicament. Britain gave honour and acknowledgement—or so he claimed—only to the "horizontal man"—the Unknown Soldier who had no further demands to make of the society he had died to protect. His still-living comrades were no longer needed and were now ignored.

Others echoed their views. "I think all this business about the unknown warrior cheap and tawdry—I would rather have spent the money on employing some live warriors, I suppose I am not as sentimental as I ought to be." Beatrice Webb acidly commented that Downing Street had been barricaded "lest there should be yet another, and still more impressive public ceremony—the funeral of an assassinated Prime Minister!" Many others, while not necessarily subscribing to such views, felt that remembrance of the dead should be combined with positive action to aid the living. Earl Haig appealed for help for "those old warriors whose only demand upon the gratitude of the nation today is that they shall be given the opportunity by their own toil to earn their daily bread."

Others echoed that call, but the government relied—not always successfully—on voluntary action through the King's National Roll Scheme to encourage employers to recruit able-bodied and disabled ex-servicemen. As a Frenchman had observed at a meeting of the war wounded in 1916, "Today we are welcome, but after the war no one will speak of us and work will be hard to find." The week surrounding Armistice Day, beginning on Monday, 8 November 1920, was also designated "Obligation Week." As the *Yorkshire Post* reported, it was "the intention during this week to make a special appeal to captains of industry and business and professional men" and, despite the saying "no sentiment in business," the effort to find openings for unemployed ex-servicemen would "touch a responsive chord in the hearts of the vast majority of employers in Northern towns. They must be all too conscious of what these men have done for them, as for the nation at large, for it to be otherwise . . . They fought for justice; we must be just."

Others went further. George Bernard Shaw argued that the disabled "drag down wages and the standard of work, and should not be employed at all industrially. The duty of the country is perfectly clear. These men were disabled in its service and should be supported unconditionally." Government support for Obligation Week was also denounced as hypocritical by munitions workers in Gretna. "The unanimous opinion of the people here is that a Government which preaches to the employers to employ all possible men, and at the same time cuts down the employees in its own factory to a most unnecessary extent is guilty both of callousness and hypocrisy." Obligation Week and other appeals to employers' patriotism met with some success but simmering discontent over the plight of unemployed and disabled ex-servicemen was to flare up at intervals right up to the Second World War. A watershed was reached in October 1920, when a march of the unemployed down Whitehall was broken up by a police baton charge. "The comradeship of the trenches was over. Ex-soldiers in blue were now ready to club down ex-soldiers in rags." It was an equally potent and long-lived issue in the United States, where in the depths of the Great Depression, during the winter of 1932–33, a protesting "Bonus Army" of unemployed ex-servicemen who had set up camp in Washington were tear-gassed and driven out of the capital by troops acting on the orders of General Douglas MacArthur.

23

MERE BONES

The funeral of the Unknown Warrior was to take place on Armistice Day, 11 November 1920. After unveiling the new Cenotaph in Whitehall, the King would walk behind the gun-carriage bearing the body of the Unknown Warrior to Westminster Abbey. Brigadier General L. J. Wyatt, DSO, General Officer Commanding British troops in France and Flanders, and director of the Army Graves Registration Service (later renamed the Imperial War Graves Commission, and now known as the Commonwealth War Graves Commission), was put in charge of the selection of the body.

Great trouble was taken to ensure that the identity and origins of the chosen soldier would remain completely unknowable. On 7 November 1920, four field ambulances, each containing an officer and two other ranks equipped with shovels and sacks, arrived at cemeteries in the four main British battle areas on the Western Front—the Aisne, the Somme, Arras and Ypres. In the lofty British tradition, the significance of the day's work they were about to undertake had not been explained to them. Their instructions were to choose a grave marked "Unknown British Soldier" and exhume the body buried there. The deliberate and apparently scrupulous selection of a random, unidentifiable body was to allow every grieving family to imagine that their missing son, husband or father could be the unknown soldier. "The Unknown Warrior whose body was to be buried may have been born to high position or to low; he may have been a sailor, a soldier or an airman; an Englishman, a Scotsman, a Welshman, an Irishman, a man of the Dominions, a Sikh, a Gurkha. No-one knows. But he was one who gave his life for the people of the British Empire." George Bernard Shaw even considered the idea of a play in which the Unknown Warrior would finally be resurrected and discovered to be German.

However, the burial parties were also privately instructed that the soldier should have fallen in the early part of the war, ensuring that decomposition was sufficiently far advanced to obviate the need for a cremation. It was felt that the public would more readily identify with the Unknown Soldier if his remains were buried without a cremation, and the church authorities—perhaps worried about the taint of putrefying flesh within Westminster Abbey—made it a condition of burial without cremation that the body dated from 1914. For military traditionalists, this also had the side benefit of ensuring that the Unknown Warrior would be an Anglo-Saxon member of the British Expeditionary Force—a regular soldier—rather than one of Kitchener's New Army of civilian volunteers or one of the hundreds of thousands of soldiers drawn from the far-flung reaches of the Empire.

The ebb and flow of the fighting and the changes in uniforms and equipment in the course of the war made it possible to distinguish at least some of the dead of 1914 from those who had fallen later. Major P. H. Pilditch, cycling through the old battlefields in search of the grave of a dead comrade, noted that "the progress of our successive attacks could clearly be seen from the types of equipment on the skeletons; soft caps denoting 1914 and early 1915, then respirators, then steel helmets marking attacks in 1916." The army had originally proposed that the body of the Unknown Warrior should be taken from a site where the Royal Naval Division had also fought, but they had not been deployed in the battle zones in 1914, and the Navy waived its rights, leaving the Army free to make its own arrangements for exhuming a body. There are, of course, no documents explicitly stating that only soldiers of the BEF were to be exhumed, but it seems clear from the minutes of the discussions that it was the tacit intention of senior Army officers to restrict the selection in this way. If so, it was an outrageous deception on the millions of relatives of servicemen who had died in the succeeding years of the war and who all, to greater or lesser degree, nurtured the belief that the Unknown Warrior might be their missing son, husband or father.

The digging parties appear to have stuck to their brief; Wyatt later described the bodies as "mere bones," but that did not necessarily preclude the soldiers from having been killed later in the war. In the rat-infested and bacteria-laden soils of Flanders and northeast France, even the bodies of the dead of 1918 would already have reached an advanced state of decomposition by the winter of 1920. Having disinterred a body, each party was then required to confirm by means of any surviving scraps of uniform fabric, boots, buttons or other distinguishing features that it was indeed that of a British soldier, and to establish that there was no means of identification upon it. If any were found, it was to be reinterred at once and a further body exhumed.

Once the party were satisfied with their choice, the empty grave was filled in and the chosen body placed in a sack, loaded into the back of the ambulance and driven to Wyatt's GHQ at St. Pol-sur-Ternoise, twenty miles west of Arras. Each of the four parties had been allocated a different and widely separated arrival time during that evening, and they were sent back to their units as soon as they had unloaded their body, ensuring that they were unable to confer or indicate to each other or to any third party the origin of any of the bodies. Each body in turn was received by the Reverend George Kendall, OBE, and re-examined to ensure that the corpse was British and that no means of identification could be found upon it. The four bodies were then covered by Union flags and laid in a row in the small corrugated iron hut that served as the chapel of St. Pol. A plain coffin of English pine was placed in front of the altar, ready to receive the remains. Kendall then left the chapel and an armed guard secured the doors.

At midnight—a time steeped in myth and ritual—Brigadier Wyatt and Lieutenant Colonel E. A. S. Gell entered the chapel and Wyatt selected one of the corpses at random. Some versions of the story suggest he was blindfolded, but Wyatt himself made no mention of that in his own account, and it is more likely that he merely pointed to one of the bodies. "I had no idea even of the area from which the body I selected had come, and no one else can know it." The two men then transferred the remains to the pine coffin standing before the altar, and screwed down the lid. Wyatt said that the other bodies were at once reinterred in the military cemetery at St. Pol, but a later and perhaps more accurate account claimed that their burial site was deliberately more obscure. The area had been the scene of heavy fighting, and there were shell-craters and "old trenches running in all directions. The burial party quickly selected a spot and . . . the three bodies were buried in a shell-hole on the road to Albert, to which the chaplain added a simple prayer."

The following morning, 8 November 1920, chaplains of the Church of England, the Roman Catholic Church and nonconformist churches held a service in the chapel, and at noon the body was sent, under escort, in "a battle-scarred ambulance" to Boulogne. At 3:30 that afternoon, after passing through ranks of troops lining the roads from the outskirts of the city, the ambulance climbed the hill overlooking the harbour and drew up at the thirteenth-century castle that served as the local headquarters of the French Army. Eight soldiers, including a sergeant-major of the Royal Army Service Corps, a sergeant of the Royal Engineers, a gunner of the Royal Field Artillery, an Australian Light Horseman, privates from the Canadian infantry and the Machine Gun Corps, and a rifleman from the 21st London Regiment (First Surrey Rifles), bore the rough coffin into the castle along stone passageways and corridors lined by French soldiers.

It was placed in the castle library, which had been converted into a temporary *chapelle ardente*, decorated with flags and palms, its floor strewn with autumn flowers and leaves. As part of France's tribute to the Unknown Warrior, a company of soldiers from the 8th Regiment—recently awarded the Légion d'Honneur en masse for their valour during the war—furnished the guard for the body throughout its last night in the country. No British troops were present. That same night, a consignment of "sixteen barrels, stated to contain fifty bags of French soil" from the Ypres Salient, was loaded onto a warship at Calais and taken across the Channel to Dover. The next morning, 10 November, "Lieutenant Swift, travelling by the 9:15 a.m. train from Dover Harbour to Victoria Station" in London, delivered the soil to Westminster Abbey, ready to be placed in the tomb, so that the Unknown Warrior "might lie in the earth so many gave their lives for."

At ten that morning, two British undertakers, Mr. Noades and Mr. Sowerbutts, entered the *chapelle ardente* in Boulogne Castle and placed the plain pine coffin, unopened, inside another casket of English oak that they had brought across the Channel during the night, then secured the lid and sealed it. Presented by the British Undertakers Association, the casket had been made from an oak that grew in the grounds of Hampton Court—"that most English of Royal palaces." It weighed almost two hundredweight and had been patterned on "the design of a sixteenth-century treasure chest, made from two-inch English oak with slightly rounded sides and lid, and a dark waxed finish." There were two pairs of hammer-wrought handles on either side of the coffin, which was bound with broad, studded bands of wrought iron. A plate of beaten iron in the shape of a sixteenth-century shield, bearing the inscription *"A British Warrior who fell in the Great War 1914–18 for King and Country"* was bolted to the lid over a "Crusader's sword" sent by the King from the royal collection at Windsor, "a soldier's gift to a soldier." "In deference to Lloyd George," the ironwork had been sent to Caernarvon to be finished by the craftsmen who made the ironwork for the investiture of the Prince of Wales.

On the previous Sunday, Mr. Noades and Mr. Sowerbutts had borne the coffin into Westminster Abbey, where they "laid it on the spot chosen for the tomb," presumably in order that the sextons should excavate no more of the sandy Thorney Island soil beneath the stone flags of the abbey floor than was necessary, for fear of disturbing the remains of other, ancient burials. However, when the sextons set to work, they found that the grave-site had "apparently been untouched since that portion of the Abbey was built. The diggers of the grave found there no remnants of other humanity." The coffin was placed in the Jerusalem Chamber of the abbey for the night, before beginning its journey to Boulogne, still accompanied by Messrs. Noades and Sowerbutts.

It was a fitting day, with a grey sky and a thick mist lying over the sea, as the coffin, draped in a Union flag, was placed on a French military wagon drawn by six black horses. With the pallbearers pacing alongside, it was taken to a "neighbouring junction of three roads," the old toll-bar known as Le Dernier Sou, where the funeral procession had assembled. At ten-thirty the church bells of Boulogne all sounded as one. The trumpets of the cavalry and the bugles of the infantry then blew the *"Aux Champs"* and the procession moved off, "as the tender melancholy of Chopin's 'Funeral March' filled the air." Escorted by a division of French troops, the casket bearing "the *'Tommy Anonyme,'* as he is dubbed in France" was borne into Boulogne at the heart of a mile-long cortège, headed by a thousand local schoolchildren given a holiday for the day, and followed by "seemingly endless ranks of cavalry," marines and infantry. Half a dozen pairs of soldiers walked directly behind the coffin, struggling with the bulk of the great wreaths they carried. The entire route had been decorated with Venetian masts, bearing tricolour streamers, trophies and flags. More French soldiers with rifles reversed and thousands of ordinary citizens lined the roads, their heads bowed in silent tribute to "the representative of the hundreds of thousands who died, as one Frenchman put it, 'for our country as much as for his own.'"

At the dockside on the Quai Carnot, Marshal Ferdinand Foch, who had attended the ceremony "entirely on his own initiative," paid an eloquent tribute on behalf of the French nation, ending with the plea that "the sacrifice symbolised by the body of the Unknown Soldier should serve to keep the two countries united in victory as they were in war." Lieutenant General Sir George MacDonogh, speaking in French, replied on behalf of King George. Their audience included General Weygand and many other senior French and British officers. As the White Ensign was slowly lowered to half-mast, the bearers who had accompanied the coffin from the castle then carried it up the gangway of the destroyer HMS *Verdun*. The bo'sun's mate piped the coffin on board with the honours normally accorded to an admiral, as sailors and marines stood at attention at the rails, presenting arms with rifles and fixed bayonets, polished till they gleamed even in the dull grey light. The ship's motto, *"On ne passe pas,"* emblazoned on the afterdeck, had been uttered by Marshal Pétain to rally and inspire his troops at Verdun. The ship had been sent by the Admiralty as a special tribute to the French people and the valour of their armies at Verdun—the symbol of French resistance during the war and the site of three-quarters of a million French and German deaths.

Marshal Foch stood at the foot of the gangway, gazing up at the coffin as it was laid on "the quarterdeck aft in front of the superstructure," and covered in wreaths of white lilies, roses and chrysanthemums. Some were so large that it took four soldiers to lift them. As the ship put out to sea a few minutes before noon, Foch, "advancing almost to the water's edge, stood alone saluting his dead comrade." A guard of Bluejackets fired a volley over the coffin, the noise drowned by a simultaneous, thunderous salute from the guns of the French shore batteries. The echoes had barely died away when HMS *Verdun* disappeared into the thick haze hanging over the water.

While the British Unknown Warrior was being selected and transported to his homeland, the French *poilu inconnu* was also being chosen and taken to Paris. At dusk on 9 November the last of eight plain oak coffins was brought into the great fortress of Verdun. Only eight bodies had been exhumed from battlefields from the Belgian frontier to the Vosges instead of the nine originally planned, because it was impossible to distinguish French from German bodies in one particularly shell-ravaged area. "The bodies were so closely intermingled that the officer in charge of the work of exhumation decided it would be unsafe to disinter a body there as the honor of burial beneath the Arc de Triomphe might quite as likely be afforded to a former enemy soldier as to a gallant *poilu*." The French military authorities refused to divulge the area in question, but some suspected it was Verdun itself.

"Military honours and the roll of muffled drums were accorded to each of the 'Unknown Dead' as the bodies were borne down a long underground passage into the heart of the citadel where in a long, low room, the coffins were placed, covered by flags and surrounded by flickering wax candles." From dawn to dusk, French people filed past the coffins in this subterranean chamber, the profound silence broken only by muffled sobs and the soft, whispering rustle of flowers as they were laid before the dead—so many that a mound of white chrysanthemums soon covered the coffins. On 9 November, Private Auguste Tain, the son of an infantryman killed at Verdun, placed a bouquet of flowers on one of the coffins. It was taken to Paris to be buried beneath the Arc de Triomphe, with an eternal flame lit over the grave.

An escort of six destroyers from the Atlantic Fleet had accompanied HMS *Verdun* across the Channel, three in line abreast ahead and another three in line abreast astern. They sailed with flags at half-mast and "stole through the last few miles so silently and solemnly that one could compare the measured progress only with the slow march of troops in a funeral procession." At about one o'clock they arrived off Dover, where the day was "admirably suited to the occasion. The sky was one solid sheet of grey, the cliffs, castle and town of Dover took their colour from the sky and the sea was so calm that it only reflected the grey of the clouds." The *Verdun* remained at anchor off Dover for two hours, but soon after three o'clock the ship "steamed slowly along the entire length of the sea wall" in order to enter by the eastern entrance, "by which many of the hospital ships used to bring back to England our wounded warriors." Well over a million wounded men had passed through Dover in the course of the war. The escort of destroyers turned back at that point, leaving the *Verdun* to steam into harbour alone. She was greeted by a nineteen-gun salute from the ramparts of the castle, a tribute normally accorded only to soldiers of the rank of Field Marshal.

Almost all the town's shops and businesses had closed to allow their workers to witness the arrival of the Unknown Warrior and groups of people were visible lining the tops of the white cliffs to east and west, while every vantage point around the harbour was packed. There was not a ripple on the water inside the harbour and the *Verdun* bore down on the Admiralty Pier "without a sound. At first all that could be seen was a dark mass with a lighter speck in the stern where the coffin stood covered in wreaths. The ship that took King Arthur to his rest was not blacker or more silent." As soon as the *Verdun* had docked, six warrant officers from the Royal Navy, Royal Marines, the Army and the Royal Air Force carried the coffin ashore while the bo'suns' pipes played "a mournful dirge."

Sir George MacDonogh led a procession including officers of the Dover garrison and the Mayor and Corporation of the city, following the coffin past a guard of honour to the Marine railway station one hundred yards away. The carriage of the South-Eastern and Chatham Railway in which the coffin was placed was "lined with purple drapery" and the sides decorated with intertwined flowers, laurel and rosemary, while a huge arrangement of white chrysanthemums stood at either end. "Two tiny electric lights shed a purple glow over the coffin." The roof of the carriage had been painted white to help spectators to identify it during the journey to London. The same carriage had been used to transport the bodies of Edith Cavell and Captain Charles Fryatt on their last journeys. Cavell, a nurse at a Brussels hospital, was charged by the Germans with aiding the escape of 200 Allied prisoners of war, and was executed on 12 October 1915, an act that caused outrage around the world and led to a significant hardening of American public opinion against Germany. Charles Fryatt was the captain of the Great Eastern Railway steamer *Brussels*, plying between Harwich and the Hook of Holland. He became a British hero after trying to ram a marauding U-boat and was given an engraved cigarette case in tribute to his bravery. It proved to be his death warrant. Two months later his ship was captured by the Germans and he was taken prisoner. When they read the inscription on his cigarette case, he was promptly charged with being a *franc tireur*—a civilian who took up arms in breach of the rules of warfare. His execution on 27 July 1916 provoked another international outcry.

The huge wreaths, once more requiring four men to carry them, had also been brought from the *Verdun* and were taken to the station and loaded into the carriage with the coffin. The officer and fifteen other ranks of the Connaught Rangers who were to mount guard on the coffin during its journey to London travelled in the adjoining saloon car, with Sir George MacDonogh and his aide, and the two undertakers, Messrs. Noades and Sowerbutts, whose formal duties would end only when they delivered the casket "to the military upon its arrival at Victoria." The two coaches were attached to the rear of the evening Dover-London boat-train.

Over an hour passed before the train departed, during which time four sentries, one from each service, stood guard in the traditional stance of military mourning, heads bowed and weapons reversed. At ten to six the train pulled slowly out of Dover. It was a cold, wet and moonless November evening, but large crowds had gathered at every station along the route. At each one, the train halted for a few moments, allowing the watchers a brief glimpse of the coffin, before the train moved on, disappearing into its own clouds of steam and smoke. At Faversham, ex-servicemen completely filled the platform. "They carried at their head a Union Jack, surmounted by a wreath of bay leaves. Boy Scouts sounded the Last Post as the train steamed out of the station." There was an honour guard from the Bluejackets at Gillingham station and another from the Royal Warwickshire Regiment at Chatham. There the crowd poured through and over the barriers, spilling on to the platform and even climbing onto the train. The miles of trackside, bridges and crossings were also lined with people, and "every street corner and road running parallel with the line held groups . . . of bareheaded watchers, peering through the darkness and rain." The majority were women, "watching and silent, many dressed in deep mourning . . . Many an upper window was open and against the golden square of light was silhouetted clear cut and black the head and shoulders of some faithful watcher. In the London suburbs there were scores of homes with back doors flung wide, light flooding out, and in the garden, figures of men, women and children gazing at the great lighted train rushing past."

The train entered Victoria Station at eight that evening, the carriage carrying the Unknown Warrior "brilliant with light and radiant with white flowers." High above, the smoke and steam "eddied and billowed round the arc lamps" in the station roof. A huge crowd was waiting and for a few moments there was chaos and something close to panic as people pushed forward, some spilling over and round the temporary barriers. A few even tried to clamber onto the engine and carriages, before police restored order and pushed the crowds back behind the barriers. The two carriages were uncoupled from the boat-train and shunted round to Platform 8, by the station exit into Buckingham Palace Road. The platform edges had been newly whitened and sand had been scattered along the length of it, ready for the morrow. From that same platform, countless men had set off for war. Some returned there in leave trains or hospital trains; many others had never come back at all.

As the train came to rest, there were no formalities other than a brief exchange of salutes between Sir George MacDonogh and his aide, and the Guards officer taking over responsibility for the coffin, but "by stripping this hour of every device of parade, they made it quick with such tragedy and such wonder as wrung the heart. Men wept as they saw the double railway carriage . . . they knew not why they wept but the great gloomy arches of the station and the rows on rows of white faces pressed to the barriers were a setting which might not be denied . . . All the while, the lights in the compartment where the dead soldier lay, glowed steadily on masses of exquisite blossoms, roses and white chrysanthemums, piled up to the windows." The wreaths were removed from the train and taken to the Jerusalem Chamber at Westminster Abbey in preparation for the next day's ceremonies, but the casket remained in the carriage overnight, watched over by a double guard of sentries from the 1st Battalion, Grenadier Guards, who stood motionless with arms reversed and heads bowed.

24

THE GREAT SILENCE

The night of 10–11 November 1920 was cold and mist crept from the river to shroud the Cenotaph and the abbey, but it thinned and lifted with the dawn and watery sunlight was filtering through the sooty glass roof of the station as the commuter trains began arriving at Victoria, where Platform 8 remained cordoned off. Crowds had begun to form outside the station as soon as it was light. At eight o'clock that November morning—a time of year long associated with the dead—the first contingents of troops and ex-servicemen began to assemble and at nine-fifteen the gun-carriage, pallbearers and the firing party that would precede the coffin formed up between Platforms 7 and 8, alongside the funeral carriage. Following them, assembling at one- or two-minute intervals, were the four massed bands of the Guards, Army, Air Force and Navy.

At nine-twenty the bearers—eight men of the Grenadier Guards—entered the carriage and draped the casket with the Union flag that David Railton had used as an altar cloth at Vimy Ridge, High

Wood, Ypres, Messines, Cambrai and Béthune, and as "the covering, often the only covering, of the slain as they were laid to rest. For all I know, it may have been used in France or Belgium when the actual 'Unknown Warrior' was slain . . . it is literally tinged with the lifeblood of fellow Britons." "Once at least it lay on the grass floor of a tent with the 'Cup of Salvation' and the bread of Communion resting upon it, for the strengthening of one who underwent sentence of death at dawn." A steel helmet, side arms and a webbing belt were placed upon the coffin, and the bearers then carried it outside and secured it on the waiting gun-carriage. The cortège was drawn up in accordance with the instructions issued "for order of precedence of Mourners on the March . . . 1. Firing Party. 2. Massed Bands, Pipes and Drums. 3. Gun Carriage and Pall Bearers. 4. Bearers. 5. Members of Royal Navy, Army and RAF—six abreast (two officers, flanked by two NCOs, flanked by two privates). 6. Ex-soldiers and sailors, four abreast, closed up." The ranks of soldiers stretched the length of the platform and back again, and right across the concourse. They stood at attention, as silent as the watching crowds, awaiting the signal to move off.

There was a pause in which the silence grew deeper and more oppressive, and even the faint dry rustle of fallen leaves in the gutters was audible, and then, at nine-forty that morning, a battery of nineteen guns stationed in Hyde Park fired a salute, while a detachment of the Household Cavalry, "detailed by Silver Stick in Waiting," kept the ground. Once more, the honours paid to the Unknown Warrior were those due to a Field Marshal. At the distant rumble of the guns, like some fading echo from the battlefield on which he died, the Unknown Warrior began his final journey through the streets of London. There was a roll on the drums of the massed bands, followed by the first chords of Chopin's "Funeral March," and "the simplest, but most impressive procession ever seen in London" began to move off. "There were no trappings of State ceremonial, no panoply of gorgeous uniforms, no cavalcade of horsemen . . . no waving flags or banners; the only flag in the long procession was the soiled and war-worn Union Jack which covered the unknown hero's coffin."

The cortège emerged from the western arch of the station into the sunlight of a perfect autumn morning, a touch of frost in the air and a blue sky veiled by the last of the morning mist that formed a halo around the sun. The air was so still that the flags at half-mast hung limp around their flagpoles and the columns of smoke from the chimneys of the surrounding houses rose in perfect vertical lines. "The Unknown

Warrior, in his daydreams in France, may have pictured his homecoming to himself, fancying how England would look on the day that he came back to it. If he did so—and who did not?—he never could have imagined a more lovely English day than the day of his homecoming. If he was a Londoner, he could not have wished to see his city looking more beautiful."

The crowds lining the route heard the continuing thunder of the guns firing the salute, "punctuating the silence and making the time of waiting more poignant. There was the sound of an order given and the Guardsmen lining the road very slowly and with an impressive accuracy of timing, reversed their arms and stood with heads bowed over them. Then faint and far away at first, then gradually nearer, with a slow, solemn throb, came the sound of the drums. Next the wail of the pipes. Now all heads were being bared . . . then came four mounted policemen, reining in their horses." Following them was the firing party and the bands of the four regiments of Foot Guards, marching in slow time, and behind them came the pipes and drums of the Scots Guards, their drums all encased in black. Then, with a space before and behind it, came the casket, drawn on the gun-carriage pulled by six horses, their jet-black coats glistening. The sun-faded crimson, white and blue of the union flag draped over the coffin was almost the only flash of colour in the whole of that sombre city. Twelve distinguished pallbearers—four Admirals of the Fleet: Sir Hedworth Meux, Earl Beatty, Sir Charles Madden and Sir Henry Jackson; four Field Marshals: Sir Henry Wilson, Earl Haig, Viscount French and Lord Methuen; three Generals: Lord Byng, Lord Horne and Albert Gatliff; and Air Marshal Sir Hugh Trenchard—accompanied the gun-carriage.

They were followed by serving troops from the Army, Navy and Air Force, all wearing dress uniform with a black crêpe mourning band around the arm, and lastly a contingent of ex-servicemen in sombre civilian clothes. The original plan for the ceremony had not included any representation by veterans, but the four major ex-servicemen's organizations had then requested that 400 to 500 be allowed to join the funeral procession, and this, coupled with a warning from another quarter that if they were excluded, "unrest among ex-servicemen would seize the opportunity to show its hand," was enough to induce a change of heart. The veterans, marching behind the uniformed seamen, soldiers and airmen, formed part of "a long river of men that changed in colour from dark blue to turbid yellow and brown and to slate colour and at last was all flecked with grey and black . . . As the river wound slowly along the road between its two black banks, the sound of the drums and the pipes grew fainter and fainter again in the distance. When the civilians passed, even the solemn thud, thud, of the drum had ceased altogether. It seemed symbolic of the fact that these men were serving no longer. The drum called them no more and, knowing that they had done their duty, they walked on in silence." The entire cortège took well over ten minutes to pass.

The procession slow-marched through Grosvenor Gardens and up Grosvenor Place, passing "between ranks, thousands strong, of silent people . . . who crowded pavements, roofs and windows, and flowed in dense, packed masses up side-streets and every open space." The majority were women, "packed together on the pavements, fatigued but bravely enduring. Wreaths large and small were clutched in trembling hands . . . The charwoman rubbed shoulders with the delicately nurtured lady of the West End mansion, the youthful hospital nurse with the pallid worker of the slums, the faded mothers from mean streets with prosperous suburban wives. All were brought together in bonds of sorrow and pride and sympathy, and each looked upon the last slow, triumphal journey of the Unknown with the tender speculation that only a woman could feel about the moving mystery of his identity."

At Hyde Park Corner, the massed, silent crowds lining the sweeping curve round to the Wellington Arch were in vivid contrast to the rumbling everyday traffic passing along Piccadilly and Knightsbridge. They watched as the procession moved on, passing down Constitution Hill and along the Mall—overlooked by the balcony of the German Embassy. If the German Chargé d'Affaires, Dr. Friedrich Sthamer, watched the procession, he must have done so with very mixed feelings. The cortège moved on to Admiralty Arch and Charing Cross, before turning into Whitehall. As the crowds waited, the silence was overpowering, almost suffocating. The "Dead March" from *Saul* sounded muted, and even the rhythmic slow tread of marching boots was muffled by the fresh sand that had been scattered on every road. From a high vantage point, a few black-clad figures could still be seen hurrying across St. James's Park towards Whitehall. "Very tiny and pathetic those figures looked . . . as they hurried across the road carrying some flowers done up in a piece of newspaper and then were swallowed up in the crowd on the other side."

The entire two-and-a-half-mile route was lined with troops—including a contingent from Alec Reader's former division, the 47th (London)—and behind them, every inch of the way, stood the countless thousands of people, all dressed in mourning black, the men standing bareheaded in the November cold. Among them were pilgrims from all over England, Scotland, Wales and Ireland, from every country of the Empire, and from all the other Allied nations, including France, Belgium and the United States. Each of them, like almost everyone else in that vast throng, was there in memory of a husband, son, friend or lover, lost in the Great War, whose last resting place remained unknown. Among them stood David Railton, the ribbon of the Military Cross upon his cassock.

Most of the crowds ten and twenty deep around Whitehall and Westminster Abbey were there by invitation only, chosen by ballot from the millions of bereaved mothers, fathers and wives. Their tickets were "personal," though they could be given to another member of the close family if the chosen individual was unable to attend. It was "a point of honour, however, that the ticket should not be transferred outside the family." The remainder of the crowd had flooded in at eight-fifteen that morning when the barriers were briefly opened and the streets around Whitehall closed to traffic. Most had queued since dawn and many all night; even some of them were to be disappointed. "When it was considered that the area allotted to the spectators was full," the barriers were closed again and the disappointed crowds locked out were advised to "make their next attempt at 2 p.m., the approximate time at which the barriers would again be opened."

All stood in utter stillness as the funeral procession moved slowly towards the new Cenotaph, "freed at last from scaffolding and tarpaulins," but still shrouded in giant Union flags. Only the sounds of horses' hooves, the creak and rattle of the gun-carriage bearing the coffin and the measured tread of the soldiers' slow-march broke the silence. At precisely ten minutes to eleven, the gun-carriage drew to a halt. King George, wearing the uniform of a Field Marshal and standing at the north end of the Cenotaph, stepped forward and placed a wreath of bay leaves and blood-red roses on the coffin—poppies were not to be adopted as the symbol of the war dead for another twelve months. The wreath was inscribed in his own hand "In proud memory of those who died unknown in the Great War. 'As unknown and yet well-known; as dying, and behold they live,'" a text from one of St. Paul's Epistles. The King reached up and, in an almost cursory way, pushed the wreath one-handed onto the coffin, gave a brief salute and then turned his back on it as he walked away.

Among the vast, hushed crowd stood a small, slight woman,

dressed all in black, her greying hair pinned under a black bonnet. She was forty-three, but with her lined, careworn face and her hollow eyes, she could have passed for sixty. Her name was Rose Reader, and in her hand she carried a wreath of laurel and the last of the summer's roses from her garden. It bore a far simpler inscription: "My Alec, Rest In Peace." For Rose, as for countless others, the burial of the Unknown Warrior, including all the traditional mourning rites, would stand for the funeral that she had been denied for her own son.

The massed bands then struck up the hymn "O God, Our Help in Ages Past," but it appeared that only the two abbey choirs stationed outside the Home Office on the west side of Whitehall sang the words. The Archbishop of Canterbury then rose to his feet and said the Lord's Prayer. Once more it appeared that few other than the choristers joined him; the rest of the vast crowds remained hushed and still. The long silence that followed was broken as Big Ben began to strike the eleventh hour of the eleventh day of the eleventh month. At the first stroke, the King turned to face the Cenotaph and, by a touch on a button, released the veiling flags. One fell to the ground, while the other caught and had to be jerked free by a scurrying official. "The memorial which authority caused to be created for a temporary occasion but which the nation, with one voice, demanded should be made permanent on its original site, stood revealed in simple grandeur."

The last stroke of eleven reverberated and then faded into the deepest silence any there had ever heard. "Nobody who stood in Whitehall during the two minutes in which the Metropolis stilled the beating of its mighty heart, will ever forget the scene or the sensation it evoked." "The complete suspension of all normal business, work and locomotion throughout the British Empire" was now in place, and the crowd, the city and the whole nation was stilled. There was no noise of traffic, no voices; nothing and nobody moved in the whole of that vast imperial capital. The central telephone switchboard later reported that not a single telephone call was made anywhere in London. The Lutine Bell silenced the 2,000 members of Lloyds of London, and the Stock Exchange ceased trading. Courts suspended their hearings—in one, a prisoner in the dock who had served in France, Egypt and Mesopotamia, and won the DCM and the Croix de Guerre, sprang "smartly to attention between the warders standing on either side of him"—and even prisoners in their cells came to attention and bowed their heads. Market-porters at Billingsgate, Covent Garden and Smithfield, and railway workers and passengers at all the mainline termini, paused and stood at attention, and ticket offices on the Underground closed. At Harrods the start of the two-minute silence was heralded by the ringing of the store's fire alarms, while Selfridge's employed a corps of buglers to play the Last Post.

The schedule of operations at the Middlesex Hospital had been arranged so that none was in progress at eleven o'clock, and surgeons, nurses and hospital porters all stood together in silence, with heads bowed. At the Crystal Palace, where the original temporary Cenotaph, installed as part of the War Museum, was decorated with flowers and flags, 2,000 ex-servicemen sitting examinations for government clerkships stood to attention when six bells (eleven o'clock) was struck on the ship's bell from HMS *Implacable*. The silence at the Zoological Gardens was "more strange and impressive because it was broken only by the familiar voices of the animals," and at Piccadilly Circus, "where traffic was doubled owing to diversion from The Strand, a man standing on the fountain started the Silence by doffing his hat. In ten seconds only the throbbing of one or two motor engines could be heard."

The scene was repeated in every town and village in the land. The firing of maroons or the ringing of church bells signalled the start of the silence. Pedestrians halted in midstride and bowed their heads, and policemen stood ready to stop all traffic, though most drivers had already pulled to the side of the road and switched off their engines. The driver of a large touring car, who ignored the two-minute silence and overtook a line of stationary traffic in Bromley in Kent, was booed by ex-soldiers standing to attention, and the offices of the *Workers' Dreadnought* newspaper were invaded by an angry mob after voices "singing, dancing and banging tin cans" were heard coming from there during the silence. The offenders were given "a good trouncing."

Such incidents were rare as the silence was almost universally observed. The naval dockyards of Devonport and Rosyth fell silent, the looms of Lancashire cotton mills were stilled and mill-workers, cotton fibres clinging like snow to their hair and clothes, spilled into the mill-yards and streets. Some 50,000 people crammed Albert Square in Manchester, where "mechanics in dungarees, working men in their working clothes and mill-girls with shawls over their heads, jostled well-to-do merchants and their clerks."

At New Street Station in Birmingham, the London and Glasgow expresses due out at eleven were delayed, "their passengers either standing up in the compartments or lining the platform"; the Cornish Riviera express halted near Taplow, and the Irish Mail near Crewe. "A quiet which could be almost felt, came over Bradford. All vehicular traffic came to a standstill, the raucous sound of the motor horn ceased to jar, the clatter of horses' feet stopped and the trams were stationary. In the crowd, women quietly wept as memories of dear ones rushed upon them, and many a man found it difficult to hide his emotions as the two minutes ticked slowly by."

At the Coal and Shipping Exchange in Cardiff, "the event was reverently observed and the members sang the *'Doxology.'*" In Sheffield, a "rocket-bomb" signalled the start of the silence "and immediately all traffic ceased, works were stilled and masses of people who had gathered in the centre of the city stood motionless." In Edinburgh the silence was signalled by the firing of a gun from the castle ramparts and "the whole city was hushed . . . trams, traincars and vehicles of all kinds came to a stand wherever they happened to be at the moment and the people in the streets . . . remaining still and reverentially uncovering or bowing their heads." Warships and Cunard liners on the high seas stopped their engines and the pilot of a Daimler Air-Express flying between Manchester and London shut off his engines and the plane glided while his four passengers stood at attention with bared heads. Even in Fenian Dublin, gripped by fervent republican and anti-British sentiment, the people seemed "to show all the reverence for the memory of the dead that could be expected of them in their present frame of mind. During the two minute silence, though most of them refrained from taking off their hats, they stood almost motionless while the tramway cars and other traffic halted and the flags on the principal buildings were half-masted."

The length and breadth of the British Isles, factories, mills, docks, mines and foundries stopped work, offices emptied, shopworkers left their tills unattended and joined the silent, motionless crowds in the streets. "More than any eloquence of tongue was this eloquence of silence." "All instruments ticking out messages to the world ceased to work. The world was for the time forgotten. The dead lived again."

There were similar scenes in almost every other combatant nation—in India, South Africa, Canada, Australia, New Zealand, in Belgium, Italy, Portugal and France. Only in the United States was it "business as usual . . . generally speaking, the observance of Armistice Day is conspicuous by its absence." And in New York, supporters of Sinn Fein burned a Union flag on Broadway, beat any Englishmen or suspected Englishmen they came across and fought running battles with police. A correspondent of the *New York Times* assured its readers that, whatever might be acceptable in New York, "Philadelphia would not stand for a second the tearing down of a flag of a nation that saved France and Belgium."

"The Great Silence," lasting two minutes—the first minute to commemorate those who fought and came home, the second to remember those who did not—was a tradition imported from South Africa. In the dark days of early 1918 when it appeared that the German offensive, Operation Michael, would sweep the Allies into the sea, the Bishop of Cape Town had suggested that a daily prayer should be offered both in commemoration of the war dead and for the safety of those still fighting. It became a daily custom that, after the firing of the midday gun, a bugler stationed on the balcony of the most prominent building in the city sounded the Last Post and when two minutes had elapsed, blew Reveille. "The Pause," as it became known, was "most solemn and inspiring . . . the effect almost magical—the city at prayer," in a "direct communion with the absent—the living and the dead."

Reuters' correspondent cabled a description to London and within a few weeks "the ceremony had been adopted in two English provincial towns and later by others, including towns in Canada and Australia." The South African leader, Sir Percy Fitzpatrick, also commended the idea to the Colonial Secretary, Lord Milner, and he enlisted the support of the King. A proposal to introduce the Great Silence to the Armistice Day commemorations was then discussed and agreed in the War Cabinet on 5 November 1919. "The advantage of the realisation by the nation of the magnitude of its deliverance from the great perils of the War outweighed the main objection that a precedent would be established which, in remote years . . . might conceivably prove inconvenient." Echoing this, the Transport Secretary commented that while all trains could be stopped on Armistice Day, just as they were for the funeral of Edward VII, he "would not promise to do it in every succeeding year until he saw what dislocation occurred."

Alongside such practical considerations, there were those who deplored the whole idea on principle. Evelyn Waugh predictably derided it as "a disgusting idea of artificial nonsense and sentimentality," while the *Daily Herald* attacked the whole commemoration. "Who organised this pageant? The people who prolonged the war and grew rich out of it and now dope the people emotionally." Peace could scarcely be said to have been achieved, when Ireland was in a ferment of armed rebellion, a British Expeditionary Force was fighting against the

Bolsheviks in Russia, RAF aircraft were bombing rebels in Iraq, and a British Army was still camped on the Rhine, while the Navy blockaded the German coast. In Ireland too, Fenian sympathizers treated the two-minute silence with some derision. A cartoon in the *Catholic Herald* showed a vicious British soldier attacking "Young Ireland," who asked his mother, "Will the brute never stop, Mother?" The answer was "Yes, my son. He will stop for two minutes on Armistice Day." Nonetheless, opponents of the Silence and of Armistice Day commemorations as a whole appeared to be a small minority. When "the hush came . . . there is nothing under heaven so full of awe as the complete silence of a mighty crowd." Almost all who witnessed it were deeply impressed and by the following year the new "tradition" was firmly established.

The silence at the Cenotaph was broken by eight buglers of the Brigade of Guards sounding the Last Post. As the echoes faded, the King, the Prime Minister and other dignitaries laid the first wreaths at the foot of the Cenotaph. Once more the King seemed almost impatient to be gone. He laid his wreath and, without even pausing to salute, turned his back and walked away. When the wreaths had been laid, the dignitaries paced behind the gun-carriage as it rumbled off towards Westminster Abbey, the Unknown Warrior's last resting place. King George, as chief mourner, took pride of place behind it, followed by the Prince of Wales, the Duke of York, Prince Henry, the Duke of Connaught and the Marquis of Milford Haven, all in full military uniform. The Archbishop of Canterbury, the Prime Minister and Ministers of State followed, with the rest of the funeral procession behind. Thousands of mourners trudged in their wake.

Those already assembled at the abbey watched as the choir moved in procession to the north porch, singing the hymn "Brief Life Is Here Our Portion." The singing grew fainter as they moved outside and then silence fell again. "There was no sound except the tolling of a bell until the words 'I am the resurrection and the life' floated to us." The bearers—NCOs of the Coldstream Guards—laid their rifles on the grass by the gates and lifted the casket from the gun-carriage. One forgot to remove his hat and, on a hissed prompt from an officer, snatched it off one-handed as he and the others bore the coffin shoulder-high through the north door of the abbey, and to the west end of the nave, passing between two lines of ninety-six men decorated for gallantry—four of the chosen one hundred were too ill to take their places—including seventy-four holders of the Victoria Cross, some in uniform, some in civilian clothes. The coffin was placed on the bars laid across the open grave, sited in front of the West Door, squarely "in the pathway of kings, for not a monarch can ever again go up to the altar to be crowned, but he must step over the grave of the man who died that his kingdom might endure."

George V took his place at the head of the grave, facing west, with the Princes, the Queen and "the other royal ladies" behind him. The Dean and the Archbishop of Canterbury faced him at the foot of the grave. Lloyd George stood to their left, in front of "row upon row of Cabinet ministers." If the royal family and the Prime Minister took centre stage among the mourners, the congregation was primarily composed of war widows and mothers who had lost sons in the Great War. Astonishingly this was at the behest of the patrician Lord Curzon, a man some felt to be obsessively concerned with rank and precedence, but who on this occasion insisted that "fashionable society be excluded" in favour of veterans of the armed forces and "the selected widows and mothers of those who had fallen, especially in the humbler ranks." There was no foreign representation. This was a private occasion "in which only the people of the British Empire should participate" and, despite the panoply of a full military funeral and the presence of the King and his ministers, for once, the King's subjects were to be given pride of place. The arrangements for Armistice Day were almost entirely of Curzon's devising and "for the only time in his career as a ceremonial impresario, Curzon had devised a ritual which caught and articulated a genuinely popular and deeply felt mood.

"A little band of about one hundred women in the Abbey received the most reverent attention. They had been selected for seats of honour because each had lost her husband and all her sons. Every woman in England so bereft who applied for a place got it . . . After the hundred had been seated, the next to be considered were those mothers who lost their only sons, or all their sons, and then came women who lost their husbands only." They were given positions in accordance with the price they had paid during the war, but the lesson from the Victory Day celebrations, when widows and mothers of dead soldiers had only been allocated seats after the Queen had personally intervened to express the hope that "the poor women will not be forgotten," had only been learned after a renewed press campaign.

The original plan for the ceremonies on Armistice Day 1920 had once more excluded war mothers and war widows. Tabloid newspapers then launched a ferocious assault, claiming that stuffed shirts and officials who had pushed pens while soldiers were "fighting and bleeding and dying" would fill the seats in Whitehall and the abbey when the Unknown Warrior went to his grave. "Irate and hysterical" women deluged the Ministry of Works with complaints, and questions were asked in Parliament, forcing the inclusion of widows and mothers. But it is noteworthy that the emphasis was entirely on widows and bereaved mothers, and no arrangements at all were made for bereaved fathers, other than the spaces allocated to MPs or members of the House of Lords who had lost either a son or a brother in the war. A girl who wrote that she had lost nine brothers killed or missing was also given a seat, as was a twelve-year-old boy who wrote, "The man in the coffin might be my daddy." "One hundred nurses wounded or blinded in the discharge of their duty" were also given places, and in all 8,000 tickets were issued for seats at the abbey or the Cenotaph.

The brief service, "the most beautiful, the most touching and the most impressive that in all its long eventful story, this island has ever seen," was conducted by Dean Ryle, his purple and gold-embroidered cape seeming almost tastelessly ostentatious at such a sombre gathering. Beethoven's "Equale for Trombones" was followed by the Twenty-third Psalm, "The Lord Is My Shepherd," and a lesson taken from the seventh chapter of the Book of Revelation. The bearers then stepped forward again and, during the singing of "Lead Kindly Light," they removed the Union flag, helmet and side arms from the casket and lowered it into the grave. Every eye in the abbey strained to catch a last glimpse of the great iron-bound coffin as it disappeared from sight forever.

As Dean Ryle recited the committal, "Earth to earth, ashes to ashes, dust to dust . . . ," the King scattered earth gathered from the battlefields out of a silver shell. It fell on the coffin with a soft, dry rattle. There were further prayers and the hymn "Abide with Me," and then the congregation sang Rudyard Kipling's Recessional, "God of Our Fathers." Originally "intended as a corrective to public rejoicing in Imperial power at the time of Queen Victoria's Diamond Jubilee . . . its performance at the burial of the Unknown Warrior . . . gave it a new significance." As they reached the closing lines—"Lest we forget, lest we forget"—"the great wave of feeling which that hymn always arouses could be felt surging through the whole congregation and, seen in many women and even some men, finding expression in tears."

Kipling's own son, John, had served with the Irish Guards and was posted missing in action at the Battle of Loos—one of 20,589 men

commemorated on the Loos Memorial to the Missing. His heartbro-
ken parents launched desperate attempts to find his body and give it a
proper burial, but John Kipling remained yet another of the war dead
with no known grave. His father is often seen as one of the most rigidly
conservative patriots and Empire loyalists, but the darkness of his
despair at the loss of his son had led him, like countless others, to question the cause and conduct of the war. In 1919 he published a bitter collection of verse, "Epitaphs of the War 1914–1918," lamenting the
needless loss of so many young men and questioning the basis on which
they had been sent to their deaths. He answered the rhetorical question
about the reason why they died with "because our fathers lied."

The Dean spoke the Blessing, then there was a pause and "from
somewhere far away in the great church, a scarcely audible whisper
began to steal upon us. It swelled with absolute smoothness until we
knew it for the roll of drums. The whole Abbey was full of the reverber-
ating roar and then it began to die away and died into a whisper so soft
that no one could say for certain when it stopped." The momentary
silence was broken by the pure silver notes of bugles echoing through
the cathedral. The Last Post was followed by the Long Reveille and as
the echoes faded, four sentries—one each from the Army, Navy, Air
Force and Marines—took up station at the four corners of the grave,
facing outwards and resting "on their arms reversed." The band of the
Grenadier Guards played Miller's "Grand Ceremonial March" and, as
the King and the other dignitaries passed out through the West Door
into the winter sunlight, the two lines of Victoria Cross holders began
to file past the grave. They were the first of millions who would do so.

As soon as the congregation had left, the great church was closed
for a few minutes. The grave was covered by "the Actors' Pall," given
by members of the Actors' Church Union in remembrance of their fellows who had died in the war, and David Railton's Union flag was
spread over it. The steel helmet, belt and side arms were placed on it,
together with a laurel wreath from the Dean, Chapter and staff of
Westminster Abbey, and one sent by the War Graves Inquiry Bureau
"composed of laurel collected from the ruined gardens of Ypres and the
cloisters of the cathedral." Four lit candles were also placed around the
grave, one at the head and foot and one at either side, and it was surrounded by low wooden barriers. The doors were then reopened to
allow the first of the endless queues of people waiting their turn to file
past the grave. They did so in two lines, parallel, unending streams
entering through the North Door, parting to pass either side of the

grave and reuniting as they exited through the West Door. "The Great Pilgrimage" had begun.

"No one could have foretold how surely the emblem to the glorious dead and the symbolic grave would capture the imagination of the people." It had been planned that the Cenotaph and the grave of the Unknown Warrior would be closed to the public almost at once, allowing just three days for mourners to visit the grave, but the response of the people, not only in London but throughout the country, forced a change of heart. During the war, Rolls of Service recording the names of those who had gone to war had been placed in public places in each community, often reinforced by small notices in the windows of individual houses. Roadside shrines, decorated with flowers, photographs and keepsakes, had also been set up throughout Britain to commemorate the dead during the war—just like the temporary mounds of cellophane-wrapped bouquets now routinely left at the death sites of car-crash victims.

The first such shrine was erected in Hackney in the spring or summer of 1916, and by the end of October of that year 250 had been established in London alone. The timing, during the Battle of the Somme, which had brought mourning into almost every British home, was by no means coincidental. Seeing an opportunity to proselytize, the churches—with the exception of hardline Protestants who objected to "idolatry"—actively supported the creation of shrines to the dead, and a widely publicized visit by Queen Mary to the Hackney shrines added further impetus. They served a dual purpose, acting as memorials to the dead while also offering the superstitious hope of protection for the living still serving at the Front, and "the roughest treat them with respect and take off their hats as they pass them." Commercially made shrines soon went on sale; a design was patented in August 1916, including a triple frame for names and photographs, and holders in which flowers and small flags could be placed.

The Cenotaph and the Grave of the Unknown Warrior were now to fulfil the same purpose for the entire nation. As Lloyd George wrote to Lutyens on 17 November 1920, "The memorial . . . has become a national shrine, not only for the British Isles, but also for the whole Empire." "The Cenotaph, it may be said, is the token of our mourning as a nation; the Grave of the Unknown Warrior is the token of our mourning as individuals." When Alderman Arthur Willey later received a letter from an anonymous "well-known Leeds man" suggesting that a Leeds Unknown Soldier should be retrieved and reinterred in the same manner as the Unknown Warrior in Westminster Abbey, there was no local support for the idea at all. The Unknown Warrior had already come to represent all the unknown soldiers, whatever their origins.

He was not merely a symbol of all the dead. The very anonymity of the body buried in Westminster Abbey allowed every person, if only in the privacy of their own thoughts, to assume a personal link with the Unknown Warrior, and many thousands of grieving people—perhaps even all of them—convinced themselves that their missing loved one really could be buried in the abbey. "One elderly man said, 'I lost two sons out there, but the other . . .' and the implied, though unuttered words, 'may be here' merely expressed the secret thoughts of many more." "The mystery as to whose son he was makes him the son and brother of us all." Elizabeth Bowes-Lyon, later Her Majesty Queen Elizabeth the Queen Mother, laid her bridal bouquet on the grave of the Unknown Warrior before walking to the altar for her wedding to the future George VI. Her tribute was in memory of her brother, the Honourable Fergus Bowes-Lyon, a captain in the Black Watch, who had been killed at Loos on 27 September 1915. Like so many hundreds of thousands of soldiers, his final resting place was also unknown. Who is to know she was not laying the flowers on his grave? For some, the intensity of emotion aroused by the sight of the grave of the Unknown Warrior and the Cenotaph was too much to bear. One man committed suicide that night; the coroner concluded that the scenes at the Cenotaph had preyed on his mind.

25

THE PEOPLE'S PILGRIMAGE

As soon as the ceremony at the Cenotaph was over, the thousands of people who had lined the streets began to queue to lay their flowers and wreaths. The first were "two legless soldiers on tricycles." Next came hundreds of policemen, and several lorries full of badly wounded men. Close behind them was a column of unemployed ex-servicemen who had been refused permission to join the main procession, but were permitted to march past it at a time when—or so it was no doubt hoped—most public and press attention would have shifted to the burial service at the abbey. They marched with the same solemn, respectful demeanour as those who came before and after them, and in doing so won some sympathy even from sections of the Conservative press. As *The Times* noted in its editorial the next day, "a quarter of a million of the comrades of the Unknown Warrior are still seeking employment." There was confirmation of that in the personal columns of its own pages, where several unemployed ex-officers had placed advertisements, seeking work.

The unemployed, the bereaved and all the rest joined the massive crowds trying to pay their respects at the Cenotaph and the abbey. There were two huge queues in Trafalgar Square, one twenty deep and stretching down Northumberland Avenue to the Victoria Embankment and then back along Northumberland Avenue to the Strand, the other reaching from the Admiralty Arch to Piccadilly Circus. There was another queue down Horse Guards Avenue and yet another on Horse Guards Parade on the other side of Whitehall. "There were many elderly people, old women so frail-looking that one wondered at their hardiness, but full of spirit and a determination that, with the help of their friends, they would reach the abbey. Many babies in arms and young children too had been brought by their mothers to take part in the nation's tribute to the Glorious Dead with whom their fathers were numbered." Most of them had brought wreaths or bunches of flowers to place at the base of the Cenotaph or on the Warrior's grave. One wreath "put down by a still young-looking woman . . . bore the inscription: 'To my only child Peter, aged nineteen. Thou shall not return to me, but I shall go to thee' . . . Another bore the words: 'To Jack, from his ever faithful wife. I know not where they have laid him, but I shall see him when the day breaks.' " Many blind ex-soldiers were among the lines filing past the Cenotaph. They saluted when they reached the monument and "their guides touched their arms and said 'Now.' "

Even in the City, where business had resumed immediately after the Great Silence, men wore "a subdued air . . . almost every person wore black. The boisterous laughter and rattle of light conversation which usually mark the luncheon hour in the restaurants were absent. Throughout the day women in deep black were to be seen in bus, in car, and on foot, on their way to the Cenotaph with wreaths—in many cases the humble tributes of the very poor." As well as individuals, many wreaths were also laid on behalf of regiments, businesses, trade unions, clubs, societies and other organizations. Some attempts were made to regulate these tributes—"The authorities wish to draw attention to the space which would be saved round the Cenotaph if bunches of flowers were brought instead of wreaths . . . it is particularly requested that no one should linger by the Cenotaph"—but such petty constraints were swept aside.

So many wreaths and bouquets were laid—100,000 in the space of the first three days—that the base of the Cenotaph was completely buried by an enormous mound rising ten feet up the sides of the memorial, covering the steps surrounding it and spilling out into the roadway on all sides. "Now only the sheer sides of the Cenotaph can be seen, and floral offerings stretch away from the obscured base like spume left on the sands by a mighty wave." There had never been an outpouring of public emotion on this scale and nothing like it has ever been seen again—the great state funeral of Queen Victoria, the later burials of George V and Winston Churchill, and even the public displays of grief at the death of Diana, Princess of Wales, were modest in comparison to the overwhelming emotional response to the burial of the Unknown Warrior.

The mass of humanity choked even the broadest thoroughfares and it took most people several hours, shuffling forward a few inches at a time, to reach the Cenotaph or the Unknown Warrior's grave. "One white-haired old woman who joined the queue in Northumberland Avenue at noon, did not reach the Cenotaph until half-past five." For many, "after long railway journeys, upset by the sorrows of the day and hours of waiting in the queues, the strain was too severe . . . many hundreds gave up, while of those who refused to give in, a large proportion" laid their wreaths or flowers at the Cenotaph and then abandoned the attempt to reach the Unknown Warrior's grave, since another queue, four-deep, stretched all the way from the Cenotaph to Westminster Abbey.

Even so, at least 40,000 people had passed through the abbey before the doors were closed at eleven o'clock that night, an hour later than the scheduled time, and tens of thousands more were locked outside. There were still long queues at midnight, and huge numbers of people continued to visit the Cenotaph throughout the night. In Whitehall, where "the whiteness of the Cenotaph gleams by day and night," "the vast sweep of the road was almost silent save for the ceaseless murmur of footsteps. Under the brilliant glare of the lamps that were softened by the foggy air, the long, dark lines of people stretched from Trafalgar Square to the Cenotaph, from whose base they could be seen vanishing in the distance, two narrow lines of slowly moving people separated by a wide pathway on which stood here and there vague figures of policemen on horseback."

The hosts of people also sought any memento or keepsake they could find. Two Army officers, Major Lionel Guest and Captain Merriman, had made sound recordings of the burial service, the first recordings ever permitted inside Westminster Abbey. The hastily pressed copies were then sold on the streets for seven shillings and sixpence (37.5p) each. The *Daily Mirror*'s special edition of 12 November sold almost 2 million copies, the highest ever sale for a single issue. Those scratched records and yellowing newspapers must have been kept and treasured for decades in thousands of homes throughout Britain. Although the general mood was one of solemn commemoration, there was no shortage of takers for a fancy-dress Victory Ball at the Albert Hall that night, where 2,000 people dined and danced to the music of the Southern Syncopated Orchestra. Had there been a prize for the most tasteless costume, the woman "dressed as an aeroplane" would have been a prime contender.

The queues at the Cenotaph and the abbey were just as long on the Friday and the pilgrimage went on throughout the weekend, with Saturday bringing huge numbers of people from outside London. "Indeed those who took part in the first two days' tribute were obviously but a small advance guard of the enormous army of silent mourners of all ages and of all classes . . . who have hungered for such an opportunity . . . thousands of poor, homely folk bereaved by the war—folk who have never been in London before—have undertaken long journeys for the purpose of joining the Great Pilgrimage."

They came in unending streams from the West Country, East Anglia, the Midlands, the North, Wales, Scotland and Ireland—from almost every community throughout the land. So wholesale had been the losses in the war that the handful of fortunate hamlets and tiny villages whose sons had all returned became known as "the thankful villages," but there were pitifully few of them. The opposite pole was represented by the thirty men from a single street of sixty houses in Altrincham, Cheshire, who were killed in the war. Several of their wives and families were among the mourners on the Great Pilgrimage. A woman whose husband was killed on the same day that she had given birth to their first child, a son, had also come to lay a wreath. A one-legged man on crutches, his face scarred by jagged shrapnel wounds, stood next to his mother, the only one of her six sons to survive the war. There, too, was Private Thomas Pestorisk of the Scottish Rifles. So badly wounded that he was "invalided out of the Service," he was "the youngest of nine brothers who joined the army and he has lost eight brothers in the war."

Two wounded soldiers had walked sixty miles to lay their wreaths. Both had lost brothers in the war. There were many men in wheelchairs, "some of whom had lost both legs." On one of their wreaths was the inscription "Lest we forget." "One policeman spoke of old women who had come from remote country villages to pay homage to the dead.

One old lady came from the far north of Scotland. She carried a bunch of withered flowers, and told me with tears in her eyes that the flowers came from a little garden which her boy had planted when he was only six." Thousands of football supporters from Blackburn, Blackpool and Sheffield, in London to support their teams that afternoon, spent the morning queueing to pass the Cenotaph.

Saturday was also "the children's day. Little ones of all ages, some war orphans, others, more fortunate, accompanied by their fathers, who have survived the great struggle, placed their simple tribute at the foot of the National Memorial." "There were little ones in their mother's arms who had never known their daddy; there were boys and girls who had only experienced during a fleeting ten days' leave all that daddy meant to them; and there were older children who remembered him before he donned the King's uniform. But each mother told her child that daddy had now returned, and hundreds of these children placed a simple bouquet at the foot of the National Monument." Among them were the orphans of fallen City and Metropolitan police, who each "laid at the base of the Cenotaph a handful of flowers 'For Daddy.' " A very small boy, seeing the carpet of flowers and wreaths as he paused to lay a small plant among them, "brought tears to the eyes even of policemen standing by and . . . caused a woman who heard him to burst out in sobs. 'Oh Mummy,' he cried. 'What a lovely garden my Daddy's got.' "

It rained steadily throughout the day, but that had no effect on the gathering queues, which lengthened even more as the day went on, and the pilgrims, though many of them were carrying children in their arms, "waited with the utmost patience." The mountain of flowers and wreaths grew ever larger and "the workmen of the Office of Works were busy during Saturday night, arranging the wreaths in order to secure the best effect possible." On the Sunday, the queues extended even further, reaching "proportions which indicated that probably the greatest pilgrimage had begun." The queue of people was reported to have stretched for seven miles and police estimated that 100,000 people had already passed the Cenotaph by noon. Many thousands more tried and failed to attend the ten o'clock service at Westminster Abbey, but joined the long lines queuing to pass the Unknown Warrior's grave during the brief intervals between services when the church was reopened to the public. One of those pilgrims left his or her own tribute on the flag covering the grave—the Mons Medal, the General Service Medal and the Victory Medal. "These eloquent symbols of gallantry could have found no more fitting resting place," and they were left undisturbed.

By Monday, 15 November, it was estimated that as many as a million and a half pilgrims had already filed past the Cenotaph and at least half a million had paid their respects at the grave of the Unknown Warrior. For four days Whitehall had been "one vast memorial to the dead. There was no sound but that of shuffling feet, as the mourners slowly advanced to the Cenotaph." On the Monday morning traffic again began to move along Whitehall, but as buses passed the Cenotaph the drivers slowed out of respect and their passengers stood and removed their hats—a habit that endured until the Second World War. Despite the traffic, the great pilgrimage still continued from early morning to midnight, with two columns of people moving slowly up the middle of the road, between the streams of vehicles. "The official mourning had finished but the tribute of the people steadily went on," and "already 100,000 wreaths have been laid." A vanload of wreaths from Drury Lane, where all the tributes from the London theatres had been gathered, was also brought to the Cenotaph that morning and "laid in the roadway" in front of the vast pyramid of flowers. Among them was a wreath bearing the inscription "In loving memory of my only boy, who enlisted at the age of thirteen and a half and was reported missing in the Battle of the Somme, July 1916, aged sixteen." He was far from the youngest to die—Private John Condon of the Royal Irish Regiment was just fourteen years old when he was killed. The oldest, Lieutenant Harry Webber of the South Lancashire Regiment, was sixty-eight.

The Dean had announced that the grave of the Unknown Warrior would be sealed after the abbey closed on the night of Wednesday, 17 November, "punctually at seven o'clock," and on the Tuesday and Wednesday the numbers visiting the grave redoubled. Even though the mourners filed past at the rate of one hundred a minute, "the queue always grew larger . . . only when the doors of the Abbey were to be closed did people begin to leave their places in order to return again today."

The numbers still visiting the grave persuaded the Dean to postpone the closure for one more day, until a quarter to four on the afternoon of 18 November. Once more, although the people queued six abreast and "passed through the Abbey at a quicker rate than on any preceding day," the queues again grew longer and longer. The closing of the abbey was postponed by a further fifteen minutes, but at four o'clock of a grey November afternoon, with dusk rapidly approaching, the great oak doors were closed and the still-lengthy queue of mourners turned away. At the very last moment a woman came to the Deanery, with a maple leaf that had been sent from Canada by a soldier who had won the Victoria Cross at Lucknow. "She asked that this be placed on the coffin before the grave was sealed up and her wish was carried out." The grave was duly filled that night with more soil from the battlefields and covered by a temporary slab of York stone with a gilded inscription:

A BRITISH WARRIOR WHO FELL IN THE GREAT WAR 1914–1918 FOR KING AND COUNTRY. GREATER LOVE HATH NO MAN THAN THIS.

Although the grave had now been closed, there was little reduction in the numbers wishing to file past it and the Cenotaph. On Sunday, 21 November, the abbey was open to pilgrims for only two hours, but in that time another 10,000 people visited the grave, while at half past three that afternoon the queue from the Cenotaph "stretched as far as the Horse Guards." The space enclosing the grave of the Unknown Warrior remained filled with "posies of flowers, with inscriptions denoting the sacrifice of precious lives," for almost a year afterwards, and in August 1921, a full nine months after Armistice Day, 300 to 400 wreaths a week were still being laid at the Cenotaph.

The flowers were cleared from the grave on 17 October 1921 when the United States of America conferred the Congressional Medal of Honor on the British Unknown Warrior, the greatest honour it was in its power to bestow, awarded only for actions performed "at the risk of life, above and beyond the call of duty." However, the honour threw the British establishment into confusion and almost led to a major diplomatic incident. The American Ambassador in London had presented a note to the Foreign Office on 24 August, informing them of the award. "Animated by the same spirit of comradeship in which we of the American forces fought alongside the Allies, we desire to add whatever we can to the imperishable glory won by the deeds of our allies and commemorated in part by this tribute to the unknown dead." He also notified them that General John J. Pershing would first visit Paris to award the Congressional Medal to the French *poilu inconnu* and would then travel on to London to make the award to Britain's Unknown Warrior. The presentation, the Ambassador concluded, would "further cement the friendly relations which have so long existed between His Majesty's government and the United States."

However, seven weeks later, on 10 October 1921, newspapers on both sides of the Atlantic were reporting that the General and the U.S. Embassy were "mystified by the silence of the British government," which had failed either to arrange a date for the ceremony or even to acknowledge the American offer. Pershing had arrived in France on 22 September and laid the Congressional Medal of Honor on the French Unknown Soldier's tomb on 2 October. He and the specially trained battalion from the American Forces on the Rhine that was also to form the guard of honour at the ceremony at Westminster Abbey had then been kept waiting in Paris for a further week, but still no reply had been received from the British War Office, "beyond a statement that such ceremonies usually take a long time to arrange."

The battalion was eventually despatched back to Coblenz and unfavourable comments from Paris were "prominently displayed in the American press," while the British attitude was the subject of "much hostile comment" in the U.S. Congress, reflecting the "unfriendly interpretation" that would be placed on the incident if it was not rapidly resolved. The best the British government could now offer by way of explanation was that "the rule regulating the acceptance of foreign decorations by British soldiers may conceivably require the untangling of an unknown quantity of red tape . . . American officials cannot refrain from pointing out that the fact that the medal was conferred by Act of Congress on behalf of the American people ought to have placed the decoration in a special category where ordinary rules and precedents do not apply."

The criticisms, and Pershing's announcement that he might not now have time to fit a visit to London into his schedule, led to a frenzy of activity in Whitehall and a humble statement within twenty-four hours, blaming "a muddle" between different government departments, though some attempt was also made to blame the U.S. Embassy because it had "failed to establish any connection between . . . the proposed visit to London of General Pershing and . . . the grant of the Congressional medal." This feeble excuse, lampooned in the British press as "a particularly tactless and stupid blunder" and "bureaucratic muddling and evasion of responsibility," was further undermined when Dean Ryle revealed that the first he had heard about the award to be made in the abbey of which he was custodian was when he read about it in the newspapers. The British statement went on to claim that the delay was not caused by any reluctance to accept the American honour, but rather by "difficult points of procedure" connected to the desire to make a simultaneous announcement of the reciprocal award that the King would make to the American Unknown Soldier on behalf of the British people.

The real source of the problem was George V. Despite Lloyd George's urging "very strongly that we shall be forced to strain a point and that no decoration but the VC [Victoria Cross] will suffice," the King flatly refused to consider it. He claimed that it would devalue an award that had only ever been given for conspicuous gallantry under enemy fire, and concluded with a disdainful dismissal of the American honour. "His Majesty considers that to compare the Victoria Cross, the highest military decoration in the world, as an equivalent to the Congress Medal, which has only now been struck and with no history behind it, is to lose sight of all proportion." His comment was not only offensive but inaccurate: Congressional Gold Medals had been awarded since 1776—the first recipient was George Washington—and the Congressional Medal of Honor had been created in 1861. The Victoria Cross had been introduced a mere five years earlier, in 1856.

On 11 October it was announced that an official explanation had at last been sent to General Pershing, but as late as 13 October, only four days before he was due to present the American medal, *The Times*, briefed by the palace, was still reporting that "some legislative action will be taken to authorise the creation of an equivalent British honour to the Congressional medal. It is quite certain that something unique will be presented" at a ceremony at Arlington Cemetery on Armistice Day. A change of heart then took place, with Lloyd George finally forcing the King's grudging acquiescence to the award of a Victoria Cross. On Monday, 17 October, the King sent U.S. President Warren G. Harding a telegram informing him that "I greatly wish [*sic*] . . . to confer on your Unknown Warrior our highest decoration for valour, the Victoria Cross." However, with further grating disdain, the King's private secretary, Lord Stamfordham, let it be known that His Majesty considered that a mere Military Cross "would be quite sufficient" for the Unknown Warrior of the Belgians.

On the same day, John J. Pershing, "the successor of Washington, Grant, Sherman and Sheridan as General of the Armies of the United States," was finally permitted to award the Congressional Medal of Honor to Britain's Unknown Warrior. He was escorted by his hand-picked battalion of 20 officers and 450 other ranks, recalled from Coblenz, and by a detachment of 25 officers and 50 sailors from the USS *Olympia*, diverted to Devonport before sailing on to Le Havre to collect the body of the American Unknown Soldier. The guard of honour was an impressive sight. "No man among the Americans was less than five feet eight inches in height and the first files were composed of giants over six feet." The troops from Coblenz "had their band and colours with them and wore their trench helmets painted with a large 'A' in a circle, to denote that they belonged to the Army of Occupation."

As he was driven from the American Embassy via the Mall and Whitehall to Westminster Abbey, "not the most direct route but it will give more people an opportunity of seeing the distinguished visitors," Pershing was cheered by densely packed crowds. Perhaps still inwardly seething, the King did not grace the occasion with his presence, but Lloyd George, Earl Haig and Winston Churchill were among the distinguished guests. To one observer "it seemed more than mere accident . . . that, just at the beginning of the ceremony, the sun should stream down in its natural gold through a window not yet painted, upon the Union Jack that was spread at the foot of the Unknown Warrior's grave."

Pershing spoke of the "overpowering emotion" he experienced on entering the abbey. "Distinguished men and women are here enshrined who, through the centuries, have unselfishly given their services and their lives . . . As they pass in memory before us, there is none whose deeds are more worthy, and none whose devotion inspires our admiration more than this Unknown Warrior." Stooping down, he then laid the medal, with its ribbon of watered blue silk, on the grave, "above the breast of the unknown hero beneath." Encased in a small frame of "old oak from the Abbey timbers," it still hangs on one of the pillars flanking the grave, "about seven feet from the ground." After leaving the abbey, Pershing also paused to lay a wreath at the foot of the Cenotaph.

On Armistice Day, 11 November 1921, the temporary stone marking the grave of Britain's Unknown Soldier was replaced by a new gravestone of black Tournai marble from Belgium. It was inscribed:

BENEATH THIS STONE RESTS THE BODY OF A BRITISH WARRIOR UNKNOWN BY NAME OR RANK, BROUGHT FROM FRANCE TO LIE AMONG THE MOST ILLUSTRIOUS OF THE LAND AND BURIED HERE ON ARMISTICE DAY 11 NOV. 1920, IN THE PRESENCE OF HIS MAJESTY, KING GEORGE V, HIS MINISTERS OF STATE, THE CHIEFS OF HIS FORCES AND A VAST CONCOURSE OF THE NATION. THUS ARE COMMEMORATED THE MANY MULTITUDES WHO, DURING THE GREAT WAR OF 1914–1918,

GAVE THE MOST THAT MAN CAN GIVE, LIFE ITSELF, FOR GOD,
FOR KING AND COUNTRY, FOR LOVED ONES, HOME AND
EMPIRE, FOR THE SACRED CAUSE OF JUSTICE AND THE FREE-
DOM OF THE WORLD.

The letters were inlaid into the marble with brass smelted from cartridge cases retrieved from the Great War battlefields.

The final part of the inscription, the famous text from the Bible
(2 Chronicles 24:16)—"They buried him among the Kings, because he
had done good toward God and toward His House"—suggested by
Dean Ryle, had originally been chosen by Richard II more than five
centuries before, as the inscription on the tomb of the Bishop of Salis-
bury in the abbey. The Dean himself appeared to be unaware of this,
however, attributing the suggestion to "a North Country archdeacon."
At the foot of the gravestone, the words "In Christ shall all be made
alive" had also been inscribed, prompting a protest from S. I. Levy,
Principal of the Liverpool Hebrew Schools. "Unknown also was the
faith of the Unknown Warrior. Heavy was the toll of Jewish life on the
battlefields of France . . . Amid the unbounded wealth of biblical inspiration, a line could have been selected which would not have offended
the living religious susceptibilities of the Unknown Warrior, whatever
his faith may have been." The Dean's reply was notably unconciliatory.
"In a Christian church, one should not be surprised to find a Christian
text and the offending lines were the only one of the five texts on the
gravestone promoting a purely Christian message." Mr. Levy's further
letter drew an even more waspish retort: The Unknown Warrior might
equally have been a Muslim or a Mormon—"we cannot hope to please
everybody."

At the conclusion of the service, the Actors' Pall was lifted from the
grave, revealing the new tombstone, and David Railton carried his
Union flag, known as the "Ypres Flag" or "Padre's Flag," to the altar to
be dedicated. Escorted by an honour guard of men of Alec Reader's former unit, the 47th (London) Division, it was then taken in procession
through the abbey and hoisted into place in St. George's Chapel, fulfilling the earlier plea of *The Times*, that it "should never leave those doubly venerable walls." "It flew at Vimy Ridge and in the Ypres salient, on
the Somme, at Messines Ridge . . . it was the frontal of rude altars
where thousands took the sacrament for the last time; it served as the
last covering for numbers of our dead; and it yet bears the glorious stain
of their blood. It has covered the grave of the Unknown Warrior and

now it is to hang near his resting-place under the venerable roof which still shelters the helmet and the blazoned shield of the Royal conqueror of Agincourt."

It was a fitting tribute to the unjustly overlooked instigator of the idea of the Unknown Warrior and the only complaint voiced about it was that there was nothing to inform the visitor of the provenance of that tattered, stained and faded flag. "How English! Most other nations would have explained somewhere for all to see that this is no ordinary flag. When they brought the Unknown Warrior through the streets, with the sombre guns booming and the troops slow marching to a wail of brass, this was the flag that covered the coffin; and there it hangs unheralded in the Abbey. In its creases you may see—ah! how many Last Suppers in Flanders fields." Almost seventy years later the brass bell from HMS *Verdun* was also hung near the grave. It is rung at noon every day, except Sunday, in memory of the dead of all wars.

Armistice Day 1921 had once more brought huge crowds to the abbey and the Cenotaph, and the two-minute silence was again observed throughout the country. The authorities had expressed the hope that "all vehicular traffic will be suspended; it does not, however, seem necessary to perpetuate the stoppage of rail and water transport," but many train drivers, bargees and ship's captains chose to ignore that advice, and even on moving trains most passengers removed their hats and rose to their feet at eleven o'clock, swaying with the motion of the train as they maintained the Great Silence.

The day did not pass without incident and popular protest. Several thousand unemployed men marched to the Cenotaph, wearing pawn tickets in place of campaign medals. Some carried placards reading, "The Dead are remembered but we are forgotten" and "To the dead victims of capitalism from the living victims of capitalism." A police inspector tore the placards from their hands before allowing them to proceed. There was a brawl in Dundee High Street between ex-servicemen and Communist demonstrators, and in Liverpool 200 unemployed men interrupted the Great Silence with cries of "Anyone want a medal?" and "What we need is food not prayers."

The government was now attempting to change the focus of Armistice Day. It was "not a day of National grief," and was "not to be kept only as a day of remembrance of the men who fell in the war and of thanksgiving for their sacrifice. It is to be marked also by rejoicings in victory. In the morning there will be religious services and observances, culminating in the Great Silence at eleven o'clock; at night there will be revelry and song." Many hotels and restaurants arranged dinners and dances, and licensing hours were extended, enabling "many who have spent the evening at the theatre to take part in a celebration supper afterwards." The London Country Club threw an Armistice Night Ball "with a 'snowstorm carnival' as a prominent feature."

Such revels were hugely controversial. Many ex-servicemen shared the view that the anniversary of victory was worthy of celebration, but many more, including the millions of still-mourning relatives of the dead, looked on such attitudes with repugnance. Sir Arthur Conan Doyle, creator of Sherlock Holmes, spoke for many when he said that Armistice Day should be "a moment for prayer," not celebration. An Edinburgh mother who had lost five sons in the war did not even leave her house on Armistice Day until 1927, when she did so only to attend the dedication of the Edinburgh Cenotaph. On the same day, many of the women at the Cenotaph and the Unknown Warrior's grave in London were still wearing "deep mourning," and a newspaper reported that "many people who danced last Armistice Day felt that they could not do so last night."

In 1921, the period of public mourning and remembrance again stretched well beyond Armistice Day itself. The following weekend was the scene of another large-scale public pilgrimage, with Saturday once more "Children's Day." "Bunch after bunch of white chrysanthemums on Saturday bore no other words than the touching phrase 'For Daddy.'" There were long queues throughout the weekend. "Some who joined the waiting lines wished simply to give a salute in honour of fallen men whom they had known only in the mass, or of comrades with whom they had fought in the war. The children and many of the women had known losses more personal and the Cenotaph to which they carried their wreaths stood for them as the symbol of a wooden cross in a cemetery of Flanders or Gallipoli. There are flowers in those cemeteries now."

Yet again there were vivid reminders that, for many pilgrims, the Unknown Warrior was not merely the symbol of their dead husband, father or son, but the actual person. An elderly woman "carrying a bunch of chrysanthemums and heather, told those about her that a clairvoyant had said that the body of her son lay under the tomb of the Unknown Warrior in the Abbey. She had travelled from the North of Scotland to see the tomb and to lay her flowers at the foot of the grave. No one disturbed her faith." The woman was far from unique. Many grieving people had turned to clairvoyants and mediums in their search for hope and consolation in their loss—there were said to be 118 mediums in Kensington alone. Conan Doyle had lost several members of his family, including his brother and brother-in-law, and his son Kingsley, and was a prominent advocate of spiritualism, which enjoyed a considerable vogue in the 1920s despite all efforts to discredit it. Many gullible people were undoubtedly fleeced but, even if fraudulent, seances and "messages from the spirit world" undoubtedly brought solace to many distraught widows and parents, giving them a ritual parting from the dead and the comforting belief that their loved ones were now "in a better place."

Another innovation on Armistice Day 1921 was much more generally accepted. Poppies first became intimately associated with the war dead in the devastated battlefields of the Somme, where the wastelands of grey-brown mud and earth erupted in vivid splashes of crimson, as numerous as the fallen soldiers who lay beneath. When the wind blew, the fallen petals carpeted the ground like the blood spilled in that same torn earth. John McRae's hugely popular poem "In Flanders' Fields" had further strengthened the association between the war dead and the flower. Of course, the poppy "also bloomed on the German, as well as the English side of the trenches, but in Germany it was ignored."

Artificial poppies were made by French women for the benefit of children living in the war-ravaged areas of France, and in August 1921 a Madame Guérin brought some to London and showed them to the Secretary of the British Legion. Four previously competing ex-servicemen's organizations had agreed to amalgamate at a meeting in Leicester on 13 November 1920. The name chosen was the Warriors' Guild, but that was changed to the British Legion on 1 July 1921. The newly formed organization readily agreed to take on the sale and distribution of the poppies in Britain and, after some deliberation, placed an initial order for one and a half million. Earl Haig, as President of the Legion, led the appeals for volunteers to help sell "Flanders poppies for the benefit of ex-Servicemen of all ranks." The minimum price at which they were sold was "one shilling for those made of silk and threepence for those of mercerised lawn [linen] but it is hoped that very few of the purchasers will be content with the minimum." As if in confirmation, a single petal from a real Flanders poppy was sold for £5 at Smithfield Market, and a basket of poppies was auctioned at Sotheby's for a total of £500, as each buyer, bidding up to £90, took a single poppy from the basket and sent the rest back to be auctioned again.

Sellers of poppies were also "stationed at practically every hotel, restaurant, club and theatre and at many large stores." "The Dowager Lady Garvagh and Lady Birch are organising a band of girls to sell poppies at all the principal restaurants and hotels," "film performers" had "a depot at St. Paul's," and "Dominion ladies resident in England will sell Flanders poppies at all the leading theatres during the evening performance." Soldiers were also given permission to wear a poppy "on their uniform head-dress, when not on duty."

Volunteers were slower to come forward in some parts of the country; the *Yorkshire Post* reported that "only three or four" had done so in the ten days since the Lord Mayor of Leeds had issued an appeal, but the public response was generally overwhelming. By the eve of Armistice Day, demand for poppies had been so great that, although 8 million had been sold, it had "only been possible to supply fifty per cent of the numbers demanded," and it was said that the British Legion had "made up with pink blotting paper what it lacked in basic material." Over £100,000 was raised for the "Haig Fund" and, perhaps for the first time in history, the majority of the money had come from "those below the traditional philanthropic classes." Not everyone trying to meet the unsatisfied demand for poppies did so from honourable motives. The British Legion had been informed that "some persons have manufactured a quantity of poppies for the purpose of selling on the street for profit. It seems inconceivable that any such attempt should be made," but people were warned only to buy poppies from vendors wearing the official badge. Even more shocking to those still nursing a hatred for "the Hun" were the reports that some of the unofficial poppies being hawked on the streets had been imported from Germany.

In subsequent years the poppies were manufactured by disabled ex-servicemen—several hundred were employed on the task—prompting one poet to muse on the symbolism of disabled soldiers making scentless, infertile, artificial flowers "of paper, tin and metal thread," in memory of once vital, now long-dead men—and the poppy rapidly became the universal symbol of remembrance. In 1927, the aviator Charles Lindbergh scattered thousands of poppy seeds from his aircraft over the American Cemetery at Waregem, and in a ceremony that continues to the present day, the annual Festival of Remembrance includes the release of a million poppy petals—one for every dead soldier of Britain and the Empire—raining down on the audience from the roof of London's Albert Hall. Originally a circulation-boosting stunt by the

Daily Express, it developed a powerful momentum of its own, helped by the BBC, which broadcast the Festival of Remembrance not only across Great Britain but throughout the countries of the Empire. From 1928 onwards, it also broadcast the Armistice Day ceremony from the Cenotaph, including the two-minute silence. It was "one of the great paradoxes of radio, that no broadcast is more impressive than the silence following the last dashing strokes of Big Ben."

The grave of the Unknown Warrior and the Cenotaph would forever remain the national sites of mourning, and "few visitors miss the opportunity of adding a handful of flowers to those at [the Cenotaph's] base. Sometimes . . . famous generals or distinguished statesmen lay a wreath with all formality . . . sometimes it is a football team, a trade union, a chamber of commerce who break away from their own business or pleasure to commemorate their own departed comrades, but far more often it is some bereaved mother, who slips quietly up, sets down a few blooms and steals away with her eyes filled with tears." A government attempt in 1923 to discontinue the annual ceremony at the Cenotaph was abandoned in the face of press and public hostility. The rituals of 11 November—"Armisticetide," as it became known, "giving it the air of an ancient religious tradition"—were already too deeply enshrined.

In 1939, on the eve of another world war and almost twenty years after the Unknown Warrior was buried, thousands were still paying their respects at his grave. Despite the opposition of the abbey authorities to the laying of any tributes on the grave, the custom had evolved among visitors and mourners of placing a single bloom, usually a poppy, there. As well as the weeklong annual pilgrimage centring on Armistice Day, there were also other, smaller pilgrimages every year— at Easter and Whitsuntide, in August, on the anniversary of the outbreak of war and at Christmas, when the tradition of laying holly wreaths was maintained. And on every day of the year, individuals would approach the Cenotaph and lay flowers or a wreath in memory of their husband, father or son who had been killed on that date.

But public demand also required the creation of purely local memorials, recognizing the sacrifice of every community from the great industrial cities to the smallest villages and hamlets. There were few precedents for this. With the exception of a handful of sites commemorating battles of the English Civil War, war memorials were almost unknown until the Boer War, when the cult of the dead fostered by Queen Victoria's prolonged public mourning for her husband,

Albert, and the memorials to him that she had constructed encouraged public displays of remembrance by her subjects. Most of the Boer War memorials were still constructed to commemorate battles and the conflict as a whole, not the 5,000 men who had perished in the fighting, but a few, paid for by communities and families, were erected in memory of civilian volunteers, who, "although needing to be commemorated as soldiers, also needed to be commemorated as citizens." Almost as an afterthought, the government provided small iron crosses to mark the graves of fallen soldiers who were not otherwise commemorated, but the Secretary of State then opposed the consolidation of scattered graves into larger cemeteries and as a result many bodies were never found and the graves never marked.

In the Great War, recognizing that the public would no longer tolerate bodies being heaped in "common graves as if they were nameless vermin," members of Red Cross units (later reorganized into the Graves Registration Commission) were for the first time given the specific duty "to search for graves, identify soldiers, mark them with a cross, register their position." But if the registration and subsequent care of war graves had assumed "a national character," and the war cemeteries and monuments commemorated rank-and-file soldiers in a way that "had never been dreamt of before," the vast majority of the dead had been civilians and not professional soldiers, and their families and communities were united in requiring that their sacrifice be acknowledged and their names recorded for posterity. As a result, the aftermath of the First World War brought a massive increase in such "civilian" monuments, recording and lamenting the sacrifice of the dead.

Fifty to sixty thousand memorials were erected in Great Britain alone, "carving in stone the names of a million dead, adding always that their lives had been given and not taken." In parallel with the widespread commemoration at home went the construction of cemeteries and memorials in the former battlefields abroad—two thousand in Belgium and France alone. The huge Thiepval Arch—like the Cenotaph, designed by Lutyens—bears the inscribed names of 73,000 missing dead from the fighting on the Somme. Some cemeteries also have a population of a small town—Tyne-Cot, the largest British military graveyard in the world, contains the bodies of almost 12,000 British dead from the Battle of Passchendaele and the inscribed names of another 35,000 who have never been found. There are hundreds of other memorials and cemeteries—almost every unit has its own individual shrine. Beginning in 1920, several thousands of tons of white Portland stone were shipped to France every week to be carved into headstones for the British known and unknown dead. By 1927, 400,000 headstones had been carved, inscribed and installed, the greatest commemoration of the dead "since Pharaonic Egypt."

Not everyone was happy to see scarce public funds devoted to the creation of memorials and monuments. As one professor complained, "Must a sort of murder be followed by a sort of suicide?" Many argued that if those dead soldiers could speak, they would urge spending money on the care and welfare of those they had left behind, rather than on "a glorified tombstone," and in some communities the commemoration of the dead took a much more utilitarian form, even if "some memorials were frankly opportunistic." According to G. K. Chesterton, some people in Beaconsfield wanted a cross, "with or without a crucified Christ, and others preferred a parish pump, a public fountain, a municipal motor bus or a club for ex-servicemen." A small island was presented to the town of Barrow-in-Furness as a war memorial and there were also hospitals, trust funds, village halls, parks, playing fields, operating theatres, cottages for district nurses, bus shelters, three railway engines, an iron girder bridge at Carlisle and, perhaps most bizarre of all, the Chiswick Rowing Tank, created "to teach the art of rowing under cover," all of which were dedicated to the war dead.

Nor was opportunism confined to local communities. An exhibition of ideas for war memorials at the Royal Academy in summer 1919 was a transparent attempt to secure lucrative commissions for academicians. The designs and maquettes were "intellectually and emotionally beneath contempt . . . it is impossible to recognise their claims to commemorate Mons and Ypres and the Somme and the piled up agony of the dark years." It is a moot point whether the academicians were more or less cynical than the sculptor Paul Auban, who created the statue of an outraged mother standing over the body of her dead son for the war memorial at Péronne on the Somme, by the simple expedient of adding a uniform to the prone figure in an unwanted pre-war memorial to the victims of a shipwreck. Auban, like many French sculptors, was benefiting from a similar boom in commemoration that saw 30,000 memorials—fifteen a day—completed in France between 1920 and 1925.

The ritual of commemoration was also fought over and adapted for propaganda purposes by those who supported the war and those who opposed it, but against a background of growing unemployment, strikes and popular discontent, and with the Bolshevik revolution in Russia casting a shadow over all Europe's monarchies, it became essential for government, military and grieving relatives alike to assert, via Remembrance Day, that the fallen had not died in vain. "The rituals of remembrance defined what was to be remembered in post-war Britain."

Forgetting his earlier opposition to the idea, the King had written to Dean Ryle shortly after the service at Westminster Abbey to say that he was "deeply impressed with today's unique ceremony, the inception of which was your own [sic]. All the arrangements and the manner in which the service was conducted were in reverence, beauty and dignity, worthy of an event unparalleled and imperishable in the Nation's life and of the Abbey's noble tradition. His Majesty sincerely thanks you and all concerned for the perfect manner in which everything was carried out." The King and Lloyd George both made use of the Cenotaph and the grave of the Unknown Warrior. The King made Armistice Day the annual focus of the "traditional" rituals and ceremonial pageants that he invented or resurrected and that have come to define the monarchy, while for Lloyd George the burial of the Unknown Warrior was almost a coronation, validating his government and his own record as a war leader.

In 1922, George V also made a pilgrimage to the battlefields and war cemeteries, doing so, like many less exalted citizens, at least partly on behalf of those who could not visit the graves for themselves. While there he made his famous observation that "the whole circuit of the earth is girdled with the graves of our dead . . . I have many times asked myself whether there can be more potent advocates of peace upon earth through the years to come, than this massed multitude of silent witnesses to the desolation of war." In what was either a heartfelt gesture or an inspired piece of public relations, the King also knelt and laid a bunch of forget-me-nots on the grave of a Sergeant Matthews in Etaples Cemetery. The flowers had been given to the Queen by Sergeant Matthews's mother, who had begged her to place them on her son's grave.

In November 1920, an English boy whose father had been killed in action in October 1914, when the boy was just six, was given a rosebud that had fallen from one of the great wreaths to the Unknown Warrior as it was unloaded at Dover harbour. The boy's uncle had stepped out of the watching crowd, retrieved the rose and later sent it to his nephew, "In Loving memory of your Dear Dad who arrived at Dover

Nov 10th 1920 in the Destroyer *Verdun*. Buried in Westminster Abbey Nov 11th 1920, the Unknown Warrior. The enclosed is a part of a rose which fell from a large wreath given by the British Army. I hope you will keep it and in years to come, you will be able to show it, in remembrance of your Dad." The boy dried the flower and kept it throughout his long life. He and his family made repeated requests to Westminster Abbey to lay the dried rosebud on the grave of the Unknown Warrior in commemoration of the father he barely remembered, but all were turned down. Sadly, he died before achieving that ambition, but on Tuesday, 19 December 2000, his daughter and other members of the family were finally permitted to place the rose on the grave, in memory of her father and that long-dead soldier of the Great War, her grandfather.

The battlefields and war cemeteries commemorating the dead continued to attract ever-growing numbers throughout the 1920s and 1930s. Some, probably the majority, were visiting the grave or the death site of a relative. Others were ex-servicemen drawn back, almost despite themselves, to the places where so many comrades had died, but still others were tourists, eager to experience something of the atmosphere—and the vicarious horror—of the trenches. As early as December 1914, a magazine had reported that civilian souvenir hunters were already active on the battlefields, and although Thomas Cook's was forced to report the following year that, because of French hostility, it would not be running sightseeing expeditions to the battlefields until the war was over, tours began almost as soon as the guns stopped firing. Cook's offered the luxury version at thirty-five guineas, or the economy model at nine and a half guineas. Even the latter was well beyond the reach of most widows and manual workers at a time when the average wage—and that barely subsistence level—was only £3 a week.

Many tourists were disappointed. "Nature herself conspires with time to cheat our recollections"; and both nature and French farmers, left to their own devices, were rapidly reclaiming what had been lost to the war. The torn and devastated earth, shattered tree-stumps, trenches, shell-craters, seas of mud and endless barbed wire were rapidly being hidden, as a writer for an Australian newspaper complained, beneath "blowing grain and nodding poppies." A keen eye could soon spot the zigzag line of filled-in trenches, and the larger craters were still there, many deep enough to have formed ponds, fringed with bullrushes and populated by croaking frogs. The only remaining trenches were those deliberately preserved as memorials, or maintained as tourist traps, guarded not by *poilus* but by French farmers charging a few francs for admission.

The villages, towns and cities of Belgium and northeast France were slowly being rebuilt. There the battlefield tourists could drink tea in the "Café des Alliés," and purchase souvenirs, either genuine battlefield detritus—buttons, badges, buckles, pistols, cartridges and shell fragments—or trashy novelties emblazoned with iron crosses, or images of the trenches and the once-ruined towns. Were these just tourist trinkets and tat, to be tossed in a drawer and forgotten, or did they perhaps help some to keep alive the fading, sepia memories of those who had fought and died there?

26

UNKNOWN BUT TO GOD

On the same day, 11 November 1920, that the British Unknown Warrior was being laid to rest, France had also buried her *poilu inconnu*. André Maginot, accompanied by five war widows, five permanently maimed soldiers, five other soldiers and five veterans of the Franco-Prussian war of 1870, had brought the chosen body from Verdun by special train. The funeral procession passed along the Boulevard St. Germain and the Champs Elyseés to the Arc de Triomphe, where the Unknown Soldier was to be laid to rest beneath the arch inscribed with the names of Napoleon's generals and victories. It was said that the fallen had picked up the laurel wreath dropped by Napoleon at Waterloo. On the casket were placed the Croix de Guerre, the Légion d'Honneur, the Military Cross—no doubt George V felt that it was "good enough" for the French as well as the Belgians—the Order of Leopold, the Distinguished Service Medal, the Greek War Cross, the Italian Military Medal, and sabres of honour from China and Japan. The ceremonies also included the laying of two wreaths on

Bartholomé's statue to the dead in Père Lachaise cemetery—one to the memory of foreigners who died in the war, and the other to the memory of French heroes. That night a torchlit procession was held through the streets. All the public buildings were illuminated and the Seine bridges "outlined with thousands of lamps."

As in Britain, the official ceremony was followed by a people's pilgrimage that brought the heart of the French capital to a standstill. But the ceremonies were not without controversy. Royalist and anti-Republican members of the Chamber of Deputies had attempted to mute celebrations of the fiftieth anniversary of the founding of the French Republic by switching the date to coincide with the burial of the Unknown Soldier. One Socialist member accused them of "hiding the Republic behind the body of a dead soldier," provoking a near-riot in the Chamber.

The French Unknown Soldier lay in state in a first-floor chamber within the Arc de Triomphe from 11 November until 28 January 1921, when he was at last laid to rest in the concrete vault prepared for him. Louis Barthou, the French Minister of War, made a brief speech, Lloyd George and the American Ambassador, Hugh C. Wallace, laid wreaths on behalf of the British and American people and the casket was then lowered into the grave and covered by a "great granite stone" with a simple inscription: "ICI REPOSE UN SOLDAT FRANÇAIS MORT POUR LA PATRIE 1914–1918."

When the barriers were removed from around the grave, a crowd poured in, "and every one threw flowers on the grave. Poor women, sobbing bitterly, laid bunches of violets, and rich women, united with them in the memory of war's griefs, kissing their flowers, laid them beside them. Soon the whole great space below the arch seemed filled with blossoms. Into the tomb, still open at one end, men who had fought beside the Unknown threw the decorations they had won for gallantry." The crowd was utterly silent, though "most of the people wept. Then Minister Barthou, who himself lost his only son in the war, stood forward once more and, bareheaded, cried in a loud voice, 'Vive la France!' The cry was taken up by thousands of voices. It gave relief at the moment of the most poignant emotion, and slowly the crowd began to melt away in the silver morning light."

For decades, the grave beneath the Arc de Triomphe remained a site of pilgrimage, arousing potent and sometimes conflicting emotions in former servicemen, bereaved parents, wives and families. The Armistice Day ceremonies in November 1921 were disrupted by a

Communist demonstration "vigourously suppressed" by police, and by the arrival of a blind war veteran bearing a wreath inscribed "War's Wrecks Present Their Compliments to the Unknown Poilu." The man, "led away at the insistence of the crowd, shouted 'Down with War' as he went." On 8 January 1922, one distraught woman, having removed all identifying marks from her clothing, climbed the Arc de Triomphe and threw herself to her death, her body falling among a crowd of mourners carrying flowers to decorate the grave of the French Unknown Soldier.

As a permanent reminder to French citizens of the sacrifice their Allies had made in defence of their lands, tablets inscribed "A LA GLOIRE DE DIEU ET A LA MEMOIRE DU MILLION DE MORTS DE L'EMPIRE BRITANNIQUE, TOMBES DANS LA GRANDE GUERRE 1914–1918 ET QUI POUR LA PLUPART REPOSENT EN FRANCE" were also erected in cathedrals and large churches all over the country. The same inscription, in Latin, to obviate the need for plaques in the twin Belgian languages of French and Flemish, was also put up in Belgian churches.

Throughout Europe, at least among the victorious Allies, each nation's unknown soldiers were exhumed and reburied with full military honours. In Belgium, the Unknown Soldier was chosen by a blinded war veteran and buried in Brussels beneath an eternal flame. The first guard on the grave was mounted by a veteran who had lost one of his arms in the fighting. An Italian Unknown Soldier, a victim of the vicious fighting between Italy and Austro-Hungary in the frozen battlefields of the Alps, was buried in Rome on 4 November 1921. The city was "overflowing with people" who had come from all over Italy to pay homage; many were "sleeping all night in the streets for need of better accommodation . . . the National Stadium, Coliseum, and any other place that affords shelter is already filled." Bitter differences were set aside for the day as "Communists wearing their badges with hammer and scythe" stood alongside "Fascisti in black shirts embroidered with skull and crossbones, mothers proudly displaying the medals won by their dead sons, little school children dressed in white, clustered around bespectacled priests, maimed soldiers who were carried on stretchers, blinded soldiers who wanted to hear, though they could not see the ceremony."

The Italian Unknown Soldier was borne through the streets in an oak coffin mounted with iron wrought from trench shells, and with "hand grenades for feet." "More than 6,000 battle flags were carried in the line of march," many showing "only a few tattered remnants hanging from the staff and many were decorated with medals won on distant battlefields." The body had lain in state in the Church of Santa Maria degli Angeli, before being interred beneath the "Altar of the Country"—the Victor Emmanuel Monument, erected eleven years earlier in celebration of Italian unity. Among the mourners was "a little white-haired peasant woman in Calabrian costume, wearing a gold medal awarded for the valour of her dead son. She is the mother of Luigi Settimo Intrieri, who, when an exploding shell tore away both his arms, refused to be removed to the rear and when, a few minutes later, another shell mangled his legs, continued to encourage his companions and insisted on dying in the captured Austrian trench . . . The throng clamouring to see the ceremonies was said to be the largest ever assembled in Rome," and once more the grave immediately became the focus of a massive and continuing popular pilgrimage.

Portugal was unique in bringing home two Unknown Soldiers—one from Flanders, one from Nyasaland in Africa—who were buried together in the Church of Belém, in Lisbon, where many Portuguese monarchs were entombed. And over the following years and decades, many other countries also followed the example inspired by Monsieur Binet-Valmer and David Railton, and erected monuments to their own unknown soldiers.

As early as 29 October 1919, American Brigadier General William D. Connor had learned of French proposals to bury an Unknown Soldier and suggested a similar ceremony for an American Unknown to the U.S. Army Chief of Staff, General Peyton C. March. March dismissed the proposal out of hand. Some idea of his reasons may be discerned from his response to another, similar proposal, when he claimed that, while France and Britain had hundreds of thousands of unknown dead, there were less than two thousand American unknowns and he believed it possible that the Army Graves Registration Service would eventually identify almost all of them. In addition, he said, the United States had no suitable national monument like Westminster Abbey or the Arc de Triomphe, where an unknown soldier could be interred.

However, moved by accounts of the ceremonies in England and France in November 1920, press and public support for the burial of an American Unknown Soldier became irresistible, though fearing congressional horse-trading and pork-barreling, the *New York Times* warned Congressmen not to allow the Unknown's tomb to be "associated with any State nor with any Army organisation. As in England and France, it is the nation that should do honor to the unidentified soldier and his tomb should be a shrine for the Americans of all the States and all the lands under the flag. And that shrine should be in the National Cemetery at Arlington, where the bravest lie, men of the South as well as men of the North, who fought for the Stars and Stripes."

On 21 December 1920, echoing that call, New York Congressman Hamilton Fish, Jr., proposed the burial of an unidentified American soldier in the new Memorial Amphitheater of Arlington National Cemetery. His proposal attracted broad support from both sides of the House, from General Pershing, the American Legion and the press, although the *New York Times* had now reversed its position on Arlington, arguing that the Rotunda of the Capitol would be a more appropriate site. "All America finds its way to the Capitol, many Americans never go to Arlington, which, being a military cemetery by dedication, can hardly be the 'Westminster Abbey of America's heroic dead.' " The Washington branch of the American Legion also favoured the Capitol, but opposition to Arlington was unavailing. On 4 March 1921, Congress approved the proposal without amendment, including the construction of a simple tomb that would eventually serve as the base of an appropriate monument.

The American Unknown Soldier would not be the first unidentified soldier to be interred at Arlington. In September 1866, the bodies or partial remains of 2,111 unidentified Civil War dead were placed in a vault at the newly opened National Cemetery, set up in the grounds of Confederate General Robert E. Lee's former mansion, confiscated at the end of the Civil War. A commemorative stone was erected, inscribed

> BENEATH THIS STONE REPOSE THE BONES OF TWO
> THOUSAND ONE HUNDRED AND ELEVEN UNKNOWN
> SOLDIERS GATHERED AFTER THE WAR FROM THE FIELDS OF
> BULL RUN, AND THE ROUTE TO THE RAPPAHANNOCK. THEIR
> REMAINS COULD NOT BE IDENTIFIED. BUT THEIR NAMES
> AND DEATHS ARE RECORDED IN THE ARCHIVES OF THEIR
> COUNTRY; AND ITS GRATEFUL CITIZENS HONOR THEM AS
> OF THEIR NOBLE ARMY OF MARTYRS. MAY THEY REST IN
> PEACE! SEPTEMBER, A.D. 1866.

However, the idea of a symbolic burial of a single Unknown Soldier from the Civil War was never raised.

On 5 March 1921, in the final hours of Woodrow Wilson's administration, the President signed into law the joint resolution from Congress authorizing the exhumation and return to the United States of one unidentified American soldier from France. A companion act conferred the award of the Congressional Medal of Honor to the French and British Unknowns. In an attempt to promote reconciliation between North and South and bury the divisive associations of Memorial Day—the annual focus of lavish commemorations by the Grand Army of the Republic—Congressman Fish had wanted the ceremony for the Unknown American Soldier to be carried out on that day. But Secretary of War Newton D. Baker, who had already intervened to veto a New York proposal to bring home another Unknown Soldier for burial in Victory Hall, the proposed (and never built) war memorial and forum in Pershing Square, now told the Senate Committee on Military Affairs that a ceremony on Memorial Day (30 May but always commemorated on the last Monday of May) would be premature. Only 1,237 dead still remained to be identified, he said (1,900, according to the Associated Press), and the majority of cases were still being investigated. To rush to inter one of those Unknowns might result in the burial of a body that could later have been identified.

A change of administration brought no change in attitude; the newly elected President Warren G. Harding's Secretary of War, John W. Weeks, also rejected Memorial Day. He opted for a ceremony on Armistice Day (now known in the United States as Veterans' Day), 11 November, with the selection of the Unknown Soldier to be carried out on 24 October. As in Britain, America's political leaders hoped that by creating monuments and rituals commemorating the military victory, they might help to heal, or at least "camouflage," the social divisions caused by the war. A reluctant and late-arriving partner in the Allied war effort, America was divided both during the fighting and in its aftermath. For the first time, the U.S. Army was manned largely by conscription rather than from volunteers. Many on the political left denounced it as a war to support capitalist interests, and many ethnic minorities, particularly German-Americans, were subject to suspicion and discrimination.

Black Americans were conscripted but found that prejudice and segregation travelled across the Atlantic with them. Their fighting qualities were unjustly disparaged and they were used mainly in menial tasks, construction, refuse disposal and its human equivalent—clearing the battlefields of the dead. Only when seconded to the far-better integrated French units did they receive anything like equal treatment. They suffered substantial casualties—the 92nd and 93rd Divisions lost more than 5,000 men between them—but when they returned to the United States after the war, they found that their war service counted for little. One infuriated black soldier sent an anonymous letter to his draft board while still in France. "You low-down Mother Fuckers can put a gun in our hands, but who is able to take it out? . . . You all can look out, for we is coming." White fears that black troops would indeed return to the United States demanding equality and using their military training to reinforce their demands led to harassment, lynchings and race riots. In the summer and autumn of 1919, white-fomented riots erupted in twenty-six American cities and there were seventy-seven documented lynchings. At least ten of the victims were ex-servicemen; some were even lynched wearing their uniforms.

During the war, the Wilson administration had used the Espionage Act to jail anti-war activists and, like the succeeding administrations, it looked the other way as waves of vigilante attacks were made on radicals, union organizers, "German sympathizers," immigrants and "slackers." As in Europe, returning servicemen found that the "world safe for democracy" that they had fought to achieve had little reward to offer them, and in 1919, there was a rash of strikes. More than 4 million men downed tools in the course of the year, including three-quarters of the Boston police force. Terrorist attacks were made against a number of politicians and, in response, hundreds of suspected foreign "radicals" were deported and a campaign of harassment was launched against their domestic allies, such as the "Wobblies"—the Industrial Workers of the World.

Like the British government, the U.S. administration was petrified that domestic unrest might fuel the growth of a domestic version of Bolshevism, and it made desperate attempts to foster a unified American identity, transcending divisions of gender, race and class. The Unknown Soldier, it was hoped, would both validate the war and provide just such a unifying symbol. Honouring him would both "acknowledge the debt owed to him by his country and . . . emphasise implicitly the duty citizen-soldiers owed their country"; "the war dead were still being pressed into service by their governments."

Like the other Allied nations, the American military authorities took extraordinary precautions to ensure that the identity of the Unknown Soldier would remain forever concealed. An unidentified body was to be exhumed from each of four military cemeteries in the four main battlegrounds in which U.S. forces had been engaged: Belleau Wood, where they suffered their first large-scale casualties and the

Marines had added another exalted chapter to their legend; Bony, on the Somme, where the New York National Guard broke through the "impregnable" Hindenberg Line; the Argonne and Thiaucourt, scene of ferocious fighting during the St. Mihiel drive; and Romagne-sous-Montfaucon, where thousands of U.S. servicemen lost their lives in the last decisive battle of the war, and where, in three hours, U.S. forces had fired more shells than had been used in the whole of the American Civil War.

Individual American combat units had been given responsibility for burying their war dead. Where they could be found, one of the two sets of dog-tags carried by soldiers was buried with them to aid later identification, and the grave marked with a wooden cross. The American Graves Registration Service, set up on 7 August 1917, had the task of consolidating these graves, scattered in hundreds of burial sites, into one of the eight newly created permanent U.S. military cemeteries. Because the bodies were almost invariably "badly decomposed, features unrecognisable," the reports on each disinterred and reburied body also included dental records. In each cemetery, every grave of an Unknown Soldier was allocated a unique number, registered at U.S. Army headquarters in Paris. Four officers—Major George F. Waugh, of the infantry, and Lieutenants John J. Powers, Hugh S. Harpole and Arthur E. Dewey, of the Quartermaster Corps—were ordered to go to their designated cemeteries on Saturday, 22 October 1921, and there open sealed orders from Lieutenant Colonel G.V.S. Quackenbush, which would indicate the number of the grave from which their Unknown Soldier was to be exhumed.

"In the preparation of the body a thorough search will be made of same for any evidence of identification, and should there be anything found on the body or in the coffin which will tend to identify this particular body, an alternate body, for which the required forms have been prepared, will be then exhumed and similarly searched. The body will be prepared according to regulations—wrapped in a blanket and placed in a special casket provided for this purpose. No marks whatsoever will be placed on the body, casket or shipping case. The metallic lining will be screwed down but no asphaltum paint will be used on the rubber gasket. The casket top will then be placed on the casket and the shipping case lid attached by only six (6) screws, which will allow the ready opening of the shipping case when the body arrives at its destination."

On Friday, 21 October, a party from Romagne travelled to Thiaucourt to prepare for the exhumation of the body there the following morning. The officer in charge, Lieutenant Arthur E. Dewey, drove in a "white observation car." A supervisory embalmer and two technical assistants travelled with him, and a checker and a convoyer followed in a truck. On his arrival at the cemetery, Dewey found that a grey steel casket in a wooden shipping case had already been delivered. Identical caskets had been sent to the other three chosen cemeteries, without any distinguishing marks that might subsequently allow identification of the cemetery from which each had come. In accordance with their orders, each casket was at once "thoroughly cleaned and polished and put in absolutely first-class condition in every particular." The surface of the outer shipping case was also "planed to a clean, new surface and the sides at the head and foot-ends reinforced with additional wood screws."

With his orders, Dewey also received two envelopes marked in red pencil "Unknown-Thiaucourt" and "Alternate-Thiaucourt." The former contained a standard U.S. Army Exhumation Form 16A, identifying the Unknown Soldier's "U" (unknown) number and the plot and the grave where the body would be found. If any means of identification whatsoever was found on the body when it was exhumed, it was to be reinterred at once, and the "alternate" envelope opened, identifying another grave. After these forms had been prepared at headquarters in Paris, all other documentation relating to the graves was burned to remove any possibility of the Unknown Soldiers or the graves from which they had been exhumed being identified at some future date. The orders concluded, "You are again cautioned to see that no records whatsoever are made of this exhumation and no marks of any kind are placed on the casket or shipping case."

Dewey identified the grave, and to speed the process of exhuming the body the next day, labourers excavated the soil to a depth of two feet. Dewey and his party then retired to Metz for the night, returning at first light the next morning to complete the task. As soon as the body was exhumed, Dewey and the supervisory embalmer began the unpleasant task of searching the remains for any form of identification. None was found. The body was then wrapped in a blanket, covered in a sheet and placed in the casket. In accordance with Dewey's orders, only six screws were used to seal the lid of the shipping case. His orders then required Dewey to go to the cemetery office, remove from the files the "pick-up card" identifying the grave-site and destroy it. He did so by burning the card and grinding the ashes into the soil with his boot. The casket was then loaded onto the truck and driven back to Romagne, where Lieutenant Harpole had already exhumed another body from that cemetery. As required by orders, both bodies were "placed in a suitable building at Romagne, aloof from the other bodies," and a guard was mounted throughout the night to keep them under constant observation "to see that they are in no way molested."

At eleven the following morning, Sunday, 23 October, the two officers left Romagne in a white Cadillac touring car at the head of a convoy of three canvas-roofed trucks. Two carried the remains of the Unknown Soldiers, the other was empty, travelling with them in case of a breakdown en route. Two civilian convoyers and a different pair of supervisory embalmers from those who had been involved in the exhumations travelled with them. Each embalmer was equipped with "two braces and screw bits, two wrenches for metallic tops and two claw hammers." They had been ordered to depart in sufficient time "travelling at moderate speed" to arrive at the Hôtel de Ville in Châlons-sur-Marne at precisely ten to three that afternoon but were ahead of schedule and halted four kilometres from the town, where the already spotless trucks were given a further cleaning and American flags were draped over the caskets.

At the designated hour, the convoy drove into the town square, lined on all sides with an honour guard "composed of *poilus* who saw action." They stood, heads bowed and rifles reversed, as the trucks pulled up outside the flag-draped Hôtel de Ville. The trucks from Bony and Belleau Wood also arrived precisely on schedule at five to three and three o'clock, respectively. Once each had pulled up, the only sounds were the creak as the tailgate of the truck was lowered, the scrape of wood on metal as the shipping case was pulled out and the shuffling feet of the eight French NCOs acting as pallbearers. They carried each casket in turn up the flight of low steps and between the lines of French infantrymen standing rigidly to attention in the entrance hall of the Hôtel de Ville, where a catafalque had been set up to receive the casket of the chosen Unknown Soldier.

The bodies were first taken into a room off the hall, draped with flags and filled with flowers and palms. The shipping cases were removed, inverted and used as biers to support the caskets, which were covered with the Stars and Stripes and arranged in a row in the middle of the room. French soldiers formed a guard of honour around the walls and from then until six that evening a steady procession of French men, women and children filed silently past the open doorway, pausing, bowing their heads and crossing themselves. Many were in tears; there was scarcely a family in France that had not lost someone—a father, son, husband, brother, uncle or cousin—in the war.

The four designated officers had meanwhile taken their exhumation forms and the alternate envelopes—none of which had been needed—to Major Robert P. Harbold, the Chief of Field Operations, who burned the papers and envelopes in front of them. Later that evening, the room housing the Unknown Soldiers was closed to the public and, acting on Major Harbold's orders, a group of French soldiers entered the room and rearranged the caskets in a different sequence, so that no one could now know from which cemetery each Unknown Soldier had been brought. A joint guard was mounted during the night by French soldiers and American troops from the Headquarters of the U.S. Army of Occupation in Coblenz.

The ceremony of selection was not scheduled to take place until eleven the following morning, Monday, 24 October, but from first light, the town square was packed with onlookers from the town and the surrounding countryside. All were dressed in their Sunday best, silent and expectant, and when they did speak it was in low, hushed tones. Inside the Hôtel de Ville, just before eleven o'clock, fifty senior Army officers and officials from the American and French governments gathered in the room where the caskets lay in state. As the bells in the clock-tower finished sounding the hour, a French military band stationed in the courtyard struck up Chopin's funeral march.

Sergeant Edward F. Younger, one of the six pallbearers sent from the U.S. Army of Occupation on the Rhine, and "a fine type of young American" "who had fought in all the American offensives and wore two wound stripes" as well as the Distinguished Service Medal, then entered the room carrying a spray of white roses, presented by a Frenchman who had lost two sons in the war. The original plan had been for a commissioned officer to make the selection, but General Rogers had changed his mind after discovering that the French had used an enlisted man to choose their Unknown Soldier. Sergeant Younger slowly circled the four caskets three times, then paused, laid the flowers on the second coffin from the right, saluted it and withdrew.

Immediately after the selection had been made, six American NCOs raised the casket onto their shoulders and carried it across the hall to another room, where Mr. Keating, the chief supervising embalmer, General Rogers and three other senior officers removed the body from its steel coffin and placed it in an ebony casket, inlaid with silver, that had been sent from the United States. It bore only the simple phrase "Unknown, but to God," echoing the inscription "A Soldier of the Great War, known unto God," coined by Rudyard Kipling.

The steel casket was then returned to the other room, by now cleared of dignitaries, where Lieutenant Dewey, Mr. Keating and his assistant removed one of the three other bodies and placed it in the steel casket that had contained America's Unknown Soldier. The caskets were then screwed shut and the rubber gaskets sealed with "asphaltum paint." At eleven o'clock that morning, they were put on trucks and transported back to Romagne-sous-Montfaucon, assigned new "Unknown Numbers" and reburied before nightfall.

Once sealed, the ebony casket containing the Unknown Soldier was draped with the Stars and Stripes, borne into the lobby of the Hôtel de Ville and placed on the catafalque, where it lay in state. The spray of white roses was placed on the casket, which was surrounded by bouquets. Some were tributes from nations, cities and great organizations, and some from individuals, including bunches of late-flowering wildflowers picked that day from the fields and lanes around Châlons. A French guard of honour lined one side of the hall, with an American guard of honour facing them. Representatives of the Veterans of Foreign Wars and the American Legion stood to attention alongside them as, once more, a column of ordinary French men and women filed past in silent tribute to America's Unknown Soldier. Many carried wreaths and "soon the coffin was buried under piled masses of flowers."

At five that afternoon, a caisson drawn by four jet-black horses pulled up outside the Hôtel de Ville. French and American officials lined the steps and, "to the crash of presented rifles and the blare of saluting bugles," eight U.S. NCOs carried the coffin out of the building into the pale winter sunshine and placed it on the caisson. The funeral procession formed up, led by the commanding officer of the U.S. 6th Division and his personal staff, all mounted on horseback. They were followed by a military band and the company of infantry forming the guard of honour. The caisson came next, flanked by two lines of pallbearers, and then a second guard of honour of twenty-four men from the Army of Occupation. Behind them came the official mourners, including Major General Henry T. Allen, commander of the American Army of Occupation in Germany, Colonel Rethers, head of the Graves Registration Service, and the Quartermaster General, Major General Rogers. The men of the 6th Division came next, and last were the representatives of numerous civilian societies, including a number of French Boy Scouts, bearing the wreaths and flowers that had been placed around the casket in the Town Hall, and many children and old people, "who had seen the war at very close hand."

As the band played the death march from *Peer Gynt*, the cortège moved off at a slow march on the two-kilometre journey along the rue de Marne to the railway station. The entire route was lined with French soldiers and dismounted French cavalrymen, and behind them were dense crowds of silent French civilians, straining for a last glimpse of America's Unknown Soldier. People stood on the tables of the street cafés for a better view and every face captured in photographs of the occasion is sombre. In their common grief for their war dead, never had Old Europe and the New World been so united. The crowds were fifty deep around the entrance to the station and the flag-draped casket remained on the caisson for almost an hour as a near-endless line of troops and societies, many carrying floral tributes, passed by in solemn procession. As each company of soldiers passed the coffin, its standard-bearer dipped their often torn and bloodied battle-colours in salute. When the last soldier had marched away, the casket was carried into the station by the U.S. NCOs and loaded aboard a special funeral train for the journey to Paris. It pulled out of the station at ten past six that evening, "in such a slow and deliberate manner as to make one believe that the train itself realised the solemnity and importance of the occasion."

The coffin remained at Batignolles Station, on the outskirts of Paris, overnight, watched over by a guard of honour of three American soldiers and a uniformed member of the American Legion. At 9:20 the following morning, Tuesday, 25 October, accompanied by U.S. Generals Allen and Rogers, and the French Minister of Pensions, André Maginot, it was taken on to Le Havre, arriving at one o'clock in the afternoon. An enormous crowd was thronging the station and the square outside, and, as the casket was carried from the train to the waiting gun-carriage, hundreds of schoolchildren, given a holiday for the day, showered it with flowers. They marched alongside it "in straggling and unceremonious order" during the funeral procession. Behind them came thirty French soldiers, carrying the wreaths and floral tributes, and one hundred representatives of *poilu* organizations, also bearing flowers. As "the solemn parade" moved off, all the church bells of the city began tolling. They continued to do so throughout the ceremonies and until the ship bearing the Unknown Soldier had steamed away from the harbour.

The procession paused briefly outside the City Hall in the Boulevard Strasbourg, where members of the city council presented another wreath, and such was the press of people in the streets that it took an hour for the cortège to reach the quayside. Every inch of the way was lined with more dense masses of French citizens, but "it was a beautiful tribute to the French people that not one policeman was used to preserve order." At the Pier d'Escale, the cruiser USS *Olympia*, Admiral Dewey's old flagship at the Battle of Manila Bay, was waiting to carry the Unknown Soldier home. Rear Admiral Lloyd H. Chandler had sailed with the ship to "represent the United States at the ceremonies." Another huge crowd had assembled, held back by a double line of troops "with swords and bayonets glinting in the mellow sunshine." A single white rose rested on the ebony coffin as Monsieur Maginot, "limping as a result of his war service," spoke on behalf of the French government, "praising the 'obscure and magnificent sacrifice' of the nameless warrior and declaring that 'France will never forget that he gave his last dream to her.' " He then placed the Croix de Chevalier de la Légion d'Honneur on the casket. The bands played "La Marseillaise" and "The Star-Spangled Banner" as the coffin was carried to the gangway of the *Olympia*.

The ship's company, in full dress uniform, lined the rails, and the twin flags—the French tricolour at the foremast and the Stars and Stripes on the main—were struck slowly to half-mast. Then, as Chopin's "Funeral March" was played once more, the American Unknown Soldier was borne aboard the ship to begin his final voyage. The casket was placed at the stern surrounded by wreaths, and, led by nuns and priests, boys and girls of the city and representatives of various organizations marched on board and threw flowers upon the coffin "until it was almost buried from sight." A "large box of earth from the American cemetery at Suresnes" had already been carried aboard. It would line the grave at Arlington, so that the American Unknown, like his British counterpart, would forever rest in the soil for which so many of his comrades had fought and died.

Soon afterwards, at three-twenty in the afternoon, the *Olympia* "slid out, dead slow," to join the flotilla of French and American warships waiting as escorts in the calm seas beyond the harbour. As the *Olympia* cleared the harbour mouth, a French battleship fired a seventeen-gun salute. The French vessels accompanied the *Olympia* and the destroyer USS *Reuben James* to the limit of French territorial waters and then with a final salute, another seventeen-gun salvo, they turned for home. The French sailors watched from the rails as the lights of the U.S. ships disappeared into the winter darkness; "the Unknown had gone home."

27

IN THE GREY DUSK

On Wednesday, 9 November 1921, the USS *Olympia* picked up a pilot off Piney Point, and then inched her way up the Potomac River, "in the grey dusk of a rainy afternoon." The original plan, announced in February by the then Secretary of War, Newton D. Baker, had been for the *Olympia* to dock at New York, where "first honors would be paid" to the Unknown Soldier, before he was brought to Washington for "the main ceremonial," but the cost, estimated by Secretary Baker at $187,000, proved too high, and there was perhaps also a fear that a ceremony in New York would only provoke a clamour from other cities and states anxious to add their own tributes to the Unknown Soldier. As a result, the plan was quietly dropped.

The cruiser had been met "far out to sea" by an escort led by the battleship *North Dakota* and the destroyer USS *Bernadou*, and ten aircraft also overflew the *Olympia* as she steamed up the Potomac. Her captain's orders were to reach Washington "after dark" to minimize the risk that the sight of the casket of the Unknown Soldier might provoke a public response that could disrupt or detract from the schedule of official arrangements.

A ceremonial guard was mounted at George Washington's home, Mount Vernon, and as the *Olympia* passed Fort Washington and Washington Barracks, twenty-one-gun salutes were fired. The salute was repeated at the Navy Yard, as the *Olympia* entered her dock at about four o'clock that dark November afternoon. General Pershing, General Harry H. Bandholtz, the commander of the Military District of Washington and the man entrusted with planning the funeral ceremonies, the Secretaries of War and the Navy, and the chiefs of the Army, Navy and Marines were at the dockside, waiting to escort the body of the Unknown Soldier to the Capitol. The absence of the chief of the U.S. Air Service indicated the low priority still accorded to this, the newest branch of the military.

As the bearers carried the casket to the gangway, the cruiser began firing minute guns and the bo'sun piped the body ashore in the manner normally accorded to a full Admiral of the Fleet. Admiral Chandler led his officers and men behind the casket, bareheaded, with their uniform hats held to their breasts. When the bearers stepped onto the dockside they paused, standing motionless as the ship's band struck up the national anthem. The naval bearers then carried the casket to a horse-drawn caisson, draped in black, where they handed over responsibility to eight bearers from the 3rd Cavalry. A cavalry band, playing "Onward Christian Soldiers," led the funeral cortège as it moved off from the Navy Yard towards the Capitol, the music punctuated by a final twenty-one-gun salute from the *Olympia*. "The open spaces of the yard were black with silent mourners and along the way taken by the solemn procession to the east plaza of the Capitol, thousands stood with uncovered heads, careless of the rain which was falling." Two squadrons of cavalry and "the military and civil dignitaries in their automobiles" followed the caisson along M Street and New Jersey Avenue to the East Plaza of the Capitol.

The casket of the American Unknown Soldier, with its simple inscription "An Unknown American who gave his life in the world war," was placed in the centre of the Capitol Rotunda, with the foot of the coffin facing the west, upon the catafalque that had formerly borne the bodies of Presidents Lincoln, Garfield and McKinley. The funeral drapes used on those occasions were "carefully reproduced" for the ceremonies for the Unknown Soldier.

In the dim light of that November evening, a small, private ceremony took place. Accompanied by the First Lady, President Harding entered the Rotunda. Mrs. Harding placed upon the coffin a wide band of white ribbon that she had herself made, and the President then pinned to it "a silver National Shield with forty-eight gold stars" representing the individual states, and laid a great wreath of crimson roses on the casket. Vice President Calvin Coolidge also laid a wreath, and Senator Cummins, "President pro tem of the Senate," and the Speaker of the House of Representatives, Frederick H. Gillette, jointly laid a wreath of red and white flowers on behalf of the Houses of Congress. Chief Justice Taft, Secretaries Weeks and Denby and General Pershing also placed their own wreaths around the catafalque.

The Unknown Warrior was then left alone, but for the guards who kept watch throughout the night, heads bowed and weapons reversed. More than an hour before the Rotunda was opened to the public the following morning, 10 November, a line had formed a block long. The rain and fog of the previous night had blown away on a brisk wind and only a few white clouds dotted the pale winter sky. Most of the flowers laid the previous night had been removed, and only "the flowers sent from France, the shield of the nation placed there by President Harding and the white ribbon tenderly tied by Mrs. Harding" lay on the American flag draping the coffin.

When the bronze doors of the Rotunda—a gift from France in the early days of the Republic—were unlocked at eight that morning, an endless stream of Americans began entering, four abreast, through the east door, filing past the casket and exiting through the west door, "with no halt to its slow march, save to permit the laying of an occasional wreath upon the growing mass of flowers." Various patriotic and fraternal organizations had also been permitted to hold brief, strictly time-tabled services or ceremonies in honour of the Unknown Soldier. A maximum of fifteen minutes was allotted to each group, as "the time for paying respects . . . does not admit of the extensive ceremonies proposed by some organizations." The only exception was for the Grand Army of the Republic, which was permitted to hold ceremonies lasting forty minutes.

There were also tributes from many foreign nations. The new French Premier, Aristide Briand, laid "a bunch of pink chrysanthemums, tied with the tricolor," and among a multitude of other tributes, the Chinese Republic sent a statue of the Angel of Peace and there were wreaths from Russia, Belgium, Japan, Czechoslovakia, Honduras and the Republic of Cuba, which sent a wreath of yellow roses. "Conspicuous among the delegations was that representing the British Empire, who came in a score of automobiles and two trucks bearing flowers." The British Ambassador, Sir Auckland Geddes, and the former Prime Minister Arthur Balfour, in Washington for the Disarmament Conference opening on 12 November, laid a wreath made of "flowers brought over from England as living plants," on behalf of the British Prime Minister and people. The wreath was inscribed "Nameless, yet his name liveth for evermore." The Earl of Cavan, representing King George V, laid "a wreath of red English roses, crowned at the top with a bunch of flowers made up from all the Dominions." The British Great War Veterans of America presented a wreath of black leaves, forming a replica of the Victoria Cross. There were tributes, too, from South Africa—"wild flowers typical of the country's unrivalled flora"— Canada, Newfoundland, India, Australia and New Zealand.

The ranks of private citizens had continued to file past the casket even as the organizations were conducting their ceremonies, but the waiting lines of individuals were still so long at the scheduled closing time of ten o'clock that night—extending "ten deep for many blocks from the Capitol"—that a two-hour extension was granted. At midnight, when the great bronze doors were closed, it was estimated that 90,000 people had already filed past the casket, but many others, disappointed, were shepherded away after the doors were shut.

Prompted by President Harding, Congress had approved a bill to declare Armistice Day 1921 a public holiday "as a mark of respect to the memory of those who gave their lives in the late World War," and the five-mile route of the funeral procession was lined with people long before the cortège set out at eight-thirty the next morning, 11 November 1921. The military escort and the dignitaries, led by President Harding, who would march behind the coffin, formed up on the East Plaza of the Capitol, all the other groups and organizations assembled in the side streets around the Capitol grounds or off Pennsylvania Avenue, ready to join the procession as it passed.

At eight that morning, as the Army band assembled on the plaza played a dirge, the "body bearers"—five soldiers, two sailors and one Marine—entered the Rotunda. One of them, Sergeant Woodfill, representing the infantry, had been hand-picked by General Pershing in tribute to Woodfill's extraordinary bravery on 12 October 1918, when three successive times he had single-handedly attacked and disabled German machine-gun nests, killing nineteen enemy soldiers and capturing three. The bearers carried the casket out of the Rotunda and down the east steps of the Capitol. Twelve honorary pallbearers—three flag officers and nine general officers, all veterans of the Great War—

followed them. As they emerged into the morning light, an artillery battery stationed near the Washington Monument began firing minute guns. It continued to do so for the next four hours, pausing only for the two-minute silence at twelve noon. The bearers placed the casket on the plain, black-draped caisson, drawn by six black horses, and the cortège moved off at once towards Pennsylvania Avenue.

Crowds 100,000 strong were spread along the entire five-mile length of the procession route, held back by infantry standing at five-yard intervals. National Guard units from New York and Pennsylvania had originally been scheduled to form part of the honour guard, but their places were taken by troops based nearer Washington. The "paucity of funds provided by Congress," which refused to "appropriate enough money for the purpose," was blamed for the change. Secretary Weeks had asked for $125,000, but Congress had voted only $50,000. "As a result," the *New York Times* complained, "the ceremonies will not be representative of the principle and object lesson which the burial of the unknown warrior implies."

General Bandholtz and three other mounted officers rode at the head of the procession, but General Pershing had declined to be a "grand marshal and ride at the head of the funeral escort. As Chief of the American Expeditionary Force, General Pershing regards himself as a mourner at the symbolic funeral and he will walk the five miles." The mounted officers were followed by a military band, a drum corps, a composite infantry regiment, a mounted battalion of field artillery and a squadron of cavalry. Four chaplains followed them, walking abreast, directly in front of the caisson. Among them was the Right Reverend Charles Henry Brent, Senior Chaplain of the American Expeditionary Force, who was to conduct the Protestant rites at the ceremony, and the Reverend Francis A. Kelley, who would perform the Catholic rituals.

Behind the caisson came the long cortège, headed by the chief mourner, President Harding, walking with the Army Chief of Staff. Vice President Coolidge and the Chief of Naval Operations came next and then the Chief Justice, walking with the Commandant of the Coast Guard, in place of the "lamed and broken" former President Wilson, who was permitted to ride in an "old-fashioned Victoria carriage" towards the rear—the only member of the cortège who was not on foot. The Chief Justice was followed by the other members of the Supreme Court, cabinet members, state governors, senators, congressmen and General Pershing.

Another drum corps followed the politicians, placed there by General Bandholtz to help maintain a brisker pace than the traditional funeral slow march, and ensure that the procession reached Arlington at the appointed time. Behind them, marching eight abreast, were soldiers who had won the Congressional Medal of Honor. All the holders of this, the highest award for valour throughout the United States had been invited to attend the ceremony, but in a further indication of congressional purse-tightening, only those who had won it in the Great War were there at government expense. The rest, although already invited, had their invitations rescinded and were forced to pay their own way, but exception was made for one Medal of Honor winner who lived in Panama and had already begun the long journey to Washington before his invitation was withdrawn.

The ailing former President Wilson came next in the procession, riding in his carriage, and following him were representatives of the Army, Navy, Marine Corps and Coast Guard—once more the USAS was slighted—and troops from every state and territory of the Union. Bringing up the rear were representatives of "forty-four patriotic, fraternal and welfare organisations," including the Grand Army of the Republic, the American Legion, the Daughters of the American Revolution, the Red Cross, the Salvation Army, the Colored Veterans of the War, the Knights of Columbus, the Jewish Veterans of the World War, the Imperial Order of the Dragon and the Gold Star Mothers. Three hundred women, "marching in the uniforms in which they served as nurses in France," represented the American Red Cross.

The crowds lining the route did not always watch in silence. They cheered the group of Medal of Honor winners and "the cheers became a roar when the Gold Star Mothers approached . . . they, like the men, followed the caisson on foot." President Wilson also received an ovation that visibly moved him. The cortège moved down Pennsylvania Avenue to the White House, where President Harding, the other politicians and the judiciary left the procession. They travelled on to Arlington by car, crossing Highway Bridge at 14th Street and entering the cemetery at Treasury Gate, but the President almost left his departure from the White House too late. He became caught in traffic and his driver had to take a short cut across an open field to get him to Arlington just in time to take his place as the Unknown Soldier was brought to his final resting place.

The procession had continued through Georgetown, crossing the river by the Aqueduct Bridge (now demolished, but then sited upstream from the present Francis Scott Key Bridge). There the four chaplains also left the procession, travelling on to Arlington by car. At the same time, the U.S. Army Band was replaced by the band of the U.S. Marines for the remainder of the journey along the Military Road of Fort Myer to the West Gate of Arlington, where most of the military escort fell out. The remainder of the procession followed the Marine Band, playing a funeral march, to the West Entrance of the Memorial Amphitheater. The caisson came to a halt at eleven-forty that morning, more than three hours after leaving the Capitol. Those members of the procession who had tickets—not all of the patriotic and fraternal representatives could be accommodated—joined the 5,000-strong crowd inside the amphitheatre. The remainder mingled with the tens of thousands of people surrounding it.

The casket was borne inside the amphitheatre and placed on a black-draped catafalque in the centre of "the great oval with walls and columns of white marble and a colonnade around the rim." To one side the audience looked out across "grassy fields with thousands of white markers over the graves of soldier and sailor dead"; on the opposite side of the auditorium was the "domed stage of marble" surrounded by deep banks of flowers. There were wreaths from every state and territory in the Union and "at the centre of every wreath was a blue star, and in the centre of the blue, a star of gold." President Harding, slightly flustered by his late arrival, hurried in at four minutes to twelve and the ceremony at once began with the playing of the national anthem. The Army Chief of Chaplains, Colonel John T. Axon, recited the invocation, "his right hand raised with dramatic intensity," and a bugler then sounded "Attention," signalling the start of the two-minute silence. Among the crowds on that cold November day were Grace Seibold and her husband, still in mourning for their son. She was one of 1,000 Gold Star Mothers allocated seats at the ceremony.

Alerted by the sound of "all public and church bells throughout the United States" tolling "at intervals between 11:45 and 12 o'clock noon," the inhabitants of every American town and city also stood in silence, responding to President Harding's "call upon all devout and patriotic citizens of the United States to pause from their accustomed occupations and labours" for a two-minute silence beginning at noon. He also requested that "they assemble in their respective houses of worship to do honour to the memory of those who died for their country in the Great War." Some may have preferred the rather more secular commemoration offered by the Keith Vaudeville Theatres across the country, which held memorial services instead of their normal programmes, where they, too, observed a two-minute silence.

(Left) Grace Seibold *(center)* with Gold Star Mothers after laying a wreath at the Tomb of the American Unknown Soldier, Arlington National Cemetery, Virginia.

(Below) George Gordon Seibold laying a wreath at the Tomb of the American Unknown Soldier in memory of his son.

(Inset) George Seibold's grandfather, Brigadier-General Edward Washburn Whitaker, a Congressional Medal of Honor winner at Reams Stations, Virginia, in June 1864.

(*Above*) "A" Flight, 148th Aero Squadron, photographed on 14 September 1918. *From left to right:* Lawrence T. Wyly, Louis W. Rabe, Field E. Kindley (holding his pet dog, Fokker), Walter B. Knox and Jesse O. Creech. Rabe had just arrived as replacement for George Seibold. Creech saw George shot down and recorded the location of the crash site. Kindley would later become engaged to George's widow, Kathryn, before dying in a crash at an air display at Kelley Field, Texas, in January 1920.

(*Right*) A marker placed on the grave of Quentin Roosevelt, killed in action in July 1918.

(*Right*) Leutnant Hermann Frommherz (*right*), Führer of Jasta 27, who shot down George Seibold on 26 August 1918, one of three American victims he claimed that day. The officer next to Frommherz is Oberleutnant Hermann Goering, Kommandeur of Jagdeschwader 1, the future Nazi Reich's marshall.

(Left) The grave of the "Red Baron," Manfred von Richthofen, at Allonville. The cross cut from a propeller was stolen from the grave in the closing week of the war.

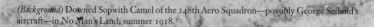

(Background) Downed Sopwith Camel of the 148th Aero Squadron—possibly George Seibold's aircraft—in No Man's Land, summer 1918.

An exhumed body being wrapped for reburial in a U.S. military cemetery. The finely woven, hard burlap used was more durable than the coarse burlap in which the bodies were transported from the battlefield.

(*Background*) Exhumed bodies from the battlefields of Romagne-sous-Montfaucon. Wrapped in burlap, they were carried by stretcher to waiting trucks, then placed in coffins and either transported to the American military cemetery for reburial or, if they could be identified and the relatives so wished it, shipped back to the United States. A disproportionately large number of the men employed on clearing the battlefields of the dead were black soldiers, the sort of menial and unpleasant task to which black troops were routinely assigned.

Sergeant Edward Younger, standing between two of the four coffins from which he chose the American Unknown Soldier.

A grave marked by the U.S. Quartermasters Corps' Graves Registration Service, showing the dead soldier's identity tag and the metal plate prepared by the Service.

(*Right*) The funeral procession of the American Unknown Soldier passing through Le Havre on 25 October 1921.

.(*Left*) The Unknown Soldier being carried aboard the *Olympia* at Le Havre.

(*Background*) The American Unknown Soldier is borne away from the train that brought him from Chalons-sur-Marne.

(*Clockwise from top right*) President Harding honouring the Unknown Soldier of World War I in the Rotunda of the Capitol, 9 November 1921.

President Harding delivering the funeral oration at Arlington National Cemetery.

Ten loudspeakers known as "projectors" and between seven and ten feet long were hung from the ceiling of Madison Square Garden, New York, to broadcast the President's speech.

President Harding and General Pershing (*center*) walk behind the coffin of the Unknown Soldier on his final journey to Arlington National Cemetery. To their left are General Pershing's aides: Colonels John McAuley Palmer, George C. Marshall and John G. Quekemeyer.

The control room at San Francisco relaying President Harding's speech through the "Bell Loud Talker."

(*Top*) General John "Black Jack" Pershing pays his tribute at the burial of the Unknown American Soldier at Arlington National Cemetery on 11 November 1921.

(*Bottom*) The British Legion's "Great March of Peace" to a ceremony of Remembrance at the Menin Gate, Ypres, 8 August 1928. The Prince of Wales led a procession of eleven thousand British pilgrims.

In New York, where "flags flew at half-mast from buildings all over the city and on ships of many nations in the port," "great crowds jammed the two cathedrals in Manhattan and overflowed onto the sidewalks." Huge crowds had also gathered to watch a parade up Fifth Avenue by the Veterans of Foreign Wars. "The Negro warriors of the Rattlesnake Division marched in a large body and were loudly cheered," but all fell quiet for the Great Silence. In Chicago, vast crowds stood bareheaded in the snow as the silence began, and in Indianapolis, crowds watched a parade by American Legionnaires and then stood bareheaded for the silence, ignoring the pouring rain. A plaque was dedicated in Louisville "under 'the naturalisation tree' where thousands of foreigners in the army took the oath of allegiance." In Philadelphia, the tolling of the old State House Bell at Independence Hall signalled the start of the silence. "On busy streets, jammed with motor cars, trucks and hurrying pedestrians, traffic policemen raised one hand in salute to the memory of the men symbolised by the Unknown Soldier whose body was honoured at Arlington, halted the hurrying throngs of humanity and quieted the roar of motors." In Brownsville, Texas, a "snow-white pigeon" flew into the Sacred Heart Church, "perched over a memorial window" and remained there throughout the silence and the rest of the Armistice Day service. On the eve of the Disarmament Conference, few could resist the symbolism. Detroit women holding a mass meeting to call for disarmament also paused in silent remembrance of the war dead. In all, more than a hundred million Americans paid "an homage of silence more eloquent than speech."

The American Army of Occupation in Coblenz and Andernach also held special services and posts of the Veterans of Foreign Wars throughout the world took part in ceremonies and commemorations. The Paris post, largely composed of members of the Graves Registration Service still involved in the task of identifying and reburying unknown American soldiers, took part in services at the Panthéon de la Guerre and the Arc de Triomphe. The Veterans of Foreign Wars also joined in commemorations in Antwerp and Brussels.

At the end of the Great Silence at Arlington, the congregation sang "America," and President Harding, having removed his overcoat, then delivered the funeral oration, praising the Unknown Soldier and calling for an end to war. Among his audience were the international delegates to the Disarmament Conference, which was to open the next morning. Although Presidents Harding and Wilson shared the platform, their visions of the means to achieve peace and the shape of the post-war world could scarcely have been more divergent. Wilson, the internationalist father of the League of Nations, had to endure the humiliation of seeing his successor destroy it, as Harding, sensing the country's isolationist mood, vetoed U.S. membership of the League as an infringement of American sovereignty.

Harding's funeral oration was captured by "a transmitter far more delicate and sensitive than . . . the ordinary telephone," and broadcast by "loud speaking apparatus hidden in and about the Arlington amphitheatre," enabling "all within half a mile of the President to hear his voice clearly and distinctly." Huge crowds at American Legion rallies in an auditorium in San Francisco and New York's Madison Square Garden, also heard a live relay of the President's speech "by means of the loud speaking telephone" or "Bell Loud Talker, as it is called." The electric current carrying the President's voice was, the *New York Times* breathlessly informed its readers, "multiplied 3,000,000,000,000,000,000,000,000,000 times." It was "the first time anything on so large a scale has been attempted in public," and his audience was "several times greater than any which ever listened all at once to a single human voice."

After the hymn, "The Supreme Sacrifice," sung by four soloists from the Metropolitan Opera, the President placed the Congressional Medal of Honor and the Distinguished Service Cross on the casket. Earl Beatty, the British Admiral of the Fleet, then laid the Victoria Cross there—"the strongest and most significant expression that Great Britain could make of her gratitude for American co-operation in the war." Premier Aristide Briand, "sturdy as the Breton fisherfolk from whom he came," was representing France at the ceremony, but Marshal Foch was also there, not, as he was careful to stress, as an official French representative but as a private citizen, a guest of the American Legion. However, it was Foch who laid the Médaille Militaire, the highest French military award, and the Croix de Guerre on the coffin.

General Diaz of the Italian Army awarded the Gold Medal for Bravery, and General Baron Alphonse Jacques placed the Belgian Croix de Guerre alongside it. Several other nations presented their country's highest awards for valour, including the Romanian Virtutea Militare and two awards from nations born out of the ruins of the Austro-Hungarian and Russian empires—the Czechoslovak War Cross and the Polish Virtuti Militari. There were further hymns and readings, and the congregation sang "Nearer My God to Thee," then the Marine Band played "Our Honored Dead" as the casket was carried to the tomb on the terrace of the amphitheatre, followed by the clergy, dignitaries and the rest of the congregation.

Bishop Brent read the burial service and then Congressman Fish, who had originally proposed the idea of burying an Unknown Soldier, laid the first wreath on the tomb. Among the wreaths were the faded white roses that Sergeant Younger had placed on the casket in Châlons-sur-Marne eighteen days earlier. They were to be buried with the Unknown Soldier. Emphasizing the theme of national reconciliation and unity, Chief Plenty Coups of the Crow Indians, wearing full war regalia and representing all American Indian tribes, placed his coup stick and war bonnet on the tomb. But despite this and the inclusion of an address by a rabbi in the funeral service, few in that vast congregation can have conceived of the American Unknown as being other than a white, Christian American. Even though a delegation of African-American leaders had laid a wreath on the casket as the Unknown Soldier lay in state at the Capitol, not a single reference was made in any speech to the possibility that he might have been black. And two years later, the President of the Jewish Welfare Board had to remind the Commission of Fine Arts that a proposed monument for the Unknown Soldier including a cross was hardly an appropriate symbol for a grave that might well have contained a Jew.

A long line of people representing various organizations also laid flowers or wreaths on the tomb. Marshal Foch laid a wreath of silver palms for French war veterans and Sergeant G. Richardson of Toronto, the oldest living holder of the Victoria Cross, who had been decorated at Cawnpore on 27 April 1859, placed a wreath of maples on behalf of the Grand Army of United Veterans of Canada. Mrs. R. Emmett Digney laid a wreath from the Gold Star Mothers and Mrs. Amelia E. McCudden presented one on behalf of British war mothers. She wore replicas of the decorations for valour, including a Victoria Cross, won by her husband and her two sons, all of whom had been killed in the war. The wreath she laid had been made from "blooms growing in boxes and pots," which had travelled with her from England in a "miniature conservatory" erected on the deck of the ship, to "ensure their perfection of bloom on their arrival in America." A florist had also made the voyage to "fashion them into the destined tribute."

After the wreath-laying had concluded, a gun battery then fired three salvos as the casket was lowered into the crypt, where it lay on the soil brought from France. A bugler sounded taps and as the last note faded, the battery fired a twenty-one-gun salute. The ceremony was over. The Unknown Soldier had gone to his last resting place, upon the hill looking out across the Potomac River to Washington, D.C.

Sir Maurice Hankey, reporting back to Lloyd George, who, like

Lord Curzon, had remained in London because of "impending developments in domestic politics" relating to "the Troubles" in Ireland, had a gratingly patronizing view of the occasion. "It was much too long, with a curious medley of prayers, hymns, long speeches, musical performances by a quartette from the New York Opera, absurd little speeches by Foreign Officers, laying decorations and repeated wreath laying. The finale was a curious function by an old Indian chief dressed up like a picture in one of Fenimore Cooper's books, but I could not see it very well because the lady in front of me had a head-dress like the Indian chief's."

Undisturbed by Old World snobbery, the streams of mourners continued to file past the tomb of the Unknown American Soldier. For some, the emotions aroused were too painful to bear. Lieutenant Colonel Charles W. Whittlesey, commander of the "Lost Battalion," which had held out alone for five days in the Argonne Forest in October 1918, and a holder of the Congressional Medal of Honor, had been one of the pallbearers at the funeral of the Unknown Soldier. He had been "deeply affected by the ceremonies" and, after leaving farewell messages, he boarded a liner outbound from New York to Havana and jumped overboard when two days out at sea.

Like its British counterpart, the Tomb of the American Unknown Soldier at once became the national symbol of mourning for the war dead, but regional and local commemoration of the war was on a more modest scale, reflecting the very different levels of losses in the two countries—from a population well under half that of the United States, Britain suffered fourteen times as many casualties. As in Britain, there were fierce arguments between advocates of utilitarian "living memorials"—schools, meeting halls, parks, libraries and community centres, rather than the rash of statuary of varying artistic merit that had been erected to commemorate the Civil War—and those who insisted that only statues and monuments were a fitting tribute to the dead. In most cases the latter argument held sway, and in communities throughout the United States, statues were erected, usually of doughboys and often accompanied by German artillery pieces, some of the captured spoils of war distributed by the U.S. government.

While the Tomb of the Unknown became the focus of pilgrimages from all over the United States, there was no common consensus on what it represented. Once more, the neutrality of the tomb allowed everyone to project onto it their own feelings, emotions and aspirations. Some saw it as a silent plea for peace and disarmament, a symbol of mourning and loss. Others, led by the American Legion, had a much more muscular, nationalist and militarist interpretation of its meaning. Both sides were united in only one thing: a deprecation of the insensitive visitors who used the tomb as either "a bench or a picnic table."

The American Legion campaigned vigourously for a ceremonial guard to be mounted to ensure that visitors showed the proper reverence for the Tomb, and in 1926, pressured by the President and Congress, the War Department agreed. The department and the legion were united in the belief that the tomb lacked a suitably patriotic monument, and two years later, after a competition to find an acceptable design, work began on replacing the original simple tomb with a far grander monument. Designed by architect Lorimer Rich and sculptor Thomas Hudson Jones, it was built at a cost of $48,000, but opened without fanfare or public ceremony on 9 April 1932. The massive sarcophagus of white Yule marble was quarried in Vermont. The front panel, facing Washington, D.C., is carved with three figures, representing "the spirit of the Allies of World War I": a female Victory figure at the centre, a male figure symbolizing Valour to the right and, at the left, Peace, offering a palm branch in reward for the soldier's devotion and sacrifice. The north and south sides contain carvings of three inverted wreaths, separated by Doric columns set into the surface, and on the west side, facing the Amphitheatre, is inscribed:

HERE RESTS IN
HONORED GLORY
AN AMERICAN SOLDIER
KNOWN BUT TO GOD

Never officially named, the Tomb of the Unknown American Soldier is now most widely known as "The Tomb of the Unknowns"—Unknown Soldiers from the Second World War and the Korean War are also buried nearby. An Unknown from the Vietnam War was also interred there, but the body was later exhumed and identified by DNA testing and that grave now stands empty. All three graves are marked with white marble slabs set into the surface of the plaza, and the site remains a place of pilgrimage for relatives of the unknown dead of all the United States' foreign wars.

The selection of Unknown Soldiers from the First World War has continued until the present day. In 1993, the body of the Australian Unknown Soldier was exhumed from the Adelaide Cemetery at Villers-Bretonneux and flown home to be interred in the Hall of Memory at the Australian War Memorial in Canberra. In 1999, the Canadian Unknown Soldier was disinterred from a cemetery near Vimy Ridge, flown to Ottawa and reburied in a sarcophagus standing in front of the Canadian War Memorial. And even more recently, on Armistice Day 2004, New Zealand's Unknown Warrior, exhumed from a cemetery in Caterpillar Valley in Longueval, just below High Wood, was buried in the National War Memorial in Wellington.

Although the development of DNA testing may now have brought an end to the process by offering the possibility of precise identification of even the most anonymous body fragment, the symbolic importance of these Unknown Soldiers remains undiminished by the passing years. The Tomb of the Unknown Warrior in Westminster Abbey, the Tomb of the Unknowns in Arlington Cemetery in Virginia, the Neue Wache in Berlin, the eternal flame burning beneath the Arc de Triomphe in Paris, the dozens of other sites in cities as far apart as Baghdad and Canberra (Australia), Ottawa and Warsaw, Athens and Kiev, Wellington (New Zealand) and Moscow, Rome and Bandung (Indonesia), and the multitude of battlefield cemeteries in Flanders and northern France remain sites of pilgrimage to this day.

In January 1946, the British government announced that all public commemoration of the dead of both world wars would in future be held on the Sunday before 11 November rather than on Armistice Day itself, and it would henceforth be known as "Remembrance Day." By this act, the Great Silence at the Cenotaph was stripped of much of its symbolism—a silence stilling the traffic and commercial activity at the height of the working week has far more impact that a silence on a day when the working heart of London is largely deserted anyway. It was perhaps expected that observance of the day would quietly fade away with the last living survivors but, after a period of steady decline, renewed interest in the Great War and the active campaigning of the Western Front Association and the British Legion has led to markedly increased attendances at Remembrance Day ceremonies in recent years and a revival of the traditional two-minute silence on Armistice Day. The dead are still with us; we shall remember them.

EPILOGUE

Long hence, when young trees are growing here and the plough has passed over shell-hole and trench, this landscape will show in the eyes of any that survive it.

ERNST JUNGER

A narrow, sinuous road cuts through the rolling farmland surrounding High Wood. The breeze confirms an American writer's observation that "when the air is damp, you can smell rusted iron everywhere, even though you see only wheat and barley." In these misleadingly placid-looking fields, the road passes cemetery after cemetery after cemetery, until High Wood at last shows itself, a long, dark mound covering the crest of a low hill. The cemetery housing those men of the 47th (London) Division whose bodies could be recovered lies to the west of the road as it passes the wood. Their modest memorial, a plain white stone cross, sits among the trees within the wood itself. After leaning at an angle for some time, slipping—appropriately enough—into a long-forgotten First World War trench, the memorial has now been righted and its foundations strengthened. One of the survivors of the Civil Service Rifles at High Wood left instructions for his ashes to be scattered here, after his death in 1976, so that he could be reunited with the comrades who had never returned.

Virtually undisturbed since the fighting ceased, High Wood remains a sombre, eerie place even today. Few birds sing there and though the wind may be whistling over the plains, it barely penetrates the heart of the wood. Dark, shadowed tracks run between the tall trees groping towards the light. In winter it seems inconceivable that those black and barren trees are not as dead as those who still lie buried beneath them. In summer, the sunlight filtering through the dense canopy of leaves is reduced to a soft green light, blurring the outlines and contours so that every shape becomes uncertain and suspicious.

As elsewhere in this war-torn land, winter ploughing in the fields around High Wood still raises an annual harvest of rusting ordnance, barbed wire, tunic buttons and fragments of bleached bone. Inside the wood, where few are permitted to wander—it is private property and the owners, living in the simple farmhouse built by their grandfather in the southern corner of the wood, give souvenir hunters short shrift—it seems that every bush and bramble conceals another rusting entrenchment tool, steel helmet, shell casing or stick grenade. Some are still live. My guide, a French armourer from the nearby village, took the cordite from one shell and ignited it with his lighter. It did not explode, but burned with a faint sizzling sound, and for a few seconds the smell of cordite again hung in the air of High Wood.

I stood at the far edge of the wood, near the summit of the hill where an icy wind was blowing up the slopes, and let my gaze travel the short arc from the Switch Line, where Alec Reader died, through Maricourt, where Paul Hub fell, to Bapaume, where George Seibold plunged to his death. At first glance, there is nothing in those bland rolling fields, ploughed and neatly furrowed and already greening with winter wheat, to hint at the multitudes still lying beneath them. Then the eye starts to pick out incongruities, faint zigzagging lines still etched in places on the landscape, a thin wavering band of deeper or paler green, a crater or a pond where none should be. And everywhere, as far as the eye can see, the fields are punctuated by walled enclosures framing neat rows of stones, white as teeth in a skull.

I turned and walked back down the hill. As I left the wood, I paused at the foot of the memorial, and laid a wreath of evergreens and—like Rose Reader—the last of the year's roses from my own garden. I placed it in tribute not only to Alec Reader, George Seibold, Paul Hub and all the numberless dead of the Great War, but to the families of all those long-dead men, who almost ninety years later are still striving to keep their memory alive.

I drove north through a landscape of sleepy villages and small towns whose names—Thiepval, Cambrai, Arras and Mons—still provoke a shudder of recognition, and arrived in Ypres just as the light was fading. At sunset, I stood before the Menin Gate. Some of the names it bears had already become illegible by the time the monument was completed in 1927, but the great arch itself will, it is claimed, stand for hundreds or even thousands of years.

Every night for over seventy-five years, a bugler has stood on this spot and played a tribute to the dead. There is now virtually no one left alive who fought in the Great War, yet crowds still gather at sunset to stand in the shadow of the great arch inscribed with the names of the myriad dead whose last resting places are unknown, and the emotional resonance of that nightly ritual at the Menin Gate remains as pure, powerful and moving as ever. We stood together in silent remembrance as the echoes of the Last Post faded and died on the cold wind blowing over that charnel land.

Notes

Unless otherwise indicated, all quotations by Paul Hub are taken from the correspondence of Paul Hub held by the Hauptstaatsarchiv Stuttgart (1351/1973 M660/019 Familienpapiere Hub); those by Alec Reader from his collected letters among the personal papers of the late Roger Goodman, copies also held by the Imperial War Museum, London (IWM 4127 83/3/1 Reader, BA); those by George Seibold from the family papers of A. Bingham Seibold, Chicago; and those of David Railton from the letters held by the Imperial War Museum (IWM 80/22/1 Reverend D. Railton).

vii: "Farewell. You have known . . . loving, faithful hearts": Otto Heinebach, *German Students' War Letters*, p. 243.

INTRODUCTION

xiii: "an echo of the Great War . . . for eighty years": Mark Derez, "A Belgian Salient for Reconstruction," pp. 443–44.

xiii: "In Memoriam" columns: Paul Fussell, *The Great War and Modern Memory*, p. 315.

xiv: "war memoirs of the dead": Samuel Hynes, *A War Imagined*, p. 209.

xiv: "people who write . . . away from the trenches": Karl Josenhans, *German Students' War Letters*, p. 41.

xv: "gone through a mirror . . . diminishing shadow": W. F. J. Harvey, *Pi in the Sky*, p. 72.

PROLOGUE: THE SOMME, 1916

3: "the usual inverted bottle . . . bearing his name": Frederick Mortimer Clapp, *History of the 17th Aero Squadron*, p. 39.

4: "came back from the line at dusk": David Railton, "The Origins of the Unknown Warrior," in *Our Empire*, vol. VII, no. 8, 1931, p. 34.

4: "only six paces . . . guns seemed to be resting": ibid.

1: THE REGIMENT OF THE DEAD

5: Whenever he went away . . . a bracelet: Interview with Frau Brigitte Kostka, January 2005.

6: He walked with a pronounced . . . shorter than the other: Interview with Frau Kostka.

6: "honourable, honest and very loyal": Interview with Frau Kostka.

6: "You must not imagine . . . stay prudently behind": Franz Blumenfeld, *German Students' War Letters*, p. 17.

6: "We had seen the generation . . . our country's greatness . . . setting out in joy . . . waiting for me later on": Otto Braun, quoted in Guy Chapman, *Vain Glory*, pp. 116–17.

6: "It is critical . . . goes up in smoke": Quoted in Holger H. Herwig, *The First World War*, p. 35.

7: "a world war . . . decades to come": Herwig, op. cit., p. 36.

7: "more smoke . . . how to annihilate one": Quoted in Michael Howard, *The Franco-Prussian War*, p. 380.

7: "The war . . . whole social organisation": M. Bloch, *Is War Impossible?*, quoted in Leon Wolff, *In Flanders Fields*, p. xiiv.

8: "we sweated like cooked herrings": GE 01 Anonymous Diary, Liddle Collection.

8: "thudding on the sand-bag . . . an angry hornet": Lance-Corporal G. E. Sedding, in Lawrence Housman (ed.), *War Letters of Fallen Englishmen*, pp. 232–33.

8: "first losses; in the first night, the first dead": GE 04 Diary of Heinrich Balters, Liddle Collection, p. 3.

8: "in an area of meadowland . . . what is to come": Herbert Sulzbach, *With the German Guns*, p. 37.

8: some likened it to siege warfare: Herwig, op. cit., p. 115.

8: "clear the houses . . . casualties are always high": ibid.

9: "Part of our trench . . . high into the air": German soldier quoted in Matthew Holden, *War in the Trenches*, p. 21.

9: "the gateway to hell": Mark Derez, "A Belgian Salient for Reconstruction," p. 437.

9: "Their shattering impact . . . locked-in concussion": Edmund Blunden, *Undertones of War*, p. 164.

9: "shrapnel bombs . . . limbs from bodies": Herwig, op. cit., p. 115.

9: "We kill and pluck . . . shells falling near them": Sulzbach, op. cit., p. 38.

9: "Before I could stop them . . . we started back": Kurt Rohrbach, *German Students' War Letters*, pp. 273–74.

10: "that louse's nest": Lothar Dietz, *German Students' War Letters*, p. 63.

10: "The breakthrough will be . . . attacked with vigour": Svetlana Palmer and Sarah Wallis, *A War in Words*, p. 33.

10: "look like a mass of poppies, intermingled with cornflowers": Quoted in Holden, op. cit., p. 24.

11: "Nobody will come through . . . a different person": Rudolf Fischer, *German Students' War Letters*, p. 14.

11: "a little wooded valley . . . in the shell-holes": Lothar Dietz, *German Students' War Letters*, pp. 62–63.

11: "First we built . . . an idyllic grove": ibid.

12: "the scabrous mud . . . fish in a basket": C. E. Montague, *Disenchantment*, p. 169.

12: "Prussian blue" peacetime uniforms: Sulzbach, op. cit., p. 39.

12: it was not defiance of the enemy . . . led them to do so: Herwig, op. cit., p. 116.

12: "a heap of rubbish": Rudolf Binding, quoted in Chapman, op. cit., p. 147.

12: killed or maimed a whole corps of German students: Williamson Murray, *War in the Air*, p. 28.

13: "march of honour to Langemark": Herwig, op. cit., p. 116.

13: "war volunteer Paul Hub . . . face of the enemy": Certificate, Paul Hub papers, Hauptstaatsarchiv, Stuttgart.

13: "recommended for the Iron Cross—for playing skat [cards] well?": GE 01 Anonymous Diary, Liddle Collection, p. 17.

13: staff officers joked that only through suicide could a soldier escape winning one: Herwig, op. cit., p. 192.

13: "in a long strange bundle . . . from the wrapping": Ernst Junger, *Copse 125*, p. 53.

13: "We fetched some large . . . from his cold cheek": Max Bassler, *German Students' War Letters*, pp. 235–36.

13: "Burying the killed . . . moving about in our trench": IWM, 5016 Misc 26 (469), German Army Officer's Recollections, p. 2.

13: "Lucky the few . . . flesh taste to rats": Hugo Muller, *German Students' War Letters*, p. 278.

14: "no rest beneath . . . blow up the graves": Gotthold von Rohden, *German Students' War Letters*, p. 160.

14: down to 30, commanded by a single officer: Herwig, op. cit., p. 119.

14: "Two cemeteries have been made . . . torn to pieces by shells": Alfons Ankenband, *German Students' War Letters*, p. 73.

14: "one good man . . . three outside of it": American veteran, quoted in Wolff, op. cit., pp. xii–xiii.

14: "become as great a necessity as the rifle": Sir John French to King George V, quoted in Harold Nicolson, *King George V*, p. 259.

14: the British Army's annual . . . four years of war: John Ellis, *Eye Deep in Hell*, p. 25.

14: war of attrition, a phrase already being used in October 1914: Captain G. Pollard, *War Letters of Fallen Englishmen*, p. 221.

15: "the principle of the gambler . . . he is a pauper": Sir William Robertson, quoted in Wolff, op. cit., pp. xii–xiii.

15: "we are a living wall . . . a fortress thousands of kilometers long": Sulzbach, op. cit., p. 138.

15: "the best trenches . . . mechanical digger had made them": A. L. Robins, Liddle GS 1368, Part 4, p. 10.

15: "as solid as a pyramid": Blunden, op. cit., p. 136.

15: floorboards, wallpaper . . . and electric light: George Coppard, *With a Machine Gun to Cambrai*, p. 87; Junger, op. cit., pp. 18–19.

15: "black lattice of flies . . . the passer-by": Blunden, op. cit., p. 242.

15: "one could traverse . . . coming to the surface": Junger, op. cit., p. 18.

15: "The result . . . lousy scratch holes": Coppard, op. cit., p. 87.

15: "a certain dampness": Quoted in Paul Fussell, *The Great War and Modern Memory*, p. 181.

15: "dread of the enemy . . . dread of the mud": Eugen Rocker, *German Students' War Letters*, p. 342.

15: "There is a soft whisper . . . oppresses one's lungs": Ludwig Fink, *German Students' War Letters*, p. 90.

16: "all that muddy brown . . . the only coloured thing": Arthur Graeme West, "God How I Hate You, You Young Cheerful Men," in *Diary of a Dead Officer*, p. 2.

16: "It was not like any mud . . . too wet to stand": John Masefield, quoted in Ione Bates, *From out of a Long Silence*.

16: "Two teams climbed . . . for sixty-four hours": GE 04, Diary of Heinrich Balters, Liddle Collection, pp. 5–6.

16: "The trench was ten feet deep . . . water and mud in addition": Norman Arnold Papers, pp. 1–14.

16: One officer reported . . . fifty-eight pounds: Ellis, op. cit., p. 48.

16: On the way up, two men . . . how pleased he was": Norman Arnold Papers, pp. 1–14.

17: "Sunrise and sunset . . . for such a land": Quoted in Ellis, op. cit., p. 9.

17: "In many places trenches . . . lower than ours": GE 04, Diary of Heinrich Balters, Liddle Collection, p. 12.

17: And in the La Bassée sector . . . emplacements were built: Ellis, op. cit., p. 12.

18: "Head-teacher Hub . . . sorrows of war": Printed card, Paul Hub papers, Hauptstaatsarchiv Stuttgart.

18: The wife of Fritz Haber . . . husband had unleashed: Joseph E. Persico, *Eleventh Month, Eleventh Day, Eleventh Hour*, p. 56.

18: Gas warfare had first been used . . . advance short of Ypres: Herwig, op. cit., p. 172; www.firstworldwar.com/battles/ypres2.htm.

19: German machine-gunners . . . pity for their enemies: Herwig, op. cit., p. 172.

2: THE PLACE WHERE THE DIRTY WORK IS DONE

20: "The Bastard . . . "like dirt" . . . "in a number of ways": Interview with the late Roger Goodman, August 2004.

21: "a splendid boy . . . a bright future": Letter in the collection of the late Roger Goodman.

21: "where recruits can join . . . or later by appointment": *London Territorials and the War*, pp. 1 and 5.

21: "recruited mainly from Civil Servants and their friends" . . . "open to all men . . . immediately on enlistment": *London Territorials and the War*, p. 19.

21: "Bank clerks and clerks . . . the quartermaster's stores": A. L. Robins, Liddle GS 1368, Part 1, p. 1.

22: Horace Iles, a member of the Leeds Pals: Richard van Emden, "Boy Soldiers" (TV).

22: John Condon . . . fourteen when he died: *The Times*, 18 November 1920.

22: "in which it was possible to drill several hundred troops": A. L. Robins, Liddle GS 1368, Part 1, p. 2.

22: "no doubt training would increase my chest measurement": ibid.

22: A soldier's pay . . . "possibly after the war": A. L. Robins, Liddle GS 1368, Part 3, p. 5.

22: "Fit was somewhat approximate . . . to be the right sizes": A. L. Robins, Liddle GS 1368, Part 1, p. 2.

22: "two in case he was killed . . . appropriate burial service": A. L. Robins, Liddle GS 1368, Part 3, p. 5.

23: "foolish patriotism": Interview with the late Roger Goodman, August 2004.

23: "Never such innocence again": Philip Larkin, "MCMXIV," in *Collected Poems*.

23: "worry caused by the feeling . . . accepted for service": *The Times*, 9 August 1914.

23: "men of handsome and boundless illusions . . . dealing with common men": C. E. Montague, *Disenchantment*, pp. 2–3.

23: "'The freedom of Europe' . . . greeds of the old": ibid., p. 180.

23: "fighting spirit . . . for ever in 1914": Quoted in *Yorkshire Observer*, 6 July 1922.

23: "the war, it was claimed . . . 'the greatest game of all'": Geoff Dyer, *The Missing of the Somme*, pp. 91–92.

23: But by the spring of 1915 . . . force them into the Army: J. M. Osborne, *The Voluntary Recruiting Movement in Britain*, pp. 24–28; C. Hughes, *The New Armies*, p. 102, quoted in Alex King, *Memorials of the Great War in Britain*, p. 224.

24: "We had not been taught . . . along the Strand": A. L. Robins, Liddle GS 1368, Part 1, p. 2.

24: "taken from Somerset House . . . handed over to the 3rd/15th CSR": ibid.

24: "was necessarily on somewhat elementary . . . arms and equipment, etc.": *The History of the Prince of Wales's Own Civil Service Rifles*, p. 373.

24: "the fine opinion of ourselves . . . true soldiering was": A. L. Robins, Liddle GS 1368, Part 1, p. 4.

24: "The joke went round . . . bows and arrows": ibid.

24: "under trying conditions of cold and wet": *The History of the Civil Service Rifles*, p. 374.

25: "a new small town . . . over 6,000 men": A. L. Robins, Liddle GS 1368, Part 2, p. 1.

25: "three long wide planks . . . served as a pillow": A. L. Robins, Liddle GS 1368, Part 2, p. 3.

25: "the whole of our Army pay . . . spent on food": ibid.

25: "there was plenty of space . . . a good miniature range": *The History of the Civil Service Rifles*, p. 375.

25: "prone, we fired five rounds . . . fifteen in one minute": A. L. Robins, Liddle GS 1368, Part 2, p. 2.

26: "right on into the docks . . . the arms to France": A. L. Robins, Liddle GS 1368, Part 3, p. 1.

26: "to see that none of the Draft ran away": ibid.

27: [The 12,400-ton P&O liner . . . sank almost at once.]: *The Times*, 28 February 1916.

27: "in fact, a town of about 10,000 men": A. L. Robins, Liddle GS 1368, Part 3, p. 3.

27: "instruction in tactics . . . time in a gas chamber": ibid.

27: "After a lecture . . . I got used to it": Revd. David Railton, IWM 80/22/1, p. 3.

28: "there we would spend . . . a trench was like": A. L. Robins, Liddle GS 1368, Part 3, p. 3.

28: "had no clue . . . Your loving son, George'": John Ewart March, IWM 292 89/21/1, p. 30.

28: "any censorable material": A. L. Robins, Liddle GS 1368, Part 4, p. 4.

29: "entrained in what seemed like a goods yard": A. L. Robins, Liddle GS 1368, Part 3, p. 6.

29: "cast away in a quarter such as goods yards inhabit": Quoted in Guy Chapman, *Vain Glory*, p. 218.

29: "hours in the train . . . trucks, poor boys": Revd. David Railton, IWM 80/22/1, p. 1.

29: "Chevaux (en long) 8" or "Hommes 37–40": *The History of the Civil Service Rifles*, p. 56.

29: "From far ahead, a crescendo . . . retired wholly from the world": Quoted in Chapman, op. cit., p. 218.

29: "packed like sardines on the floor of the van" . . . "accordingly rather cramped." . . . "bully beef and dog biscuits": A. L. Robins, Liddle GS 1368, Part 3, p. 6.

29: "inches deep in mud . . . feet get less blistered": Revd. David Railton, IWM 80/22/1, p. 2.

29: "cheered on our way . . . as if we didn't know": F. de Margry, IWM 4410 82/22/1, p. 6.

30: "The stench of the front . . . before you could see it": Paul Fussell, *The Great War and Modern Memory*, p. 49.

30: "splashed with blood": Major A. Anderson, IWM 3608 85/23/1, p. 7.

30: "a weird, pale-green glow . . . are pretty busy": Major A. Anderson, IWM 3608 85/23/1, p. 6.

30: "The Colonel appears up the dugout steps . . . for a moment and revives": Major A. Anderson, IWM 3608 85/23/1, pp. 3–5.

30: "To feel the kind . . . felt like home": H. Todd, IWM 7152 77/164/1, p. 22.

31: "to accustom them . . . being under fire": Major A. Anderson, IWM 3608 85/23/1, p. 5.

31: "would herd together like sheep when under fire": F. de Margry, IWM 4410 82/22/1.

31: "distinguish among the hubbub . . . its whole trajectory": Ernst Junger, *Copse 125*, p. 47.

31: "pair of boots, still containing someone's feet": Edmund Blunden, *Undertones of War*, p. 68.

31: "watched all day . . . met with fire": Captain T. P. C. Wilson, in Lawrence Housman (ed.), *War Letters of Fallen Englishmen*, p. 297.

31: One officer of the West Yorkshire Regiment . . . two different enemy snipers: John Ellis, *Eye Deep in Hell*, p. 68.

31: "Trench Requisites" departments of the larger London stores: Fussell, op. cit., p. 42.

31: "stood beside Sniper McDonald . . . bagged that morning": Thomas McCall, "A Highland Battalion at Loos," p. 72.

32: An officer of the 4th Oxfordshire . . . until 3 August: Ellis, op. cit., p. 30.

32: "a brownish-yellow fleeting shadow" ... "puzzled over as though ... mighty and unknown beast": Ernst Junger, *Storm of Steel*, p. ix.

32: "like that of slum life ... in an urban cellar": Montague, op. cit., p. 35.

32: Troop reliefs were made ... saps and tunnels constructed: A. L. Robins, Liddle GS 1368, Part 4, p. 13.

32: "usually undrinkable ... not being washed properly": R. E. Harris, IWM 3392 86/66/1.

32: "if you'd been there long enough ... Shell or BP tin": Harry Patch interview, *Sunday Times* magazine, 7 November 2004.

32: "through so many dead being buried about": R. E. Harris, IWM 3392, 86/66/1.

32: "One day the water ... chased him along the trench": McCall, op. cit., pp. 72–73.

33: "A second man ... in which they were carried": A. L. Robins, Liddle GS 1368, Part 4, p. 13.

33: "you could cup your hand ... couldn't see any light": Harry Patch interview, *Sunday Times* magazine, 7 November 2004.

33: "much of the time was occupied ... frenzy by a louse": IWM 6434 97/10/1.

33: In frosty weather ... returned almost at once: H. Todd, IWM 7152 77/164/1, p. 21.

34: "and when this got too bad ... sleep on the bare earth": A. L. Robins, Liddle GS 1368, Part 4, p. 3.

34: "pretty primitive ... conversed with us": A. L. Robins, Liddle GS 1368, Part 4, p. 7.

35: "along which the Boche ... almost impassable barrage": Alan H. Maude, *The History of the 47th (London) Division*, p. 50.

35: "a vividly painted crucifix ... protected from direct fire": Major A. Anderson, IWM 3608 85/23/1, p. 2.

36: "poisoned with human relics ... reeks to heaven of mortality": Lieutenant Bernard Pitt, in Housman (ed.), op. cit., p. 216.

3: THE SUICIDE SQUAD

38: "the whites of their pockets ... slower and more methodical": Leon Wolff, *In Flanders Fields*, p. 287.

38: "We thought that was terrible ... gold teeth for souvenirs": Jensen, "War Log of an Underdog," pp. 182–97, quoted in Joseph E. Persico, *Eleventh Month, Eleventh Day, Eleventh Hour*, p. 278.

39: "No one wants to go back ... sampled it properly": Norman Arnold Papers, p. 14.

39: "risk the Zeps ... if we could only return": Captain E. E. Simeons, IWM 2808 94/28/1.

39: "like the poor ... take them for granted": H. G. R. Williams, Liddle GS 1745, quoted in Liddle, *A Soldier's War*, p. 67.

39: "A sentry on guard . . . nettles and grass": C. E. Montague, *Disenchantment*, p. 154.

40: "Having attached themselves to us . . . as well be included": IWM 12667 Misc 235 (3341), Records of the 279th Siege Battery, pp. 35–36.

40: "I was soundly asleep . . . if not too cosy": F. de Margry, IWM 4410 82/22/1.

40: One sleeping corporal's nose . . . dispatched by a bayonet: Brigadier F. P. Roe, Liddle GS 1377, quoted in Liddle, op. cit., p. 67.

40: "eat through anything . . . stood still long enough": Harry Patch interview, *Sunday Times* magazine, 7 November 2004.

40: "they would eat a wounded man . . . defend himself": Canadian soldier quoted in Ellis, *Eye Deep in Hell*, p. 54.

40: "they favoured the eyeballs and the liver of the dead": Matthew Holden, *War in the Trenches*, p. 11.

40: "We borrowed a large cat . . . dragged it to their holes": P. H. Pilditch, IWM Con Shelf.

40: "The front and back of the trenches . . . didn't do any good": H. Todd, IWM 7152 77/164/1, p. 21.

40: "The old saying . . . dogs met them. Bon!" IWM 12667 Misc 235 (3341), Records of the 279th Siege Battery, pp. 35–36.

41: "a great rat hunt" . . . "We shake the powder . . . killed with sticks": Ernst Junger, *Copse 125*, p. 85.

41: "the continuation of labouring . . . conditions routinely flouted": Geoff Dyer, *The Missing of the Somme*, p. 59.

41: In November 1915 the British High Command . . . replaced by "working party": Ellis, op. cit., p. 40.

41: "Passing through the remains . . . keep proper cover": Major A. Anderson, IWM 3608 85/23/1, p. 2.

41: "We made our way in the darkness . . . observation from the Boche": Revd. David Railton, IWM 80/22/1, p. 7.

42: "uneven and full of holes . . . half hour trudge": Ione Bates, *From Out of a Long Silence*.

42: "close together . . . barbed wire" . . . "working feverishly in the chalk . . . blow their opponents sky-high": John Ewart March, IWM 292 89/21/1, p. 18.

42: "Out in the tall grasses . . . letters and personal effects": E. G. de Caux, IWM 564 88/46/1, p. 7.

42: "Little wooden crosses increased . . . impossible to bear him away": G. Skelton, IWM 6597 79/17/1, p. 54.

42: In factories in the towns . . . wooden crosses: Persico, op. cit., p. 107.

42: "I watched the men . . . they all saw and understood": Paul Maze, quoted in James Hannah (ed.), *The Great War Reader*, p. 86.

42: Even more chilling . . . 1917 had even begun: Dyer, op. cit., p. 12.

42: "a good padre who was often seen in the trenches": A. L. Robins, Liddle GS 1368, Part 4, p. 6.

42: and largely responsible ... adopted by the organization: Michael Moynihan, *God on Our Side*, p. 46.

43: "disturbingly conscious ... great mass of people" ... "disguised as a tramp" ... sleeping in doss-houses: Andrew Railton, quoted in Moynihan, op. cit., p. 75.

43: Like his brother, Nathaniel ... Territorial Chaplain to the Forces: John Hundevad, "The Unknown Warrior," in the *Legionary*, vol. 30, no. 3, August 1955, p. 20.

43: "There is only one Front ... not during engagements": Revd. David Railton, IWM 80/22/1, p. 14.

43: "Why should these men ... go through its gates?": Albert Marrin, *The Last Crusade*, p. 191.

43: "declaimed with an almost Mohammedan ... awaiting the dying warrior": Quoted in Alan Wilkinson, *The Church of England and the First World War*, p. 182.

43: "MOBILISE THE NATION FOR A HOLY WAR": *Manchester Guardian*, 10 June 1915.

43: "prayed for victory ... the smiting themselves": Frank Richards, *Old Soldiers Never Die*, p. 301.

43: Increasing numbers of clergy ... in a poison gas factory: Wilkinson, op. cit., p. 40.

43: "They have turned their churches ... commission in a regiment'": George Bernard Shaw, postscript to *Androcles and the Lion*.

44: "It made us think ... the slow-moving wounded": www.hellfire -corner.demon.co.uk/coulson.htm.

44: "What on earth ... felt to be his duty": Canon E. C. Crosse, IWM 4772 80/22/1, Part 2, pp. 4–5.

44: "a stretcher case": ibid.

44: "in the very forefront ... Jesus squandered his": Canon E. C. Crosse, IWM 4772 80/22/1, Part 2, pp. 5–6.

44: Another chaplain, the forty-four-year-old ... the Somme in September 1916: Wilkinson, op. cit., p. 42.

44: awarded a Military Cross: It was gazetted on 6 November 1916.

44: "Yesterday I took my first burial ... back along the trench": Revd. David Railton, IWM 80/22/1, pp. 3–4.

44: "bury for choice between ... chances of being shelled": Moynihan, op. cit., p. 135.

44: "many on both sides ... sniping at burial parties": Wolff, op. cit., p. 9.

44: "two by two and each file ... recent shell-hole." ... "(I stuffed my pockets ... penny-in-the-slot machines at home": Revd. Maurice Murray, quoted in Moynihan, op. cit., pp. 135–37.

45: "as reverently as we can ... squabbling with each other": Revd. David Railton, IWM 80/22/1, p. 7.

45: At other times, fierce fighting . . . flat on their stomachs: Wilkinson, op. cit., p. 138.

46: "Bennett the RC . . . it is done reverently": Revd. David Railton, IWM 80/22/1, p. 20.

46: "a violent bombardment . . . heard or seen" . . . "All of us noticed at 3:30 a.m. . . . whole of the bombardment" . . . "one of our officers . . . and several men": Revd. David Railton, IWM 80/22/1, pp. 7–8.

46: the still-smoking crater . . . fortifying the far lip: Alan H. Maude, *The History of the 47th (London) Division*, p. 51.

46: "murderous instrument . . . fall almost vertically": Karl Josenhans, *German Students' War Letters*, p. 39.

46: "an explosive called ammonal . . . the Day of Judgement" . . . "apparently collected by French villagers . . . set of false teeth" . . . "the canister could easily be heard . . . flying in all directions": Robert Graves, *Goodbye to All That*, p. 161.

47: "When on leave, acquaintances . . . that he learns caution": Junger, op. cit., p. 46.

47: "Crater Jumping Parties": John Ewart March, IWM 292 89/21/1, p. 18.

47: a General Order required . . . occupied at once: Ellis, op. cit., p. 15.

48: "All worked themselves dead beat": Maude, op. cit., p. 52.

48: "such expressions as 'You never hear . . . from a stray shell": F. de Margry, IWM 4410 82/22/1, pp. 12–13.

48: "the broad fact remained . . . no attempt to justify them": Canon E. C. Crosse, IWM 4772 80/22/1, Part 3, pp. 9–10.

50: "Ignoring all that at Aldershot . . . from your hole into his": Montague, op. cit., p. 38.

50: "The most agile and daring . . . ahead as bomb-throwers": Junger, op. cit., p. 247.

50: "old ham tins . . . with earth to fill in": Montague, op. cit., p. 40.

51: "our new piece of front . . . our unprotected troops": Maude, op. cit., p. 52.

51: "came suddenly with a shriek . . . rocked the earth and air": Edmund Blunden, *Undertones of War*, p. 221.

51: "the main work of an infantry soldier": Louis Simpson, quoted in Dyer, op. cit., p. 47.

51: "the great leveller . . . like being under anaesthetic": John Keegan, *The First World War*, p. 398.

51: "I *adore* the war. It is like a big picnic . . ." . . . "I can understand now . . . shock to me at first": Captain the Hon. J. H. F. Grenfell, in Lawrence Housman (ed.), *War Letters of Fallen Englishmen*, pp. 117–19.

52: "hanging over the area . . . a beautiful, still evening": *The History of the Prince of Wales's Own Civil Service Rifles*, p. 94.

52: "no sooner in position . . . a barrage of tear gas": ibid.

52: "the most intense bombardment . . . chance of finding out": Regimental Diary of the Civil Service Rifles, 22 May 1916.

52: "at once loaded up with bombs . . . ammunition per man" . . ."where any of these troops were . . . was supposed to capture": *The History of the Civil Service Rifles*, p. 95.

53: "fitful glare of Very lights": ibid., p. 96.

53: "Moonlight on bayonets . . . yards from the Boche": Francis Alfred Martin, quoted in Ione Bates, *From out of a Long Silence*.

53: "ordinary wire-cutters were useless": F. de Margry, IWM 4410 82/22/1, p. 14.

53: "the ordinary Army issue would cut only British wire": Graves, op. cit., p. 194.

53: "I saw by the light . . . 'Get out you b——ds!'": F. W. Watts, "A Night Counter-Attack," quoted in Jill Knight, *The Civil Service Rifles in the Great War*, p. 72.

54: the German 49th Field Artillery . . . its shells fell short: Ellis, op. cit., p. 62.

54: "great execution among the enemy . . . our old front line": Maude, op. cit., p. 56.

54: "the ground was covered . . . among the burial party": Canon E. C. Crosse, IWM 4772 80/22/1, Part 3, p. 27.

54: "remained a long time . . . not worth another life": Guy Chapman, *A Passionate Prodigality*, p. 252.

54: "Burying a dead man . . . those with weak stomachs": Letter from a soldier with the Civil Service Rifles, quoted in Ione Bates, *From out of a Long Silence*.

55: "I once fell and put . . . nostrils, as you approached": Stuart Cloete, quoted in David Cannadine, "(War and) Death, Grief and Mourning in Modern Britain," p. 204.

55: "shimmering cloud" of flies . . . with its fetid odour": Quoted in Ellis, op. cit., p. 58.

55: "a noise like rustling silk . . . dead man's guts": Quoted in ibid.

55: "We worked with sandbags . . . and then to puke": Stuart Cloete, quoted in Cannadine, op. cit., p. 204.

55: "to drown . . . with rum": Wilkinson, op. cit., p. 162.

55: "In some places the bodies . . . shell-fire behind them": Richard Schmeider, *German Students' War Letters*, p. 209.

55: "buried in the trench, wrapped in an old blanket": R. A. Walker, IWM 977 88/11/1.

55: "swampy nature of the ground" . . . "melancholy task [of burial] . . . filled up with water": IWM 12667 Misc 235, (3341) Records of the 279th Siege Battery, p. 35.

55: "twenty-five of us . . . No Man's Land to be brought in": H. R. Butt, IWM 6771 97/26/1, p. 37.

56: "It seems doubtful now . . . incurring the resulting losses?": Maude, op. cit., p. 57.

4: ONE GREAT CRY OF AGONY AND HORROR

57: "determined and assured . . . array of solid skills": Certificate of Good Conduct, Hub family papers.

58: "Up till recently I encouraged . . . the joy-life of marriage": Revd. David Railton, IWM 80/22/1, p. 16.

58: "our old bloodbath—the Somme": German letter, quoted in Philip Gibbs, "The Battle of the Somme."

59: "The fields over which the scythe . . . a hot stream of scent": Ernst Junger, *Copse 125*, p. 28.

59: "smelling to heaven like incense in the sun": Captain T. P. C. Wilson, in Lawrence Housman (ed.), *War Letters of Fallen Englishmen*, pp. 296–97.

59: "Brimstone butterflies . . . ooze of the shell-holes": Junger, op. cit., p. 38.

59: "Then a bare field strewn . . . then barbed wire again": Captain T. P. C. Wilson, in Housman (ed.), op. cit., pp. 296–97.

60: "To inspire the German troops . . . speedy ending to the war": Gibbs, op. cit.

60: "We, who have seen the dark . . . but willingly, is not easy": Johannes Philippsen, *German Students' War Letters*, p. 369.

60: an average of one ton . . . every square yard: Holger H. Herwig, *The First World War*, p. 199.

60: "During that week the earth shook . . . South-East England": W. F. J. Harvey, *Pi in the Sky*, p. 9.

60: "Some of the shells burst upwards . . . scoured earthwards by a storm": Junger, op. cit., p. 230.

60: "Heavy shells pass so high . . . the crashes ring out": ibid., p. 38.

60: "Speech was of course impossible . . . enormous waves on a beach": Lieutenant Christian Creswell Carver, in Housman (ed.), op. cit., p. 62.

60: "a hurricane of hoarse and hollow banging . . . and beast-like screams": Henri Barbusse, quoted in John Ellis, *Eye Deep in Hell*, p. 63.

61: "To have to crouch . . . limits of human endurance": Junger, op. cit., p. 20.

61: "by the ninth day, almost every soldier was crying": Quoted in Ellis, op. cit., p. 65.

61: "so that at the moment of assault . . . a gas attack, also of an improved kind": Lieutenant Alfred Dambitsch, *Destructive Technology at the Somme*.

61: "People seven to eight kilometres behind . . . continuous bombardment are indescribable": Letter written by a German soldier, IWM SS 473, p. 3.

62: "unlimited amounts of ammunition . . . life or death for the Army": Herwig, op. cit., p. 166.

62: Even though output rose . . . the German armies were demanding: ibid., p. 167.

62: "an alarmingly large number . . . field guns": Gibbs, op. cit.

62: "You have to stay . . . our airmen are a rotten lot": Anonymous Soldier on the Somme, IWM SS 473, p. 4.

62: "The English are always flying . . . idea where the enemy line is": Letter of a Man of the 24th Division, IWM SS 473, p. 3.

62: "It is absolutely necessary . . . barricade and others the trench": Morning Report 3rd Platoon, IWM SS 473, p. 3.

62: "over what miserable traces . . . grown in a cellar": Junger, op. cit., p. 55.

62: "grey dust that has settled . . . drunk up their blood": ibid., p. 239.

62: "pitiful letters" . . . "We are quite shut off . . . shot to pieces": Gibbs, op. cit.

63: "shook all over . . . released from this hell": IWM SS 473, p. 2.

63: "Young recruits who had just come . . . stood the test so well": Dambitsch, op. cit.

63: "not even a rat" . . . authorized for army mules: Harvey, op. cit., p. 9.

63: This may also have reflected . . . behind a creeping barrage: Paul Fussell, *The Great War and Modern Memory*, p. 13.

63: "very surprised to see them walking . . . we just fired into them": Quoted in Ellis, op. cit., p. 94.

64: "one could walk across . . . foot on the ground": Joseph E. Persico, *Eleventh Month, Eleventh Day, Eleventh Hour*, p. 112.

64: 1 July is still a day of mourning in Newfoundland: Herwig, op. cit., p. 202.

64: out of 900 men of the "Leeds Pals" . . . the roll-call that night: Derek Boorman, *At the Going Down of the Sun*, p. 137.

64: As a military consequence . . . attack were left behind: Fussell, op. cit., p. 82.

64: "three-quarters of their number . . . heaps of killed and wounded": Gibbs, op. cit.

64: "of considerable intensity . . . dropped by day and night": Divisional Order of the 53rd Division, IWM SS 473, p. 3.

64: "I stood on the brink . . . We were that handful": Gibbs, op. cit.

64: "heaps of corpses—a stench; I have to lie amid corpses": Letter from a Soldier [probably] of the 84th Reserve Infantry, IWM SS 473, p. 2.

64: "but that is the same . . . wound to send me home": Letter from a Man of the 86th Reserve Regiment, IWM SS 473, p. 2.

64: *"Heimatschuss"*—literally a "home shot": My thanks to Christian Kuhrt for unearthing this term.

64: "We meet parties of wounded . . . they jog along quite merrily": Friedrich Oehme, *German Students' War Letters*, p. 288.

65: "Our losses in territory . . . pay a bitter price": Crown Prince Rupprecht, "The Battle of the Somme."

65: "The only thing that really troubles . . . longing for peace": Alfred E. Vaeth, *German Students' War Letters*, p. 175.

65: "All the Bavarian troops . . . and it's a swindle": German letter, quoted by Gibbs, op. cit.

65: "I collect my men . . . occupy our 200-yard sector": Friedrich Oehme, *German Students' War Letters*, p. 291.

5: A NEW WORLD OF WAR

67: one German officer expressed . . . women in negligees": Holger H. Herwig, *The First World War*, p. 246.

67: "stood a good chance . . . want to die virgins": Robert Graves, *Goodbye to All That*, p. 195.

67: "saved the life of scores . . . combatant officers treated there": ibid.

67: American troops with venereal disease . . . punishment and deterrent": Gary Mead, *The Doughboys*, p. 114.

68: "The French equivalent . . . letters home were often written": A. L. Robins, Liddle GS 1368, Part 4, p. 3.

70: Each balloon was accompanied . . . trying to shoot it down: Martin Marix Evans, *American Voices of World War I*, pp. 61–62.

71: "in the whole vocabulary . . . stomach of ordinary mortals": Edmund Blunden, *Undertones of War*, p. 36.

71: "stars and wet grass . . . movement gives you away": Captain T. P. C. Wilson, in Lawrence Housman (ed.), *War Letters of Fallen Englishmen*, p. 301.

71: "We advance slowly . . . the clatter of metal": Ernst Junger, *Copse 125*, p. 249.

71: "getting nearer than bomb-throwing distance": Alan H. Maude, *The History of the 47th (London) Division*, p. 58.

71: "a dismal failure . . . in CSR circles": *The History of the Prince of Wales's Own Civil Service Rifles*, p. 103.

72: "prodigious dugouts, arranged even in two storeys": Blunden, op. cit., p. 136.

72: "the cubby-hole . . . direct hit by a shell": A. L. Robins, Liddle GS 1368, Part 4, p. 11.

75: "one of the most important . . . attention of the enemy": A. L. Robins, Liddle GS 1368, Part 4, p. 8.

75: "frost-blue" streams . . . the church always emerges": E. G. de Caux, IWM 564 88/46/1, p. 23.

75: "The monotonous rolling . . . sullen and menacing air": Junger, op. cit., p. 231.

75: "In the Angres sector . . . our normal dwelling-place": Maude, op. cit., p. 60.

76: "We halted at the outskirts . . . moving out again": J. H. Moore, Memoirs, Bradford Archives, 67D84/1, pp. 104–5.

76: "in the state of a horse . . . but not to rise": C. E. Montague, *Disenchantment*, p. 52.

76: "Our doctor is a terror . . . know he is behind": Revd. David Railton, IWM 80/22/1, p. 2.

76: At the end of a march . . . barracks for eight days: John Ellis, *Eye Deep in Hell*, p. 32.

76: "Orders were that no one . . . they were just raw": Revd. David Railton, IWM 80/22/1, p. 9.

77: "We had hot summer weather . . . These were pleasant days": Maude, op. cit., p. 61.

77: "a delightful bathing place . . . the River Canche": *The History of the Civil Service Rifles*, p. 105.

78: "examine without prejudice . . . the sick and wounded": Canon E. C. Crosse, IWM 4772 80/22/1, Part 3, pp. 53–54.

78: "an army of Crusaders . . . almost a humiliation": Canon E. C. Crosse, ibid., pp. 3–5.

78: "It is always assumed . . . other than physical help": ibid., Part 3, pp. 53–54.

79: "The early part of the day . . . marched, marched, marched": Revd. David Railton, IWM 80/22/1, pp. 10–11.

79: "considered by many to be . . . the flies on the Western Front": *The History of the Civil Service Rifles*, p. 107.

79: "the untended bushes . . . no breath of air": Leon Wolff, *In Flanders Fields*, p. 8.

79: "the scuttling of hundreds . . . ammunition, relief parties": Quoted in Michael Moynihan, *God on Our Side*, p. 137.

80: "not a single parcel . . . their hands rot off": GE 01 Anonymous Diary, Liddle Collection.

81: "on a flagged course": Maude, op. cit., p. 62.

81: "A kind of 'finishing school' . . . battle of the Somme": *The History of the Civil Service Rifles*, p. 107.

81: "a certain wood . . . so far kept secret": ibid., p. 108.

81: "Wet weather set in . . . as noiselessly as possible": E. G. de Caux, IWM 564 88/46/1, p. 24.

81: "the horizon was lit . . . a day fed the guns": *The History of the Civil Service Rifles*, p. 108.

81: "power-driven, bullet-proof . . . and climbing earthworks": Quoted in Joseph E. Persico, *Eleventh Month, Eleventh Day, Eleventh Hour*, pp. 117–18.

81: "Covered entirely with tarpaulins . . . new and formidable weapon": Anthony French, *Gone for a Soldier*, p. 67.

81: "walls were no obstacles . . . nor any ordinary trench": E. G. de Caux, IWM 564 88/46/1, p. 24.

82: "it was the widespread impression . . . better prepared for battle": Terry Norman, *The Hell They Called High Wood*, p. 217.

82: "rejoiced at having got . . . the song of the lark": Territorial soldier, quoted in Ellis, op. cit., p. 112.

82: "I used to hear the larks . . . anything else out here": Sergeant-Major F. H. Keeling in Housman (ed.), op. cit., p. 164.

83: "six field guns . . . and a Zeppelin": George L. Mosse, *Fallen Soldiers*, p. 60.

83: [Field Service postcards . . . crossed out as appropriate.]: A. L. Robins, Liddle GS 1368, Part 4, p. 4.

84: "fastened to a tree . . . Holy Table as usual": Revd. David Railton, IWM 80/22/1, p. 10.

84: "a bloodthirsty sermon . . . from the New Testament": Quoted in Alan Wilkinson, *The Church of England and the First World War*, p. 152.

84: "walked into a new world of war": Maude, op. cit., pp. 62–63.

84: "Dawn had come . . . its shattered tower": E. G. de Caux, IWM 564 88/46/1, p. 24.

84: "holding out her child . . . endless procession below": Maude, op. cit., pp. 62–63.

85: "when this figure falls . . . with iron girders": Lance Corporal C. H. Morden, 2476 93/25/1, p. 1.

85: "a city of empty and ruined . . . taken off the population": *The History of the Civil Service Rifles*, p. 109.

85: "Beyond the valley . . . chalk of the old front lines": E. G. de Caux, IWM 564 88/46/1, p. 24.

85: "a vast armed camp . . . well within shell-fire": Corporal De Ath, quoted in *The History of the Civil Service Rifles*, p. 109.

85: "As far as the eye could see . . . the target was too vast": E. G. de Caux, IWM 564 88/46/1, p. 25.

85: "wearing the uniform . . . same helplessness individually": E. G. de Caux, letter to Eric Gore-Brown, IWM 256 88/52/1.

85: "in any old corner . . . monsters roaring incessantly": Corporal De Ath, quoted in *The History of the Civil Service Rifles*, p. 109.

85: "Guns were put in shell-holes . . . at night and covered over": Harry Smith Diary, Bradford Archives, 66D81/1.

85: "making an ominous roar . . . rushing through a tunnel": F. de Margry, IWM 4410 82/22/1, p. 5.

85: "scarcely concealed positions . . . tanks fed by pipelines": E. G. de Caux, IWM 564 88/46/1, p. 25.

85: "Up near the line . . . anything quite like High Wood": Maude, op. cit., pp. 62–63.

85: "It was a scene of desolation . . . was to be our goal": Corporal De Ath, quoted in *The History of the Civil Service Rifles*, pp. 109–10.

86: "splintered to matchwood": Graves, op. cit., p. 183.

86: "barely two feet above the ground": J. H. Moore, Memoirs, Bradford Archives, 67D84/1, p. 29.

86: "like a sea all heaving in anger": Revd. David Railton, IWM 80/22/1, p. 15.

86: "poisoned with fumes . . . a mass of corruption": Maude, op. cit., pp. 62–63.

86: "small lakes of what was . . . foul semblance of blood": Blunden, *Undertones of War*, p. 134.

86: "After weary weeks of training . . . was near at hand": Lance Corporal C. H. Morden, IWM 2476 93/25/1, p. 1.

86: "to get possession of the key to the ridge": E. G. de Caux, IWM 564 88/46/1, p. 23.

86: "it looked terrible country . . . German science and skill": Corporal De Ath, quoted in *The History of the Civil Service Rifles*, p. 110.

86: "The place stank of death . . . a hand and forearm": Anthony French, *Gone for a Soldier*, p. 68.

87: "boots and bones protruding from one's dugout walls": Sergeant E. B. Nottingham, in Housman (ed.), op. cit., p. 202.

87: "You can't *face* death . . . one would go mad": Captain T. P. C. Wilson, ibid., p. 296.

87: "In one deep, sandy trench . . . interfere with the head": Revd. Maurice Murray, quoted in Moynihan, op. cit., p. 137.

87: "more or less a graveyard . . . to laugh or cry": Letter from Colonel Fielding, 8 October 1917, quoted in Ione Bates, *From out of a Long Silence*.

87: "Even the great shell-hole . . . hooking the handle of a bomb": Blunden, op. cit., p. 132.

87: "it was literally true . . . bodies of the dead": Canon E. C. Crosse, IWM 4772 80/22/1, Part 2, pp. 5–6.

87: "Dead bodies were used . . . protection to those inside": R. E. Harris, IWM 3392 86/66/1, pp. 29–30.

87: "burying a man who has been killed . . . are often left exposed": ibid., pp. 29–30.

88: Every morning for several weeks . . . English upper-class accent: Ronald Blythe, *Akenfield*, p. 40.

88: "Everywhere like a pall . . . disinfect them": Matthew Holden, *War in the Trenches*, p. 11.

6: A STORM OF SHRAPNEL

93: "You don't really think any more . . . to be peace again": Herbert Sulzbach, *With the German Guns*, p. 86.

99: "under constant gunfire . . . one shell-hole to another": Letter from a Man of the 119th Regiment, IWM SS 473, p. 2.

99: "hardly endurable . . . water is to be had": Diary of a Man of the 28th Regiment, IWM SS 473, p. 1.

101: Some men said "it was shooting" . . . "it was raining": Ernst Junger, *Copse 125*, p. 55.

103: "nothing but the drumfire . . . night after night": Gerhard Gurtler, *German Students' War Letters*, p. 363.

104: "I looked around me . . . for night or the enemy": Karl Gorzel, *German Students' War Letters*, p. 373.

7: THE ROTTENEST PLACE ON THE SOMME

105: "Greatcoats and packs . . . entrenching tools were carried": E. G. de Caux, IWM 564 88/46/1, p. 25.

105: "including a biscuit," and "wire-cutters, as many as possible": Robert Graves, *Goodbye to All That*, pp. 123–24.

105: "It was almost dusk . . . at the sheltered approach": Anthony French, *Gone for a Soldier*, p. 69.

106: "The stench of dead mule . . . wide berth to any dud shell": ibid., pp. 69–70.

106: "I wondered . . . whatever else might happen": Private Fred Ball, in C. B. Purdom, *Everyman at War*.

107: "Stretcher bearers . . . garments brushed against our hands": French, op. cit., p. 70.

107: "ghastly by day . . . the rottenest place on the Somme": Corporal H. F. Hooton, quoted in Terry Norman, *The Hell They Called High Wood*, p. 83.

107: "who got any sleep . . . lie down in shellholes": *The History of the Prince of Wales's Own Civil Service Rifles*, p. 111.

107: "One by one they realised . . . where no help was": English soldier, quoted in John Ellis, *Eye Deep in Hell*, p. 97.

108: The Mills bombs for Alec . . . two at a time: Edmund Blunden, *Undertones of War*, p. 96.

108: "felt for their grenades . . . if anyone knew the time": French, op. cit., p. 72.

108: The 15th Battalion . . . attack at zero hour, 6:20 a.m.: The majority of sources, including Maude, op. cit., p. 64, and Norman, op. cit., p. 219, and a number of individual diaries and testimonies, put zero hour at 6:20 a.m. *The History of the Civil Service Rifles*, p. 110, gives it as 5:50 a.m., but is probably referring to the time at which the men of "B," "C" and "D" Companies moved out of the trenches to align themselves with "A" Company.

108: The fact that this was written . . . how strong that probability was: PRO WO95/2727.

108: "The postmen . . . was quietly ignored": E. G. de Caux, IWM 564 88/46/1, p. 24.

109: "All along the skyline . . . the heavy 'crump' of the Hun shells": Corporal De Ath, quoted in *The History of the Civil Service Rifles*, p. 110.

109: "over badly crumped ground": Norman, op. cit., p. 214.

110: The London Division's commander . . . either side of the wood: ibid., p. 217.

110: "the cold disturbing air . . . the approach of the morning": Blunden, op. cit., p. 96.

110: "the heaviest sick-list . . . ever known": Graves, op. cit., p. 196.

110: "the rum ration . . . won the war": Quoted in William Moore, *The Thin Yellow Line*, p. 203.

110: "by way of reward . . . even proving fatal": F. de Margry, IWM 4410 82/22/1, p. 13.

110: "After a few glasses . . . he was rat-hunting": Ernst Junger, *Copse 125*, p. 85.

110: "as the sky was turning grey . . . hand to hand": French, op. cit., p. 72.

110: "It'll last about twenty minutes . . . Senior man present takes charge" . . . "When you get the first line . . . over together; and good luck": ibid.

111: "in a few minutes . . . peace of mind was short-lived": Private Fred Ball, in Purdom, op. cit.

111: "breaking the deadly stillness . . . one huge earthquake": J. H. Moore, Memoirs, Bradford Archives, 67D84/1, p. 29.

111: "Out of the void . . . monotonous roar": French, op. cit., p. 73.

111: "a murderous fire . . . on the assembly trenches": *The History of the Civil Service Rifles*, p. 111.

112: The tanks were then to continue . . . zero plus thirty-two minutes—6:52 a.m.: Norman, op. cit., p. 219.

112: Forty-two tanks . . . before the attack had even begun: ibid., p. 218.

112: "company commanders . . . neither seen nor heard": *The History of the Civil Service Rifles*, p. 112.

112: Like a bemused motorist . . . to ask the way to High Wood: Norman, op. cit., p. 220.

113: "materially interfered with the removal of the wounded": *The History of the Civil Service Rifles*, p. 113.

113: After almost being shot . . . dig out their useless tank: Norman, op. cit., pp. 222–23.

113: "thus disappointed . . . afraid to fire near the tanks": Maude, op. cit., p. 64.

113: "The fury of our barrage . . . roaring sound before us": Private Fred Ball in Purdom, op. cit.

113: "By some means the signal . . . every scrap of shelter?": ibid.

113: "So many men strolling . . . a paddock in New Zealand": R. E. Harris, IWM 3392 86/66/1.

113: "as a bridegroom who goes to meet his bride": Quoted in David Cannadine, "(War and) Death, Grief and Mourning in Modern Britain," p. 196.

113: "stumbled into a mist . . . machine-gun and rifle-fire": Private Fred Ball in Purdom, op. cit.

114: "The din must have been deafening . . . associate no sound with it": Second Lieutenant A. D. Young, in Lawrence Housman (ed.), *War Letters of Fallen Englishmen*, pp. 313–14.

114: "in reduced condition . . . crouched there awaiting orders": French, op. cit., p. 76.

114: "Sackfuls of bombs are passed . . . you have never seen alive": Junger, op. cit., pp. 250–53.

115: "so that they must either choke . . . held up their hands in horror?": Captain J. E. Crombie, in Housman (ed.), op. cit., 82–83.

115: "No man in this war . . . had his hands up first": General Harper, quoted in Ellis, op. cit., p. 78.

115: "a German staff officer working round . . . shot the German in the head: Robert Graves, op. cit., p. 186.

116: "full of German stick-bombs . . . suffice to ward off their fate": Junger, op. cit., p. 241.

117: all three lost four-fifths . . . and most of their NCOs: *The History of the Civil Service Rifles*, p. 113.

8: A MILLION BLOODY RUGS

118: "the falling and burning trees . . . the defences obliterated": G. Skelton, IWM 6597 79/17/1, pp. 50–51.

118: "Assembly trenches . . . almost untenable": Terry Norman, *The Hell They Called High Wood*, p. 224.

119: "The yells were soon death-screams . . . friend and foe alike": Rifleman Don Cree, quoted in ibid., p. 225.

119: "clockwork warfare . . . mathematically worked out": Quoted in Guy Chapman, *Vain Glory*, p. 424.

119: "fine powder . . . no trace": Lance-Corporal W. Robertson, quoted in Norman, op. cit., p. 222.

119: The artillery laid down a barrage . . . sustained rapid fire: *The History of the Prince of Wales's Own Civil Service Rifles*, p. 118.

119: One soldier even claimed . . . the carriages of a train: Norman, op. cit., p. 229.

120: "The German Switch Line . . . by the British artillery": E. G. de Caux, IWM 564 88/46/1, p. 25.

120: "just as if they were on parade": Major Lord Gorell, quoted in Norman, op. cit., p. 232.

120: "a mere handful . . . they had it rough": Rifleman Don Cree, quoted in ibid., p. 233.

120:    "No man was to halt . . . look after themselves": IWM 97/10/1.

120:    "I saw men in their madness . . . deaf at the time": Corporal M. J. Guiton, quoted in *The History of the Civil Service Rifles*, p. 115.

120:    "the melancholy work . . . buried side by side there": ibid., pp. 114–15.

120:    "As one looked on . . . war was at an end": Canon E. C. Crosse, IWM 4772 80/22/1, Part 3, p. 28.

121:    "Many men who have stood . . . the battlefield in general": Revd. David Railton, IWM 80/22/1, pp. 13–14.

121:    "almost impossible for an armed man . . . a wounded comrade" . . . "many a time . . . reasonable chance of survival": G. Skelton, IWM 6597 79/17/1, pp. 53–54.

121:    "In many cases . . . stretchers and carrying parties": ibid., p. 53.

121:    "A couple of Sappers . . . war then started again": John Ewart March, IWM 292 89/21/1, pp. 19–20.

121:    "the ceaseless wail . . . terrible nights in High Wood": *The History of the Civil Service Rifles*, pp. 114–15.

121:    "The trailing processions . . . marked for miles across country": C. E. Montague, *Disenchantment*, pp. 164–65.

122:    "The dead lay where . . . found out that he survived": G. Skelton, IWM 6597 79/17/1, p. 53.

122:    "the best part of three days": E. G. de Caux, letter to Eric Gore-Brown, IWM 256 88/52/1.

122:    "We are now burying . . . it is dreadful": Revd. David Railton, IWM 80/22/1, p. 13.

122:    "His eyes seemed a bit full . . . over the top with me' " . . . "The sprig of white heather . . . brought him no luck": Revd. David Railton, IWM 80/22/1, pp. 11, 13.

122:    "lay three or four deep . . . made their faces black": John Masefield, in Peter Vansittart (ed.), *John Masefield's Letters from the Front*, p. 209.

122:    "I was attached to a company . . . in the last great sleep" . . . "often have I picked up . . . dead was in my nostrils": J. McCauley, IWM 6434 97/10/1, pp. 92–93.

123:    "Number, Rank, Name . . . Graves Registration Units": IWM SS 456 Burial of Soldiers.

124:    His amateur "Graves Registration Commission" . . . cash-starved organization: Samuel A. Hynes, *A War Imagined*, pp. 270–71.

124:    "Everything is done as tenderly . . . an English churchyard": Directorate of Graves Registration, *The Care of the Dead*.

124:    "continually reminding padres . . . trench for the purpose": Canon E. C. Crosse, IWM 4772 80/22/1, Part 3, pp. 30–31.

124:    By nightfall on 15 September . . . another issue of rum: Ione Bates, *From out of a Long Silence*, entry for 16 September 1916.

124:    "small reinforcement of fifty-three men": ibid.

124: "dirty cartridges . . . make them fire": John Ellis, *Eye Deep in Hell*, p. 47.

124: "a skeleton of a battalion . . . running out of the trenches": Private Fred Ball, in Purdom, op. cit., 149–50

124: "a hollow square . . . remaining Sergeant Majors": E. G. de Caux, letter to Eric Gore-Brown, IWM 256 88/52/1.

125: In all, 380 of the 450 . . . had not returned: *The History of the Civil Service Rifles*, p. 117.

125: "hundreds of wounded men . . . but unable to move": J. H. Moore, Memoirs, Bradford Archives, 67D84/1, pp. 108–9.

125: "shuffling past . . . supported by listless cripples": Henry Williamson, quoted in Ellis, op. cit., pp. 120–21.

125: "It has been a great victory . . . too much to bear": Revd. David Railton, IWM 80/22/1, p. 13.

125: The London Division was officially criticized . . . entrusted to his command: Norman, op. cit., p. 235.

125: "to their great joy . . . a whops' [wasp's] nest' ": *The Times*, September 1916, quoted in ibid., p. 242.

126: "Now and then we heard . . . in mid-Victorian days": Lord Northcliffe's War Book, quoted in Paul Fussell, *The Great War and Modern Memory*, p. 88.

126: "little it mattered . . . was not evidence": Montague, op. cit., p. 177.

126: "when autumn twilight came . . . the stuff open-mouthed": ibid., pp. 97–98.

127: "It is rubbish like this . . . war is a great sport": Second Lieutenant A. C. Young, in Lawrence Housman (ed.), *War Letters of Fallen Englishmen*, p. 312.

127: Widespread distrust of the media . . . Charles a Court Repington in 1920: Hynes, op. cit., p. 288.

127: Very few photographs . . . might prove too graphic: cf. Geoff Dyer, *The Missing of the Somme*, pp. 38–39.

127: "Runlets of news . . . no bombs to throw back": Montague, op. cit., p. 25.

127: "The Great Advance" . . . British troops who survived it: Fussell, op. cit., p. 12.

127: "Let us not hesitate . . . do that in as many hours": Lieutenant A. C. Stephen, in Housman (ed.), op. cit., p. 262.

127: "Despite the optimistic public claims . . . every household in Britain": Philip Dutton, *The Dead Man's Penny*, p. 61.

127: "in modern warfare . . . made to do just as well": Lieutenant L. Y. Sanders, in Housman (ed.), op. cit., p. 228.

128: Of men aged between thirteen . . . 20 percent disabled: Jay M. Winter, *Britain's Lost Generation of the First World War*, p. 450.

128: "In the school library . . . a pyramid of corpses": George Orwell, *Collected Essays, Journalism and Letters*, vol. 1, p. 537.

128: "those indelible days . . . Thanksgiving for Victory": John Anthony Crosse, Epilogue, IWM 4772 80/22/1, p. 16.

128: "the appalling weather . . . throughout the winter": Ellis, op. cit., p. 22.

128: "In the training camps . . . as long as you let him": Montague, op. cit., p. 63.

128: "a year ago, it was very exceptional . . . the daily average": Quoted in Edmund Blunden, *Undertones of War*, pp. 288–89.

128: Severe cases . . . Not Yet Diagnosed (Nervous): Ellis, op. cit., p. 117.

129: three times as many men . . . Passchendaele the following year: Chaplain, quoted in ibid., p. 119.

129: the deliberate killing of officers by their own men: Thaer, Generalstabdienst, pp. 80–92, quoted in Holger H. Herwig, *The First World War*, p. 203.

129: "a new spirit . . . few rifles being fired": Quoted in Richard Garrett, *The Final Betrayal*, p. 138.

129: The "lions led by donkeys" . . . Franco-Prussian War: Richard Holmes, *The Western Front*, p. 13.

129: "it is easy to make a fool . . . still a fool": S. H. Raggett, IWM 1027 90/1/1.

129: "When you are given . . . not carry you too far": Montague, op. cit., p. 79.

130: "cannot be considered severe . . . the front attacked": R. Blake (ed.), *The Private Papers of Douglas Haig*, p. 54.

130: "The men are much too keen . . . complete indifference": Canon E. C. Crosse, IWM 4772 80/22/1.

130: "Generals dealt with war . . . troops fought it retail": Joseph E. Persico, *Eleventh Month, Eleventh Day, Eleventh Hour*, p. 83.

130: "much overrated" weapons: Quoted in ibid., p. 128.

130: "to thank it . . . congratulations in the graveyard": Stephen Graham, *A Private in the Guards*.

130: "Our battalion attacked . . . I suppose it was worth it": NCO, 22nd Manchester Rifles, quoted in Guy Chapman, *Vain Glory*, p. 325.

131: "aeroplanes and tanks . . . the man and the horse": Quoted in Ellis, op. cit., p. 84.

131: "overestimated the ability . . . run before they could walk": Gary Sheffield, *The Somme*, p. 160.

131: "a whole empire walking . . . a million bloody rugs": F. Scott Fitzgerald, *Tender Is the Night*, pp. 124–25.

9: THE PLACE OF JUDGEMENT

134: "It was a horrid feeling . . . crying 1like a child": S. H. Raggett, IWM 1027 90/1/1, p. 18.

135: "Everybody who looks daily . . . old, very old": Kurt Rohrbach, *German Students' War Letters*, p. 269.

135:　"We stood and sat on bodies . . . gradually became quite blunted": August Hopp, ibid., p. 50.

136:　"The night passed . . . have to sit in the mud": ibid., p. 59.

136:　"Life here isn't worth a damn . . . one or two cigarettes": Fritz Meese, ibid., p. 120.

136:　"suffocated in swamp and blood": German Werth, *Flanders 1917 and the German Soldier*, pp. 327–38.

136:　"Soldiers! Conscious of the victory . . . to stand firm!": Quoted in Herbert Sulzbach, *With the German Guns*, p. 96.

136:　"snap their fingers . . . lying in front of him": ibid., p. 97.

136:　"lying at each listening post . . . avoid becoming casualties": Edmund Blunden, *Undertones of War*, p. 167.

137:　"a lull in the fighting . . . neither gun, machine or rifle": Revd. David Railton, IWM 80/22/1, p. 38.

137:　"never stopped for one moment—ever": Robert Graves, *The Listener*, 15 July 1971, p. 74.

137:　"this bitter, bitter winter . . . degrees of frost out here": Revd. David Railton, IWM 80/22/1, pp. 27, 29.

137:　"had to light a fire . . . as one could acquire": A. L. Robins, Liddle GS 1368, Part 1, p. 3.

137:　"a 'rabbit-hole'—a burrow under the firing step": Helmut Zschuppe, *German Students' War Letters*, p. 365.

137:　"only just managed . . . how long it will last": GE 01 Anonymous Diary, Liddle Collection, pp. 1–16.

137:　Instead he was cold . . . anywhere but there . . . "our watchword is still . . . however cold it is": ibid.

138:　"The men always got . . . put new life into them": Thomas McCall, "A Highland Battalion at Loos."

138:　"the Tommies started . . . lasted till midnight" . . . "with several of my company . . . prison at Bapaume" . . . "went sick . . . in this cold weather": GE 01 Anonymous Diary, Liddle Collection, pp. 1–16.

138:　"was suffering badly . . . they could fight no longer": J. McCauley, IWM 6434 97/10/1, p. 89.

139:　By 1918, the rate . . . 33 percent: *Economist* annual reports, cited in Guy Chapman, *Vain Glory*, p. 127.

139:　"the fortunes from swords . . . shares and honours": Ronald Blythe, *The Age of Illusion*, p. 6.

139:　"All we want to hear . . . simply unimaginable": Captain E. E. Simeons, IWM 2808 94/28/1.

139:　"There are moments when . . . would be peace tomorrow": Richard Schmeider, *German Students' War Letters*, p. 209.

139:　when resting on the march . . . the road from their men: Paul Fussell, *The Great War and Modern Memory*, p. 82.

139:　"GHQ had heard of the trenches . . . common people lived": Philip Gibbs, *Realities of War*, p. 245.

139:   "Battalion commanders did not soon . . . had been moulders": C. E. Montague, *Disenchantment*, p. 43.

139:   "your old mare . . . attack of the strangles": John Ellis, *Eye Deep in Hell*, p. 42.

140:   "five a side in badly-lit . . . taking orders for drinks": Herbert Essame, quoted in Fussell, op. cit., p. 83.

140:   "London to any open eye . . . disguised as a soldier": Montague, op. cit., p. 26.

140:   "The Duke of —— . . . ammunition and war matériel": F. de Margry, IWM 4410 82/22/1, pp. 7–8.

140:   "There was a bad smell . . . we've got to win first' ": Montague, op. cit., pp. 46–48.

140:   "The war will end . . . at home? They will": Wilfred Owen, *Letters of Wilfred Owen.*

140:   "They were almost exactly . . . old rulers of Germany": Montague, op. cit., pp. 46–48.

140:   "I will go on fighting . . . soldier or fighter for that": Sergeant-Major F. H. Keeling, in Lawrence Housman (ed.), *War Letters of Fallen Englishmen*, pp. 161–62.

141:   "for the Hun, I feel nothing . . . wife and his books": Captain A. G. West, ibid., p. 290.

141:   "thought us all equally fools . . . pasturing lice": Montague, op. cit., p. 128.

141:   "the same mixture . . . wife and children": Charles Masterman, *England After War*, p. 11.

141:   The Kaiser's alleged description . . . War Office civil servant: Fussell, op. cit., p. 116.

141:   A British ship . . . between the two countries: Gary Mead, *The Doughboys*, p. 21.

141:   The *New York Herald* . . . serialized in American newspapers: Joseph E. Persico, *Eleventh Month, Eleventh Day, Eleventh Hour*, p. 91.

141:   "never contained the right things . . . the wife's letters": Montague, op. cit., p. 143.

10: THE FURNACE

143:   "Through all those wet, snowy . . . ourselves in the ground": Willi Bohle, *German Students' War Letters*, p. 331.

143:   "every village was reduced . . . advance into a wasteland": Ernst Junger, *Storm of Steel*, p. 139.

144:   "A new shovel lying . . . pens on a desk": Leon Wolff, *In Flanders Fields*, pp. 55–56.

144:   "We all had on us the stench . . . stuffed with corpses": Anonymous French soldier, quoted in John Ellis, *Eye Deep in Hell*, p. 59.

145:   It is claimed . . . Verdun after the war: Holger H. Herwig, *First World War*, p. 184.

145: a thousand soldiers had died per square metre: German Werth, *Verdun*, p. 396, quoted in George L. Mosse, *Fallen Soldiers*, p. 93.

145: "Our dugout . . . where the explosive was stored": Kurt Rohrbach, *German Students' War Letters*, p. 276.

145: "a great, bloody heap . . . in each other's bodies": Walter Ambroselli, *German Students' War Letters*, p. 190.

145: "The air was suffocating . . . took our breath away": Werth, *Verdun*, pp. 202–6, quoted in Holger H. Herwig, *The First World War*, p. 189.

146: The dead were walled up . . . abandoned passageways: Herwig, op. cit., pp. 297–99.

146: One Württemberg unit . . . camped at Montfaucon: ibid., p. 189.

146: "Heroes become victims . . . nobody knows where to": Quoted in ibid., p. 198.

146: At the height of the mutiny . . . were involved: Wolff, op. cit., p. 64.

147: over a hundred ringleaders . . . death by their own artillery: Richard Garrett, *The Final Betrayal*, p. 137.

147: So disciplined at the start . . . senior officer approached: Matthew Holden, *War in the Trenches*, p. 46.

147: 18,000 Prussian soldiers . . . carrying them to the front lines: Herwig, op. cit., p. 325.

147: "deadly attack": Ludwig Finke, *German Students' War Letters*, p. 92.

147: "a sea of mud . . . adds a finishing touch!": Gerhard Gurtler, *German Students' War Letters*, p. 359.

148: "One could see nothing anywhere . . . into the prevailing haze": Captain D. G. Browne, quoted in Guy Chapman, *Vain Glory*, p. 456.

148: Attempts by the Tank Corps . . . no more of these ridiculous maps": Quoted in Wolff, op. cit., p. 135.

148: "I had a certain feeling . . . drown or get out of this hole?' ": Von Hindenburg, quoted in ibid., pp. 141–42.

148: "Every brook is swollen . . . had declared against us": Quoted in ibid., p. 150.

149: "Boots were torn . . . remained to die, stuck fast": G. Skelton, IWM 6597 79/17/1, p. 54.

149: "We produced ropes . . . just below the knee": John Ewart March, IWM 292 89/21/1, p. 22.

149: "sunk lower in the mud and with their minds gone": G. Skelton, IWM 6597 79/17/1, p. 54.

149: "one of his comrades mercifully put a bullet through his skull": Quoted in Mark Derez, "A Belgian Salient for Reconstruction," p. 442.

149: A Guards battalion lost sixteen men to the mud in a single month: Ellis, op. cit., p. 45.

149: "They drowned in mud . . . pulled them down": Geoff Dyer, *The Missing of the Somme*, p. 83.

149: "a khaki-clad leg . . . above the rising water": Ellis, op. cit., p. 47.

149: "From a tank point of view . . . for little gain": Quoted in Wolff, op. cit., p. 151.

150: "like men . . . dug up again": Quoted in ibid., p. 215.

150: Douglas Haig's sole concession . . . during his morning canter: Joseph E. Persico, *Eleventh Month, Eleventh Day, Eleventh Hour*, p. 189.

150: "simply a desolation . . . a big heap of bricks": Lieutenant G. W. L. Talbot, in Lawrence Housman (ed.), *War Letters of Fallen Englishmen*, p. 273.

150: "Scarcely any stone . . . the municipal cemetery": Derez, op. cit., p. 440.

150: "During the whole battle . . . attrition on the Western Front": Quoted in Wolff, op. cit., p. 262.

150: "The War Cabinet felt . . . 'Keep back the men' ": Quoted in ibid., p. 267.

151: Churches also gave up . . . "donated" 10,312: Herwig, op. cit., p. 256v.

151: Petrol stocks were a third . . . billiard tables: ibid., p. 354.

151: When the war . . . fell by a quarter: ibid., p. 272v.

151: "The women who stood . . . death of their husbands": Ernst Glaeser, quoted in ibid., p. 292.

151: "In earlier days, when a horse . . . We found it excellent": Ernst Junger, *Copse 125*, pp. 141–42.

152: There had been food shortages . . . "turnip winter" of 1916–17: Herwig, op. cit., p. 3.

152: Albert Speer was . . . left over from peacetime": Quoted in Garrett, op. cit., p. 242.

152: Government action often made . . . the *"Schweinemord"* (pig murder): Herwig, op. cit., p. 285.

152: "Faces like masks . . . worthy of comment: Blucher, *An English Wife in Berlin*, quoted in ibid., p. 290.

152: "One of the most terrible . . . clothing seems to alleviate": Quoted in Wolff, op. cit., p. 21.

153: Order was restored . . . strike leaders to the front lines: Herwig, op. cit., p. 292.

153: By the end of the month . . . Hamburg and Brandenburg: ibid., pp. 378–79.

153: The new territories were plundered . . . the former Russian territories: ibid., p. 386.

11: A TEST TO DESTRUCTION

154: Prominent in Republican politics . . . Rock Creek Road: Interview with Teddy Westlake, September 2004.

154: "no siblings anywhere can have been as close": Interview with Grace "Bambi" Williams, September 2004.

155: After working at the Government . . . patent law firm: *Washington Post*, 29 September 1918.

155: Patent law was evidently . . . from 1913 to 1917: PRO AIR76/453.

155: "had to know somebody . . . at least a judge": Kenneth Baker, *Oatmeal and Coffee*, pp. 31–32, quoted in Joseph E. Persico, *Eleventh Month, Eleventh Day, Eleventh Hour*, p. 162.

155: "naturally athletic . . . candidates are not desired": Alan Clark, *Aces High*, p. 162.

155: "the first member . . . flying alone is called": *Washington Sunday Star*, 15 December 1918.

156: "tall and beautiful": Interview with Grace "Bambi" Williams, September 2004.

156: "quietly married . . . the bride's mother": *Washington Post*, 30 July 1917.

156: The wedding was arranged . . . did not attend: Interview with Teddy Westlake, September 2004.

156: "would not have been thrilled . . . was an Episcopalian": Conversation with Teddy Westlake, September 2004.

156: "pseudo-Canadians" . . . Fifth Avenue, New York: W. F. J. Harvey, *Pi in the Sky*, p. 71.

156: "feeling controls": Peter H. Liddle, *The Airman's War*, p. 79.

156: "other schools in different parts of Canada": *Washington Sunday Star*, 15 December 1918.

156: On 2 September 1914 . . . Schlieffen plan had required: Williamson Murray, *War in the Air*, p. 26.

157: Bréguet's report . . . value of air observation: ibid.

157: Its authorized strength . . . in the pay scale: Clark, op. cit., p. 161.

157: When the United States actually . . . 1,000 enlisted men: ibid.

157: One bizarre British experiment . . . enemy aircraft's propeller: Murray, op. cit., p. 34.

157: "adversely affected their performance": Christopher Shores, Norman Franks and Russell Guest, *Above the Trenches*, p. 11.

157: A Frenchman, Roland Garros . . . aircraft with this system: ibid., pp. 11–12; Murray, op. cit., p. 35.

157: By the late summer of 1915 . . . British and French aircraft: Harvey, op. cit., p. 2.

158: As the losses of the RFC . . . Romanian engineer, Constantinescu: Shores, Franks and Guest, op. cit., pp. 11–12.

158: "When correctly adjusted . . . striking the blades": Harvey, op. cit., p. 60.

158: "British gun-sights . . . 100 mph targets": ibid., p. 33.

158: In November 1917 . . . during a training flight: *Washington Sunday Star*, 15 December 1918.

158: That crash may have been . . . in his military records: Seibold family papers.

159: "we passed, some hundreds of yards . . . straight down into it": Irvin S. Cobb, *Saturday Evening Post*, 9 March 1918.

160: "We could feel our ship throb . . . what succour we could": ibid.

160: "paid the munificent sum . . . we had just completed": Oliver Bennett, "Words from a War Bird," in *Cross and Cockade International*, 2, No. 4.

160: "a mental and physical strain . . . more being failures": Harvey, op. cit., p. 71.

160: The belief that American pilots . . . instructor earlier that year: Marvin L. Skelton, *Callahan: The Last War Bird*, pp. 141–42.

160: "didn't have any sense . . . everybody wanted to fly": ibid., pp. 8–10.

161: "were to endure . . . with the enemy": Harvey, op. cit., p. 71.

161: One hapless group . . . with some hyperbole: Skelton, op. cit., pp. 12–13.

161: "The plane proceeded . . . directly over the hole": ibid.

161: "sheer murder" . . . "short training was a consequence . . . shortness of training": Murray, op. cit., pp. 38, 42.

161: "quite inadequate . . . their new element": Harvey, op. cit., p. 71.

161: Even in April 1917 . . . one hundred a month: ibid., p. 2.

161: "a bias towards horsemen and countrymen": ibid., p. 71.

161: "a barber's lather boy": ibid., p. 73.

162: "the two situations . . . so deep and bitter": ibid.

162: "like a stone . . . just like a carpet": Robert Cude, IWM Con Shelf, p. 97.

162: "'considered attitude . . . doctrinaire opinion": A. Boyle, *Trenchard*, quoted in Harvey, op. cit., p. 73.

162: "In common with neglect . . . daily weather forecast": Harvey, op. cit., p. 71.

162: "very spotty . . . not many instructors": Bennett, op. cit.

162: The huge losses . . . rushed to the Front: Harvey, op. cit., p. 28.

162: "like when you got up . . . how they did it": Skelton, op. cit., p. 8.

162: "can't even fly, let alone fight": Arthur Gould Lee, *No Parachute*, p. 4.

162: "1. Undergone instruction . . . assisted by flares": Peter H. Liddle, *The Airman's War*, p. 79.

163: "There's no way to check . . . suited to fighter work": Skelton, op. cit., p. 13.

163: "aim might have been helped . . . marked with "rude crosses"": W. P. Taylor and F. L. Irvin, *The History of the 148th Aero Squadron*, p. 9.

163: "proved most costly . . . fire near the front lines": Francis L. "Spike" Irvin, "War Diary," p. 3.

163: The death toll . . . months of combat ahead: Taylor and Irvin, op. cit., p. 5.

12: VANISHED FROM THE FACE OF THE EARTH

165: The civilian populations . . . massing of German reserves: Holger H. Herwig, *The First World War*, p. 397.

165: "We are already imagining . . . not for a second": Herbert Sulzbach, *With the German Guns*, p. 149.

165: "Handed in our one blanket . . . to get through the mud": GE 01 Anonymous Diary, Liddle Collection.

165: "a green Very light . . . 'annihilation fire'": Ernst Junger, *Copse 125*, p. 204.

165: "with a crash . . . were coming to an end": Sulzbach, op. cit., p. 150.

166: "The gunners stand . . . salvo after salvo is fired": ibid.

166: Some spoke of trenches . . . any day of the entire war: Herwig, op. cit., p. 403.

166: "However did we people . . . fifty pitched battles?": Sulzbach, op. cit., p. 151.

166: "If there does not exist . . . this never occurred again": William Moore, *The Thin Yellow Line*, p. 143.

167: "Better homes where the children . . . the ideal of family life": Quoted in Alan Wilkinson, *The Church of England and the First World War*, pp. 280–81.

167: The monthly average . . . 75,000 in 1918: Matthew Holden, *War in the Trenches*, p. 36.

169: "Living like princes . . . we eat mostly meat": GE 01 Anonymous Diary, Liddle Collection.

169: "Plenty of oats . . . whisky and English cigarettes": Sulzbach, op. cit., p. 153.

170: Finally they reached Bazentin . . . retreated the previous day: Jill Knight, *The Civil Service Rifles in the Great War*, p. 124.

171: "In an advance . . . casualties were correspondingly higher": Sulzbach, op. cit., p. 154.

172: Scavenging stocks of food . . . German advance in its tracks: Bruce I. Gudmundsson, *Stormtroop Tactics*, p. 145.

172: "on account of shortage of food . . . caught out by the company commander": GE 01 Anonymous Diary, Liddle Collection.

172: "entire divisions had totally gorged themselves on food and liquor": Quoted in Herwig, op. cit., p. 410.

172: "looked very little like soldiers . . . Men who could hardly walk": Rudolf Binding, quoted in Paul Fussell, *The Great War and Modern Memory*, p. 18.

172: "Repulsive scenes of drunkenness": Quoted in Herwig, op. cit., p. 410.

174: "Stacks and stacks . . . waistcoats, silk socks": Quoted in ibid.

174: "It is no longer possible . . . troops from the villages": IWM SS 472, p. 1.

175: "ritualisation of fire": Herwig, op. cit., p. 246.

175: "the sanatorium of the West": John Ellis, *Eye Deep in Hell*, p. 169.

175: "An English officer . . . chuck the whole business!": Karl Aldag, *German Students' War Letters*, pp. 34–36.

176: "an English officer came across . . . without inflicting any casualties": ibid., p. 36.

176: "At first we threw bombs . . . left and right of the trench": Oskar Meyer, ibid., p. 182.

176: "When one labours for four years . . . energy, initiative and individualism": Gary Mead, *The Doughboys*, p. 87.

176: "This was really a place . . . unworthy of the human race": Sulzbach, op. cit., pp. 167–68.

178: "Every battalion and company . . . has been dashed": Quoted in Herwig, op. cit., p. 409.

180: "He died two days ago . . . in Flanders in the trenches": Kurt Rohrbach, *German Students' War Letters*, pp. 273–74.

13: THE LONESOMEST FEELING

181: "an inconspicuous office in Mason's Yard, off St. James": W. F. J. Harvey, *Pi in the Sky*, p. 72.

181: "It is the lonesomest feeling . . . a very welcome sight": John Grider, quoted in Marvin Skelton, *Callahan: The Last War Bird*, p. 8.

182: A former Harvard quarterback and "an older man than the average flyer": Burke Davis, *War Bird*, p. 73; W. P. Taylor and F. L. Irvin, *The History of the 148th Aero Squadron*, p. 56.

182: All the pilots had trained . . . any combat experience: A. Bingham Seibold and Marvin L. Skelton, "The Search for Lt. Seibold," in *Over the Front*, 6, 1991.

182: "Like all mechanisms of its day . . . putting one through a blade": Robert E. Rogge, *A History of the 148th Aero Squadron*, p. 165.

182: "unforgiving handling characteristics": Len Cacutt, *Great Aircraft of the World*, p. 38.

182: "coarse use": ibid., p. 31.

183: "Always wear a belt . . . stall on a left hand turn": Chaz Bowyer, *Sopwith Camel: King of Combat*, p. 168.

183: " 'Don't get into a right-hand climbing turn.' That's all they told you": Oliver Bennett, "Words from a Warbird," in *Cross and Cockade International*, 2, No. 4, p. 86.

183: "constant blipping with the cut-out button": Joe Christy and Leroy Cook, *American Aviation*, p. 38.

183: The position of the top wing . . . the guns often froze: Ray Sturtivant and Gordon Page, *The Camel File*, p. 7.

183: This had an unfortunate side-effect . . . a spoonful taken orally: Rogge, op. cit., p. 159.

183: "it could bite its own tail": Christy and Cook, op. cit., p. 38.

183: "Not only did they believe . . . confusing to an enemy": Norman Franks, *American Aces of World War I*, p. 16.

183: "unquestionably the greatest . . . includes the German planes": A. J. Lynch, interview with Lieutenant Richmond Viall, pp. 243–44.

183: they were responsible for more "kills" of enemy aircraft—1,694: Rogge, op. cit., p. 160.

183: "could turn inside a stairwell" and "was deadly below 5,000 feet": Davis, op. cit., p. 74.

183: "a Camel pilot had to shoot down . . . out-run a Fokker": Rogge, op. cit., p. 160.

183: That view was confirmed . . . tight circle and dogfight": Lawrence Wyly interview, History of Aviation Collection, University of Texas at Dallas.

184: "When we thought we were good enough . . . back to our airdrome": Davis, op. cit., p. 74.

184: George Seibold reported . . . on 4 July 1918: PRO AIR76/453.

184: A grainy, black and white film . . . is George: Hugh Wynne Film No. 10, History of Aviation Collection, University of Texas at Dallas.

184: "'very slow on learning . . . destroyed more Allied or German planes": users.aristotle.net/~russjohn/warriors/ace.html.

184: After he wrecked his fifth aircraft . . . Dover in dense fog: James J. Hudson, "Air Knight of the Ozarks," in *American Aviation Historical Society Journal*, Winter 1959, pp. 240–41.

184: "no less a fine pilot . . . the first to commence one": Taylor and Irvin, op. cit., p. 22.

184: "Because of his wonderful knowledge . . . or the lower flight": ibid.

184: "The Knights of the White Triangle": ibid., p. 7.

184: The three flights were distinguished . . . "C" Flight's were blue: Sturtivant and Page, op. cit., p. 253; Franks, op. cit., pp. 58–60.

185: "various coloured silk stockings": Bennett, op. cit., p. 323.

185: "very comfortably and attractively arranged": Taylor and Irvin, op. cit., p. 25.

185: "They must have a great outfit . . . all over the world": Elliot Springs, *Warbirds*, p. 242.

185: The U.S. High Command . . . squadron on the Western Front: Davis, op. cit., p. 80.

185: "an immense, irregular patchwork . . . well-tilled fields": Frederick Mortimer Clapp, *History of the 17th Aero Squadron*, p. 18.

185: "the spire of St. Eloi . . . on the Yser canal": ibid.

185: George was one of two pilots . . . both escaped unhurt: Francis L. "Spike" Irvin, "War Diary," p. 10.

185: "no pilot was to cross . . . into a fixed target": Clapp, op. cit., p. 16.

186: "diving and firing . . . nearby at St. Pol": Taylor and Irvin, op. cit., p. 21.

186: "there was nothing left of it but shreds": Clapp, op. cit., p. 17.

186: "saw a rotten attempt . . . emptied my guns into it": Springs, op. cit., pp. 164–65.

186: "after two to four hours . . . ground in semi-darkness": Harvey, op. cit., p. 29.

186: Before taking off . . . the enemy: Franks, op. cit., p. 32.

186: "The way the earth looked . . . the dive; machine guns": Alan Clark, *Aces High*, p. 185.

186: "Although 17,000 to 18,000 feet . . . blood round the lips": Harvey, op. cit., pp. 31–32.

187: "took their charges . . . them look it over": Taylor and Irvin, op. cit., p. 23.

187: The majority of U.S. pilots . . . under the mental strains: Springs, op. cit., p. vii.

187: According to one pilot . . . average man could stand: Arthur Gould Lee, *No Parachute*, p. 7.

187: "My ears are afire . . . I have to live": Davis, op. cit., p. 79.

187: "war flying exposes the human . . . exposed to before": Medical Research Committee report, June 1918.

187: "a lot of fellows . . . at least half-drunk": Tom L. Moore interview, History of Aviation Collection, University of Texas at Dallas.

187: "wonderful game . . . injuries to the players": John H. Morrow, *The Great War in the Air*, p. 239.

187: "playing for one's school . . . fighting for the Empire": George L. Mosse, *Fallen Soldiers*, p. 142.

187: He was killed while the ball was still in the air: Robert Cude, IWM Con Shelf, pp. 36–38.

188: "at full throttle to remain on the ground": Harvey, op. cit., p. 32.

188: "half the fragile aircraft . . . flying field in France": Williamson Murray, *War in the Air*, p. 30.

188: "flitting around like the bats in a belfry tower" . . . "firing Very lights . . . large gasoline flares": Taylor and Irvin, op. cit., p. 24.

188: "no attempt yet at offensive work": ibid., p. 23.

188: "like snakes' tongues as they burst": Eduard Offenbacher, *German Students' War Letters*, p. 223.

188: "A burst near you . . . deflection for the next shot": Springs, op. cit., pp. 168–69.

188: "for marking up the first point . . . American Air Service": Irvin, "War Diary," p. 10; Taylor and Irvin, op. cit., p. 23.

188: Despite the occasional wail . . . Coudekerque and St. Pol-sur-Mer: Clapp, op. cit., p. 19.

189: "You watched the sky . . . be over tonight'": Irvin, "War Diary," p. 12.

189: "every clear night . . . tiresome already" . . . "just as easy to find . . . as in the daylight": Springs, op. cit., p. 165.

189: "The strictest rules . . . regard to lights": Irvin, "War Diary," p. 12.

189: "on which hospital trains . . . that part of the Front": Clapp, op. cit., p. 18.

189: "a little water . . . from the feet up": Irvin, "War Diary," p. 12.

189: "real war flying started today": ibid.

189:   "twelve, fourteen, even sixteen" . . . 15,000 feet over Dunkirk: Clapp, op. cit., p. 21.

189:   The bombers flew on . . . as high as 19,000 feet: Bennett, op. cit., p. 318; Rogge, op. cit., p. 162, puts the Camel's ceiling at 16,000 feet.

189:   "the best and most accurate that the 148th ever encountered": Taylor and Irvin, op. cit., p. 24.

189:   "the white blossoms . . . ever-drooping star-shells": Paul Bewsher, quoted in Guy Chapman, *Vain Glory*, p. 617.

189:   "the two British concrete-laden battleships": Taylor and Irvin, op. cit., p. 24.

189:   "which they bombed twice a day regularly for weeks": Clapp, op. cit., p. 21.

190:   "a pretty sorry lot . . . two flight and squadron shows": Bennett, op. cit.

190:   "a reckless waste of human life": Morrow, op. cit., p. 238.

190:   "Lt. Forster's machine . . . hit by German AA": Irvin, "War Diary," p. 13.

190:   On the same patrol . . . more than slight injuries: ibid.

190:   "If you heard reports . . . crackling, only more so": Bennett, op. cit., p. 319.

14: GOING OUT LIKE CANDLES

192:   "the silent crowds . . . galloping through the night": C. E. Montague, *Disenchantment*, p. 163.

192:   On 11 June . . . "superior" American forces would rescue the "tired Europeans": General John J. Pershing, quoted in David F. Trask, *The AEF and Coalition Warmaking*, p. 77.

192:   "the U.S. regular army . . . Denmark or the Netherlands": Gary Mead, *The Doughboys*, p. 13.

192:   "lay in beautifully . . . machine-guns had caught them": A. J. Smithers, *Sir John Monash*, p. 197, quoted in Mead, op. cit., p. 180.

192:   "dig a trench shoulder-high . . . guns at close range": Barrie Pitt, *1918: The Last Act*, p. 8, quoted in Joseph E. Persico, *Eleventh Month, Eleventh Day, Eleventh Hour*, p. 67.

192:   "While the French army bled . . . anything about trench warfare": Stephen Ambrose, *Duty, Honor, Country*, p. 251, quoted in Mead, op. cit., p. 172.

192:   "carrying rifles over open ground . . . and the students deaf": Persico, op. cit., p. 254.

193:   in the closing stages of the war . . . against the Allies' 3,500: Holger H. Herwig, *The First World War*, pp. 418–20.

194:   Half the British infantry . . . had been when he died: Paul Fussell, *The Great War and Modern Memory*, p. 18.

194:   "the terrible brazen roar . . . thousands of guns" . . . "It looks as though . . . this would happen—never": Herbert Sulzbach, *With the German Guns*, p. 204.

194:   "You shouted into the darkness . . . fourteen whole kilometres": ibid., p. 206.

194:   "skeletal [German] divisions . . . and on the ground": Herwig, op. cit., p. 418.

194:   "The word 'hell' . . . world were coming to an end": Sulzbach, op. cit., pp. 207–8.

195:   reserves taking their places . . . shouts of "strike-breakers": Herwig, op. cit., p. 419.

195:   "Planes are coming over . . . drawing to its close": Sulzbach, op. cit., p. 207.

195:   "dying off in the hospitals . . . no physical reserves": Ernst Junger, *Copse 125*, p. 79.

197:   *"der schwarze Tag . . . der Geschichte dieses Krieges"*: Ludendorff, *Memoirs*, quoted in Harold Nicolson, *King George V*, p. 323.

198:   "direct evidence . . . considerable numbers": J. F. C. Fuller, *Evidence of the Shell Shock Enquiry*, 1922, quoted in John Ellis, *Eye Deep in Hell*, p. 185.

198:   "In almost every single order . . . issued for deserters": GE 13 Karol Lubinski, Liddle Collection.

198:   "unmolested by the authorities": Herwig, op. cit., p. 325.

198:   Trains carrying wounded men . . . commandeered by rebellious troops: ibid., p. 420.

198:   An entire trainload . . . advancing American troops: Ellis, op. cit., p. 181.

198:   "feared the shame of ridicule" . . . "from a simple sense of duty . . . [but] most of us from habit" . . . "not a man would have remained voluntarily at the Front": Quoted in Herwig, op. cit., p. 193.

198:   "men endured the horrors . . . allow them to give in": Christopher Dowling, introduction to George Coppard, *With a Machine Gun to Cambrai*.

15: GROUND ATTACK

200:   They were faced . . . only in concentrated formations: Williamson Murray, *War in the Air*, p. 70.

201:   Whether in celebration . . . champagne party that evening: Francis L. "Spike" Irvin, "War Diary," p. 13.

201:   They were accordingly transferred . . . northeast of Amiens: PRO AIR76/453.

201:   "got busy with the war again": Irvin, "War Diary," p. 13.

201:   "no words will suffice . . . this national hero": Herbert Sulzbach, *With the German Guns*, p. 166.

201: "it was no strange sight . . . about the grave": Irvin, "War Diary," p. 13.

201: "a hot spot . . . based in this area": James J. Hudson, "Air Knight of the Ozarks," in *American Aviation Historical Society Journal*, Winter 1959, p. 243.

201: as soon as they arrived . . . Albert and Roye: Irvin, "War Diary," p. 14.

201: "up and down the lines . . . ready for battle": Burke Davis, *War Bird*, p. 80.

202: "Nobody in the squadron . . . how they must feel": Elliot Springs, *Warbirds*, pp. 239, 253.

202: "My eyes are so sore . . . they ache all night": ibid., pp. 256–57.

202: "It was not long before . . . recorded with increased frequency": Alan Clark, *Aces High*, p. 176.

202: "about the colour of veinous blood": Oliver Bennett, "Words from a Warbird," in *Cross and Cockade International*, 2, No. 4, p. 320.

203: "fired 150 rounds . . . when I saw him crash": PRO AIR1/1228/204/5/2634.

203: "and was about to finish off his opponent" . . . "suddenly there was a terrible pain . . . free with both hands": Peter Kilduff, *Richthofen*, pp. 210–11; Norman Franks and Greg Van Wyngarden, *Fokker D VII Aces of World War I*, p. 19.

203: "Unknown. Two-seater . . . like Fokker biplane": PRO AIR1/1228/204/5/2634.

203: "It was the most dangerous . . . that seemed an age": Elliot Springs, foreword to Clayton Knight, *Pilot's Luck*.

204: On George's return . . . confirming the kill: PRO AIR1/1228/204/5/2634.

204: "obliged to dead-stick to the ground": Robert E. Rogge, *A History of the 148th Aero Squadron*, p. 164.

204: "was having the time . . . that fascinating machine-gun": W. P. Taylor and F. L. Irvin, *The History of the 148th Aero Squadron*, p. 27.

204: "came down like a ton . . . top flight came in": Davis, op. cit., p. 81.

204: Waggling his wings as the signal to go: James J. Hudson, "Captain Field E. Kindley," in *Arkansas Historical Quarterly*, 1959, No. 2, p. 103.

204: "fired about 200 rounds . . . edge of the scrap": PRO AIR1/1228/204/5/2634.

204: "I turned up at them . . . while gliding down": PRO AIR1/1228/204/5/2634.

205: To everyone's delight . . . the right forearm: Irvin, "War Diary," p. 14; Taylor and Irvin, op. cit., p. 29, suggests that it was three days before Wyly returned.

205: "through the constant work . . . good for landing": Taylor and Irvin, op. cit., p. 43.

205: "a most disagreeable place": ibid.

205: Like his comrades . . . first combat missions: ibid., p. 32.

206: "If you have ever seen . . . foliage and branches": ibid., p. 42.

206: "low work, the most dangerous of any": Letter from James A. Keating to Mrs. Grace Darling Seibold, Seibold family papers.

206: "an expensive business . . . a vital objective": W. F. J. Harvey, *Pi in the Sky*, p. 28.

206: "a severer test . . . fitting of his machine": Frederick Mortimer Clapp, *History of the 17th Aero Squadron*, p. 39.

206: "an aircraft was an offensive . . . and make him fight": Peter Daybell, *Some Aspects of the Aircrew Experience During the Great War*, p. 3.

206: "Trenchard's policy . . . cumulus cloud cover": Harvey, op. cit., pp. 2–3.

207: "just because I'm condemned . . . think I don't understand": Daybell, op. cit., p. 3.

207: "It was hardly surprising . . . uselessly high casualties": Harvey, op. cit., pp. 2–3.

207: Of 1,437 British pilots . . . time of the Armistice: Murray, op. cit., p. 17.

207: it was claimed that pilots . . . during heavy fighting: ibid., p. 41.

207: "206 flying crew . . . strength of thirty-six": Harvey, op. cit., p. 2.

207: "Whether or not the air casualties . . . may be argued": H. A. Jones, *The War in the Air*, vol. V, quoted in ibid., p. 3.

207: "Most leading German pilots . . . many were its victim": Harvey, op. cit., pp. 2–3.

207: "a proof of the low altitude . . . shot down by infantry": IWM SS472, p. 1.

208: "gave us an opportunity . . . to his scouts [fighters]": Clapp, op. cit., p. 38.

208: "without cessation . . . inflicting on them many casualties": ibid., p. 39.

208: "During the day one hardly dares . . . nerves this costs us": Diary of a Prisoner of the 125th Regiment, IWM SS473, p. 4.

208: "they fly around . . . heroes of the war": Harry S. Truman to Bess Truman, quoted in Joseph E. Persico, *Eleventh Month, Eleventh Day, Eleventh Hour*, p. 289.

208: "in pairs or alone and make three or four trips a day": Springs, op. cit., p. 257.

208: A modified version . . . underneath the pilot's seat: Ray Sturtivant and Gordon Page, *The Camel File*, p. 7.

209: Aircraft were then kept flying . . . focus of the Allied attack: Jones, op. cit., vol. VI, p. 470.

210: all pilots were directed . . . targeting anti-tank guns: ibid., p. 475.

210: "until the tanks . . . periodically bombed": J. F. C. Fuller, *Tanks in the Great War*, pp. 247–48.

210: "big drive towards Bapaume . . . a terrific barrage": Irvin, "War Diary," p. 14.

210: "each got a Hun": ibid.

210: "would rise about twenty feet . . . dead horses and tanks": Springs, op. cit., pp. 257–58.

210: "the force of the gas . . . a hissing sound": Captain E. E. Simeons, IWM 2808 94/28/1.

210: "curious greenish-yellow clouds . . . a frosty night": Quoted in Guy Chapman, *Vain Glory*, p. 136.

211: "The gas was so strong . . . holes by the score": Captain E. E. Simeons, IWM 2808 94/28/1.

211: "squares of blue flannel . . . a temporary palliative": Quoted in Chapman, op. cit., p. 142.

211: The night was fine . . . Cambrai railway junction: Jones, op. cit., vol. VI, p. 472.

211: "obtaining much relief": Irvin, "War Diary," p. 15.

16: THE LOSSES WE HAVE SUFFERED

214: "night and day aircraft . . . seventeen men killed here": GE 01 Anonymous Diary, Liddle Collection.

214: "a slope of the Somme valley": Footnotes by Alfred Hub, correspondence of Paul Hub.

214: They had paused for the distribution . . . He died soon afterwards: Footnotes by Alfred Hub, correspondence of Paul Hub.

17: A DIMINISHING SHADOW

215: "a Bavarian Division . . . advancing to its support" . . . "the most resolute offensive . . . exposed for the time being": H. A. Jones, *The War in the Air*, vol. VI, p. 473.

215: "low strafing all day . . . in and around Bapaume": Francis L. "Spike" Irvin, "War Diary," p. 15.

216: This crude method . . . squadrons to bear on targets: Jones, op. cit., pp. 474–75.

216: "hitting ground troops . . . vicinity of Bapaume": Irvin, "War Diary," p. 15.

216: "fired into infantry and horses" . . . "dropped bombs . . . Thinks he killed two": A. Bingham Seibold and Marvin L. Skelton, "The Search for Lt. Seibold," in *Over the Front*, 6, 1991.

216: "fearsome devices . . . fire around the balloons": Joe Christy and Leroy Cook, *American Aviation*, p. 38.

217: "probably a Hannoveraner" . . . "The flight below us dived . . . ammunition was all gone": PRO AIR1/1228/204/5/2634.

217: It was George's fourth victory . . . "distinguished service": *Washington Post*, 29 September 1918.

217: one more confirmed kill . . . pilots until much later: PRO AIR1/1228/204/ 5/2634.

217: "starring their airmen . . . mockery in the RFC": W. F. J. Harvey, *Pi in the Sky*, p. 73.

217: "grew stronger and gustier . . . eighty miles an hour": Frederick Mortimer Clapp, *History of the 17th Aero Squadron*, p. 40.

217: it was so windy . . . into the wind for takeoff: James J. Hudson, *Hostile Skies*, p. 216.

217: "blowing furiously into Hunland": Clapp, op. cit., p. 41.

218: "George spied three Huns . . . gotten another Hun": Letter from James A. Keating to Mrs. Grace Darling Seibold, Seibold family papers.

218: "a chestful of decorations": Norman Franks and Greg Van Wyngarden, *Fokker D VII Aces of World War I*, pp. 81–82.

218: "a gaudy Fokker . . . as a Staffelführer": ibid.

218: "after an engagement . . . down in a slow spin": Account of James Bruce Edwards, in Seibold and Skelton, op. cit.; E. H. Zistel to M. L. Newhall, 1 November 1918, Seibold family papers.

218: "About 7:30 p.m. an aeroplane . . . burst into a cheer": Canon E. C. Crosse, IWM 4772 80/22/1, p. 13.

218: "some of our 'low-strafers' . . . the Cambrai-Bapaume road": Clapp, op. cit., p. 40.

219: "five Fokkers, climbing east . . . came down from higher up": Combat reports of Lt. R. M. Todd and Lt. W. D. Tipton, quoted in ibid., pp. 74–75.

219: "First sortie of the whole *Geschwader* . . . plunged down burning": "Diary of Lt. Friedrich Noltenius," in *Cross and Cockade International*, 7, No. 4, Winter 1966.

219: "a cloud of fifty to sixty German machines": James J. Sloan, *148th American*, p. 257.

219: "11 Camels and Fokkers . . . four others crash": PRO AIR1/1228/204/5/2634.

219: "The pilot lived and died . . . a diminishing shadow": Harvey, op. cit., p. 72.

18: AT THE ELEVENTH HOUR

220: On or soon after . . . as his regiment retreated: Footnotes by Alfred Hub, correspondence of Paul Hub.

221: "There can be no conclusion . . . brought to her knees": Joseph E. Persico, *Eleventh Month, Eleventh Day, Eleventh Hour*, p. 313.

221: "thin, crescent-shaped mouth . . . smiled in his life": Quoted in Gary Mead, *The Doughboys*, p. 110.

222: By the time the guns finally fell silent . . . D-Day in Normandy in 1944: Persico, op. cit., frontispiece.

222: "The retaking of Mons . . . 700,000 lives later": ibid., p. 354.

222: "Their proximity in dust . . . futility of their actions": Thomas W. Laqueur, "Memory and Naming in the Great War," p. 150.

223: "The soldiers marched quickly . . . this was a whole regiment": Ernst von Salomon, quoted in Guy Chapman, *Vain Glory*, p. 709.

224: "neither at the German military cemetery . . . the lists of dead soldiers": Footnotes by Alfred Hub, correspondence of Paul Hub.

224: Maria remained childless . . . Paul had hoped to share: Interview with Frau Brigitte Kostka, January 2005.

224: "workers of war": The phrase is Ernst Junger's in *Storm of Steel*.

224: Until the Great War . . . retreat from Moscow: George L. Mosse, *Fallen Soldiers*, pp. 3–4.

224: That massive death toll . . . decade prior to the war: A. J. P. Taylor, *English History, 1914–45*.

224: Almost half of the British dead . . . found but not identified: *The Times*, 10 November 1928.

224: Those unknown dead had "given even their names": S. MacHaughtan, quoted in Laqueur, op. cit., p. 158.

224: "associated with punishment, barbarity and victimisation": Catherine Moriarty, "The Absent Dead and Figurative First World War Memorials," *Transactions of the Ancient Monuments Society*, 1, 1995, p. 9.

224: Over 2 million German . . . fatherless children in Germany: Holger H. Herwig, *The First World War*, p. 444.

225: In total, over 9 million . . . listed as missing: Microsoft Encarta, 2002.

225: Shell-shock also affected . . . every four combatants: Herwig, op. cit., p. 2.

225: In total perhaps 12 million . . . by the wartime conditions: ibid., p. 1.

225: It says much for the grief . . . any supporting evidence: cf. Jean Yves Naour, *The Living Unknown Soldier*.

19: THE COINAGE OF REMEMBRANCE

226: "killed in action in the field . . . in due course": Papers of the late Roger Goodman.

226: "The King commands me . . . Freedom and Justice": A. Clayden, IWM 1782 92/3/1, p. 3.

227: It was a form of words . . . "worthy" of the dead: Mark Connelly, *The Great War, Memory and Ritual*, p. 1.

227: "the sacrifices were like the stockyards . . . except bury it": Ernest Hemingway, *A Farewell to Arms*, p. 196.

227: "Whatever pride I had . . . Now all that is gone": Quoted in David Cannadine, "(War and) Death, Grief and Mourning in Modern Britain," p. 216.

227: "It is with extreme sorrow . . . Graves Registration Committee": Papers of the late Roger Goodman.

227: "If an officer was killed . . . the War Office": Canon E. C. Crosse, IWM 4772 80/22/1, Part 3, p. 28.

227: "three stock messages . . . died painlessly": Jay Winter, *Sites of Memory, Sites of Mourning*, p. 35.

228: "very careful in writing . . . claims on the War Office": Canon E. C. Crosse, IWM 4772 80/22/1, Part 3, p. 29.

228: Despite the need for accuracy . . . Robert Graves among them: Robert Graves, *Goodbye to All That*, p. 182.

228: "they almost invariably write . . . buried respectable?' ": K. E. Luard, *Unknown Warrior*, p. 93.

228: An order had been issued . . . in force until the 1960s: Philip Longworth, *The Unending Vigil*, p. 14.

229: "the sight of hundreds . . . sickening horror": Caroline Playne, quoted in Alan Wilkinson, *The Church of England and the First World War*, p. 170.

229: "In the absence of corpses . . . death and killing": Bernd Huppauf, *War and Death: The Experience of the First World War*, quoted in Catherine Moriarty, "Christian Iconography and First World War Memorials," *Imperial War Museum Review*, 6, 1992, p. 73.

229: "a tragic, almost frightening figure . . . frequent in the streets": Geoffrey Gorer, *Death, Grief and Mourning*, p. 4.

229: A *Times* reporter . . . in mourning dress: Wilkinson, op. cit., p. 169.

229: Although, as early as the opening days . . . killed in action: *Pall Mall Gazette*, 1 September 1914.

229: "followed scrupulously . . . woman to do otherwise": Gorer, op. cit., p. 4.

229: "mourning succumbed . . . an insufficient comment": Quoted in Cannadine, op. cit., p. 218.

229: "the full panoply . . . leave from the trenches": Gorer, op. cit., p. 6.

229: "identified these practices . . . exhausted with death": David W. Lloyd, *Battlefield Tourism*, p. 4.

230: at the war's end . . . graves in France alone: Samuel A. Hynes, *A War Imagined*, p. 271.

230: On 29 December 1915 . . . all her war dead: George L. Mosse, *Fallen Soldiers*, p. 46.

230: "came in great numbers to dig up their dead": Mark Derez, "A Belgian Salient for Reconstruction," p. 451.

230: some entrepreneurial Frenchmen . . . plus a handling charge: Winter, op. cit., p. 24.

230: "this form of private enterprise . . . crassness of the rich": ibid., p. 26.

230: "For miles these graves occur . . . in decent order": Quoted in Eric Homberger, *The Story of the Cenotaph*, p. 1430.

231: "Private BA Reader . . . a more satisfactory reply": Papers of the late Roger Goodman.

231: "The Command Paymaster . . . Bertram Alec Reader": ibid.

231: "I am much afraid . . . transmitted to you": ibid.

231: "In the newspapers . . . of the dead soldier": Gerhard Gurtler, *German Students' War Letters*, p. 364.

232: "ascertain as far as possible . . . has been done": *The Times*, 9 December 1919.

232: "We must make every effort . . . a tendency to erect": Ministry of Works to Sir Sydney Greville, quoted in Thomas W. Laqueur, "Memory and Naming in the Great War," p. 155.

232: An Army General Routine Order . . . Parliament in May 1920: Paul Gough, *Loci Memoriae*, p. 6.

232: "At the going down of the sun . . . early as September 1914: *The Times*, 21 September 1914. The actual lines are: "At the going down of the sun and in the morning, We will remember them"—the times of the twice-daily "Stand-To."

232: cost a bereaved . . . sevenpence halfpenny: Gough, op. cit., p. 8.

232: "the Dead Man's Penny" . . . freedom and honour: Philip Dutton, "The Dead Man's Penny," *Imperial War Museum Review*, 3, 1988, p. 66.

232: Others undoubtedly felt . . . been more appropriate: Walter Eberbach, *Verdun: Die Weltblutpumpe*, IWM MED/733.

233: "I join with my grateful people . . . others in the Great War": Dutton, op. cit., p. 66.

233: "the sovereign be specifically mentioned . . . irritation at the amendment": ibid.

233: "He whom this scroll commemorates . . . be not forgotten": A. Clayden, IWM 1782 92/3/1, p. 5.

233: There was outrage . . . lying on a rubbish heap: *Daily Sketch*, 30 November 1926.

233: "I regret to have to inform you . . . the place of the memorial": Papers of the late Roger Goodman.

234: "the coinage of remembrance . . . crossed all borders": Gough, op. cit., p. 1.

234: 100,000 other people . . . that year alone: Imperial War Graves Commission, Annual Report, 1929–30, p. 6.

235: Ten years later . . . sacrifice had been forgotten: Interview with the late Roger Goodman, August 2004; Doug Goodman, "Pilgrimage for an Unknown Soldier," *The Times*, 14 September 1991. Rose should have been able to identify the memorial on which her son's name was inscribed by contacting the Imperial War Graves Commission, but she evidently did not know this and no one informed her.

20: MISSING IN ACTION

236: The Squadron War Diary . . . "not returned at 7:30 p.m.": PRO AIR1/1228/204/5/2634.

236: "Major General, Commanding...Chicago IL, USA": PRO AIR1/ 984/ 204/5/1175.

237: "On the 26th of August... when I touched him": Account of James Bruce Edwards, in A. Bingham Seibold and Marvin L. Skelton, "The Search for Lt. Seibold," in *Over the Front*, 6, 1991.

237: "could not look into his pockets... other person's initials": ibid.

238: "if by giving his life... glad to do so": *Washington Sunday Star*, 15 December 1918.

238: In fact, although his plane... the end of the war: home.indy.rr.com/ johnstons/wwi.htm

238: Even more appalling... left on his doorstep: *Gold Star Mothers: Pilgrimage of Remembrance*, DVD.

239: "last seen flying east of Bapaume": Seibold family papers; *Washington Post*, 16 December 1918.

239: It was not until 13 December... in the enemy lines": Seibold and Skelton, op. cit.

239: this was confirmed in a letter... received on Christmas Eve: Seibold family papers.

239: "I cannot imagine... bravely and well": Seibold family papers.

240: He kept the flag... his daughter, Grace Seibold: Grace Seibold obituary, *Washington Star*, 13 June 1947.

240: "Sir, I have the honour... at muster out in 1865": Seibold family papers.

240: "1st. Lieut. Seibold... place where it crashed": Seibold family papers.

241: Some funeral industry organizations... dead U.S. servicemen: "Paris Director in League with Purple Cross (?)," in *Embalmers' Monthly*, 33, January 1920, and "Rid the Profession of Odium That Has Come to It," in *Embalmers' Monthly*, 33, February 1920.

241: "a sanitary and recognizable condition... years after death": Quoted in G. Kurt Piehler, *Remembering War the American Way*, p. 94.

242: The Bring Home the Soldier Dead... died on foreign soil": Quoted in ibid., p. 96.

242: As the architect of the chapel... "they were Christian": Quoted in ibid., p. 100.

242: Private or state monuments... "from a particular locality": American Battle Monuments Commission, quoted in ibid., p. 99.

243: "monuments shot up like mushrooms... made the supreme sacrifice": Mark Derez, "A Belgian Salient for Reconstruction," p. 455.

243: It was a process that occupied... the former battlefields: *New York Times*, 16 April 1921.

243: In so doing, she was consciously... Thomas Nelson Page: *New York Times*, 21 April 1921.

243: "Mrs. Roosevelt and I . . . let it lay": John W. Graham, unpublished paper, "Quentin Roosevelt and the Gold Star Mothers' Pilgrimages," quoted in Lisa M. Budreau, "Mourning and the Making of a Nation," p. 4.

244: "I protest against the remains . . . back to the U.S.": Kathryn Benson Seibold to the Adjutant General, War Department, 8 April 1919, Seibold family papers.

244: "It seems incredible . . . an investigation and report?": General Whitaker to U.S. Secretary of War, 26 August 1919, Seibold family papers.

244: "commune list 1144-2670 . . . Bapaume (Pas de Calais)": Chief, Cemeterial Division, to Chief, American Graves Registration Service, 29 March 1920, Seibold family papers.

244: It was "thought likely . . . nearest to the Commune of Bapaume" . . . "Sgt. Young states that he remembers . . . the British Air Service probably knows something about this matter": Chief, Cemeterial Division, to Chief, American Graves Registration Service, 29 March 1920, Seibold family papers.

244: "careful search was also made . . . Cemetery near Bapaume": Seibold family papers.

245: "This is not an unusual case . . . some definite information": Charles J. Wynne to George G. Seibold, 18 September 1920, Seibold family papers.

245: "to include fillings . . . matters of identification": Cemeterial Division to George G. Seibold, 27 September 1920, Seibold family papers.

245: "It is now the opinion . . . Villers Tournelle, Somme": Chief, Cemeterial Division, to Chief, American Graves Registration Service, October 1920, Seibold family papers.

245: He had done his ground training . . . Illinois at Champaign: James J. Hudson, "Air Knight of the Ozarks," in *American Aviation Historical Society Journal*, Winter 1959, p. 237.

245: his wartime instructions to his cousin . . . Lake Park Avenue in Chicago: James J. Hudson, "Captain Field E. Kindley," in *Arkansas Historical Quarterly*, 1959, No. 2, p. 115.

246: "just about everything you'd want . . . made up for in common sense": users.aristotle.net/~russjohn/warriors/ace.html.

246: His resourcefulness and self-reliance . . . grandmother and two aunts: users.aristotle.net/~russjohn/warriors/ace.html.

246: "It is not a lasting proposition . . . feel like taking it": Hudson, "Kindley," p. 129.

246: "aerobatics, mock dogfighting . . . target shooting": Hudson, "Air Knight," pp. 250–51.

246: "To avoid hitting the crowd . . . plane was a washout": Hudson, "Kindley," pp. 128–29.

247: Kindley was probably killed . . . the burning wreckage: Conversation between Arthur Brooks and A. Bingham Seibold; Hudson, "Kindley," p. 130; Hudson, "Air Knight," p. 252.

247: There were to be no open displays . . . the end of her life: Interview with A. Bingham Seibold, October 2004.

247: "a very giving and kind woman": Interview with Teddy Westlake, September 2004.

247: "A shell came over us . . . not a shred": Harry Patch interview, *Sunday Times* magazine, 7 November 2004.

247: "Ground troops and artillery men . . . there were no remains": Interview with A. Bingham Seibold, October 2004.

248: "the serial numbers of fuselages . . . point of origin": Notebook of Miss C. M. Marx, IWM 86/75/1.

248: "Grave 29, Plot 8 . . . Department of Pas-de-Calais": H. J. Conner to Chief, American Graves Registration Service, 17 May 1923, Seibold family papers.

248: "an unknown American aviator . . . having such dental work": H. J. Conner to Mrs. George Gordon Seibold, 17 May 1923, Seibold family papers.

248: "My late husband . . . entitled to one": Kathryn B. (Seibold) Sutherland to H. J. Conner, 11 May 1923, Seibold family papers.

248: According to members . . . after her mother's death: Interview with Teddy Westlake, October 2004.

249: "his machine landed on its back . . . mangling the pilot": A. R. C. Berne Report B758, Seibold family papers.

249: "Do not know what further to do . . . suggest what to do?" Scott to Mr. Davis, 5 July 1923, Seibold family papers.

249: "There seems nothing further . . . doubtless George Seibold": Scott to Mr. Davis, 5 July 1923, Seibold family papers.

249: "The headless aviator . . . they will agree with us": C.S. to Mr. Davis, 6 July 1923, Seibold family papers.

250: The American Graves Registration Service . . . location is furnished": F. W. Van Doyne to Quartermaster General, 19 April 1927, Seibold family papers.

250: "totally devastated . . . got over his death": Interview with Teddy Westlake, September 2004.

250: "had we not known . . . guessed from her actions": Interview with Teddy Westlake, September 2004.

250: "Had his body been returned . . . memento of my son's service": Grace Seibold to John W. Weeks, 4 August 1924, Seibold family papers.

250: "I always expected that one day . . . there would be Uncle George": Interview with Grace "Bambi" Williams, September 2004.

250: "helping the returning veterans . . . the loss of her son": Theodosia

Nelson, *History of the Gold Star Mothers*, quoted in *Chronicle Telegram*, Elyria, Ohio, 3 July 1988.

21: A HOUSE FOREVER DESOLATE

251: On 28 May 1918 . . . supreme sacrifice for the nation: Lisa M. Budreau, "Mourning and the Making of a Nation," p. 2.

251: "They have issued special rules . . . much curiosity and vain labour": Elliot Springs, *Warbirds*, pp. 254–55; Budreau, op. cit., p. 2.

252: "the last full measure . . . in this sacrifice": Gold Star Mothers Web site.

252: Some congressional opponents . . . mothers and war widows: Budreau, op. cit., p. 3.

252: "nothing but a deserted sea . . . corpses are sleeping": David W. Lloyd, *Battlefield Tourism*, p. 114.

252: "The emptied land . . . churches or farmsteads": Paul Gough, *Loci Memoriae*, p. 5.

252: "the pestle and mortar of war . . . from which it had come": C. E. Montague, *Disenchantment*, p. 204.

253: in the summer of 1919 . . . picnicking in the uncleared battlefields: *Illustrated London News*, 14 June 1919.

253: All solitary graves . . . permanent cemetery would be forty: *The Times*, 10 November 1928.

253: "when the burial party came along . . . as an unknown soldier: John Sheen, *Tyneside Irish*.

253: "He had sent for me to ask . . . but I was adamant": J. McCauley, IWM 6434 97/10/1, pp. 92–93.

254: most had been kept away . . . equipment from the battlefields: Jami L. Bryan, "Fighting for Respect," *Stand To*, 72, January 2005, p. 22.

254: Even with 30,000 workers . . . "ghost employees": Mark Derez, "A Belgian Salient for Reconstruction," p. 441.

254: "as much as 5,000 kilos . . . the shells and larger pieces": ibid., pp. 442–44.

254: "I want to begin by telling you . . . lying over there": Mrs. Eddie Vedder of New York City, Testimony Before the House Committee on Military Affairs, 1924, quoted in *Gold Star Mothers: Pilgrimage of Remembrance*, DVD.

255: "It was the mothers who suffered . . . enriched the foreign soil": Mathilda Burling, Testimony Before the House Committee on Military Affairs, 1928, quoted in *Gold Star Mothers: Pilgrimage of Remembrance*, DVD.

255: "Without Mothers, America would have had . . . beautiful flag in the world": Mathilda Burling, quoted in Budreau, op. cit., p. 6.

255: "Every spare farthing . . . left forever desolate": Charles F. G. Masterman, *England After the War*, p. 79.

255:   "interested in every movement . . . their families sustained": Pershing Papers, Container 37.

255:   But he abhorred . . . a glorified "sightseeing tour": Pershing Papers, Container 37.

255:   "a picture of a drunken American . . . kissing a naked Frenchwoman": Harvey Levenstein, *Seductive Journey*, p. 274.

256:   These would enable mothers . . . buried or commemorated: Budreau, op. cit., p. 2.

256:   "Widows who had not remarried . . . only as an afterthought": ibid.

256:   The St. Barnabas Society . . . sign-posts to guide them": Quoted in Jay Winter, *Sites of Memory, Sites of Mourning*, p. 52.

256:   "devoid of comfort and luxury . . . talking about the war": Quoted in George L. Mosse, *Fallen Soldiers*, p. 154.

256:   The St. Barnabas Society ended . . . pilgrims could afford: ibid., p. 155.

257:   "As the Act of March 2, 1929 . . . eligible to make the pilgrimage": Constance Potter, "World War I Gold Star Mothers' Pilgrimages," *NARA Prologue (Washington)*, vol. 31, no. 2, Summer 1999, p. 3.

257:   "granted membership only . . . the Caucasian race": G. Kurt Piehler, *The War Dead and the Gold Star*, p. 177.

257:   One shipping line even claimed . . . consider using them again: *Gold Star Mothers: Pilgrimage of Remembrance*, DVD.

257:   The first one drawn was Nebraska . . . make the pilgrimage: U.S. Quartermaster Museum, www.qmmuseum.lee.army.mil/historyweek/5–11 feb.htm.

257:   Many of their sons and husbands . . . to go to war: Budreau, op. cit., p. 1.

257:   "meals and incidental expenses . . . OTHER THAN THAT SPECI-FIED": A. D. Hughes to Mrs. Geo. Gordon Seibold, 8 May 1931, Seibold family papers.

257:   "prevent over-emphasis . . . upon the least provocation": Colonel Richard T. Ellis, quoted in Budreau, op. cit., p. 8.

258:   Nineteen more vessels—all ships of the United States Lines: Major Louis C. Wilson, "The War Mother Goes over There," in *Quartermaster Review*, May–June 1930.

258:   over the next four years . . . see their men's graves: Gold Star Pilgrimage Web site; NARA Prologue, 9 March 2004; Budreau, op. cit., p. 1.

258:   There were seven days in Paris . . . visiting the battlefields and cemeteries: Party "F" itinerary, Somme Group, Seibold family papers.

258:   "nuisances of a difficult kind": Liaison report, "F" Party West, 1931, Seibold family papers.

258:   "for purposes of organising . . . excluded from her organisation": Liaison report, "F" Party West, 1931, Seibold family papers.

258:   "loyal, capable and patriotic . . . the pain of others": American Gold Star Mothers Web site.

258: "a lifelong devotion . . . "Oh! There he is": Conversation with Grace "Bambi" Williams, September 2004.

259: His name does not appear . . . attached to the RFC and RAF: PRO AIR2/219/6103585.

259: "we never knew where he was": Interview with Teddy Westlake, October 2004.

259: Perhaps all traces of his aircraft . . . still continuing the search: Interview with A. Bingham Seibold, October 2004.

22: THE CENOTAPH

260: "How that grave caused me to think . . . happy for a few minutes": David Railton, "The Origins of the Unknown Warrior," in *Our Empire*, vol. VII, no. 8, 1931, p. 34.

260: "told nobody; yet I could not . . . never let it drop": ibid.

261: "If God spares me . . . men who fought out here": Revd. David Railton, IWM 80/22/1, p. 24.

261: "devote much time . . . Industrial Christian Fellowship": Andrew Railton, quoted in Michael Moynihan, *God on Our Side*, p. 75.

261: The first monument to dead soldiers . . . 10 August 1792: Thomas W. Laqueur, "Memory and Naming in the Great War," p. 159.

261: The last rites for the Duke . . . lavish as those for a king: David Cannadine, "(War and) Death, Grief and Mourning in Modern Britain," p. 189.

261: 200,000 filing past the body . . . Great Hall in Chelsea: David W. Lloyd, *Battlefield Tourism*, p. 76.

262: At Waterloo and in the Crimean . . . the ground and forgotten": W. M. Thackeray, quoted in Laqueur, op. cit., p. 151.

262: Monsieur Binet-Valmer . . . Section Heads and War Veterans: www.trussel.com/maig/lacas2e.htm.

262: a journalist, Gabriel Boissy . . . to symbolize remembrance: Richard Garrett, *The Final Betrayal*, p. 178.

262: "the dust of one soldier . . . so great a monument": *Daily Express*, 16 September 1919.

262: "consonant with the symbolic character of the monument": PRO WORK 20/139; cf. also Lloyd, op. cit., pp. 63–64.

262: "great men would be likely to heed . . . might be final": Railton, "Origins of the Unknown Warrior," p. 34.

262: "who is there that would risk . . . a newspaper 'stunt'?" ibid., p. 35.

262: "I felt somehow sure . . . Parish Church of the Empire": ibid.

263: "Death's Cathedral Palace . . . keep their court": Herbert Jeans, "In Death's Cathedral Palace," *British Legion Journal*, vol. 9, no. 5, November, 1929, p. 118.

263: "Now or never" . . . "made bold to suggest . . . no 'Service' experience": Railton, "Origins of the Unknown Warrior," p. 35.

263: "warmly inclined to favour . . . idea shall germinate": ibid.

263:   "ecclesiastical misgivings" . . . Cenotaph designed by Lutyens: Ken
       Inglis, "The Homecoming," *Journal of Contemporary History*, 27, 1992,
       quoted in Paul Gough, *Loci Memoriae*, p. 12.

263:   "I am desirous to approach the King . . . interred in Westminster
       Abbey": Dean Ryle to Lord Stamfordham, 4 October 1920, Westmin-
       ster Abbey, 58666.

263:   "it is not possible to say . . . such a service": Ronald Blythe, *The Age of
       Illusion*, p. 13.

263:   "the idea of paying the last honour . . . the Dean of Westminster": *The
       Times*, 12 November 1920.

263:   "His Majesty is inclined to think . . . time is gradually healing": Lord
       Stamfordham to Dean Ryle, 7 October 1920, Westminster Abbey, 58667.

263:   "Nations must justify mass killings . . . sanity of the survivors":
       P. Berton, *Vimy*, p. 307, quoted in Adrian Gregory, *The Silence of Mem-
       ory*, p. 8.

264:   "by themselves remain inert . . . they finally produce": James E. Young,
       The Texture of Memory, p. xiiiv.

264:   "a war-torn and hungry proletariat . . . preponderance of voting
       power": Wheeler-Bennett, *King George VI*, quoted in Eric Hobsbawm
       and Terence Ranger, *The Invention of Tradition*, p. 141.

264:   Labour unrest had led to strikes . . . averted only by the outbreak of
       war: Samuel A. Hynes, *A War Imagined*, p. 6.

264:   The minister, Winston Churchill . . . strike that summer: Garrett, op.
       cit., p. 135.

264:   "like the noise of the machines . . . the silence of the guns": Charles
       Masterman, *England After War*, p. 7.

264:   "We had beaten the Germans . . . Haig was a great hero": B. Bond (ed.),
       The First World War and British Military History, p. 274, quoted in Greg-
       ory, op. cit., p. 37.

264:   Ezra Pound's conviction . . . "a botched civilisation": Ezra Pound,
       "Hugh Selwyn Mauberley," in *Personae*, p. 200.

264:   "The land for heroes . . . vain search for work": Graham Wootton,
       quoted in Garrett, op. cit., p. 227.

265:   "The fight that always occurs . . . the slogans of 1914": George Orwell,
       Collected Essays, Journalism and Letters, vol. I, p. 505.

265:   "the inadequacy of his present position . . . more than recompensed":
       Masterman, op. cit., p. 6.

265:   "Many sanguine well-to-do people . . . followed, feared and loved":
       C. E. Montague, *Disenchantment*, p. 211.

265:   "flame might still flicker . . . Flanders and Picardy": ibid., p. 179.

265:   "the pre-war virilists . . . was seated an earwig": ibid., p. 40.

265:   "the ancient trappings of throne and sceptre": *The Times*, 21 April 1917.

265:   "cities pounded to rubble . . . irksome or worthless": Montague, op.
       cit., p. 88.

265: "we are passing through dreadful days . . . darkness and hopelessness": Letter to André Gide, quoted in Hynes, op. cit., p. 288.

266: burning shops with Germanic names . . . dogs in the streets: Graham Greene, *A Sort of Life*, quoted in Paul Fussell, *The Great War and Modern Memory*, p. 176.

266: "the one good word . . . touched and astonished": Montague, op. cit., p. 192.

266: "daily growing more anxious . . . possibly revolution": Stamfordham to Lloyd George, quoted in J. Gore, *George V*, p. 224.

266: "dimly aware how surprisingly little . . . a piece of food": Montague, op. cit., pp. 196–97.

266: "Seven hundred thousand . . . transitory is the life of man": Masterman, op. cit., pp. 11–14.

266: "Civilisation itself . . . air of precariousness": Montague, op. cit., pp. 193–95.

266: "the hills about Verdun . . . anybody is sane": Mr. Page, U.S. Ambassador in London, to Mr. Aldermen, in Hampton, Virginia, 1916, quoted in Masterman, op. cit., p. 2.

267: Some 2.7 million Germans . . . the end of the war: Holger H. Herwig, *The First World War*, p. 297.

267: In 1928, 2.5 million . . . issued to war-wounded men: Michael Gavaghan, *The Story of the Unknown Warrior*, p. 3.

267: A further ten years . . . service in the Great War: Lyn Macdonald, *The Roses of No Man's Land*, p. 303.

267: During the war, a German widow's pension . . . skilled worker's wage: Jay Winter, *Sites of Memory, Sites of Mourning*, p. 47.

267: "be found serving ribbons . . . aid of artificial light": Masterman, op. cit., p. 5.

267: "threatening, insubordinate and mutinous": Haig to Churchill, 30 January 1919, quoted in Eric Homberger, *The Story of the Cenotaph*, p. 1429.

268: "the guardian of the peace was hunger": Garrett, op. cit., p. 100.

268: "When all the great and good . . . poor devil like everyone else": Montague, op. cit., pp. 144–45.

268: [250,000 Germans died of malnutrition in 1918 alone]: Herwig, op. cit., p. 433.

268: "felt to be dangerously rapid": Homberger, op. cit., p. 1429.

268: Many ex-servicemen returned home . . . armed insurrection: Wal Hannington, quoted in Gregory, op. cit., p. 55.

268: "There was a notice . . . and then the miners": Mr. Hills, quoted in Garrett, op. cit., p. 98.

268: "we dare not give an unpopular order . . . a thing of the past": Quoted in Homberger, op. cit., p. 1429.

269: The ringleaders were arrested . . . having them all shot: ibid.

269: Two-thirds of the male unemployed were ex-servicemen: Graham Wootton, *Official History of the British Legion*, p. 31.

269: ex-gratia payments of twenty-nine shillings . . . an end in March 1921: Gregory, op. cit., p. 55.

269: "the greatest indignity . . . soup kitchens": Lance-Corporal W. J. Evans, quoted in Martin Middlebrook, *The First Day on the Somme*, p. 309.

270: "We remember it always . . . the heart of life": Montague, op. cit., quoted in Guy Chapman, *Vain Glory*, p. 115.

270: "everlastingly differentiated . . . except his fellow soldiers": Siegfried Sassoon, *Memoirs of an Infantry Soldier*.

270: "between you and us, there hangs a veil": Quoted in Hynes, op. cit., p. 243.

270: "The dead are less dead . . . it has slain": Quoted in ibid., p. 238.

270: Despite the unrest among troops . . . was well known: "Suggestions to Prevent the Spread of Revolutionary Ideas in the United Kingdom," PRO CAB 24/GT 8335.

270: "To me the most contemptible cur . . . die in his place": Elliot Springs, *War Birds*, p. 269.

270: the term H.S.B.—Home Service Bastard . . . not in the front lines: A. L. Robins, Liddle GS 1368, Part 2, p. 4.

270: "to the highest pitch . . . high patriotic feeling": Quoted in Homberger, op. cit., p. 1429.

271: "a servants' festival . . . these peace rejoicings": Virginia Woolf, *Diary* vol. I, *1915–1919*, p. 292.

271: "deprecated a national rejoicing . . . tribute to the dead": Cannadine, op. cit., p. 220.

271: the erection of a temporary "catafalque" . . . lying in state: War Cabinet Peace Celebrations Committee, Minutes of Meeting, 1 July 1919, 8 PRO CAB 52/27.

271: In Britain, virtually the only pre-war precedent . . . died in the fighting: Alex King, *Memorials of the Great War in Britain*, p. 44.

271: In many areas a commemorative element . . . such as Trafalgar Day: ibid., pp. 44–45.

271: "rather foreign to the spirit . . . the Latin temperament": Quoted in Homberger, op. cit., p. 1429.

271: "too Germanic": Michele Fry, "Lutyens's Cenotaph," footnote.

272: The Greeks also attached . . . an empty grave: Alan Borg, *War Memorials*, p. 67.

272: At the turn of the century . . . "The Cenotaph of Sigismunda": Christopher Hussey, *Life of Sir Edwin Lutyens*, p. 25.

272: In 1916 it had been agreed . . . war dead of the city: Alan Wilkinson, *The Church of England and the First World War*, p. 296.

272: Charles Sargeant Jagger's Royal Artillery Memorial . . . terror of war":

James Stevens Curl, "The Royal Artillery Memorial at Hyde Park Corner," p. 92.

272: Haig chose to describe it . . . an Empire's unity": *The Times*, 10 November 1920.

272: "it speaks of the qualities of the race": *The Times*, 11 November 1920.

272: "THE GLORIOUS DEAD" . . . coined by Lloyd George: Gavaghan, op. cit., p. 3.

272: On May Day 2000 . . . in red paint: Fry, op. cit., p. 6.

272: Lutyens was given . . . Vita Sackville-West, that night: Hussey, op. cit., p. 392.

273: By ten o'clock the following morning . . . full-size working drawings: ibid.

273: Based on the Greek principle of *entasis* . . . distance above the ground: Fry, op. cit., p. 4.

273: The detailed technical drawings . . . thirty-three pages: Hussey, op. cit., p. 392.

273: "mathematical precision" . . . evoked by that empty tomb: Winter, op. cit., p. 104.

273: It was so fragile . . . erect the banners adorning it: Garrett, op. cit., p. 160.

273: "an Imperial monument . . . races and creeds": Lord Ronaldshay, *The Life of Lord Curzon*, vol. III, p. 200.

273: Lutyens's design was deliberately non-denominational . . . pagan and an insult: Gregory, op. cit., p. 199.

273: "our pals died to kill militarism, not to establish it here": Quoted in Homberger, op. cit., p. 1430.

273: In Luton, ex-servicemen . . . military occupation for several days: ibid.

274: So dense were the crowds . . . actually saw the parade: Garrett, op. cit., p. 124.

274: Lutyens's "temporary but fitting monument": *The Times*, 18 July 1919.

274: "the most impressive sight I ever saw": Harold Nicolson, *King George V*, p. 338.

274: When the Americans passed the Treasury . . . more easily explained": Garrett, op. cit., p. 129.

274: Each serviceman was rewarded . . . for their homeward journeys: ibid., p. 123.

274: Within an hour, they were piled high around its base: *Manchester Guardian*, 21 July 1919.

274: Press reports the following day . . . mystical significance: King, op. cit., pp. 142–43.

274: "a light was shining . . . light on an altar": *Manchester Guardian*, 21 July 1919.

274: "you could scarce see the Cenotaph . . . that encompassed it": *Daily Mail*, 12 November 1919.

274: "moments of silence . . . they had died to win?": *Morning Post*, 21 July 1919.

275: "The Cenotaph grows in beauty . . . so noble a thing": Hussey, op. cit., p. 393.

275: Over the succeeding days . . . "a cult" and "cenotapholatry": *Church Times*, 21 November 1919.

275: "a desecration of a sacred spot": Lloyd, op. cit., p. 77.

275: Several applications for permission . . . the Department of Works: PRO WORK 20/139.

275: The subject of a permanent memorial . . . erected on the same site: PRO WORK 20/139.

275: "Simple, grave and beautiful . . . appeal to the imagination": *The Times*, 26 July 1919.

275: "of too mournful a character . . . victory of our arms": PRO CAB 24.84, GT7784, 23 July 1919.

275: "qualified by the salute . . . would give this pertinence": Cenotaph, Office of Works File No. 1126, 2, PRO WORK 20/139.

275: "consecrated by the tears of many mothers": *Daily Mail*, 23 July 1919.

275: "the Cenotaph in its present position . . . could not be uprooted": *The Times*, 31 July 1919.

275: "The plain fact . . . the Cenotaph should be as it now is": Quoted in Cannadine, op. cit., p. 221.

276: It was estimated . . . the temporary Cenotaph: *Evening Standard*, 1 August 1919.

276: so many flowers were laid . . . "custodians" to deal with them: *Daily Express*, 31 December 1919.

276: "a large, white Maltese Cross . . . with a spire twenty-four feet high": Quoted in King, op. cit., p. 56.

276: On the first day, 4 August . . . tributes had been laid there: Quoted in ibid.; others put the number at 70,000, cf. *The Times, Daily Express*, 5 August 1918.

276: "outrage on this small sacred spot . . . Mothers are to be treated?": Quoted in King, op. cit., p. 57.

276: "the war was an experience . . . a whole community": W. Lloyd Warner, *American Life: Dream and Reality*, quoted in Robert Bocock, *Ritual in Industrial Society*, pp. 109–10.

276: "universal ritual . . . a particular nation state": Bocock, op. cit., p. 110.

276: "the placing of flowers . . . should be discountenanced": PRO CAB 24/GT8335.

276: "exalt the dignity of sacrifice without the tears": Quoted in Lloyd, op. cit., p. 77.

276: The crowds were even bigger . . . help maintain order: ibid., p. 56.

277: In Manchester, the organizer of the local branch . . . honour of the dead": *Manchester Guardian*, 12 November 1919.

277: "utterly without soul or sentiment or understanding": *Daily Express*, 14 January 1920.

277: "to spare the feelings of those to whom the structure is especially sacred": PRO WORK 20/139.

277: "since the ground upon which the Cenotaph . . . that portion of the road": PRO WORK 20/139.

277: The stones were cut . . . one-sixteenth of an inch wide: Hussey, op. cit., p. 392.

277: He felt that this figurative element . . . the monument itself: Lutyens to Sir Alfred Mond, 29 July 1919, PRO WORK 20/139.

277: "prevent living sentries being posted on days of ceremony": Sir Edwin Lutyens, quoted in Hussey, op. cit., p. 394.

277: The Cenotaph "could refer to the dead . . . itself was not doubted": Fry, op. cit., p. 5; King, op. cit., p. 144.

277: "the specificity of patriotic and nationalistic sentiment": Lutyens to Sir Alfred Mond, 29 July 1919, PRO WORK 20/139; cf. Homberger, op. cit., pp. 1429–30; Allan Greenberg, "Lutyens' Cenotaph," in *Journal of the Society of Architectural Historians*, 1989, vol. XLVIII, no. 1, pp. 9–12; King, op. cit., pp. 142–44.

278: Sir Henry Wilson . . . initially sceptical Cabinet: Lloyd, op. cit., p. 65.

278: "After some discussion . . . Colonel Storr (Cabinet Office) as Secretary": Cabinet Memorial Services (November 11th) Committee, Westminster Abbey 58671.

278: "one of the most solemn . . . ceremonials ever held": Quoted in David Cannadine, *Aspects of Aristocracy*, p. 107.

278: "possessed unrivalled skill . . . an inventor of traditions": Cannadine, *Aspects of Aristocracy*, p. 78.

278: "Your memorandum. . . . this impressive suggestion": M. P. A. Hankey to Dean Ryle, 15 October 1920, Westminster Abbey 58669.

278: "objection has been made . . . no memorial of the Great War": Cabinet Memorial Services (November 11th) Committee, Westminster Abbey 58671B.

279: Railton's recommendation . . . by one of his relatives: Railton, "Origins of the Unknown Warrior," p. 36.

279: Railton found it "more homely and friendly": ibid.

279: "warmly supported" . . . as well as Army": Cabinet Memorial Services (November 11th) Committee, Westminster Abbey 58671B.

279: "The remains of one of the numerous unknown men . . . in all future times": Cabinet Memorial Services (November 11th) Committee, Westminster Abbey 58671B.

279: "I am heartily glad . . . honour you are doing to the Army": Sir Henry Wilson to Dean Ryle, Westminster Abbey 58672A.

279: "the silent ambassador . . . to the courts of the living": Blythe, op. cit., p. 8.

279:   "an emblem of 'the plain man' . . . the illustrious dead": *The Times*, 11 November 1920.

280:   ("strange" as Andrew Kelly . . . would be more universal"): Andrew Kelly, preface to Gough, op. cit.

280:   "Those mourning at home . . . a last farewell": Bernd Huppauf, *War and Death: The Experience of the First World War*, quoted in Catherine Moriarty, "Christian Iconography and First World War Memorials," *Imperial War Museum Review*, 6, 1992, p. 66.

280:   "The Prince of Darkness . . . I heard him laugh": Siegfried Sassoon, "At the Cenotaph," in *Collected Poems*, p. 201.

280:   In his poem . . . were now ignored: W. H. Auden, "The Horizontal Man," in *Poems*, p. 6.

280:   "I think all this business . . . sentimental as I ought to be": Correspondence of W. C. Bridgeman, 6 November 1920, Shropshire Record Office.

280:   "lest there should be yet another . . . assassinated Prime Minister": *Diary of Beatrice Webb*, vol. III, p. 371, quoted in Hynes, op. cit., p. 281.

280:   "those old warriors . . . earn their daily bread": IWM 70295 Remembrance Day, Poppy Day, frontispiece.

281:   "Today we are welcome . . . work will be hard to find": Quoted in Winter, op. cit., p. 46.

281:   "the intention during this week . . . we must be just": *Yorkshire Post*, 8 November 1920.

281:   "drag down wages . . . be supported unconditionally": Quoted in Gregory, op. cit., p. 53.

281:   "The unanimous opinion . . . callousness and hypocrisy": *Yorkshire Post*, 10 November 1920.

281:   "The comradeship of the trenches. . . . ex-soldiers in rags": Wal Hannington, *Struggles*, pp. 13–14, quoted in Gregory, op. cit., p. 56.

281:   It was an equally potent . . . General Douglas MacArthur: Janet Maslin, "Home from the War," *New York Times*, 21 February 2005; *Gold Star Mothers: Pilgrimage of Remembrance*, DVD.

23: MERE BONES

283:   "The Unknown Warrior . . . people of the British Empire": *The Times*, 12 November 1920.

283:   George Bernard Shaw . . . discovered to be German: "The Unknown Warrior," in *After the Battle*, 6, 1974, p. 48.

283:   It was felt that the public . . . body dated from 1914: PRO WORK 20/1/3; David W. Lloyd, *Battlefield Tourism*, p. 67.

283:   "the progress of our successive attacks . . . marking attacks in 1916": Major P. H. Pilditch, IWM Con Shelf.

283:   There are, of course, no documents . . . restrict the selection in this way: PRO CAB 27/99; Adrian Gregory, *The Silence of Memory*, p. 46.

284: The digging parties . . . the bodies as "mere bones": Brigadier General L. J. Wyatt, letter to the *Daily Telegraph*, 11 November 1939.

284: The four bodies: The number of bodies exhumed varies in different accounts between four and six, but there seems no reason to doubt the version of events given by Brigadier General L. J. Wyatt himself.

284: the small corrugated iron hut . . . chapel of St. Pol: Rose E. Coombs, *Before Endeavours Fade*, p. 131.

284: "I had no idea . . . no one else can know it": Brigadier General L. J. Wyatt, letter to the *Daily Telegraph*, 11 November 1939.

285: Wyatt said that the other bodies . . . cemetery at St. Pol: Brigadier General L. J. Wyatt, letter to the *Daily Telegraph*, 11 November 1939.

285: "old trenches running . . . added a simple prayer": Sir Cecil Smith to the Dean of Westminster, July 1978, Westminster Abbey.

285: "a battle-scarred ambulance": Clive Parson, "Bringing Home the Unknown Warrior," in *Ingall's Magazine*, vol. 1, no. 3, September 1951, p. 4.

285: It was placed in the castle library . . . autumn flowers and leaves: *The Times*, 11 November 1920; *Yorkshire Post*, 10 November 1920.

285: "sixteen barrels, stated to contain fifty bags of French soil": IWM Misc 7/143; several sources, including Brigadier General L. J. Wyatt (letter to the *Daily Telegraph*, 11 November 1939), mention "six barrels," and David Railton ("The Origins of the Unknown Warrior," in *Our Empire*, vol. VII, no. 8, 1931, pp. 34–36) talks of "100 sandbags of soil, but there seems no reason to doubt the veracity of the official Army documents covering the transport of sixteen barrels containing fifty bags of soil.

285: "Lieutenant Swift . . . Victoria Station": IWM Misc 7/143.

285: "might lie in the earth so many gave their lives for": Brigadier General L. J. Wyatt, letter to the *Daily Telegraph*, 11 November 1939.

285: At ten that morning, two British undertakers . . . secured the lid and sealed it: IWM Misc 200/2938.

286: "that most English of Royal palaces": Herbert Jeans, "In Death's Cathedral Palace," *British Legion Journal*, vol. 9, no. 5, November 1929, p. 118.

286: "the design of a sixteenth-century treasure chest . . . dark waxed finish": Parson, op. cit., p. 4.

286: A plate of beaten iron . . . "a soldier's gift to a soldier": *Yorkshire Post*, 11 November 1920.

286: "In deference to Lloyd George": Parson, op. cit., p. 4.

286: "laid it on the spot chosen for the tomb": ibid.

286: "apparently been untouched . . . no remnants of other humanity": *The Times*, 12 November 1920.

286: "neighbouring junction of three roads . . . Chopin's 'Funeral March' filled the air": *The Times*, 11 November 1920.

286: "the '*Tommy Anonyme*,' as he is dubbed in France": *Yorkshire Post*, 11 November 1920.

286: borne into Boulogne . . . endless ranks of cavalry," marines and infantry: *Yorkshire Post*, 11 November 1920; *The Times*, 11 November 1920.

286: Half a dozen pairs of soldiers . . . great wreaths they carried: IWM 505, Pathé Newsreel, Armistice Day 1920.

287: The entire route had been decorated . . . trophies and flags: *Yorkshire Post*, 10 November 1920.

287: "the representative of the hundreds . . . as for his own'": *Yorkshire Post*, 8, 11 November 1920.

287: "entirely on his own initiative": Michael Gavaghan, *The Story of the Unknown Warrior*, p. 81.

287: "the sacrifice symbolised . . . as they were in war": *The Times*, 11 November 1920.

287: "the quarterdeck aft in front of the superstructure": *Yorkshire Post*, 12 November 1920.

287: covered in wreaths of white lilies, roses and chrysanthemums: *The Times*, 11 November 1920.

287: Some were so large that it took four soldiers to lift them: Gavaghan, op. cit., p. 30.

287: "advancing almost to the water's edge . . . saluting his dead comrade": *Yorkshire Post*, 11 November 1920.

287: The echoes had barely died . . . hanging over the water: *The Times*, 11 November 1920.

288: "The bodies were so closely intermingled . . . a gallant *poilu*": *New York Times*, 10 November 1920.

288: "Military honours and the roll of muffled drums . . . flickering wax candles": *Yorkshire Post*, 10 November 1920.

288: "stole through the last few miles . . . a funeral procession": *The Times*, 11 November 1920.

288: "admirably suited to the occasion . . . grey of the clouds": *The Times*, 11 November 1920.

288: "steamed slowly along the entire length . . . our wounded warriors": *The Times*, 11 November 1920.

289: "without a sound . . . blacker or more silent": *The Times*, 11 November 1920.

289: "a mournful dirge": *Yorkshire Post*, 11 November 1920.

289: "lined with purple drapery" . . . "Two tiny electric lights . . . glow over the coffin": *Yorkshire Post*, 11 November 1920.

289: The roof of the carriage . . . the journey to London: Gavaghan, op. cit., p. 36.

290: "to the military upon its arrival at Victoria": IWM Misc 200/2938.

290: "They carried at their head . . . steamed out of the station": *Yorkshire Post*, 11 November 1920.

290: There was an honour guard . . . climbing onto the train: *Daily Graphic*, 11 November 1920.

290:   "every street corner and road . . . the darkness and rain": *Yorkshire Post*, 11 November 1920.

290:   "watching and silent . . . the great lighted train rushing past": *Daily Mail*, 11 November 1920.

290:   "brilliant with light and radiant with white flowers": *The Times*, 11 November 1920.

290:   "eddied and billowed round the arc lamps": *The Times*, 11 November 1920.

291:   "by stripping this hour . . . piled up to the windows": *The Times*, 11 November 1920.

291:   The wreaths were removed . . . arms reversed and heads bowed: *The Times*, 10 November 1920.

24: THE GREAT SILENCE

292:   At eight o'clock that November morning . . . alongside the funeral carriage: IWM 94/3/1.

293:   "the covering, often the only covering . . . lifeblood of fellow Britons": David Railton, "The Origins of the Unknown Warrior," in *Our Empire*, vol. VII, no. 8, 1931, p. 36.

293:   "Once at least it lay on the grass floor . . . death at dawn": *The Times*, 10 November 1920.

293:   "for order of precedence . . . four abreast, closed up": IWM 94/3/1. Major C. J. Saunders: Orders by Major General G. D. Jeffreys, CCB, CMG, Commanding London District, on the Occasion of the Burial in Westminster Abbey of the Body of an Unknown British Warrior, p. 3.

293:   "detailed by Silver Stick in Waiting" . . . Once more, the honours paid . . . due to a Field Marshal: ibid.

293:   "the simplest, but most impressive procession ever seen in London": *Yorkshire Post*, 12 November 1920.

293:   "There were no trappings of State ceremonial . . . unknown hero's coffin": *Yorkshire Post*, 12 November 1920.

293:   "The Unknown Warrior, in his daydreams in France . . . city looking more beautiful": *The Times*, 12 November 1920.

294:   "punctuating the silence . . . reining in their horses": *The Times*, 12 November 1920.

294:   The original plan for the ceremony . . . to show its hand": PRO WORK 20/1/3; David W. Lloyd, *Battlefield Tourism*, p. 78.

294:   "a long river of men . . . they walked on in silence": *The Times*, 12 November 1920.

295:   "between ranks, thousands strong . . . every open space": *The Times*, 12 November 1920.

295:   "packed together on the pavements . . . the moving mystery of his identity": *Yorkshire Post*, 12 November 1920.

295:    "Very tiny and pathetic . . . on the other side": *The Times*, 12 November 1920.

296:    "a point of honour . . . transferred outside the family": *The Times*, 8 November 1920.

296:    The remainder of the crowd . . . Whitehall closed to traffic: *The Times*, 8, 10 November 1920.

296:    "When it was considered . . . barriers would again be opened": *The Times*, 12 November 1920.

296:    "freed at last from scaffolding and tarpaulins": *The Times*, 12 November 1920.

296:    "In proud memory of those who died . . . behold they live'": IWM 81/3675.

296:    The King reached up . . . as he walked away: IWM 505, Pathé Newsreel, Armistice Day 1920.

297:    One fell to the ground . . . a scurrying official: IWM 505, Pathé Newsreel, Armistice Day 1920.

297:    "The memorial which authority caused to be created . . . revealed in simple grandeur": *The Times*, 12 November 1920.

297:    "Nobody who stood in Whitehall . . . the sensation it evoked": *Yorkshire Post*, 12 November 1920.

297:    "The complete suspension . . . throughout the British Empire": *The Times*, 8 November 1920.

297:    The central telephone switchboard . . . anywhere in London: Richard Garrett, *The Final Betrayal*, p. 162.

297:    "smartly to attention . . . either side of him": *Manchester Evening News*, 11 November 1920.

298:    At the Crystal Palace . . . HMS *Implacable*: *Yorkshire Post*, 10 November 1920.

298:    "more strange and impressive . . . motor engines could be heard": *The Times*, 12 November 1920.

298:    The driver of a large touring car . . . booed by ex-soldiers standing to attention: Garrett, op. cit., p. 171.

298:    the offices of the *Workers' Dreadnought* . . . "a good trouncing": *Daily Mail*, 12 November 1920.

298:    "mechanics in dungarees . . . merchants and their clerks": *The Times*, 12 November 1920.

298:    "their passengers either standing up . . . lining the platform": *The Times*, 12 November 1920.

298:    the Cornish Riviera express . . . the Irish Mail near Crewe: Terry Cave, *The Unknown Warrior*, Western Front Association Bulletin, No. 17, p. 24.

298:    "A quiet which could be almost felt . . . minutes ticked slowly by": *Yorkshire Post*, 12 November 1920.

299:    At the Coal and Shipping Exchange . . . passengers stood at attention with bared heads: Eric Homberger, *The Story of the Cenotaph*, p. 1430.

299:     "to show all the reverence . . . principal buildings were half-masted": *The Times*, 12 November 1920.

299:     "More than any eloquence of tongue was this eloquence of silence": *Yorkshire Post*, 12 November 1920.

299:     "All instruments ticking out messages . . . The dead lived again": *The Times*, 12 November 1920.

299:     "business as usual . . . conspicuous by its absence": *The Times*, 12 November 1920.

299:     And in New York, supporters of Sinn Fein . . . running battles with police: *The Times*, 12 November 1920.

300:     "Philadelphia would not stand . . . saved France and Belgium": *New York Times*, 16 November 1920.

300:     "most solemn and inspiring . . . the city at prayer": "The Origin of the Two Minutes' Silence," in *Our Empire*, vol. VI, no. 8, 1931, p. 27.

300:     "direct communion with the absent—the living and the dead": Owen Chadwick, "Armistice Day," *Theology*, 79, 1976, p. 323.

300:     "the ceremony had been adopted . . . towns in Canada and Australia": "The Origin of the Two Minutes' Silence," p. 27.

300:     The South African leader . . . Colonial Secretary, Lord Milner: PRO CAB24/CP45.

300:     "The advantage of the realisation . . . conceivably prove inconvenient": PRO CAB/21/160.

300:     "would not promise to do it . . . what dislocation occurred": Chadwick, op. cit., p. 324.

300:     "a disgusting idea of artificial nonsense and sentimentality": R. Davie (ed.), *The Diaries of Evelyn Waugh*, p. 37, quoted in David Cannadine, "(War and) Death, Grief and Mourning in Modern Britain," p. 222.

300:     "Who organised this pageant . . . dope the people emotionally": *Daily Herald*, 11 November 1920.

301:     A cartoon in the *Catholic Herald* . . . "two minutes on Armistice Day": Quoted in Adrian Gregory, *The Silence of Memory*, p. 42.

301:     "the hush came . . . silence of a mighty crowd": *Daily Express*, 12 November 1919.

301:     Once more the King . . . turned his back and walked away: IWM 505, Pathé Newsreel, Armistice Day 1920.

301:     "There was no sound . . . floated to us": *The Times*, 12 November 1920.

301:     The bearers . . . on the grass by the gates: Michael Gavaghan, *The Story of the Unknown Warrior*, p. 54.

301:     One forgot to remove his hat . . . snatched it off one-handed: IWM 505, Pathé Newsreel, Armistice Day 1920.

301:     seventy-four holders of the Victoria Cross . . . some in civilian clothes: Cave, op. cit., p. 24.

302:     "in the pathway of kings . . . his kingdom might endure": *New York Times*, 12 November 1920.

302: "the other royal ladies" . . . "row upon row of Cabinet ministers": *The Times*, 12 November 1920.

302: "fashionable society be excluded . . . especially in the humbler ranks": Lord Curzon, quoted in Garrett, op. cit., pp. 102–3.

302: "in which only the people of the British Empire should participate": PRO WORK 20/1/3.

302: "for the only time in his career . . . deeply felt mood": Garrett, op. cit., p. 106.

302: "A little band . . . lost their husbands only": PRO WORK 21/74.

302: "the poor women will not be forgotten": Lloyd, op. cit., pp. 78–79.

302: Tabloid newspapers then launched a ferocious assault . . . went to his grave: *Daily Graphic*, 13, 15 October 1920; Lloyd, op. cit., p. 79.

303: "Irate and hysterical": Quoted in Lloyd, op. cit., p. 79.

303: "the man in the coffin . . . discharge of their duty": M. H. Fitzgerald, *Herbert Edward Ryle*, p. 311.

303: 8,000 tickets were issued for seats at the abbey or the Cenotaph: *New York Times*, 12 November 1920.

303: The brief service, "the most beautiful . . . such a sombre gathering: *The Times*, 12 November 1920; *New York World*, 11 November 1920.

303: "intended as a corrective . . . gave it a new significance": Bob Bushaway, *Name upon Name*, p. 145.

303: "the great wave of feeling . . . finding expression in tears": *The Times*, 12 November 1920.

304: In 1919 he published . . . "because our fathers lied": Rudyard Kipling, "Common Form," from "Epitaphs of the War," in *The Years Between*.

304: "from somewhere far away . . . for certain when it stopped": *The Times*, 12 November 1920.

304: The Last Post was followed . . . resting "on their arms reversed": IWM 94/3/1 Major C. J. Saunders: Orders by Major General G. D. Jeffreys, CCB, CMG, Commanding London District, on the Occasion of the Burial in Westminster Abbey of the Body of an Unknown British Warrior, p. 7.

304: "composed of laurel . . . cloisters of the cathedral": *The Times*, 10 November 1920.

305: "No one could have foretold . . . the imagination of the people": *Yorkshire Post*, 13 November 1920.

305: During the war, Rolls of Service . . . windows of individual houses: Bushaway, op. cit., p. 139.

305: They served a dual purpose . . . still serving at the Front: Mark Connelly, *The Great War, Memory and Ritual*, p. 25.

305: "the roughest treat them with respect . . . as they pass them": *Evening News*, 7 October 1916.

305: Commercially made shrines . . . small flags could be placed: Alex King, *Memorials of the Great War in Britain*, p. 48.

305: "The memorial . . . for the whole Empire": Lloyd George, quoted in Christopher Hussey, *The Life of Sir Edwin Lutyens*, p. 394.

305: "The Cenotaph, it may be said . . . mourning as individuals": Herbert Jeans, "In Death's Cathedral Palace," *British Legion Journal*, vol. 9, no. 5, November 1929, p. 118.

305: When Alderman Arthur Willey . . . Unknown Warrior in Westminster Abbey: *Yorkshire Post*, 18 November 1920.

306: "One elderly man said . . . secret thoughts of many more": *The Times*, 12 November 1920.

306: "The mystery as to whose son . . . son and brother of us all": Jeans, op. cit., p. 118.

306: One man committed suicide . . . preyed on his mind too much: *Daily Express*, 16 November 1920.

25: THE PEOPLE'S PILGRIMAGE

307: "two legless soldiers on tricycles": David W. Lloyd, *Battlefield Tourism*, p. 71.

307: Close behind them was a column . . . burial service at the abbey: Adrian Gregory, *The Silence of Memory*, p. 59.

307: As *The Times* noted in its editorial . . . still seeking employment": *The Times*, 12 November 1920; cf. *Daily Mail* and *Daily Express*, 12 November 1920.

308: "There were many elderly people . . . their fathers were numbered": *The Times*, 12 November 1920.

308: "put down by a still young-looking woman . . . 'when the day breaks'": *Yorkshire Post*, 13 November 1920.

308: Many blind ex-soldiers . . . touched their arms and said 'Now'": *New York Times*, 12 November 1920.

308: "a subdued air . . . the humble tributes of the very poor": *Yorkshire Post*, 12 November 1920.

308: "The authorities wish to draw attention . . . linger by the Cenotaph": *The Times*, 10 November 1920.

309: "Now only the sheer sides . . . sands by a mighty wave": *Yorkshire Post*, 15 November 1920.

309: "One white-haired old woman . . . the Cenotaph until half-past five": *The Times*, 12 November 1920.

309: "after long railway journeys . . . the Cenotaph to Westminster Abbey: *The Times*, 12 November 1920.

309: "the whiteness of the Cenotaph gleams by day and night": *Yorkshire Post*, 13 November 1920.

309: "the vast sweep of the road . . . policemen on horseback": *Daily Mail*, 12 November 1920.

310: "dressed as an aeroplane": Richard Garrett, *The Final Betrayal*, p. 163.

310: "Indeed those who took part . . . joining the Great Pilgrimage": *The Times*, 15 November 1920.

310: The opposite pole . . . were killed in the war: Derek Boorman, *At the Going Down of the Sun*, p. 108.

310: There, too, was Private Thomas Pestorisk . . . eight brothers in the war": Matthew Holden, *War in the Trenches*, p. 11.

310: Two wounded soldiers . . . lost brothers in the war: *Daily Express*, 15 November 1920.

310: There were many men in wheelchairs . . . "Lest we forget": *The Times*, 19 November 1920.

310: "One policeman spoke of old women . . . when he was only six": *Daily Telegraph*, 12 November 1920.

311: Thousands of football supporters . . . to pass the Cenotaph: *Daily Mail*, 15 November 1920.

311: "the children's day . . . foot of the National Memorial": *The Times*, 15 November 1920.

311: "There were little ones in their mother's arms . . . the National Monument": *Yorkshire Post*, 15 November 1920.

311: "laid at the base of the Cenotaph . . . 'For Daddy'": *Yorkshire Post*, 15 November 1920.

311: "brought tears to the eyes . . . 'garden my Daddy's got'": *Daily Herald*, 13 November 1920.

311: the pilgrims . . . "waited with the utmost patience": *The Times*, 15 November 1920.

311: "the workmen of the Office of Works . . . the best effect possible" . . . "proportions which indicated . . . greatest pilgrimage had begun": *The Times*, 15 November 1920.

311: The queue of people . . . seven miles: *Daily Mirror*, 15 November 1920.

311: "These eloquent symbols of gallantry . . . fitting resting place": *The Times*, 15 November 1920.

312: By Monday, 15 November . . . grave of the Unknown Warrior: *Yorkshire Post*, 15 November 1920.

312: "one vast memorial to the dead . . . advanced to the Cenotaph": *The Times*, 16 November 1920.

312: "The official mourning had finished . . . 100,000 wreaths have been laid": *The Times*, 16 November 1920.

312: A vanload of wreaths . . . vast pyramid of flowers: *Yorkshire Post*, 17 November 1920.

312: "In loving memory of my only boy . . . July 1916, aged sixteen": *The Times*, 18 November 1920.

312: "punctually at seven o'clock": *Yorkshire Post*, 17 November 1920.

312: "the queue always grew larger . . . return again today": *The Times*, 17 November 1920.

312: "passed through the Abbey at a quicker rate . . . preceding day": *The Times*, 19 November 1920.

312: The closing of the abbey was postponed . . . mourners turned away: *The Times*, 18 November 1920.

313: "She asked that this be placed on the coffin . . . wish was carried out": *The Times*, 18 November 1920.

313: On Sunday, 21 November . . . "as far as the Horse Guards": *The Times*, 22 November 1920.

313: "posies of flowers . . . sacrifice of precious lives": *Yorkshire Post*, 13 November 1920.

313: in August 1921, a full nine months . . . laid at the Cenotaph: *The Times*, 24 August 1921.

313: "at the risk of life, above and beyond the call of duty": *The Times*, 18 October 1921.

313: "Animated by the same spirit of comradeship . . . the unknown dead": *New York Times*, 11 October 1921.

313: "further cement . . . the United States": *New York Times*, 11 October 1921.

314: "mystified by the silence of the British government": *New York Times*, 11 October 1921.

314: "beyond a statement that such ceremonies . . . time to arrange": *The Times*, 11 October 1921.

314: "prominently displayed in the American press" . . . "much hostile comment" . . . "unfriendly interpretation": *The Times*, 11 October 1921.

314: "the rule regulating the acceptance . . . precedents do not apply": *The Times*, 11 October 1921.

314: The criticisms . . . into his schedule: *New York Times*, 10 October 1921.

314: "failed to establish any connection . . . the Congressional medal": *New York Times*, 12 October 1921.

314: "a particularly tactless and stupid blunder": *Daily News*, 12 October 1921.

314: "bureaucratic muddling and evasion of responsibility": *The Times*, 12 October 1921.

314: Dean Ryle revealed . . . about it in the newspapers: *New York Times*, 12 October 1921.

314: "difficult points of procedure": *New York Times*, 12 October 1921.

315: "very strongly . . . lose sight of all proportion": Stamfordham to Curzon, quoted in J. Gore, *George V*, p. 262.

315: On 11 October it was announced . . . to General Pershing: *New York Times*, 12 October 1921.

315: "some legislative action . . . Arlington Cemetery on Armistice Day: *The Times*, 13 October 1921.

315: "I greatly wish [*sic*] . . . the Victoria Cross": *The Times*, 18 October 1921.

315: "would be quite sufficient" . . . Warrior of the Belgians: Stamfordham to War Office, quoted in Gore, op. cit., p. 262.

315:   "the successor of Washington, Grant, Sherman ... Armies of the United States": *The Times*, 18 October 1921.

315:   He was escorted ... American Unknown Soldier: *The Times*, 15 October 1921.

316:   "No man among the Americans ... giants over six feet": *New York Times*, 17 October 1921.

316:   "had their band and colours ... Army of Occupation": *New York Times*, 17 October 1921.

316:   "not the most direct route ... the distinguished visitors": *The Times*, 17 October 1921.

316:   Perhaps still inwardly seething ... the distinguished guests: *The Times*, 18 October 1921.

316:   "it seemed more than mere accident ... foot of the Unknown Warrior's grave": *The Times*, 18 October 1921.

316:   Pershing spoke of the "overpowering emotion" ... "this Unknown Warrior": *The Times*, 18 October 1921.

316:   "above the breast of the unknown hero beneath": *The Times*, 18 October 1921.

316:   "old oak from the Abbey timbers" ... "about seven feet from the ground": *The Times*, 7 November 1921.

317:   "Unknown also was the faith ... whatever his faith may have been": Quoted in Ronald Blythe, *The Age of Illusion*, p. 12.

317:   "In a Christian church ... Christian message": Quoted in ibid.

317:   "we cannot hope to please everybody": Quoted in ibid.

317:   Escorted by an honour guard ... the 47th (London) Division: John Hundevad, "The Unknown Warrior," in the *Legionary*, vol. 30, no. 3, August 1955, p. 21.

317:   "should never leave those doubly venerable walls": *The Times*, 12 November 1920.

317:   "It flew at Vimy Ridge ... conqueror of Agincourt": *The Times*, 11 November 1921.

318:   "How English! Most other nations ... Last Suppers in Flanders fields": H. V. Morton, "Among the Kings," from *The Spell of London*, pp. 17–18.

318:   "all vehicular traffic ... rail and water transport": *The Times*, 17 October 1921.

318:   Several thousand unemployed men ... in place of campaign medals: Alan Wilkinson, *The Church of England and the Great War*, p. 305.

318:   "The Dead are remembered but we are forgotten": *The Times*, 11 November 1921.

318:   "To the dead victims of capitalism from the living victims of capitalism": Owen Chadwick, "Armistice Day," *Theology*, 79, 1976, p. 327.

318:   There was a brawl in Dundee ... Communist demonstrators: ibid.

318:   "Anyone want a medal?" and "What we need is food not prayers": *Liverpool Courier*, 12 November 1920; *Liverpool Weekly Post*, 12 November 1920.

318: "not a day of National grief": PRO HO45/11557/20.

318: "not to be kept only as a day of remembrance . . . revelry and song": *The Times*, 7 November 1921.

319: "many who have spent the evening . . . celebration supper afterwards" . . . "with a 'snowstorm carnival' as a prominent feature": *The Times*, 7 November 1921.

319: Many ex-servicemen shared the view . . . worthy of celebration: cf. *Yorkshire Post*, *The Times*, *Daily Mirror*, 12 November 1919.

319: Sir Arthur Conan Doyle . . . "for prayer," not celebration: Quoted in Stanley Weintraub, *A Stillness Heard Round the World*, p. 262.

319: An Edinburgh mother . . . the Edinburgh Cenotaph: *Scotsman*, 12 November 1927.

319: On the same day, many of the women . . . "deep mourning": *Scotsman*, 12 November 1927.

319: "many people who danced last Armistice Day . . . not do so last night": *Daily Express*, 12 November 1926.

319: "Bunch after bunch . . . 'For Daddy'": *The Times*, 14 November 1921.

319: "Some who joined the waiting lines . . . in those cemeteries now": *The Times*, 14 November 1921.

319: "carrying a bunch of chrysanthemums . . . disturbed her faith": *The Times*, 14 November 1921.

320: there were said to be 118 mediums in Kensington alone: Wilkinson, op. cit., p. 179.

320: "also bloomed on the German . . . it was ignored": George L. Mosse, *Fallen Soldiers*, p. 111.

320: in August 1921, a Madame Guérin . . . Secretary of the British Legion: *The Official History of the British Legion*, p. 39.

320: The name chosen was the Warriors' Guild . . . Legion on 1 July 1921: IWM 81/3675.

320: "Flanders poppies for the benefit of ex-Servicemen of all ranks": *The Times*, 7 November 1921.

320: "one shilling for those made of silk . . . content with the minimum": *The Times*, 10 November 1921.

320: As if in confirmation . . . £5 at Smithfield Market: Chadwick, op. cit., p. 326.

320: a basket of poppies was auctioned . . . to be auctioned again: *Daily Mail*, 12 November 1920.

321: "stationed at practically every hotel . . . many large stores": *The Times*, 10 November 1921.

321: "The Dowager Lady Garvagh . . . the evening performance": *The Times*, 7 November 1921.

321: "on their uniform head-dress, when not on duty": *The Times*, 7 November 1921.

321: "only three or four" . . . an appeal: *Yorkshire Post*, 5 November 1921.

321: By the eve of Armistice Day . . . 8 million had been sold: *The Times*,
      11 November 1921.

321: "only been possible to supply . . . the numbers demanded": *The Times*,
      10 November 1921.

321: "made up with pink blotting paper what it lacked in basic material": *The
      Official History of the British Legion*, p. 40.

321: "those below the traditional philanthropic classes": Gregory, op. cit.,
      p. 107.

321: "some persons have manufactured . . . attempt should be made" . . .
      imported from Germany: ibid., p. 108.

321: several hundred were employed on the task: *The Official History of the
      British Legion*, p. 40.

321: "of paper, tin and metal thread": Herbert Read, "A Short Poem for
      Armistice Day," in David Roberts, *Minds at War*.

321: In 1927, the aviator Charles Lindbergh . . . American Cemetery at
      Waregem: Paul Gough, *Loci Memoriae*, p. 7.

322: "one of the great paradoxes . . . strokes of Big Ben": *Radio Times*,
      8 November 1935.

322: "few visitors miss the opportunity . . . her eyes filled with tears": *New
      York Times*, 8 May 1921.

322: A government attempt in 1923 . . . press and public hostility: Lloyd, op.
      cit., pp. 88–89.

322: "Armisticetide," as it became known . . . "an ancient religious tradi-
      tion": Alex King, *Memorials of the Great War in Britain*, p. 21.

323: "although needing . . . commemorated as citizens": Catherine Mori-
      arty, "Christian Iconography and First World War Memorials," *Imper-
      ial War Museum Review*, 6, 1992, p. 65.

323: Almost as an afterthought . . . the graves never marked: Thomas W.
      Laqueur, "Memory and Naming in the Great War," p. 152.

323: "common graves as if they were nameless vermin": Vera Brittain, *Testa-
      ment of Youth*, p. 97.

323: "to search for graves . . . register their position": "War Diary" of Regi-
      nald Bryson, quoted in Laqueur, op. cit., pp. 152–53.

323: But if the registration . . . "a national character": Field Marshal Sir John
      French, PRO WO 32/5847.

323: "had never been dreamt of before": Sir Reginald Blomfield, *Memoirs of
      an Architect*, p. 176.

323: "carving in stone . . . given and not taken": Blythe, op. cit., p. 7.

324: By 1927, 400,000 headstones . . . "since Pharaonic Egypt": Gough,
      op. cit., p. 8.

324: "Must a sort of murder be followed by a sort of suicide?" W. R.
      Lethaby, quoted in Bob Bushaway, "Name upon Name," p. 146.

324: "a glorified tombstone": *Carlisle Journal*, 20 June 1919.

324: "some memorials were frankly opportunistic": Eric Homberger, *The
      Story of the Cenotaph*, p. 1430.

324: "with or without a crucified Christ . . . club for ex-servicemen": Quoted in K. S. Inglis, "The Homecoming," *Journal of Contemporary History*, [month unknown] 27, 1992, p. 585.

324: "to teach the art of rowing under cover": Alan Borg, *War Memorials from Antiquity to the Present*, p. 140.

324: "intellectually and emotionally beneath contempt . . . the dark years": *Athenaeum*, 31 October 1919.

324: the sculptor Paul Auban . . . victims of a shipwreck: Annette Becker, *Les Monuments aux Morts*, quoted in Jay Winter, *Sites of Memory, Sites of Mourning*, p. 94.

324: 30,000 memorials—fifteen a day . . . between 1920 and 1925: Geoff Dyer, *The Missing of the Somme*, p. 64.

325: "The rituals of remembrance . . . post-war Britain": Bushaway, op. cit., p. 161.

325: "deeply impressed with today's unique ceremony . . . everything was carried out": Lord Stamfordham to Dean Ryle, Westminster Abbey 58675.

325: "the whole circuit of the earth . . . the desolation of war": www.cwgc.org/cwgcinternet.

325: The flowers had been given to the Queen . . . place them on her son's grave: F. Fox, *The King's Pilgrimage*, Part IV, p. 4.

325: "In Loving memory of your Dear Dad . . . in remembrance of your Dad": IWM, EPH 3232, Dried Rosebud on a Stem from the Army wreath surmounting the coffin of the Unknown Soldier.

326: Sadly, he died before achieving that ambition . . . Great War, her grandfather: ibid. Names withheld at the request of the deceased's daughter.

326: As early as December 1914 . . . active on the battlefields: *The War Illustrated*, 1, December 1914.

326: Thomas Cook's was forced to report . . . until the war was over: *The Times*, 31 March 1915.

326: Even the latter was well beyond . . . only £3 a week: Lloyd, op. cit., p. 38.

326: "Nature herself conspires with time to cheat our recollections": Vera Brittain, quoted in Mosse, op. cit., p. 112.

326: "blowing grain and nodding poppies": Quoted in ibid., p. 113.

26: UNKNOWN BUT TO GOD

328: It was said that the fallen . . . Napoleon at Waterloo: quoted in George L. Mosse, *Fallen Soldiers*, p. 94.

328: The ceremonies also included . . . the memory of French heroes: *New York Times*, 8 November 1920.

329: "outlined with thousands of lamps": *New York Times*, 12 November 1920.

329:    "hiding the Republic behind the body of a dead soldier": *New York Times*, 9 November 1920.

329:    "and every one threw flowers . . . they had won for gallantry" . . . "most of the people wept . . . silver morning light": *New York Times*, 29 January 1921.

330:    "led away at the insistence of the crowd, shouted 'Down with War' as he went": *New York Times*, 14 November 1921.

330:    On 8 January 1922, one distraught woman . . . the French Unknown Soldier: *New York Times*, 9 January 1922.

330:    The first guard on the grave . . . one of his arms in the fighting: Richard Garrett, *The Final Betrayal*, p. 179.

330:    "overflowing with people" . . . "sleeping all night in the streets . . . shelter is already filled": *New York Times*, 2 November 1921.

330:    "Communists wearing their badges . . . they could not see the ceremony": *New York Times*, 3 November 1921.

330:    "hand grenades for feet": *New York Times*, 3 November 1921.

330:    "More than 6,000 battle flags were carried in the line of march": *New York Times*, 5 November 1921.

330:    "only a few tattered remnants . . . won on distant battlefields": *New York Times*, 3 November 1921.

331:    "a little white-haired peasant woman . . . largest ever assembled in Rome": *New York Times*, 5 November 1921.

331:    As early as 29 October 1919 . . . General Peyton C. March: B. C. Mossman and M. Warner Stark, *The Last Salute*, p. 3.

331:    he claimed that, while France and Britain . . . an unknown soldier could be interred: ibid.

331:    "associated with any State . . . fought for the Stars and Stripes": *New York Times*, 9 December 1920.

331:    "All America finds its way to the Capitol . . . 'America's heroic dead.' ": *New York Times*, 12 June 1921.

333:    A companion act agreed . . . French and British Unknowns: *New York Times*, 6 March 1921.

333:    But Secretary of War Newton D. Baker . . . forum in Pershing Square: *New York Times*, 27 November 1920.

333:    (1,900, according to the Associated Press): *New York Times*, 14 September 1921.

333:    To rush to inter one of those unknowns . . . later have been identified: Mossman and Stark, op. cit., pp. 3–4.

333:    He opted for a ceremony . . . carried out on 24 October: *New York Times*, 17 March 1921.

333:    As in Britain, America's political leaders . . . social divisions caused by the war: G. Kurt Piehler, *Remembering War the American Way*, p. 94.

333:    the 92nd and 93rd Divisions lost more than 5,000 men between them: Jami L. Bryan, *Fighting for Respect*, p. 25.

334:    "You low-down Mother Fuckers . . . we is coming": Quoted in Gary Mead, *The Doughboys*, p. 76.

334:    At least ten of the victims . . . lynched wearing their uniforms: Bryan, op. cit., p. 25.

334:    "acknowledge the debt owed . . . owed their country": G. Kurt Piehler, *Remembering War the American Way*, p. 117.

334:    "the war dead were still being pressed into service by their governments": G. Kurt Piehler, *The War Dead and the Gold Star*, p. 168.

334:    An unidentified body was to be exhumed . . . whole of the American Civil War: Arthur E. Dewey, *Selection of the Unknown Soldier*, pp. 1–2.

335:    The American Graves Registration Service, set up on 7 August 1917: Constance Potter, *World War I Gold Star Mothers Pilgrimages*, p. 1.

335:    "badly decomposed, features unrecognisable": ibid.

335:    "In the preparation of the body . . . the body arrives at its destination": Operations Division to Officer in Charge of Operations, Romagne-sous-Montfaucon, 5 October 1921, AMHI.

336:    "white observation car" . . . "thoroughly cleaned . . . in every particular" . . . "planed to a clean . . . additional wood screws": ibid.

336:    With his orders, Dewey . . . and "Alternate-Thiaucourt": Dewey, op. cit., p. 2; Operations Division to Officer in Charge of Operations, Romagne-sous-Montfaucon, 15 October 1921, AMHI.

336:    "You are again cautioned . . . casket or shipping case": Operations Division to Officer in Charge of Operations, Romagne-sous-Montfaucon, 15 October 1921, AMHI; Dewey, op. cit., pp. 2–3.

337:    "placed in a suitable building . . . no way molested": Operations Division to Officer in Charge of Operations, Romagne-sous-Montfaucon, 15 October 1921, AMHI; Dewey, op. cit., pp. 3–4.

337:    "two braces and screw bits . . . two claw hammers": Officer in Charge of Operations, Romagne, to Supervisory Embalmers, 20 October 1921, AMHI.

337:    They had been ordered to depart . . . draped over the caskets: Operations Division to Officer in Charge of Operations, Romagne-sous-Montfaucon, 15 October 1921, AMH.

337:    "composed of *poilus* who saw action": *New York Times*, 24 October 1921.

337:    French soldiers formed a guard . . . cousin—in the war: Dewey, op. cit., pp. 5–6.

338:    "a fine type of young American": *The Times*, 25 October 1921.

338:    "who had fought in all the American offensives and wore two wound stripes": *New York Times*, 25 October 1921.

338:    carrying a spray of white roses . . . lost two sons in the war: Mossman and Stark, op. cit., p. 5.

338:    The original plan . . . choose their Unknown Soldier: ibid.

338:    Sergeant Younger slowly circled . . . saluted it and withdrew: Dewey, op. cit., pp. 5–6; the *New York Times*, 25 October 1921, stated that it was "the furthest coffin to the right."

339: "soon the coffin was buried under piled masses of flowers": *The Times*, 25 October 1921.

339: "to the crash of presented rifles and the blare of saluting bugles": *The Times*, 25 October 1921.

339: The men of the 6th Division . . . "who had seen the war at very close hand": Dewey, op. cit., pp. 8–9; *The Times*, 25 October 1921.

340: "in such a slow and deliberate manner . . . importance of the occasion": Dewey, op. cit., p. 9.

340: "in straggling and unceremonious order": *The Times*, 26 October 1921.

341: "it was a beautiful tribute . . . used to preserve order": *New York Times*, 26 October 1921.

341: "represent the United States at the ceremonies": *The Times*, 3 October 1921.

341: "with swords and bayonets glinting in the mellow sunshine": *The Times*, 26 October 1921.

341: A single white rose rested on the ebony coffin: *New York Times*, 26 October 1921.

341: "limping as a result of his war service" . . . "praising the 'obscure and magnificent sacrifice' . . . his last dream to her": *The Times*, 26 October 1921.

341: He then placed the Croix . . . gangway of the Olympia: *The Times*, 3 October 1921.

341: "until it was almost buried from sight": *New York Times*, 26 October 1921.

341: "large box of earth from the American cemetery at Suresnes": *New York Times*, 25 October 1921.

341: "slid out, dead slow": *The Times*, 26 October 1921.

342: "the Unknown had gone home": *The Times*, 26 October 1921.

27: IN THE GREY DUSK

342: On Wednesday 9, November 1921 . . . a pilot off Piney Point: *New York Times*, 8 November 1921.

342: "in the grey dusk of a rainy afternoon": *The Times*, 11 November 1921.

342: "first honors would be paid" . . . "the main ceremonial": *New York Times*, 10 February 1921.

342: the cost, estimated by Secretary Baker at $187,000: *New York Times*, 10 February 1921.

342: "far out to sea": *New York Times*, 3 November 1921.

342: Her captain's orders . . . "after dark": *New York Times*, 2 October 1921.

343: General Pershing . . . Unknown Soldier to the Capitol: B. C. Mossman and M. Warner Stark, *The Last Salute*, pp. 9–10.

343: "The open spaces of the yard . . . rain which was falling": *The Times*, 11 November 1921.

343: "the military and civil dignitaries in their automobiles": Mossman and Stark, op. cit., p. 11.

343: The funeral drapes. . . . ceremonies for the Unknown Soldier: *New York Times*, 23 October 1921.

344: "a silver National Shield with forty-eight gold stars": Mossman and Stark, op. cit., p. 11.

344: "President pro tem of the Senate": *New York Times*, 9 November 1921.

344: "the flowers sent from France . . . tenderly tied by Mrs. Harding": *New York Times*, 11 November 1921.

344: "with no halt to its slow march . . . growing mass of flowers": *The Times*, 11 November 1921.

344: "the time for paying respects . . . proposed by some organisations": *New York Times*, 29 October 1921.

344: The only exception . . . ceremonies lasting forty minutes: *New York Times*, 3 November 1921.

344: "a bunch of pink chrysanthemums" . . . a wreath of yellow roses: *New York Times*, 11 November 1921.

344: "Conspicuous among the delegations . . . two trucks bearing flowers": *New York Times*, 11 November 1921.

345: "flowers brought over from England" . . . "liveth for evermore." *The Times*, 11 November 1921.

345: "a wreath of red English roses . . . from all the Dominions": *New York Times*, 11 November 1921.

345: "wild flowers typical of the country's unrivalled flora": *New York Times*, 8 October 1921.

345: "ten deep for many blocks from the Capitol": *New York Times*, 11 November 1921.

345: Prompted by President Harding: *New York Times*, 21 September 1921.

345: "as a mark of respect . . . the late World War": Presidential proclamation, 5 November 1921.

345: The military escort and the dignitaries . . . the procession as it passed: Mossman and Stark, op. cit., p. 13.

345: One of them, Sergeant Woodfill . . . and capturing three: *New York Times*, 1 November 1921.

346: Crowds 100,000 strong . . . five-yard intervals: *New York Times*, 2 October 1921.

346: The "paucity of funds provided by Congress": *New York Times*, 20 October 1921.

346: "appropriate enough money for the purpose" . . . "As a result . . . the unknown warrior implies": *New York Times*, 24 October 1921.

346: "grand marshal and ride . . . walk the five miles": *New York Times*, 9 November 1921.

346: Among them was the Right Reverend . . . perform the Catholic rituals: *New York Times*, 15 October 1921.

346: "lamed and broken": *New York Times*, 12 November 1921.

346: "old-fashioned Victoria carriage": *New York Times*, 12 November 1921.

347: "forty-four patriotic, fraternal and welfare organisations": Mossman and Stark, op. cit., p. 14.

347: "marching in the uniforms in which they served as nurses in France": *New York Times*, 3 November 1921.

347: "the cheers became a roar . . . the caisson on foot": *New York Times*, 12 November 1921.

347: He became caught in traffic . . . his final resting place: Mossman and Stark, op. cit., p. 16.

348: "the great oval . . . colonnade around the rim": *New York Times*, 12 November 1921.

348: "grassy fields with thousands . . . domed stage of marble": *New York Times*, 12 November 1921.

348: "at the centre of every wreath was a blue star, and in the centre of the blue, a star of gold": *New York Times*, 12 November 1921.

348: "his right hand raised with dramatic intensity": *New York Times*, 12 November 1921.

348: She was one of 1,000 . . . seats at the ceremony: *New York Times*, 25 October 1921.

348: "all public and church bells . . . and 12 o'clock noon": Presidential proclamation, 5 November 1921.

348: "call upon all devout . . . country in the Great War": *New York Times*, 23 October 1921.

348: Some may have preferred . . . observed a two-minute silence: *New York Times*, 17 October 1921.

349: "flags flew at half-mast . . . many nations in the port": *New York Times*, 12 November 1921.

349: "great crowds jammed the two cathedrals . . . overflowed onto the sidewalks": *New York Times*, 12 November 1921.

349: "The Negro warriors . . . were loudly cheered": *New York Times*, 12 November 1921.

349: "under 'the naturalisation tree' . . . oath of allegiance": *New York Times*, 12 November 1921.

349: In Philadelphia, the tolling . . . start of the silence: *New York Times*, 12 November 1921.

349: "On busy streets . . . quieted the roar of motors": *New York Times*, 12 November 1921.

349: "snow-white pigeon" . . . "perched over a memorial window": *New York Times*, 12 November 1921.

349: "an homage of silence more eloquent than speech": *New York Times*, 11 November 1921.

349: The Veterans of Foreign Wars . . . Antwerp and Brussels: *New York Times*, 10 November 1921.

350: "a transmitter far more delicate and sensitive than . . . the ordinary telephone": *New York Times*, 6 November 1921.

350: "loud speaking apparatus . . . clearly and distinctly": *New York Times*, 23 October 1921.

350: "by means of the loud speaking telephone": *New York Times*, 6 November 1921.

350: "Bell Loud Talker, as it is called": *New York Times*, 11 November 1921.

350: "multiplied 3,000,000,000,000,000,000,000,000,000 times": *New York Times*, 13 November 1921.

350: It was "the first time . . . attempted in public": *New York Times*, 6 October 1921.

350: "several times greater than any which ever listened all at once to a single human voice": *New York Times*, 6 November 1921.

350: "the strongest and most significant . . . co-operation in the war": *New York Times*, 19 October 1921.

350: "sturdy as the Breton fisherfolk from whom he came": *New York Times*, 12 November 1921.

350: Marshal Foch was also there . . . guest of the American Legion: *New York Times*, 2 September 1921 and 4 October 1921.

351: Among the wreaths were the faded . . . buried with the Unknown Soldier: Mossman and Stark, op. cit., p. 7.

351: Chief Plenty Coups . . . war bonnet on the tomb: Michael Gavaghan, *The Story of the Unknown Warrior*, p. 70.

351: And two years later . . . might well have contained a Jew: Irving Lehman to Charles Moore, quoted in G. Kurt Piehler, *Remembering War the American Way*, p. 121.

351: Marshal Foch laid a wreath of silver palms . . . United Veterans of Canada: *The Times*, 11 November 1921; *New York Times*, 29 October 1921.

351: "blooms growing in boxes and pots": *New York Times*, 29 October 1921.

351: "miniature conservatory . . . on their arrival in America": *New York Times*, 22 October 1921.

351: "fashion them into the destined tribute": *New York Times*, 29 October 1921.

352: "impending developments in domestic politics": *New York Times*, 21 September 1921.

352: "It was much too long . . . head-dress like the Indian chief's": Quoted in J. Gore, *George V*, p. 262.

352: Lieutenant Colonel Charles W. Whittlesey . . . two days out at sea: *New York Times*, 27 November 1921.

352:    in communities throughout the United States . . . distributed by the U.S. government: Piehler, op. cit., p. 111.

353:    "a bench or a picnic table": ibid., p. 122.

EPILOGUE

355:    "Long hence, when young trees are growing . . . any that survive it": Ernst Junger, *Copse 125*, p. 58.

355:    "when the air is damp . . . wheat and barley": Paul Fussell, *The Great War and Modern Memory*, p. 69.

355:    One of the survivors . . . who had never returned: Jill Knight, *The Civil Service Rifles in the Great War*, p. 94.

357:    the great arch . . . thousands of years: Alan Wilkinson, *The Church of England and the First World War*, p. 303.

357:    Every night for over seventy-five years: Except for the period of the Nazi occupation during the Second World War.

357:    a bugler . . . tribute to the dead: A ritual some claim was first suggested by Rudyard Kipling, cf. Geoff Dyer, *The Missing of the Somme*, pp. 101–2.

Bibliography

———————

Primary Sources

FAMILY PAPERS

Roger Goodman, Wandsworth, London
Brigitte Kostka, Stetten-im-Remstal, Germany
A. Bingham Seibold, Chicago
Theodosia "Teddy" Westlake, Yellow Springs, Ohio
Grace "Bambi" Williams, Granville, Ohio

IMPERIAL WAR MUSEUM
DEPARTMENT OF DOCUMENTS

Con Shelf, Major P. H. Pilditch
Con Shelf, Robert Cude
80/22/1 Reverend D. Railton
86/75/1 Miss C. M. Marx
94/3/1 Major C. J. Saunders: Orders by Major General G. D. Jeffreys, CCB,
   CMG, Commanding London District, on the Occasion of the Burial in Westminster Abbey of the Body of an Unknown British Warrior, Thursday,
   11 November 1920

97/10/1 John McCauley, "A Manx Soldier's War Diary"

140 89/19/1

256 88/52/1 Gore-Browne, Colonel Sir Eric, DSO OBE TD ADC

292 89/21/1 March, John Ewart

564 88/46/1 Caux, E. G. de, MM

565 88/52/1

925 88/11/1

977 88/11/1 Walker, R. A.

978 88/11/1

1027 90/1/1 Raggett, S. H.

1506 90/40/1

1782 92/3/1 Clayden, A.

2342 93/20/1

2476 93/25/1 Morden, C. H.

2523 93/25/1

2783 86/48/1 Leather, J. H.

2808 94/28/1 Simeons, Captain E. E.

2895 94/46/1

2902 P374 Munro, Lieutenant H. A.

2944 Misc 175 (2656)

3392 86/66/1 Harris, R. E.

3608 85/23/1 Anderson, Major A.

4127 83/3/1 Reader, B. A.

4410 82/22/1 Margry, F. de

4772 80/22/1 Crosse, Canon E. C., DSO MC

4774 80/19/1

4931 Misc 139 (2165)

5016 Misc 26 (469) "German Army Officer's Recollections . . ."

5373 Misc 134 (2071)

5606 96/38/1

6434 97/10/1 McCauley, J.

6444 97/17/1 and Con Shelf

6597 79/17/1 Skelton, G.

6771 97/26/1 Butt, H. R.

6972 77/8/1

6999 Misc 195 (2892) "Letter from a Wounded Soldier . . ."

7002 Misc 195 (2894) Notes Concerning War Memorials and Cemeteries of the First World War

7152 77/164/1 Todd, H.

7378 76/171/1 & PP/MCR/60

7594 Misc 200 (2938) Correspondence concerning the escort of the body of the Unknown Warrior to Britain, 1920

7830 98/24/1

8178 99/13/1

8192 99/13/1

8210 99/22/1
8514 99/54/1
8572 Con Shelf
8632 Con Shelf
8782 Misc 25 (426)
9886 01/5/1
9932 Misc 85 (1285)
10407 Misc 128 (1979)
10746 Misc 7 (143) Two papers relating to the soil for the burial of the Unknown
    Warrior, 10 November 1920
10819 P443
11342 01/38/1
11461
11601 01/38/1
11668 01/51/1
11686 01/46/1
11731 01/52/1
11811 02/31/1
11847 Misc 223 (3210)
11905 02/4/1
12122 P275
12324 P265
12553 03/15/1
12667 Misc 235 (3341) Records of the 279th Siege Battery
Misc 7/143
Misc 200/2938

IWM Sound Archive
36
7363
9339
9422
10168
10441
14599

IWM Film Archive
IWM 505 Armistice Day 1920—Homecoming of an Unknown Warrior

IWM Department of Printed Books
81/3675 Revd. Canon F. B. MacNutt (senior chaplain to the forces in the BEF),
    The Unknown Warrior's Call to Living Warriors
93/86 Bringing Home the Unknown Warrior
333 (41) K. 60791. *The Unknown Warrior: A Symposium of Articles on How the
    Unknown Warrior Was Chosen*

70295 Remembrance Day, Poppy Day

CDS 82, November 1915, Instructions Regarding the Construction of Trenches and Shelters

K98/378 2/15 Battalion, County of London Regiment

SS 455 Preventative Measures Against Lice

SS 456 Burial of Soldiers

SS 472 German Documents on the Battle of the Somme

SS 473 German Documents on the Battle of the Somme

SS 478 German Documents on the Battle of the Somme

SS 3444 Abolition of Flies in Camps, Billets and Hospitals

IWM Department of Exhibits

EPH 3232 Dried Rosebud on a Stem from the Army wreath surmounting the coffin of the Unknown Soldier

MED/733 Walter Eberbach, *Verdun: Die Weltblutpumpe*

NATIONAL ARCHIVES (FORMERLY PUBLIC RECORD OFFICE)

ADM242/10 War Graves Roll

ADM242/11 Statistical Casualty Book

AIR/959/204/5/1036 Miscellaneous correspondence with American squadrons in France

AIR1/984/204/5/1175 Casualties of the American Flying Corps

AIR1/1073/204/5/1647 Supply of Sopwith Camel Aeroplanes: American squadrons

AIR1/1187/204/5/2595 RFC War Diaries

AIR1/1228/204/5/2634 Combat Reports 148 USA Squadron

AIR2/219 List of American personnel who lost their lives while attached to the RCF and RAF

AIR 76/453 Records of Service, RFC Officers

CAB 21/160

CAB 24/109

CAB 24/CP45

CAB 24/GT 8335

CAB 24/84/GT 7784

CAB 27/99

CAB 52/27

HO 45/11557/20

Leaflet No. 37, June 1983, Operation Records of the British Army in the War of 1914–1919

WO 30/3000

WO 32/5847

WO 95/2727

WORK 20/1/3

WORK 20/139

WORK 21/74

WESTMINSTER ABBEY MUNIMENT ROOM AND LIBRARY

58667 Lord Stamfordham to Dean Ryle, 7 October 1920
58669 M. P. A. Hankey, Secretary to the Cabinet, to Dean Ryle, 15 October1920
58671 Cabinet Memorial Services (November 11th) Committee, 19 October 1920
58671B Cabinet Memorial Services (November 11th) Committee
58672A Sir Henry Wilson to Dean Ryle, 16 October 1920
58675 Lord Stamfordham to Dean Ryle, 11 November 1920
Sir Cecil Smith to the Dean of Westminster, July 1978

BODLEIAN LIBRARY, DEPARTMENT OF WESTERN MANUSCRIPTS

MSS.Eng.hist.c.88-177c
MSS.Eng.misc.e.265-329

CAMBRIDGE UNIVERSITY LIBRARY, DEPARTMENT OF
MANUSCRIPTS AND UNIVERSITY ARCHIVES

ADD.MS7509/466 Papers of E. H. Blakeney

UNIVERSITY OF LEEDS, BROTHERTON LIBRARY,
LIDDLE COLLECTION

GE 01 Anonymous
GE 04 Balters, Heinrich
GE 09 Kalepky, L.
GE 13 Lubinski, Karol
GS 0029 Amsden, C. S.
GS 0591 French, H. J. A.
GS 0710 Harford, Sir James
GS 1317 Radice, F. R.
GS 1368 Robins, A. L.
GS 1377 Roe, Brigadier F. P.
GS 1745 Williams, H. G. R.

LIDDELL HART CENTRE FOR MILITARY STUDIES

Capt. Gerard Gavin

NATIONAL WAR MUSEUM OF SCOTLAND

3.G.915.1 Letter from K. A. Bippes

NATIONAL ARMY MUSEUM

6111-146 Wiley West
7402-29 Mary Frances Maxwell

ROYAL ARTILLERY INSTITUTION LIBRARY

552 Letters to the Misses Hughes

SHROPSHIRE RECORD OFFICE

4629/1/1920/125 Correspondence of William Clive and Caroline Beatrix
  Bridgeman

SUFFOLK RECORD OFFICE

GB 554/Z3/4 Orders of GOC London District for the burial of the Unknown
  Warrior and the unveiling of the Cenotaph

WEST YORKSHIRE ARCHIVE SERVICE, BRADFORD DISTRICT ARCHIVES

10D76/3/27/58 Norman Arnold, Papers
66D81/1 Harry Smith, Diary
67D84/1 J. H. Moore, Memoirs
67D89/1 John H. Taylor, Diary

WEST YORKSHIRE (PRINCE OF WALES'S OWN)
REGIMENT MUSEUM, YORK

253 Conan Doyle's account of the Battle of the Aisne
262
264

AMERICAN MILITARY HISTORY INSTITUTE

Dewey, Arthur E., *Selection of the Unknown Soldier*
Operations Division to Officer in Charge of Operations, Romagne-sous-
  Montfaucon, 5 October 1921
Operations Division to Officer in Charge of Operations, Romagne-sous-
  Montfaucon, 15 October 1921
Officer in Charge, Operations, Romagne, to 1st Lieutenant Arthur E. Dewey,
  QMC, 18 October 1921
Officer in Charge, Operations, Romagne, to Camp Quartermaster, Meuse-
  Argonne Cemetery, 20 October 1921
Officer in Charge, Operations, Romagne, to Supervisory Embalmers, 20 October
  1921
Officer in Charge, Operations, Romagne, to Civilian Employees, 20 October
  1921

UNIVERSITY OF DALLAS

George H. William World War I Aviation Library
Ola Sater Collection: World War I
Box 2, Box 28, Box 29, Box 74, Box 75

Olive Senn Collection: World War I
Box 1

George H. Williams Collection: World War I
Box 145, Box 146, Box 150

Hugh Wynne Collection: World War I
Film No. 10

U.S. LIBRARY OF CONGRESS

Manuscript Division
Pershing Papers
Container No. 37

U.S. NATIONAL ARCHIVES

120.5.1 Records of the Chief of the Air Service

BIBLIOTHEK FÜR ZEITGESCHICHTE, STUTTGART

Paul Knoch Collection, Diary of Ernst Knopper

HAUPTSTAATSARCHIV STUTTGART

1351/1973 M660/019 Familienpapiere Hub

Secondary Sources

NEWSPAPERS, MAGAZINES

After the Battle: 6, 1974, pp. 48–53, "The Unknown Warrior."
Air Power Historian: July 1962, p. 157, Robert E. Rogge, "A History of the 148th Aero Squadron."
American Aviation Historical Society Journal: Winter 1959, James J. Hudson, "Air Knight of the Ozarks," James J. Sloan, "The 148th American"; 28, Fall/Winter 1983, pp. 181–89, Geoffrey Rossano, "Doing Their Duty Side by Side: American Aviation Personnel in Allied Service."
Arkansas Historical Quarterly: 1959, No. 2, James J. Hudson, "Captain Field E. Kindley, Arkansas' Air Ace of the First World War."
Barnsley Chronicle: 24 July 1920.
British Legion Journal: Vol. 9, No. 5, November 1929, Herbert Jeans, "In Death's Cathedral Palace (The Story of the Unknown Warrior)"; Vol. 10, No. 5, 1939, E. E. R. Tiddall, "How They Chose the Unknown Warrior."
Carlisle Journal: 20 June 1919.

Church Times: 21 November 1920.

Cross and Cockade International: 1, Autumn 1961, A. J. Lynch, "Interview with Lieutenant Richmond Viall"; 2, No. 4, Oliver Bennett, "Words from a War-bird"; 7, No. 4, Winter 1966, "Diary of Lt. Friedrich Noltenius"; 33, No. 1, 2002, J. Stirling Hallstead, "A Mission to the Royal Flying Corps"; 33, No. 2, 2002, Ken Slocombe, "What Goes Up: Experiments with the Observation Balloon"; 34, No. 1, 2003, Peter Daybell, "Some Aspects of the Aircrew Experience During the Great War, Part 2"; 35, No. 1, 2004, Peter C. Ford, "The Practical Training of Kite Balloon Observers."

Daily Express: 1, 5, 7 August 1918; 16 September, 12 November, 31 December 1919; 14 January, 11, 12, 16 November 1920.

Daily Graphic: 11, 12 November 1920.

Daily Herald: 11, 13 November 1920.

Daily Mail: 23 July, 12 November 1919; 11, 12, 13, 15 November 1920.

Daily Mirror: 28 February 1916; 9–12, 15 November 1920.

Daily Sketch: 30 November 1926.

Daily Telegraph: 9–12 November 1920; 11 November 1939 (letter from Brigadier General L. J. Wyatt); 14 October 1993 (obituary of Lt. Col. H. Williams); 11 November 2000 (obituary of Andrew Railton).

Dover News: 10–11 November 1920.

Embalmers' Monthly: 33, January 1920, "Paris Director in League with Purple Cross (?)"; 33, February 1920, "Rid the Profession of Odium That Has Come to It."

Evening News: 7 October 1916.

Evening Standard: 1 August 1919; 7 May 1923.

Federal Register: Vol. 68, No. 189, Tuesday, 30 September.

Great War Magazine: 1, September 2001, Ray Westlake, "The U.K. National Inventory of War Memorials"; 4, June 2002, Peter M. Smith, "In Memory of the Nameless Fallen: The Story of the Unknown Soldier"; 9, September 2003, Sandra Gittins, "Lutyens."

Guardian: 10 November 2003.

History and Memory: 5, 1993, pp. 7–31, Ken S. Inglis, "Entombing Unknown Warriors: From London and Paris to Baghdad."

Imperial War Museum Review: 3, 1988, pp. 60–68, P. Dutton, "The Dead Man's Penny: A History of the Next of Kin Memorial Plaque"; 6, 1992, pp. 63–75, Catherine Moriarty, "Christian Iconography and First World War Memorials."

Independent: 18 February 1999, Alex King, "The Iconography of War Memorials"; 23 March 1999, Alex King, "Monuments with No Fixed Meaning."

Ingall's Magazine: Vol. 1, No. 3, September 1951, Clive Parson, "Bringing Home the Unknown Warrior."

Journal of Contemporary History: 27, 1992, pp. 583–605, Ken S. Inglis, "The Homecoming: The War Memorial Movement in Cambridge, England."

Journal of the Society of Architectural Historians: 1989, Vol. XLVIII, No. 1, pp. 5–23, Allan Greenberg, "Lutyens' Cenotaph."

Legionary: Vol. 30, No. 3, August 1955, John Hundevad, "The Unknown Warrior."

Listener: 15 July 1971.

Liverpool Courier: 12 November 1920.

Liverpool Weekly Post: 12 November 1920.

Manchester Evening News: 11 November 1920.

Manchester Guardian: 10 June 1915; 21 July, 11, 12 November 1919.

Morning Post: 21 July 1919.

NARA Prologue (Washington): Vol. 31, No. 2, Summer 1999, Constance Potter, "World War I Gold Star Mothers' Pilgrimages, Part I"; 9 March 2004.

New York Times: 2, 8–12, 15–17, 27 November, 9 December 1920; 12, 21, 22, 29 January, 2, 3, 10 February, 4, 6, 17, 18 March, 16, 17 April, 5, 8, 30 May, 12 June, 7 July, 13 August, 2, 11, 14, 18, 21–25 September, 2–6, 8–12, 15–20, 22–29 October, 1–15, 17–20, 22–24, 29 November, 6, 11, 16, 27 December 1921; 12 May 1945.

Our Empire: Vol. VI, No. 8, pp. 26–27, "The Origin of the Two Minutes' Silence"; Vol. VII, No. 8, 1931, pp. 34–36, the Reverend David Railton, "The Origins of the Unknown Warrior"; Vol. IX, No. 5, p. 118.

Over the Front: 6, 1991, A. Bingham Seibold and Marvin L. Skelton, "The Search for Lt. Seibold"; 10, No. 4, 1995, Karl B. Ogilvie, "A Chat with Lothar"; 11, No. 1, 1996, Douglas V. Fant and Dr. Ing. Niedermeyer, "The End of an Action-Filled Life: Leutnant Erwin Böhme's Final Letters"; 12, No. 1, 1997, Stewart K. Taylor, "The Silent Volunteers," "Pranged," "Unsung Sextet," "In Case I Should Not Return"; 13, No. 2, 1998, Robert B. Gill, "WWI Flying on the Texas Gulf Coast"; 13, No. 3, 1998, Christopher Lew, "Bloody April," S. A. H. Henderson, "One Step Closer to Hauptmann: The Last Flight of Oberleutnant Kurt Wolff"; 14, No. 3, 1999, Jan Hayzlett, "My Last Time at the Front, July–August 1918"; 15, No. 2, 2000, Dr Achim Fuchs, "The Bavarian War Archive in Munich"; 17, No. 3, 2002, Hptm. A. D. Robert Ritter von Greim, "During the Defensive Battle on the Somme"; 19, No. 1, 2004, Stephen Miller, "Jesse Orin Creech."

Pall Mall Gazette: 1 September 1914.

Picture Postcard Monthly: November 1992, B. Drinkwater, "The Day They Buried the Unknown Warrior."

Population Studies: 31, 1977, Jay M. Winter, "Britain's 'Lost Generation' of the First World War."

Quartermaster Review (Fort Lee, Virginia): May–June 1930.

Radio Times: 8 November 1935.

Reveille (Sydney): November 1967, E. C. Sier, "How They Chose the Unknown Warrior."

Saturday Evening Post: 9 March 1918, Irvin S. Cobb, "The Sinking of the *Tuscania*."

Scotsman: 12 November 1920; 12 November 1927.

Stand To: 72, January 2005, Jami L. Bryan, "Fighting for Respect: African-Americans in World War I."

Sunday Times: 7 November 2004.

Theology: 64, 1961, pp. 442–45, N. Annan, "Remembrance Sunday"; 68, 1965,

pp. 525–39, R. Coppin, "Remembrance Day"; 79, 1976, pp. 322–29, O. Chadwick, "Armistice Day."

The Times: 9 August, 21 September 1914; 31 March 1915; 28 February 1916;
21 April, 5 August 1917; 19, 21, 26, 31 July 1919; 5, 15 October, 8, 10–12,
15–19, 22, 27 November 1920; 24 August, 3, 8, 11–15, 17–20, 22, 25–27 October, 4, 7, 10–12, 14 November 1921; 10 November 1928; 14 September 1991.

Times Literary Supplement: 12 November 1976, pp. 1429–30, Eric Homberger,
"The Story of the Cenotaph."

Transactions of the Ancient Monuments Society: 1, 1995, pp. 3–39, Catherine Moriarty, "The Absent Dead and Figurative First World War Memorials."

War Illustrated: 1 December 1914.

Washington Post: 18, 30 July 1917; 29 September, 16 December 1918; 5 July 1919;
13, 15, 16 June 1947; 2 June 1955; 1 November 1972; 7 September 1973.

Washington Star: 11 May 1945; 13 June 1947; 28 May 1955.

Washington Sunday Star: 15 December 1918.

Western Front Association Bulletin: 17 October 1986, Terry Cave, "The Unknown
Warrior."

Yorkshire Observer: 6 July 1922.

Yorkshire Post: 8–13, 15, 17, 18, 26 November 1920; 5, 12 November 1921.

BOOKS

Unless otherwise indicated, the place of publication is London.

Andrews, William Linton, *Haunting Years*, Naval & Military Press, Uckfield, East
Sussex, 2001.

Andriessen, J. H. J. (ed.), *World War I in Photographs*, Grange Books, Hoo,
Rochester, Kent, 2003.

Anon, *The War the Infantry Knew*, P. S. King & Son, 1938.

Ariès, Philippe, *Western Attitudes Towards Death from the Middle Ages to the Present*,
Johns Hopkins University Press, Baltimore, 1976.

Arthur, Max, *Forgotten Voices of the Great War: A New History of WWI in the Words
of the Men and Women Who Were There*, Ebury Press, 2003.

Ashworth, Tony, *Trench Warfare 1914–1918*, Pan Macmillan, 1980.

Auden, W. H., *Poems*, 1930.

Bairnsfather, Bruce, *Bullets and Billets*, 1916.

Barnett, Correlli, *The Great War*, Penguin, 2000.

Barrie, Alexander, *War Underground: The Tunnellers of the Great War*, Tom Donovan Publishing, 1988.

Bates, Ione, *Out of a Long Silence*, privately published, 2002.

Bayliss, Gwyn M., *Bibliographic Guide to the Two World Wars: An Annotated Survey
of English Language Reference Materials*, Bowker, 1977.

Baynes, John, *Morale*, Cassell, 1967.

Beckett, Ian F. W., *The First World War: The Essential Guide to Sources in the
National Archives*, Naval & Military Press, Uckfield, East Sussex, 2002.

Beckett, Ian F. W., and Simpson, Keith (eds.), *A Nation in Arms: A Social History of
the British Army in the First World War*, Manchester University Press, 1985.

Bergerac, B. de, *The Oxford Victory Pageant 1919*, Oxford, 1919.

Blake, R. (ed.), *The Private Papers of Douglas Haig, 1914–1919*, Eyre & Spottis-woode, 1952.

Blomfield, Sir Reginald, *Memoirs of an Architect*, 1932.

Blunden, Edmund, *Undertones of War*, 1930.

Blythe, Ronald, *Akenfield*, Allen Lane, 1970.

Blythe, Ronald, *The Age of Illusion*, Penguin, 1963.

Bocock, Robert, *Ritual in Industrial Society*, Allen & Unwin, 1974.

Boorman, Derek, *At the Going Down of the Sun: British First World War Memorials*, Ebor Press, York, 1988.

Boraston, J. H. (ed.), *Sir Douglas Haig's Despatches*, Naval & Military Press, Uck-field, East Sussex, 2001.

Borg, Alan, *War Memorials from Antiquity to the Present*, Leo Cooper, 1991.

Bowyer, Chaz, *Sopwith Camel: King of Combat*, Aston, Bourne End, 1988.

Bracco, M., *Merchants of Hope: British Middlebrow Writers and the First World War, 1919–1939*, Oxford, 1993.

Brittain, Vera, *Testament of Youth*, Penguin, 1989.

British Legion Album, In Aid of Field Marshal Haig's Appeal for Ex-Servicemen of All Ranks, London, nd, 1923?.

British Legion Annual, 1924.

British Legion: Ten Memorable Days, 1938.

Brook-Shephard, Gordon, *November 1918*, Collins, 1981.

Brown, Malcolm, *The Imperial War Museum Book of the First World War*, 1991.

Brown, Malcolm, *The Imperial War Museum Book of the Somme*, 1996.

Brown, Malcolm, *The Imperial War Museum Book of the Western Front*, 1993.

Brown, Malcolm, *Tommy Goes to War*, Tempus, 1999.

Buchan, J., and Newbolt, H., *Days to Remember*, 1923.

Budreau, Lisa M., "Mourning and the Making of a Nation: The Gold Star Pil-grimages, 1930–1933," unpublished thesis, Vanderbilt University, Nashville, Tenn., 2002.

Bushaway, Bob, "Name upon Name: The Great War and Remembrance," in Roy Porter (ed.), *Myths of the English*, Polity, Cambridge, 1992.

Butler, A. S. G., *The Architecture of Sir Edwin Lutyens*, Country Life, 1950.

Cacutt, Len, *Great Aircraft of the World*, Colour Library Books, Godalming, 1988.

Cannadine, David, *Aspects of Aristocracy*, Penguin, 1998.

Cannadine, David, "(War and) Death, Grief and Mourning in Modern Britain," in Joachim Whaley (ed.), *Mirrors of Mortality: Studies in the Social History of Death*, Europa, 1984.

Cannadine, David, and Price, S. (eds), *Rituals of Royalty: Power and Ceremonial in Traditional Societies*, Cambridge, 1987.

Carpenter, E. (ed.), *A House of Kings*, Baker, 1966.

Castelbled, Maurice de, *History of the AEF*, New York, 1937.

Cecil, Hugh, and Liddle, Peter H., *Facing Armageddon: The First World War Expe-rienced*, Leo Cooper, 2003.

Chambrun, Colonel de, and Marenches, Colonel de, *The American Army in the European Conflict*, New York, 1939.

Chapman, Guy, *A Passionate Prodigality*, 1953.

Chapman, Guy (ed.), *Vain Glory*, 1937.

Charteris, J., *Field Marshal Earl Haig*, 1929.

Christy, Joe, and Cook, Leroy, *American Aviation*, McGraw Hill, New York, 1993.

Clapham, H. S., *Mud and Khaki: The Memories of an Incomplete Soldier*, Naval & Military Press, Uckfield, East Sussex, 2003.

Clapp, Frederick Mortimer, *A History of the 17th Aero Squadron*, New York, 1920.

Clark, Alan, *Aces High: The War in the Air over the Western Front, 1914–1918*, Weidenfeld & Nicolson, 1973.

Clark, Alan, *The Donkeys*, Pimlico, 1991.

Clark, Don, *Wild Blue Yonder: An Air Epic*, Seattle, 1972.

Cole, Christopher, *RAF Communiqués, 1918*, Kimber, 1988.

Connelly, Mark, *The Great War, Memory and Ritual: Commemoration in the City and East London, 1916–1939* (Royal Historical Society Studies in History New Series), Boydell Press, 2002.

Connerton, Paul, *How Societies Remember*, Cambridge, 1989.

Cooke, James J., *The U.S. Air Service in the Great War: 1917–1919*, Praeger, Westport, Conn., 1996.

Coombs, Rose E. B., *Before Endeavours Fade*, After the Battle Publications, 1976.

Cooper, C. S., *Outdoor Monuments of London*, 1928.

Cooper, Duff, *Haig*, 2 vols, 1935–36.

Coppard, George, *With a Machine Gun to Cambrai*, Imperial War Museum, 1969.

Corns, Cathryn, and Hughes-Wilson, John, *Blindfold and Alone: British Military Executions in the Great War*, Cassell, 2001.

Curl, James Stevens, "The Royal Artillery Memorial at Hyde Park Corner," in Ann Compton (ed.), *Charles Sargeant Jagger, War and Peace Sculpture*, Imperial War Museum, 1985.

Dambitsch, Lieutenant Alfred, *Memoirs and Diaries: Destructive Technology at the Somme*, www.firstworldwar.com/diaries/somme-dambitsch.htm.

Davis, Burke, *War Bird: The Life and Times of Elliot White Springs*, University of North Carolina, Chapel Hill, 1987.

DeGroot, Gerard J., *Blighty: British Society in the Era of the Great War*, Longman, 1996.

Derez, Mark, "A Belgian Salient for Reconstruction: People and Patrie, Landscape and Memory," in Peter H. Liddle (ed.), *Passchendaele in Perspective*, Leo Cooper, 1997.

Directorate of Graves Registration, *The Care of the Dead*, 1916.

Dyer, Geoff, *The Missing of the Somme*, Weidenfeld & Nicolson, 2001.

Edmonds, Charles, *A Subaltern's War*, 1929.

Edmonds, Sir James E. (ed.), *Military Operations: France and Belgium, 1915: Battles of Aubers Ridge*, Festubert and Loos, 1928.

Eksteins, Modris, *Rites of Spring*, Bantam, 1989.

Ellis, John, *Eye Deep in Hell: Trench Warfare in World War I*, Penguin, 2002.

Enser, A. G. S., *A Subject Bibliography of the First World War: Books in English 1914–78*, Deutsch, 1979.

Evans, Martin Marix, *American Voices of World War I: Primary Source Documents, 1917–1920*, Fitzroy Dearborn Publishers, 2001.

Fielding, Rowland, *War Letters to a Wife*, Naval & Military Press, Uckfield, East Sussex, 2001.

Fitzgerald, M. F., *Herbert Edward Ryle*, Macmillan, 1928.

Flex, Walter, *The Wanderer Between Two Worlds*, 1917.

Fox, F., *The King's Pilgrimage*, 1921.

Franks, Norman, *American Aces of World War I (Aircraft of the Aces No. 42)*, Osprey, Oxford, 2001.

Franks, Norman, and Bailey, Frank, *Over the Front: A Complete Record of the Fighter Aces and Units of the United States and French Air Services, 1914–*, Grub Street, 1992.

Franks, Norman, Bailey, Frank, and Guest, Russell, *Above the Lines, A Complete Record of the Fighter Aces of the German Air Service, Naval Air Service and Flanders Marine Corps, 1914–1918*, Grub Street, 1993.

Franks, Norman, and Van Wyngarden, Greg, *Fokker D VII Aces of World War I (Part 1) (Aircraft of the Aces No. 53)*, Osprey, Oxford, 2003.

French, Anthony, *Gone for a Soldier*, Warwick, 1972.

Fry, Michele, "Lutyens's Cenotaph: Inscribing the First World War onto London's Political Landscape," unpublished essay, 2001.

Fussell, Paul, *The Bloody Game*, Scribners, 1971.

Fussell, Paul, *The Great War and Modern Memory*, Oxford University Press, 1975.

Gaffney, Angela, *Aftermath: Remembering the Great War in Wales*, University of Wales Press, Cardiff, 1998.

Gammage, Bill, *The Broken Years: Australian Soldiers in the Great War*, Penguin, Harmondsworth, 1975.

Garrett, Richard, *The Final Betrayal: Armistice 1918 . . . and Afterwards*, Buchan & Enright, Southampton, 1989.

Gavaghan, Michael, *The Story of the Unknown Warrior*, M & L Publications, Preston, 1997.

Gibbs, Sir Philip, "The Battle of the Somme," in Charles F. Horne (ed.), *Source Records of the Great War*, Vol. IV, National Alumni, 1923.

Gibbs, Sir Philip, *Realities of War*, 1920 (published as *Now It Can Be Told*, New York, 1920).

Gibson, Edwin, and Ward, G. Kingsley, *Courage Remembered: The Story Behind the Construction and Maintenance of the Commonwealth's Military Cemeteries and Memorials of the Wars of 1914–1918 and 1939–1945*, HMSO, 1989.

Gilbert, Martin, *The Routledge Atlas of the First World War*, 2002.

Giles, J., *The Ypres Salient*, Leo Cooper, 1970.

Gilmour, David, *Curzon*, John Murray, 1994.

Gore, J., *King George V: A Personal Memoir*, 1941.

Gorer, Geoffrey, *Death, Grief and Mourning in Contemporary Britain*, Cresset Press, 1965.

Gough, Paul, *Loci Memoriae*, The Architecture Centre, Bristol and the Centre for Contextual, Public and Commemorative Art at UWE, Bristol, 2001.

Graham, Stephen, *The Challenge of the Dead: A Vision of the War and the Life of the Common Soldier in France*, Cassell, 1921.

Graham, Stephen, *A Private in the Guards*, 1919.

Graves, Robert, *Goodbye to All That*, 1929.

Graves, R., and Hodges, A., *The Long Weekend: A Social History of Great Britain, 1918–1939*, 1940.

Green Cross Society, *Roads of Remembrance as War Memorials*, 1920.

Gregory, Adrian, *The Silence of Memory: Armistice Day, 1919–1946*, Berg Publishers, Oxford, 1994.

Gudmundsson, Bruce I., *Stormtroop Tactics*, Westport, New York, 1989.

Haig, Dorothy, *Douglas Haig: The Man I Knew*, 1936.

Haigh, R. H., and Turner, P. W., *Not for Glory*, Robert Maxwell, 1969.

Hannah, James (ed.), *The Great War Reader*, Texas A & M University Press, 2000.

Harbord, James G., *The American Army in France, 1917–1919*, New York, 1936.

Harries, Meirion, and Harries, Susie, *The War Artists: Official Art of the Twentieth Century*, Michael Joseph, 1983.

Harvey, W. F. J., *Pi in the Sky: A History of No. 22 Squadron*, Colin Huston, Leicester, 1971.

Hay, Ian, and Beith, John H., *Their Name Liveth: The Book of the Scottish War Memorial*, Bodley Head, 1931.

Haythornthwaite, Philip J., *The World War One Source Book*, Arms and Armour Press, 1992.

Henig, R., *Versailles and After*, New York, 1995.

Herwig, Holger H., *The First World War: Germany and Austria-Hungary, 1914–1918*, Hodder Arnold, 1997.

Hill, A. W., *Our Soldiers' Graves*, 1920.

The History of the Prince of Wales's Own Civil Service Rifles, 1921.

Hitchcock, F. C., *Stand To: A Diary of the Trenches, 1915–1918*, 1937.

Hobsbawm, Eric, and Ranger, Terence (eds.), *The Invention of Tradition*, Cambridge, 1983.

Hoffmann, Max, *War Diaries and Other Papers*, Vol. 1, 1929.

Holden, Matthew, *War in the Trenches*, Wayland, 1973.

Holmes, Richard (ed.), *The First World War in Photographs*, Sevenoaks, 2001.

Holmes, Richard, *The Western Front*, BBC, 1999.

Horne, Charles F. (ed.), *Source Records of the Great War*, Vol. IV (of 7 vols.), The American Legion, Indianapolis, 1930 (National Alumni, New York, 1923).

Horne, Cyril Morton, *Songs of the Shrapnel Shell and Other Verses*, Harper & Brothers, New York & London, 1918.

Houlbrooke, Ralph (ed.), *Death, Ritual and Bereavement*, Routledge, 1989.

Housman, Lawrence (ed.), *War Letters of Fallen Englishmen*, 1930.

Howard, Michael, *The Franco-Prussian War: The German Invasion of France, 1870–1871*, Methuen, 1961.

Hudson, James J., *Hostile Skies: A Combat History of the American Air Service in World War I*, Syracuse University Press, New York, 1968.

Hudson, James J., *In Clouds of Glory: American Airmen Who Flew with the British During the Great War*, Arkansas University Press, Fayetteville, 1990.

Huntington, R., and Metcalfe, P. (eds.), *Celebrations of Death: The Anthropology of Mortuary Ritual*, Cambridge, 1991.

Hurst, Sydney Cecil, *Silent Cities: An Illustrated Guide to the War Cemeteries and Memorials of the Missing in France and Flanders*, 1929.

Hussey, Christopher, *The Life of Sir Edwin Lutyens*, Country Life, 1953.

Hynes, Samuel, *A War Imagined: The First World War and English Culture*, Bodley Head, 1990.

Imperial War Graves Commission, *Annual Reports, 1921–1930*.

Inglis, Ken S., *Sacred Places: War Memorials in the Australian Landscape*, Melbourne University Press, 1998.

Irvin, Francis L. "Spike," "War Diary of Sergeant Major F. L. Irvin," in W. P. Taylor and F. L. Irvin (eds.), *History of the 148th Aero Squadron Aviation Section, U.S. Army Signal Corps, AEF–BEF, 1917–1918*, Sunflower UP, Manhattan, Kansas, 1957.

Jackson, J. Hampden, *The Post-War World*, Gollancz, 1935.

Jones, Henry Albert, *The War in the Air* (6 vols.), Oxford, 1922–37.

Jukes, Geoffrey, *The First World War: The Eastern Front*, Fitzroy Dearborn, 2003.

Junger, Ernst, *Copse 125*, Naval & Military Press, Uckfield, East Sussex.

Junger, Ernst (trans. Michael Hofmann), *Storm of Steel*, Allen Lane, 2003.

Keegan, John, *The First World War*, Hutchinson, 1998.

Kilduff, Peter, *Richthofen: Beyond the Legend of the Red Baron*, Arms & Armour, 1994.

King, Alex, *Memorials of the Great War in Britain: The Symbolism and Politics of Remembrance (The Legacy of the Great War)*, Berg Publishers, 1998.

Kipling, Rudyard, *The Years Between*, 1919.

Knight, Jill, *The Civil Service Rifles in the Great War: "All Bloody Gentlemen,"* Pen & Sword, 2004.

Konody, P. G., and Dark, Sidney, *Sir William Orpen*, 1932.

Laqueur, Thomas W., "Memory and Naming in the Great War," in *Commemorations: The Politics of National Identity*, Princeton University Press, 1994.

Larkin, Philip, *Collected Poems*, Faber, 2003.

Lee, Arthur Gould, *No Parachute: A Fighter Pilot in World War One*, Jarrold, 1968.

Levenstein, Harvey, "Seductive Journey: American Tourists in France," in *Jefferson to the Jazz Age*, Macmillan, 1997.

Liddle, Peter H., *The Airman's War, 1914–1918*, Blandford, Poole, Dorset, 1987.

Liddle, Peter H., "Passchendaele Experienced: Soldiering in the Salient During the Third Battle of Ypres," in *Passchendaele in Perspective*, Leo Cooper, 1997.

Liddle, Peter H. (ed.), *Passchendaele in Perspective*, Leo Cooper, 1997.

Liddle, Peter H., *The Soldier's War, 1914–1918*, Blandford, 1988.

Liddle, Peter H., *Voices of War*, Leo Cooper, 1988.

Liddle, Peter H., and Cecil, Hugh, *At the Eleventh Hour: Reflections, Hopes and Anxieties at the Closing of the Great War, 1918*, Leo Cooper, 1998.

Lloyd, Alan, *The War in the Trenches*, Hart Davis, MacGibbon, 1976.

Lloyd, David W., *Battlefield Tourism*, Berg Publishers, 1998.

Lloyd George, David, *War Memoirs*, 1936.

London Territorials and the War, date unknown.

Longstreet, Stephen, *The Canvas Falcons: The Story of the Men and Planes of World War I*, World, New York, 1970.

Longworth, Philip, *The Unending Vigil: A History of the Commonwealth War Graves Commission*, Constable 1967.

Low, A. M., *Benefits of War*, 1943.

Lowe, T. A., *The Western Battlefields: A Guide to the British Line*, 1920.

Luard, K. E., *Unknown Warriors: Extracts from the Letters of a Nursing Sister in France*, 1930.

McCall, Thomas, "A Highland Battalion at Loos," in C. B. Purdom (ed.), *Everyman at War*, 1930.

Macdonald, Lyn, *The Roses of No Man's Land*, Penguin, 1993.

Macgill, Patrick, *The Great Push: An Episode of the Great War*, Caliban Press, 1984.

McIntyre, Colin, *Monuments of War: How to Read a War Memorial*, Hale, 1990.

Mackintosh, Ewart Alan, *A Highland Regiment*, John Lane, 1917.

Mackintosh, Ewart Alan, *War, the Liberator and Other Pieces*, John Lane, 1918.

McLaughlin, Redmond, *The Royal Army Medical Corps*, Leo Cooper, 1972.

Major and Mrs. Holt's Battlefield Guide—Somme, Leo Cooper, 2000.

Marrin, Albert, *The Last Crusade: The Church of England in the First World War*, Duke University Press, Durham, North Carolina, 1974.

Marwick, A., *The Deluge: British Society and the Great War*, 1965.

Masterman, Charles Frederick Gurney, *England After War*, 1922.

Maude, Alan H. (ed.), *The 47th (London) Division, 1914–1919*, Naval & Military Press, Uckfield, East Sussex, 2000.

Mayer, S. L., and Koenig, W. J., *The Two World Wars: A Guide to Manuscript Collections in the United Kingdom*, Bowker, 1976.

Mayo, James M., *War Memorials as Political Landscape: The American Experience and Beyond*, Praeger, New York, 1988.

Mead, Gary, *The Doughboys, America and the First World War*, Allen Lane, 2000.

Middlebrook, Martin, *The First Day on the Somme*, Allen Lane, 1971.

Middlebrook, Martin, and Middlebrook, Mary, *The Somme: A Battlefield Guide*, Viking, 1991.

Milner, Laurie, *Leeds Pals*, Leo Cooper, 1991.

Mitchell, T. J., and Smith, G. M., *Casualties and Medical Statistics of the Great War*, 1931.

Montague, C. E., *Disenchantment*, 1922.

Morgan, Kenneth Owen, *Consensus and Disunity: The Lloyd George Coalition Government*, Clarendon Press, Oxford, 1979.

Moore, William, *The Thin Yellow Line*, Leo Cooper, 1974.

Morrow, John H., *The Great War in the Air*, Airlife, Shrewsbury, 1993.

Morton, H. V., "Among the Kings," from *The Spell of London*, 1926.

Mosier, John, *The Myth of the Great War*, Profile, 2001.

Mosse, George L., *Fallen Soldiers: Reshaping the Memory of the World Wars*, Oxford University Press, New York, 1990.

Mossman, B. C., and Stark, M. Warner, *The Last Salute*, Washington, 1971.

Moult, T. (ed.), *Cenotaph: A Book of Remembrance in Poetry and Prose*, 1923.

Moynihan, Michael (ed.), *God on Our Side: The British Padre in World War One*, Leo Cooper, 1983.

Moynihan, Michael (ed.), *People at War, 1914–1918*, David & Charles, 1973.

Mullins, C. F., *Shocked and Disillusioned*, 1919.

Murphy, Jack, *History of the U.S. Marines*, Bison Books, 1984.

Murray, Williamson, *War in the Air, 1914–45*, Cassell, 1999.

Murray, W. W., *The Epic of Vimy*, Ottawa, 1936.

Naour, Jean Yves, *The Living Unknown Soldier*, Heinemann, 2005.

Nicolson, Harold, *Curzon: The Last Phase*, 1937.

Nicolson, Harold, *King George the Fifth*, Constable, 1952.

Norman, Terry (ed.), *Armageddon Road: A VC's Diary, 1914–16*, William Kimber, 1982.

Norman, Terry, *The Hell They Called High Wood: The Somme, 1916*, Leo Cooper, 2003.

Orwell, George, *The Collected Essays, Journalism and Letters*, Vol. 1, *An Age Like This, 1920–1940*, Secker & Warburg, 1968.

Owen, Wilfred, *Collected Letters*, ed. Harold Owen and John Bell, Oxford University Press, 1967.

Palmer, Alan, *Victory 1918*, Weidenfeld and Nicolson, 1998.

Palmer, Svetlana, and Wallis, Sarah, *A War in Words*, Simon & Schuster, 2003.

Panichas, George A., *Promise of Greatness: 50th Anniversary of the Armistice*, John Day, New York, 1968.

Parker, Peter, *The Old Lie: The Great War and the Public School Ethos*, Constable, 1987.

Percy, Clayre, and Ridley, Jane (eds.), *The Letters of Sir Edwin Lutyens*, Collins, 1985.

Pershing, John J., *My Experiences in the World War*, 1931.

Persico, Joseph E., *Eleventh Month, Eleventh Day, Eleventh Hour: Armistice Day, 1918, World War I and Its Violent Climax*, Random House, 2004.

Piehler, G. Kurt, *Remembering War the American Way*, Smithsonian, Washington, 1995.

Piehler, G. Kurt, "The War Dead and the Gold Star: American Commemoration of the First World War," in Gillis, John R. (ed.), *Commemorations: The Politics of National Identity*, Princeton University Press, 1994.

Plowman, Max, *A Subaltern on the Somme*, Naval & Military Press, Uckfield, East Sussex, 2001.

Porter, Roy (ed.), *Myths of the English*, Polity, Cambridge, 1992.

Pound, Ezra, *Personae*, 1926.

Purdom, C. B. (ed.), *Everyman at War*, 1930.

Quinn, Tom, *Tales of the Old Soldiers*, Sutton, Stroud, Glos, 1993.

Register of the Victoria Cross, This England, Cheltenham, 1988.

Renn, Ludwig, *War*, Naval & Military Press, Uckfield, East Sussex, 2001 (fiction).

Richards, Frank, *Old Soldiers Never Die*, 1933.

Richardson, F. M. F., *Remembrance Wakes*, 1934.

Roberts, David, *Minds at War: The Poetry and Experience of the First World War*, Saxon Books, 1996.

Ronaldshay, Lord, *Life of Lord Curzon*, 1928.

Rose, Kenneth, *King George V*, Weidenfeld & Nicolson, 1983.

Rupprecht, Crown Prince, "The Battle of the Somme," in Charles F. Horne (ed.), *Source Records of the Great War*, Vol. IV, National Alumni, New York, 1923.

Sassoon, Siegfried, *Collected Poems*, Faber and Faber, 1947.

Scott, W. H., *Leeds in the Great War*, Leeds, 1923.

Shakespear, Lt. Col. John, *The 34th Division, 1915–1919: The Story of Its Career from Ripon to the Rhine*, 1921.

Shaw, George Bernard, *Androcles and the Lion*, Longman, Harlow, 1997.

Sheen, John, *Tyneside Irish, 24th, 25th & 26th & 27th (Service) Battalions of the Northumberland Fusiliers: A History of the Tyneside Irish Brigade Raised in the North East in World War One*, Pen & Sword, Barnsley, Yorkshire, 1998.

Sheffield, Garry, *Forgotten Victory: The First World War: Myths and Realities*, Review, 2002.

Sheffield, Garry, *The Somme: A New History*, Weidenfeld & Nicolson, 2003.

Sherren, W., *The Rights of the Ex-Service Man and Woman*, 1921.

Shipley, Robert, *To Mark Our Place: A History of Canadian War Memorials*, NC Press, Toronto, 1987.

Shores, Christopher, Franks, Norman, and Guest, Russell, *Above the Trenches: A Complete Record of the Fighter Aces and Units of the British Empire Air Forces, 1915–1920*, Grub Street, 1990.

Shores, Christopher, Franks, Norman, and Guest, Russell, *Above the Trenches— Supplement*, Grub Street, 1996.

Skelton, Marvin L., *Callahan: The Last War Bird*, Air Force Historical Foundation, Manhattan, Kansas, 1980.

Spears, E. L., *Prelude to Victory*, 1939.

Springhall, J., *Youth, Society and Empire: British Youth Movements, 1880–1940*, 1977.

Springs, Elliot White, *War Birds: Diary of an Unknown Aviator*, 1926.

Stallings, Laurence, *The Doughboys: The Story of the AEF, 1917–1918*, Harper & Row, 1966.

Stone, Norman, *The Eastern Front, 1914–1917*, Penguin, 1998.

Strachan, Hew, *The First World War*: Vol. 1, *To Arms*, Oxford University Press, 2001.

Sturtivant, Ray, and Page, Gordon, *The Camel File*, Air Britain, Tonbridge, 1993.

Sulzbach, Herbert (trans. Richard Thonger), *With the German Guns: Four Years on the Western Front, 1914–1918*, Leo Cooper, 1973.

Swift, Earl, *Where They Lay*, Bantam Press, 2003.

Tawney, R. H., *The Attack and Other Essays*, 1929.

Taylor, W. P., and Irvin, F. L. (eds.), *History of the 148th Aero Squadron Aviation Section, U.S. Army Signal Corps, AEF–BEF, 1917–1918*, Sunflower University Press, Manhattan, Kansas, 1957.

Terraine, J., *Douglas Haig: The Educated Soldier*, Leo Cooper, 1990.

Thorpe, Barrie, *Private Memorials of the Great War on the Western Front*, Western Front Association, Reading, Berkshire, 1999.

Toland, John, *No Man's Land: 1918, the Last Year of the Great War*, Doubleday, New York, 1980.

Trask, David F., *The AEF and Coalition War Making*, University Press of Kansas, Lawrence, 1993.

U.S. Air Force Historical Research Center, *Air Force Victory Credits: World War I, World War II, Korea and Vietnam*, USAF, Maxwell AFB, AL, 1988.

U.S. Quartermaster Museum, *This Week in Quartermaster History: 5–11 February*, Fort Lee Virginia, 2004.

Vance, Jonathan F., *Death So Noble: Memory, Meaning and the First World War*, UBC Press, Vancouver, 1997.

Vansittart, Peter (ed.), *John Masefield's Letters from the Front*, Constable, 1984.

Ward, Stephen R., *The War Generation: Veterans of the First World War*, Kennikat Press, New York, 1975.

Watrin, Janine, *The British Military Cemeteries in the Region of Boulogne-sur-Mer*, Book Club Ltd., 1977.

Webb, Beatrice, *Diaries*, ed. Margaret I. Cole, Longmans, Green, 1952.

Webb, M. de P., *Britain Victorious: A Plea for Sacrifice*, 1920.

Wedd, A. F. (ed.), *German Students' War Letters*, 1929.

Weintraub, Stanley, *A Stillness Heard Around the World: November 1918*, Allen & Unwin, 1986.

Werth, German, "Flanders 1917 and the German Soldier," in Peter H. Liddle (ed.), *Passchendaele in Perspective*, Leo Cooper, 1997.

West, Arthur Graeme, *The Diary of a Dead Officer*, 1918.

W. G. T., *For Those Who Mourn*, 1917.

Whaley, Joachim (ed.), *Mirrors of Mortality: Studies in the Social History of Death*, Europa, 1984.

Whitehead, Ian, "Third Ypres—Casualties & British Services: An Evaluation," in Peter H. Liddle (ed.), *Passchendaele in Perspective*, Leo Cooper, 1997.

Whittick, Arnold, *War Memorials*, Country Life, 1946.

Wilkinson, Alan, *The Church of England and the First World War*, SPCK, 1978.

Williams, John, *The Home Front: Britain, France and Germany, 1914–1918*, Constable, 1972.

Williamson, Henry, *The Power of the Dead*, Macdonald, 1963.

Williamson, Henry, *Wet Flanders Plain*, Gliddon, Norwich, 1989.

Winnington-Ingram, A. F., *Victory and After*, 1919.

Winter, Denis, *Death's Men: Soldiers of the Great War*, Allen Lane, 1978.

Winter, Denis, *Haig's Command*, Viking, 1991.

Winter, Jay M., *The Experience of World War I*, Macmillan, 1988.

Winter, Jay M., *The Great War and the British People*, Macmillan, 1986.

Winter, Jay M., and Baggett, Blaine, *The Great War and the Shaping of the 20th Century*, BBC Books, 1996.

Winter, Jay M., *Sites of Memory, Sites of Meaning* (Studies in the Social and Cultural History of Modern Warfare), Cambridge University Press, 1995.

Wolff, Leon, *In Flanders Fields*, Penguin, 1979.

Wood, Herbert Fairlie, and Swettenham, John, *Silent Witnesses*, Hakkert, Toronto, 1974.

Woolf, Virginia, *Diary*, Vol. I, *1915–1919*, Hogarth Press, 1977.

Wootton, Graham, *Official History of the British Legion*, 1956.

Wootton, Graham, *The Politics of Influence: British Ex-Servicemen, Cabinet Decisions and Cultural Change (1917–1957)*, Cambridge, Mass., 1963.

Young, James E., *The Texture of Memory: Holocaust Memorials and Meaning*, Yale University Press, New Haven, 1993.

Ziegler, Philip, *Crown and People*, Collins, 1978.

TELEVISION PROGRAMMES/DVDS

Van Emden, Richard, "Boy Soldiers," *Secret History*, Channel 4, 14 June 2004.

Wood, Alison Davis, *Gold Star Mothers: Pilgrimage of Remembrance*, WILL-TV, University of Illinois, 2004.

WEB SITES

www.acepilots.com/wwi/us_brit.html

www.afa.org/magazine/july2001/0701kelly.asp

www.theaerodrome.com/isearch/index.php

www.aftermathww1.com/warrior.asp

www.bbc.co.uk/history

berlin1.btm.de/infopool/jsp/e_sw_neue-wache.jsp

chadwyck.com (U.S. archive of 146,000 collections, 5,500 repositories)

cs02.com/whiteflags/pdf/locimemoriae.pdf

www.cwgc.org

www.firstworldwar.com

www.geocities.com/isanders_2000/neuewache.htm

www.goldstarmoms.com

www.hellfire-corner.demon.co.uk/coulson.htm

home.indy.rr.com/johnstons/wwi.htm

www.homeofheroes.com/gravesites/unknowns/foreign_greatbritain.html

www.lib.byu.edu/~rdh/wwi/1914.html

www.mdw.army.mil/fs-a04.htm

news.bbc.co.uk/1/hi/special_report/1998/10/98/world_war_i/194164.stmwww.ezboard.com

www.qmmuseum.lee.army.mil/historyweek/5–11feb.htm

www.rnzrsa.org.nz/review/art2002august/article_%203a.html

www.sassoonery.demon.co.uk/cenotaph.htm

www.trussel.com/maig/lacas2e.htm

users.aristotle.net/~russjohn/warriors/ace.html

www.vanderbilt.edu/rpw_center/pdfs/BUDREAU.PDF

www.veteransagency.mod.uk/remembrance/unknown_warrior.shtml

www.westminster-abbey.org/library/burial/warrior.htm

Index

Illustration Credits

The author and publisher are grateful to the institutions and individuals listed below for the right to reprint the images included in this book:

Page 4: (top and background) Library of Congress
Page 5: (top) *The New York Times;* (bottom) U.S. Army Quartermaster Museum
Page 6: (top left, top right, and background) Library of Congress
Page 7: (top right, center right, and bottom left) Library of Congress; (center left and bottom right) AT&T archives
Page 8: (all) Getty Images